KEY MATHS 9²

▶ **David Baker**
The Anthony Gell School, Wirksworth

▶ **Paul Hogan**
Fulwood High School, Preston

▶ **Barbara Job**
Christleton County High School, Chester

▶ **Renie Verity**
Pensby High School for Girls, Heswall

First published in 1997 by:
Stanley Thornes (Publishers) Ltd

Second edition published in 2001 by:
Nelson Thornes Ltd
Delta Place
27 Bath Road
CHELTENHAM
GL53 7TH
United Kingdom

12 / 15 14 13 12

A catalogue record for this book is available from the British Library.

ISBN 978 0 7487 5988 0

Illustrations by Maltings Partnership, Hugh Neill, David Oliver, Angela Lumley, Jean de Lemos, Clinton Banbury
Page make-up by Tech Set Ltd

Printed and bound in China

Acknowledgements

The publishers thank the following for permission to reproduce copyright material:
Adams Picture Library: 316 (B Hodgson); Allsport: 59 (Mike Cooper), 63, (Mike Powell), 59, 60, 63 (Mike Hewitt), 66 (Steven Dunn); 66 (Simon Brut); Barnaby's Picture Library: 101 (David Kirby); Coloursport: 104 (Andrew Cowie); Empics: 51; Esher Cordon Art: 257; J Allan Cash Photo Library: 22, 116; Janine Weidel: 86; Leslie Garland Picture Library: 123; Martyn Chillmaid: 16, 23, 25, 26, 42, 45, 46, 50, 55, 82, 83, 93, 108, 110, 111, 112, 113, 123, 142, 144, 147, 151, 198, 199, 200, 201, 233, 306, 318, 326, 327, 332; Palais de la decouverte: 41; Photostage: 54 (Donald Cooper); Robert Harding: 107 (D Furlong); Science Photo Library: 252 (Dick Luria); Sylvia Cordaiy: 251 (Patrick Partington); Tony Stone Imaging: 109; Telegraph Colour Library: 104 (S Hutchings); Topham Picturepoint: 47; Zefa Pictures: 219 (P Menzel); All other photographs STP Archives

Cover photographs: Tony Stone Images (front);
Pictor International (spine); Tony Stone Images (back)

The publishers have made every effort to contact copyright holders but apologise if any have been overlooked.

Contents

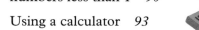

iii

1 Pythagoras

Pythagoras was a Greek philosopher and mathematician who lived in the sixth century BC.

Apart from his famous theorem, Pythagoras also discovered the mathematical basis of music. For example, that an octave can be expressed as the ratio 1:2. (A string stopped at half its length will sound the octave above the full length.)

CORE

1 Pythagorean triples

The Ancient Egyptians used ropes to make sure that their buildings had square corners.

Exercise 1:1

1 Look at this sequence of squares:

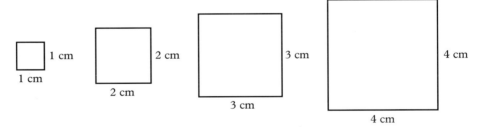

The areas of the squares are $1 \times 1, 2 \times 2, 3 \times 3, 4 \times 4$

The areas of these squares give you the first four square numbers: 1, 4, 9, 16

Write down the first 16 square numbers.

2 Look at these square numbers:

9   16   25

These three square numbers are special because

$9 + 16 = 25$

There are other sets of square numbers which work like this.

a How many can you find?

b You can write

$$9 + 16 = 25$$

as $3^2 + 4^2 = 5^2$

When you do this the numbers 3, 4 and 5 are called a **Pythagorean triple**.

Use your answers to **a** to write your own Pythagorean triples.

3 Look at the Pythagorean triple 3, 4 and 5.

Here is a triangle with sides of
length 3 cm, 4 cm and 5 cm:

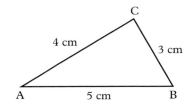

You are going to draw this triangle.

a Draw a line AB 5 cm long.

Open your compasses to 4 cm.
Put the point on A.
Draw an arc.

b Open your compasses to 3 cm.
Put the point on B.
Draw an arc.

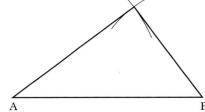

c The two arcs cross at a point.
Mark this point C.
Draw in AC and BC.

d Measure the largest angle of your triangle.
Mark the size of this angle on your triangle.

4 Draw two more triangles using your triples from question **2**.
Measure the largest angle of each triangle.
Mark the size of this angle on the triangle.

5 What do your three triangles have in common?

6 Draw three more right angled triangles.
Choose any lengths you like for the sides.
For each triangle:
a Measure the lengths of the sides.
b Square these numbers.
c Is the square of the largest number equal to the sum of the squares
of the other two numbers?

2 Finding the hypotenuse

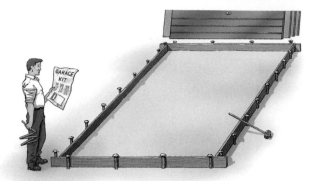

It is very important to have the right angles of the base correct before putting up the garage or it will not fit together properly. Mr Evans is going to measure the sides and a diagonal of this garage base.
He will use the lengths to make sure that he has a right angle in each corner.

| **Hypotenuse** | The longest side of a right angled triangle is called the **hypotenuse**. |

| **Pythagoras' theorem** | In this right angled triangle: |

$$c^2 = a^2 + b^2$$

The square of the = the sum of the squares of
hypotenuse   the other two sides

This is called **Pythagoras' theorem** after the Greek mathematician, Pythagoras.

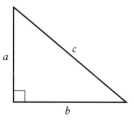

Example

a Write down the letter of the hypotenuse in this triangle.
b Write down Pythagoras' theorem for this triangle.

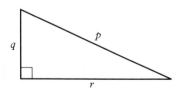

a The hypotenuse is p.
b $p^2 = q^2 + r^2$

Exercise 1:2

   a Write down the letter of the hypotenuse in each of these triangles.
   b Write down Pythagoras' theorem for each triangle.

1

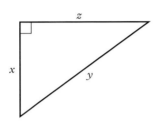

5

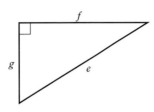

2

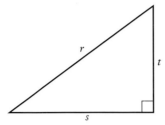

6

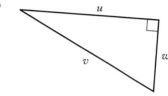

3

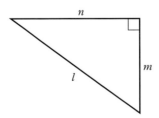

7

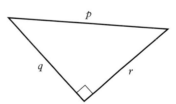

4

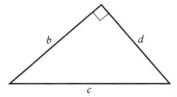

8

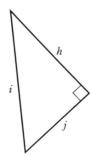

◄◄REPLAY►

Example　　　Use x^2 on your calculator to find 3.7^2

Key in:　　　3 $.$ 7 x^2 $=$

Answer:　　　13.69

Exercise 1:3

1 Use x^2 on your calculator to find each of these.
 a 7^2 　　　**c** 45^2 　　　**e** 7.3^2 　　　**g** 32.8^2
 b 27^2 　　　**d** 2.6^2 　　　**f** 5.36^2 　　　**h** 1.67^2

Example　　　Solve this equation: $x^2 = 54$
Give x correct to 1 dp.

You use $\sqrt{}$ to find the value of x:　　$x = \sqrt{54}$

Key in:　　$\sqrt{}$ 5 4 $=$

This gives:　7.3484692

Answer:　　7.3 correct to 1dp.

Remember the rule for rounding to 1 dp:
Look at the *second* figure after the decimal point.
If the second figure is 0, 1, 2, 3 or 4, miss off the unwanted figures.
If the second figure is 5, 6, 7, 8 or 9, add one to the number in the first decimal place.

2 Solve these equations.
 a $x^2 = 81$ 　　　**b** $v^2 = 196$ 　　　**c** $p^2 = 361$ 　　　**d** $r^2 = 184.96$

3 Solve these equations.
Give your answers correct to 1 dp.
 a $n^2 = 35$ 　　　**c** $m^2 = 75$ 　　　**e** $q^2 = 80$ 　　　**g** $s^2 = 146$
 b $y^2 = 56.8$ 　　　**d** $x^2 = 45.1$ 　　　**f** $w^2 = 9.07$ 　　　**h** $k^2 = 166.3$

You can use Pythagoras' theorem to find the length of the hypotenuse
if you know the lengths of the other two sides.

Example

Find the length of the hypotenuse
of this triangle.
Give your answer correct to 1 dp.

Using Pythagoras' theorem:
$p^2 = 7^2 + 10^2$
$p^2 = 49 + 100$
$p^2 = 149$
$p = \sqrt{149}$
$p = 12.2$ cm correct to 1 dp.

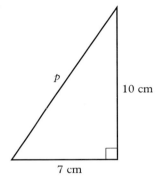

Check: Look at the triangle.
12.2 cm seems a reasonable length for the longest side.

Exercise 1:4

1 Find the length of the hypotenuse in each of these triangles.
Look at the triangle each time to check that your answer is reasonable.

a

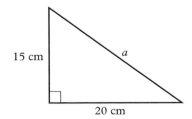

c

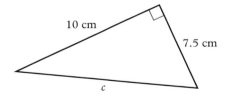

b

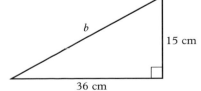

d

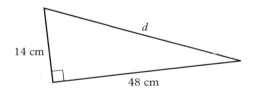

2 Find the length of the hypotenuse in each of these triangles.
Give your answers correct to 1 dp.

a

8 cm

5 cm

a

c

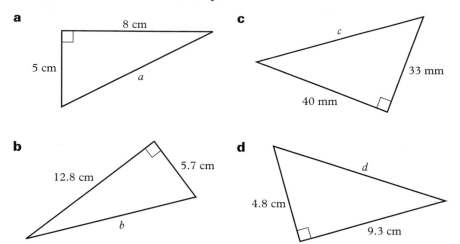

c

33 mm

40 mm

b

12.8 cm

5.7 cm

b

d

d

4.8 cm

9.3 cm

For the rest of this exercise, give your answers correct to 1 dp when
you need to round.

3 The diagram shows a ramp for wheelchairs.
Find the length of the ramp.

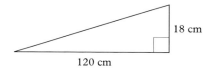

18 cm

120 cm

4 Here is Sinita's scarf.
It is a large triangle.
The two shorter edges are each 60 cm.
Find the length of the longest edge.

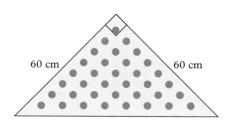

60 cm

60 cm

5 Alan is orienteering.
He travels cross country as
shown in the diagram.
He finishes 145 m north and
50 m west from his starting
point.
How far is Alan from his
starting point?

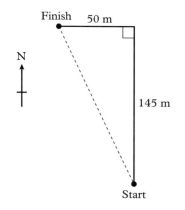

Finish 50 m

N

145 m

Start

6 Here is an isosceles triangle.
The base of the triangle is 8 cm.
Its height is 6 cm.
Use the red triangle to find the
length of one of the equal sides.

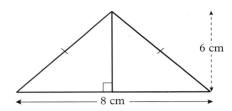

7 A mast is held in place by two
equal wires as shown.
The height of the mast is 70 m.
Find the length of each wire.

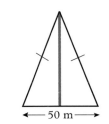

8 This is Gavin's tent.
It is 80 cm high and 120 cm wide.
Find the length of one of the
sloping sides of the tent.

9 The diagram shows the
triangle EFG.
a EG = 6 units
Write down the length of FG.
b Use Pythagoras' theorem to
find the length of EF.

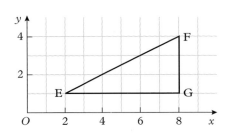

● **10** You cannot draw a right angled triangle with edges 7 cm, 9 cm and 21 cm.
Use Pythagoras' theorem to show this.

● **11** Mr Evans is making a base for a garage.
The sides of the base measure 3.5 m
and 5 m.

The base should be a rectangle.
Mr Evans finds a diagonal measures
6.5 m.

Use Pythagoras' theorem to decide
if the base is a rectangle.

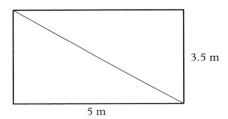

3   Finding any side

Mark has to clean the gutter at the edge of the roof.
He wants to know if his ladder will reach the gutter.

Pythagoras' theorem can be used to find one of the shorter sides of a triangle.

Example   Mark's ladder is leaning against a wall.
Find the height h that the ladder reaches up the wall.
Give your answer correct to 1 dp.

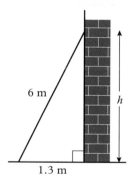

6 m

h

1.3 m

Using Pythagoras' theorem.

$$6^2 = h^2 + 1.3^2$$ Write the equation the other way round.

$$h^2 + 1.3^2 = 6^2$$ The unknown, h, is now on the left hand side.

$$h^2 + 1.69 = 36$$

$$h^2 + 1.69 - \mathbf{1.69} = 36 - \mathbf{1.69}$$ Subtract 1.69 from *both* sides.

$$h^2 = 34.31$$

$$h = \sqrt{34.31}$$

$$h = 5.9 \text{ m correct to 1 dp}$$

Check: 5.9 m is less than the hypotenuse, 6 m. It looks like a reasonable answer.

Exercise 1:5

Look at the triangle in each question to check that your answer is reasonable.

1 Find the missing lengths in each of these triangles.

a

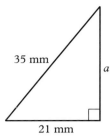

c

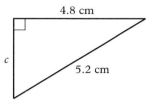

b

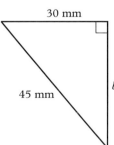

d

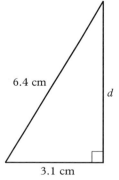

2 Find the missing lengths in each of these triangles.
Give your answers correct to 1 dp when you need to round.

a

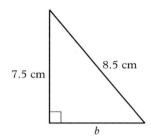

c

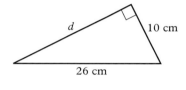

b

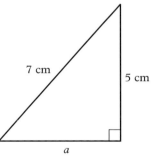

d

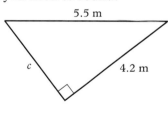

For the rest of this exercise, give your answers correct to 1 dp when you need to round.

3 Sally has leant her ladder against the wall.
How far up the wall does the ladder reach?

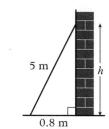

4 The picture shows a slide in a children's playground.
The length of the slide is 6 m.
The horizontal distance is 4 m.
Find the height of the slide.

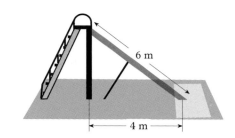

5 This is a diagram of the water chute in a theme park.
The chute is 20 m long.
The horizontal distance travelled is 15.4 m.
 a Find the vertical distance travelled.
● **b** Each step is 18 cm high.
How many steps will be needed to reach the top of the water chute?

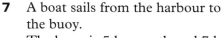

● **6** Two sides of a right angled triangle are 14 cm and 18 cm.
How long will the third side be if
 a it is the longest side
 b it is the shortest side?

7 A boat sails from the harbour to the buoy.
The buoy is 5 km south and 7 km west of the harbour.
 a How far has the boat travelled?
 b The boat is now 4.9 km from the tip of the headland.
The tip is 2 km west of the boat.
How far north of the boat is it?

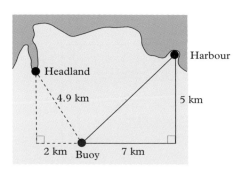

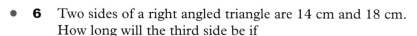

Exercise 1:6

Give your answers correct to 1 dp when you need to round.

1 A gate needs to be strengthened by fixing a strut across the diagonal.
Calculate the length of the strut.

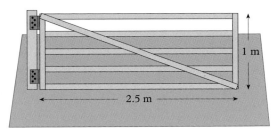

2 The diagram shows a shelf support.
Find the height of the support.

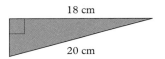

3 The positions of three houses are marked on the diagram.
House A is 7 km from B and 7 km from C.
The distance between B and C is 10 km along a straight road.
What is the shortest distance from A to the road?

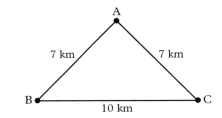

4 Sonya is training for her Duke of Edinburgh Award. She is improving her fitness by running in the local park. She uses two different routes.
  a Sonya's first route is to run the perimeter of the park.
How long is this route?
  b Sonya's second route is shown by the arrows in the diagram.
How long is this route?

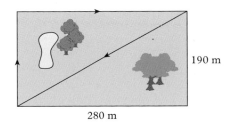

5 Rajiv is moving a fridge into his kitchen. He is using a trolley to wheel the fridge. The diagram shows the fridge when it is being moved by the trolley.
  a Find the total height of the fridge plus the trolley.
  b The kitchen door is 2 m high.
Will Rajiv get the fridge through the door?

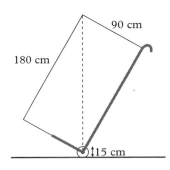

1 One of these sets of three numbers does not obey the rule $c^2 = a^2 + b^2$
Find the odd one out.

   a 10, 24, 26   **b** 8, 15, 17   **c** 4, 5, 6   **d** 6, 8, 10

2 Find the length of the hypotenuse in each of these triangles.
Give your answers correct to 1 dp when you need to round.

   a   **b**   **c**

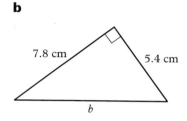 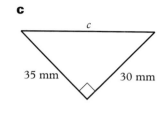

3 A rectangle has length 24 cm and width 15 cm.
Find the length of a diagonal.

4 An aircraft flies 260 km due north, and
then 340 km due east.
How far is the aircraft from its starting point?

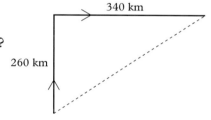

5 The diagram shows how a ramp for
wheelchairs is to be put over some
steps.
How long will the ramp need to be?
Give your answer correct to the
nearest centimetre.

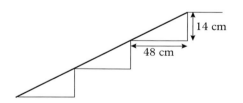

6 Use squared paper to draw an x axis from 0 to 6 and a y axis from
0 to 8.
Plot points P (2, 1), Q (5, 8) and R (5, 1).

   a Find the length PR.
   b Find the length RQ.
   c Use Pythagoras' theorem to find the length PQ.

7 Find the lengths of the sides marked with letters in these triangles.

a

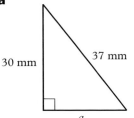

30 mm   37 mm

a

b

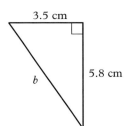

3.5 cm

5.8 cm

b

c

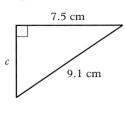

7.5 cm

c 9.1 cm

8 Jason has a theory that if he moves a ladder 1 m closer to a wall, it will reach 1 m further up the wall. The diagrams show the two positions of Jason's ladder.
  a Find the distance up the wall that the ladder reaches in the two positions.
    Give your answer correct to 2 dp.
  b How much further up the wall does the ladder reach in position (2)?
    Is Jason's theory correct?

(1)   (2)

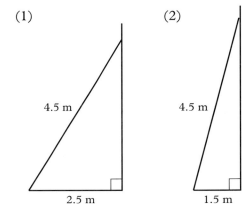

4.5 m   4.5 m

2.5 m   1.5 m

9 The triangle shown is isosceles.
  a Calculate the height of the triangle. correct to 1 dp.
  b Work out the area of the triangle.

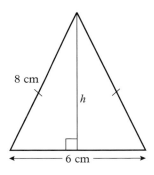

8 cm h

6 cm

10 Jane is flying a kite.
Nathan is standing directly below the kite.
He is 14 m from Jane.
The kite string is 30 m long.
Work out the height of the kite.
Give your answer correct to the nearest metre.

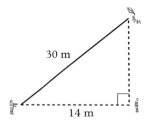

30 m

14 m

15

1   Alisha is using a glass rod to stir
the liquid in this beaker.
The rod is 25 cm long.
The beaker is 14 cm high and has
a diameter of 10 cm.
How long is the part of the glass
rod outside the beaker?

2   This is a picture of a rubber.
Find the length of a sloping
edge of the rubber.

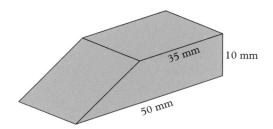

3   The diagram shows a shed.
a   Find the length of the edge of the
sloping roof of the shed.
b   Find the area of the roof of the shed.

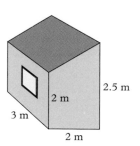

4   Look at this spiral.
a   Use Pythagoras' theorem to find p^2.
b   Use Pythagoras' theorem and your
value of p^2 to find q^2.
c   Use Pythagoras' theorem and your
value of q^2 to find r^2.
d   Use the pattern to find the length
marked s.

5   The end of this prism is an equilateral
triangle of side 8 cm.
a   Calculate the height of the triangle, h.
b   Calculate the area of the triangle.
c   Calculate the volume of the prism.

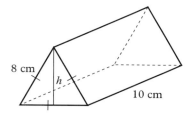

- **Hypotenuse**   The longest side of a right angled triangle is called the **hypotenuse**.

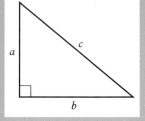

Pythagoras'   In this right angled triangle:
theorem $c^2 = a^2 + b^2$

The square of the = the sum of the squares of
  hypotenuse   the other two sides

- *Example*   Find the length of the hypotenuse
    of this triangle correct to 1 dp.

    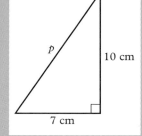

    Using Pythagoras' theorem:
    $p^2 = 7^2 + 10^2$
    $p^2 = 49 + 100$
    $p^2 = 149$
    $p = \sqrt{149}$
    $p = 12.2$ cm correct to 1 dp.

    Check: Look at the triangle.
        12.2 cm seems a reasonable
        length for the longest side.

- *Example*   Mark's ladder is leaning
    against a wall.
    Find the height h that the
    ladder reaches up the wall.
    Give your answer correct
    to 1 dp.

    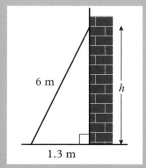

Using Pythagoras' theorem.

$6^2 = h^2 + 1.3^2$ Write the equation the other way round.

$h^2 + 1.3^2 = 6^2$ The unknown, h, is now on the left hand side.
$h^2 + 1.69 = 36$
$h^2 + 1.69 - \mathbf{1.69} = 36 - \mathbf{1.69}$ Subtract 1.69 from *both* sides.
$h^2 = 34.31$
$h = \sqrt{34.31}$
$h = 5.9$ m correct to 1 dp

Check: 5.9 m is less than the hypotenuse, 6 m. It looks like a reasonable answer.

1 Calculate the lengths of the sides marked with letters in these triangles.
Give your answers correct to 1 dp when you need to round.

a

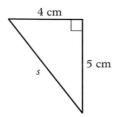

4 cm

5 cm

s

c

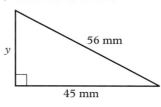

56 mm

y

45 mm

b

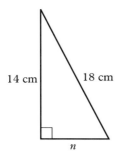

14 cm

18 cm

n

d

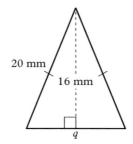

20 mm

16 mm

q

2 Use Pythagoras' theorem to test whether this triangle has a right angle.

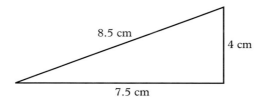

8.5 cm

4 cm

7.5 cm

3 A ladder 3.5 m long, leans against the wall of a house.
The foot of the ladder is 1.2 m from the wall.
Calculate how far the ladder reaches up the wall.
Give your answer correct to 1 dp.

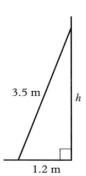

3.5 m

h

1.2 m

2 Formulas

For a moving object

$E = mc^2$

where E = energy,

c is the velocity of light

and m is mass

In simple terms this states that all energy has mass. It was devised by the German-born scientist Albert Einstein.

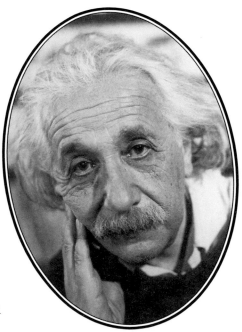

1 ◀◀ REPLAY ▶

Colin is going to paper his bedroom.
He needs to know how many rolls of wallpaper to buy.
Colin has found a formula for estimating the number of rolls of wallpaper:

$$R = \frac{H \times P}{5}$$

H = **H**eight of room in metres
P = **P**erimeter of room in metres

Colin's room is about 2 m high and the perimeter is 16 m.

Colin needs $\dfrac{2 \times 16}{5} = 6.4$ rolls

Colin decides to buy 7 rolls of paper.

Exercise 2:1

Here are some formulas used in maths for finding perimeters and areas.

1 $P = 4l$ gives the perimeter of a square.
    a Find P when $l = 5$ cm.
    b Find P when $l = 7$ cm.

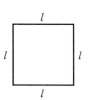

2 $A = l^2$ gives the area of a square.
    Remember: $l^2 = l \times l$
    a Find A when $l = 4$ cm.   **b** Find A when $l = 9$ cm.

3 $P = 2l + 2w$ gives the perimeter of a rectangle.
    a Find P when $l = 6$ cm and $w = 4$ cm.
    b Find P when $l = 8$ m and $w = 5$ m.

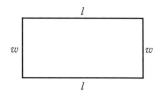

4 $A = lw$ gives the area of a rectangle.
    Find A when $l = 7$ cm and $w = 5$ cm.

5 $P = 2 \times (l + w)$ is another way of writing the perimeter of a rectangle.
Find P when $l = 4.5$ cm and $w = 2.5$ cm.

6 $A = 6l^2$ is a formula for finding the
surface area of a cube of side l.
Remember: $A = 6 \times l^2$
a Find A when $l = 3$ cm.
b Find A when $l = 5$ cm.

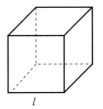

7 $A = \frac{1}{2}bh$ gives the area of a triangle.
Find A when $b = 30$ mm and $h = 20$ mm.

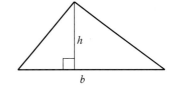

8 $A = bh$ gives the area of a parallelogram.
Find A when $b = 7$ cm and $h = 4$ cm.

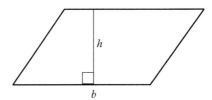

9 $C = 3d$ is a formula for estimating the
circumference of a circle.
a Estimate C when $d = 15$ mm.
b Estimate C when $d = 8$ cm.

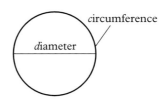

10 $A = \dfrac{a + b}{2} \times h$ is a formula for

finding the area of a trapezium.
Find A when $a = 5$ cm, $b = 7$ cm
and $h = 4$ cm.

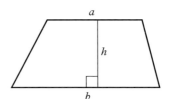

You can write formulas to work things out in everyday life.

Examples **1** Mr Patel uses his car to tow a boat.
The *t*otal length is the length of the *c*ar plus the length of the *b*oat.
In algebra this is written $t = c + b$

You can use the formula to find the total length if the car is 4 m long and the boat is 5 m long.
$t = 4 + 5 = 9$
The total length is 9 m.

2 A £50 prize is shared by some children.
They each get an equal amount of *m*oney.

In algebra this is written $m = \dfrac{50}{c}$

You can use the formula to find the amount if four children share the prize.

$m = \dfrac{50}{4} = 12.5$

The children get £12.50 each.

Exercise 2:2

Use the red letters and numbers to write each of your formulas in these questions.

1 **a** Write down a formula to find the total *l*ength of a *c*ar towing a *b*oat.
   b Use your formula to find *l* when $c = 3$ m and $b = 4$ m.

2 **a** Write down a formula to find the *m*oney received by some *p*eople when a £100 prize is shared between them.
   b Use the formula to find *m* when 5 people share the prize.

3 **a** Write down a formula to find the *t*otal length of some *s*tring after a piece **5** m long has been cut off.
b Use the formula to find *t* when *s* = 20 m.

4 **a** Write down a formula to find the number of *f*ree seats left in a theatre seating **450** when some *s*eats have been sold.
b Use the formula to find *f* when *s* = 390.

5 **a** Write down a formula to find the total *c*ost of **9** *d*isco tickets.
b Use your formula to find *c* when *d* = £5.50.

6 **a** Write down a formula to find the *w*eight of each piece of fudge when a *b*lock is cut into **15** pieces.
b Use your formula to find *w* when *b* = 240 g.

7 **a** Write down a formula to find the total *c*ost of a *d*rink and a *b*iscuit.
b Use your formula to find *c* when *d* = 60 p and *b* = 35 p.

8 **a** Write down a formula to find the *a*mount per person when a *t*axi fare is shared between **3** people.
b Use your formula to find *a* when *t* = £6.

9 **a** Write down a formula to find the *w*ages of somebody who earns £5 per *h*our.
b Use your formula to find *w* when *h* = 3 hours.

10 **a** Write down a formula to find the *w*eight of a 5 kg bag of potatoes when some *p*otatoes have been used.
b Use your formula to find *w* when *p* = 1.75 kg.

Some formulas are in two parts.
One part is an amount that varies, and the other part stays the same.

Example The Green family hire a car for their holiday.
For each day of the holiday they must pay £50. They also pay a fixed amount of £40 for insurance.
a Write down a formula for the total cost (**T** = total, **d** = days).
b Use your formula to find T when $d = 12$ days.

a

Number of days **d**	Hire charge	Insurance	Total **T**
1	$50 \times 1 = 50$	40	$50 + 40 = 90$
2	$50 \times 2 = 100$	40	$100 + 40 = 140$
3	$50 \times 3 = 150$	40	$150 + 40 = 190$
4	$50 \times 4 = 200$	40	$200 + 40 = 240$

$T = 50 \times d + 40$ or $T = 50d + 40$

b When $d = 12$, $T = 50 \times 12 + 40 = 640$ Answer: £640

Exercise 2:3

1 The Jones family have one newspaper delivered to their house each day.
The newspaper costs 40 p. There is also a fixed delivery charge of 50 p per week.
a Copy the table and fill it in.

Number of days **d**	Cost of papers	Delivery charge	Total **T**
1	$40 \times 1 = 40$	50	$40 + 50 = 90$
2	$40 \times 2 = 80$	50	$80 + 50 = \ldots$
3			
4			

b Find a formula for the total cost of the papers.
(**T** = total cost in pence, **d** = number of days)
Use the table to help you.
c Use your formula to find T when (1) $d = 6$ days (2) $d = 4$ days

2 For each day's work in a shop, the manager is paid £60 and each of the assistants is paid £35.
a Copy the table and fill it in.
Go as far as 4 in the first column.

Number of assistants **n**	Assistants' wages	Manager's wages	Total **T**
1	$35 \times 1 = 35$	60	$35 + 60 = 95$

b Find a formula for the total amount paid to the staff for one day's work in the shop (**T** = total, **n** = number of assistants).
c Use your formula to find T when (1) $n = 7$ (2) $n = 10$

In each of these questions you have to find a formula.
You can make a table to help you find the formula.
You may be able to write the formula down without using a table.

3 Year 9 are having a party. It costs a fixed amount of £90 to hire a disco
and £3 per pupil for refreshments.
  a Find a formula for the total cost of the party.
  (T = total cost, n = number of pupils)
  b Use your formula to find T when 120 Year 9 pupils go to the party.

4

A goods train has an engine 6 m long. Each wagon is 8 m long.
  a Write down a formula for the total length of the goods train.
  (T = total length, n = number of wagons)
  b Use your formula to find the total length of a train with 20 wagons.

5 9W are going to the theatre.
The cost of hiring the coach is £55 and the theatre tickets are £4 each.
  a Write down a formula for the total cost of the outing.
  (T = total cost in £, n = number of pupils going on the outing)
  b Use your formula to find the total cost when 30 pupils go on the
  outing.

6 Charlene has joined a swimming club. She had to pay £25 to join
the club.
She also pays £1.50 every time she goes swimming.
  a Write down a formula for the total cost of Charlene's swimming
  sessions.
  (T = total cost in £, n = number of times Charlene goes swimming)
  b Use your formula to find the total cost if Charlene goes swimming
  30 times.

7 The Northern Electricity Board charges customers 8 p per unit of
electricity that they use, plus a fixed charge of £12.
  a Write down a formula for the total cost of electricity used.
  (T = total cost in £, n = number of units of electricity used)
  b The Suresh family have used 1200 units of electricity.
  Use your formula to work out the total cost of their electricity bill.

2 Patterns

Gavin is making patterns using green and yellow tiles.

Exercise 2:4

1

a Use squared paper to copy these patterns.
b Draw pattern number 4.

2 How many tiles will there be altogether in pattern number 5?

3 Gavin's rule to work out the total number of tiles is $3n + 4$, where n is the number of the pattern.
a What does the 4 stand for in the $3n + 4$ rule?
b What does the $3n$ stand for in the $3n + 4$ rule?

4 a Gavin wants to make pattern number 11.
How many yellow tiles does he need?
b How many tiles does Gavin need altogether to make pattern number 11?

5 Gavin makes a pattern using 34 tiles altogether.
How many yellow tiles does he use?

6 Gavin has 8 green tiles and 36 yellow tiles.
What is the number of the biggest pattern that Gavin can make?

Exercise 2:5

Lucy is making patterns using beads and matchsticks.

1   Draw pattern number 4.

2   **a**   How many extra beads does Lucy add each time she makes a new
        pattern?
     b   How many beads will there be in pattern number 5?
     c   How many beads will there be in pattern number 10?

3   Lucy's rule for the number of beads is '2 times the number of the
        pattern add 2'.
        Write Lucy's rule using algebra. Use *n* for the number of the pattern.

4   Lucy uses 22 beads to make a pattern.
        Write down the number of the pattern.

5   **a**   How many extra matchsticks does Lucy add each time she makes a
        new pattern?
     b   How many matchsticks will there be in pattern number 5?

6   **a**   Copy this and fill it in:
        The rule for the total number of matchsticks is ... times the
        number of the pattern add ...
     b   Write down the rule using algebra. Use *n* for the number of the
        pattern.

7   Lucy uses 31 matchsticks to make a pattern.
        Write down the number of the pattern.

◀◀ **REPLAY** ▶

Exercise 2:6

1 These patterns are made from beads and matchsticks.

Pattern number 1   Pattern number 2   Pattern number 3

a Draw the next two patterns.
b Copy this table and fill it in:

Number of matchsticks	1	2	3	4	5
Number of beads	2	4			

2   ?   ?   ?

c How many beads do you add each time?
d Copy this and fill it in:
   number of beads = ... × number of matchsticks

2 These patterns are made from yellow and blue counters.

Pattern number 1   Pattern number 2   Pattern number 3

a Draw the next two patterns.
b Copy this table and fill it in:

Number of blue counters	1	2	3	4	5
Number of yellow counters	4	6			

2   ?   ?   ?

c How many yellow counters do you add each time?

The first part of the formula is:
   number of yellow counters = 2 × number of blue counters +...

d Copy this table. It is to help you find the rest of the formula.

Number of blue counters	1	2	3	4	5
	2 + ?	4 + ?	+ ?	+ ?	+ ?
Number of yellow counters	4	6			

Use the first part of the formula to finish the row of green numbers.
Then finish filling in the table.

e What do you add to the green numbers to get the number of yellow counters?

f Copy this and fill in the formula for the number of yellow counters.
number of yellow counters = ... × number of blue counters + ...

g Write down the formula using algebra. Use y for the number of yellow counters and b for the number of blue counters.

3 These hexagon patterns are made from matchsticks.

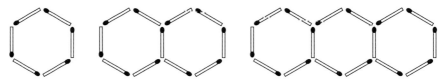

Pattern number 1   Pattern number 2   Pattern number 3

a Draw the next two hexagon patterns.

b Copy this table and fill it in.

Number of hexagons	1	2	3	4	5
Number of matchsticks	6	11			

? ? ? ?

c How many matchsticks do you add each time?

The first part of the formula is:
number of matchsticks = 5 × number of hexagons + ...

d Copy this table. It is to help you find the rest of the formula.

Number of hexagons	1	2	3	4	5
	5 + ?	10 + ?	+ ?	+ ?	+ ?
Number of matchsticks	6	11			

Use the first part of the formula to finish the row of green numbers.
Then fill in the rest of the table.

e What do you add to the green numbers to get the number of matchsticks?

f Copy this and fill in the rule for the number of matchsticks.
number of matchsticks = ... × number of hexagons + ...

g Write down the formula using algebra. Use m for the number of matchsticks and h for the number of hexagons.

◄◄REPLAY►

Number sequence	A **number sequence** is a pattern of numbers.
Term	Each number in the sequence is called a **term**.

Example   Here is a number sequence: 7, 9, 11, 13, 15, ...
   a   Describe the sequence in words.
   b   Find the formula for the nth term of the sequence.

a   The sequence goes up in 2's starting from 7.

b   7   9   11   13   15

         +2   +2   +2   +2

Number of term	1	2	3	4	5	n
2 times table	2 + 5	4 + 5	6 + 5	8 + 5	10 + 5	$2n$ + 5
Sequence	7	9	11	13	15	$2n + 5$

The formula for the nth *term* = $2n + 5$

Exercise 2:7

1   Here is a number sequence: 5, 8, 11, 14, 17, ...
   a   Describe the sequence in words.
   b   Copy this table for the number sequence and fill it in.

Number of term	1	2	3	4	5	n
... times table	... + ?	... + ?	... + ?	... + ?	... + ?	...n + ...
Sequence	5	8	11	14	17	...n + ...

   c   Write down the nth term of the sequence.

You can also have sequences where you need to take away a number.

2 Here is a number sequence: 1, 4, 7, 10, 13, ...
  a Describe the sequence in words.
  b Copy this table for the number sequence and fill it in.

Number of term	1	2	3	4	5	n
... times table	... − ?	... − ?	... − ?	... − ?	... − ?	...n −...
Sequence	1	4	7	10	13	...n − ...

  c Write down the formula for the nth term of the sequence.

For the sequences in questions **3** to **10**:
  a Describe the sequence in words.
  b Find a formula for the nth term of the sequence.
    You may be able to find the formula without drawing a table
    every time.

3 7, 11, 15, 19, 23, ...

4 2, 9, 16, 23, 30, ...

5 11, 14, 17, 20, 23, ...

6 2, 7, 12, 17, 22, ...

7 4, 15, 26, 37, 48, ...

8 1, 3, 5, 7, 9, ...

9 10, 16, 22, 28, 34, ...

10 2, 10, 18, 26, 34, ...

● **11** These patterns are made of blue tiles.

 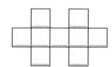 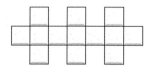

Pattern number 1   Pattern number 2   Pattern number 3

  a Draw the next two patterns.
  b How many blue tiles do you add each time?
  c Find a formula for the number of blue tiles in the nth pattern.
  d Use your formula to find the number of tiles in the 25th pattern.
  e A pattern uses 49 blue tiles.
    What is the number of this pattern?

Exercise 2:8

1 Here is a sequence of equilateral triangles.
You can find the perimeter of each of the triangles.

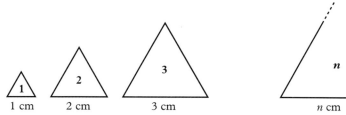

a Draw and label the diagrams for triangles 4 and 5 of the sequence.
b Copy the table and fill it in for the first 5 triangles.

Number of triangle	1	2	3	4	5	n
Perimeter in cm	3×1	3×2	3×3	$\ldots \times \ldots$	$\ldots \times \ldots$	?

c Describe the number pattern shown in the table in words.
d Fill in the nth term for the pattern using algebra.

2 Here is a sequence of squares.
1 cm is added to the sides of the squares each time.

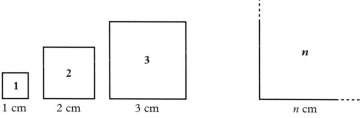

a Draw and label the diagrams for squares 4 and 5 of the sequence.
b Copy this table.
Fill it in for the perimeters of the first 5 squares.

Number of square	1	2	3	4	5	n
Perimeter in cm	4×1	4×2	4×3	$\ldots \times \ldots$	$\ldots \times \ldots$	?

c Describe the number pattern shown in the table in words.
d Fill in the nth term using algebra.
e The areas of the squares are $1 \times 1 = 1^2$, $2 \times 2 = 2^2$, $3 \times 3 = 3^2$ etc.
Copy this table and fill it in for the areas of the squares.

Number of square	1	2	3	4	5	n
Area in cm^2	1^2	2^2				?

3 Here is a sequence of cubes.

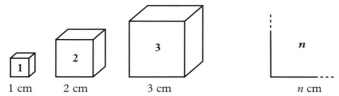

The volumes of the cubes are $1 \times 1 \times 1 = 1^3$ etc.

a Draw and label the diagrams for cubes 4 and 5 of the sequence.

b Copy the table and fill it in for the first 5 cubes.

Number of cube	1	2	3	4	5
Volume of cube in cm^3	1^3				

c Describe the number pattern shown in the table in words.

d Fill in the nth term using algebra.

Solar panels

This space station is made of lots of small cubes fixed together.
It has $4 \times 4 \times 4 = 64$ small cubes altogether.

The small cubes on the outside of the space station have circular solar panels. There is one solar panel fitted on every outside face.

1 **a** How many small cubes have 3 solar panels?
b How many small cubes have exactly 2 solar panels?
c How many small cubes have exactly 1 solar panel?
d How many small cubes have no solar panels?

2 Another space station is a cube with edges 3 small cubes long.
a Sketch this space station.
b How many small cubes of this space station have 3 solar panels?
c How many small cubes have exactly 2 solar panels?
d How many small cubes have exactly 1 solar panel?
e How many small cubes have no solar panels?

3 Investigate the numbers of solar panels in other sizes of space station.

You can make sequences of numbers from powers higher than 3.
These do not have special names like square and cube.

Remember that when you write 2^5, the 5 is called a **power**.
The power tells you how many 2s to multiply together.
So $2 \times 2 \times 2 \times 2 \times 2 = 2^5$.
This means that $2^5 = 32$.

Example Work out 4^3.
$4^3 = 4 \times 4 \times 4 = 64$

Exercise 2:9

1 Write these numbers using a power.
   a 3×3
   c $6 \times 6 \times 6 \times 6 \times 6$
   e $9 \times 9 \times 9 \times 9 \times 9 \times 9$
   b $5 \times 5 \times 5$
   d $8 \times 8 \times 8 \times 8$
   f $4 \times 4 \times 4 \times 4 \times 4 \times 4 \times 4$

You can use the $\boxed{y^x}$ button on your calculator to work out powers.

Example Work out 5^6.

Key in:

The answer is 15625.

2 Work these out. Use the $\boxed{y^x}$ button on your calculator.
   a 5^4
   d 6^4
   g 8^3
   j 15^3
   b 3^6
   e 4^7
   h 6^5
   k 4.1^3
   c 7^3
   f 2^8
   i 21^2
   l 3.7^5

3 **a** Work out 0.5^3.
   b Compare the size of the answer with the size of the number you
      started with.
      Write down what you notice.

4 **a** Work out 3^4
   b Work out 3^7
   c Work out 3^{11}
   d Multiply your answer to **a** and **b** together.
      Write down what you notice.

Look at your answers to question **4**.
You should have noticed that $3^4 \times 3^7 = 3^{11}$

Now look at the powers. Notice that $4 + 7 = 11$.
This is not a coincidence.
It is because $3^4 = 3 \times 3 \times 3 \times 3$
and $3^7 = 3 \times 3 \times 3 \times 3 \times 3 \times 3 \times 3$

If you multiply these together you get $3 \times 3 \times 3 \times 3 \times 3 \times 3 \times 3 \times 3 \times 3 \times 3 \times 3$
which is 3^{11}

So when you **multiply** two powers of the same number together you **add** the powers.

Example   Work out   **a** $5^6 \times 5^8$ **b** $17^3 \times 17^5$

a $5^6 \times 5^8 = 5^{6+8} = 5^{14}$

b $17^3 + 17^5 = 17^{3+5} = 17^8$

5 Write each of these as a single power.
   a $5^4 \times 5^3$ **d** $6^4 \times 6^5$ **g** $8^3 \times 8^3 \times 8^2$
   b $3^6 \times 3^4$ **e** $4^7 \times 4^{10}$ **h** $6^5 \times 6^2 \times 6$
   c $7^3 \times 7^7$ **f** $2^8 \times 2^3$ **i** $21^2 \times 21 \times 21^4$

This rule also works with algebra.

Example   Simplify these expressions as much as possible.
   a $y^2 \times y^7$ **b** $a^2 b^3 \times a^4 b^4$

a $y^2 \times y^7 = y^{2+7} = y^9$.

b $a^2 b^3 \times a^4 b^4 = a^{2+4} b^{3+4} = a^6 b^7$.

6 Simplify each of these as much as possible.
   a $t^4 \times t^3$ **d** $a^4 b^2 \times a^5$ **g** $c^5 \times c^3 \times c^6$
   b $y^8 \times y^6$ **e** $s^7 t^3 \times s^6 t^2$ **h** $n^5 \times n^2 \times n$
   c $p^3 \times p^9$ **f** $y^3 \times z^8$ ● **i** $a^2 b^3 \times a^4 b^4 \times a^4 b^2$

1 $P = 5l$ is a formula for the perimeter of a regular pentagon of side l. Use the formula to find P when
  a $l = 9$ cm **b** $l = 3.5$ cm

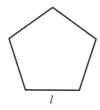

2 Paul has hired a bicycle for his holiday.
The bicycle costs £8 for the insurance plus £5 a day.
  a Write down a formula for the total cost of the hire.
      (T = total cost, n = number of days)
  b Use your formula to work out the total cost for 7 days hire.

3 Rani is making these patterns using red and yellow tiles.

Pattern number 1   Pattern number 2   Pattern number 3

  a Draw pattern number 4.
  b How many more yellow tiles does Rani add each times she makes a new pattern?
  c How many tiles will there be altogether in pattern number 5?
  d Rani's rule to work out the total number of tiles is $2n + 1$ where n is the number of the pattern.
      What does the 1 stand for in the $2n + 1$ rule?
  e What does the $2n$ stand for in the $2n + 1$ rule?
  f Rani wants to make pattern number 9.
      How many yellow tiles does she need?
  g Rani makes a pattern using 23 tiles altogether.
      How many red tiles does she use?
  h Rani makes a pattern using 31 tiles altogether.
      How yellow tiles does she use?
  i Rani has 5 red tiles and 38 yellow tiles.
      What is the number of the biggest pattern that Rani can make?

4 Describe each of these sequences in words.
Write down a formula for the nth term of each sequence.
  a 8, 13, 18, 23, 28, ...
  b 12, 14, 16, 18, 20,...
  c 1, 5, 9, 13, 17,...
  d 3, 11, 19, 27, 35,...
  e 9, 15, 21, 27, 33,...
  f 5, 16, 27, 38, 49,...

5 These triangle patterns are made of matchsticks.

Pattern number 1 Pattern number 2 Pattern number 3

a Draw the next two patterns.
b Copy this table and fill it in.

Number of triangles	1	2	3	4	5
Number of matchsticks	3	5			

c How many matchsticks do you add each time?

The first part of the formula is:
   number of matchsticks = 2 × number of triangles + ...

d Copy this table. It is to help you write the rest of the formula.

Number of triangles	1	2	3	4	5
	2 + ?	4 + ?	+ ?	+ ?	+ ?
Number of matchsticks	3	5			

Use the first part of the formula to finish the row of green numbers.
Fill in the rest of the table.
e Write down a formula in algebra for the number of matchsticks
   when there are n triangles.

6 This is a sequence of triangles.

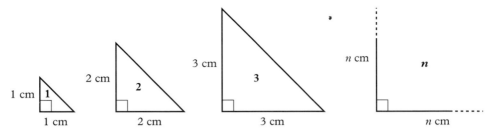

a Sketch diagrams for triangles 4 and 5 of the sequence.
b The areas of the triangles in the sequence are:
   $\frac{1}{2} \times 1 \times 1 = \frac{1}{2} \times 1^2$, $\frac{1}{2} \times 2^2$, $\frac{1}{2} \times 3^2$, ...
   Copy the table and fill it in.

Number of triangle	1	2	3	4	5	n
Area of triangle in cm²	$\frac{1}{2} \times 1^2$					

1 An expression for finding the surface area of a cube
is $6l^2$, where l is the length of an edge of the cube.
Find the surface area when
a $l = 2$ cm   **b** $l = 5$ cm

2 Les buys a cookery magazine every week for £1.50
A binder for the set of magazines costs £4.
a Write down a formula for the total cost of the magazines and the
binder.
(T = total cost, n = number of weeks)
b Use your formula to find the total cost of the binder and the
magazines for 12 weeks.

3 These pentagon patterns are made with matchsticks.

Pattern number 1   Pattern number 2   Pattern number 3

a Draw the next two pentagon patterns.
b Make a table to show the number of matchsticks needed for each
pattern.
c How many matchsticks do you add each time?
d How many matchsticks are there in the 20th pentagon pattern?
e Write down a formula in algebra for the number of matchsticks in
the nth pattern.

4 Here is a sequence of rectangles:

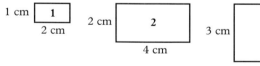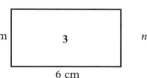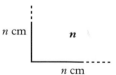

a Sketch and label rectangles 4 and 5.
b The table shows how to find the area of each rectangle.
Copy the table and fill it in.
c Find the nth term.

Number of rectangle	1	2	3	4	5	n
Area of rectangle in cm²	1×2	2×4	3×6	$\ldots \times \ldots$	$\ldots \times \ldots$	$n \times \ldots$

- You can write formulas to work things out in everyday life.

  Example   A £50 prize is shared by some children.
  They each get an equal amount of money.

  In algebra this is written $m = \dfrac{50}{c}$

  You can use the formula to find the amount if four children share the prize.

  $m = \dfrac{50}{4} = 12.5$ The children get £12.50 each.

- Some formulas are in two parts.
  One part is an amount that varies, and the other part stays the same.

  Example   The Green family hire a car for their holiday.
  For each day of the holiday they must pay £50. They also pay a fixed amount of £40 for insurance.

  a Write down a formula for the total cost (T = total, d = days).
  b Use your formula to find T when $d = 12$ days.

a

Number of days d	Hire charge	Insurance	Total T
1	$50 \times 1 = 50$	40	$50 + 40 = 90$
2	$50 \times 2 = 100$	40	$100 + 40 = 140$
3	$50 \times 3 = 150$	40	$150 + 40 = 190$
4	$50 \times 4 = 200$	40	$200 + 40 = 240$

$T = 50 \times d + 40$ or $T = 50d + 40$

b When $d = 12$, $T = 50 \times 12 + 40 = 640$ Answer: £640

- *Example*   Here is a number sequence: 7, 9, 11, 13, 15,…
  a Describe the sequence in words.
  b Find the formula for the nth term of the sequence.

a The sequence goes up in 2s starting from 7.

b

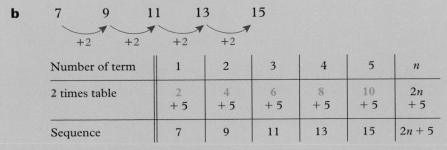

Number of term	1	2	3	4	5	n
2 times table	2 + 5	4 + 5	6 + 5	8 + 5	10 + 5	$2n$ + 5
Sequence	7	9	11	13	15	$2n + 5$

The formula for the nth term $= 2n + 5$

1   **a**   Use the red letters to write down a formula for the *t*otal cost of a *s*andwich and a *c*up of coffee.

    b   Use your formula to find the total cost when the sandwich is £1.50 and the cup of coffee is 70 p.

2   Some of Year 9 go on an outing to a castle. It costs £70 for the hire of the coach and £2 per pupil to go in the castle.

    a   Write down a formula for the total cost of the outing.
      (***T*** = total cost, ***n*** = number of pupils on the outing)

    b   Use your formula to find the total cost of an outing for 54 pupils.

3   These patterns are made of square tiles.

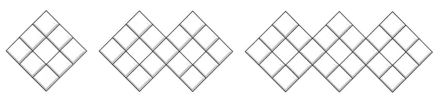

Pattern number 1   Pattern number 2   Pattern number 3

    a   Draw the next two patterns.

    b   Copy this table and fill it in.

Number of pattern	1	2	3	4	5
Number of tiles	8	15			

The first part of the formula is:
    number of tiles = 7 × number of pattern + …

    c   Copy this table. It is to help you find the rest of the formula.

Number of pattern	1	2	3	4	5
… times table	7 + ?	… + ?	… + ?	… + ?	… + ?
Number of tiles	8	15			

Use the first part of the formula to finish the row of green numbers. Fill in the rest of the table.

    d   Write down a formula for the number of tiles in the *n*th pattern.

    e   Use your formula to find the number of tiles in the 20th pattern.

4   **a**   Describe each of these sequences in words.

    b   Write down a formula for the *n*th term of each sequence.
      (1)   6, 10, 14, 18, 22,…   (2)   1, 8, 15, 22, 29,…

3 Circles

Here is a photograph taken in the Palais de la découverte, a science museum in Paris. The photograph shows the value of π, written to 706 decimal places, around the walls of the museum. Try to find out what the world record for calculating π is.

1 How long is a circle?

Kiran has just bought a new bike.
He wants to set up the computer
to be able to see how far he rides.
He enters the distance across the
wheel into the computer.
This is because the distance
round a circle depends on the
distance across the circle.

Exercise 3:1

W 1 You need worksheet 3:1.

2 The distance across each circle is 5 cm.
    a Divide each of your estimates by 5.
       Use a calculator and write down all the numbers on the calculator
       display.
    b What do you notice about these answers?

Circumference   The **circumference** of a circle
is the distance around the circle.
The circumference depends on
the distance across the circle.

Diameter   The distance across a circle is
called the **diameter**.
A diameter must pass through
the centre of the circle.

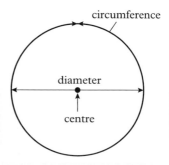

The circumference divided by the diameter always gives the same
answer.
This answer is a special number in maths.
It is called **pi** (which you say as 'pie') and it is written as π.

π

For all circles

Circumference = $\pi \times$ *d*iameter

This rule is often written $C = \pi d$

There should be a π key on your calculator.

Key in π on your calculator.

You should get   3.1415927

You might get more digits than this. It depends which calculator you have.

Example

Find the circumference of this circle.

$C = \pi d$
$\quad = \pi \times 8$

Key in: $\boxed{\pi}$ $\boxed{\times}$ $\boxed{8}$ $\boxed{=}$

You should get   25.132741

$\quad = 25.1$ cm to 1 dp

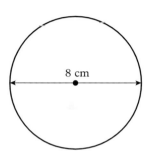

Exercise 3:2

Give all your answers in this exercise correct to 1 dp.

1 Find the circumferences of these circles.

a

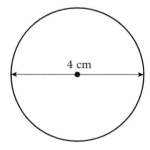

4 cm

c

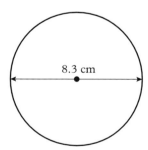

8.3 cm

b

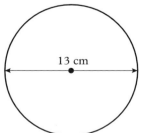

13 cm

d

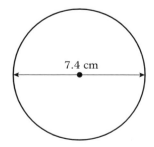

7.4 cm

e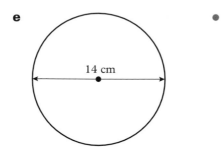

f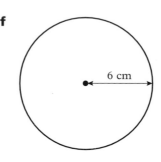

2 The diameter of each wheel on Kiran's bike is 70 cm.
What is the circumference of a wheel?

3 This circular mirror is edged with
decorative plastic tape.
What is the length of the tape?

4 This plate is edged with gold trim.
What is the length of the gold trim?

5 Janet is making a lampshade.
The top of the lampshade has a
diameter of 20 cm.
The bottom has a diameter of 32 cm.
Janet wants to decorate the top and
bottom of the lampshade by putting
braid around the edges.
What length of braid does she need to buy?

6 The diagram shows a roll of sticky tape.
The diameter of the cardboard ring is 3.4 cm.
The tape on the roll is 1.7 cm thick.
What is the outer circumference of the tape?

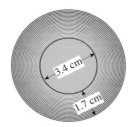

7 The regions on this dartboard are separated using lengths of wire.

   a How many straight pieces of wire are there?

   b The length of each straight piece of wire is 15.6 cm.
      What is the total length of all the straight pieces?

There are 6 wire circles.

The diameters of these are 33.6 cm, 31.6 cm,
21 cm, 19 cm, 2.4 cm and 1.3 cm.

   c Find the length of each circular wire.

   d What is the total length of all the circular
      pieces of wire?

   e What is the total length of wire on the dartboard?

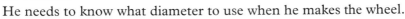

John is making a trundle wheel for his
Technology project.
He wants each turn of the wheel to
measure 1 metre on the ground.
The circumference of the wheel must
be 1 metre.

He needs to know what diameter to use when he makes the wheel.
He needs a formula for the diameter.

The formula for finding the circumference is

$$C = \pi \times d$$

The inverse of multiplying by π is dividing by π.
Divide both sides by π:

$$\frac{C}{\pi} = \frac{\pi \times d}{\pi}$$

$$\frac{C}{\pi} = d$$

The formula for finding the diameter is $\quad d = \dfrac{C}{\pi}$

Example   The circumference of a circle is 40 cm.
                Find the diameter.

$$d = \frac{C}{\pi}$$

$$d = \frac{40}{\pi}$$

Key in: **4** **0** **÷** **π** **=** 12.732395

= 12.7 cm to 1 dp

Exercise 3:3

Give all your answers in this exercise correct to 1 dp.

1 Find the diameters of these circles.

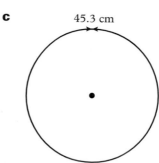

a 15 cm

c 45.3 cm

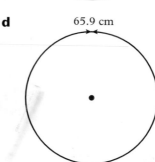

b 26 cm

d 65.9 cm

2 Find the diameter that John must use to make his trundle wheel the right size.
Use 100 cm as the circumference.
Give your answer in centimetres.

3 A roundabout has a circumference of 220 m.
What is the diameter of the roundabout?

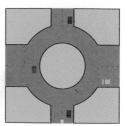

4 What is the diameter of a circular mirror with circumference 250 cm?

5 When you are using your calculator you know that it is a good idea to check your answers by estimation.
Use $\pi = 3$ to *estimate* the answers to questions **1** to **4**.

| **Radius** | The **radius** of a circle is the distance from the centre to the circumference.
The radius is half the diameter. |

6 For each of these circles find:
  a the diameter
  b the radius

(1)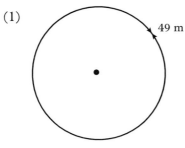
49 m

(3)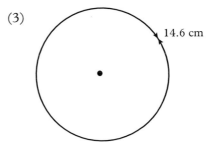
14.6 cm

(2)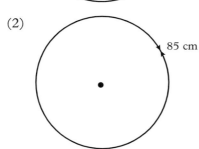
85 cm

(4)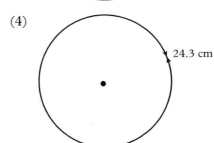
24.3 cm

7 The largest big wheel in the world is in Kobe in Japan.
The circumference is 200 m.
Find the radius of the wheel.

8 The distance around a circular running track is 400 m.
Find the radius of the track.

9 The perimeter of this track is 400 m.
  a What is the total length of the straight parts of the track?
  b What is the total length of the curved parts?
  c What is the diameter of the semi-circular ends?
  d What is the radius of the semi-circular ends?

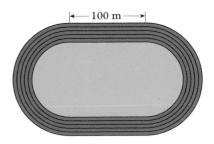
←—— 100 m ——→

2 Area of a circle

Fred the farmer is annoyed about this crop circle.
His crop has been destroyed.
He wants to know how much of the crop has been lost.
He needs to know the area of the circle.

Area of a circle
The **area of a circle** depends on the radius of the circle.
The formula is

$$Area \ of \ circle = \pi \times radius \times radius$$

This rule is often written $A = \pi \times r \times r$

or $\quad A = \pi r^2 \quad$ (r^2 means $r \times r$)

Example
Find the area of this circle.

$$
\begin{aligned}
A &= \pi r^2 \\
&= \pi \times 4^2 \\
&= \pi \times 4 \times 4 \\
&= \pi \times 16 \\
&= 50.3 \text{ cm to 1 dp}
\end{aligned}
$$

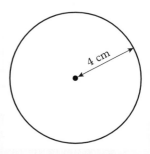

4 cm

Exercise 3:4

Give all your answers in this exercise correct to 1 dp.

1   Find the areas of these circles.

a
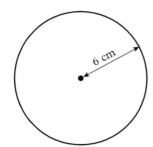

e
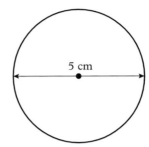

b
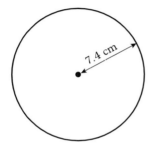

f
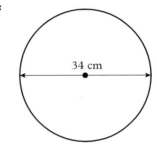

c
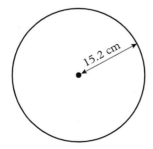

g
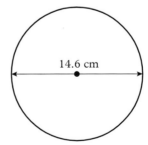

d
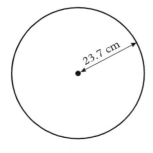

h
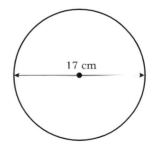

2 Use $\pi = 3$ to *estimate* the areas of the circles in question **1**.

3 The radius of the centre circle on a soccer pitch is 5 yds.
What is the area of the circle?

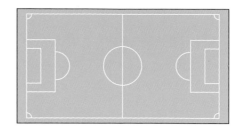

4

The diameter of a 10 p coin is 24 mm.
Find the area of one face of the coin.

5 Find the area of this circular table.

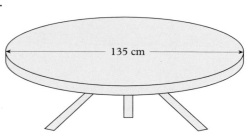

6 Find the areas of each of these plates:

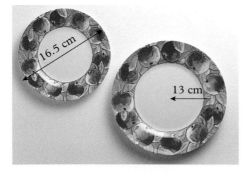

7 A CD is made from plastic.
The radius of a CD is 6 cm.
The hole in the middle has a radius of 0.75 cm.
  a Find the area of the hole.
  b Find the area of the plastic.

Exercise 3:5

Give all your answers in this exercise correct to 1 dp.

1 Find the areas of these shapes.

a

8 cm

d

10 cm

12 cm

b

4 cm

e

20 cm

8 cm

c

7 cm

12 cm

f

8 cm

10 cm

6 cm

2 The goal area on an ice hockey rink is a semi-circle.
The diameter is 3.6 m.
Find the area.

51

3 Find the area of this brooch.

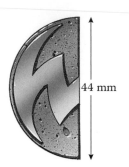

44 mm

4 This table is a rectangle with a semi-circle
at each end.
  a Find the area of the rectangular top.
  b Find the area of one of the semi-circles.
  c Find the total area when all of the table
  is being used.

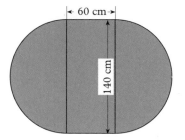

← 60 cm →

140 cm

5 The floor of a disco is a circle with radius 4.5 m.
The floor needs polishing.
  a What is the area of the floor?
  b Polishing costs £2.50 for every square metre.
  Any extra part of a square metre also costs £2.50.
  How much does it cost to have the floor polished?

6 Rachel makes covers for circular paddling pools.
This is how she charges:

Area of pool	Cost
Up to 10 000 cm²	£7
Between 10 000 cm² and 20 000 cm²	£12.50
Over 20 000 cm²	£15

How much would she charge for each of these pools?

a

35 cm

b

120 cm

c

180 cm

Give all answers correct to 1 dp.

1 Find the circumferences of these circles.

a

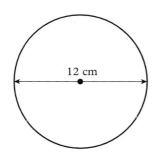

12 cm

c

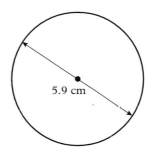

5.9 cm

b

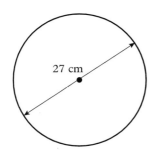

27 cm

d

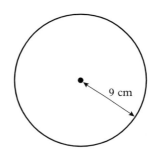

9 cm

2 Jack wants to put fencing around this pond.
He measures all round the pond.
He says the circumference is 7.2 m.
How do you know this is wrong?

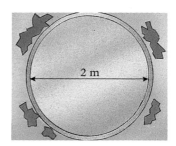

2 m

3 Jill runs around a circular lake 7 times.
The lake has a radius of 38 m.
How far does she run?

4 Mr Patel is fitting glass in this window frame.
He has to put putty all round the outside.
What is the length all round the outside?

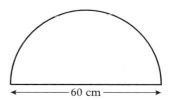

60 cm

5 The circumference of this
circular stage is 28.5 m.
What is the diameter of the stage?

6 The circumference of a lake is 440 m.
How far is it straight across the lake?

7 The perimeter of this track is 500 m.
  a What is the total length of the straight parts?
  b What is the total length of the curved parts?
  c What is the diameter of the semi-circular ends?

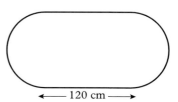

← 120 cm →

8 Find the diameter of the circle that has the
same perimeter as this rectangle.

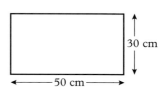

30 cm

← 50 cm →

9 Find the areas of these circles.

a

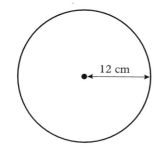

12 cm

b

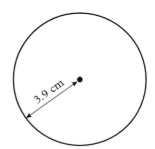

3.9 cm

10 Which of these two shapes has the shorter perimeter?

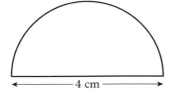

← 4 cm →

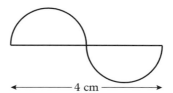

← 4 cm →

11 Find the areas of these shapes.

a

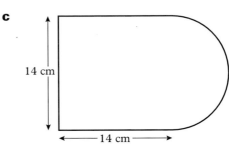

26 cm

c

14 cm

14 cm

b

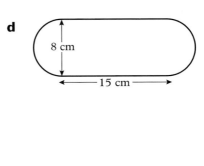

11 cm

d

8 cm

15 cm

12 This is the value of π to 21 decimal places:

3.141 592 653 589 793 238 462

Mathematicians have used fractions to give the value of π.
Here are some of the fractions:

Mathematician	Fraction
Archimedes	$\frac{22}{7}$
Ptolemy	$\frac{377}{120}$
Tsu Ch'ung-Chih	$\frac{355}{113}$

Use your calculator to find out whose fraction was most accurate.

13 This circular pond has a diameter of 25 m.
There are 3 circular islands in the pond.
Each island has a radius of 2.5 m.
Find the area of the surface of the water.

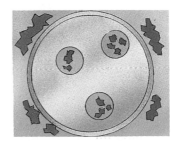

1 The wheel of a bike has a diameter of 50 cm.
  a Find the circumference of the wheel in metres.
  b How far has the bike moved when the wheel has made 1 turn?
  c How many complete turns will the wheel have made when the bike has travelled 1 km?

2 The minute hand of this clock is 9 cm long.
  a How far does the tip of the minute hand travel in 1 hour?
    The tip of the hour hand travels 38 cm in 24 hours.
  b How long is the hour hand?

3 Find the area of this shape:

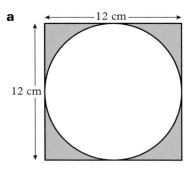

2 cm   2 cm   2 cm

4 Find the shaded areas.

  a

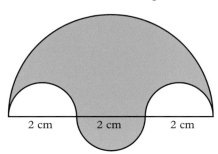

12 cm, 12 cm

  b

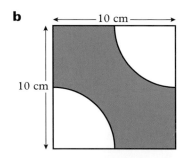

10 cm, 10 cm

5 Paul has hit a cricket ball through this circular window.
The diameter of the window is 56 cm.
The glass to repair the window costs 50 p for 250 cm².
The beading around the window also needs to be replaced.
This costs £1.50 per metre.
How much does Paul have to pay for the materials to fix the window?

- **Circumference** The **circumference** of a circle is the distance around the circle.
  The circumference depends on the distance across the circle.

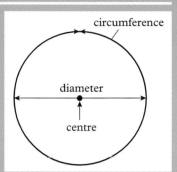

  Diameter The distance across a circle is called the **diameter**.

  Example Find the circumference of this circle.

  $$C = \pi d$$
  $$= \pi \times 8$$

  Key in: | π | $\times$ | 8 | = |
  You should get 25.132741
  $= 25.1$ cm to 1 dp

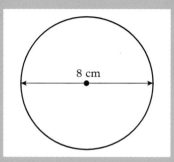

8 cm

- *Example* The circumference of a circle is 40 cm.
  Find the diameter.

  $$d = \frac{C}{\pi} \qquad \therefore \quad d = \frac{40}{\pi}$$

  Key in: | 4 | 0 | $\div$ | π | = | 12.732395
  $= 12.7$ cm to 1 dp

- **Radius** The **radius** of a circle is the distance from the centre to the circumference.
  The radius is half the diameter.

- **Area** The **area of a circle** depends on the radius of the circle.

  Example Find the area of this circle.

  $$A = \pi r^2$$
  $$= \pi \times 4^2$$
  $$= \pi \times 4 \times 4$$
  $$= \pi \times 16$$
  $$= 50.3 \text{ cm to 1 dp}$$

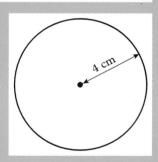

4 cm

1 Find the circumferences of these circles.

a

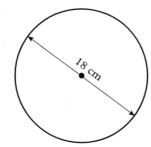

18 cm

b

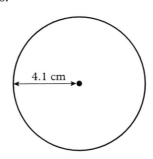

4.1 cm

2 The circumference of this pie dish is 82 cm. What is the diameter of the pie dish?

3 Find the areas of these circles.

a

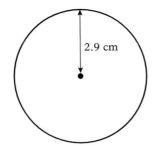

2.9 cm

b

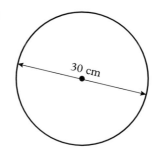

30 cm

4 Find the areas of these shapes.

a

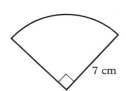

7 cm

b

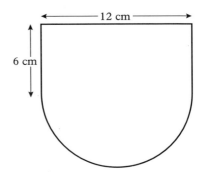

12 cm

6 cm

4 Statistics

Michelle Smith won three gold medals for Ireland in swimming events at the 1996 Olympics in Atlanta:

200-metres individual medley

400-metres individual medley

400-metres freestyle

1 Looking at data

This photo shows the men's 100 m final from the 1996 Olympic Games.
In 1956, the winning time in this event was 10.5 s.
The winning time in 1996 was 9.84 s.
This is an improvement of only 0.66 seconds, nearly $\frac{2}{3}$ of a second, in 40 years.

▼ You need worksheet 4 : 1, **Olympic men's 100 m winners**.

In this section you are going to look at data from the 1996 Olympic Games.

You will collect information and draw diagrams to show the data that you have collected.

You are going to start by looking at discrete data.

Discrete data	When data can only take certain individual values it is called **discrete**.
Example	Shoe size is an example of discrete data. The values can only be 1, $1\frac{1}{2}$, 2, $2\frac{1}{2}$, etc. There are no shoe sizes between these.

Exercise 4:1

▼ You need worksheet 4 : 2, **Final medals table**. It shows the number of medals that each country won in the 1996 Olympic Games.

In this exercise you need to use the worksheet to find the information needed for each question.

1 Look at the gold medals that each country won.
  a Copy this tally-table. Fill it in.

Number of gold medals	Tally	Number of countries
0–9		
10–19		
20–29		
30–39		
40–49		

  b Copy these axes on to graph paper.

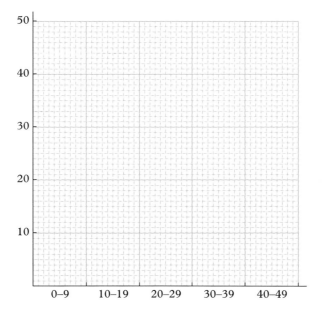

  c Draw a bar-chart to show this information.
    Remember not to leave gaps between the bars for grouped data.

2 Look again at the number of gold medals.
  a Copy this tally-table. Fill it in.

Number of gold medals	Tally	Number of countries
0–4		
5–9		
10–14		
15–19		
20–24		
25–29		
30–34		
35–39		
40–44		

b Draw a bar-chart to show this information.
● **c** You have now drawn two bar-charts showing the gold medal information.
Which one shows the data more clearly? Explain your answer.

3 Look at the silver medals that each country won.
  a Copy this tally-table. Fill it in.

Number of silver medals	Tally	Number of countries
0–4		
5–9		
10–14		
15–19		
20–24		
25–29		
30–34		

  b Draw a bar-chart to show this information.

4 Look at the bronze medals that each country won.
  a Choose sensible groups for the data.
    Draw a tally-table to show the information.
  b Draw a bar-chart to show the information.

5 Look at the total number of medals that each country won.
  a Choose sensible groups for the data.
    Draw a tally-table to show the information.
  b Draw a bar-chart to show the information.

Exercise 4:2

▼ You need worksheet 4 : 3, **Decathlon – final summary**.
It shows the number of points that the top 30 competitors scored in the decathlon final of the 1996 Olympic Games.
A competitor gets a points score for each of the 10 events in the decathlon. The gold medal winner in 1996 scored 8824 points.

In this exercise you need to use the worksheet to find the information needed for each question.

1 Look at the points scored for the 100 m.
  a What is the highest score?
  b What is the lowest score?
  c Choose sensible groups for the data.
     Draw a tally-table to show the information.
  d Draw a bar-chart to show the information.

2 Look at the points scored for the 1500 m.
  a What is the highest score?
  b What is the lowest score?
  c Choose sensible groups for the data.
     Draw a tally-table to show the information.
  d Draw a bar-chart to show the information.

3 Look at the two bar-charts that you have drawn.
   Which event do you think that the competitors find harder?
   Explain your answer.

4 Look at the points scored for the discus.
  a Choose sensible groups for the data.
     Draw a tally-table to show the information.
  b Draw a bar-chart to show the information.

5 Look at the points scored for the javelin.
  a Choose sensible groups for the data.
     Draw a tally-table to show the information.
  b Draw a bar-chart to show the information.

6 Look at the bar-charts you have drawn for the last two questions.
   Which of these two events do you think that the competitors find harder?
   Explain your answer.

7 Look at the total points scored.
  a Choose sensible groups for the data.
     Draw a tally-table to show the information.
  b Draw a bar-chart to show the information.

Now you are going to look at continuous data.

Continuous data	Data is **continuous** when it can take *any* value in a certain range.
Examples	The lengths of earthworms, the heights of pupils in Year 9, and the weights of hamsters are all examples of continuous data.

Exercise 4:3

W You need worksheet 4 : 4, **Swimming: men's and women's 400 m freestyle**.
It shows the times of the competitors in the preliminary rounds of the 1996 Olympic 400 m freestyle for men and women.
Danyon Loader won his final in 3 minutes 47.97 seconds.
Michelle Smith won her final in 4 minutes 7.25 seconds.
These times are both faster than any of the times in the preliminary rounds.

1 Look at the times in the men's preliminary rounds.
   a Copy this tally-table. Fill it in.

Time	Tally	Number of competitors
3 m 40 s but less than 3 m 50 s		
3 m 50 s but less than 4 m 00 s		
4 m 00 s but less than 4 m 10 s		
4 m 10 s but less than 4 m 20 s		
4 m 20 s but less than 4 m 30 s		
4 m 30 s but less than 4 m 40 s		
4 m 40 s but less than 4 m 50 s		

   b Draw a bar-chart to show this information.

2 Look at the times in the women's preliminary rounds.
   a Draw a tally-table for this information.
      Use the same groups as for the men.
   b Draw a bar-chart to show this information.

● **3** Look at your two bar-charts.
      Describe the differences between the two bar-charts.

2 Averages and range

A famous politician once said, 'We want everyone to be better than average'.

Why is this impossible?

There are 3 different types of average. One type of average is the **mean**.

Mean

To find the **mean** of a set of data:
(1) Find the total of all the data values.
(2) Divide by the number of data values.

Example

Here are the weights of 6 sprinters in kilograms:

88   90   79   94   86   91

Find their mean weight.

The total is:

$$88 + 90 + 79 + 94 + 86 + 91 = 528 \, \text{kg}$$

The mean is $528 \div 6 = 88 \, \text{kg}$

Exercise 4:4

1 These are the weights and heights of 5 sprinters.

Weight (kg)	85	91	74	68	82
Height (cm)	170	190	185	178	188

Find:
a the mean height of the sprinters,
b the mean weight of the sprinters.

2 These are the weights and heights of 5 weightlifters.

Weight (kg)	104	108	112	107	104
Height (cm)	168	188	187	175	182

a Find:
  (1) the mean weight of the weightlifters,
  (2) the mean height of the weightlifters.
b Do you think that the weightlifters would make good sprinters? Explain your answer.

3 This table shows the medals won at the Olympic Games by the USA.

Year	Gold	Silver	Bronze	Total
1996	44	32	25	101
1992	37	33	37	107
1988	35	31	27	93

Use this information to find:
a the mean number of gold medals that the USA has won in the last 3 Olympics,
b the mean of the total number of medals that the USA has won in the last 3 Olympics.
  Give your answers correct to 1 dp.

· ·

Another type of average is the **mode**.
It is easy to find.
It is often used when the average has to be a whole number.

Mode	The **mode** is the most common or most popular data value. This is sometimes called the **modal value**. The mode does not have to be a number. For example it could be the most common type of medal.

Example

These are the winning distances in the men's javelin for the Olympics from 1968 to 1992. They are given to the nearest metre. Find the modal distance.

90 **90** 95 91 89 84 **90**

There have been more **90** m winning throws than anything else. The mode is **90** m.

Exercise 4:5

1 These are the silver medal and bronze medal throws in the same seven men's Olympic javelin competitions. They are rounded to the nearest metre.

Silver	89	90	88	90	86	84	87
Bronze	87	84	87	87	84	83	83

a What is the mode of the silver distances?
b What is the mode of the bronze distances?

2 The distances in the men's javelin in the 1996 Olympics were:

Gold:	88 m
Silver:	87 m
Bronze:	87 m

a If you include these distances, which mode changes?
b What would you do about this problem?

3 Here are the results for the women's javelin for the same years. They have been rounded to the nearest metre.

Year	Gold	Silver	Bronze
1968	60	60	58
1972	64	63	60
1976	66	65	64
1980	68	68	67
1984	70	69	67
1988	75	70	67
1992	68	68	67

a Write down the modal distance for each medal.

b The women's results for 1996 were:

Gold: 68 m
Silver: 66 m
Bronze: 65 m

Do these results change any of the modes?

4 These pie-charts show the medals won by the UK and Poland in the 1996 Olympics. You can't see how *many* medals they won.

UK

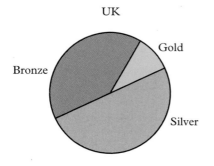

Poland

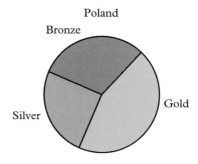

a What is the modal type of medal for the UK?
b What is the modal type of medal for Poland?
c Explain how you found the answer.

• •

Sometimes the mode is not a useful average to find. The most common data value could be the smallest or the biggest number. It is often more useful to have a middle value.
This is the third type of average. It is called the **median**.

Median

To find the **median,** put all the data values in order of size. The **median** is then the middle value.

Example

These are the numbers of medals won by Japan at the Olympics from 1972–1996:

29   25   0   32   14   22   14

Find the median number of medals that Japan has won.
Write the numbers in order. Start with the smallest.

0   14   14   (22)   25   29   32

Find the middle number. It is **22**.
The median number of medals is **22**.

Exercise 4:6

1 Here are the number of Olympic medals won by Italy from 1972–1996.

18   13   15   32   14   19   34

Find the median number of medals won by Italy.

Europe
Italy
Africa
Kenya

2 Here are the number of Olympic medals won by Kenya from 1972–1996.

9   0   0   3   9   8   8

Find the median number of medals won by Kenya.

3 Here are the number of Olympic medals won by Australia from 1972–1996.

17   5   9   24   14   27   40

a Find the median number of medals won by Australia.
b Find the mean number of medals that they have won.
c Explain why you can't find the mode.

If you have an even number of data values then there will not be one exactly in the middle.
When this happens you should find the mean of the middle two numbers.

Example

These are the winning distances in the men's javelin for the past few Olympics. They are given to the nearest metre. Find the median distance.

95   91   89   84   90   88

Write the numbers in order.

84   88 | 89   90 | 91   95

Find the middle two numbers: 89   90

Find the mean: $\dfrac{89 + 90}{2} = 89.5$

The median distance is 89.5 m.

---

4 These are the winning distances in the men's discus for the past few Olympics. They are given to the nearest metre.

   61   65   64   68   67   67   69   65

   a Write these numbers in order. Start with the smallest.
   b Find the median distance.

5 These are the silver medal distances in the men's discus for the past few Olympics. They are given to the nearest metre.

   61   63   64   66   66   66   67   65

Find the median distance.

6 These are the winning times in the women's 100 m for the past few Olympics. They are given to the nearest tenth of a second.

   11.4   11.0   11.1   11.1   11.1   11.0   10.5   10.8

Find the median time.

7 These are the silver medal times in the women's 100 m for the past few Olympics. They are given to the nearest tenth of a second.

   11.6   11.1   11.2   11.1   11.1   11.1   10.8   10.8

Find the median time.

. . . .

The range

Cars travel a total of 270 000 million kilometres in the UK every year. The average for the UK, France, Germany and Spain is 255 000 million km.

This average does not tell the whole story. There is a big difference between the countries.

Germany's total is the biggest at 376 000 million. Spain's total is the smallest, at only 70 000 million.

The difference of 306 000 million km is called the **range** of the data.

Range	The **range** of a set of data is the biggest value take away the smallest value.

Exercise 4:7

1 These are the average ages that people live to in different countries.
This is called 'life expectancy'.

Country	Life expectancy	
	Men	Women
UK	72	78
Angola	43	46
Brazil	62	68
Kenya	57	61
Iceland	75	80
Turkey	63	66

a Work out the range for men.
b Work out the range for women.

2 Look at this data. It is about 10 pupils in Year 11.
The data was taken when they were in Year 7, Year 9 and Year 11.
The heights are to the nearest centimetre.

Pupil	Sex	Y7 height	Y7 shoe size	Y9 height	Y9 shoe size	Y11 height	Y11 shoe size
1	F	145	2	154	3	160	4
2	F	153	3	160	5	167	5
3	F	137	1	147	3	154	4
4	F	141	2	156	4	165	6
5	F	149	2	160	3	170	4
6	M	131	3	157	5	165	7
7	M	151	5	159	7	175	9
8	M	141	3	155	5	171	8
9	M	150	4	165	5	180	10
10	M	129	3	135	4	155	7

a Find the range of the boys' heights in Year 7.
b Find the mean of the boys' heights in Year 7.
c Find the range of the boys' shoe sizes in Year 7.
d Find the mode of the boys' shoe sizes in Year 7.

3 **a** Find the range of the boys' heights in Year 9.
    b Find the mean of the boys' heights in Year 9.
    c Find the range of the boys' shoe sizes in Year 9.
    d Find the mode of the boys' shoe sizes in Year 9.

4 Do the same calculations for the girls.

5 **a** Which sex had the larger modal shoe size?
    b Which sex had the larger mean height?
    c Which sex had the larger range of heights?
    d Compare your answers for Year 9 with Year 7.
       Write down what you notice.

6 Do some calculations to see how the averages and ranges have changed by Year 11.
Use the questions in this exercise to help you.

◀◀REPLAY▶

Sometimes data is given in a table.

Class 9T counted the number of Smarties found in 100 tubes chosen at random.
Many tubes contained the same number of Smarties.
They put their data in a table.

Number of Smarties in a tube	Number of tubes	
34	13 ◀———	This row shows that 13 of the
35	24	tubes had 34 Smarties in them.
36	27	This is a total of
37	22	$13 \times 34 = 442$ Smarties
38	14	

To work out the total number of Smarties they need to find the total for each row. They add another column to the table so it looks like this:

Number of Smarties in a tube	Number of tubes	Number of Smarties
34	13	13 × 34 = 442
35	24	24 × 35 = 840
36	27	27 × 36 = 972
37	22	22 × 37 = 814
38	14	14 × 38 = 532
		Total = 3600

Mean number of Smarties $= \frac{3600}{100} = 36$

The modal number of Smarties in a tube is 36. This is because there are more tubes with 36 Smarties than any other number.

Exercise 4:8

1 Another 100 tubes of Smarties are chosen at random. The number of Smarties in each tube is shown in the table.

Number of Smarties in a tube	Number of tubes
34	12
35	24
36	31
37	18
38	15

a Copy this table. Fill it in.

Number of Smarties in a tube	Number of tubes	Number of Smarties
34	12	12 × 34 =
35	24	24 × 35 =
36	31	... × ... =
37	18	... × ... =
38	15	... × ... =
		Total =

b Work out the mean number of Smarties.
c Write down the modal number of Smarties.

2 Ramesh has bought 50 CDs. This is how much they cost.

Cost (£)	Number of CDs
11.99	8
12.49	12
12.99	17
13.49	7
13.99	6

a Find the mean cost of a CD.
b Write down the modal cost of a CD.

3 The number of matches in 60 boxes is shown in the table.

Number of matches	Number of boxes
46	14
47	15
48	22
49	6
50	3

The makers claim that the average contents is 48. Is this a fair claim?
Explain your answer.

Mean, mode, median and range for grouped data

It is not easy to work out averages for grouped data. Here are the boys'
results in a Year 9 maths test. The results have been grouped in tens.

Mark	31 to 40	41 to 50	51 to 60	61 to 70	71 to 80	81 to 90	91 to 100
Number of boys	5	14	28	35	24	16	8

Look at the first column.
You can see that these boys scored between 31 and 40 but you do not know
exactly what each of them scored.
To work out an **estimate** for the mean, you have to assume that all
5 of them scored the mark in the middle of the group.

This middle value is $\dfrac{31 + 40}{2} = 35.5$

In the same way you have to assume that the 14 people in the second column all scored the middle of that group which is $\dfrac{41 + 50}{2} = 45.5$

You can work out all the mid-points. You can do a new table which looks like this:

Mark (mid-point)	35.5	45.5	55.5	65.5	75.5	85.5	95.5
Number of boys	5	14	28	35	24	16	8

Now you can work out the mean as if these were the scores that everybody got.

$$\text{Mean} = \frac{35.5 \times 5 + 45.5 \times 14 + 55.5 \times 28 + 65.5 \times 35 + 75.5 \times 24 + 85.5 \times 16 + 95.5 \times 8}{130}$$

$$= \frac{8605}{130}$$

$$= 66.2 \ (1 \ \text{dp})$$

This is only an **estimate** for the mean.

You have assumed that all the people in each group have scored the middle mark in each group. This may not be true, so your mean may well be wrong!

When data is grouped you cannot tell which data value is the most common. You cannot find the mode. You can only say which group has the most values in it. This group is called the **modal group**. For the boys' test marks the modal group is 61 to 70 marks.

You cannot find the median either! You cannot write out the values in order so you can find the middle one. You can estimate the median value and you will see this done next year.

You can only estimate the range too!

An **estimate** for the range is the *biggest possible* value take away the *smallest possible* value.

For the boys' marks the biggest possible value is 100 and the smallest is 31.
An estimate for the range is 69 marks.

Exercise 4:9

1 Here are the Year 9 girls' scores in the same maths test.

Mark	31 to 40	41 to 50	51 to 60	61 to 70	71 to 80	81 to 90	91 to 100
Number of girls	4	17	23	26	21	19	10

a Copy this table. Fill in the mid-points for each group of marks.

Mark (mid-point)	35.5						
Number of girls	4	17	23	26	21	19	10

b Work out an estimate for the mean. Give your answer to 1 dp.
c Write down the modal group for the girls' marks.
d Write down an estimate for the range of the marks.

2 Eve asked all the people in her class how much money they get each week. Here are her results:

Amount	0 p–99 p	£1–£1.99	£2–£2.99	£3–£3.99	£4–£4.99
Number of people	3	7	9	7	4

a Copy this table. Fill in the mid-points for each group.

Amount (mid-point)					
Number of people	3	7	9	7	4

b Work out an estimate for the mean.
   Give your answer to the nearest penny.
c Write down the modal group for the amount of money received.
d Write down an estimate for the range of the amount of money received.

1 Joanna can catch either of two buses to get home.
This is how long she had to wait on the last 5 times that she used Bus 1.

   10 mins   14 mins   13 mins   12 mins   11 mins

This is how long she had to wait on the last 5 times that she used Bus 2.

   10 mins   8 mins   17 mins   9 mins   16 mins

a Work out the mean of the waiting time for each bus.
b Work out the range of the waiting time for each bus.
c Which bus do you think that Joanna should catch?
Explain your answer using the mean and the range of the waiting times.

2 Asha is doing a survey of how much people earn in a week.
She has drawn this bar-chart to show her results:

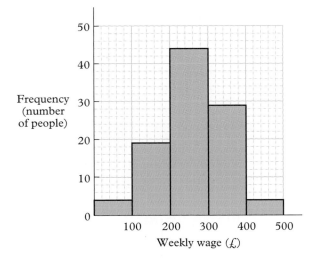

a Copy this table. Fill it in.

Mid-point	Frequency	Mid-point × Frequency
50	4	
150	19	
Total =	Total =	

b Work out an estimate for the mean weekly wage.
c Write down the modal group.
d Write down an estimate of the range of the weekly wages.

1 The graph shows the number of hours that men and women in the UK worked in 1990.

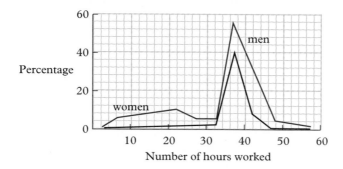

a Write down one thing that is similar about the pattern in the number of hours worked by men and women.
b Write down one thing that is different about the pattern in the number of hours worked by men and women.

2 There are 29 pupils in 9X. Jason is away when there is a test.
The mean test score for the other 28 pupils is 76.5
Jason takes the test late and gets 86.
What is the new mean score for 9X?

3 Ellen measures the weight of crisps in 30 bags. The bags were marked 'Average contents 25 g'. She used a very accurate electronic balance.
Here are her results.

24.498	24.531	25.014	25.367	24.487
25.571	25.274	24.985	24.361	25.184
25.367	25.148	25.178	24.257	24.568
24.759	24.589	26.010	25.451	24.856
24.968	25.374	25.984	26.357	24.168
26.254	23.987	24.591	24.367	25.684

a Choose sensible groups for this data.
Draw a tally-table for these groups. Fill it in.
b Draw a diagram of your results.
c Write down the modal group for the weight of crisps.
How can you see the modal group from your diagram?
d Work out an estimate for the mean from the groups that you have just made up.
e Work out the mean from the original data.
f How accurate is the estimate for the mean?
g Is the average contents claim correct?

- **Mean** To find the **mean** of a set of data:
  (1) Find the total of all the data values.
  (2) Divide by the number of data values.

- **Mode** The **mode** is the most common or most popular data value.
  This is sometimes called the **modal value**.
  The mode does not have to be a number.
  For example it could be the most common type of medal.

- **Median** To find the **median** put all the data values in order of size.
  The **median** is then the middle value.
  If you have an even number of data values then there will not be
  one exactly in the middle. To find the median when this happens,
  you should work out the mean of the middle two numbers.

- **Range** The **range** of a set of data is the biggest value take away the
  smallest value.

- **Grouped data** It is not easy to work out averages for grouped data.

  To work out an estimate for the **mean**, use the middle of the
  group and then work out the mean as if this was the value that
  everybody got.

Example Here are the results in a Year 9 maths test.

Mark	31–40	41–50	51–60	61–70	71–80	81–90	91–100
Mark (mid-point)	35.5	45.5	55.5	65.5	75.5	85.5	95.5
Number of boys	5	14	28	35	24	16	8

$$\text{Mean} = \frac{35.5 \times 5 + 45.5 \times 14 + 55.5 \times 28 + 65.5 \times 35 + 75.5 \times 24 + 85.5 \times 16 + 95.5 \times 8}{130}$$

$$= \frac{8605}{130} \quad = 66.2 \ (1 \ dp)$$

This is only an **estimate** for the mean.
You cannot find the **mode**. You can only say which group has the most values
in it.
This group is called the **modal group**.
An estimate for the **range** is the *biggest possible* value take away the *smallest
possible* value.

1 These are the amounts of money that 12 friends spend when they go to the cinema.

£3.20   £2.40   £3.50   £2.40   £2.40   £3.40
£3.70   £2.40   £2.80   £2.60   £2.40   £2.90

a Work out the mean amount of money to the nearest penny.
b Work out the median amount of money.
c Write down the modal amount of money.
d Work out the range of the amount of money.

2 The data shows the amount of rain in millimetres that fell on each day in November.

3.5   16.4   6.4   3.7   14.2   8.9
22.9   2.9   7.8   18.9   0.1   2.6
9.4   14.2   4.5   11.6   15.9   6.1
13.7   13.9   3.1   2.5   5.6   1.4
6.9   4.1   17.9   19.2   10.7   7.2

a Copy this tally-table. Fill it in.

Amount of rain (mm)	Tally	Number of days
0–5		
5–10		
10–15		
15–20		
20–25		

b Draw a bar-chart to show this information.
Don't leave gaps between the bars.
This graph shows the rainfall in April.

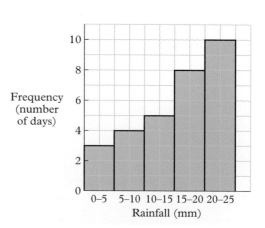

c How many days are there in the month shown on this graph?
d Look at the bar-chart you have drawn and the one given in this question. Which one shows the wetter month? Explain how you can tell.
e Work out an estimate of the mean amount of rain in each month. You need to write down the mid-points of the groups first.

5 Accuracy

The number 10^{100} is called a googol. This is 1 with one hundred zeros.

10^{100} = 10 000 000 000 000 000 000 000 000 000 000 000 000 000 000 000 000 000 000 000 000 000 000 000 000 000 000 000 000 000 000 000 000 000 000 000 000

The number 10^{googol} or $10^{10^{100}}$ is called a googolplex.

This is 1 with a googol zeros.

It takes Kerry $\frac{1}{4}$ second to write a zero and $\frac{1}{5}$ second to write the 1.

How many years would it take her to write a googolplex?

CORE

1 Rounding

Sarah has measured how long it takes for 60 swings of the pendulum.
She has worked out the time for one swing of the pendulum.
This is her answer:

Time for one swing = 1.036 251 seconds

This is not a sensible answer. She cannot measure this time accurately.
She needs to round off her answer.

◄◄REPLAY►

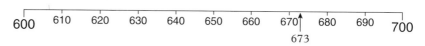

673 is nearer to 670 than to 680. It is 670 to the nearest ten.
673 is nearer to 700 than to 600. It is 700 to the nearest hundred.

8.39 is closer to 8.4 than to 8.3. It is rounded to 8.4 to 1 decimal place.

You can use this **rule of rounding**.
Look at the first 'unwanted' digit.
If it is 5, 6, 7, 8 or 9, add one to the last digit that you want to keep.
If the first 'unwanted' digit is 0, 1, 2, 3 or 4, you do not add one.

Examples   2.4761 correct to 1 dp is 2.5   4.0275 correct to 3 dp is 4.028

Exercise 5:1

1 Round these numbers correct to the nearest whole number.
    a 7.1   **b** 4.8   **c** 14.45   **d** 367.6   **e** 2.09

2 Round these numbers correct to the nearest ten.
    a 58   **b** 25   **c** 294   **d** 199   **e** 431

3 Round these numbers correct to the nearest hundred.
    a 361   **b** 209   **c** 3829   **d** 4780   **e** 999

4 Round these numbers correct to 1 dp.
    a 4.682   **b** 10.147   **c** 21.846   **d** 2.053   **e** 47.98

5 Round these numbers correct to 2 dp.
    a 73.592   **b** 4.3554   **c** 18.339   **d** 0.308   **e** 7.899

6 Round these numbers correct to 3 dp.
    a 5.6682   **b** 37.0745   **c** 0.8591   **d** 0.3499   **e** 0.9995

Sally is 153 cm tall correct to the nearest centimetre.

153 cm = 1.53 m
1.53 m is correct to the nearest centimetre.

Sally is 1.53 m tall correct to the nearest centimetre.

You can give a length in metres correct to 2 dp.
The length is then correct to the nearest centimetre.

Example Give these lengths correct to the nearest centimetre:
    a 347.9 cm   **b** 1.426 m

    a 347.9 cm correct to the nearest centimetre is 348 cm.
    b 1.426 m correct to the nearest centimetre is 1.43 m.

7 Give each of these lengths correct to the nearest centimetre.
    a 8.3 cm   **c** 4.132 m   **e** 0.318 m   **g** 0.167 m   **i** 13.205 m
    b 127.9 cm   **d** 11.037 m   **f** 9.214 m   **h** 12.325 m   **j** 5.009 m

This rock weighs 1235 g correct
to the nearest gram.
1235 g = 1.235 kg

The rock weighs 1.235 kg correct
to the nearest gram.

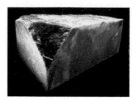

You can give a weight in kilograms correct to 3 dp.
The weight is then correct to the nearest gram.

Example   Give these weights correct to the nearest gram.
    a 41.2 g   **b** 0.8047 kg

    a 41.2 g correct to the nearest gram is 41 g.
    b 0.8047 kg correct to the nearest gram is 0.805 kg.

---

8   Give these weights correct to the nearest gram.
    a 56.8 g   **c** 7.2031 kg   **e** 3.5024 kg   **g** 0.0259 kg
    b 129.4 g   **d** 1.2578 kg   **f** 0.3219 kg   **h** 2.1798 kg

---

Significant figure

In any number the first **significant figure** is the first digit which is not a 0
For most numbers this is the first digit.

The first significant figure is the red digit:
   37.8   650   7.961   0.0538   0.002 004

Rounding to 1 significant figure (1 sf)

To **round to 1 significant figure (1 sf)**:
a Look at the first digit after the first significant one.
b Use the normal rules of rounding.
c Be careful to keep the number about the right size.

Examples   64.9 to 1 sf is **60**   It is *not* 6!   5.06 to 1 sf is 5
              284 to 1 sf is **300**   0.0381 to 1 sf is 0.04

Exercise 5:2

1   Round these numbers correct to 1 sf.
    a 7.25   **c** 264   **e** 508.2   **g** 37 821
    b 48   **d** 95   **f** 999   **h** 460 097

2   Round these numbers correct to 1 sf.
    a 0.084   **b** 0.0035   **c** 0.070 94   **d** 0.005 55

It is easy to hit the wrong key when using a calculator.
It is a good idea to check that your answer is about right.

Estimate

To get an **estimate** we round each number to one significant figure.

Example

Work out 362×24

Use a calculator to get $362 \times 24 = 8688$
Estimate: $362 \times 24 \approx 400 \times 20 = 8000$
8000 is near to 8688 so the answer is probably right.

Exercise 5:3

Work these out.
Check each answer by doing an estimate.

1 **a** 74×31 **c** 866×62 **e** 6.9×3.4 **g** 2.3×9.8
    b $544 - 206$ **d** $832 + 365$ **f** 3.06×7.5 **h** 4.24×6.29

Example

Work out $30.45 \div 8.7$

Use a calculator to get $30.45 \div 8.7 = 3.5$
Estimate: $30.45 \div 8.7 \approx 30 \div 9$

9 goes into 27 three times so $30 \div 9 \approx 3$

3 is near to 3.5 so the answer is probably right.

Work these out.
Check each answer by doing an estimate.

2 **a** $21.28 \div 2.8$ **c** $94.38 \div 3.9$ **e** $129.6 \div 2.7$ **g** $377.3 \div 4.9$
    b $30.94 \div 9.1$ **d** $43.07 \div 7.3$ **f** $431.6 \div 8.3$ **h** $495.6 \div 1.4$

3 Each of these rolls of wallpaper costs £6.75
How much will 9 rolls cost?

4 A machinist makes 87 pockets every hour. He worked 38 hours during one week. How many pockets did he make?

5 Sian goes shopping at the supermarket.
This list shows what she bought.
How much did she have to pay?

| loaf | 67p | jam | 52p |
| butter | 89p | apples | 53p |

6 The crowd at a football match was 27 645.
There were 3594 less at the previous game.
What was the attendance at the previous game?

7 The table shows the number of people visiting a candle factory.

Week one	361
Week two	279
Week three	198
Week four	340
Week five	512

a What was the total number of visitors during the 5 week period?
b What was the mean number of visitors per week?

8 The number of pupils that went on a school trip was 1274.
Each coach carried 49 pupils. How many coaches were used?

Rounding to any number of significant figures	To **round to any number of significant figures**: **a** Look at the first unwanted digit. **b** Use the normal rule of rounding. **c** Be careful to keep the number about the right size.

A zero is only significant when it appears to the **right** of the first significant figure.

Examples   253.7 to 2 sf is 250. It is *not* 25!   52 780 to 3 sf is 52 800
6739 to 3 sf is 6740   0.036 28 to 2 sf is 0.036

0.008 047 1 to 3 sf is 0.008 05   Here the 0 after the 8 is significant.

Exercise 5:4

1 Round these calculator displays correct to 2 sf.

a 23.444444   **c** 90.666667   **e** 0.40752

b 1657.3917   **d** 12089   **f** 8.05737

2 Round these calculator displays correct to 4 sf.

a 12.333333   **c** 0.32475   **e** 31.423704

b 7.1090909   **d** 0.0181818   **f** 99.999999

Do these calculations on a calculator.
Round the answers correct to 3 sf.

3 7.34×3.18 **8** $34 \div 7$ **13** $\sqrt{8}$

4 11.9×0.213 **9** $25 \div 9$ **14** $\sqrt{14}$

5 0.913×0.648 **10** $0.58 \div 6$ **15** $\sqrt{35}$

6 314.5×670 **11** $0.09 \div 11$ **16** $\sqrt{0.06}$

7 0.2009×0.405 **12** $7.3 \div 1.2$ **17** $\sqrt{0.17}$

18 Round these numbers.
   a 5.067 to 2 sf   **d** 23.56 to 1 sf   **g** 108.4 to 1 sf
   b 863.4 to 3 sf   **e** 20 785 to 3 sf   **h** 4555 to 2 sf
   c 2.0472 to 2 sf   **f** 0.059 82 to 2 sf   **i** 0.404 040 to 4 sf

• 19 Write down how many significant figures there are in each of these
   numbers.
   a 34.5   **d** 304   **g** 1100   **j** 0.08   **m** 0.003
   b 17   **e** 75   **h** 0.24   **k** 0.901   **n** 0.4005
   c 3.152   **f** 270   **i** 0.319   **l** 0.0404   **o** 4.0

Sensible rounding

Exercise 5:5

1 Look at this question $\dfrac{600.1 \times 565.1}{42}$

   a Round each number in the question to 1 sf.

   b Use this to estimate the answer to the question.

   c Work out the answer to the question using your calculator.
Give your answer to the nearest whole number.

   d Work out the error in your estimate.
Do you think your estimate is good?

When you are estimating the answer to a question that involves a fraction there is often a way of getting a much better estimate than by rounding to 1 sf.

Example   Estimate the answer to $\dfrac{65.9 \times 56.1}{42}$

If you do this question by rounding each number to 1 sf you get

$$\frac{65.9 \times 56.1}{42} \approx \frac{70 \times 60}{40} = \frac{4200}{40} = 105$$

The actual answer is 88.0 to 3 sf.

105 may not seem too far from 88 but you can get much closer!

Start by rounding all of the numbers to the nearest whole number.

$$\frac{65.9 \times 56.1}{42} \approx \frac{66 \times 56}{42}$$

Now you need to be clever and see that you can split the 42 in the denominator into 6×7 and cancel the fraction like this:

$$\frac{66 \times 56}{42} = \frac{66 \times 56}{6 \times 7} = \frac{66}{6} \times \frac{56}{7} = 11 \times 8 = 88$$

This gives an excellent approximation!

For questions **2** to **7**:

a Estimate the answer by splitting the denominator so the fraction cancels.

b Work out the exact answer using your calculator. Give your calculator answer to 3 significant figures.

2 $\dfrac{24.8 \times 41.8}{35}$

4 $\dfrac{21.8 \times 41.9}{12}$

6 $\dfrac{14.8 \times 4.8}{25}$

3 $\dfrac{16.3 \times 35.8}{24}$

5 $\dfrac{35.8 \times 56.1}{48}$

7 $\dfrac{19.8 \times 63.8}{40}$

To use this method you have to try to cancel parts of the fraction. This won't always happen like in the questions you have seen. You may have to round the numbers in the numerator so that the fraction will cancel.

Example   Estimate the answer to $\dfrac{78 \times 41}{6.9 \times 8.4}$

The numbers in the denominator round to 7×8 so round the numbers in the numerator to multiples of 7 and 8.

$$\frac{78 \times 41}{6.9 \times 8.4} \approx \frac{77 \times 40}{7 \times 8} = 11 \times 5 = 55$$

The exact answer is 55.2 (3 sf) so this method gives a really good estimate.

For questions **8** to **16**:

a Estimate the answer by rounding so that the fraction will cancel.

b Work out the exact answer using your calculator. Give your calculator answer to 3 significant figures.

8 $\dfrac{15.8 \times 40}{35}$

11 $\dfrac{36.2 \times 38.9}{4.7 \times 8.1}$

14 $\dfrac{46.7 \times 50.1}{7.89 \times 3.15}$

9 $\dfrac{12.7 \times 102.5}{30}$

12 $\dfrac{18.1 \times 33.4}{2.66 \times 6.89}$

15 $\dfrac{26.7 \times 50.4}{3.19 \times 12.1}$

10 $\dfrac{32.1 \times 17}{45}$

13 $\dfrac{39.1 \times 43.4}{5.3 \times 6.8}$

16 $\dfrac{86.7 \times 26.1}{12.89 \times 7.15}$

2 Multiplying and dividing by numbers less than 1

Saleem takes tablets for his hay fever.
The dose is half a tablet each day.
Saleem has five tablets.
How many days will they last?

Saleem needs to work out how many halves there are in 5.
The sum he has to do is $5 \div \frac{1}{2}$

The tablets will last 10 days.

Exercise 5:6

When you have to explain an answer, an example or a diagram often helps to show what you mean.

1 Den and Sally are doing this question:
$3 \div \frac{1}{2} = ?$
Den said that the answer was $1\frac{1}{2}$
Sally drew this diagram to help her find the answer.

Sally said there are 6 halves in 3 so the answer is 6.
a Which is the right answer?
b Can you see where the wrong answer came from?

2 Rob and Ceri are doing this question.
$10 \div 0.5 = ?$
Rob says that the answer is 2 as numbers always get smaller when they are divided.
Ceri says that the answer is 20 as 0.5 is the same as a half and there are 20 halves in 10 whole ones.
a Which is the right answer?
b Can you see where the wrong answer came from?

3 $8 \times \frac{1}{2} = ?$
Les drew this diagram
to find the answer.

Les says the answer is 4.
Sonya says Les must be wrong as numbers always get bigger when
they are multiplied.
a Who is right?
b Why is the other person wrong?

4 Jen and Nathan are doing this question.
$12 \times 0.2 = ?$
Jen says the answer must be 24 because $12 \times 2 = 24$ and numbers
always get bigger when they are multiplied.
Nathan says that the answer is 2.4 because 0.2 is less than 1 so the
answer should be less than 12.
a Who is right?   **b** Why is the other person wrong?

In questions **5–11** decide on the correct answer without using a
calculator.

5 $16 \div \frac{1}{2} = ?$
A 8   **B** 20   **C** 32   **D** 80

6 $14 \times 0.1 = ?$
A 14   **B** 140   **C** 1.4   **D** 0.14

7 $0.2 \times 6 = ?$
A 12   **B** 1.2   **C** 3   **D** 0.3

8 $15 \div 0.3 = ?$
A 5   **B** 0.5   **C** 50   **D** 1.5

9 $4 \div 0.5 = ?$
A 2   **B** 20   **C** 8   **D** 0.8

10 $(0.5)^2 = ?$
A 25   **B** 2.5   **C** 0.10   **D** 0.25

11 $0.6 \div 0.3 = ?$
A 0.2   **B** 2   **C** 20   **D** 1.8

Check your answers using a calculator.

Game: Four in a line

This is a game for 2 players.
You need two colours of counters. Each player uses a different colour.

Player 1   Pick one whole number, × or ÷ and one fraction or decimal.
Example   2 × **0.3**   Answer: 0.6
Work out your choice of question **without** your calculator.

Player 2   Do the same question **without** a calculator as a check.
If you get different answers check using a calculator.

Player 1   Cover up your answer on the board with a counter.
If you get an answer that is not on the board, you cannot
put a counter down.

Player 2   Now have a turn like player 1.

The first player to get four counters in a row in any direction is the winner.

1, 2, 3, 4, 5   **× or ÷**   **0.1, 0.2, 0.3**
6, 7, 8, 9, 10   **0.4, $\frac{1}{2}$**

100	3	2.1	0.7	90	14
18	70	0.5	40	1	60
0.9	0.2	2	12	8	10
1.2	0.8	30	5	0.6	1.5
1.8	4	0.1	50	6	0.3
0.4	16	1.6	20	1.4	80

3   Using a calculator

Kevin and two friends have bought a tent for £129.95
They are sharing the cost equally between them.
Kevin works out the three shares on his calculator like this: 129.95 ÷ 3
Here is the calculator display of the answer:

$$43.31666667$$

Kevin says that he can get the calculator to round the answer to 2 dp.

Using fix mode on a calculator

Example

You can use the **fix mode** to round 43.316 66667 to 2 dp.

Key in: **2nd F**   **FSE**   **2nd F**   **TAB**   **2**
            Fix mode   Number of decimal places

The display now shows 43.32 Answer: £43.32

To change the calculator back to normal key in

2nd F   **FSE**   **2nd F**   **FSE**   **2nd F**   **FSE**

Exercise 5:7

For questions **1–4** round your answers correct to 2 dp.

Set your calculator in fix mode by keying in   **2nd F**   **FSE**   **2nd F**   **TAB**   **2**

1 Work these out:
    a   £34.65 ÷ 4   **b** £21.99 ÷ 7   **c** £3.20 ÷ 6   **d** £123.50 ÷ 16

2 A pack of 8 sausages costs £1.55
    What does one sausage cost?

3 A pack of 12 bread rolls costs £1.06
    What does one roll cost?

4 The school canteen sells 702 lunches. They take £658.45
    What is the mean amount spent on one lunch?

For questions 5–7, set your calculator in fix mode to round to 3 dp
by keying in **2nd F** **FSE** **2nd F** **TAB** **3**

The calculator display should look like this   FIX   DEG
                                              0.000

5 A pack of 8 chicken breasts weighs 1.75 kg.
What is the mean weight of one chicken breast?
Give your answer correct to 3 dp.
This means your answer is correct to the nearest gram.

6 Seven friends share a 1.5 litre bottle of coke.
How much do they each get?
Give your answer correct to the nearest
millilitre.
(This means the answer must be correct
to 3 dp.)

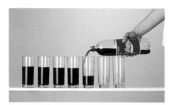

7 Seven identical kitchen cupboards standing side by side measure 3 m.
How wide is one cupboard?
Give your answer correct to the nearest millimetre.

The calculator will round to any number of decimal places using the fix mode.

Press **2nd F** **FSE**

For **one** decimal place key in   **2nd F** **TAB** **1**

For **two** decimal places key in   **2nd F** **TAB** **2**

For **three** decimal places key in   **2nd F** **TAB** **3**

For the nearest whole number key in   **2nd F** **TAB** **0**

---

8 Set your calculator to round to 1 dp.
Round these numbers to 1 dp.
a 35.583   **b** 7.3495   **c** 21.947   **d** 8.091   **e** 50.607

9 Set your calculator to round to 3 dp.
Round these numbers to 3 dp.
a 3.5694   **b** 6.0287   **c** 46.5589   **d** 30.3521   **e** 9.758 53

10 Set your calculator to round to 0 dp.
Round these numbers to the nearest whole number.
a 61.93   **b** 204.488   **c** 19.093   **d** 39.51   **e** 299.99

Remember: To change the calculator back to normal key in

2nd F **FSE** **2nd F** **FSE** **2nd F** **FSE**

Very large numbers on a calculator

Exercise 5:8

1 **a** Copy this number pattern and fill it in.
$$1^2 = 1 \times 1 \qquad = \ldots$$
$$10^2 = 10 \times 10 \qquad = \ldots$$
$$100^2 = 100 \times 100 \qquad = \ldots$$
$$1000^2 = 1000 \times 1000 = \ldots$$
  b Use the number pattern to write down the answer to $1\,000\,000^2$

2 **a** Copy this number pattern and fill it in.
$$4^2 = 4 \times 4 \qquad = \ldots$$
$$40^2 = 40 \times 40 \qquad = \ldots$$
$$400^2 = 400 \times 400 \qquad = \ldots$$
$$4000^2 = 4000 \times 4000 = \ldots$$
  b Use the number pattern to write down the answer to $4\,000\,000^2$

3 Write down the answers to these.
  a 3000^2 **c** 500^2 **e** $700\,000^2$
  b $20\,000^2$ **d** $60\,000^2$ **f** $8\,000\,000^2$

4 **a** Copy this table.
    Fill in the (Number)^2 column using the patterns that you found in questions **1**, **2** and **3**.

Number	(Number)^2	Calculator display
1 000 000 2 000 000 3 000 000		

  b Use a calculator to fill in the last column. Use the $\boxed{x^2}$ key.

    For the first line key in $\boxed{1}\ \boxed{0}\ \boxed{0}\ \boxed{0}\ \boxed{0}\ \boxed{0}\ \boxed{0}\ \boxed{x^2}\ \boxed{=}$

    Leave two more lines in your table for adding extra numbers.
  c Look at columns two and three of your table.
    Explain what you think the calculator display means.

5 **a** Add the numbers $4\,000\,000$ and $5\,000\,000$ to your table.
    Fill in the table.
  b What happens to the calculator display for these two numbers?

The calculator is using a method for writing numbers which are very large.

Standard form   A very large number can be written as **a number between 1 and 10 multiplied by a power of 10**. This is called **standard form**.

4 000 000 000 = 4 multiplied by 10 nine times = 4×10^9
3 600 000   = 3.6 multiplied by 10 six times = $\mathbf{3.6 \times 10^6}$

$\mathbf{1.6 \times 10^8}$ is standard form.
It means 1.6 multiplied by 10 eight times = $1.6 \times 100\,000\,000$
                                          = $160\,000\,000$

16×10^7 is not standard form because 16 is not between 1 and 10.

Example   Write each calculator display as an ordinary number.

  a 8.1^{03} **b** 7.28^{05} **c** 2.06^{08}

  a $8.1 \times 10^3 = 8.1 \times 1000 = 8100$
  b $7.28 \times 10^5 = 7.28 \times 100\,000 = 728\,000$
  c $2.06 \times 10^8 = 2.06 \times 100\,000\,000 = 206\,000\,000$

Exercise 5:9

1 Write each calculator display as an ordinary number.

  a 2.9^{04} **c** 9.0^{07} **e** 8.03^{01}

  b 5.78^{06} **d** 1.57^{05} **f** 9.8374^{03}

2 Write each calculator display as an ordinary number.

  a 2.8^{02} **c** 7.1^{06} **e** 7.37^{01}

  b 1.65^{04} **d** 2.09^{08} **f** 3.425^{05}

3 Which of these numbers are not written in standard form?
  a 3.05×10^2 **c** 0.6×10^5 **e** 9.2×10^3
  b 49×10^6 **d** 495×10^9 **f** 3×10^6

4 These numbers are written in standard form.
Write them as ordinary numbers.

a 2.34×10^4 **c** 5.83×10^8 **e** 7.48×10^9
b 5.7×10^3 **d** 8.215×10^2 **f** 1.0×10^5

Examples   **1** Write these numbers in standard form.

     a 40 000 000   **b** 350 000   **c** 2 830 000

     a 40 000 000 = 4 multiplied by 10 seven times = 4×10^7
     b 350 000 = 3.5 multiplied by 10 five times = 3.5×10^5
     c 2 830 000 = 2.83 multiplied by 10 six times = 2.83×10^6

    2 2.81^{03} on a calculator *must* be written as $\mathbf{2.81 \times 10^3}$

     Never use the calculator display method to write a number in standard form.

---

5 Write these numbers in standard form.

     a 4000   **c** 300   **e** 2 000 000
     b 70 000   **d** 900 000   **f** 500 000 000 000

6 Write these numbers in standard form.

     a 70 000   **c** 378 000 000   **e** 700 000 000
     b 450 000   **d** 560 000 000   **f** 10 000 000 000

7 The average distance from the Sun to Earth is 93 000 000 miles.
Write this number in standard form.

8 This table shows the distances of planets from the Sun in kilometres.

Planet	Distance from the Sun (km)
Earth	1.5×10^8
Jupiter	7.78×10^8
Mars	2.28×10^8
Mercury	5.8×10^7
Pluto	5.92×10^9
Saturn	1.43×10^9
Uranus	2.87×10^9
Venus	1.08×10^8
Neptune	4.5×10^9

     a Write down each distance as an ordinary number.
     b Which planet is closest to the Sun?
        Explain how you can tell this from the standard form.
     c Which planet is furthest from the Sun?

4 Error in measurement

Peter is having some new furniture for his bedroom.
He is measuring the space to see if a new computer desk will fit.
Peter is using a measuring tape marked in centimetres.
He can only measure to the nearest centimetre.
Peter measures the space as 98 cm.

Lower and upper limits

The length of the space for Peter's computer can be any value between 97.5 and 98.5 cm.
This can be shown on a number line.

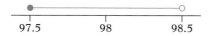

97.5   98   98.5

97.5 is the smallest length that rounds to 98.
97.5 is called the **lower limit**.
98.5 is halfway between 98 and 99.
The length cannot be exactly 98.5 but this is used as the upper limit.
98.5 is called the **upper limit**.

Exercise 5:10

1 This catalogue has three different computer desks for sale.
The widths are correct to the nearest centimetre.

10 "OXFORD" COMPUTER DESK. Black ash effect finish. Complete with pull out shelf and two drawers. Size (W)109, D(48), (H)81 cm. Weight in excess of 20 kg.
Cat. No. 610/8621   £39.99

11 Ⓢ SUPERSTORES ONLY
STUDENT DESK. Mahogany effect finish. Cupboard with lockable door and two drawers. Size (W)127, D(55), (H)75 cm.
Cat. No. 611/4622   £37.99

12 "OXFORD" COMPUTER DESK. Mahogany effect finish. Complete with pull out shelf and two drawers. Size (W)110, D(50), (H)82 cm. Weight in excess of 20 kg.
Cat. No. 610/8528   £39.99

a What is the width of the desk, cat.no.610/8621?
Copy and complete this number
line to show all the possible
real widths.

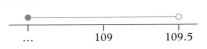

b What is the width of the desk, cat.no.611/4622?
Show all the possible real widths on a number line.

c What is the width of the desk, cat.no.610/8528?
Show all the possible real widths on a number line.

Example

Lisa has measured her pencil.
It is 8.3 cm correct to 1 dp.
What are the upper and lower limits of the length?

The lower limit is 8.25
The upper limit is 8.35

---

2 Lorna has measured her form room. It is 12.3 m long and 6.7 m
wide correct to 1 dp.
a What are the lower and upper limits of the length?
b What are the lower and upper limits of the width?

3 The capacity of a fridge is 5.2 cubic feet correct to 1 dp.
What are the upper and lower limits for the capacity of the fridge?

4 Write down the upper and lower limits for each of these:
a The length of a pencil is 16 cm correct to the nearest centimetre.
b The weight of a box is 23.6 lb correct to 1 dp.
c The weight of a baby is 4.2 kg correct to one tenth of a kilogram.
d A journey took 75 minutes correct to the nearest minute.

5 **a** The length of an envelope is 25 cm to the nearest centimetre.
Show all the possible real lengths using a number line.
b Mary has made a card.
It is 24.5 cm long correct to 1 dp.
Show all the possible real lengths using a number line.
c Can Mary be sure that the card will fit in its envelope?

● **6** The school record for the discus was measured as 33.51 m correct to the nearest centimetre.
What are the upper and lower limits for the throw?

● **7** A scientist weighs a moon rock as 2.452 kg correct to the nearest gram.
What are the upper and lower limits of the weight?

● ●

You can also have lower and upper limits for area and perimeter.

Example The school playground is to be resurfaced and a fence is to be built.

The length and width of the playground have been measured correct to the nearest metre.

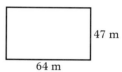

To find the minimum area you take the lowest values for the length and width.
For the **maximum** area you take the highest values.

Minimum area = 63.5 × 46.5   Maximum area = 64.5 × 47.5
          = 2952.75 m²   = 3063.75 m²
The lower limit is 2952.75 m² and the upper limit is 3063.75 m²

Similarly, for the perimeter:
Minimum perimeter = 63.5 + 46.5 + 63.5 + 46.5 = 220 m
Maximum perimeter = 64.5 + 47.5 + 64.5 + 47.5 = 224 m
The lower limit is 220 m and the upper limit is 224 m.

Exercise 5:11

1 The sides of a rectangular field are measured correct to the nearest metre. The length is 329 m and the width is 251 m.
  a Write down the lower and upper limits of the length.
  b Write down the lower and upper limits of the width.
  c Use the lower limits to find the minimum value of the area.
  d Use the upper limits to find the maximum value of the area.
  e Use the lower limits to find the minimum value of the perimeter.
  f Use the upper limits to find the maximum value of the perimeter.

2 The sides of a rectangular skating rink are 96 m and 43 m to the nearest metre.
  a Write down the lower and upper limits of the length and width.
  b Work out the minimum area of the ice rink.
  c Work out the maximum area of the ice rink.

3 Asha uses a metre rule to measure the length of her garden.
  She measures the length as 17 m exactly.
  The metre rule is only accurate to the nearest centimetre.
  a Find the lower and upper limit of the length of the metre rule.
  b Use the lower limit to find the minimum length of the garden.
  c Use the upper limit to find the maximum length of the garden.

4 The length of the side of a square carpet tile is 30.0 cm correct to 1 dp.
  Rudi lays 25 of the tiles in a row.
  Find the lower and upper limits for the length of the 25 tiles.

5 The sides of a box are 6 cm, 8 cm and 10 cm correct to the nearest centimetre.
  a Write down the lower and upper limits of each dimension of the box.
  b Use the lower limits to find the minimum volume of the box.
  c Use the upper limits to find the maximum volume of the box.

6 This rectangular sand pit has dimensions 109 cm by 81 cm by 18 cm. All lengths are correct to the nearest centimetre.
  a Find the lower and upper limits of the area of the sand pit.
  b Find the lower and upper limits of the volume of the sand pit.

7 Greg is fitting kitchen units.
  Each unit is 1.68 m long correct to the nearest centimetre.
  He wants to fit 4 of these units into a space 6.73 m long.
  Will the units fit? Explain your answer.

1 The price for printing a motif on to a sweatshirt is:

   up to 5000 mm² £2
   5000 mm² and over £3

This motif is 138 mm by 37 mm.

   a Estimate the area of the motif.
   b Use your estimate to find the cost of printing the motif.
   c Work out the actual area of the motif.
   d Use your answer to **c** to find the actual cost of printing.
   e Explain why the two costs are different.

2 Round these numbers.
   a 2.599 78 to 3 dp   **c** 24.3753 to 3 dp   **e** 3.999 to 2 dp
   b 3.576 to 1 dp   **d** 0.006 to 2 dp   **f** 0.899 95 to 4 dp

3 Give each of these lengths correct to the nearest centimetre.
   a 13.7 cm   **b** 4.232 m   **c** 5.0375 m   **d** 0.807 m

4 Give each of these weights correct to the nearest gram.
   a 90.4 g   **b** 7.1054 kg   **c** 6.3855 kg   **d** 0.5139 kg

5 Round these numbers.
   a 3.582 to 2 sf   **d** 7.386 to 1 sf   **g** 403.8 to 1 sf
   b 48.395 to 3 sf   **e** 95 723 to 3 sf   **h** 8697 to 2 sf
   c 34.354 to 2 sf   **f** 0.005 82 to 2 sf   **i** 0.040 067 1 to 4 sf

6 Work these out. Check each answer with an estimate.
   Give your answers correct to 3 sf when you need to round.
   a 6.7×5.8 **c** $459 - 187$ **e** $914 \div 291$ **g** $724 \div 6.7$
   b $178 + 94$ **d** $366 \div 3.7$ **f** $379 \div 9.8$ **h** 14.8×38

7 Write each calculator display as an ordinary number.

   a 5.7^{04} **c** 9.2^{03} **e** 6.5^{01}

   b 5.482^{06} **d** 3.06^{03} **f** 1.1156^{05}

8 These numbers are written in standard form.
   Write them as ordinary numbers.
   a 8.483×10^3 **c** 4.3981×10^9 **e** 3.375×10^6
   b 3.8×10^4 **d** 7.8×10^5 **f** 7×10^{10}

9   A room is 3.93 m long and 2.89 m wide correct to the nearest centimetre.
Find the lower and upper limits of the area of the room.

10   A section of fencing is 2 m long correct to the nearest centimetre.
What is the maximum length of 6 sections of fencing fixed together?

11   This playground has been measured
to the nearest metre.
  a Write down the lower and upper
limits for the length and width.
  b Calculate the minimum area.
  c Calculate the maximum area.
  d Calculate the minimum perimeter.
  e Calculate the maximum perimeter.

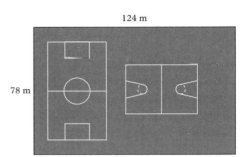

124 m

78 m

12   John is 166 cm tall and his sister Ann is 158 cm tall.
Both heights are correct to the nearest centimetre.
  a Write down the lower and upper limits of John's height.
  b Write down the lower and upper limits of Ann's height.
  c What is the maximum difference in their heights?
  d What is the minimum difference in their heights?

13   A child's temperature rose from 37.7 °C to 38.8 °C.
Both temperatures are correct to 1 dp.
Find the lower and upper limits of the rise in temperature.

14   Rhian and Petra each have a pet stick insect. They both say that
the length of their stick insect is 5 cm to the nearest centimetre.
Does this mean that the insects are the same length?
Explain your answer.

15 $p = 5.2$ cm, $r = 1.9$ cm and $s = 2.0$ cm correct to 1 dp.
Find the largest possible value of:
  a $p + r + s$ **b** $p - r$ **c** $p - s$ **d** $s - r$

16 $p = 5.2$ cm, $r = 1.9$ cm and $s = 2.0$ cm correct to 1 dp.
Find the least possible value of:
  a $p + r + s$ **b** $p - r$ **c** $p - s$ **d** $s - r$

1   Theo and Mandeep are doing this question:

$(0.4)^2 = ?$

Theo says that the answer is 1.6 because 0.4 is a decimal and 1.6 has a decimal as part of it.

Mandeep says that the answer is 0.16 because 0.4 is less than 1 so the answer must be less than 1.

a   Who is right?   **b**   Why is the other person wrong?

2   The diameter of this paddling pool is 183 cm correct to the nearest centimetre.

a   Find the lower and upper limits of the area.

b   The depth of the pool is 38 cm correct to the nearest centimetre.
Find the lower and upper limits of the volume in litres.

3   Pat does 30 mental calculations in 248 seconds to the nearest second. What are the limits of the mean time for Pat to do one calculation?

4   The weights of four rowers are 86.3 kg, 89.2 kg, 85.0 kg and 93.9 kg correct to 1 dp.

a   Find the upper limit of their total weight.

b   Use your answer to **a** to find the maximum value of the mean weight.

c   Find the minimum value of the mean weight.

5   The rainfall for five separate months was 13.5 cm, 15.1 cm, 17.2 cm, 14.0 cm and 13.9 cm correct to 1 dp.

a   Find the minimum total rainfall.

b   Find the minimum mean rainfall.

c   Find the maximum mean rainfall.

- **Rounding to any number of significant figures**

  To **round to any number of significant figures**:
  a Look at the first unwanted digit.
  b Use the normal rule of rounding.
  c Be careful to keep the number about the right size.

  Examples   253.7 to 2 sf is 250.   It is *not* 25!   0.036 28 to 2 sf is 0.036
  52 780 to 3 sf is 52 800   0.008 047 1 to 3 sf is 0.008 05

- **Standard form**   A very large number can be written as **a number between 1 and 10 multiplied by a power of 10**. This is called **standard form**.

  $$4\ 000\ 000\ 000 = 4 \text{ multiplied by 10 nine times} = 4 \times 10^9$$
  $$3\ 600\ 000 \quad = 3.6 \text{ multiplied by 10 six times} = 3.6 \times 10^6$$

  1.6×10^8 is standard form.
  It means 1.6 multiplied by 10 eight times = $1.6 \times 100\ 000\ 000 = 160\ 000\ 000$

  16×10^7 is not standard form because 16 is not between 1 and 10.

- **Lower and upper limits**   A space has length 98 cm correct to the nearest centimetre. The length of the space can be any value between 97.5 and 98.5 cm.

  This can be shown on a number line:

  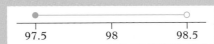

  97.5 is the smallest length that rounds to 98.
  97.5 is called the **lower limit**.
  98.5 is halfway between 98 and 99. The length cannot be exactly 98.5 but this is used as the upper limit.
  98.5 is called the **upper limit**.

  You can also have lower and upper limits for area and perimeter.

  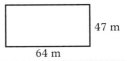

  To find the **minimum** area you take the lowest values for the length and width. For the **maximum** area you take the highest values.

  Lower limit $= 63.5 \times 46.5$ Upper limit $= 64.5 \times 47.5$
  $\qquad\qquad = 2952.75 \text{ m}^2$ $\qquad\qquad = 3063.75 \text{ m}^2$

  To find the minimum perimeter you take the lowest values for the length and width. For the maximum perimeter you take the highest values.

  Lower limit $= 63.5 + 46.5 + 63.5 + 46.5 = 220 \text{ m}$
  Upper limit $= 64.5 + 47.5 + 64.5 + 47.5 = 224 \text{ m}$

1 Round these numbers:
   a 23.52 to the nearest whole number   **b** 349 to the nearest ten
   c 35.572 to 1 dp   **e** 39.4729 to 3 dp   **g** 0.037 56 to 2 sf
   d 75.043 to 2 sf   **f** 27.462 to 3 sf   **h** 0.007 008 9 to 3 sf

2   **a** Give 5.649 m correct to the nearest centimetre.
   b Give 0.3782 kg correct to the nearest gram.

3 Pat and Peter are doing this question: $20 \times 0.3 = ?$
Pat says the answer must be 60 because $20 \times 3 = 60$ and numbers
always get bigger when they are multiplied.
Peter says that the answer is 6 because 0.3 is less than 1 so the answer
should be less than 20.
   a Who is right?   **b** Why is the other person wrong?

4 Write each calculator display as an ordinary number.

   a 3.67^{03} **b** 6.293^{06}

5 Write these standard form numbers as ordinary numbers.
   a 1.647×10^2 **b** 7.32×10^5

6 Tanya has measured her pen.
The pen is 15.7 cm long correct to 1 dp.
Write down the lower and upper limits of the length of Tanya's pen.

7 John has measured the sides of his desk to the nearest centimetre.
The length is 130 cm and the width is 52 cm.
   a Write down the lower and upper limits of the length and width.
   b Find the minimum and maximum values of the perimeter.
   c Find the minimum and maximum values of the area.

8   **a** Estimate the area of this poster.
       Show the numbers you are using for
       your estimate.
   b Work out the actual area of the poster.

78.5 cm

44.5 cm

6 Volume

Many scientists believe that global warming is melting the polar ice caps.

A study by the Inter-governmental Panel for Climate Change estimates that by the year 2070 global sea level could be as much as 71 cm higher than it is now.

Find out which parts of the UK would be underwater.

1 Units of capacity

Concrete is used to make the foundation of a house.
The builder needs to know how much concrete to mix.
He works out the volume of the hole that he needs to fill.

◄◄ REPLAY ►

Capacity

The **capacity** of a hollow object is the volume of space inside it.

This cube is filled with water.
The capacity of the cube is 1 millilitre.
1 ml is the same as 1 cm³.

1 cm
1 cm 1 cm

Large volumes are measured in litres.
1 litre = 1000 ml
This lemonade bottle holds 2 litres.

Exercise 6:1

1 Look at these objects.
List the objects in order of capacity.
Start with the smallest.

2 This bottle of cough mixture contains 120 ml.
  a How many 5 ml spoons will it fill?
  b Gemma has to take one 5 ml spoonful
    of cough mixture three times a day.
    How many days will the bottle last?

3 A factory makes silver medals.
Each medal needs 10 ml of molten
silver.

How many medals can you make from:

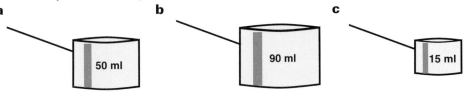

a 50 ml   **b** 90 ml   **c** 15 ml

  d 25 ml of molten silver   **e** 1000 ml of molten silver?

4 Barbara fills her car with petrol. Her car's petrol tank has a capacity of
45 litres. The car uses 11 litres of petrol for a journey.
  a How much petrol is left in the tank?
  b How many more times can Barbara make the same journey before
    she needs to fill up with petrol?

5 Sam's water pump can pump
water at the rate of 2 litres per
second.
How many litres of water can it
pump in two minutes?

6 Ben has bought a bottle of car shampoo. The label on the bottle says
that the contents are enough for 25 shampoos.
The bottle contains 750 ml.
How many millilitres should Ben use for one shampoo?

Sometimes you need to convert units. *Remember*: 1 l = 1000 ml

---

Examples **1** Convert 8500 ml to litres
           8500 ml = 8500 ÷ 1000 l
                 = 8.5 l

  2 Convert 2.6 litres to ml
      2.6 l = 2.6 × 1000 ml
          = 2600 ml

---

7 Change these capacities to litres.
  a 5000 ml   **c** 2500 ml   **e** 250 ml
  b 7000 ml   **d** 6750 ml   **f** 700 ml

8 Change these capacities to millilitres.
  a 9 l   **c** 1.75 l   **e** 4.25 l
  b 2.7 l   **d** 6.5 l   **f** 4.025 l

9 Greg is getting lemonade for a disco.
The lemonade comes in 2 litre bottles.
Each glass has a capacity of 300 ml.
  a How many glasses can Greg pour
      from each bottle?
  b Greg estimates that he will need
      40 glasses of lemonade.
      How many bottles does he need
      to buy?

10 A bottle of orange squash contains 800 ml.
The instructions say: 'One part squash to five parts water.'
How much orange drink will the bottle make
  a in millilitres   **b** in litres?

11 Sara is buying shampoo.
She likes two brands.
  a How much does 100 ml
      of Hairclean shampoo cost?
  b How much does 100 ml
      of Nostrum shampoo cost?
  c Which shampoo is the cheaper?

Nostrum
£2.16
300 ml

Hairclean
£1.40
200 ml

2 Volume of a cuboid

The builder needs to know how many bricks there are in each pack.

◄◄REPLAY►

When we need to know the volume we use cm^3.

1 cm^3

A cube that has sides of 1 cm is called a 1 cm cube.
You say that it has a volume of 1 cm cubed.
You write this as **1 cm^3**.

Example

This shape is made from 5 cubes.
Its volume is 5 cm^3.

Exercise 6:2

Jenny made these shapes with 1 cm cubes.
What is the volume of each shape?

1

2

3

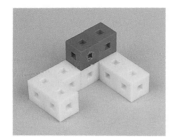

4

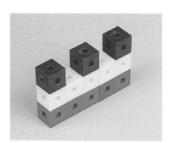

| Volume of a block | Look at this block of 1 cm cubes. There is a fast way to find the **volume of a block**. |

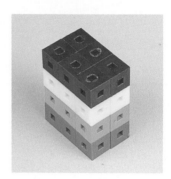

Count the number of cubes along the length, width and height.

Volume = length × width × height
$$= 3 \times 2 \times 4$$
$$= 24 \text{ cm}^3$$

Exercise 6:3

Find the volumes of these blocks of 1 cm cubes.
Write your answers in cm³.

1

2

3

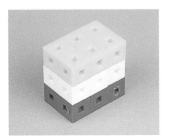

4

The blocks of cubes in the last exercise are all in the shape of a cuboid. You can measure the length of each side of the cuboid instead of counting cubes.
These lengths are used to calculate the volume.

Volume of a cuboid

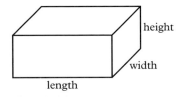

Volume of a cuboid = length × width × height

Example   Find the volume of this cuboid.

Volume = length × width × height
$$= 3 \times 5 \times 2$$
$$= 30 \text{ cm}^3$$

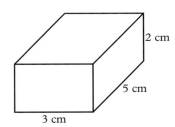

Exercise 6:4

Work out the volumes of these cuboids.

1

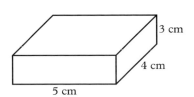

2

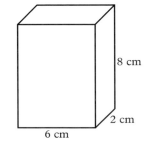

3

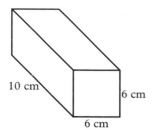

10 cm 6 cm 6 cm

4

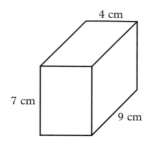

4 cm 7 cm 9 cm

Work out the volumes of these containers.

5

15 cm 10 cm 30 cm

7

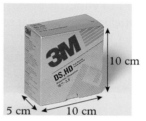

10 cm 5 cm 10 cm

6

40 cm 21 cm 7 cm

8

10 cm 8 cm 2 cm

9 **a** Work out the volume of this cube.
  b What is the volume of 4 of these cubes?

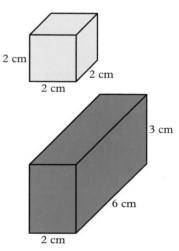

2 cm 2 cm 2 cm

  c Work out the volume of this box.
  d Which has the greater volume,
       the 4 cubes or the box?

  e Will the cubes fit into the box?
       Explain your answer.

3 cm 6 cm 2 cm

Example   Peter wants to find the
length of this cuboid.
The volume is 224 cm³.

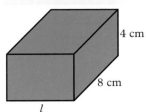

4 cm

8 cm

l

$$\text{Volume} = \textbf{\textit{l}}\text{ength} \times \text{width} \times \text{height}$$
$$224 = \textbf{\textit{l}} \times 8 \times 4$$
$$224 = \textbf{\textit{l}} \times 32 \qquad \textit{The inverse of } \times 32 \textit{ is } \div 32$$
$$224 \div 32 = \textbf{\textit{l}} \qquad \textit{You divide both sides by 32}$$
$$\textbf{\textit{l}} = 7 \text{ cm}$$

The length is 7 cm.

Exercise 6:5

Find the lengths marked with a letter.

1   Volume = 135 cm³

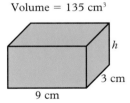

h

3 cm

9 cm

3   Volume
= 3840 cm³

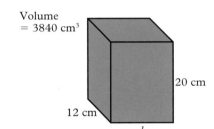

20 cm

12 cm

l

2   Volume = 693 cm³

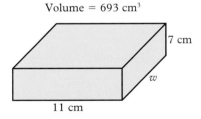

7 cm

w

11 cm

● **4**

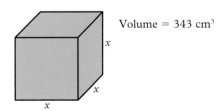

Volume = 343 cm³

x

x

x

5   This is a picture of Judy's new fish tank.
   a   Find the volume of the tank in cm³.
   b   What is the capacity of the tank
      in litres?
      Remember: 1 ml = 1 cm³
   c   Judy puts 51 litres of water into
      the tank.
      Find the depth of water in the tank.

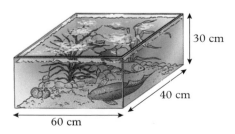

30 cm

40 cm

60 cm

3   Volumes of prisms and cylinders

Gas is stored in holders like this.
The holder is a cylinder.
The height of the cylinder changes
as the volume of gas stored changes.

◀◀ REPLAY ▶

| **Prism** | A **prism** is a solid which is exactly the same shape all the way through. Wherever you cut a slice through the solid it is the same size and shape. |

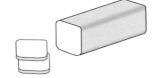

| **Cross section** | The shape of the slice is called the **cross section** of the solid. A prism has a polygon as its cross section. |

| **Cylinder** | A **cylinder** is like a prism but it has a circle as its cross section. |

Exercise 6:6

1   Look at these solids.

   a   Write down the letters of the solids that have the same cross section all the way through.

   b   Write down the name of the shape of the cross section for each solid in part **a**.

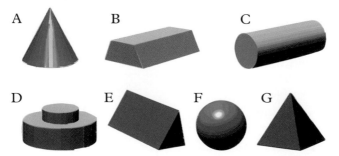

A   B   C

D   E   F   G

Volume of a prism	The volume of a prism or cylinder is **area of cross section × length**

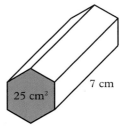

Example

Find the volume of this prism.

Area of cross section = 25 cm²

Volume = 25 × 7
    = 175 cm³

Work out the volumes of these prisms and cylinders.

2

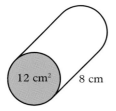

12 cm²   8 cm

5

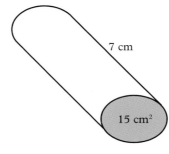

7 cm

15 cm²

3

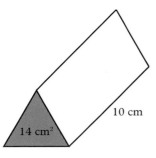

7 cm²   9 cm

6

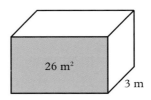

26 m²

3 m

4

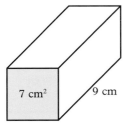

10 cm

14 cm²

7

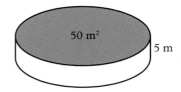

50 m²

5 m

You can find the length of a prism if you know its volume.

Example　The volume of this prism is 208 cm³.
The area of the triangle is 26 cm².

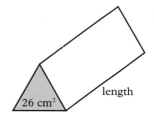

Volume = area of cross section × length
$$208 = 26 \times \text{length}$$ 　　*The inverse of ×26 is ÷26*
$$208 \div 26 = \text{length}$$ 　　*Divide each side by 26*
$$\text{length} = 8 \text{ cm}$$

Find the length of each of these shapes.

8

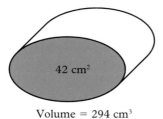

42 cm²

Volume = 294 cm³

9

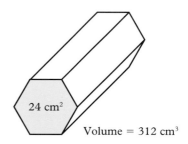

24 cm²

Volume = 312 cm³

Sometimes you have to work out the area of the cross section first.

Example　Find the volume of this prism.

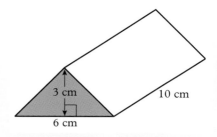

Area of cross section = $\dfrac{\textbf{base} \times \textbf{height}}{\textbf{2}}$

$$= \frac{6 \times 3}{2}$$

$$= 9 \text{ cm}^2$$

3 cm　　10 cm

6 cm

Volume = area of cross section × length
$$= 9 \times 10$$
$$= 90 \text{ cm}^3$$

Exercise 6:7

Work out the volume of each of these prisms.

1

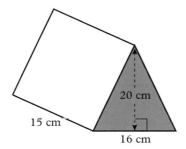

3

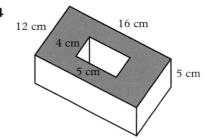

2

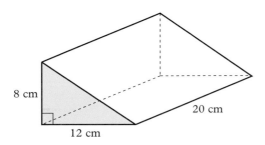

4

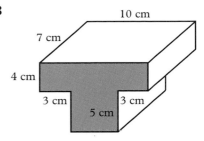

5 Kiran is making a ramp for a wheel chair.
What volume of concrete does he need?

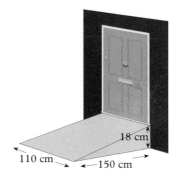

6 Harry has built a coal bunker.
The picture shows the lengths of the sides.
What is the volume of Harry's coal bunker?

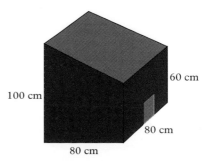

119

7 Find the lengths marked with a letter.

a

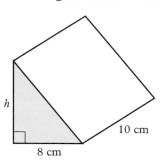

10 cm

8 cm

Volume = 880 cm³

b

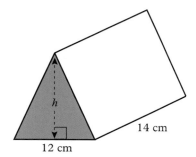

14 cm

12 cm

Volume = 1176 cm³

Volume = area of cross section × length

The cross section of a cylinder is a circle.
The area of a circle is $\pi \times$ radius $\times$ radius

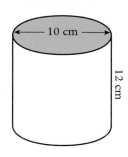

10 cm

12 cm

Example   **Area of cross section = $\pi \times$ radius $\times$ radius**
$$= 3.14 \times 5 \times 5$$
$$= 78.5 \text{ cm}^2$$
Volume of cylinder $= 78.5 \times 12$
$$= 942 \text{ cm}^3$$

Exercise 6:8

Work out the volumes of these cylinders.
Give your answers correct to 1 dp.

1

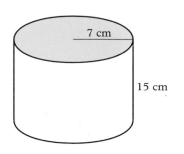

7 cm

15 cm

2

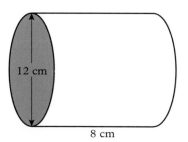

12 cm

8 cm

3

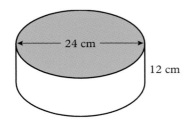

24 cm

12 cm

5

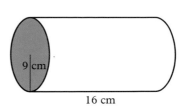

9 cm

16 cm

4

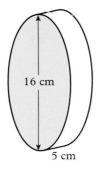

16 cm

5 cm

6

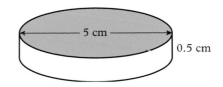

5 cm

0.5 cm

Exercise 6:9

1 Dale is buying corned beef.
These tins cost the same.
Dale has to decide which of
the two tins is the better value.
  a Find the volume of each tin.
  b Which tin gives the better value?

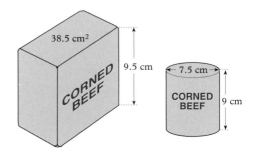

38.5 cm²

9.5 cm

CORNED BEEF

7.5 cm

CORNED BEEF

9 cm

2 Sinita has two cake tins. They are both 10 cm high.
One tin has a circular base. The other tin has a square base.

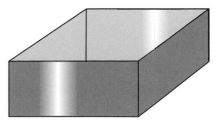

20 cm

  a Find the volume of the tin with the circular base.
  The two tins have the same volume.
  b Find the length of the side of the square for the square based tin.
  Give your answer correct to 3 sf.

3 This cylindrical bottle contains water to a depth of 15 cm.
The diameter of the bottle is 10 cm.

The water is poured into ice cube moulds.
The cubes have sides 3 cm long.

a Find the volume of the water in the bottle.
b How many moulds will the water fill?

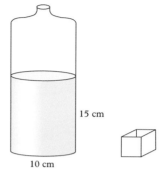

4 A wire has a circular cross section.
The diameter is 0.4 cm.
The wire is 150 cm long.
Find the volume of the wire.
Give your answer correct to 1 dp.

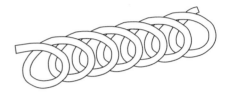

5 This peg is made from two
cylinders.
One cylinder has diameter
8 cm and height 2 cm.
The other cylinder has height
10 cm and diameter 2 cm.

Find the volume of the peg
correct to 1 dp.

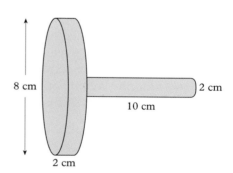

6 What is the capacity of this
cylindrical water heater?

Give your answer in litres correct
to the nearest litre.

Remember: 1 ml = 1 cm³

7 This drum has a capacity of 70 litres.
The height is 50 cm.

Find:
a the capacity of the drum in cm³,
b the area of the circular base in cm².

8 A garden roller has a circular cross section.
The radius is 24 cm.
a Find the area of the circle.

b The volume of the roller is 226 080 cm³.
Find the length of the roller correct to
the nearest centimetre.

9 These two cylinders have the
same volume.
a Find the volume of cylinder A.
b Find the length of cylinder B.
Give your answers correct to 1 dp.

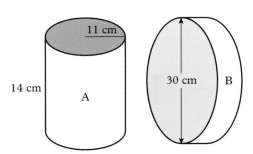

10 The photo shows the dimensions of
a cylindrical gas holder.
a Find the number of litres of gas
stored in the holder.
b 1 million litres of gas are used
during one day.
How much does the height of the
holder fall?
Give your answer correct to the
nearest metre.

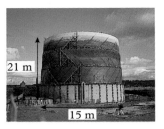

Design a presentation box

A company that makes cheese wants a presentation box for three cheeses.

Each of the three cheeses is in the shape of a cylinder.
The radius of each cheese is 2 cm and the height is 3 cm.

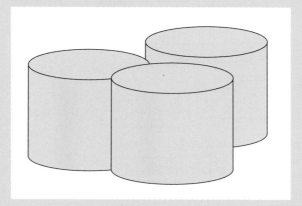

The box must have these design features:

- It must not collapse when one or two cheeses are removed from the box.
- You must be able to see how many cheeses are in the box at any time.

Other things to consider are:

- The box needs to be simple to make.
- The box should not use too much card.
- Several of the boxes will need to be packaged together to send to the shops.
- The shops will want to stack the cheese boxes on shelves.

Design a suitable presentation box for the cheeses.
You will need to consider different arrangements for the cheeses.

Choose the final design and give reasons for your choice.

1 Jenny can buy oil in these sizes.

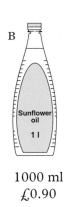

A

B

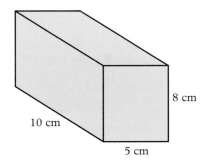

C

500 ml
£0.50

1000 ml
£0.90

3000 ml
£2.80

    a How much does 100 ml cost for size A?
    b How much does 100 ml cost for size B?
    c How much does 100 ml cost for size C?
    d Which size gives the best value for money?

2 Find the volumes of these cuboids.

a

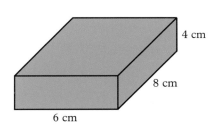

4 cm
8 cm
6 cm

b

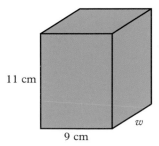

8 cm
10 cm
5 cm

3 Find the lengths marked with a letter.

a

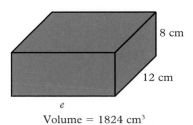

8 cm
12 cm
e
Volume = 1824 cm³

b

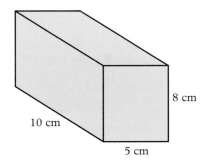

11 cm
9 cm
w
Volume = 742.5 cm³

125

4 This is a net of a cuboid.

What is the volume of the cuboid?

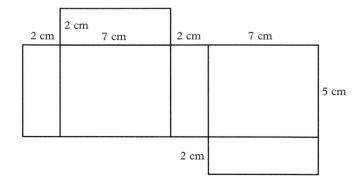

5 Glenda is making a wall for the school play. She uses 50 of these polystyrene blocks.
What volume of polystyrene does she use?

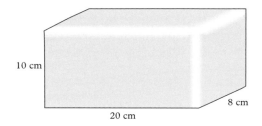

6 John is making a wedding cake with three tiers.
He uses three square based tins.

The tins all have a height of 8 cm.
The lengths of the sides of the tins are 20 cm, 30 cm and 40 cm.

What is the total volume of the three tins?

7 Work out the volumes of these prisms.

a

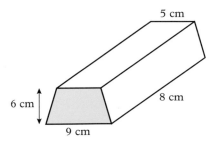

b

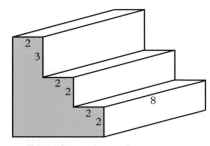

all lengths are in centimetres

8 Find the lengths marked with a letter.

a

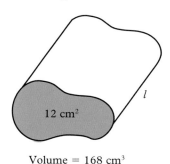

12 cm²

Volume = 168 cm³

b

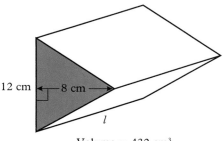

12 cm 8 cm

l

Volume = 432 cm³

9 Find the volumes of these cylinders correct to 1 dp.

a

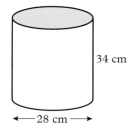

34 cm

←—28 cm—→

b

8.5 cm

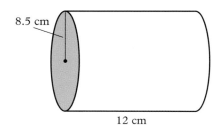

12 cm

10 a What is the volume of this tin of cat food?

b The tins of cat food are packed into boxes like this one.
How many tins will fit into the box?

c What is the volume of the wasted space inside the box?
Give your answer correct to the nearest whole number.

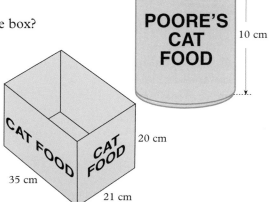

7 cm

POORE'S
CAT
FOOD

10 cm

20 cm

CAT FOOD   CAT FOOD

35 cm

21 cm

11 Rajiv has bought a 100 ml tube of toothpaste.
Rajiv uses a small cylinder of toothpaste each time that he cleans his teeth.
The circular cross section has a diameter of 0.5 cm.
He cleans his teeth twice a day.
How long will the tube last?

3 cm

1 Ellen has made a device that collects rainfall.
The rain is collected in a rectangular tray 3 m long and 2 m wide.
It then runs into the measuring cylinder underneath.
The diameter of the cylinder is 40 cm.
What is the depth of water in the cylinder after 1 cm of rain has fallen into the tray?
Give your answer correct to the nearest centimetre.

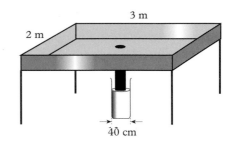

2 Richard is making glass fibre.
He starts with a cylinder of glass as shown in the diagram.
He spins this into glass fibre with a circular cross section of diameter 0.1 cm.
What length of glass fibre does he make?
Give your answer correct to the nearest metre.

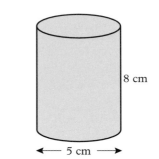

3 The diagram shows 25 cm of rubber tubing.
The inner radius is 2 cm and the outer radius is 5 cm.
Find the volume of rubber used to make the tubing.
Give your answer correct to 1 dp.

4 This diagram shows the cross section of a hosepipe.
Water flows through the pipe at a speed of 14 cm each second.
What volume of water will flow through the pipe in one minute?
Give your answer in litres correct to 1 dp.

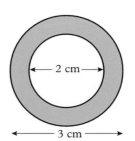

- **Capacity**   The **capacity** of a hollow object is the volume of space inside it.

  This cube is filled with water.
  The capacity of the cube is 1 millilitre.
  1 ml is the same as 1 cm³.

- **Volume of a cuboid**   Find the volume of this cuboid.

  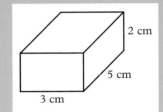

  Volume = length × width × height
  $$= 3 \times 5 \times 2$$
  $$= 30 \text{ cm}^3$$

- **Prism**   A **prism** is a solid which is exactly the same shape all the way through. Wherever you cut a slice through the solid it is the same size and shape.

  Cross section   The shape of the slice is called the **cross section** of the solid.

  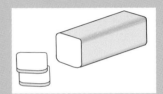

- **Volume of a prism**   The volume of a prism or cylinder is **area of cross section × length**

  Example   Find the volume of this prism.

  Area of cross section = 25 cm²

  Volume = 25 × 7
         = 175 cm³

  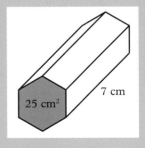

- *Example*   Find the volume of this cylinder.

  Area of cross section = π × radius × radius
  $$= 3.14 \times 5 \times 5$$
  $$= 78.5 \text{ cm}^2$$

  Volume of cylinder = area of cross section × length
  $$= 78.5 \times 12$$
  $$= 942 \text{ cm}^3$$

  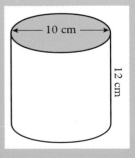

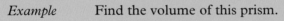
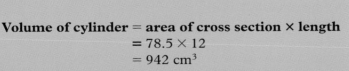

Find the volume of each of these solids.

1

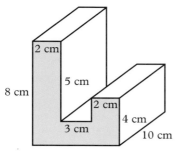

42 cm²   5 cm

3

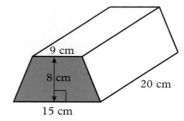

9 cm
8 cm
15 cm
20 cm

2

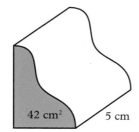

2 cm
5 cm
8 cm
2 cm
3 cm
4 cm
10 cm

4

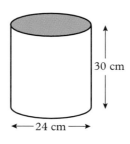

30 cm
24 cm

5 The volume of a cuboid is 1287 cm³. The area of the base is 33 cm².
Find the height of the cuboid.

6 **a** Find the area of the circular base
of this container.
b Jim pours 5 litres of water into it.
Find the depth of water in the container.
Give your answer correct to 1 dp.

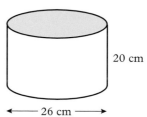

20 cm
26 cm

7 A semi-circular tunnel is dug through a hillside.
The diagram shows the cross section of the tunnel.
The length of the tunnel is 250 m.
Find the volume of earth that was removed to
make the tunnel.

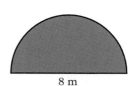

8 m

8 Which of these two bottles of shampoo
is the better value for money?

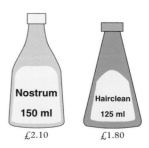

Nostrum
150 ml
£2.10

Hairclean
125 ml
£1.80

7 Number revision

At sea level sound travels at 333.15 metres per second.

Light travels at 299 800 000 metres per second.

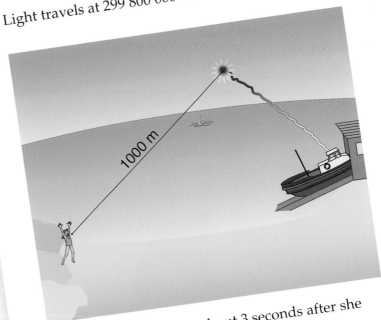

1000 m

The girl hears the bang about 3 seconds after she sees the flare explode.

1 ◄◄REPLAY►

71% of the surface of the earth is covered by water.

This pie-chart has been divided into
100 equal parts.
Each part is 1% of the pie-chart.

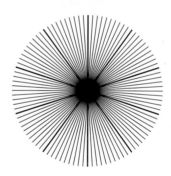

Exercise 7:1

For each diagram write down
a the percentage that is coloured,
b the percentage that is not coloured.

1

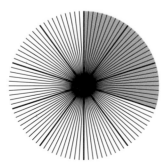

2

3 The human body is about 70% water.
What percentage is not water?

4 Cara has done 82% of her homework.
What percentage does she still have to do?

5 Mark has coloured in
35% of his picture.
What percentage does
he still have to colour?

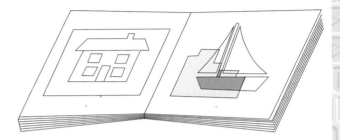

6 12% of year 9 at Stanthorne High go home to lunch.
What percentage stay at school for lunch?

7 The percentage of homes that have a telephone is 87%
What percentage of homes do not have a telephone?

1% of this pie-chart is coloured red.

$1\% = \dfrac{1}{100} = 0.01$ is coloured red.

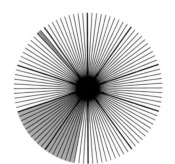

17% is coloured blue.

$17\% = \dfrac{17}{100} = 0.17$ is coloured blue.

Exercise 7:2

1 Copy these and fill them in with a fraction and with a decimal number.

  a 43% = ... = ...   **d** 91% = ... = ...   **g** 11% = ... = ...

  b 79% = ... = ...   **e** 7% = ... = ...   **h** 9% = ... = ...

  c 3% = ... = ...   **f** 67% = ... = ...   **i** 41% = ... = ...

You can write percentages as fractions of 100.
Sometimes you can simplify the fractions.

10% is coloured blue.

$$10\% = \frac{10}{100} = \frac{1}{10}$$ is coloured blue.

2 Copy these and fill them in.

a $30\% = \frac{\cdots}{100} = \frac{\cdots}{10}$

b $90\% = \frac{\cdots}{100} = \frac{\cdots}{10}$

3 **a** How many parts are green?
b What percentage is green?
c Write the percentage as a decimal.
d Write the percentage as a fraction of 100.
e Write the percentage as a fraction in its simplest form.

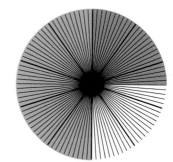

4 **a** How many parts are purple?
b What percentage is purple?
c Write the percentage as a decimal.
d Write the percentage as a fraction of 100.
e Write the percentage as a fraction in its simplest form.

5 **a** How many parts are yellow?
b What percentage is yellow?
c Write the percentage as a decimal.
d Write the percentage as a fraction of 100.
e Write the percentage as a fraction in its simplest form.
f Copy these and fill them in.

$$40\% = \frac{\cdots}{5}, \quad \cdots\% = \frac{4}{5}$$

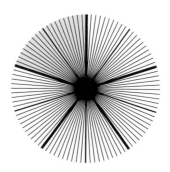

Here are two flow charts to help you to remember how to work with percentages, fractions and decimals.

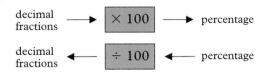

Examples

1 Change these to percentages:
a 0.65   **b** $\frac{3}{5}$

☐ × 100

a $0.65 \times 100 = 65\%$

b $\frac{3}{5} \times 100 = (3 \div 5) \times 100 = 60\%$

2 Change 14% to:
a a decimal
b a fraction in its lowest terms.

☐ ÷ 100

a $14\% = 14 \div 100 = 0.14$ **b** $14\% = \frac{14}{100} = \frac{7}{50}$ (÷ 2)

Exercise 7:3

1 Change these decimal numbers to percentages.
a 0.38   **b** 0.07   **c** 1.5   **d** 0.8   **e** 0.005

2 Change these fractions to percentages.
a $\frac{4}{5}$ **b** $\frac{3}{8}$ **c** $\frac{11}{20}$ **d** $\frac{16}{25}$ **e** $\frac{1}{3}$

3 Change these percentages to decimals.
a 79%   **b** 21%   **c** 7%   **d** 90%   **e** 30%

4 Change these percentages to fractions of 100.
a 57%   **b** 9%   **c** 81%   **d** 3%   **e** 17%

5 Change these percentages to fractions.
Give the fractions in their lowest terms.
a 75%   **d** 5%   **g** 2%   **j** 4%   **m** 36%
b 70%   **e** 15%   **h** 22%   **k** 8%   ● **n** $12\frac{1}{2}\%$
c 60%   **f** 55%   **i** 26%   **l** 24%   ● **o** $33\frac{1}{3}\%$

Robert, Chris and Fiona are comparing their test marks.
Robert got $\frac{63}{75}$, Chris got $\frac{51}{60}$ and Fiona got $\frac{65}{80}$.
They are going to change each mark to a percentage.
They can then see who got the highest mark.

Example

Fiona got $\frac{65}{80}$. Change $\frac{65}{80}$ to a percentage.

To change a fraction to a percentage you multiply by 100.

$$\frac{65}{80} = \frac{65}{80} \times 100\% = (65 \div 80) \times 100\% = 81.25\%$$

Fiona got 81% correct to the nearest whole number.

Exercise 7:4

1 Change Robert's and Chris' marks to percentages.
Who got the higher mark?

2 Change these fractions to percentages.
Give your answers correct to the nearest whole number.

a $\frac{71}{80}$ **c** $\frac{4}{5}$ **e** $\frac{23}{36}$ **g** $\frac{27}{55}$ **i** $\frac{96}{120}$

b $\frac{16}{40}$ **d** $\frac{56}{60}$ **f** $\frac{15}{48}$ **h** $\frac{23}{28}$ **j** $\frac{112}{125}$

To work out what percentage one number is of another:
(1) Write the number as a fraction.
(2) Convert the fraction to a percentage.

Example

A 35 g slice of wholemeal bread contains 3 g of fibre.
What percentage of the bread is fibre?

The fraction of bread that is fibre is $\dfrac{3}{35}$

Convert the fraction to a percentage.

$$\frac{3}{35} \times 100 = (3 \div 35) \times 100 = 8.5714 \dots$$

$$= 8.6\% \text{ correct to 1 dp}$$

3 This is what Ellen did during one 24 hour period:

sleeping	8 hours	school	6 hours
eating	2 hours	watching TV	3 hours
at a disco	4 hours	other	1 hour

Work out the percentage of her time that Ellen spent:
a sleeping   **c** at a disco
b watching TV   **d** eating
Give each percentage correct to the nearest whole number.

4 Rajiv is looking at the populations of the villages in his local area.
This is his data:

Village	Barrow	Manley	Ashton	Sately
Population	928	735	1035	1256

a What is the total population?
b What percentage of the population live in Barrow?
c What percentage of the population live in Sately?
d What percentage of the population live in either Manley or Ashton?
Give each percentage correct to the nearest whole number.

5 George received £40 for his birthday.
He spent £24 and saved the rest.
a What percentage did George spend?
b What percentage did he save?

6 Martin and Claire each have a
packet of peanuts weighing 30 g.
a Martin eats all his peanuts.
What percentage has he eaten?
b Claire eats 18 g of her peanuts.
What percentage has Claire
eaten?

7 Sinita opened a 750 g packet of cornflakes for breakfast.
After breakfast she found there were 525 g of cornflakes remaining.
a How many grams of cornflakes were eaten?
b What percentage of the cornflakes were eaten?

8 Theo works 40 hours each week.
His working hours are reduced to 38 hours a week.
What is the percentage reduction in the hours that Theo works?

CORE

2   Increase and decrease

● ●

Fishing rod £20
Tackle box £12
Football £10
Football pump £6
Dartboard £12.20
Darts £8
Tennis racket £45
Cricket bat £28.50
Tennis balls £7
Cycling helmet £24.80
Cycle computer £16.80
Cycle lights £10.40

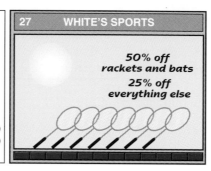

27   WHITE'S SPORTS

50% off rackets and bats

25% off everything else

Lisa wants to know how much she will save if she buys a dartboard.

Remember: $50\% = \frac{1}{2}$ and $25\% = \frac{1}{4}$

Example

Lisa is buying a dartboard. It costs £12.20.
The shop has reduced the price by 25%.
a How much does Lisa save?
b How much does Lisa pay for the dartboard?

a Lisa knows that $25\% = \frac{1}{4}$ and that $\frac{1}{4}$ of £12.20 = £3.05
Lisa saves £3.05.

b Lisa pays £12.50 − £3.05 = £9.45

Exercise 7:5

Use the prices given in the picture to answer the questions in this exercise.
For each item give:
a the amount saved   **b** the reduced price.

1 a tackle box   **6** a football pump

2 a fishing rod   **7** a cycling helmet

3 a tennis racket   **8** a cricket bat

4 the tennis balls   **9** a cycle computer

5 a football   **10** cycle lights

29   CAMPING STORES

Tent £108
Sleeping bag £32
Airbed £12
Camping mat £4
Folding table
and stool set £30.50
Lantern £24
Camp cookset £12
Gas cooker £16
Water carrier £5.50
Cool box £12.30

**10% off
marked prices**

Example

Alan is buying a tent. It costs £108.
The shop has reduced the price by 10%.
  a How much does Alan save?
  b How much does Alan pay for the tent?

a Alan knows that 10% = $\frac{1}{10}$ and that $\frac{1}{10}$ of 108 = $\frac{108}{10}$ = 10.8

Alan saves £10.80

Remember:

b Alan pays £108 − £10.80 = £97.20

Exercise 7:6

Use the prices given in the picture for questions **1** to **8**.
For each item give:
  a the amount saved   **b** the reduced price.

1 a sleeping bag   **5** an airbed

2 a gas cooker   **6** a cool box

3 a lantern   **7** a water carrier

4 a camp cookset   **8** a folding table and stool set

9 A mountain bike costs £120.
The shop is selling the bike at 10% off the full price.
What is the reduced price?

10 Huw gets £12 per week for his paper round.
The shopkeeper is going to increase his money by 10%.
How much will Huw get at this new rate of pay?

11 This box of tea contains 200 teabags.
A special offer pack contains 10% more.
  a How many extra tea bags is this?
  b How many tea bags in total are in
     the special offer pack?

12 A packet of sweets contains 200 g.
A special offer pack contains 20% more.
  a How many extra grams of sweets is this?
  b How many grams are there altogether in the special offer pack?

• •

Sometimes you need a calculator to work out the percentage.

Example   Sian is buying a computer.
                   It costs £960.
                   The shop reduces the price by 12%.
                   How much does Sian save?

                   Sian needs to work out 12% of 960.

                                      Step 1   Step 2   Step 3

                   This can be written: $\dfrac{12}{100}$ ×   960

                   Step 1   This changes the percentage to a decimal.
                            The decimal appears when you press ✕ at Step 2.
                   Step 2   'Of' is the same as multiply so use the ✕ key.
                   Step 3   You are finding the percentage of this amount.

                   Key in:
                                Step 1   Step 2   Step 3

                   【1】【2】【÷】【1】【0】【0】【✕】【9】【6】【0】【=】 115.2
                   Answer: £115.20

140

Exercise 7:7

1 Find 12% of 300 g.

2 Find 18% of 250 cm.

3 Find 8% of 600 cm.

4 Find 45% of 120 g.

5 Find 34% of 350 m.

6 Find 12% of £150.

7 Find 15% of £450.

8 Find 9% of £420.

9 There are 40 ink cartridges in a standard packet.
A special offer packet contains 15% more.
How many cartridges are there in the special offer packet?

10 The volume of a standard size bottle of bath oil is 320 ml.
A special offer bottle contains 8% more.
  a How much more bath oil is in the special offer bottle?
  b What is the total amount of bath oil in the special offer bottle?

11 A packet contains 660 g of coffee.
The larger size packet holds 35% more.
  a How much more coffee is in the larger packet?
  b How much coffee is there altogether in the larger packet?

• **12** Helen's family went out for a meal.
The bill came to £32.50.
They gave the waitress a $12\frac{1}{2}$% tip.
  a How much was the tip?
  b What was the total cost of the meal?

• **13** A shop had a sale. For each day of the sale the prices were reduced by
15% of the prices on the day before.
  a A sweater sold for £28 before the sale.
    Find its selling price after:
    (1) one day in the sale,
    (2) two days in the sale.
  b Find the selling price of each of these after two days in the sale.
    (1) A jacket with a price of £46.50 before the sale.
    (2) A pair of jeans with a price of £32.95 before the sale.

Example Pierre wants a computer game for his birthday.
The computer game cost £54.
His parents agree to pay $\frac{3}{4}$ of the cost.
How much do Pierre's parents pay?

$\frac{3}{4}$ of £54 = $\frac{3}{4} \times 54$

Key in: 3 ÷ 4 × 5 4 =

or if you have a $a\frac{b}{c}$ key:

3 $a\frac{b}{c}$ 4 × 5 4 =

Press $a\frac{b}{c}$ again to convert to a decimal.

Pierre's parents pay £40.50

Exercise 7:8

1 Use a calculator to find:
  a $\frac{3}{4}$ of £22
  b $\frac{3}{5}$ of 375 houses
  c $\frac{5}{8}$ of 400 people
  d $\frac{3}{20}$ of £6.80

2 Use a calculator to find each of these.
Give each answer correct to the nearest penny.
  a $\frac{2}{3}$ of £50
  b $\frac{3}{7}$ of £20
  c $\frac{4}{11}$ of £5.60
  d $\frac{4}{5}$ of 32p
  e $\frac{5}{9}$ of £2.75
  f $\frac{7}{12}$ of 85p

3 Danny is going to the sports centre. All prices are reduced by $\frac{1}{3}$.
Danny is going to the gym first and then he is going swimming.
Swimming usually costs £1.35 and the gym usually costs 75 p.
How much will Danny have to pay in total at the reduced price?

4 A flask can hold up to 750 ml of coffee. The flask is $\frac{7}{8}$ full.
How much coffee does it contain?

5 Barbara is buying a new tennis racket.
Shop A offers a 15% discount.
Shop B offers to cut the price by $\frac{1}{8}$.
Which shop gives the lower price?
Show all your working.

142

3 Ratio

There are the same number of girls as boys at Stanthorne High. The **ratio** of girls to boys is 1 : 1

◀◀ REPLAY ▶

Here are six counters.

There are 2 red counters out of a *total* of 6 counters.

The **fraction** of the counters that are red is $\dfrac{2}{6} = \dfrac{1}{3}$

There are 2 red counters and 4 blue counters.

The **ratio** of red counters to blue counters is   2 : 4
You simplify ratios like fractions.   2 : 4 = 1 : 2

The ratio 1 : 2 tells you that there is 1 red counter for every 2 blue counters.
The ratio *compares* the number of red counters with the number of blue counters.

Ratio	**Ratio** is a measure of the relative size or quantity of things.

Exercise 7:9

Give your answers in their simplest form in this exercise.

1 Look at the red and blue counters in the example.
   a What fraction of the counters are blue?
   b What is the ratio of blue counters to red counters?

2 Lucy is threading beads in a pattern.

   a What fraction of the beads are yellow?
   b What fraction of the beads are green?
   c What is the ratio of green beads to yellow beads?
   d What is the ratio of yellow beads to green beads?
   e Lucy continues her pattern.
      (1) If Lucy uses 3 more greens, how many more yellows will she use?
      (2) If Lucy uses 21 yellows altogether, how many greens will she use?

3 Liam is making this pattern with cubes.

   a Copy and complete these ratios for the colours in the pattern.
      (1) red : blue : yellow = 4 : 2 : ... = 2 : ... : ...
      (2) blue : red : yellow = 1 : ... : ...
      (3) yellow : red : blue = ... : ... : 1
   b Liam continues his pattern. He uses 6 more reds.
      (1) How many more blues does Liam use?
      (2) How many more yellows does he use?
   c Liam uses 30 yellows altogether.
      (1) How many blues does he use?
      (2) How many reds does he use?

4 Sonja is making an orange drink. She uses 4 parts water to 1 part orange squash.
   a Write down the ratio of squash to water.
   b She uses 200 ml of squash. How much water does she use?
   c What fraction of the dilute drink is squash?
   d If the jug contains 1500 ml of the dilute drink, how much of the squash has Sonja used?

Exercise 7:10

Simplifying ratios

Example Write these ratios in their lowest terms. **a** $8 : 12$ **b** $24 : 6 : 12$

a 4 goes into 8 and 12 $8 : 12 = \dfrac{8}{4} : \dfrac{12}{4} = 2 : 3$

b 6 goes into 24, 6 and 12 $24 : 6 : 12 = \dfrac{24}{6} : \dfrac{6}{6} : \dfrac{12}{6} = 4 : 1 : 2$

---

1 Simplify these ratios.
a	$10 : 15$	**d**	$30 : 10$	**g**	$12 : 6 : 6$	**j**	$40 : 20 : 60 : 20$
b	$20 : 5$	**e**	$10 : 5$	**h**	$7 : 7 : 14$	**k**	$9 : 3 : 6 : 3$
c	$5 : 5$	**f**	$33 : 22$	**i**	$6 : 4 : 2$	**l**	$24 : 16 : 8 : 80$

Example Carl, Rani and Katy win a prize of £60. They decide to share the prize in the ratio of their ages. Carl is 15, Rani is 10 and Katy is 5. How much does each of them get?

The ratio of their ages is $15 : 10 : 5 = \dfrac{15}{5} : \dfrac{10}{5} : \dfrac{5}{5} = 3 : 2 : 1$

$3 + 2 + 1 = 6$ shares are needed.

One share is £60 ÷ 6 = £10   Carl gets £10 × 3 = £30
Rani gets £10 × 2 = £20
Katy gets £10 × 1 = £10

Check: £30 + £20 + £10 = £60

---

2 Share these amounts in the ratios given.
You may need to simplify the ratio first.
Check your answer each time.
a	£25	$2 : 3$	**d**	£100	$5 : 3 : 2$	**g**	£4.40	$2 : 8 : 10$
b	£27	$2 : 7$	**e**	£30	$1 : 2 : 3$	**h**	45 p	$10 : 20$
c	£34	$7 : 10$	**f**	£21	$2 : 1 : 4$	**i**	70 p	$18 : 9 : 3$

Sometimes ratios are written in the form $1 : n$
You can see this form on maps.

Example   Convert the ratio $2 : 9$ into the form $1 : n$

To convert $2 : 9$ into the form $1 : n$ you need to change the 2 to a 1.
This means you divide by 2.

$$2 : 9 = \frac{2}{2} : \frac{9}{2} = 1 : 4.5$$

3   Convert these ratios into the form $1 : n$
Copy these and fill in the numbers.

a $2 : 5 = \dfrac{2}{2} : \dfrac{5}{2} = 1 : \ldots$ b $4 : 3 = \dfrac{4}{4} : \dfrac{3}{\ldots} = 1 : \ldots$

4   Convert these ratios into the form $1 : n$

a $2 : 7$ c $10 : 17$ e $2 : 1$ g $10 : 3$ i $10 : 7$
b $4 : 11$ d $6 : 15$ f $4 : 1$ h $6 : 3$ j $3 : 1$

5   a   Cake mixture A uses four parts fat to seven parts flour.
    (1) Write the ratio of fat to flour in figures.
    (2) Convert the ratio to the form $1 : n$
  b   Cake mixture B uses five parts fat to nine parts flour.
    (1) Write the ratio of fat to flour in figures.
    (2) Convert the ratio to the form $1 : n$
  c   Saleem prefers a diet with less fat and more flour.
    Compare the two ratios in the form $1 : n$
    Which cake mixture should Saleem choose?

Suppose you know how much a certain number
of items costs.
You can find the cost of one item. Then you can
find the cost of any number of the items.

Example   Four peaches cost 80 p.
Find the cost of seven peaches.

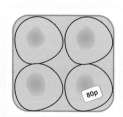

4 peaches cost 80 p, so 1 peach costs $80 \div 4 = 20$ p
7 peaches cost 7×20 p $= 140$ p $= £1.40$

Exercise 7:11

1 **a** If four oranges cost 60 p, what does one orange cost?
   b How much do six oranges cost?

2 **a** Marie gets paid £20 for 5 hours work.
       What does she get paid for working 1 hour?
   b How much does Marie get for 7 hours work if she is paid at the
       same rate?

3 **a** Three tea bags contain 7.5 g of tea.
       How much tea does one tea bag contain?
   b How much tea do 10 tea bags contain?

4 Three melons cost £2.40. How much do five melons cost?

5 Four lemons cost 64 p. How much do seven lemons cost?

6 Six grapefruit cost £1.56. How much do five grapefruit cost?

7 Ian earns £10.50 for 3 hours work.
   How much does he get for 5 hours work paid at the same rate?

8 4 cm^3 of copper weigh 35.68 g.
   a The mass of 1 cm^3 of a material is called its **density**.
       Find the density of copper in g/cm^3.
   b Find the mass of 15 cm^3 of copper.

9 10 cm^3 of iron weigh 78.6 g.
   a Find the density of iron in g/cm^3.
   b Find the mass of 2.5 cm^3 of iron.

10 A car travels 150 miles in 3 hours.
   a How far does the car travel in 1 hour?
   b Write down the speed of the car in miles per hour.
   c How far does the car travel in 4 hours at the same speed?

11 A plane flies 2500 km in 5 hours.
   a How far does the plane fly in 1 hour?
   b Write down the speed of the plane in kilometres per hour.
   c How far does the plane fly in 7 hours at the same speed?

12 A plane flies 1290 miles in 3 hours.
   How far does it fly in 5 hours at the same speed?

....

There are some formulas you can use for questions on speed, distance and time.

$$\textbf{S}\text{peed} = \frac{\textbf{D}\text{istance}}{\textbf{T}\text{ime}} \qquad \textbf{T}\text{ime} = \frac{\textbf{D}\text{istance}}{\textbf{S}\text{peed}} \qquad \textbf{D}\text{istance} = \textbf{S}\text{peed} \times \textbf{T}\text{ime}$$

Here is an easy way to remember the formulas.

Look at this triangle:

Cover **S**

$$S = \frac{D}{T}$$

Cover **T**

$$T = \frac{D}{S}$$

Cover **D**

$$D = S \times T$$

Examples   **1** A train travels for 210 miles at a speed of 70 miles per hour.
   How long does the train take?

   You need to find the **time** so you use $\textbf{T} = \dfrac{\textbf{D}}{\textbf{S}} = \dfrac{210}{70} = 3$ hours

   2 A plane flies at 600 km per hour for 2 hours and 15 minutes.
   How far does it fly?
   You need to find the **distance** so you use $\textbf{D} = \textbf{S} \times \textbf{T}$

   15 minutes is $\frac{1}{4}$ of an hour or 0.25 of an hour.
   $2\frac{1}{4}$ hours = 2.25 hours
   $\textbf{D} = \textbf{S} \times \textbf{T} = 600 \times 2.25 = 1350$ km

   If you have a **DMS** key, you can key in hours and minutes.

   6 **0** **0** **×** **2** **DMS** **1** **5** **2nd F** **DMS**
   Answer: 1350 km

Exercise 7:12

1 A plane flies 1800 km at a speed of 450 km per hour.
How long does the plane journey take?

2 A train travels for 3 hours 30 minutes at a speed of 90 miles per hour.
How far does the train travel?

3 A runner runs 1500 m in 4 minutes.
What is the runner's speed in metres per minute?

4 Kevin sees a flash of lightning.
He starts counting and counts
7 seconds until he hears the
thunder. Kevin knows that the
speed of sound is 360 metres
per second. He works out how
far the noise of the thunder
travelled to reach him.
Work out Kevin's answer in
a metres,
b kilometres.

5 A plane flies from London to Edinburgh in 1 hour 15 minutes.
The plane flies at 320 miles per hour.
Find the distance from London to Edinburgh.

6 In the United States, pronghorn antelopes have been timed running
4 miles in 6.8 minutes.
a Work out the speed of the antelopes in miles per minute.
Give your answer correct to 3 dp.
b Convert the speed to miles per hour.
Give your answer correct to the nearest whole number.

7 The fastest speed recorded for a spider running across a flat surface is
53 cm per sec.
How long would the record breaking spider take to run across a room
5 m wide? Give your answer in seconds correct to 1 dp.

1 Rachel has dug 42% of her vegetable garden.
What percentage does she still have to dig?

2 When peeling potatoes 8% of the mass is cut off as peel.
What percentage is left?

3 This table shows the membership of a sports club.

Type of membership	Adult	Student	Child
Number of members	245	78	92

a What is the total number of members?
b What percentage of the membership are adults?
c What percentage of the membership are children?
Give answers correct to 1 dp.

4 There are 900 pupils in Lisa's school.
a About 44% of all people have blood group A.
How many of the pupils should have blood group A?
b About 4% of people have blood group AB.
How many of the pupils should have blood group AB?

5 Michael says that 15% of 60 is the same as 60% of 15.
Is Michael correct?
Show your working.

6 A television costs £380.
It is reduced by 25%.
What is the new price?

25% off

7 A standard packet of soap powder contains 2 kg.
A special offer pack is made giving an extra 15%.
How much powder does the special offer pack contain?

8 The price of a ticket to go bowling has been increased by $\frac{1}{5}$.
What is the new price if a ticket used to cost £4.80?

9 Nathan buys some furniture in a sale.
The prices are reduced by $\frac{2}{5}$.
The old price of the items was £390.
How much does Nathan pay?

10 Give each answer in its simplest form in this question.
Andy is making this pattern with counters.

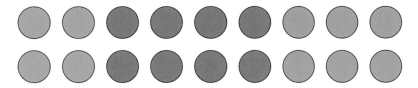

   a What fraction of the counters are red?
   b Write down the ratio of green counters : red counters : blue counters.
   c Write down the ratio of red counters : green counters : blue counters.
   d Andy continues his pattern.
      If he uses 10 more green counters how many more blue counters will he need?

11 Sally, Khalid and Mary help in a cafe.
Sally works 3 hours, Khalid works 2 hours and Mary works 4 hours.
The owner of the cafe is prepared to pay £27.
Share the money between the three people in the ratio of the hours they
have worked.

12 Approximately 350 of the people who went to a concert were women.
200 were men and 150 were children.
   a Write down the ratio of women : men: children.
      Simplify the ratio.
   b What fraction of the total number of people were children?

13 8 video cassettes put side by side on a
shelf measure 20 cm. How many
centimetres would 11 video cassettes
placed side by side measure?

14 A plane flies at 450 miles per hour for 3 hours and 15 minutes.
How far does the plane fly?

15 A hiker walks at an average speed of $2\frac{1}{2}$ miles per hour.
   a How long will it take the hiker to do a walk of 14 miles?
   b Your answer to **a** contains a decimal of an hour.
      How many minutes are there in an hour?
      Multiply the decimal part of the time by this number.
   c Write down the time the hiker takes in hours and minutes.

1 What percentage is X of Y if:
   a X is the same size as Y
   b X is twice as big as Y
   c X is half as big as Y
   d X is one and a half times as big as Y?

2 Alison puts £125 in a savings account paying 5.9% interest per year.
   The interest on the account is added at the end of each year.
   Alison does not intend to draw any money out.
   Work out the amount she will have in the account after:
   a 1 year   **b** 2 years

3 An insect repellant contains 15% active
   ingredient and the rest is a cream base.
   a What percentage of the product is
      the cream base?
   b Write down the ratio of active
      ingredient to cream base.
   c Write the ratio of active ingredient
      to cream base in the form $1 : n$
      Give your answer correct to 3 sf.

4 Sapna is making some lemon and blackcurrant drink.
   She uses three parts lemon squash, one part blackcurrant syrup and
   ten parts water.
   Sapna has made 3.5 litres of the drink.
   a How much lemon squash has Sapna used?
   b How much blackcurrant syrup has she used?
   c Sapna makes some more of the drink.
      She uses 450 ml of lemon squash.
      What is the total volume of the second lot of drink?

5 **a** A train travels at 110 miles per hour for $2\frac{1}{2}$ hours.
      How far does the train travel in this time?
   b The train continues for a further half an hour at 50 miles per hour.
      How far does the train travel in this time?
   c Find the average speed for the whole journey.
$$\left(\text{Average speed} = \frac{\text{total distance}}{\text{total time}} \right)$$

- To work out what percentage one number is of another:
  (1) Write the number as a fraction.
  (2) Convert the fraction to a percentage.

  Example   A 35 g slice of wholemeal bread contains 3 g of fibre.
  What percentage of the bread is fibre?

  $$\frac{3}{35} \times 100 = 3 \div 35 \times 100 = 8.5714 \ldots = 8.6\% \text{ correct to 1 dp}$$

- *Examples*   **1**   Change these to percentages: **a** 0.65   **b** $\frac{3}{5}$

  $\boxed{\times 100}$

  a $0.65 \times 100 = 65\%$

  b $\frac{3}{5} \times 100 = 3 \div 5 \times 100 = 60\%$

  2   Change 14% to: **a** a decimal   **b** a fraction in its lowest terms

  $\boxed{\div 100}$

  a $14\% = 14 \div 100 = 0.14$ **b** $14\% = \frac{14}{100} = \frac{7}{50}$ $\overset{\div 2}{\underset{\div 2}{}}$

  Remember: $50\% = \frac{1}{2}$ $25\% = \frac{1}{4}$ $10\% = \frac{1}{10}$ $20\% = \frac{1}{5}$ $75\% = \frac{3}{4}$

- *Example*   Sian is buying a computer. It costs £960.
  The shop reduces the price by 12%. How much does Sian save?

	Step 1	Step 2	Step 3
Sian needs to work out 12% of 960.	$\dfrac{12}{100}$	$\times$	960

	Step 1		Step 2	Step 3

  $\boxed{1}\ \boxed{2}\ \boxed{\div}\ \boxed{1}\ \boxed{0}\ \boxed{0}\ \boxed{\times}\ \boxed{9}\ \boxed{6}\ \boxed{0}\ \boxed{=}$ £115.20

- **Ratio**   **Ratio** is a measure of the relative size or quantity of things.

  Example   Share £60 in the ratio of the ages of Carl, Rani and Katy. They are aged 15, 10 and 5 years respectively.

  The ratio of their ages is $15 : 10 : 5 = \dfrac{15}{5} : \dfrac{10}{5} : \dfrac{5}{5} = 3 : 2 : 1$

  $3 + 2 + 1 = 6$ shares are needed.   Carl gets £10 × 3 = £30
  One share is £60 ÷ 6 = £10   Rani gets £10 × 2 = £20
  Katy gets £10 × 1 = £10

  Check: £30 + £20 + £10 = £60

- Sometimes ratios are written in the form $1 : n$

  Example   Convert the ratio $2 : 9$ into the form $1 : n$
  To convert $2 : 9$ into the form $1 : n$ you need to divide by 2. $2 : 9 = \dfrac{2}{2} : \dfrac{9}{2} = 1 : 4.5$

1 Sam has used 46% of a video tape.
What percentage is left?

2 A primary school has 250 pupils.
35 pupils go to visit a local secondary school.
What percentage is this?

3 Change these to percentages.
a $\frac{4}{5}$ **b** 0.39

4 Convert 16% to:
a a decimal   **b** a fraction in its lowest terms.

5 A salesman earns £240 a week.
He gets a rise of 5%.
What is his new salary?

6 The total prize money for a
marathon run is £360.
The money is shared between
1st, 2nd and 3rd prizes in the
ratio 5 : 3 : 1. How much is
each prize worth?

7 Three model cars cost £2.61
How much do 7 cars cost?

8 5 cm³ of mercury weigh 67.7 g.
a Find the density of mercury.
b Find the mass of 12 cm³ of mercury.

9 A plane travels 2320 km at a speed of 580 km per hour.
How long does the plane take to fly this distance?

10 The speed of light is about 300 000 km per second.
How far will light travel in 6 seconds?

8 Algebra

QUESTIONS

EXTENSION

SUMMARY

TEST YOURSELF

In 3 years' time, Nishi's father will be 4 times as old as Nishi.

In 3 years' time, Nishi's father will be 40.

How old is Nishi now?

1 Brackets

... continued on page 161 ...

◀◀ **REPLAY** ▶

Collecting terms	$a + a + a + a + a = 5a$ This is called **collecting terms**. *Remember*: $5a = 5 \times a$
Power	$a \times a \times a = a^3$ The **power** '3' tells you how many *a*s are multiplied together.

Exercise 8:1

Write each of these expressions in a shorter form by collecting terms or using a power.

1 $b + b + b + b + b + b$

2 $m \times m$

3 $g + g + g + g$

4 $y \times y \times y \times y \times y$

5 $t + t + t$

6 $n + n + n + n + n + n + n$

7 $k + k$

8 $r \times r \times r \times r$

9 $j \times j \times j \times j \times j \times j \times j$

10 $p + p + p + p + p$

11 $h \times h \times h$

12 $q \times q \times q \times q \times q$

Sometimes you have more than one letter or number to collect.

Examples   **1** $f + f + f + g + g = 3f + 2g$ **3** $4t + 2 + 3t = 7t + 2$

   2 $2a + 4a + 3b = 6a + 3b$ **4** $3g - g + 2h + 4h = 2g + 6h$

Exercise 8:2

Collect these terms.

1 $j + j + k + k + k + k$ **7** $4g + 3g + 5h + 2h$

2 $p + p + q + q + q$ **8** $2p + 4p + 3q - 3q$

3 $h + h + h + h + i$ **9** $3a + b + a + 2b$

4 $5f + 2f + g + g$ **10** $7r + 2s + r - s$

5 $r + 2r + 3s + 2s$ **11** $5p + 6 + 2p - 5$

6 $7y - 5y - y$ **12** $3t + 6s - 4s + t$

Sometimes you have more than one letter or number to multiply.

Examples   **1** $f \times g = fg$ **3** $4r \times 2s = 8rs$

   2 $g \times 3h = 3gh$ **4** $(2p)^2 = 2p \times 2p = 4p^2$

Exercise 8:3

Simplify these expressions.

1 $c \times d$ **5** $4 \times 2w$ **9** $4s \times 3s$ **13** $(3p)^2$

2 $2 \times 4c$ **6** $3s \times 3t$ **10** $3a \times 2a$ **14** $k \times 6k$

3 $2 \times r \times s$ **7** $4b \times 5c$ **11** $(4k)^2$ **15** $j \times 3j$

4 $5 \times 3c$ **8** $2d \times 6e$ **12** $(2q)^2$ ● **16** $4r \times 2rs$

Multiplying out brackets

You can use BODMAS to remind you what to do first.

You do   **B**rackets first
then powers   **O**f
Next you do   **D**ivision
and   **M**ultiplication
Then you do   **A**ddition
and   **S**ubtraction

Example   Work these out using the rules of **BODMAS**.
         a $3 \times (5 + 9)$ **b** $2 \times 4 + 3 \times 5$

         a $3 \times (5 + 9) = 3 \times 14$ **b** $2 \times 4 + 3 \times 5 = 8 + 15$
                               $= 42$ $= 23$

Exercise 8:4

1   Work out part (1) and part (2) of **a** to **e** using the rules of BODMAS.
    a   (1) $2 \times (3 + 7)$ (2) $2 \times 3 + 2 \times 7$
    b   (1) $5 \times (9 - 4)$ (2) $5 \times 9 - 5 \times 4$
    c   (1) $10 \times (7 + 8)$ (2) $10 \times 7 + 10 \times 8$
    d   (1) $7 \times (6 - 5)$ (2) $7 \times 6 - 7 \times 5$
    e   (1) $4 \times (8 - 3)$ (2) $4 \times 8 - 4 \times 3$

2   Write down what you notice about the answers in question **1**.

If you have a letter in the bracket, you cannot work out the bracket first.
You have to *multiply out* the bracket.

         Using the rules of algebra $2(3j + 4)$ means $2 \times (3j + 4)$
         $2 \times (3j + 4)$ means $2 \times 3j + 2 \times 4 = 6j + 8$

Example   Multiply out the bracket $7(10 - r)$

         $7(10 - r) = 7 \times 10 - 7 \times r$ The sign in $7(10 - r)$ is minus
                 $= 70 - 7r$ so the sign in $70 - 7r$ is also minus.

---

3 Copy these expressions and fill them in.

a $4 \times (3 + a) = 4 \times 3 + 4 \times a$
$ = 12 + \ldots$

d $2 \times (s - 3) = 2 \times \ldots - 2 \times \ldots$
$ = \ldots - \ldots$

b $5 \times (2 + y) = 5 \times \ldots + 5 \times \ldots$
$ = \ldots + 5y$

e $5 \times (2p - 3) = 5 \times \ldots - 5 \times \ldots$
$ = \ldots - \ldots$

c $7 \times (t - 3) = 7 \times \ldots - 7 \times \ldots$
$ = 7t - \ldots$

f $10 \times (2 + 3h) = 10 \times \ldots + 10 \times \ldots$
$ = \ldots + \ldots$

Exercise 8:5

Multiply out these brackets.

1 $4(3 + t)$

5 $9(2s - 3)$

9 $6(5 + j + k)$

2 $6(1 - s)$

6 $4(2t + s)$

10 $8(2 + m + n)$

3 $4(p + q)$

7 $3(10j - 4k)$

11 $7(3 + 2a + b)$

4 $5(3y + 2)$

8 $5(4x + 5y)$

12 $9(r - s - t)$

You can have letters outside the bracket.
Remember: $d \times 5 = 5 \times d = 5d$ and $d \times d = d^2$

Example   Multiply out: **a** $d(5 + c)$ **b** $f(2f + 3)$

a $d(5 + c) = d \times 5 + d \times c$
$ = 5d + cd$

b $f(2f + 3) = f \times 2f + f \times 3$
$ = 2f^2 + 3f$

You write cd and not dc. The letters go in alphabetical order.

---

13 $a(5 + b)$

17 $m(2n + 5)$

21 $e(f + 2g - h)$

14 $f(g - 3)$

18 $r(3 - 2s)$

22 $w(7 + 3x - y)$

15 $c(c + 2)$

19 $t(s + t)$

23 $p(p - q + 4r)$

16 $e(5 - e)$

20 $x(x - y)$

● **24** $5a(3a + 4b - 7c)$

You can have more than one bracket.

Example   Multiply out these brackets: $5(3 + 2x) + 3(4 - x)$
Give your answer in its simplest form.

$$5(3 + 2x) + 3(4 - x) = 15 + 10x + 12 - 3x$$
$$= 27 + 7x$$

Exercise 8:6

Multiply out these sets of brackets.
Give your answers in their simplest form.

1 $2(3 + y) + 5(4 + y)$

2 $3(4 + d) + 4(2 + d)$

3 $5(3 + x) + 5(7 + x)$

4 $3(8 + f) + (4 + f)$

5 $11(5 + 3k) + 5(7 + 4k)$

6 $2(7 + 2y) + 5(4 + 3y)$

7 $2(10 + e) + (6 + e)$

8 $2(r + 9) + 6(r + 2)$

9 $2(q + 5) + 4(q + 7)$

10 $2(t + 3) + 5(2t + 5)$

11 $3(4r + 1) + 5(r + 2)$

12 $3(4r + 5) + 5(r - 2)$

13 $6(s + 1) + 5(s - 1)$

14 $12(2x + y) + 2(3x - y)$

15 $4(a + 2b) + (a - b)$

16 $3(s + 2t) + 2(2s + 3t)$

17 $6(s + t) + 3(s - t)$

18 $5(q + r) + 2(q - r)$

19 $4(3 + y) + 3(4 - y)$

● **20** $4(5 + 2y) + y(3 + y)$

● **21** $s(4 + s) + 2(3 + 2s)$

● **22** $x(x + 3) + 4(x - 2)$

2 Equations

. . .

Linear equations	Equations with simple letters and numbers are called **linear equations**. Linear equations must not have any terms with powers like x^2 or x^3

Remember: When you are solving equations you *must* do the same thing to both sides of the equation.

Examples

The inverse of × 5 is ÷ 5 so divide both sides by 5.

1 Solve $5x = 60$

$$\frac{5x}{5} = \frac{60}{5}$$

$$x = 12$$

2 Solve $3x + 4 = 19$

The inverse of + 4 is − 4 so first subtract 4 from both sides.

$$3x + 4 - 4 = 19 - 4$$

Now divide both sides by 3.

$$3x = 15$$

$$x = 5$$

Exercise 8:7

Solve these equations.

1 $4x = 16$

2 $3x = 21$

3 $x + 6 = 12$

4 $x + 12 = 45$

5 $x - 7 = 23$

6 $\dfrac{x}{5} = 12$

7 $\dfrac{x}{7} = 2$

8 $0.5x = 3$

9 $3x + 1 = 16$

10 $5x - 3 = 27$

11 $3x + 7 = 16$

12 $\dfrac{x}{5} - 1 = 12$

13 $\dfrac{x}{3} + 2 = 10$

● **14** $4x - 6 = 16$

● **15** $\dfrac{2x}{3} = 6$

● **16** $\dfrac{3x}{2} + 5 = 26$

Look at the equation $7x = 4x + 9$
It has letters on both sides.
To solve it, you start by changing the equation so that x is only on one side.

Example   Solve $7x = 4x + 9$

Look to see which side has the *least* x.
Take this number of x's from both sides.
In this example the right-hand side has only $4x$.
Subtract $4x$ from each side. $7x - 4x = 4x - 4x + 9$
$$3x = 9$$
Divide both sides by 3. $x = 3$

Exercise 8:8

Solve these equations.

1 $6x = 4x + 8$ **5** $4x + 8 = 6x$

2 $9x = 6x + 24$ **6** $12x = 6 + 10x$

3 $10x = 5x + 45$ **7** $2.5x = 1.5x + 6$

4 $7x = x + 42$ ● **8** $3.5x = x + 10$

Sometimes, the side with the least x will be the left-hand side. You can still solve the equation in the same way.

Example   Solve $3x + 6 = 6x$

Take $3x$ from both sides. $3x + 6 - 3x = 6x - 3x$
$$6 = 3x$$

Divide by 3. $2 = x$

It is usual to write this
the other way around. $x = 2$

---

9 $4x + 3 = 5x$ **12** $5x + 21 = 12x$

10 $3x + 6 = 5x$ **13** $0.5x + 15 = 2.5x$

11 $2x + 17 = 4x$ ● **14** $3x - 6 = 5x$

Some equations have letters and numbers on both sides.
First, change the equation so it has x on only one side.

Example $5x + 3 = 2x + 15$

The right-hand side has least x.
Subtract $2x$ from each side. $5x - 2x + 3 = 2x - 2x + 15$
$$3x + 3 = 15$$

Now remove the numbers from the side with the x.
The left-hand side has a 3.
Subtract 3 from each side. $3x + 3 - 3 = 15 - 3$
$$3x = 12$$

Divide both side by 3. $x = 4$

Exercise 8:9

Solve these equations.

1 $6x + 2 = 3x + 5$

2 $9x + 1 = 5x + 13$

3 $5x - 5 = 2x + 4$

4 $10x - 12 = 3x + 16$

5 $13x - 15 = 12x + 19$

6 $8x + 12 = 3x + 57$

7 $12x - 1 = 7x + 19$

8 $5x - 4 = 4x + 3$

9 $2.5x + 10 = 1.5x + 17$

● **10** $3.5x - 12 = x + 3$

The method does not alter if you have a minus sign in front of one of the letters.
A negative number is always less than a positive number.
This means that the side with the minus sign has the least x.
To remove the x from this side, **add** the same number of xs on to each side.

Example   Solve $5x + 3 = 21 - x$

First, remove the x from the right-hand side.
To do this, add x to each side. $5x + x + 3 = 21 - x + x$

Now solve the equation as before. $6x + 3 = 21$

Subtract 3 from each side. $6x = 18$

Divide both sides by 6. $x = 3$

---

11 $5x + 3 = 15 - x$

12 $7x + 2 = 20 - 2x$

13 $2x + 4 = 13 - x$

14 $4x - 3 = 12 - x$

15 $10x - 5 = 31 - 2x$

16 $2x - 7 = 3 - 8x$

17 $2.6x + 10 = 23 - 1.3x$

● **18** $0.5x - 5 = 15 - x$

If equations have brackets in them, you should remove the brackets first.

Example   Solve $3(2x + 1) = 27$

Remove the bracket.
Now solve the equation as usual.

$$3(2x + 1) = 27$$
$$3 \times 2x + 3 \times 1 = 27$$
$$6x + 3 = 27$$
$$6x = 24$$
$$x = 4.$$

Exercise 8:10

Solve these equations.

1 $3(2x + 2) = 24$

2 $5(6x - 2) = 50$

3 $4(3x - 7) = 20$

4 $6(7x - 1) = 36$

5 $10(3x - 4) = 80$

6 $12(3x + 2) = 36$

7 $2(x + 1) = 8$

8 $6(3x + 5) = 30$

9 $7(2x - 16) = 0$

10 $\frac{1}{2}(x + 5) = 20$

Exercise 8:11

Solve these equations.

1 $6x = 3x + 99$

2 $3x - 4 = x + 8$

3 $6(2x - 4) = 36$

4 $5x + 10 = 2x + 16$

5 $11x + 90 = 20x$

6 $\frac{1}{2}x + 10 = 23$

7 $6 - x = 1 + 4x$

8 $\frac{x}{5} + 3 = 12$

9 $\frac{2x}{3} - 4 = 19$

10 $\frac{1}{2}x + 3 = \frac{1}{4}x + 12$

1 Simplify these expressions.
  a $h + h + h + h + h$
  b $k \times k \times k \times k \times k \times k$
  c $a + a + a + b + b$
  d $6v + 2w + v + 3w$
  e $5t + 4s + 2t - 3s$
  f $5x + 7 - 4x + 3$

2 Simplify these.
  a $4 \times 3f$
  b $3s \times 4t$
  c $(4e)^2$
  d $r \times 5r$

3 Multiply out these brackets.
  a $5(2t + 5)$
  b $7(3r - 1)$
  c $4(3 + 5f)$
  d $10(6x - 5y)$
  e $4(3e - 5g)$
  f $5(2r + 3s)$

4 Multiply out these brackets.
  a $t(4t + 5)$
  b $a(3a + 2)$
  c $w(1 - 5w)$
  d $c(3 - 5c)$
  e $r(3r - 2s)$
  f $p(p + 2q)$

5 Multiply out these brackets.
Give each answer as simply as possible.
  a $2(r + 3) + 5(2r - 1)$
  b $3(4 + 2g) + 2(1 + 3g)$
  c $7(2t + 1) + 3(t - 2)$
  d $4(e + f) + 3(2e + f)$
  e $3(s + 2t) + 4(s - t)$
  f $11(3p + 2q) + 2(5p - 3q)$

6 Solve these equations.
  a $3x = 18$
  b $x - 6 = 17$
  c $\frac{x}{3} = 7$
  d $x + 6 = 6$
  e $2x + 3 = 9$
  f $5x - 1 = 24$

7 Solve these equations.
  a $5x + 3 = 2x + 18$
  b $12x - 4 = 7x + 31$
  c $8x + 5 = 3x + 25$
  d $4x - 5 = x + 1$
  e $7x + 1 = 5x + 9$
  f $10x - 17 = 6x + 3$

8 Solve these equations.
  a $3x + 24 = 7x$
  b $2x + 16 = 6x$
  c $6x + 16 = 10x$
  d $4.5x + 20 = 6.5x$

9 Solve these equations.
  a $5(x + 3) = 25$
  b $6(2x + 2) = 24$
  c $3(3x - 2) = 30$
  d $5(2x + 1) = 35$

10 Vali, Sharon, Jon and Mandy each start a game with one or more boxes of counters. There are c counters in each box.

| 2 boxes
Vali | 1 box
Sharon | 3 boxes
Jon | 4 boxes
Mandy |

The table shows what happens during the game.

a Write an expression to show the number of counters that Jon and Mandy have at the end of the game.
Write each expression as simply as possible.

	Start	During game	End of game
Vali	2 boxes	lost 7 counters	$2c - 7$
Sharon	1 box	won 5 counters	$c + 5$
Jon	3 boxes	won 6 counters	
Mandy	4 boxes	won 8 counters and lost 4 counters	

b At the end of the game Vali and Sharon have the same number of counters. Write an equation to show this.
c Solve your equation to find the value of c.

11 The length of a side of this square is x cm.
  a Copy and fill in:
  The perimeter of the square is $x + x + x + x = \ldots x$
  The perimeter of the square is 52 cm.
  b Write down an equation $4x = \ldots$
  c Solve your equation to find the length of a side of the square.

x

1 Multiply out these brackets.
   a $3r(4r - 3s)$ **b** $7t(3r + 4s)$ **c** $5g(3g + 2)$

2 Solve the following equations.
   a $6x + 5 = 3x + 2$ **c** $5x - 5 = 2x + 4$
   b $9x + 1 = 5x + 13$ **d** $10x - 12 = 3x + 16$

3 Solve the following equations
   a $6(3x + 1) = 3(4x + 2)$ **c** $3(6x - 5) = 5(x + 10)$
   b $2(7x - 3) = 3(2x + 6)$ **d** $2(5x - 9) = 3(x + 1)$

4 Four people each have a card.

$5a - 1$	$a + 5$	$a - 4$	$3a + 7$
Ann	Bob	Cath	David

   a Ann and David decide to find the value of a that makes their cards
      have the same value. They write this equation: $5a - 1 = 3a + 7$
      Find the value of a that makes Ann and David's cards the same.
   b Ann and Bob decide to find the value of a that makes their cards
      have the same value. Find this value of a.
   c There are two people whose cards will never be worth the same as
      each other. Who are the two people?
      Explain why their cards cannot be the same.

5

   The length of this train's engine is 12 m.
   The length of each carriage is 15 m.
   a Work out the length of a train with 8 carriages.
   b Write down a formula for the length of a train with n carriages.
   c The length of a train with n carriages is 177 m.
      (1) Write down an equation using your answer to **b**.
      (2) Solve the equation to work out the number of carriages.

- **Collecting** $a + a + a + a + a = 5a$
  This is called **collecting terms**. *Remember*: $5a = 5 \times a$

  Power $a \times a \times a = a^3$
  The **power** '3' tells you how many *as* are multiplied together.

- Sometimes you have more than one letter or number to collect.

  Examples   **1** $f + f + f + g + g = 3f + 2g$ **3** $4t + 2 + 3t = 7t + 2$

  2 $2a + 4a + 3b = 6a + 3b$ **4** $3g - g + 2h + 4h = 2g + 6h$

- Sometimes you have more than one letter or number to multiply.

  Examples   **1** $f \times g = fg$ **3** $4r \times 2s = 8rs$

  2 $g \times 3h = 3gh$ **4** $(2p)^2 = 2p \times 2p = 4p^2$

- *Examples*   Multiply out these brackets.

  1 $7(10 - r)$
  $7(10 - r) = 7 \times 10 - 7 \times r$
  $= 70 - 7r$

  2 $5(3 + 2x) + 3(4 - x) = 15 + 10x + 12 - 3x$
  $= 27 + 7x$

- *Examples*   Solve these equations.

1 $7x = 4x + 9$ **3** $5x + 3 = 21 - x$
$7x - 4x = 4x - 4x + 9$ First, remove the x from the
$3x = 9$ right-hand side.
Divide both sides by 3. $x = 3$ To do this, add x to each side.
                                          $5x + x + 3 = 21 - x + x$
                                          $6x + 3 = 21$
                                          $x = 3$

2 $3x + 6 = 6x$ **4** $3(2x + 1) = 27$
Take $3x$ from both sides.   Remove the bracket.
$3x + 6 - 3x = 6x - 3x$ $3 \times 2x + 3 \times 1 = 27$
$6 = 3x$ $6x + 3 = 27$
Divide by 3. $2 = x$ $6x = 24$
Write this the other way round. $x = 2$ $x = 4$

1   Simplify these expressions.

    a $e + e + e + e$ **d** $q \times q \times q$

    b $f \times f \times f$ **e** $h \times h \times h \times h \times h$

    c $g + g + g + g + g + g$ **f** $k + k$

2   Collect like terms.

    a $2f + 3g + 5f + g$ **d** $4g + 4 - 3g - 2$

    b $8r + s + 3r - s$ **e** $5x + 4y - 3y + 2x$

    c $4u + 5u + 7v - 5v$ **f** $5r + 2r - 4r + 6$

3   Simplify, these expressions.

    a $4 \times 3a$ **c** $3 \times c \times d$

    b $5r \times 2r$ **d** $(3y)^2$

4   Multiply out these brackets.

    a $3(2r - 5)$ **c** $d(2e - 5)$

    b $t(t + 4)$ **d** $6r(s + 2r)$

5   Multiply out each of these sets of brackets.
    Give your answers as simply as possible.

    a $7(f + 3) + 2(5f - 4)$ **b** $4(p + 2q) + 3(p - 2q)$

6   Solve these equations.

    a $x + 5 = 17$ **c** $\dfrac{x}{3} = 11$

    b $5x = 35$ **d** $x - 5 = 22$

7   Solve these equations.

    a $3x + 15 = 8x$ **b** $5x - 7 = 18$

8   Solve these equations.

    a $6x - 3 = 4x + 5$ **b** $4x + 6 = 21 - x$

9   Solve these equations.

    a $5(x + 4) = 35$ **b** $3(x - 2) = 18$

9 Statistics

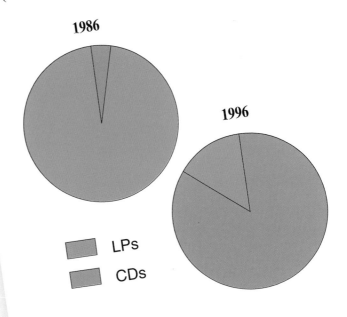

Relative share of retail sales in UK held by LPs and CDs (albums only) in 1986 and 1996.

1986

1996

LPs

CDs

Source: unpublished data.

CORE

1 Scatter diagrams

Mammals have different average life spans.
A horse is expected to live about 20 years.
A dog is expected to live about 12 years.
Pregnant mammals carry their unborn young for different lengths of time.
This length of time is called the gestation period.
There is a relationship between the lifespan and the gestation period.

Fiona has found the lifespans and gestation periods for different pet animals.
She has drawn this graph using her data.

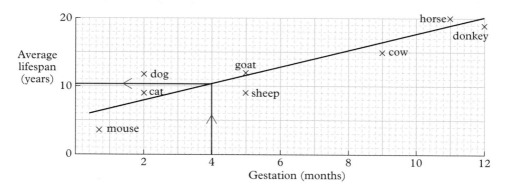

| **Correlation** | Fiona's graph shows that as the lifespan increases so does the gestation period. There is **correlation** between the two. |

| **Scatter graphs** | Graphs like this are called **scatter graphs**. |

| **Line of best fit** | The points seem to lie roughly in a straight line. Fiona has drawn in the line that best fits the points. This line is called the **line of best fit**. |

Fiona knows that the gestation period for a pig is 4 months.
She uses the line of best fit to estimate the average lifespan of a pig.
The red line starts at 4 months. Follow the red line to find an estimate for the average lifespan of a pig.
The estimate is $10\frac{1}{2}$ years.

Exercise 9:1

1 Mr Lawson has plotted the marks for his maths group in the end of term exams.
The pupils sat two papers.

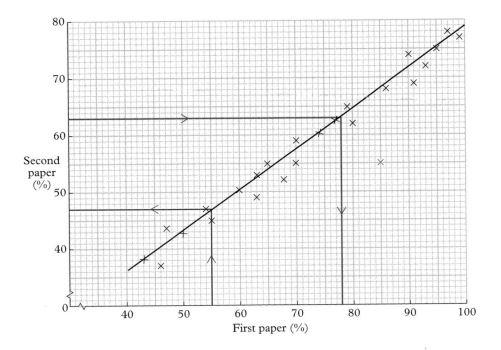

a Joshua scored 55% on the first paper but he was ill for the second paper. Use the line of best fit to estimate what his mark would have been for the second paper.
The red line starts at 55% on the axis for the first paper.
Follow the red line to find the estimated mark for the second paper.

b Marie missed the first paper but scored 63% on the second paper.
Use the line of best fit to estimate her mark for the first paper.
Follow the blue line to help you.
Would you expect Marie to get this mark if she sat the paper?
Explain your answer.

c Which paper do you think was harder? Explain your answer

d One of the students was not well when he took the second paper.
His marks are shown by the green cross.
Explain why this cross is well below the line of best fit.
Write down his mark on the first paper.
Use the line of best fit to estimate the mark he was expected to get on the second paper.

2 Alan is looking to see if there is correlation between the lengths and widths of leaves from a bush. These are his measurements in centimetres.

Length	7.4	6.9	5.0	6.3	6.6	6.5	5.0	6.3
Width	3.5	3.2	2.1	2.8	2.9	3.0	1.8	2.5

a Use graph paper to plot Alan's data.
b Is there correlation?
   Explain your answer.
c Draw the line of best fit.
d Estimate the width of a leaf when the length is 6.0 cm.
   Use the line of best fit.

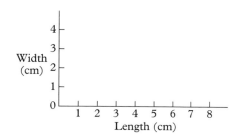

3 Sinita is writing up the results of a scientific experiment.
For part of her experiment she heated a beaker of liquid and measured the temperature every minute.
This is a graph of her results.

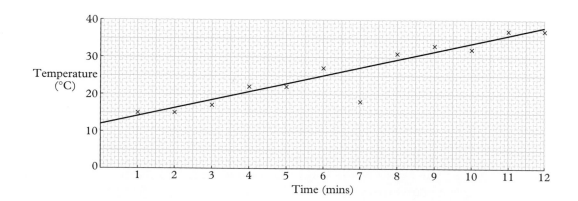

a Sinita misread the thermometer for one of the readings.
   Write down the time of this reading.
b What would you expect the temperature to be at $10\frac{1}{2}$ minutes?
c Write down the temperature of the liquid at the beginning of the experiment.

4 A doctor is checking the weights of babies at a clinic. He is using this scatter graph to help him identify any babies who are underweight or overweight for their height.

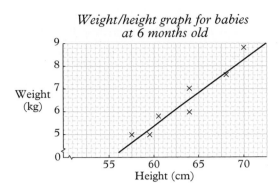

Weight/height graph for babies at 6 months old

Write down for each of these babies whether you think they are underweight, overweight or about the correct weight

Baby	Rashid	Jane	Louise	Sam
Height (cm)	66	63	69	65
Weight (kg)	7.2	5.0	7.9	8.4

There are different types of correlation in these graphs.

Positive correlation

This scatter graph shows the weights and heights of 10 children. As the weight increases so does the height. This is called **positive correlation**.

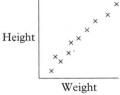

Negative correlation

This scatter graph shows sales of gloves and daily temperatures. As the temperature increases so the sales of gloves decrease. This is called **negative correlation**.

No correlation

This scatter graph shows the salaries and heights of teachers. There is no relationship between the two. The points are scattered all over. There is **no correlation**.

175

Correlation can be strong or weak.

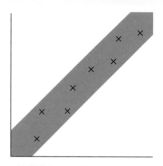

Strong positive correlation
The crosses lie in a narrow band.

Weak negative correlation
The crosses lie in a broad band.

5 Look at each of these scatter graphs.
Describe the type of correlation you can see.

a

Sales of umbrellas

Rainfall

c

Average test mark

Number of days absent

b

Maths mark for Year 9

Height for Year 9

d

Sales of suntan cream

Temperature

6 Laura is doing a survey. She asks eight of her friends how much time they spent on homework last night and how long they watched the television. These are her results. The times are in minutes.

Homework	65	120	85	35	160	100	70	95
Television	190	90	150	210	85	250	150	140

   a Draw a scatter diagram to show Laura's data.
   b Does your graph show any correlation?
   If it does, describe the type of correlation.

7 Jack and Sara manage eight paper shops.
Jack thinks that the weekly sales of papers depend on the size of the shop.
Sara thinks that the sales depend on the number of houses within 3 miles.

They used their sales figures to draw these two scatter graphs.

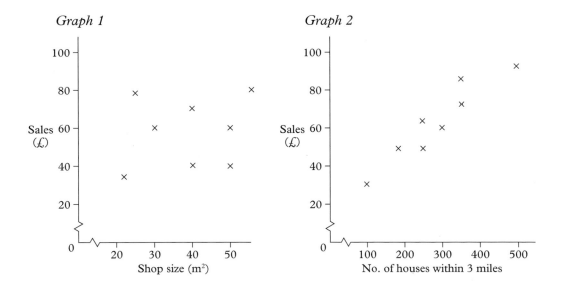

   a What does graph 1 show about the relationship between weekly sales and shop size?
   b What does graph 2 show?
   c Jack and Sara are asked to manage another paper shop.
   It has a floor area of 28 m² and there are 450 houses within 3 miles.
   Use one of the graphs to estimate the sales that the shop is likely to make.
   Write down which graph you used. Explain how you made your estimate.

2 Pie-charts

The land in Holland is mostly flat.
The small number of hills are not very high.
The pie-chart shows how the land is divided between below sea level, at sea level, and above sea level.

Exercise 9:2

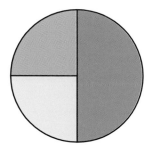

1 The whole circle is 100%.
  a What percentage of the circle is red?
  b What percentage of the circle is green?
  c (1) What fraction of the circle is red or yellow?
    (2) What percentage is this?

You may have to *estimate* the percentages shown by 'slices' of pie-charts.

Example This pie-chart shows what pupils in a school do for lunch.
  a Estimate the percentage that buy lunch in the school canteen.
  b Estimate the percentage that bring a packed lunch.

  a The 'slice' for school canteen is a bit less than half.
    It is a bit less than 50%.
    An estimate is 45%.
  b The 'slice' for packed lunch is a bit more than a quarter.
    It is a bit more than 25%.
    An estimate is 30%.

---

2 Estimate the percentage of each of these pie-charts that is coloured red.

a 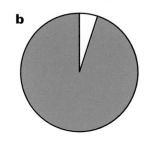 **b** 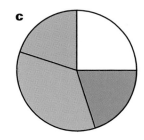 **c**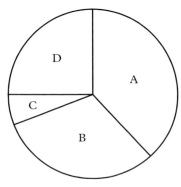

3 This pie-chart shows the balance of food recommended for a healthy diet.
  a Copy the table below.
  b Estimate the percentage in each section of the pie-chart.
  Fill in the table with your estimates.
  c Find the total of your estimates.
  Do they add up to 100%?

Balance of food for a healthy diet

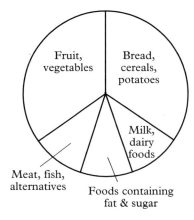

Item of diet	Percentage
fruit/veg	
bread/cereals/pots	
milk/dairy foods	
foods with fat/sugar	
meat/fish/alternatives	

4 This pie-chart shows the contents of a type of cheese.

Contents	Percentage
fat	31%
water	38%
protein	25%
carbohydrate	

Contents of a type of cheese

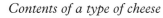

  a What does part A of the pie-chart represent?
  Use the contents table to help you.
  b What does part D represent?
  c Use the contents table to find the percentage part C represents.

5 These pie-charts show the percentages of Year 9 girls and boys at Stanthorne High who go home to lunch.

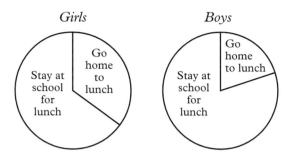

Girls   Boys

a Estimate the percentage of girls who go home to lunch.
b Estimate the percentage of boys who go home to lunch.
c The number of girls in Year 9 is approximately equal to the number of boys. Sketch a new pie-chart for the whole of Year 9 to show the percentage who go home to lunch.

◀◀REPLAY▶

Example   The table gives the type of fish bought by 60 customers of a fish and chip shop one evening.

Type of fish	cod	plaice	scampi	haddock
Number of customers	28	9	6	17

Show these results in a pie-chart.

1 There are 60 people in the survey, and $360° ÷ 60 = 6°$
This means that each person gets 6° of the circle.

2 Work out the angle for each fish. This is easy to do in a table.

Fish	Number of people	Working	Angle
cod	28	28 × 6°	168°
plaice	9	9 × 6°	54°
scampi	6	6 × 6°	36°
haddock	17	17 × 6°	102°
Total	60		360°

3 Check that the angles add up to 360°.

4 a Draw a circle. Mark the centre.
Draw a line to the top of the circle.
Draw the first angle (168°).

b Measure the next angle from
the line that you have just
drawn (54°).

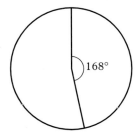

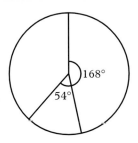

Type of fish bought by 60 customers

c Carry on until you
have drawn all the angles.
Label the pie-chart.

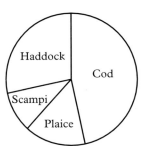

Exercise 9:3

1 Nayreen asks 9W what school clubs they belong to.
  a Copy this table.

Club	Number of pupils	Working	Angle
chess	5	5 × ...°	
gym	12	12 × ...°	
drama	10		
none	3		
Total			

  b How many pupils did Nayreen ask?
  c Copy and fill in:
    There are ... pupils and 360° ÷ ... = ...°
    Each pupil gets ...° of the circle.
  d Fill in the working and angle columns of the table.
  e Draw and label a pie-chart.

2 The school canteen supervisor recorded the vegetarian meals sold in a week. The results are shown in the table.

Meal	cheese flan	vegeburger	vegetable curry	bean casserole
Number sold	31	12	22	25

   a How many vegetarian meals were sold?
   b Work out the angle of the circle each meal will get.
   c Draw a pie-chart to show the meals sold.
   Remember to label the pie-chart.

3 *Teen Style* magazine asked their readers to name their favourite type of feature in the magazine. The results are shown in the table.

Type of feature	fiction	fashion	health	sport	travel
Number of people	270	216	42	123	69

   a Write down how many people took part in the survey.
   b Find the angle for each sector of the pie-chart.
   c Draw a pie-chart for the data.

4 Rajiv is doing a survey on cars that fail their MOT.
He has collected data on cars that failed for just one reason.

Reason	brakes or lights	tyres	mechanical	exhaust gas
Number of cars	33	21	51	9

   a Write down the total number of cars surveyed.
   b Find the angle for each sector of the pie-chart.
   Round each angle to the nearest degree.
   c Draw a pie-chart for the data.

3 Misleading diagrams

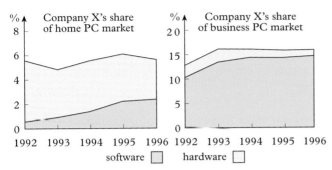

Sometimes charts are used to mislead people.
Changing the scale of a diagram can have a big effect on its appearance. When you read statistical diagrams, you should always look carefully at the scale.

Exercise 9:4

1 Robert sells mountain bikes. He wants to expand his business.
He needs to borrow money from the bank. He wants to show the bank manager that his sales are growing fast. These are the sales for the last 6 months.

Month	Jan	Feb	Mar	Apr	May	June
Number of bikes sold	26	27	29	34	44	55

Robert draws two bar-charts. Chart A uses the whole scale.
In chart B the scale starts at 25.
The two graphs show exactly the same information.
They look very different because the scales are different.

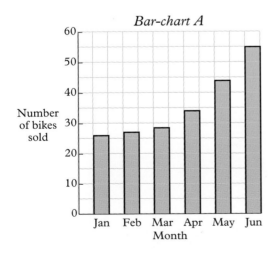

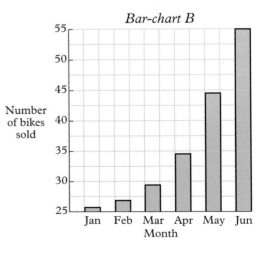

Which chart should Robert show the bank manager?
Explain your answer.

2 This table shows the sales of a company which provides take-away meals. It lists the number of meals sold in the last eight weeks.

Week 1	440	Week 5	465
Week 2	455	Week 6	485
Week 3	450	Week 7	490
Week 4	460	Week 8	495

The manager of the company wants to employ more staff. She wants to show that sales are increasing.

The owner of the company does not want to pay for any more staff. She wants to show that the sales are about the same level.

Draw one graph for each person.
Choose your scale carefully and say who would use each graph.

3 Richard started a part time window cleaning business eight years ago. He now wants to sell the business. He wants to make it look as successful as possible. Here are his profits for the eight years.

Year	1	2	3	4	5	6	7	8
Profit	£200	£225	£235	£270	£290	£330	£370	£335

Draw a bar-chart that would help Richard to make his business look very successful.

4 A computer company is advertising its products. It uses this graph in its advert to show how successful the company is. How is the graph misleading?

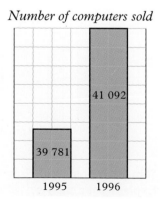

Number of computers sold

41 092

39 781

1995   1996

5 This chart shows a company's profits in 1995 and 1996. Why is the chart misleading?

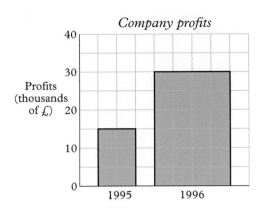

6 The Sunshine Holiday Company uses these diagrams to show how its sales are increasing.

Year	1995	1996
Sales	42 000	80 000

1995

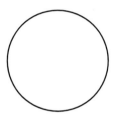

1996

Measure the diameters of these circles. How are these diagrams misleading?

7 A farm selling cheese uses these diagrams to show that sales of cheese have doubled in the last year. What comments can you make about the diagrams?

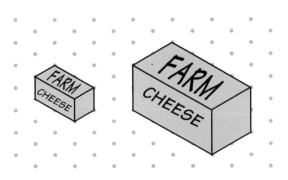

Spending time

Melissa is interested in the way teenagers spend their time.
She guesses that *the more money teenagers get the more time they spend shopping.*
This guess is called a hypothesis.

Investigate the way teenagers spend their time.
Include in your data some information to test Melissa's hypothesis
on shopping.

Make a hypothesis of your own and test it.

Write a report about how teenagers spend their time.
You should include diagrams and calculations.

Remember these rules for questionnaires from last year.

- Questions should not be biased or upset people.

- Questions should be clear and useful to your survey.

- Don't ask questions that give a lot of different answers.

- Put your questions in a sensible order.

1 Steven sells cold drinks in the park.
He recorded the temperature and the number of drinks he sold each day for two weeks. This is his data.

Number of drinks sold	40	50	85	90	100	125	115
Temperature °C	8	9	10	11	11	12	12

Number of drinks sold	150	160	200	255	250	275	290
Temperature °C	13	14	16	18	18	19	20

a Use graph paper to plot Steven's data.
b Describe the correlation.
c Draw the line of best fit.
d Estimate the sales on a day when the temperature is 15°C.
   Use the line of best fit.

2 This pie-chart shows what Michael did during 24 hours last weekend.
a What fraction of his time did he spend playing with his friends?
b How many hours did he play with his friends?
c He spent about the same length of time on another activity. What was it?
d Estimate the percentage of his time that he spent sleeping.

How Michael spent 24 hours

3 A cafe recorded the number of drinks sold during one day.
The results are shown in the table.

Drink	Number of people
tea	38
coffee	43
cold drinks (fizzy)	23
cold drinks (still)	16

Draw a pie-chart to show this data.

4 Jason carried out a survey of taxi drivers.
He drew these graphs to show his results.

a What does this graph show about the relationship between the numbers of hours worked and the amount of money earned?

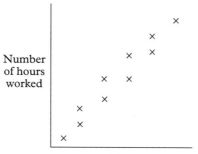

b What does this graph show about the relationship between the number of hours worked and the number of hours spent watching television?

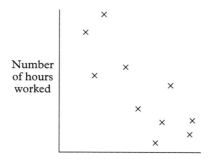

c This table shows Jason's data on the number of hours worked and the number of miles driven. Draw a scatter graph to show this data.

Hours worked	23	29	20	33	35	25
Miles driven	690	826	640	974	980	763

Hours worked	28	32	30	24
Miles driven	850	928	1020	672

Draw the line of best fit on your graph.
Estimate the number of miles driven by a driver who works 27 hours.
Use your line of best fit.

5 Stacey's parents have told her that if there is a great improvement in her test marks then they will buy her a computer game. These are Stacey's marks in her last five monthly tests.

Jan	Feb	Mar	Apr	May
50%	58%	61%	66%	69%

a Stacey decides to use a graph to show off the increase in her marks. Draw a suitable graph for Stacey. Choose your scale carefully.
b Stacey's rotten brother doesn't want Stacey to have a computer game. He draws a different graph to show Stacey's marks. Draw the graph that Stacey's brother would draw.

6 Sandhills golf club runs a tournament each year.
Last year the prize money was £2000. This year it is £4000. The club uses this poster to advertise the tournament.
Why is the poster misleading?

7 This graph shows the monthly profits of the school enterprise company.
Explain why the graph is misleading.

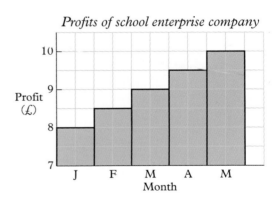

8 This table shows how the value of a car changes as it gets older.

Age (years)	1	2	3	5	6	7
Value (£)	9500	7800	7100	4000	3100	1700

a Draw a scatter graph to show this data.
b Describe the correlation.
c Draw the line of best fit.
d Estimate the value of the car when it is 4 years old.

1 The table shows the fuel consumption in miles per gallon of different size car engines.

Fuel consumption (mpg)	Engine (cc)	Fuel consumption (mpg)	Engine (cc)	Fuel consumption (mpg)	Engine (cc)
33	1250	35	1300	32	1400
30	1500	32	1500	29	1600
30	1600	27	1800	28	1800
24	1900	25	1900	22	2000
25	2000	23	2000	20	2200
22	2200	20	2500		

a Use graph paper to draw a scatter diagram of this data.
b Describe the correlation.
c Draw the line of best fit.
d Use the line of best fit to estimate the fuel consumption of a 1700 cc engine.

2 Jean did a traffic survey outside her school.
She recorded how many people were in each car.
These pie-charts show her data for two times of the day.

Between 8.15 and 9.00 am   *Between 9.00 and 9.45 am*

a Estimate what percentage of cars between 8.15 and 9.00 am contained one person.
b Jean surveyed 80 cars between 8.15 and 9.00 am. About how many contained one person?
c Jean surveyed another 80 cars between 9.00 and 9.45 am. Estimate the percentage of cars with just one person.
d How did the number of cars with one person alter between the two times?
Can you suggest a reason for this?
e Sketch a new pie-chart showing the percentage of cars containing one person for the total time from 8.15 to 9.45 am.

- **Correlation**
  This graph shows that as the lifespan increases so does the gestation period. There is correlation between the two.

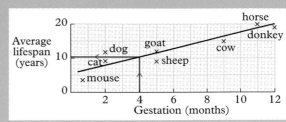

  Scatter graphs
  Graphs like this are called **scatter graphs**. The points seem to lie roughly in a straight line.

  Line of best fit   The line is called the **line of best fit**.

- Correlation can be strong or weak.

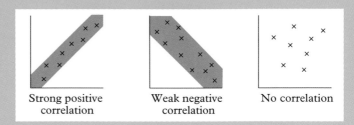

Strong positive correlation   Weak negative correlation   No correlation

- You can use a pie-chart to show the results of a survey.

Example

Type of fish	cod	plaice	scampi	haddock
Number of customers	28	9	6	17

Show these results in a pie-chart.

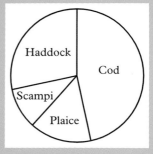

1 There are 60 people in the survey, and $360° ÷ 60 = 6°$
This means that each person gets $6°$ of the circle.

2 Work out the angle for each fish.
This is easy to do in a table.
e.g. The angle for cod is $28 × 6° = 168°$

3 Check that the angles add up to $360°$.

4 Draw and label the pie-chart.

- Sometimes charts are used to mislead people.
  Changing the scale of a diagram can have a big effect on its appearance. When you read statistical diagrams, you should always look carefully at the scale.

1 The table gives the marks of 12 pupils in their Year 9 examination papers for maths. Both papers are marked out of 50.

a On graph paper draw a Paper 1 axis across the page and a Paper 2 axis up the page.
Make both axes go up to 50.

Paper 1	14	36	25	48	39	28	47	40	26	34	18	32
Paper 2	12	37	20	46	40	23	41	35	19	21	19	29

b Plot the data. Draw the line of best fit.
c Which paper do you think is easier?
d Murray got a worse mark than expected for Paper 2.
What is Murray's Paper 2 mark?
e Brenda was absent for Paper 1 and got 30 on Paper 2.
Estimate a Paper 1 mark for Brenda.

2 Penny asked her class where they would like to go on holiday.
She drew this pie-chart to show her results.

Where my class want to go on holiday

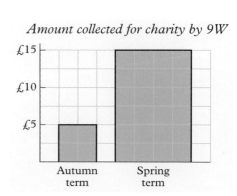

a What fraction of her class chose Australia?
b About what percentage of her class chose Europe?
c There are 28 pupils in Penny's class. How many chose America?
d Pritesh did a similar survey for his class.

Holiday choice	Europe	Australia	America	Africa	Asia
Number of pupils	10	6	8	2	4

Draw a pie-chart to show Pritesh's results.

3 Sandra has drawn this graph to show the amount collected for charity by 9W in the Autumn Term and the Spring Term.
Why is Sandra's graph misleading?

Amount collected for charity by 9W

10 The best chapter, probably

A hurricane is an intense, devastating tropical storm caused by a low-pressure weather system. Hurricanes occur in tropical regions usually between July and October.

Weather forecasters try to warn people of the approach of a hurricane. The forecasters use probabilities to give an idea of the likelihood of a hurricane striking a particular area.

1 ◀◀REPLAY▶

Rudi has bought a raffle ticket.
The prize is a holiday.
The supermarket has sold
thousands of tickets.
Rudi knows his chance of
winning the holiday is very small.

Probability

Probability tells us how likely something is to happen.
All probabilities must be between 0 and 1.

Examples

1 In a raffle 100 tickets are sold.
What is the probability of Alex winning first prize if she has
bought:

a 1 ticket   **b** 5 tickets?

a Probability of winning $= \dfrac{1}{100}$

b Probability of winning $= \dfrac{5}{100}$

$= \dfrac{1}{20}$

2 Andrew throws a dice.
a What is the probability that
Andrew throws a three?
b Show the probability of a three
on a probability scale.

a Probability of a three $= \dfrac{1}{6}$

b

0     $\frac{1}{6}$ 1

Exercise 10:1

1 500 tickets are sold in a raffle.
What is the probability of Brian winning first prize if he has bought:
  a 1 ticket   **b** 5 tickets   **c** 10 tickets?

2 Sahid chooses one letter at random from the word SUCCESS.
  a What is the probability that the letter he chooses is
    (1) the E   (2) an S?
  b Copy this probability scale.

   Show the probability of choosing a C on the scale.

3 Sam chooses a number at random from this list.
    5, 6, 7, 8, 9, 10, 11, 12
  a What is the probability that the number she chooses is
    (1) a two-digit number   (2) a number less than 7?
  b Copy this probability scale.

   Mark the probability that Sam chooses an even number on the scale.

4 A box contains 3 red, 5 green and 4 blue pencils.
Pat chooses a pencil at random. What is the probability that it is:
  a red   **c** either green or blue
  b green   **d** neither red nor green?

5 The table shows the membership of a youth club.
  a How many members are under 16?
  b How many members are female?
  c How many members of the club are there altogether?
  d A member is chosen at random.
   What is the probability that the member is:
    (1) female   (2) under 16
    (3) male and over 16?

	Under 16	16 and over
Male	18	26
Female	21	25

6 Katy has done a survey on the favourite sports of her friends.
She has drawn a bar-chart to show her data.

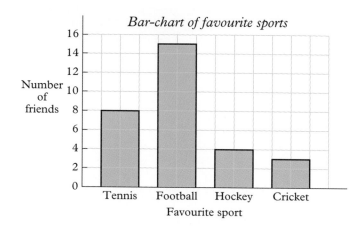

a How many of Katy's friends took part in her survey?
b One of Katy's friends is chosen at random.
What is the probability that the friend's favourite sport is:
(1) tennis   (2) hockey or cricket?
c Copy this probability scale.

0   1
├──┤

Mark the probability that the friend's favourite sport is football on
your scale.

7 Michael has 7 white beads and 1 black bead
in a bag.
He picks out a bead without looking.

His father says the probability of the
bead being black is $\frac{1}{7}$ because there are
7 white beads and one black bead.
His mother says the probability is $\frac{1}{8}$ because there
are 8 beads and just one is black.

a Whose answer is correct?
Why is the other answer wrong?
b Michael changes the number of beads in the bag.
The probability of choosing a black bead is now $\frac{3}{11}$.
How many black beads and how many white beads could be in
the bag now?
Is this the only possible answer? Give your reasons.

Probabilities always add up to 1.

Example

The probability that Peter will go bowling sometime during this week is $\frac{3}{5}$.

What is the probability that Peter will not go bowling?

Probability that Peter will not go bowling $= 1 - \dfrac{3}{5}$

$$= \dfrac{2}{5}$$

Exercise 10:2

1 The probability that the Khan family will go to France for their holiday is $\frac{8}{9}$. What is the probability that they will not go to France for their holiday?

2 Out of every 100 people, 13 are left handed.
   What is the probability that a person chosen at random is:
   a left handed   **b** not left handed?

3 Liam has to decide what sport to choose for his activity afternoon. The probability of each of his choices is given in the table.

Football	Climbing	Swimming
0.40	0.25	0.35

   a Write down the probability that he chooses
       (1) football
       (2) climbing or swimming.
   b What is the probability that he does not choose swimming?

4 Mark says the probability that his team will win their match is 0.6
   The probability that they will lose is 0.3
   Find the probability that the team will draw the match.

5 The probability that Samina goes home from the disco by bus is 0.35 and by taxi it is 0.45
   What is the probability that Samina will go home by another method?

Katie is running in a 100 metre race.
There are six runners.

The runners are **not all equally likely**
to win.

The probability that Katie wins is **not** $\frac{1}{6}$

The probability depends on how fast
Katie can run.

Exercise 10:3

Decide if each of these statements is true or false.
Write down your reason in each case.

1   The school canteen sells milk and cola.

 There are 2 drinks so the probability of a person having cola is $\frac{1}{2}$

2   A coin has 2 sides, heads or tails.

 The probability of getting tails if you toss the coin is $\frac{1}{2}$

3   In the summer, Year 9 pupils can choose to do athletics, cricket or tennis.

 There are 3 sports so the probability that a pupil chooses tennis is $\frac{1}{3}$

4   This spinner has 3 sections.

 The probability of it landing on blue is $\frac{1}{3}$

5   A shop sells balls in 3 colours, red, blue and yellow.

 The probability of a person choosing to buy a red ball is $\frac{1}{3}$

6   A cafe sells 2 hot snacks, hot dogs and beefburgers.
 David wants a hot snack.

 The probability that he chooses a beefburger is $\frac{1}{2}$

2 Relative frequency

There are 10 beads in a bag. Some of the beads are red and the rest are black. David and Pavneet have to find out how many beads of each colour are in the bag without looking. They take one bead out of the bag, note its colour and replace it. They do this lots of times.

Challenge

This is for 2 or more people.

You need a bag containing 10 beads.
Do not look inside the bag.

Choose a bead from the bag without looking.

Note the colour of the bead on a copy of this tally-table. Replace the bead. A second person has a go, notes the colour and replaces the bead. This is done 10 times.

Colour	Tally	Total

Use the data collected to guess the contents of the bag.

Now repeat the sampling another 10 times.
Use both sets of data to improve your guess.

Repeat the experiment several times until you think that you have worked out the correct contents of the bag.
Is your final answer more reliable than your first answer?
Give a reason why.

Check your answer by looking at the contents of the bag.

Ask your teacher for another bag.
Find the contents of the bag using the method above.

Jane has thrown her dice 100 times.
She has recorded the number each
time using tally marks.

Number	Tally	Frequency
1	ⷶ ⷶ ⷶ ||||	19
2	ⷶ ⷶ ⷶ	15
3	ⷶ ⷶ ⷶ |	16
4	ⷶ ⷶ ⷶ |||	18
5	ⷶ ⷶ ⷶ ||	17
6	ⷶ ⷶ ⷶ	15

Jane has labelled the total column 'Frequency'.

Frequency   The **frequency** of an event is the number of times that the event happens.

Jane thinks that the dice is fair.
If it is fair, the probability of getting each number is $\frac{1}{6}$

She checks her data to see if the dice is fair.
She uses the relative frequency from her experiment.

Relative frequency   The **relative frequency** of an event $= \dfrac{\text{frequency of the event}}{\text{total frequency}}$

The relative frequency gives an *estimate* of the probability.

Jane's data shows that the frequency of getting 1 on her dice is 19.
The total of all the frequencies is 100.

The relative frequency of $1 = \dfrac{19}{100}$

Jane wants to see if $\frac{1}{6}$ and $\frac{19}{100}$ are approximately the same value.

She converts them both to decimals.

$$\frac{1}{6} = 0.17 \text{ (2 dp)} \qquad \frac{19}{100} = 0.19$$

The two values are very close.

Jane can get a better estimate for the probability by repeating the experiment more times.

Exercise 10:4

1 Ceri tossed two coins 100 times.
This is her data.

Outcome	Tally	Frequency
2 heads	||| ||| ||| ||| ||	22
2 tails	||| ||| ||| ||| ||| ||	27
head, tail	||| ||| ||| ||| ||| ||| ||| ||| ||| |||		51

Find the relative frequency of
a 2 heads   **b** 2 tails   **c** a head and a tail
Give your answers as decimals.

2 Simon collected data on the colours of cars passing the school gate.
His results are shown in the table.

Colour	Tally	Frequency
black	||| ||||	9
red	||| ||| ||| ||| ||| |||	30
white	||| ||| ||| ||| |||		26
blue	||| ||| ||	12
green	||| ||| ||| ||||	19
other	||||	4

a How many cars did Simon include in his survey?
b What is the relative frequency of white?
   Give your answer as (1) a fraction (2) a decimal (3) a percentage.
c What is the relative frequency of black?
   Give your answer as (1) a fraction (2) a decimal (3) a percentage.
d What is the most likely colour of the next car passing the school gate?
e Write down an estimate for the probability that the next car will be green. Give your answer as a fraction.
f How can the estimate for the probability of green be made more reliable?

3 Jennie has carried out an experiment to see which way a drawing pin lands when it is dropped on to the floor. Here is her data.

Position	Tally	Frequency
pin up	ЖЖ ЖЖ ЖЖ ЖЖ ЖЖ ЖЖ ЖЖ I	36
pin down	ЖЖ ЖЖ ЖЖ ЖЖ IIII	24

a How many times has Jennie dropped the pin?
b Work out the relative frequencies of each way the pin lands. Give your answers as decimals.
c Which way is the pin more likely to land?
d How could Jennie be more sure of her prediction?

4 Jason is designing a game for his school charity day.
Pupils pay to take part.
They roll a penny on to this board and win prizes depending on where the penny ends up.
If the penny lands completely inside a red square they win the amount of money written in that square.

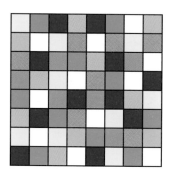

Jason needs to know how often pupils will win.
He can then decide on an entry fee and the value of the prizes.
He decides to roll pennies and record the outcomes.
Here is his data.

Outcome	Tally	Frequency
win	ЖЖ ЖЖ II	12
lose	ЖЖ ЖЖ ЖЖ ЖЖ ЖЖ ЖЖ ЖЖ III	38

a Give an estimate for the chance that a pupil will win with one go.
b Jason decides to charge pupils 5 p to take part in his game.
How much should he give as a prize?
Remember that he is trying to raise money for charity.

3   Listing outcomes

Rupert and Mary have organised a game for the school fair.
Pupils have to throw two dice.
If they get two sixes then they win a model car.

Rupert and Mary need to work out the probability of somebody winning a prize.
They do this by using a sample space diagram.

◀◀REPLAY▶

Sample space	A **sample space** is a list of all the possible outcomes.
Sample space diagram	A table which shows all of the possible outcomes is called a **sample space diagram**.

Example   John tosses this coin and spins this spinner.

  a   Draw a sample space diagram.

  b   Write down the probability that John gets a tail and a 3.

a

		Number on spinner			
		1	2	3	4
Coin	H	H, 1	H, 2	H, 3	H, 4
	T	T, 1	T, 2	T, 3	T, 4

b   There are eight possible outcomes shown in the diagram.
T, 3 appears once. The probability of a tail and a 3 is $\frac{1}{8}$

Exercise 10:5

1   Copy this sample space diagram.
Fill it in to show all the possible outcomes of tossing two coins.

		50 p coin	
		H	T
20 p coin	H	…	…
	T	T, H	…

2 A coin is tossed and a dice thrown.
Copy and complete this sample space diagram to show all the possible outcomes.

		Dice					
		1	2	3	4	5	6
Coin	H						
	T						

a What is the total number of possible outcomes?
b What is the probability of getting a head and a three?
c What is the probability of getting a tail and an even number?

3 Alan and Fatima are doing a probability experiment.
Alan picks a bead at random from his bag.
Alan's bag contains 2 red and 4 blue beads.
Fatima picks a bead at random from her bag.
Fatima's bag contains 1 red and 2 blue beads.
a Copy and complete this sample space diagram.

		Alan					
		R	R	B	B	B	B
Fatima	R						
	B						
	B						

b What is the total number of possible outcomes?
c What is the probability of getting two blue beads?
d What is the probability of getting one blue and one red bead?

4 Melanie uses these two spinners.

a Draw a sample space diagram to show all the possible outcomes.
b What is the probability of Melanie getting a white and a 2?

5 Joshua sees a game at a school fair,
'Throw two sixes to win a model car'.
Joshua decides to have a go.
He throws the two dice.

    a Draw a sample space diagram to show all the possible outcomes.
    b Use your diagram to write down the probability that Joshua gets:
        (1) two sixes   (3) two even numbers
        (2) a six and a four   (4) two numbers that add up to eight

---

Example   Peter has to pick two counters from a bag
containing these four coloured counters.
    a List all the ways that Peter can pick
       two counters.
    b If Peter picks the counters without
       looking, what is the probability he
       gets a red and a yellow?

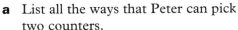
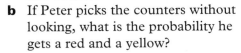

    a   red, blue   red, green   red, yellow
        blue, green   blue, yellow   green, yellow

    b There are six ways that Peter can pick the counters.
       The probability of a red and a yellow is $\frac{1}{6}$

---

6 Marie has to choose one boy and one girl from these pupils:
Rajiv   Jim   David   Karen   Sapna   Jane
List all her possible choices.

7 Kate, Pam and Wendy take part in a quiz. To decide the order in
which they answer questions, their names are put into a bag.
The names are taken out of the bag one at a time.
    a List all the ways the names could be drawn out.
    b Write down the probability that Wendy is last.

8 Andrew chooses a meal and a
drink from this menu.
    a Write down all Andrew's choices.
    b Explain why the probability that
       Andrew chooses fish and chips
       and tea is not $\frac{1}{6}$

Menu

Chicken & chips
Fish & chips

Tea
Coffee
Coke

4 Probability methods

Karen and Rob want an estimate of the probability that it will rain on the day of the school fair in June.

They need to look at *data* for the weather in June in past years.

There are three methods of finding probabilities.

Method 1   Use equally likely outcomes
e.g. the probability of getting a 4 on a dice is $\frac{1}{6}$

Method 2   Use a survey or do an experiment
e.g. to find the probability that a car passing the school is red, do a survey of the colours of cars passing the school.

Method 3   Look back at data
e.g. to find the probability that it will rain on a day in June, look at the number of days it rained in June in past years.

Exercise 10:6

Look at each of the situations in questions **1–10**.
Decide whether you would use *method 1*, *method 2* or *method 3* to estimate the probabilities.

If your answer is *method 1*, write down the probability.
If your answer is *method 2*, describe the survey or the experiment you would do.
If your answer is *method 3*, describe the data you would need.

1   The probability that you will win a raffle if you buy one ticket and there are 100 tickets sold.

2   The probability that a dropped piece of toast will land butter side up.

3   The probability that a pupil chosen at random from your school has cereal for breakfast.

4   The probability that it will snow in London on 25th December this year.

5   The probability that this spinner will land on red.

6   The probability that the next car to come down a road will be green.

7   The probability that from a choice of athletics, cricket or tennis, a pupil will choose tennis.

8   The probability that there will be no pieces of litter in your school hall at the end of an afternoon.

9   The probability that a pupil chosen at random from your school will choose maths as their favourite subject.

10 The probability that there will be a flu epidemic next winter.

1 Harriet puts these beads in a bag.
She picks out a bead without looking.
  a Which colour is Harriet most likely
   to choose?
  b Which colour is Harriet least likely
   to choose?
  c Harriet wants all the colours to
   have an equal chance.
   What beads does Harriet need to add to her bag?

2 David has 14 socks in his drawer. Eight are black and the rest are white.
David picks out a sock at random. What is the probability that the
sock is
  a black   **b** white   **c** blue?

3 Carol puts 12 counters in a bag.
She takes out one counter at random and records the colour.
Carol then replaces the counter.
She does this 12 times.
Here is Carol's tally-table:

Colour	Tally	Total
green	|||| |	6
yellow	||||	4
red	||	2

  a Carol says, 'There must be 6 green counters in my bag because
      there are 6 greens in my table'.
   Explain why Carol is wrong.
  b What is the smallest number of red counters that can be in the bag?
  c Carol says, 'There cannot be any blue counters in my bag because
      there are no blues in my table'.
   Explain why Carol is wrong.

4 Make three copies of this spinner.
  a Shade the copies so that each shaded portion
   has the probability given.
   (1) Shaded has double the chance of unshaded.
   (2) Probability of shaded is 75%.
   (3) Probability of shaded is about 40%.
  b Copy this probability scale.

   0   1
   ├──┤

   Show the probability of shaded for each of your three spinners on
   your scale.

5 a The probability of getting a 6 on a biased dice is $\frac{1}{4}$
Write down the probability of not getting a 6.

b The probability of at least one person in 9M forgetting their maths books is 90%.
What is the probability of all of 9M remembering their maths books?

6 The school tuck shop sells these crisps: salt and vinegar, smoky bacon, cheese and onion.
Chris says that as there are 3 flavours, the probability of a person buying cheese and onion is $\frac{1}{3}$
Explain why Chris is wrong.

7 Denis has done a survey on the type of vehicles passing the school.
His results are given in the table.

Vehicle	Frequency
car	64
lorry	12
bus	15
motorcycle	9

a How many vehicles are there altogether in the survey?
b Write down the relative frequency of each type of vehicle as:
(1) a fraction   (2) a decimal   (3) a percentage
c Denis can hear another vehicle coming. What is it most likely to be?

8 Pam shuffles a pack of cards. She chooses a card, notes the suit and replaces the card. Pam then offers the pack to Saleem who also chooses a card.
a Copy this sample space diagram.
Fill it in.

		Pam's card			
		C	D	H	S
Saleem's	S				
card	H				
	D				
	C				

b Write down the probability that the cards are:
(1) a heart and a club   (3) both the same colour
(2) both red cards   (4) both from the same suit

1 Mandy has 20 beads of three different colours in a bag.
She wants to find out how many beads there are of each colour
without looking.
Mandy takes out a bead and writes down the colour.
Mandy then puts the bead back in the bag.
She repeats this 60 times.

The table shows Mandy's results.

Colour	Frequency
red	29
white	11
yellow	20

a Write down the relative frequency of each colour as a fraction.
b How many beads of each colour do you think Mandy has?
c How could Mandy improve her chance of being right about the
numbers of beads?

2 This drinks machine is broken.
You cannot choose which drink you get!

Jane likes all the drinks.
Paul only likes chicken soup.

Jane and Paul buy one drink each.

a Write down the probability that:
(1) Jane will get a drink she likes,
(2) Paul will get a drink he likes.

b Copy this probability scale.

Mark the probabilities from part **a** on your scale.

c Anne buys a drink. The arrow shows the probability that Ann will
get a drink that she likes.

(1) How many of the drinks does Ann like?
(2) Draw a new probability scale.
    Mark the probability that Ann will get a drink that she does
    not like.

- **Probability** **Probability** tells us how likely something is to happen. All probabilities must be between 0 and 1.

  Example   In a raffle 100 tickets are sold.
  What is the probability of Alex winning first prize if she has bought:
  a 1 ticket   **b** 5 tickets?

  a Probability of winning $= \dfrac{1}{100}$ **b** Probability of winning $= \dfrac{5}{100} = \dfrac{1}{20}$

  Probabilities always add up to 1.

  Example   The probability that Peter will go bowling sometime during this week is $\frac{3}{5}$

  What is the probability that Peter will not go bowling?

  Probability that Peter will not go bowling $= 1 - \dfrac{3}{5} = \dfrac{2}{5}$

- **Relative frequency** The **relative frequency** of an event $= \dfrac{\text{frequency of the event}}{\text{total frequency}}$

  The relative frequency gives an *estimate* of the probability.

  Jane has tossed a dice 100 times.
  Jane's data shows that the frequency of getting 1 on her dice is 19.
  The total of all the frequencies is 100.

  The relative frequency of $1 = \dfrac{19}{100}$

- **Sample space** A **sample space** is a list of all the possible outcomes of an experiment.

  Sample space diagram A table which shows all of the possible outcomes is called a **sample space diagram**.

  Example   John tosses this coin and spins this spinner.
  Draw a sample space diagram.

		Number on spinner			
		1	2	3	4
Coin	H	H, 1	H, 2	H, 3	H, 4
	T	T, 1	T, 2	T, 3	T, 4

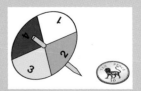

1 These beads are put in the bag.
Debbie then chooses a bead from
the bag without looking.

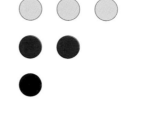 

   a What is the probability
that Debbie gets:
(1) a red bead
(2) a green bead
(3) a black bead?

   b Debbie wants to make all the colours have equal chances.
What beads does she need to add to the bag?

2 Decide whether each of these statements is true or false:
   a Year 9 can choose to study French or German.
There are 2 choices so the probability that a pupil chooses French is $\frac{1}{2}$
   b An ordinary dice is thrown. There are 6 numbers so the probability
of getting 5 is $\frac{1}{6}$

3 The probability that a Year 9 pupil chosen at random has a scientific
calculator is 0.8. Write down the probability that the same Year 9
pupil does not have a scientific calculator.

4 A take-away has noted the first 100 meals bought one Saturday evening.
Here are their results:

Meal	Frequency
chicken and chips	35
fish and chips	31
chicken curry	14
prawn fried rice	20

   a Write down the relative frequency of fish and chips as:
(1) a fraction   (2) a decimal   (3) a percentage
   b A new customer comes in to buy a meal.
What meal is the customer most likely to choose?

5 Kamal spins this spinner.
She also throws a dice.

   a Draw a sample space diagram to show
the possible outcomes.
   b Use your diagram to write down the
probability of getting:
(1) red and a 6   (2) green and a 1

11 Algebra: getting closer

When a rocket is launched, it has to escape from the Earth's gravity. To do this, the rocket must work up to escape velocity, which is 11 km/s. It must do this gradually, to avoid being burned by the heat generated through air resistance.

1 Trial and improvement

Paul is making a curry.
He is adding the curry powder.
Paul wants the curry to be neither
too mild nor too spicy.
He can taste the curry to see if it is hot
enough.
He can add more curry powder if necessary.
If it is too spicy he can make it milder next
time.

You can solve equations by trying different values to get closer to the
right answer.
This is called trial and improvement.

Example $x^2 + x = 37$
The value of x lies between a pair of 1 decimal place numbers.
Find these numbers using trial and improvement.

Value of x	Value of x^2	Value of $x^2 + x$	
5	25	30	too small
6	36	42	too big
5.5	30.25	35.75	too small
5.6	31.36	36.96	too small
5.7	32.49	38.19	too big

x lies between 5.6 and 5.7

Exercise 11:1

1 Look at the equation $x^2 + x = 60$
The value of x lies between a pair of 1 decimal place numbers.
Find these numbers by trial and improvement using this table.

Value of x	Value of x^2	Value of $x^2 + x$	

2 Look at the equation $x^2 + x = 95$
The value of x lies between a pair of 1 decimal place numbers.
Find these numbers by trial and improvement using this table.

Value of x	Value of x^2	Value of $x^2 + x$	

For each of the equations in questions **3–6**:
The value of x lies between a pair of 1 decimal place numbers.
Find these numbers using trial and improvement.

3 $x^2 + x = 53$

5 $x^2 + x = 134$

4 $x^2 + x = 18$

6 $x + x^2 = 77$

Example Solve $x^2 + 3x = 82$
Use trial and improvement.
Give your answer correct to 1 dp.

Value of x	Value of x^2	Value of $3x$	Value of $x^2 + 3x$	
8	64	24	88	too big
7.5	56.25	22.5	78.75	too small
7.6	57.76	22.8	80.56	too small
7.7	59.29	23.1	82.39	too big: x between 7.6 and 7.7

Try 7.65 to see if x is between 7.6 and 7.65 or between 7.65 and 7.7

7.65	58.5225	22.95	81.4725	too small

x lies between 7.65 and 7.7
x rounds to 7.7
Answer: $x = 7.7$ to 1 dp

Solve the equations in questions **7–11** by trial and improvement.
Give each answer correct to 1 dp.

7 $x^2 + 2x = 82$

9 $x^2 + 3x = 145$

8 $2x + x^2 = 115$

10 $x^2 + 4x = 71$

11 $x(x + 1) = 48$ *Remember:* $x(x + 1) = x \times (x + 1)$

Use this table:

Value of x	Value of $x + 1$	Value of $x(x + 1)$	
6	7	42	too small

● **12** Keith is investigating rectangles that have a perimeter of 20 cm.

a Keith draws one of the rectangles.
It has a length of 7 cm.
(1) What is its width?
(2) What is its area?

? cm

7 cm

b Keith draws a second rectangle with a perimeter of 20 cm.
It has a length of 9 cm.
(1) What is its width?   (2) What is its area?

c Copy this table to find more of Keith's rectangles.
Fill in the table.

Width (cm)	Length (cm)	Area (cm²)
1	9	9
2		
3	7	
4		
5		

d What does the width plus the length add up to each time?

Keith wants a rectangle with perimeter 20 cm and area 22 cm².
Keith calls the width of his rectangle x. The length is $10 - x$.
Keith writes the equation $x(10 - x) = 22$

e Find x using trial and improvement.
Give the value of x correct to 1 dp.

Value of x	Value of $10 - x$	Area	
3	7	21	

f Write down the lengths of the two sides of the rectangle for this
value of x.

You can solve equations using trial and improvement correct to as many decimal places as necessary.

Example $x^2 + x = 49$ x lies between 6 and 7.
The value of x lies between a pair of 2 decimal place numbers. Find these numbers using trial and improvement.

Value of x	Value of x^2	Value of $x^2 + x$	
7	49	56	too big
6.5	42.25	48.75	too small
6.6	43.56	50.16	too big: x between 6.5 and 6.6
6.55	42.9025	49.4525	too big
6.52	42.5104	49.0304	too big
6.51	42.3801	48.8901	too small

x lies between 6.51 and 6.52

Exercise 11:2

For each of the equations in questions **1**–**4**:
The value of x lies between a pair of 2 decimal place numbers.
Find these numbers using trial and improvement.

1 $x^2 + x = 79$

2 $x^2 + 2x = 19$

3 $x^2 + 4x = 93$

4 $x^2 + 3x = 39$

5   Look at this equation: $x(24 + x) = 110$
The value of x lies between a pair of 2 decimal place numbers.
Find these numbers using trial and improvement.

Value of x	Value of $24 + x$	Value of $x(24 + x)$	

6   Look at this equation: $x^2 + x = 65$
The value of x lies between a pair of 3 decimal place numbers.
Find these numbers using trial and improvement.

Exercise 11:3

1 The  key on Kiran's calculator is broken.
Kiran is using trial and improvement to find $\sqrt{11}$.
Here is Kiran's working:

1st try $3 \times 3 = 9$
2nd try $3.4 \times 3.4 = 11.56$
3rd try $3.3 \times 3.3 = 10.89$

  a Continue Kiran's trials.
      Give at least 4 more sensible trials.
      Try to get as close to 11 as you can.
  b Solve the equation $x^2 - 3 = 8$.
      You can use your working in part **a** to help you.

2 Lesley wants to find the values of x which make the equation
$x^2 = 5x - 3$ correct.
Lesley works out the values of x^2 and $5x - 3$.
She subtracts the value of $5x - 3$ from the value of x^2.
This gives Lesley the *difference* between each pair of values.
Lesley writes down whether the difference is positive or negative.

x	x^2	$5x - 3$	Difference	
-2	4	-13	17	positive
-1	1	-8	9	positive
0	0	-3	3	positive
1	1	2	-1	negative
2	4	7	-3	negative

  a Lesley knows there is a value of x between 0 and 1 which makes the
      equation correct.
      Use Lesley's table to explain why.
  b Lesley tries some 1 decimal place numbers for x.

x	x^2	$5x - 3$	Difference	
0.1	0.01	-2.5	2.51	positive
0.2	0.04	-2	2.04	positive

      Copy Lesley's table.
      The value of x lies between a pair of 1 decimal place numbers.
      Continue Lesley's table to find these numbers.

2   Inequalities

Eggs are packed according to their weight.
They are extra small, small, medium, large or extra large.
An extra large egg weighs at least 73 g.
You can write 'mass of an extra large egg $\geqslant$ 73 g'.

◀◀REPLAY▶

Inequalities using whole numbers

Inequalities	The signs $<$ $\leqslant$ $>$ $\geqslant$ are called **inequality** signs.

Examples   **1**   Write down the first five possible values of x if x is a whole number and $x < 2$

$x < 2$ means *x is less than* 2
x is *not equal to* 2, so 2 is not included   Answer: $-3, -2, -1, 0, 1$

2   Write down the possible values of x if x is a whole number and $-2 < x \leqslant 4$

-2 *is less than* x, so -2 is not included   The possible values of x are:
x *can be equal to* 4, so 4 is in the answer $-1, 0, 1, 2, 3, 4$

Exercise 11:4

Write down the first five possible values of x if x is a whole number.

1 $x > 4$ **3** $x \leqslant 7$ **5** $x \geqslant -4$ **7** $x < 3$

2 $x \geqslant 5$ **4** $x < 0$ **6** $x \leqslant -3$ **8** $x \leqslant -10$

Write down all the values of x if x is a whole number.

9 $-4 \leqslant x < 2$

11 $0 \leqslant x \leqslant 6$

13 $-7 < x \leqslant -3$

10 $-5 < x < 4$

12 $-10 < x < -5$

14 $-1 < x < 1$

15 Write down the lowest value that x can have if $x > -1$ and x is a whole number.

16 Write down the highest value that x can have if $x \leqslant -3$ and x is a whole number.

17 $-12 \leqslant x < 16$ and x is a whole number.
   a Write down the lowest value that x can have.
   b Write down the highest value that x can have.

Inequalities where x can be any number

Jason is writing down some values of x for the inequality $x \geqslant 3$
Jason knows it is difficult because x is not a whole number.

Some of the numbers Jason writes down are:

   3, 3.1, 3.25, 3.33333..., $3\frac{1}{2}$, 4.6

Jason draws a number line because it includes all the values of x *between* 3 and 4, and all the values of x *between* 4 and 5 and so on.

Here is Jason's number line.

Jason has coloured in the circle above the 3.
This shows that 3 is a possible value of x.

Example   Draw a number line to show $-1 \leqslant x < 4$

The circle above the 4 is not coloured in.
This shows that 4 is not a possible value of x.

Exercise 11:5

Write down the inequality shown on each of these number lines.

1

5

2

6

3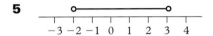

7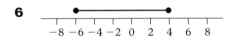

4

8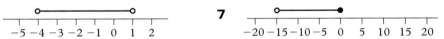

Draw number lines to show these inequalities.

9 $x > 0$

11 $-2 \leqslant x < 1$

13 $x \geqslant 3$

10 $x \leqslant 2$

12 $0 < x < 5$

14 $-3 \leqslant x \leqslant 1$

You may need to solve an inequality.
You do this in the same way as you solve an equation.

Examples   Solve these inequalities.

1 $\dfrac{x}{3} \geqslant 5$ **2** $2x + 13 < 21$

1

$\dfrac{x}{3} \geqslant 5$

Multiply both sides by 3 $\dfrac{x}{3} \times 3 \geqslant 5 \times 3$

$x \geqslant 15$

2 $2x + 13 < 21$

Subtract 13 from both sides $2x + 13 - 13 < 21 - 13$

$2x < 8$

Divide both sides by 2 $\dfrac{2x}{2} < \dfrac{8}{2}$

$x < 4$

Exercise 11:6

Solve these inequalities.

1 $x + 4 < 6$ **7** $5x > 20$ **13** $2x + 1 < 5$

2 $x - 1 \geqslant 1$ **8** $x + 3 \geqslant 12$ **14** $3x - 4 < 20$

3 $\dfrac{x}{5} \geqslant 2$ **9** $x + 11 < 16$ **15** $5x + 1 \leqslant 26$

4 $\dfrac{x}{2} \geqslant 10$ **10** $\dfrac{x}{10} \leqslant 7$ **16** $3x - 10 > 5$

5 $3x < 9$ **11** $x + 25 < 30$ **17** $4x + 3 > 27$

6 $x - 6 > 0$ **12** $6x > 12$ ● **18** $2(3x - 1) \geqslant 10$

1 A chef slices a pizza into six slices.
Each slice must weigh at least 250 g.
Solve this inequality to find the
minimum weight of the whole pizza.

$$\frac{\text{weight of pizza}}{6} \geqslant 250$$

2 Sinita's luggage allowance for her
holiday is 20 kg.
Sinita's empty suitcase weighs 2.8 kg.
Solve this inequality to find the
maximum weight that Sinita can
pack in her suitcase.

weight of Sinita's packing $+ 2.8 \leqslant 20$

3 This car has luggage on its roof rack.
The height of the car without the
roof rack is 1.5 m.
Solve the inequality to find the
maximum height that the roof rack
and luggage can be for the car to get
into the car park.

MAXIMUM HEIGHT 2.2 M

$1.5 +$ height of the roof rack and luggage < 2.2

● **4** Alec is fencing a square field for some sheep.
Alec wants the field to have an area of
at least 576 m^2.
Here is Alec's working:

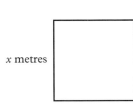

x metres

x metres

Area of field $=$ length $\times$ width
$\qquad = x \times x$
$\qquad = x^2$

Area of field $\geqslant 576$
$\qquad x^2 \geqslant 576$

Solve the inequality to find the smallest possible value of x.
You can use trial and improvement.

1 Solve these equations using trial and improvement.
Give each answer correct to 1 dp.

   a $x^2 + x = 26$ **b** $x^2 + 2x = 37$ **c** $x^2 + 5x = 61$

2 The value of x lies between a pair of 2 decimal place numbers.
Find these numbers using trial and improvement.

   a $x^2 + x = 15$ **b** $x^2 + 2x = 105$ **c** $x^2 + 3x = 34$

3 Look at this equation: $x(17 + x) = 75$
The value of x lies between a pair of 2 decimal place numbers.
Find these numbers using trial and improvement.

Value of x	Value of $17 + x$	Value of $x(17 + x)$	

4 Jane is trying to solve the equation $x^3 = 50$
Here is Jane's working:

    1st try $3 \times 3 \times 3 = 27$
    2nd try $4 \times 4 \times 4 = 64$
    3rd try $3.5 \times 3.5 \times 3.5 = 42.875$

Continue Jane's trials.
Give at least 4 more sensible trials.
Try to get as close to 50 as you can.

5 Colin wants to find the radius of this circle.
He knows that the area of the circle is 73 cm².
Colin knows that the formula for the area of
a circle is: Area = πr^2.
Colin uses 3.14 as the value of π.
Here is Colin's working:

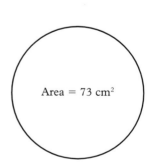

Area = 73 cm²

    1st try $3.14 \times 4 \times 4 = 50.24$
    2nd try $3.14 \times 5 \times 5 = 78.5$
    3rd try $3.14 \times 4.5 \times 4.5 = 63.585$

   a Continue Colin's trials.
Find the radius of Colin's circle correct to one decimal place.

   b Fiona wants to find the radius of a circle of area 138 cm².
Use trial and improvement to find the radius of Fiona's circle
correct to 1 dp.

6 Write down the first five possible values of x if x is a whole number.
    a $x > -9$ **b** $x \leqslant 1$ **c** $x \geqslant -8$ **d** $x < -4$

7 Write down all the values of x if x is a whole number.
    a $-3 < x < 4$ **b** $-1 \leqslant x \leqslant 6$ **c** $-2 \leqslant x < 1$

8 Draw a number line to show each of these inequalities.
    a $x \leqslant 1$ **b** $-5 \leqslant x \leqslant 0$ **c** $x > -3$ **d** $-1 < x \leqslant 4$

9 Solve these inequalities.

    a $x + 5 > 7$ **c** $\dfrac{x}{4} \geqslant 8$ **e** $3x < 21$ **g** $\dfrac{x}{6} > 4$

    b $x - 7 \leqslant 1$ **d** $8x < 16$ **f** $x - 4 \geqslant 3$ **h** $x + 12 < 20$

10 Solve these inequalities.
    a $7x - 4 < 38$ **b** $5x + 9 > 24$ **c** $4x - 13 \leqslant 23$

11 Which of these values of x make the inequality $3x + 4 > 10$ true?
    a $x = 2$ **b** $x = 15$ **c** $x = 0$ **d** $x = 3.5$

12 Write down a value of x that makes both of these inequalities true.
    $x + 5 < 17$ $3x > 33$

13 Write down a value of x that makes both of these inequalities true.
    $x - 16 > 7$ $4x < 96$

14 George does a paper delivery round.
He gets £9.45 a week.
George is to have a rise in his wages.
His new wages will be at least £10.37.
Solve this inequality to find the smallest
rise that George is likely to get.

$9.45 + \text{rise} \geqslant 10.37$

1 Find the value of x in these equations correct to 2 dp.
Make a table and use trial and improvement.
   a $x^2 + 5x = 75$ **b** $x^2 + 3x = 17$

2 The value of x lies between a pair of 2 decimal place numbers.
Find these numbers using trial and improvement.
Make a table and use trial and improvement.
   a $x^3 = 95$ ($x^3 = x \times x \times x$)   **b** $x^2 + \sqrt{x} = 30$

3 Here are the triangle numbers.

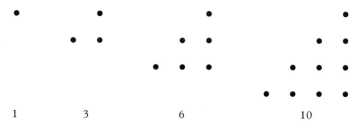

1   3   6   10

   a Draw diagrams to find the 5th and 6th triangle numbers.
   b The formula for the triangle numbers is $\frac{1}{2}(n^2 + n)$.
      Test that the formula works for the 6th triangle number.
   c Use your formula to work out the 31st triangle number.
   d Use trial and improvement to find the first triangle number over 1000.

4 The value of x lies between a pair of 3 decimal place numbers in the equation
$x(20 + x) = 58$
Find these numbers using trial and improvement.
Use this table.

Value of x	Value of $20 + x$	Value of $x(20 + x)$	

5 Steve has drawn a rectangle
8 cm long and 5 cm wide.
Steve decides that the rectangle needs
to be larger. He wants it to have an
area of at least 68 cm².
Steve writes:
    Area $= 8 \times (5 + x)$
    $8(5 + x) \geqslant 68$
Solve Steve's inequality to find the
extra length that Steve needs.

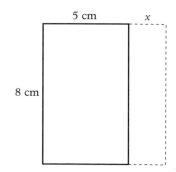

- *Example*   Solve $x^2 + 3x = 82$
  Use trial and improvement.
  Give your answer correct to 1 dp.

Value of x	Value of x^2	Value of $3x$	Value of $x^2 + 3x$	
8	64	24	88	too big
7.5	56.25	22.5	78.75	too small
7.6	57.76	22.8	80.56	too small
7.7	59.29	23.1	82.39	too big: x between 7.6 and 7.7

Try 7.65 to see if x is between 7.6 and 7.65 or between 7.65 and 7.7

| 7.65 | 58.5225 | 22.95 | 81.4725 | too small |

x lies between 7.65 and 7.7   so x rounds to 7.7
Answer: $x = 7.7$ to 1 dp

- *Example*   Write down the possible values of x if x is a whole number
  and $-2 < x \leqslant 4$

  The possible values of x are $-1, 0, 1, 2, 3, 4$
  (-2 is less than x, so -2 is not included. x can be equal to 4,
  so 4 is in the answer)

- You can draw a number line to show an inequality.

  Example   Draw a number line to show $-1 \leqslant x < 4$

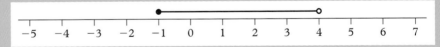

  The circle above the 4 is not coloured in.
  This shows that 4 is not a possible value of x.

- *Example*   Solve the inequality $2x + 13 < 21$

  $$2x + 13 < 21$$
  Subtract 13 from both sides $$2x + 13 - 13 < 21 - 13$$
  $$2x < 8$$
  Divide both sides by 2 $$\frac{2x}{2} < \frac{8}{2}$$
  $$x < 4$$

1 Solve these equations using trial and improvement.
Give each answer correct to 1 dp.

   a $x^2 + x = 46$ **b** $x^2 + 3x = 21$

2 Look at this equation: $x(x + 5) = 34$
The value of x lies between a pair of 2 decimal place numbers.
Find these numbers using trial and improvement.

Value of x	Value of $x + 5$	Value of $x(x + 5)$	

3 Rachel is using trial and improvement to find $\sqrt{19}$.
Here is Rachel's working:

    1st try $4 \times 4 = 16$
    2nd try $4.3 \times 4.3 = 18.49$
    3rd try $4.4 \times 4.4 = 19.36$

   a Continue Rachel's trials.
       Give at least 4 more sensible trials.
       Try to get as close to 19 as you can.
   b Solve the equation $x^2 + 4 = 23$
       You can use your working in part **a** to help you.

4 Write down the first five possible values of x for these inequalities.
x is a whole number.

   a $x > -8$ **b** $x < -5$ **c** $x \geqslant -6$ **d** $x \leqslant 7$

5 Write down all the values of x for these inequalities.
x is a whole number.

   a $-3 < x < 6$ **b** $-3 \leqslant x \leqslant 1$ **c** $0 \leqslant x < 5$

6 Draw a number line to show each of these inequalities.

   a $x \leqslant 3$ **c** $x > -5$
   b $-4 \leqslant x \leqslant 1$ **d** $-1 \leqslant x < 2$

7 Solve these inequalities.

   a $x + 1 > 7$ **d** $4x < 16$

   b $\dfrac{x}{7} > 4$ **e** $2x + 5 \leqslant 17$

   c $3x < 21$ **f** $4x - 12 \geqslant 20$

12 Decimals

In printed maths we don't use commas in numbers. Why is this?

1 Using a calculator

'When I said put brackets on your calculator ...'

Bracket key

Example

Work out: 35 (14 + 9)

You need to use the bracket keys to do this.
Remember: 35 (14 + 9) means $35 \times (14 + 9)$

3 5 × (1 4 + 9) =

Answer: 805

Exercise 12:1

Work these out using the bracket keys on a calculator.

1 6 (24 + 11)

2 67 − (76 − 34)

3 24 (45 + 57)

4 (34 × 5) − (23 + 44)

5 102 ÷ (38 + 13)

6 (86 − 21) × (45 − 39)

7 25 (22 − 9)

8 (87 − 63) − (54 − 49)

Exercise 12:2

Try each of the key sequences in this exercise yourself.
Use a scientific calculator.

1 Paul and Katie are working out $25 - 8 \times 2$

Paul does it in his head like this: $25 - 8 \times 2 = 17 \times 2 = 34$

Katie does the working on her scientific calculator.

| **2** | **5** | **−** | **8** | **×** | **2** | **=** | Answer: 9

   a Which answer is correct?
   b What has the other person done wrong?

2 Gary and Rita are working out $\dfrac{12 + 15}{3}$

Gary works the answer out on his scientific calculator.

| **1** | **2** | **+** | **1** | **5** | **÷** | **3** | **=** | Answer: 17

Rita works the question out in her head like this: $\dfrac{12 + 15}{3} = \dfrac{27}{3} = 9$

   a Which answer is correct?
   b What has the other person done wrong?

3 Jason and Sally have to work out $\dfrac{12}{2 \times 3}$

Jason works it out in his head like this: $\dfrac{12}{2 \times 3} = \dfrac{12}{6} = 2$

Sally does the working on a calculator.

| **1** | **2** | **÷** | **2** | **×** | **3** | **=** | Answer: 18

   a Which answer is correct?
   b What has the other person done wrong?

You may need to put brackets into a calculation before you work it out.

Example   Work out: **a** $\dfrac{12 + 15}{3}$ **b** $\dfrac{12}{2 \times 3}$

a Put brackets round the top. $\dfrac{12 + 15}{3} = \dfrac{(12 + 15)}{3}$

Key in: **(** **1** **2** **+** **1** **5** **)** **÷** **3** **=**

Answer: 9

b Put brackets round the bottom. $\dfrac{12}{2 \times 3} = \dfrac{12}{(2 \times 3)}$

Key in: **1** **2** **÷** **(** **2** **×** **3** **)** **=**

Answer: 2

Exercise 12:3

For each of these questions:
a Copy the question.
b Put brackets in the correct place.
c Work out the answer using a calculator.

1 $\dfrac{54 + 42}{12}$ **5** $\dfrac{57}{181 - 162}$ **9** $\dfrac{3.7 - 2.9}{0.16}$

2 $\dfrac{67 + 115}{7}$ **6** $\dfrac{81}{157 + 167}$ **10** $\dfrac{0.72}{0.31 + 1.13}$

3 $\dfrac{126 - 108}{9}$ **7** $\dfrac{345 - 263}{8}$ **11** $\dfrac{7.29 + 4.71}{18.8 + 5.2}$

4 $\dfrac{91}{142 - 135}$ **8** $\dfrac{98}{136 - 87}$ **12** $\dfrac{5.6 - 3.2}{2.5 + 2.3}$

Give your answers correct to 1 dp when you need to round.

13 $\dfrac{75}{7 \times 12}$
  15 $\dfrac{7.3 + 5.8}{2.9^2}$
  17 $\dfrac{314 - 142}{3.9 \times 9.6}$

14 $\dfrac{15^2}{12 \times 2.5}$
  16 $\dfrac{5.65^2}{9.3 - 6.17}$
  18 $\dfrac{26^2 - 49}{13 + 14^2}$

Example $m = \dfrac{I}{v - u}$ is a formula used in physics.

Use the formula to find m when $I = 300$, $v = 125$, $u = 85$.

Write the value of each letter in the formula.	$m = \dfrac{300}{125 - 85}$
Put brackets in the correct place.	$m = \dfrac{300}{(125 - 85)}$
Work out the answer.	$m = 7.5$

Exercise 12:4

1 Use the formula in the example to find m when $I = 450$, $v = 63$, $u = 48$.

2 The formula $w = \dfrac{P - 2l}{2}$ gives the width
of a rectangle. P is the perimeter and
l is the length.
Find w for this rectangle.

Perimeter = 42 cm

Length = 14.8 cm

3 The formula $6r(r + h)$ gives an
estimate for the *total* surface area
of a cylinder. h is the height of the
cylinder and r is the radius.
Use the formula to estimate the
area of aluminium sheet used to
make this can. The height of the
can is 11.5 cm, and the radius is
3.8 cm.

233

4 Pritesh throws a ball straight up in the air with a speed of u m/s.

t seconds later the speed is v m/s.

t is given by the formula $t = \dfrac{u - v}{9.8}$

Find the value of t when $u = 22$ m/s and $v = 17.1$ m/s

5 $h = \dfrac{2A}{a + b}$ gives the height of a trapezium.

A is the area and a and b are the parallel sides.
Find h for this trapezium.
The area of this trapezium is 273 cm².

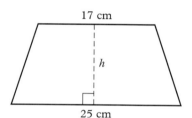

17 cm

h

25 cm

6 ABCD is called a golden rectangle.
It is a shape that artists like.
The length of a golden rectangle is

found by multiplying the width by $\dfrac{2}{\sqrt{5} - 1}$

Find the length of the golden rectangle
that has a width of 7 cm.
Give your answer correct to 1 dp.

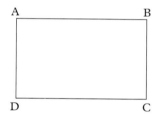

A   B

D   C

It is helpful to use brackets if you have more than one term under a square root.

Example   Work out $7\sqrt{4^2 + 3^2}$

Put brackets in under the square root:

$7\sqrt{4^2 + 3^2} = 7\sqrt{(4^2 + 3^2)}$

You start by working out the brackets:

$\boxed{\sqrt{}}$ $\boxed{(}$ $\boxed{4}$ $\boxed{x^2}$ $\boxed{+}$ $\boxed{3}$ $\boxed{x^2}$ $\boxed{)}$ $\boxed{\times}$ $\boxed{7}$ $\boxed{=}$

Answer: 35

Exercise 12:5

1 Work through the example.
Make sure you know how to get the correct answer.
You may need a different key sequence.

Work these out.
Give your answers correct to 3 significant figures (sf) when you need
to round.

2 $\sqrt{56 + 44}$ **6** $\sqrt{7^2 + 24^2}$ **10** $6\sqrt{61^2 - 60^2}$

3 $\sqrt{236 - 40}$ **7** $\sqrt{1 + 34^2}$ **11** $1 + \sqrt{4.8^2 + 3.6^2}$

4 $\sqrt{457 + 168}$ **8** $2\sqrt{6^2 - 3^2}$ **12** $2\sqrt{2 + \dfrac{14^2}{2}}$

5 $\sqrt{180 - 11}$ **9** $\frac{1}{2}\sqrt{17^2 - 12^2}$ ● **13** $\dfrac{16}{\sqrt{1 - 0.6^2}}$

Exercise 12:6

1 The formula $c = \sqrt{a^2 + b^2}$ gives
the length of side c of this
triangle.
Use the formula to calculate c
correct to 2 dp.

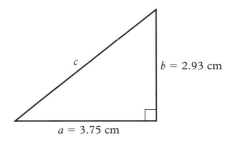

$b = 2.93$ cm

$a = 3.75$ cm

2 Jane hits a ball straight up in the
air at a speed u of 15 m/s.
After one second the height of the
ball, h, is 10 m.
Jane has a formula for finding the
velocity v of the ball.

$v = \sqrt{u^2 - 20h}$

Use Jane's formula to find v.

2 Mental decimals

Sometimes we have to do calculations without using a calculator.

Adding and subtracting decimals

Examples   **1** $2 + 3.75 = 5.75$ **3** $5.63 + 0.04 = 5.67$

2 $4.27 + 0.1 = 4.37$ **4** $4.6 - 1.2 = 3.4$

Exercise 12:7

Work these out in your head.
Write down the answers.

1 Add 3 to each of these numbers.
   a 4.5   **b** 7.62   **c** 18.59   **d** 24.7   **e** 0.164

2 Add 0.1 to each of these numbers.
   a 7.1   **b** 2.04   **c** 21.63   **d** 12.325   **e** 0.53

3 Add 0.05 to each of these numbers.
   a 0.7   **b** 8.04   **c** 35.2   **d** 0.62   **e** 1.9

4 Subtract 2 from each of these numbers.
   a 5.8   **b** 2.09   **c** 19.6   **d** 5.32   **e** 8.04

5 Subtract 0.5 from each of these numbers.
   a 0.6   **b** 2.73   **c** 21.9   **d** 0.83   **e** 4.51

6 **a** $3 + 1.2$ **c** $2.6 + 8$ **e** $7.8 + 4$ **g** $12 + 4.7$
  b $5 + 2.4$ **d** $0.4 + 6$ **f** $9 + 1.8$ **h** $5.6 + 21$

7 **a** $1.2 + 0.5$ **c** $4.7 - 1.2$ **e** $6.7 - 1.5$ **g** $12.4 + 5.3$
  b $4.3 + 1.1$ **d** $2.1 + 3.4$ **f** $7.8 - 1.6$ **h** $14.6 - 12.3$

Examples

1 Look at $1 - 0.3$
 You can write this as $1.0 - 0.3$
 $10 - 3 = 7$ so $1.0 - 0.3 = 0.7$

2 Look at $10 - 4.3$
 'Borrow' 1 from the 10 to get 9.
 Use the 1 to take away the decimal: $1 - 0.3 = 0.7$
 Now take the 4 from the 9: $9 - 4 = 5$
  $10 - 4.3 = 5.7$

---

8 Subtract each of these numbers from 1.
  a 0.1   **b** 0.4   **c** 0.8   **d** 0.9   **e** 0.2

9 Subtract each of these numbers from 10.
  a 8.5   **b** 6.8   **c** 4.9   **d** 1.7   **e** 6.2

● **10** Subtract each of these numbers from 1.
  a 0.18   **b** 0.34   **c** 0.68   **d** 0.09   **e** 0.72

Look at the red numbers in 0.5×3
Work the red numbers out first: $5 \times 3 = 15$ so $0.5 \times 3 = 1.5$
There is one number after the decimal point in the question, so there
is one number after the decimal point in the answer.

Examples   **1** $7 \times 0.2 = 1.4$ **2** $0.3 \times 8 = 2.4$

Exercise 12:8

Work these out in your head.
Write down the answers.

1 0.6×3 **4** 6×0.8 **7** 7×0.9 **10** 4×0.8

2 5×0.5 **5** 7×0.6 **8** 6×0.9 **11** 0.7×4

3 5×0.6 **6** 8×0.9 **9** 0.9×5 **12** 0.8×7

Examples   **1** $0.5 \times 0.9 = 0.45$ There are **two** numbers after the decimal points in the questions, so there are **two** numbers after the decimal points in the answers.

  2 $1.2 \times 0.2 = 0.24$

---

13 0.6×0.3 **16** 0.5×0.8 **19** 0.7×1.2 **22** $(0.9)^2$

14 0.5×0.7 **17** 1.1×0.8 **20** 1.3×0.3 **23** $(0.8)^2$

15 0.4×0.5 **18** 0.8×0.7 **21** $(0.7)^2$ **24** $(0.6)^2$

Example $1.2 \div 3$ You can work it out like this $\begin{array}{r} 0.4 \\ 3\overline{)1.^12} \end{array}$

  or you can work it out in your head. $1.2 \div 3 = 0.4$

Exercise 12:9

Work these out in your head if you can.
You can use paper if you need to.
Write down the answers.

1 $1.6 \div 4$ **4** $0.08 \div 2$ **7** $0.48 \div 8$ **10** $0.21 \div 7$

2 $2.4 \div 3$ **5** $0.12 \div 4$ **8** $8.1 \div 9$ **11** $4.5 \div 9$

3 $2.5 \div 5$ **6** $0.27 \div 3$ **9** $2.4 \div 6$ **12** $5.6 \div 8$

Exercise 12:10   Game: Four in a row

This is a game for two players.
You will need several counters of two different colours.

Above the board is a set of numbers.
All the numbers on the board can be made by multiplying two of these numbers together.

Player 1
(1) Choose two numbers from the list.
(2) Multiply the numbers together.
Do not use a calculator.
(3) If your answer appears on the board cover it with a counter.
You may not get an answer on the board.
You cannot put a counter down if this happens.

Player 2
Start by checking Player 1's answer. You can use a calculator.
Now have a go yourself.
Use a different colour for your counters.

The winner is the first person to get four counters in a straight line.
The line can be in any direction.

1	2	3	4	5	6	7	8	9
0.1	0.2	0.3	0.4	0.5	0.6	0.7	0.8	0.9

4.9	0.24	7.2	4.8	0.24	1.8
0.56	2	0.08	0.4	3	2.8
1.2	2.4	4.2	0.18	24	0.2
0.42	0.3	0.72	3.6	1.6	72
2.7	0.7	1	0.32	2.5	4
0.1	0.8	0.12	0.6	1.4	0.48

Sometimes you have to put decimals in order of size.

◀◀REPLAY▶

Example Put these in order of size. Start with the smallest.
4.615   3.842   4.67

3 is smaller than 4.   4.615   3.842   4.67
3.842 is the smallest number.

The first numbers after   4.615   4.67
the decimal point are the same.

1 is smaller than 7.   4.615   4.67
4.615 is smaller than 4.67

The numbers in order are: 3.842   4.615   4.67

Exercise 12:11

In questions **1** to **10** put the numbers in order of size, smallest first.

1 5.378   5.3542   **6** 5.98   5.9321   3.901

2 4.723   4.7   **7** 12.256   12.2581   12.14

3 3.37   3.356   **8** 32.1   32.12   32.103

4 1.334   2.541   1.36   **9** 26.245   26.2   26.251

5 2.65   4.6781 4.651 **10** 3.2356   3.234   3.2349

11 Year 9 have a discus competition. These are the five longest throws.

8.78 m   8.5 m   8.14 m   9.3 m   9.287 m

a Put these distances in order of size. Start with the biggest.
b Which of these distances would be very hard to measure?

3 Multiplying and dividing decimals

Liam and his grandmother
are out for a walk.
Liam suggests a short cut.
He says that the short cut saves 2 km.
His grandmother wants to know how
far that is in miles.
Liam knows that 1 km is about 0.6 miles.
Liam works out:
$$2 \text{ km} = 2 \times 0.6 \text{ miles}$$
$$= 1.2 \text{ miles}$$
He tells his grandmother that the short
cut saves a little more than a mile.

Short multiplication of decimals

◄◄REPLAY►

Example   Work out 0.25×7

Start with   0.25   →   0.25
$7 \times 5 = 35$ ×   7   ×   7
                           5   **1.75**   The decimal point in 1.75
                           3   3   goes under the point in 0.25

$7 \times 2 = 14$
Then add the 3 to give **17**

Estimate: $0.25 \times 7 \approx 0.3 \times 7 = 2.1$ Answer: 1.75
The estimate is not the same as the answer but it is quite close.

Exercise 12:12

Work these out using short multiplication.
Do estimates to check your working.

1	1.4	**2**	2.4	**3**	0.26	**4**	4.7
	× 5		× 4		× 3		× 2

Set these out in the same way as questions **1** to **4**.
Work out the answers.

5 3.4 × 5   **7** 2.72 × 7   **9** 0.637 × 9   **11** 40.3 × 7

6 0.48 × 4   **8** 3.62 × 8   **10** 0.814 × 6   **12** 0.246 × 9

Long multiplication of decimals

Example   Work out   **a** 1.63 × 42   **b** 3.64 × 52

a
```
      1.63
   ×    42
     3 26   → (163 × 2)
    65 20   → (163 × 40)
    68.46
```

b
```
      3.64
   ×    32
     7 28   ← (364 × 2)
   109 20   ← (364 × 30)
   116.48
```

Estimates: **a** 1.63 × 42 ≈ 2 × 40 = 80   **b** 3.64 × 32 ≈ 4 × 30 = 120

Exercise 12:13

Work these out using long multiplication.
Do estimates to check your working.

1 1.42 × 34   **4** 6.8 × 82   **7** 0.67 × 29   **10** 0.34 × 27

2 2.43 × 52   **5** 3.08 × 62   **8** 5.12 × 38   **11** 3.65 × 56

3 3.12 × 67   **6** 4.16 × 91   **9** 4.06 × 84   **12** 0.129 × 36

Short division of decimals

Example   9.6 ÷ 4   4)9.6

First do the 9 ÷ 4. This is 2 with 1 left over.   2
Put the 2 on top of the 9 and carry the 1 like this: 4)9.¹6

Now do 16 divided by 4.   2.4
The decimal point goes between the 2 and the 4,   4)9.¹6
above the decimal point in the 9.6

So 9.6 ÷ 4 = 2.4   Estimate: 9.6 ÷ 4 ≈ 10 ÷ 4 = 2.5

Exercise 12:14

Work these out using short division.
Do estimates to check your working.

1 $5\overline{)6.5}$.   **3** $3.18 \div 2$ **5** $0.738 \div 9$ **7** $0.534 \div 6$

2 $3\overline{)5.7}$ **4** $1.32 \div 3$ **6** $0.312 \div 4$ **8** $0.0535 \div 5$

Sometimes the divisions do not work out exactly.

Example   **a** $13.7 \div 4$ **b** $5.3 \div 8$

Add as many 0s   **a** $\dfrac{3.\,4\,2\,5}{4\overline{)13.^17^10^20}}$ **b** $\dfrac{0.6\,6\,2\,5}{8\overline{)5.3^50^20^40}}$
as you need

Estimates: **a** $13.7 \div 4 \approx 12 \div 4 = 3$ **b** $5.3 \div 8 \approx 5 \div 8 \approx 0.6$

Work these out.
Add as many 0s as you need.

9 $3.7 \div 2$ **11** $14.6 \div 8$ **13** $30.1 \div 8$ **15** $475 \div 4$

10 $1.36 \div 5$ **12** $154 \div 4$ **14** $507 \div 2$ **16** $829 \div 8$

Sometimes you need to round.

Example   **a** $43.1 \div 6$ **b** $23 \div 7$
Round the answers correct to 3 dp.

You need to find the **fourth**   **a** $\dfrac{7.\,1\,8\,3\,3}{6\overline{)43.^15^20^20^20}}$ **b** $\dfrac{3.\,2\,8\,5\,7}{7\overline{)23.^20^60^40^50}}$
decimal place to round to
three places.

Answers: **a** 7.183 **b** 3.286

Estimates: **a** $43.1 \div 6 \approx 40 \div 6 \approx 7$ **b** $23 \div 7 \approx 20 \div 7 \approx 3$

Work these out.
Round the answers correct to 3 dp.

17 $4.7 \div 3$ **19** $6.21 \div 11$ **21** $5.47 \div 6$ **23** $0.327 \div 7$

18 $1.86 \div 7$ **20** $3.79 \div 6$ **22** $25.3 \div 9$ **24** $0.859 \div 9$

Long division of decimals

Example $60.2 \div 14$

14 will not go into 6 so first do $60 \div 14$

$$14\overline{)60.2}$$

You need to find out how many times 14 goes into 60.

$14 \times 2 = 28$
$14 \times 3 = 42$
$14 \times 4 = 56 \leftarrow$
$14 \times 5 = 70$

14 will go in 4 times. Put the 4 above the 0.

$$\begin{array}{r} 4 \\ 14\overline{)60.2} \end{array}$$

$14 \times 4 = 56$ Put this answer under the 60.

$$\begin{array}{r} 4 \\ 14\overline{)60.2} \\ 56 \end{array}$$

Now subtract 56 from 60.

$$\begin{array}{r} 4 \\ 14\overline{)60.2} \\ 56 \\ \hline 4 \end{array}$$

The 4 is the 'carry'.
Bring down
the 2 to the 4

$$\begin{array}{r} 4 \\ 14\overline{)60.2} \\ 56 \downarrow \\ \hline 4\,2 \end{array}$$

Now do $42 \div 14$

$14 \times 2 = 28$
$14 \times 3 = 42 \leftarrow$

14 will go 3 times exactly.
Put the 3 in after the 4.
Put the decimal point in 4.3
above the decimal point in 60.2

$$\begin{array}{r} 4.3 \\ 14\overline{)60.2} \\ 56 \\ \hline 4\,2 \end{array}$$

$14 \times 3 = 42$
Put the answer under the 42.
When you subtract this time there is no remainder.

$$\begin{array}{r} 4.3 \\ 14\overline{)60.2} \\ 56 \\ \hline 4\,2 \end{array}$$

This is what the working looks like
when you have finished!

$$\begin{array}{r} 4.3 \\ 14\overline{)60.2} \\ 56 \\ \hline 4\,2 \\ 4\,2 \\ \hline - \end{array}$$

Answer: 4.3

Exercise 12:15

Work these out by long division. They should all work out exactly.

1 3.12 ÷ 12   **5** 48.1 ÷ 13   **9** 6.72 ÷ 14

2 55.5 ÷ 15   **6** 14.72 ÷ 32   **10** 85.1 ÷ 23

3 71.4 ÷ 21   **7** 81 ÷ 18   **11** 14.28 ÷ 42

4 6.5 ÷ 25   **8** 17.68 ÷ 34   **12** 233.7 ÷ 19

Exercise 12:16

1 A chair costs £49.85
Find the cost of 24 chairs.

2 Jenny buys a bag of fun size Mars bars.
She pays £2.16
There are 18 Mars bars in the bag.
How much is one Mars bar?

3 Lil makes purses to sell.
She sells the purses for **£2.65** each.
  a Lil sells **27** purses.
     How much does she get for the **27** purses?
     Write down enough working to show
     that you have not used a calculator.
  b Lil has a box of **300** beads.
     She uses **14** beads to make a pattern on each purse.
     How many complete purses can she make using the **300** beads?
     Write down enough working to show
     that you have not used a calculator.

1 Work these out.
Give your answer correct to 3 sf when you need to round.

a $\dfrac{6.7 + 2.4}{13}$ **b** $\dfrac{56}{7 \times 1.6}$ **c** $\dfrac{6.6 + 8.5}{9.2 - 3.9}$ **d** $\dfrac{1.8^2 + 2.4^2}{0.85}$

2 Work these out.
Give your answer correct to 3 sf when you need to round.

a $\sqrt{8.5^2 + 7.2^2}$ **b** $4\sqrt{1 - 0.24^2}$ **c** $\tfrac{1}{2}\sqrt{5.2^2 - 2.5^2}$ **d** $\dfrac{10}{\sqrt{14^2 - 9^2}}$

3 Work these out in your head.
Write down the answers.
a $21.8 + 3$ **c** $2.3 + 1.6$ **e** $1.8 - 0.7$ **g** $10 - 4.8$
b $0.6 + 4.3$ **d** $4.5 - 3.4$ **f** $3 - 2.4$ **h** $20 - 14.1$

4 Work these out in your head.
Write down the answers.
a 0.8×0.9 **c** 0.7×8 **e** 1.1×0.7 **g** 6×1.2
b 0.6×7 **d** 0.7×6 **f** $(0.4)^2$ **h** 9×0.7

5 Write these decimals in order, smallest first.
a 4.15, 4.1, 4.105   **c** 14.505, 14.005, 14.05
b 0.213, 0.231, 0.23   **d** 8.97, 8.907, 8.097

6 Work these out.
a 7.18×7 **b** 6.25×6 **c** 9.084×4 **d** 26.73×9

7 Work these out.
a 6.34×45 **b** 71.62×28 **c** 8.074×17 **d** 84.62×39

8 Work these out.
Give your answer correct to 3 sf when you need to round.
a $2.835 \div 7$ **b** $517.5 \div 9$ **c** $14.16 \div 8$ **d** $7.13 \div 6$

9 Work these out.
a $105.4 \div 17$ **b** $2360.6 \div 29$ **c** $100.8 \div 32$ **d** $180.44 \div 52$

1 When water falls over a waterfall it starts going faster. The formula for the energy that the water gains because it goes faster is

$$E = \frac{m(v^2 - u^2)}{2}$$

m is the mass of the water
u is the speed of the water at the top of the fall
v is the speed of the water at the bottom
Find E when $m = 1000$, $v = 8$ and $u = 2.5$

2 Here is a way of finding the triangle numbers.

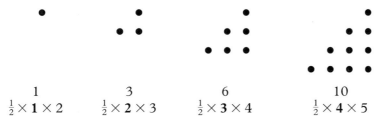

1	3	6	10
$\frac{1}{2} \times 1 \times 2$	$\frac{1}{2} \times 2 \times 3$	$\frac{1}{2} \times 3 \times 4$	$\frac{1}{2} \times 4 \times 5$

a Write down the expressions for the fifth and sixth numbers.
Work them out.

b The formula for the nth triangle number is $\frac{1}{2}n(n + 1)$.
Use the formula to work out these triangle numbers:
(1) 12th   (2) 20th   (3) 31st   (4) 100th

3 The area of this triangle
can be found using the formula
Area $= \frac{1}{2}q\sqrt{p^2 - q^2}$

a Calculate the area when
$p = 0.25$ m and $q = 0.07$ m

b Calculate the area when
$p = 4.6$ cm and $q = 3.7$ cm
Give this answer correct
to 1 dp.

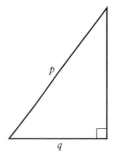

4 Rob has these number cards:

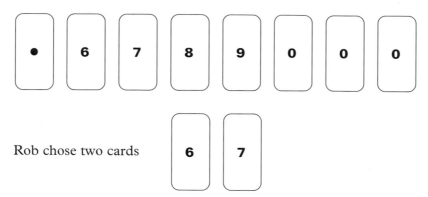

Rob chose two cards

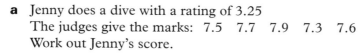

He made the number 67 with his two cards.

a Rob then made a number 1000 times as big as 67
Write down the number that Rob made.

b Rob made the number 69.8 with his cards.
Rob then made a number that was 10 times as big as 69.8
Write down the number that Rob made.

c Rob then used the cards to make a number 100 times bigger than 69.8
Show the number that Rob made.

5 Jenny, Harneet and Tracy have
entered a diving competition.
Each of their dives will have a
dive rating. The harder the dive
the higher the rating.
Here are the rules for working out a score:
(1) Remove the highest and lowest marks.
(2) Add together the middle three marks.
(3) Multiply the answer to (2) by the dive rating.
Each mark is out of 10.

a Jenny does a dive with a rating of 3.25
The judges give the marks: 7.5   7.7   7.9   7.3   7.6
Work out Jenny's score.

b Harneet's marks are: 8.2   8   8.1   7.9   7.8
Harneet's score is 80.88.
What is the dive rating of her dive?

c Tracy has chosen a dive with a rating of 3.34
Tracy's score is 81.83.
Here are four of the judges marks: 8.2   8.2   7.9   8.3
Find the missing mark.

- **You may need to put brackets into a calculation before you work it out.**

  Examples   Work out: **a** $\dfrac{12+15}{3}$ **b** $7\sqrt{4^2+3^2}$

  a Put brackets round the top. $\dfrac{12+15}{3} = \dfrac{(12+15)}{3}$

  $\boxed{(}\ \boxed{1}\ \boxed{2}\ \boxed{+}\ \boxed{1}\ \boxed{5}\ \boxed{)}\ \boxed{\div}\ \boxed{3}\ \boxed{=}$ Answer 9

  b Put in brackets. $7\sqrt{4^2+3^2} = 7\sqrt{(4^2+3^2)}$

  $\boxed{\sqrt{\ }}\ \boxed{(}\ \boxed{4}\ \boxed{x^2}\ \boxed{+}\ \boxed{3}\ \boxed{x^2}\ \boxed{)}\ \boxed{\times}\ \boxed{7}\ \boxed{=}$ Answer 15

- ## *Adding, subtracting, multiplying and dividing decimals*

  Examples   **1** $4.27 + 0.1 = 4.37$ **2** $4.6 + 1.2 = 3.4$

  3 $0.5 \times 0.9 = 0.45$ There are **two** numbers after the decimal points
  in the questions, so there are **two** numbers after
  4 $1.2 \times 0.2 = 0.24$ the decimal points in the answers.

  5 $1.2 \div 3 = 0.4$ **6** $0.15 \div 5 = 0.03$

- ## *Short and long multiplication of decimals*

  Examples   Work out: **1** 0.25×7 **2** 3.64×52

  1 $\begin{array}{r} 0.25 \\ \times\ \ \ 7 \\ \hline 1.75 \\ \scriptstyle 3 \end{array}$ **2** $\begin{array}{r} 3.64 \\ \times\ \ \ 32 \\ \hline 7\ 28 \\ \scriptstyle 1 \\ 109\ 20 \\ \scriptstyle 1\ 1 \\ \hline 116.48 \\ \scriptstyle 1 \end{array}$ $\leftarrow (364 \times 2)$
    $\leftarrow (364 \times 30)$

  Estimates: **1** $0.25 \times 7 \approx 0.3 \times 7 = 2.1$ **2** $3.64 \times 32 \approx 4 \times 30 = 120$

- ## *Short and long division of decimals*

  Examples   **1** $43.1 \div 6$ **2** $60.2 \div 14$

  Round the answer correct
  to 3 decimal places.

  You need to find the **fourth** $6\overline{)43.^15^10^20^20}$ with quotient 7.1833
  decimal place to round to
  three places.   Answer: 7.183

  Estimate: $43.1 \div 6 \approx 40 \div 6 \approx 7$

  $\begin{array}{r} 4.3 \\ 14\overline{)60.2} \\ 56\downarrow \\ \hline 42 \\ 42 \\ \hline - \end{array}$

  Answer: 4.3

1 Work these out.
Give your answer correct to 3 sf when you need to round.

   a $\dfrac{3.4 + 5.5}{3.7}$ **b** $\dfrac{5.6}{1.4 \times 8}$ **c** $\dfrac{67 - 14.6}{4.3 + 5.9}$ **d** $4\sqrt{4.5^2 + 6^2}$

2 Find out the value of p in this formula.

   $p = \dfrac{q^2 + r^2}{q - r}$ $q = 14.8$ $r = 12.3$

3 Work these out in your head.
Write down the answers.
   a $6.7 + 3$ **c** $3.62 - 0.5$ **e** $2 - 1.6$
   b $0.45 + 0.2$ **d** $7.4 + 1.3$ **f** $10 - 3.7$

4 Work these out in your head.
Write down the answers.
   a 3×0.7 **c** 1.2×5 **e** $3.5 \div 7$
   b 0.4×0.6 **d** 0.3×1.1 **f** $0.64 \div 8$

5 Write these decimals in order, smallest first.
   a $8.19, \quad 8.019, \quad 8.109$ **b** $1.2, \quad 1.02, \quad 1.002$

 6 Work these out.
   a 7.62×5 **b** 34.8×6

 7 Work these out.
   a 6.74×36 **b** 74.8×27

 8 Work these out.
Give your answer correct to 3 dp if you need to round.
   a $4.56 \div 8$ **b** $7.59 \div 7$

 9 Work these out.
   a $59.2 \div 16$ **b** $88.4 \div 26$

13 Try angles

QUESTIONS

EXTENSION

SUMMARY

TEST YOURSELF

These satellite dishes are set at a precise angle of elevation and direction (east) to receive TV broadcasts from a satellite orbiting the Earth. Find out what the angle is.

1   ◀◀REPLAY▶

The instrument showing the wings of a plane against a horizontal line tells the pilot if the plane is flying straight or making a turn. The instrument shows an acute angle between the wings and the horizontal line. The greater the angle, the tighter the turn.
The horizontal line is called an artificial horizon.

Angles on a straight line	**Angles on a straight line** add up to **180°**
Example	$a = 180° - 30° - 65°$ $a = 85°$

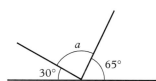

Angles at a point	**Angles at a point** add up to **360°**
Example	$b = 360° - 130° - 155°$ $b = 75°$

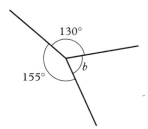

Opposite angles	**Opposite angles** are **equal**
Example	c is opposite 125° and d is opposite 55°. $c = 125°$ $d = 55°$ (notice that c and d add up to 180°)

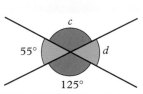

Exercise 13:1

Calculate the angles marked with letters.

1

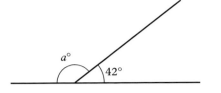

5

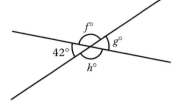

2

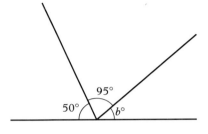

6

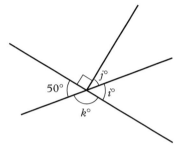

3

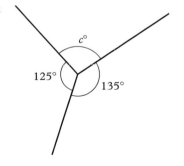

7

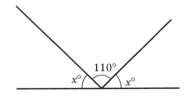

4

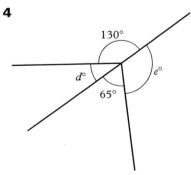

8

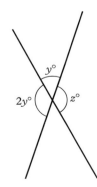

Angles of a triangle	**The angles of a triangle** add up to **180°**

Example

$x = 180° - 40° - 75°$
$x = 65°$

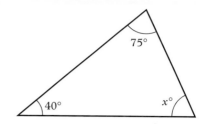

Angles of a quadrilateral	**The angles of a quadrilateral** add up to **360°**

Example

$y = 360° - 90° - 130° - 60°$
$y = 80°$

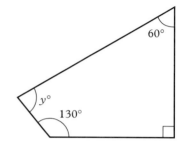

9

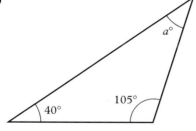

11

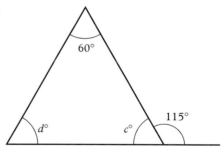

10

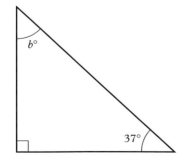

● 12

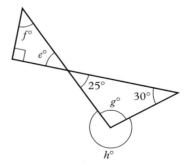

13

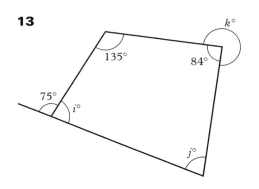

● **14**

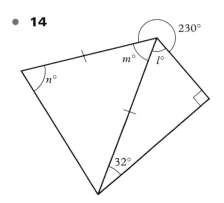

Angles and parallel lines

Alternate angles	Angles on opposite sides of the intersecting line are called **alternate angles.** They are found in **Z** shapes. **Alternate angles are equal**.	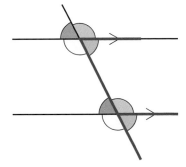
Corresponding angles	Angles on the same place in 'top' and 'bottom' sets of angles are called **corresponding angles**. They are found in **F** shapes. **Corresponding angles are equal**.	
Interior angles	Angles between parallel lines are called **interior angles**. **Interior angles add up to 180°.**	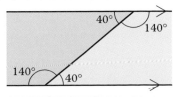

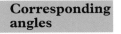

Exercise 13:2

1 Find the angles marked with letters.
Write down which rules you have used.

a

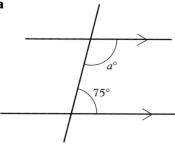

c

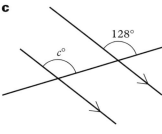

b

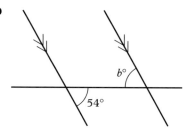

d

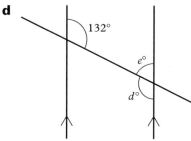

Find the angles marked with letters.

2

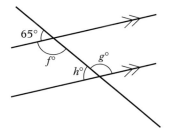

4

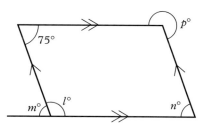

3

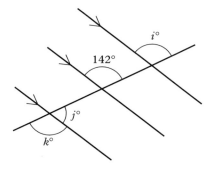

5

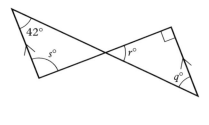

2 Polygons

· ·

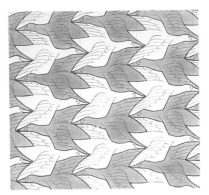

This tessellation is based on a rectangle. Pieces of the rectangle are cut out and moved. The new shape still tessellates.
These pictures were drawn by M C Escher (1898–1970), a famous artist and mathematician.

Polygon	A **polygon** is a shape with straight sides.
Regular polygon	**Regular polygons** have all their sides the same length. All the angles are also equal.

Exercise 13:3

1 Copy this table. Fill it in.

Number of sides	Name of polygon
3	
4	
5	
6	
7	
8	
9	
10	

Choose from: decagon, hexagon, triangle, heptagon, quadrilateral, pentagon, octagon, nonagon.

2 In this question you are going to draw a regular pentagon.
   You will need a protractor or angle measurer.

   a Draw a horizontal line 10 cm long, with 5 cm solid and 5 cm dotted.
   Leave some space above it.

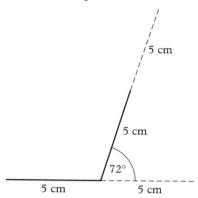

   b Put the centre of your protractor on the end of the solid line.
   Measure 72° from the dotted line.

   c Draw another line 10 cm long.
   Draw 5 cm solid and 5 cm dotted.

   d Repeat **b** and **c** on your new line.

   e Keep going until you complete the pentagon.

3 Draw a regular hexagon.
   You can do this in the same way, but use an angle of 60°.

4 Draw a regular octagon.
   The angle you will need is 45°.

| Exterior angle | The angle you used to draw the shapes is called an **exterior angle**. It is outside the shape. |

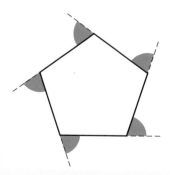
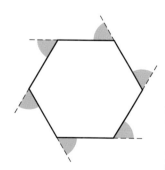

Look at this large pentagon marked out in a school yard.
Peter walks along the first side.
To walk along the second side he has to turn through the angle marked in red.
To walk along the third side he has to turn through the angle marked in blue.

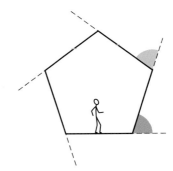

When he has walked all the way around the shape he is back facing in the same direction that he started.
He has turned through 360°.
The exterior angles of a pentagon must add up to 360°.

The exterior angles of any polygon add up to 360°.

Example

Work out the size of the exterior angle of a regular hexagon.

The angles add up to 360°.
If the hexagon is regular all its exterior angles will be equal.

External angle $= \dfrac{360°}{6} = 60°$

Exercise 13:4

1 Work out the exterior angle of a regular octagon.

2 Work out the exterior angle of a regular nonagon.

3 Work out the exterior angle of a regular decagon.

4 Copy this sentence. Fill in the gaps.
As the number of sides gets _____ the exterior angles get
_____ but they always add up to _____ .

5 Work out the exterior angle of a regular heptagon.
Round your answer to 2 dp.

6 Work out the exterior angles for regular polygons with the following
numbers of sides.
a 12
b 15
c 20
d 30

7 a Copy these pentagons. They do not have to be exact.

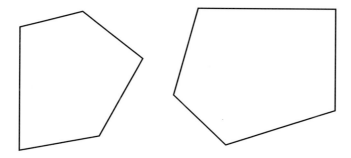

b Mark on the exterior angles of each pentagon.
c Measure the 5 exterior angles of each pentagon.
d Add up the angles and check that the total is 360°.

8 Four of the exterior angles of a pentagon are 56°, 47°, 103° and 67°.
What is the size of the fifth angle?

9 The exterior angle of a regular polygon is 36°.
How many sides has it got?

Interior angles The angles inside a polygon are called **interior angles**. They always make a straight line with the exterior angle.

exterior angle + interior angle = 180°

interior angle = 180° − exterior angle

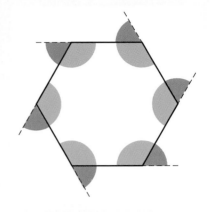

Example Work out the interior angle of a regular hexagon.

$$\text{Exterior angle} = \frac{360°}{6} = 60°$$

$$\text{Interior angle} = 180° - 60° = 120°$$

Exercise 13:5

1 Work out the interior angle of a regular pentagon.

2 Work out the interior angle of a regular octagon.

3 Copy this table. Fill it in.

Number of sides	Name of polygon	Exterior angle	Interior angle
3	equilateral triangle		
4	square		
5	regular pentagon		
6	regular …		
7	regular …		
8	regular …		
9	regular …		
10	regular …		

4 Tessellations

You will need a polygon stencil or some templates of regular polygons.

Squares tessellate.
They fit together without any gaps.

The angles around a
point total 360°.

If a regular polygon tessellates with itself you have a
regular tessellation.
If two regular polygons tessellate together you have a
semi-regular tessellation.

a Find as many regular tessellations as you can.
Mark on the interior angles and show that they all add
up to 360° around a point.

b Find as many semi-regular tessellations as you can.
Mark on the interior angles and show that they add up
to 360° around a point.
Try not to repeat any of your tessellations.

5 Explain why regular pentagons do not tessellate.
Use the angles to help you.

6 a 'All triangles tessellate'.
Is this true or false?
Draw some triangle tessellations. Measure and mark the angles.

b 'All quadrilaterals tessellate'.
Is this true or false?
Draw some quadrilateral tessellations. Measure and mark the
angles.

Sum of the interior angles

You already know that the angles in a triangle add up to 180°. This is the **sum of the interior angles** of a triangle.

It is possible to find the sum of the interior angles of any polygon.

(1) Draw the polygon.

(2) Mark all the interior angles.

(3) Join one vertex to all the others. All the interior angles are now inside one of the triangles.

(4) Count the number of triangles. Multiply by 180° to find the total.

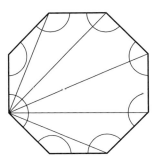

Example

Find the sum of the interior angles of an octagon.

The octagon splits into 6 triangles.
Total = 6 × 180° = 1080°

If it is a regular octagon, each interior angle = $\dfrac{1080°}{8}$

$= 135°$

Exercise 13:6

For each of these polygons:

a Draw a sketch.

b Split it into triangles.

c Work out the sum of the interior angles.

d Work out the size of each interior angle if the polygon is regular.

e Check your answers to **d** with your table from Exercise 13:5.

1 Square

2 Pentagon

3 Heptagon

4 Nonagon

5 Decagon (10 sides)

6 Dodecagon (12 sides)

3 Angles and transformations

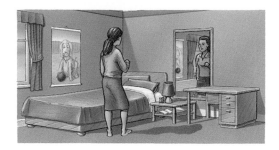

Sian has moved the furniture in her bedroom. She has turned the bed 90° so that it fits into the corner.
The desk has been moved along the wall.
The poster on the wall is an enlargement of a photograph Sian took of her dog.
The mirror shows Sian's reflection.

Any movement of a shape is called a transformation in mathematics.
There are four types of transformations:

reflection   translation   rotation   enlargement

◀◀ REPLAY ▶

Object	The shape you start with is called the **object**.
Image	The transformed shape is called the **image**.
Congruent	When shapes are identical they are called **congruent**.
	This shape has been reflected.
	The object and image are congruent.
Line of reflection	The mirror line is called a **line of reflection**.

Exercise 13:7

Copy each diagram.
Draw the image of each pattern in the line of reflection.

1   a   **b**

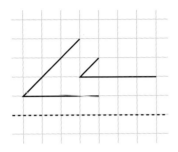   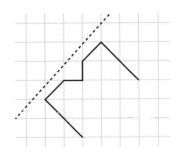

Copy each diagram.
Complete it so that the dotted line is a line of reflection.

2   a   **b**

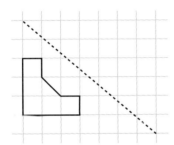   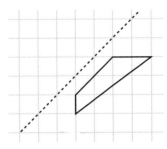

Translation	A **translation** is a movement in a straight line.

Example

This object and image
show a translation.
Describe the translation.

Mark a point P on the
object.
Mark the corresponding
point on the image.
Label it P′.

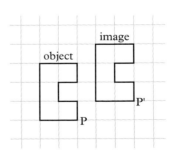

P has moved 3 units to
the right and 1 unit up.
This means that the whole shape has moved 3 units to the
right and 1 unit up.
The object and image are congruent.

Exercise 13:8

1 Describe the translation for each pair of shapes.

a

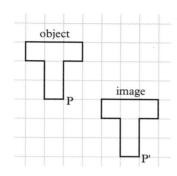

b

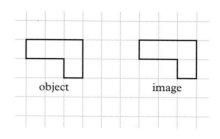

2 For parts **a** to **d**, describe the translation that is needed to move the object to the image.

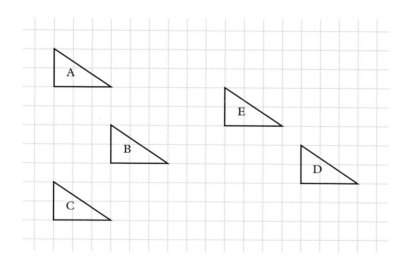

	Object	Image
a	A	B
b	C	D
c	B	E
d	E	C

Rotation

A **rotation** turns a shape through an angle about a fixed point.

Centre of rotation

The fixed point is called the **centre of rotation**.

Nina is going to rotate this rectangle through 90° clockwise.
The origin is the centre of rotation.
Nina puts some tracing paper on top of the diagram. She traces the rectangle and marks a cross at the centre of rotation.

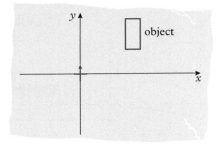

Nina uses the cross to help her to rotate the tracing paper through 90° clockwise.
She marks the new position of the rectangle on her axes. She labels this the image.
The object and image are congruent.

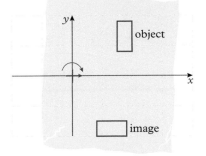

Exercse 13:9

1 Copy the axes and the shape S on to squared paper.

2 Rotate S 90° clockwise about the origin.
Use tracing paper to help you.
Label the image A.

3 Rotate S 180° anticlockwise about the origin.
Label the image B.

4 Rotate S 90° anticlockwise about the origin.
Label the image C.

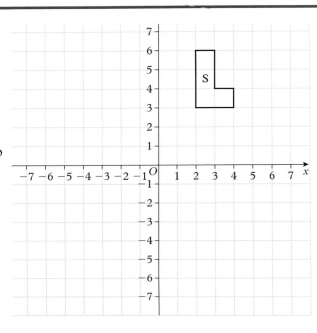

Example

The red shape has been reflected vertically.
The blue shape has been rotated 90° anticlockwise.

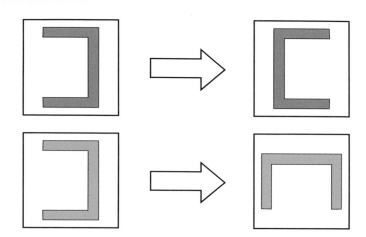

Exercise 13:10

1 Draw a diagram to show the position of this
shape after it has been
  a reflected vertically
  b reflected horizontally
  c rotated 90° clockwise
  d rotated 180° anticlockwise.

2 Richard is making patterns using this shape.

He made this pattern by
translating the shape.

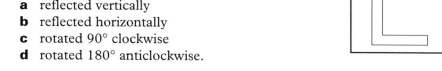

He made this pattern by
reflecting the shape
vertically.

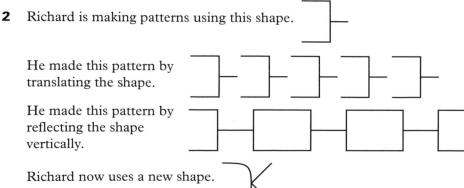

Richard now uses a new shape.

  a Draw the pattern he would get by translating the new shape.
  b Draw the pattern he would get by reflecting the new shape vertically.

3 Tara had made a puzzle for her
brother Chris.
The puzzle has four cards placed
like this.

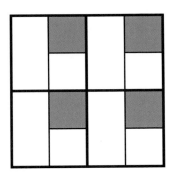

Chris can only move the cards in three ways:
(1) He can reflect a card vertically.

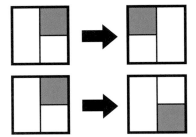

(2) He can reflect a card horizontally.

(3) He can rotate a card through any angle.
Chris has to transform the cards in the first pattern to make the
second pattern.

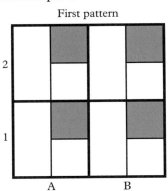

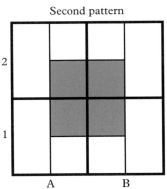

Copy this table. It shows the transformations needed for cards A1 and
B1 to make the second pattern.
Fill in the transformations needed for A2 and B2.

Card	Transformation
A1	none – card is in correct position
B1	reflect vertically
A2	
B2	

◀◀ **REPLAY** ▶

| **Enlargement** | An **enlargement** changes the size of an object. The change is the same in all directions. |

| **Scale factor** | The **scale factor** tells us how many times bigger the enlargement is. |

Example   Enlarge the triangle by a scale factor of 2.

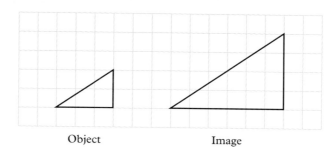

Object   Image

The image is **2** times as long and **2** times as high as the object. The object and the image are not congruent because they are different sizes.

Exercise 13:11

1 Copy these shapes on to squared paper.
Enlarge each shape by a scale factor of 2.

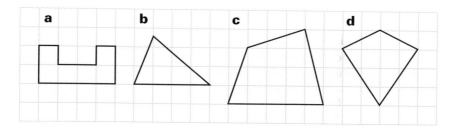

2 Enlarge the shapes in question **1** by a scale factor of 3.

The word **enlarge** normally means to make something **bigger**.
In maths, enlargements can also make objects **smaller**!
This happens when the scale factor is less than one.

Example

Enlarge this shape by a scale factor of $\frac{1}{2}$.

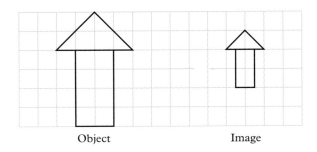

Object   Image

Each length of the image is $\frac{1}{2}$ the length of the object.

3 Copy these shapes on to squared paper.
Enlarge each shape by a scale factor of $\frac{1}{2}$.

a 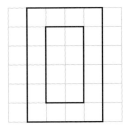   **b** 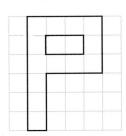   **c**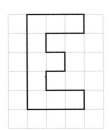

4 For each of these pairs of shapes, write down the scale factor of the
enlargement that transforms:
a S into T   **b** T into S
Make any measurements that you need to help you.

(1)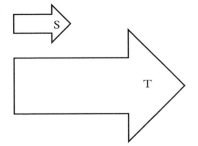

(2)

1 Calculate the angles marked with letters.

a

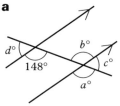

b

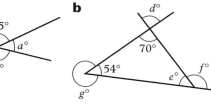

c

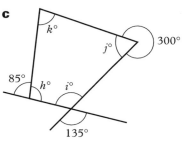

2 Calculate the angles marked with letters.

a

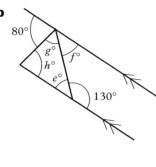

b

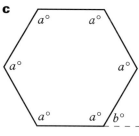

c

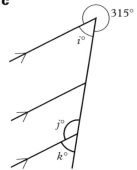

3 Calculate the angles marked with letters.

a

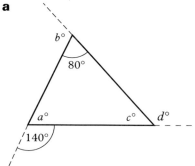

c

b

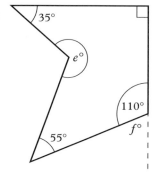

d

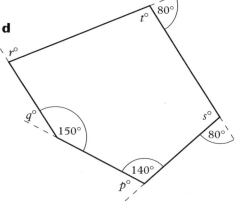

4 **a** Draw any heptagon.

    b Mark and measure all the interior angles.

    c Find the total of all the interior angles.

    d Divide your heptagon into triangles. Calculate the total of the interior angles. Is your answer the same as part **c**?

5 Copy the axes and the shape P on to squared paper.

    a Rotate P 180° anticlockwise about the origin. Label the image R.

    b Rotate P 90° anticlockwise about the origin. Label the image R.

    c What would happen if you rotated shape P 270° clockwise about the origin?

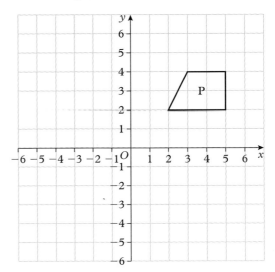

6 Enlarge each shape by the scale factor given.

    a scale factor 2   **c** scale factor $\frac{1}{4}$

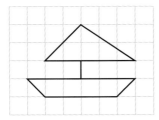

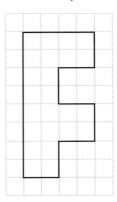

    b scale factor 3   **d** scale factor $2\frac{1}{2}$

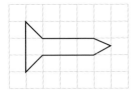

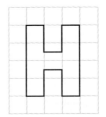

1 Work out the angles marked in this regular pentagon.

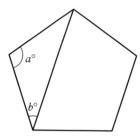

2 A regular polygon has n sides.
  a Write down a formula to work out the exterior angle.
  b Use your answer to **a** to write down a formula for the interior angle.

3 What other shape will fit with two regular dodecagons to form a tessellation?

4 Gavin has a photo of his dog.
It measures 14 cm wide by 10 cm high.

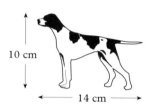

Gavin wants to enlarge the photo so that it just fits into this frame. The frame measures 35 cm wide by 25 cm high. What scale factor should Gavin use to enlarge his photo?

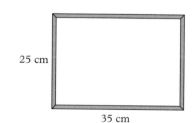

5 Alisha has enlarged this rectangle using different scale factors.
These are the sizes of her enlarged rectangles.
For each one find the scale factor that Alisha used.

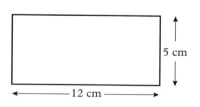

a

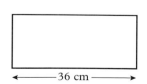

b

c

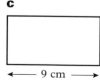

- **Polygon**　A **polygon** is a shape with straight sides.

  Regular polygon　**Regular polygons** have all their sides the same length. All the angles are also equal.

- **Exterior angles**　The angles outside a polygon are called **exterior angles**. The **exterior angles** of any polygon add up to 360°.

  Interior angles　The angles inside a polygon are called **interior angles**. They always make a straight line with the exterior angle. This means that

  exterior angle + interior angle = 180°

  interior angle = 180° − exterior angle

  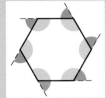

- **Sum of the interior angles**　It is possible to find the **sum of the interior angles** of any polygon.

  Example　Find the sum of the interior angles of an octagon.
  The octagon splits into 6 triangles.
  Total = 6 × 180° = 1080°
  If it is a regular octagon, each

  interior angle = $\dfrac{1080°}{8}$ = 135°.

- **Line of reflection**　The mirror line is called a **line of reflection**.

  Translation　A **translation** is a movement in a straight line.

  Rotation　A **rotation** turns a shape through an angle about a fixed point.

  Centre of rotation　The fixed point is called the **centre of rotation**.

- **Congruent**　When shapes are identical they are called **congruent**. For reflection, translation and rotation the object and the image are always congruent. For enlargement they are not congruent.

- **Enlargement**　An **enlargement** changes the size of an object. The change is the same in all directions.

  Scale factor　The **scale factor** tells us how many times bigger the enlargement is.

1 Calculate the angles marked with letters.

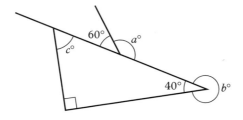
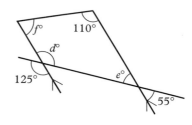

2 Work out the size of the exterior angle of a regular polygon with
   a 6 sides   **b** 9 sides   **c** 10 sides   **d** 7 sides

3 Copy this table. Fill it in.

Number of sides	Name of polygon	Exterior angle	Interior angle
3	equilateral triangle		
5	regular pentagon		
8	regular octagon		
12	regular dodecagon		

4 The sum of the interior angles of a polygon is 1620°. How many sides does the polygon have?

5 **a** Copy the axes and the shape A on to squared paper.
   b Reflect A in the *y* axis. Label the image B.

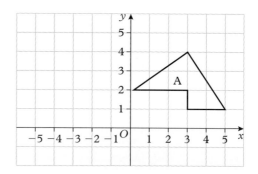

6 Enlarge this shape using a scale factor of $1\frac{1}{2}$.

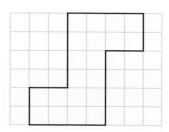

14 Algebra: two at a time

These two discs each have a different number on their reverse side.

Adding any pair of the four numbers gives these totals:

27, 23, 32, 18

Find the two numbers.

1 ◀◀REPLAY▶

The gradient tells you how steep the hill is.
We use the word gradient in mathematics. It tells you about the steepness of straight lines.

| **Equation** |

The rule of a line is called the **equation** of the line.

This line has the rule:
y co-ordinate = **x** co-ordinate + 2
The equation is **y = x + 2**

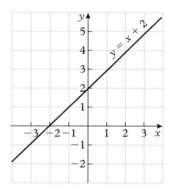

Exercise 14:1

1 a Copy the axes on to squared paper.
   b The point (1, 1) lies on the line $y = x$
      Its y co-ordinate is equal to its
      x co-ordinate.
      These points also lie on the line $y = x$
      (2, ...) (..., 3) (4, ...) (..., 5)
      Copy these points and fill in the missing
      numbers.
   c Mark the points on your grid.
      Join them with a straight line.
      Label the line with its equation
      y = x

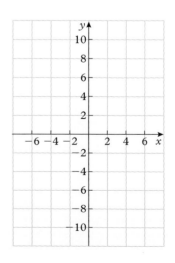

2 Draw these lines on the same axes that you used for question **1**.
Label each line with its equation.
   a   *y* co-ordinate = **2** × *x* co-ordinate $y = 2x$
   b   *y* co-ordinate = **3** × *x* co-ordinate $y = 3x$
   c   *y* co-ordinate = *x* co-ordinate ÷ **2**

$$y = \frac{x}{2} \quad \text{or} \quad y = \tfrac{1}{2}x$$

3 You have drawn the lines
   $y = x$ $y = 2x$ $y = 3x$ $y = \tfrac{1}{2}x$
   a   Which line is the steepest?
   b   Which line is the least steep?
   c   Which part of the equation tells you how steep the line is?

4 Which line is the steeper in each of these pairs?

   a $y = 4x$ or $y = 8x$ **c** $y = \dfrac{x}{3}$ or $y = x$

   b $y = 7x$ or $y = 2x$ **d** $y = \dfrac{x}{5}$ or $y = \dfrac{x}{4}$

5 The diagram shows three graphs.
Write down the equation of each graph.
Choose from these equations.

$$y = 5x \quad y = 2\tfrac{1}{2}x \quad y = \frac{x}{3}$$

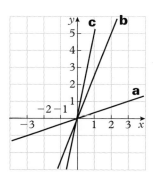

Exercise 14:2

You will need squared paper for this exercise.

1   **a**   Copy the axes on to squared paper.
     b   Draw and label the line $y = x$
     c   Copy and fill in this table for the line $y = x + 1$
        Draw and label the line $y = x + 1$

x	1	2	3	4
y	2	...	4	...

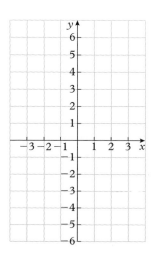

     d   Copy and fill in this table for the line $y = x + 3$
        Draw and label the line $y = x + 3$

x	1	2	3	4
y	...	5	...	...

2 Make a table for each of these lines.

x	1	2	3	4	5
y	...	...	...	...	...

   a $y = x - 1$

   b $y = x - 2$

   c $y = x - 3$

   d Draw and label each line on the same axes that you used for question **1**.

3 Look at the lines on your axes.

   a What do you notice about all the lines?

   b Which part of the equation tells you where the line will cross the y axis?

4 Where will these lines cross the y axis?

   a $y = x + 7$ **c** $y = x + \frac{1}{2}$

   b $y = x - 5$ **d** $y = x - \frac{3}{4}$

Example

Draw the line $y = 2x + 1$

Use your line to find the value of x when $y = -3$

Find the value of y when $x = 0$

$y = 2 \times 0 + 1$

   $= 1$

x	0	1	2
y	1	3	5

Similarly when $x = 1$

$y = 2 \times 1 + 1$

   $= 3$

and when $x = 2$

$y = 2 \times 2 + 1$

   $= 5$

Now draw the graph.
The points to plot are (0, 1), (1, 3) and (2, 5).
The point on the graph where the y co-ordinate is -3 has an x co-ordinate of -2.
So when $y = -3$, $x = -2$

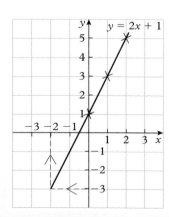

Exercise 14:3

1 **a** Copy and fill in this table for $y = x + 2$

x	0	1	2
y	...	3	...

   b Draw a set of axes on squared paper.
   Use values of x from -4 to 4 and values
   of y from -4 to 8.

   c Draw and label the line $y = x + 2$

   d Is the point (4, 7) above or below the line?

   e The point (..., -1) lies on the line.
   What is the missing x co-ordinate?

2 **a** Copy and fill in this table for $y = 2x - 3$

x	0	1	2
y	...	-1	...

   b Draw a set of axes on squared paper.
   Use values of x from -4 to 4 and values of y
   from -8 to 6.

   c Draw and label the line $y = 2x - 3$

   d Is the point (-1, -2) above or below the line?

   e The points lie on the line. Fill in the missing co-ordinates.
   (3, ...) (-2, ...) (..., -3) (..., 0)

3 This is the graph of $y = \frac{1}{2}x - 1$
   Use the graph to answer these
   questions.

   a What is the value of y when $x = 4$?

   b What is the value of x when $y = -3$?

   c Which of these points lie below the
   line?
   (2, -1) (3, 3) (1, -2)

   d These points lie on the line.
   Fill in the missing co-ordinates.
   (..., -2) (0, ...)

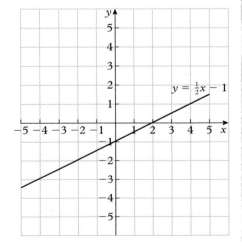

Example

Does the point (2, 5) lie on the line $y = x + 4$?
When $x = 2$ $y = 2 + 4 = 6$
When $x = 2$, $y = 6$, so:
The point (2, 6) lies on the line.
The point (2, 5) does not lie on the line.

4 Each of parts **a** to **f** has a point and a line.
Does the point lie on the line?
a (3, 7) $y = x + 4$
b (2, 8) $y = 3x$
c (2, 6) $y = 2x + 3$
d (1, 6) $y = 3x - 1$
e (0, −5) $y = 2x - 5$
f (4, 16) $y = 5x - 3$

Exercise 14:4

1 a Draw a set of axes on squared paper.
Use values of x from −4 to 4 and values
of y from −4 to 8.

x	−1	0	1	2
y	1	0	...	−2

b Copy and fill in this table for $y = -x$

c Draw and label the line $y = -x$

2 a Copy and fill in this table for $y = -2x$

b Use the same set of axes you used for
question **1**.
Draw and label the line $y = -2x$

x	−1	0	1	2
y	2	0	−2	...

3 a Copy and fill in this table for $y = -3x$

b Use the same set of axes you used for
question **1**.
Draw and label the line $y = -3x$

x	−1	0	1	2
y	...	...	−3	−6

c Look at the three graphs you have drawn.
Describe the graphs.
Does the rule for steepness still work?

Gradient

The **gradient** of a line tells you how steep the line is.
Both these lines have a '3' to tell you how steep they are.
They have **gradient** 3.
The lines are parallel because they have the same gradient.
The +2 and the −4 tell you where the lines cross the y axis.

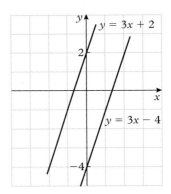

Both these lines have gradient −2.
They are parallel.
They cross the y axis at 0 and −1.

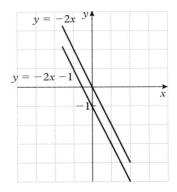

Example

Find the equation of the red line.
The red line is parallel to the line $y = 5x + 2$
Part of the equation must be $y = 5x$ ...
The red line crosses the y axis at **−3**.
The equation of the red line must be $y = 5x - 3$

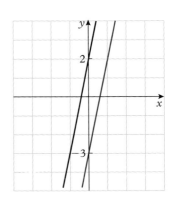

Exercise 14:5

Write down the equation of each red line.

1

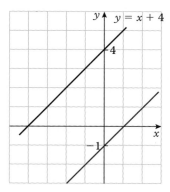

$y = x + 4$

4

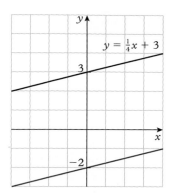

$y = \frac{1}{4}x + 3$

2

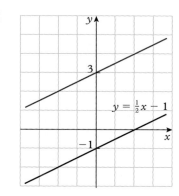

$y = \frac{1}{2}x - 1$

5

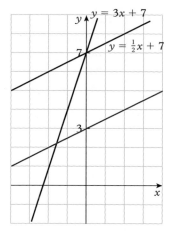

$y = 3x + 7$

$y = \frac{1}{2}x + 7$

3

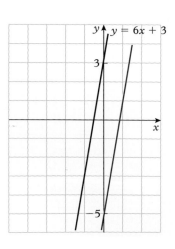

$y = 6x + 3$

6

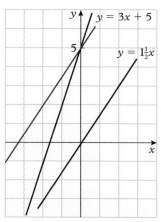

$y = 3x + 5$

$y = 1\frac{1}{2}x$

Point of intersection

The point where two lines cross is called the **point of intersection**.

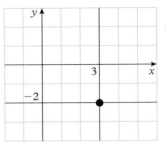

Example

a Write down the equation of the vertical line.

b Write down the co-ordinates of the point of intersection of the two lines.

a All points on the vertical line have *x* co-ordinates of **3**. The equation of the line is **x = 3**

b The co-ordinates of the point of intersection are (3, −2).

Exercise 14:6

1 a Write down the equations of these lines.

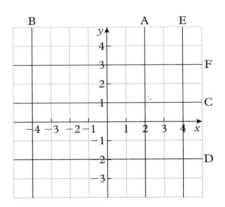

Write down the co-ordinates of the points of intersection of these pairs of lines.

b E and C   **c** A and D   **d** B and F

2 Write down the co-ordinates of the point of intersection of each pair of lines.

a x = 3 and y = 2   **d** x = −3 and y = 4
b x = 8 and y = 1   **e** x = −7 and y = −2
c x = 4 and y = −6   **f** x = 6 and y = 0

3 Which vertical and horizontal lines have the following points of intersection?

a (3, 5)   **c** (4, −3)   **e** (−1, −5)
b (6, 9)   **d** (0, −5)   **f** (−5, −6)

The equations of lines are not always written in this form.

Example

Draw the line $2x + y = 6$

There is a quick method to draw a line like this.
You find the points when $x = 0$ and $y = 0$

When $x = 0$	When $y = 0$
$0 + y = 6$	$2x + 0 = 6$
$y = 6$	$2x = 6$
	$x = 3$

This gives $(0, 6)$ This gives $(3, 0)$

Both of these points lie on the line.

Now plot these two points and join them up to give the line $2x + y = 6$

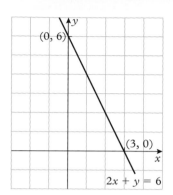

Exercise 14:7

1 Copy the axes on to squared paper.
  a Find the co-ordinates of two points on the line $x + y = 3$
  b Plot the points.
  Draw and label the line $x + y = 3$

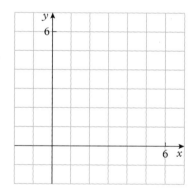

2 Make another copy of the axes from question **1**.
  a Find the co-ordinates of two points on the line $x + 2y = 6$
  b Plot the points.
  Draw and label the line $x + 2y = 6$

3 Make another copy of the axes from question **1**.
  a Find the co-ordinates of two points on the line $2x + 3y = 12$
  b Plot the points.
  Draw and label the line $2x + 3y = 12$

2 Simultaneous equations

It is easy to see where these two lines of gymnasts cross at the box. In mathematics you have to find where two lines cross.
You can do this by drawing lines or by using algebra.

Example

Alex and Tom are buying some food at the youth club.
Alex buys two **b**iscuits and one **d**rink for 10 p.
Tom buys one **b**iscuit and two **d**rinks for 14 p.
Find the cost of a **b**iscuit and the cost of a **d**rink.

Alex's equation is $2b + d = 10$
When $b = 0$ $d = 10$
When $d = 0$ $2b = 10$
                     $b = 5$
Two points on this line
are (0, 10) and (5, 0).

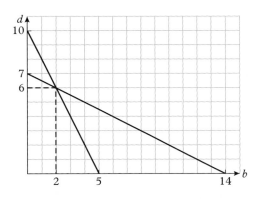

Tom's equation is $b + 2d = 14$
When $b = 0$ $2d = 14$
                     $d = 7$
When $d = 0$ $b = 14$
Two points on this line are (0, 7)
and (14, 0).

The lines intersect at (2, 6).
This means that $b = 2$ and $d = 6$
So a biscuit costs 2 p and a drink costs 6 p.

Check: $2b + d = 2 \times 2 + 6 = 10$ ✓ $b + 2d = 2 + 2 \times 6 = 14$ ✓

| Simultaneous equations | When you solve two equations at the same time you are solving **simultaneous equations**. |

Exercise 14:8

Draw graphs to solve these problems.
Check your answers in the original problem each time.

1 Solve these pairs of simultaneous equations.

a $x + y = 5$
$2x + 4y = 12$

● **b** $x + y = 7$
$3x + y = 11$

2 John and Alisha took part in a school quiz. They had to choose a *s*tandard or a *h*ard question on each turn.
John answered 3 *s*tandard and 2 *h*ard questions correctly and scored 12 points.
Alisha answered 1 *s*tandard and 4 *h*ard questions correctly and scored 14 points.
Find the points awarded for a *s*tandard question and for a *h*ard question.

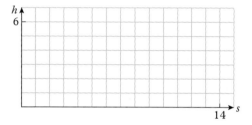

● **3** A school sells two types of calculator. One is a *b*asic model and the other is a *s*cientific model.
The cost of one *b*asic and one *s*cientific calculator is £10.
The cost of 3 *b*asic and 2 *s*cientific calculators is £24.
Find the cost of a *b*asic model and the cost of a *s*cientific model.

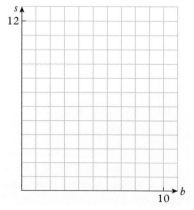

You can also solve simultaneous equations using algebra.

Example

Solve this pair of simultaneous equations $\quad 5x + y = 20$
$\qquad\qquad\qquad\qquad\qquad\qquad\qquad\qquad\quad 2x + y = 11$

Number the equations

(1) $5x + y = 20$
(2) $2x + y = 11$

Subtract to get rid of y
This finds x

$3x \quad = 9$
$x = 3$

Use equation (1) to find y

Put $x = 3$ in equation (1)
$5 \times 3 + y = 20$
$15 + y = 20$
$y = 5$
The answer is $x = 3$, $y = 5$

Use equation (2) to check your answer
$2x + y = 2 \times 3 + 5 = 6 + 5 = 11$ ✓

Exercise 14:9

Solve these pairs of simultaneous equations.
Start by subtracting the equations each time.

1 $\quad 5x + y = 13$
$\qquad x + y = 5$

5 $\quad 5x + y = 23$
$\qquad 2x + y = 14$

2 $\quad 3x + y = 22$
$\qquad x + y = 12$

6 $\quad 3x + 2y = 16$
$\qquad x + 2y = 12$

3 $\quad 5x + y = 28$
$\qquad 2x + y = 13$

7 $\quad 4x + 3y = 25$
$\qquad x + 3y = 13$

4 $\quad 7x + y = 18$
$\qquad 3x + y = 10$

8 $\quad 5x + 2y = 19$
$\qquad x + 2y = 15$

Example

Solve this pair of simultaneous equations $3x + y = 19$
$x - y = 1$

Number the equations

(1) $3x + y = 19$
(2) $x - y = 1$

Add to get rid of y
This finds x

$4x = 20$
$x = 5$

Use equation (1) to find y

Put $x = 5$ in equation (1)
$3 \times 5 + y = 19$
$15 + y = 19$
$y = 4$

The answer is $x = 5$, $y = 4$

Use equation (2) to check your answer
$x - y = 5 - 4 = 1$ ✓

Exercise 14:10

Solve these pairs of simultaneous equations.
Start by adding the equations each time.

1 $2x + y = 12$
$x - y = 3$

4 $4x + y = 12$
$3x - y = 2$

2 $4x + y = 7$
$5x - y = 2$

5 $3x + 2y = 17$
$5x - 2y = 7$

3 $3x + y = 18$
$x - y = 2$

6 $4x + 3y = 26$
$5x - 3y = 19$

Exercise 14:11

Solve these pairs of simultaneous equations.
You need to decide whether to add or subtract the equations.

1 $2x + y = 11$
$3x - y = 9$

4 $4x + 2y = 38$
$3x - 2y = 11$

2 $3x + 2y = 16$
$x + 2y = 12$

5 $5x + 3y = 19$
$2x + 3y = 13$

3 $4x + 2y = 28$
$x - 2y = 2$

6 $5x + 3y = 27$
$4x - 3y = 0$

You sometimes have to multiply one of the equations before adding or subtracting.

Example

Solve this pair of simultaneous equations $\quad 2x + 3y = 13$
$$4x - y = 5$$

Number the equations $\qquad\qquad$ (1) $\quad 2x + 3y = 13$
(2) $\quad 4x - y = 5$

You need to multiply equation (2) by **3**
so that you have $3y$ in $\qquad\qquad\qquad\qquad 2x + 3y = 13$
each equation $\qquad$ (2) $\times$ **3** $\quad 12x - 3y = 15$

Add to get rid of y $\qquad\qquad\qquad\qquad\quad 14x \quad\; = 28$
This finds x $\qquad\qquad\qquad\qquad\qquad\qquad x = 2$

Use equation (1) to find y $\qquad$ Put $x = 2$ in equation (1)
$$2 \times 2 + 3y = 13$$
$$4 + 3y = 13$$
$$3y = 9$$
$$y = 3$$
The answer is $x = 2$, $y = 3$

Use equation (2) to check your answer
$4x - y = 4 \times 2 - 3 = 8 - 3 = 5$ ✓

Exercise 14:12

Solve these pairs of simultaneous equations.
You will need to multiply one equation by a number.

1 $\quad 3x + 2y = 16$
$\qquad x + y = 7$

4 $\quad 5x + 3y = 36$
$\qquad x + y = 10$

2 $\quad 4x - 2y = 6$
$\qquad 3x + y = 17$

5 $\quad 3x + 2y = 9$
$\qquad 4x - y = 1$

3 $\quad 7a - 3b = 17$
$\qquad 2a + b = 16$

● **6** $\quad f + 4g = 7$
$\qquad 5f - 2g = 24$

Sometimes both equations have to be multiplied before adding or subtracting.

Example

Solve this pair of simultaneous equations $3x + 5y = 30$
$2x + 3y = 19$

Number the equations

(1) $3x + 5y = 30$
(2) $2x + 3y = 19$

Multiply equation (1) by 2 $6x + 10y = 60$
Multiply equation (2) by 3 $6x + 9y = 57$

You can now subtract to get rid of x $y = 3$
Put $y = 3$ in equation (1) $3x + 15 = 30$
$3x = 15$
$x = 5$

The answer is $x = 5$, $y = 3$

Check using equation (2)
$2x + 3y = 2 \times 5 + 3 \times 3 = 10 + 9 = 19$ ✓

Exercise 14:13

Solve these pairs of simultaneous equations.
You will need to multiply both equations.

1 $2x + 3y = 11$
$5x + 4y = 24$

5 $4x + 3y = 12$
$5x + 7y = 15$

2 $3x - 2y = 13$
$4x + 3y = 40$

6 $7p - 3q = 5$
$3p + 2q = 12$

3 $7a + 4b = 41$
$2a + 5b = 31$

7 $5x - 3y = 24$
$3x - 2y = 14$

4 $3x + 2y = 33$
$7x + 5y = 79$

8 $2c - 3d = 6$
$5c - 7d = 17$

1 Which line is steeper in each of these pairs?

   a $y = 3x$ or $y = 5x$

   b $y = 6x$ or $y = x$

   c $y = \frac{3}{4}x$ or $y = 4x$

   d $y = \frac{1}{2}x$ or $y = \frac{1}{4}x$

2 Where does each of these lines cross the y axis?

   a $y = x + 6$ **d** $y = 4x - 1$

   b $y = x - 3$ **e** $y = 2x - 5$

   c $y = 3x + 2$ **f** $y = x + 1$

3 **a** Copy and complete this table for $y = 2x - 1$

x	0	1	2
y	...	...	3

   b Draw a set of axes on squared paper.
       Use values of x from -3 to 3 and values of y from -7 to 5.

   c Draw and label the line $y = 2x - 1$

   d Is the point (2, 1) above or below the line?

   e The point (..., -3) lies on the line.
       What is the missing x co-ordinate?

   f What is the value of y when $x = -2$?

   g What is the value of x when $y = 0$?

4 Each of parts **a** to **d** has a line and some points.
   The points lie on the line.
   Find the missing co-ordinates.

   a $y = x + 5$ (3, ...)   (0, ...)   (-1, ...)

   b $y = x - 3$ (5, ...)   (3, ...)   (1, ...)

   c $y = 2x + 4$ (2, ...)   (0, ...)   (-1, ...)

   d $y = 3x - 4$ (4, ...)   (1, ...)   (-2, ...)

5 Write down the equation of each red line.

a

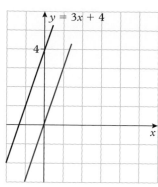

$y = 3x + 4$

c

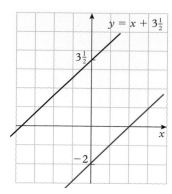

$y = x + 3\frac{1}{2}$

b

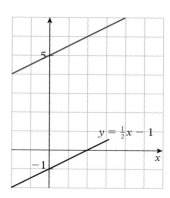

$y = \frac{1}{2}x - 1$

d

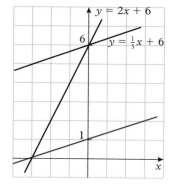

$y = 2x + 6$

$y = \frac{1}{3}x + 6$

6 Write down the equations of these lines.

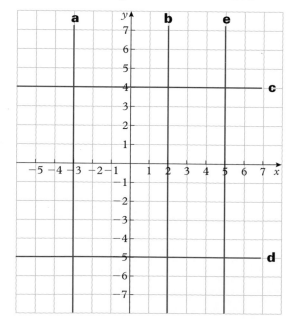

7 Draw a graph to solve this problem. Check your answer in the original problem.

Lucy bought two *a*pples and one *b*iscuit for 22 p.
Sandeep bought one *a*pple and three *b*iscuits for 21 p.
Find the cost of one *a*pple and the cost of one *b*iscuit.

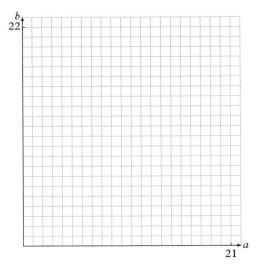

8 Solve these pairs of simultaneous equations.
Start by subtracting the equations each time.

a $5x + y = 17$
$4x + y = 15$

c $5x + 3y = 33$
$x + 3y = 21$

b $6x + 2y = 20$
$4x + 2y = 14$

d $6x + 4y = 28$
$2x + 4y = 20$

9 Solve these pairs of simultaneous equations.
Start by adding the equations each time.

a $4x + y = 27$
$2x - y = 3$

c $7x + 3y = 65$
$4x - 3y = 23$

b $5x + 2y = 36$
$4x - 2y = 18$

d $6x - y = 20$
$3x + y = 25$

10 Solve these pairs of simultaneous equations.
You need to decide whether to add or subtract the equations.

a $2x - 3y = 4$
$x + 3y = 11$

c $7x + 3y = 13$
$4x + 3y = 10$

b $4x + 2y = 22$
$x + 2y = 10$

d $2x - y = 4$
$x + y = 11$

295

1 Find two points on each of these lines.
Do not draw the graph.

a $2x + 3y = 12$ **c** $3x + 4y = 24$

b $x + 3y = 9$ **d** $5x + 4y = 20$

2 The points $(1, 5)$ and $(2, 7)$ lie on the line $y = ax + b$

a Substitute the values of x and y into the equation of the line.
$\ldots = \ldots a + b$ and $\ldots = \ldots a + b$

You now have two simultaneous equations.

b Solve the two simultaneous equations to find the values of a and b.

3 The points $(1, 7)$ and $(2, 12)$ lie on the line $y = ax + $ b.

a Substitute the values of x and y into the equation of the line to get two simultaneous equations.

b Solve the two simultaneous equations to find the values of a and b.

4 The sum of two numbers is 12.
The difference is 2.
Let the two numbers be x and y.
The sum of the two numbers is $x + y$.
The difference of the two numbers is $x - y$.
Write down two equations $x + y = \ldots$
$$x - y = \ldots$$
Find the two numbers by solving this pair of simultaneous equations.

5 The sum of two numbers is 22.
The difference is 4.
Find the two numbers by solving a pair of simultaneous equations.

- **Point of intersection**   The point where two lines cross is called the **point of intersection**

  Equation   The rule of a line is called the **equation** of the line

- **Gradient**   The **gradient** of a line tells you how steep the line is. Both these lines have a '3' to tell you how steep they are. They have a **gradient** 3. The lines are parallel because they have the same gradient. The +2 and the −4 tell you where the lines cross the y axis.

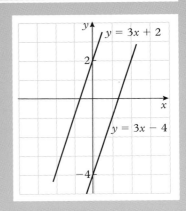

- **Simultaneous equations**   When you solve two equations at the same time you are are solving **simultaneous equations.**

  Example   Solve this pair of simultaneous equations

  $$5x + y = 20$$
  $$2x + y = 11$$

  Number the equations

  (1) $5x + y = 20$
  (2) $2x + y = 11$

  Subtract to get rid of y
  This finds x

  $$3x = 9$$
  $$x = 3$$

  Use equation (1) to find y

  Put $x = 3$ in equation (1)
  $$5 \times 3 + y = 20$$
  $$15 + y = 20$$
  $$y = 5$$
  The answer is $x = 3$, $y = 5$

  Use equation (2) to check your answer
  $$2x + y = 2 \times 3 + 5 = 6 + 5 = 11 \checkmark$$

1 Look at these three lines.

$$y = 2x + 5 \qquad y = 5x - 2 \qquad y = 4x + 3$$

a Which line is the steepest?
b Which line is the least steep?
c Which line crosses the y axis at 5?

2 Each of these points lies on one of the lines.
Match the points with the lines.

$$(3, 7) \qquad (9, 5) \qquad (3, 2)$$
$$y = 2x - 4 \qquad y = x - 4 \qquad y = 3x - 2$$

3 Write down the equation of each red line.

a

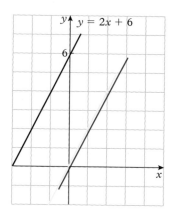

b

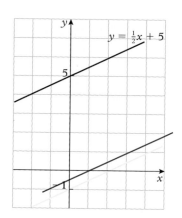

4 Draw a graph to solve this problem.
Check your answer in the original problem.
Tim buys two *a*pples and one *p*ear for 20 p.
Andrea buys one *a*pple and two *p*ears for 22 p.
Find the cost of one *a*pple and the cost of one *p*ear.

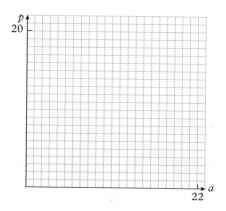

5 Solve these pairs of simultaneous equations.
You need to decide whether to add or subtract the equations.

a $2x + y = 11$
$5x - y = 17$

b $7x + y = 44$
$3x + y = 20$

15 Loci: know your place

In maths an ellipse is defined as the locus of a point which moves so that the sum of its distances from two fixed points remains constant.

To draw an ellipse you need two nails fixed to paper on a board, a piece of string tied into a loop and a pencil. Keep the string taut and move the pencil around the two nails until you end up where you started.

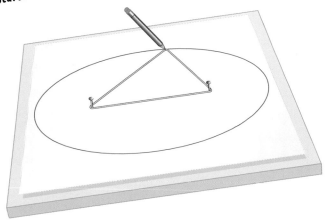

1 Locus of a point

Exercise 15:1

You will need a sheet of paper and some counters.

1 a Mark a point in the centre of your paper.
Label it A.
 b Put a counter on the paper 7 cm from A.
Put some more counters on your paper so
that they are also 7 cm from A.
 c All your counters should lie on a curve.
Descibe this curve.

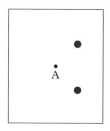

2 a Mark two points on your paper.
Label them B and C.
 b Put a counter on the paper so that it is the
same distance from both B and C.
Put more counters on the paper so that they
are all the same distance from both B and C.
 c All your counters should lie on a straight line.
Describe the position of this line.

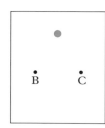

3 **a** Draw a line 7 cm long in the middle of your paper.

b Put a counter on the paper so that it is 5 cm from the line.
Put more counters on the paper so that they are all 5 cm from the line.

c Describe where your counters can be. This should include some straight parts and some curved parts.

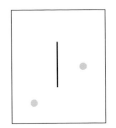

Locus

The position of an object can be given by a rule.
The **locus** is all the possible positions that the object can take that satisfy the rule.
The locus can either be described in words or by drawing.

Example

Describe the locus of an object that is always 2 cm from a point D.

The locus is a circle. The centre is D and the radius is 2 cm.

---

4 **a** Describe in words the locus of an object that is always 4 cm from a point R.

b Sketch the locus of the object.

5 **a** Copy this line on to paper.

A ———————————————— B

b Draw a sketch of the locus of a point that is always 8 cm away from the line AB.

6 Describe the locus of the tip of the minute hand as it moves around the clock face.

7 Describe the locus of the tip of the arrow as it moves over the scale of this ammeter.

Example   John's house is 2 km from
the school and 3 km from
the motorway.
Where could John's house
be?

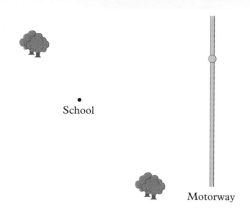

John's house is 2 km from
the school.
His house lies on a circle
whose centre is the school.
The radius is 2 km.

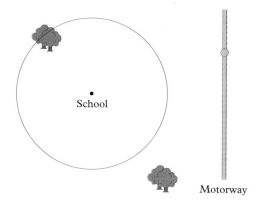

The house is 3 km from
the motorway.
It lies on a line 3 km from
the motorway.
This line is parallel to the
motorway.

John's house must be at
one of the points where
the circle and the line
cross.
These are marked with a
cross

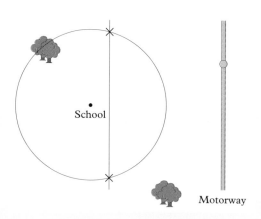

Scale: 1 cm to 1 km

Exercise 15:2

Use tracing paper to copy these maps.
The scale of each map is 1 cm to 1 km.

1 Katy's house is 3 km from school and
4 km from the motorway.
  a Copy the diagram.
  b Find the two possible positions of
     Katy's house.

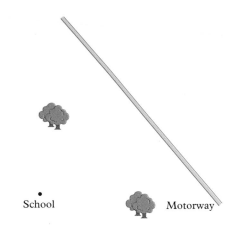

School   Motorway

2 Brian lives 1 km from the motorway
and 2 km from the edge of the forest.
  a Copy the diagram.
  b Find the position of Brian's house.

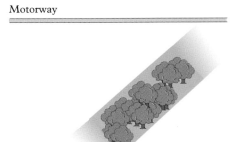

Motorway

3 Parvit lives 4 km from the school and
3 km from the hospital.
  a Copy the diagram.
  b Find the two possible positions of
     Parvit's house.

School

Hospital

4 Sam lives 2 km from the school and 5 km from the hospital.
  a Make another copy of the map in question **3**.
  b Mark the two possible positions of Sam's home.

Example   A goat is tethered to a ring
in the ground.
The rope is 3 m long.
Draw a diagram to show the
area where the goat can graze.

The point R is the ring.
The red shading shows the
area where the goat can graze.
The radius of the circle is the
length of the rope.

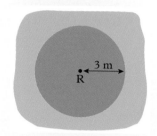

You should always say which part of the shading is your answer.
A key is useful when there are two or more types of shading.

Exercise 15:3

1   The horse is tied to a wall as shown.
The length of the rope is 4 m.
Make a sketch showing the area
where the horse can reach.

2   This bull is tethered to a ring in
the farmyard.
The rope is 5 m long.
Make a sketch showing the area
where the bull can reach.

W   You will need worksheet 15:1 for the rest of
this exercise.

3   The guard dog is on a chain of length 3 m.
The other end of the chain is fixed
to a ring.
The ring can move along the rail.
The rail is 7 m long.
Use shading to show the area where the dog can reach.

4 A and B show the positions of
two radio transmitters.
Each transmitter can cover a
distance of 40 km.

a Draw the locus of the area
covered by transmitter A.

b Draw the locus of the area
covered by transmitter B.

c Use shading and a key to show
the area covered by both
transmitters.

A •

B •

Scale: 1 cm to 10 km

5 The diagram shows the floor
area of a room. The points A
and B show the positions of
alarm sensors. Each sensor
can cover a distance of up
to 4 m.

a Draw the locus of the area
covered by sensor A.

b Draw the locus of the area
covered by sensor B.

c Use shading and a key to
show the area covered by
both sensors.

d Draw a new diagram showing the floor area
of a room 7 m by 4 m.
Use the same sensors.
Shade the floor area not covered by either of the two sensors.

A •

B •

Scale: 1 cm to 1 m

6 Laura plugs her electric
mower into the socket on the
side of the house.
The mower lead is 5 m long.
Shade the part of the lawn
that Laura can reach with the
mower.

Scale: 1 cm to 1 m

Example

Kay wants to sketch the locus of the valve on the rim of a bicycle wheel as the bike moves forward.

Kay uses a piece of paper and a circle of card to help her.
She makes a mark on the edge of the circle.

Kay rolls the circle along the ruler bit by bit.
Each time, she makes a mark on the paper beside the mark on the circle.

Kay joins up the marks.

The curve is the locus of a point on a wheel as it moves forward.

Exercise 15:4

1 Patrick has put a mark on
the corner of this box.
He finds the locus of this
corner as the box rolls over.

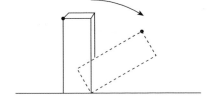

Use a ruler and a rectangular
piece of card.
Mark a corner of the card.
Roll the card along the ruler. Mark the paper as the box rolls bit by bit.
Join up your marks with a curve.

2 **a** Use a ruler and a circle made out of card like Kay's.
Make a sketch of the locus of a point on the circle as the circle
moves forward.
  b Find the locus of the corner
of this square as it rolls forward.
  c Investigate what happens with
other regular shapes.

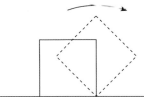

3 Rolf rolls a coin around the inside
edges of a box.
Sketch the locus of the centre of
the coin as it moves around the box.

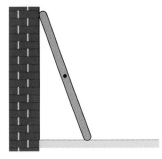

4 Mark puts his ladder against the house.
The ground is slippery.
The ladder slides down until it is lying
on the ground.
Draw the locus of the centre of the
ladder as it slides down the wall.

Hint: Use the edges of a piece of paper
to be the wall and the ground.
Use a ruler for the ladder.

2 Constructions

This aircraft is flying exactly down the middle of two cliffs. It keeps exactly between the two cliffs to stay on course.

Bisecting an angle	**Bisecting an angle** means splitting it exactly in half. You do not need an angle measurer to do this. It is more accurate to do it with compasses.

Exercise 15:5

1 **a** Draw a 60° angle.

b Open your compasses a small distance. You **must** keep your compasses fixed from now on.

c With the compass point on the corner of the angle, draw a small arc which crosses both arms of the angle. Label these points A and B.

d Place your compasses on point A and draw another arc in the middle of the angle.

e Now place your compasses on point B. Draw another arc in the middle of the angle. It should cross the first one.

f Finally, draw a line from the corner of the angle through the point where your two arcs cross. This line bisects the angle.

g Measure the two parts of the angle to check that it is correct.

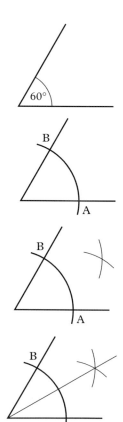

2 **a** Draw a 45° angle.
   b With your compass point at the corner of the angle,
      draw an arc crossing both arms .
      Label the crossing points A and B.
   c Draw arcs from points A and B.
   d Draw the line which bisects the angle.
   e Measure the two parts of the angle to check that it is correct.

3 **a** Draw a right angle. (90°)
   b Bisect the angle.
      Use the instructions in question **2** to help you.

4 **a** Draw an angle of 120°.
   b Bisect this angle.

| **Equidistant from two lines** | All the points on the line bisecting an angle are **equidistant** from the two arms of the angle. |

This means that they are always the same distance from the two lines. Both the blue lines are the same length. So are both the red ones.

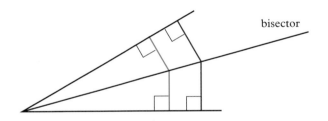

bisector

---

5 **a** Draw two lines AB and AC which are at 48° to each other.
   b Draw the locus of the points which are equidistant from AB and AC.

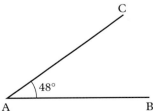

6 **a** Draw two lines PQ and PR which are at 130° to each other.
   b Draw the locus of the points which are equidistant from PQ and PR.

Exercise 15:6

1 a Draw a horizontal line 8 cm long.
Leave some space above it.
Label the ends of the line A and B.

b Set your compasses to 6 cm.
Draw an arc, centre A (blue arc).

c Set your compasses to 7 cm.
Draw an arc, centre B (red arc).

d Join A and B to the point where
your arcs cross.
Label this point C. You should now have a triangle.
You will need this triangle for question **2**.

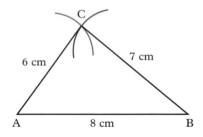

2 a Bisect the angle at vertex (corner) A of the triangle.

b Bisect the angle at vertex B of the triangle.

c Bisect the angle at vertex C of the triangle.
The three bisectors should cross at one point.

3 a Construct an equilateral triangle with
sides 10 cm.

b Label your triangle PQR.

c Bisect all three angles of the triangle.

d Mark the point X at the middle of PR.

e Place the point of your compasses on
the point where the bisectors cross.
Carefully move your pencil point until
it touches point X.

f Draw a circle with your compasses.
This circle should just touch all three sides of the triangle.
This is called the **inscribed circle**.

4 A wall and a fence are at 50° to each other.
A farmer wants to put a path exactly in the middle of the two.

a Draw a diagram to show where the path would go.

b Shade the area which is nearer to the wall than the fence.

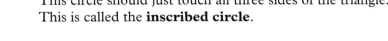

Bisecting a line	**Bisecting a line** means cutting it exactly in half.

Perpendicular bisector	Two lines which are at right angles are called perpendicular. On this diagram, CD is perpendicular to AB and CD bisects AB. CD is called the **perpendicular bisector** of AB. CD crosses AB at the midpoint of the line AB.

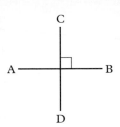

Exercise 15:7

1 a Draw a line 10 cm long. Label the ends A and B.
 b Put your compass point on A. Move your pencil until you can tell it is more than half way along the line.
 c Draw an arc from above the line to below it.
 d **Without changing your compasses,** move the compass point to B.
 e Draw another arc from B.
 f Your arcs should cross above and below the line. Label these points C and D.
 g Join C to D. Use a ruler. Line CD bisects line AB at right angles. Label the point where CD and AB cross. Call it X. Measure AX and BX with a ruler to check that they are equal.

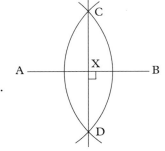

2 a Draw a line 8.5 cm long.
 b Label your line AB.
 c Draw arcs from A and B.
 d Label the crossing points of the arcs C and D.
 e Join C to D to bisect the line at right angles.
 f Check that CD bisects AB by measuring.

3 a Draw a line 6.4 cm long.
 b Label the line AB.
 c Bisect the line using a ruler and compasses.

Equidistant from two points	All the points on the perpendicular bisector of a line are **equidistant from the two points** at the ends of the original line. Every point on CD is the same distance from A and B. You can describe CD as the locus of the points that are equidistant from A and B.	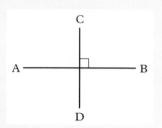

4 **a** Draw points A and B which are 7 cm apart.

    b Join the points with a straight line.

    c Draw the locus of the points which are equidistant from A and B.

5 The diagram shows the position of two buoys near a harbour. The buoys are 20 m apart. Ships follow a path exactly between the two buoys to make sure they are in the deepest water.

    a Using a scale of 1 cm to 2 m, draw the position of the two buoys.

    b Draw the path a ship should take through the buoys.

6 The diagram shows a plan of a rectangular park.

A and B are two drinking fountains.

    a Using a scale of 1 cm to 50 m, draw a scale plan of the park.

    b Draw a line on your diagram to help you show the area of the park which is nearer to fountain A.

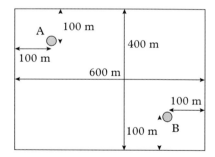

7 **a** Make a rough copy of this treasure map.

       It does not have to be exact.

    b The treasure is buried at a point which is equidistant from A and B. It is also equidistant from C and D. Find the treasure!

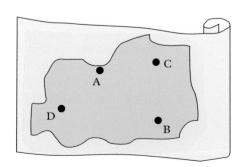

Exercise 15:8

1 **a** Construct a triangle with sides 10 cm,
8 cm and 7 cm.
Start by drawing a horizontal line
10 cm long.
b Label your triangle PQR.
c Draw the perpendicular bisectors of all
three sides of the triangle.
d Place the point of your compasses on the
point where the bisectors cross.
Carefully move your pencil point until it
touches point P.
e Draw a circle with your compasses.
This circle should just touch all three points P, Q and R.
This is called the **circumscribed circle** or the **circumcircle**.

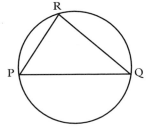

2 **a** Construct a triangle with sides 9 cm, 7 cm and 8 cm.
Start by drawing a horizontal line 9 cm long.
Label your triangle PQR.
b Draw the perpendicular bisectors of all three sides of the triangle.
Label the point where the bisectors cross X.
c Draw the circumcircle of the triangle.

3 **a** Draw a rectangle 12 cm by 8 cm.
b Draw in the diagonals.
c Draw the perpendicular bisector of each diagonal.
d Colour in the pattern you have made.

4 **a** Draw a circle of radius 6 cm.
b Mark 4 points W, X, Y and Z
around the circumference of the
circle.
c Draw in the lines WY and XZ.
d Draw the perpendicular bisectors
of WY and XZ.
The crossing point of these
bisectors should be the centre of
the circle.

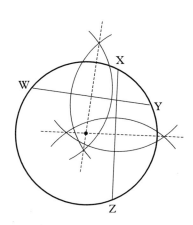

You also need to know how to construct a perpendicular from a point to a line.

You want to construct the perpendicular from P onto AB.

Put your compass point on P and make sure your compasses are open wide enough to be able to draw an arc that crosses AB at two points.
Label these points C and D.

Now put your compass on C and then D and draw two arcs that cross below the line.
Call this point Q.

Now join P to Q.
The line PQ will be perpendicular to AB.
The bold part of the line is the line you need.

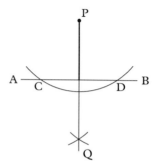

You also need to know how to construct a perpendicular from a point on a line.

You want to construct the perpendicular from P.

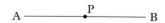

Put the compass pont on P and draw arcs on both sides of P.
Call the points where these arcs meet the line C and D.

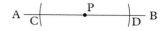

Now draw the perpendicular bisector of CD.
This line will pass through P.
This is the perpendicular from P that you need. You may only need to draw the part of the line from P above AB or below AB.

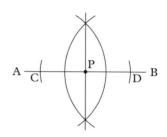

Exercise 15:9

1 **a** Copy the diagram.
It does not have to be exact.
b Construct the perpendicular from P
onto AB.

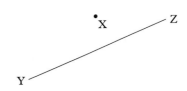

2 **a** Copy this diagram.
It does not have to be exact.
b Construct the perpendicular from
X onto YZ.

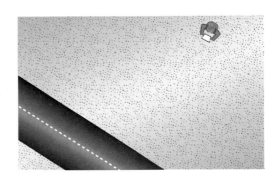

3 Adam is orienteering.
He sees a road and wants to get
there as quickly as possible.
Draw a diagram to show this.
Mark a point for Adam. Label it A.
Draw a line for the road.
Construct the route that Adam
should take.

4 **a** Copy the diagram.
It does not have to be exact.
b Construct the perpendicular
from K.

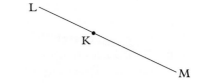

5 Leah is playing with a tennis ball.
She has dropped it onto the ground.
Construct the locus of the ball as it
bounces up.
You will need to draw a horizontal
line for the court and label the point
where the ball starts on the ground B.

1 Describe the locus of each of these:
  a a door handle as the door opens,
  b the foot of a person running,
  c a chair on this fairground ride.

2 There are two footpaths in the area shown in the diagram.

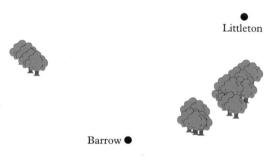

Tarvin ●

● Littleton

Barrow ●

  Scale: 1 cm to 1 km

  a Copy the diagram.
  b One footpath is always the same distance from Tarvin and
    Littleton. Sketch this footpath on your diagram.
  c Another footpath is always 1 km from the road between Tarvin and
    Barrow. This footpath is on the same side of the road as Littleton.
    Sketch this footpath on your diagram.
  d Mark on your diagram the point where the two footpaths cross.

3 This dog is chained to a ring in
  the wall.
  The length of the chain is
  3 m.
  Make a sketch showing the area
  where the dog can reach.

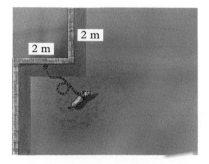

316

4 **a** Draw a 70° angle.
   b With your compass point on the corner,
       draw an arc crossing both arms of the angle.
       Label the crossing points A and B.
   c Draw arcs from points A and B.
   d Draw the line which bisects the angle.
   e Measure the two parts of the angle to check that it is correct.

5 **a** Draw two lines AB and AC which are at 64° to each other.
   b Draw the locus of the points which are equidistant from AB
       and AC.

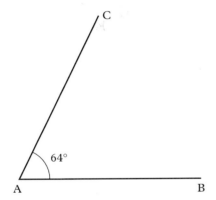

6 **a** Draw this triangle accurately.
   b Bisect the angle at vertex A.
   c Bisect the angle at vertex B.
   d Bisect the angle at vertex C.
       The three bisectors should
       cross at one point.

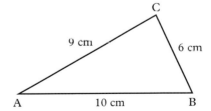

7 **a** Draw a line 5 cm long.
   b Label the end points A and B.
   c Draw the locus of the points which are equidistant from A and B.

1   Asha rolls the smaller coin around the larger coin.
    Sketch the locus of:
    a the centre of the smaller coin,
    b a point on the edge of the smaller coin.

2   Keith is rowing across a river 30 m wide.
    There is a strong current downstream.
    For each complete stroke of the oars Keith moves 2 m across and 1 m
    down the river.
    a Draw a line on your
        paper to represent the
        bank of the river.
    b Mark Keith's starting
        point.
    c Mark his position after
        one stroke of the oars.
    d Do this for three more
        strokes of the oars.
    e How far down the river
        will Keith have moved by
        the time he reaches the
        opposite bank?

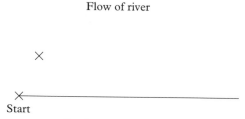

Flow of river

Start

Scale: 1 cm to 2 m

3   A small rectangular flag measures 10 cm by 5 cm.
    Its design is created by bisecting each angle and drawing the bisector
    to the edge of the rectangle.
    Make an accurate drawing of the flag and colour it as you wish.

4   The diagram shows a large room and the position of three TV
    monitors.
    a Make a rough copy of the
        diagram.
    b Lightly shade the area which is
        nearer to monitor A than to
        monitor B.
    c Shade the area which is nearer to
        monitor A than monitor C.
    d Show the area which is closer to
        monitor A than either of the other
        two monitors.

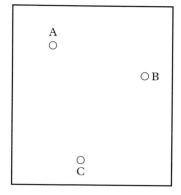

- **Locus**

The position of an object can be given by a rule.
The **locus** is all the possible positions that the object can take that satisfy the rule.
The locus can either be described in words or by drawing.

Example

Describe the locus of an object that is always 2 cm from a point D.

The locus is a circle. The centre is D and the radius is 2 cm.

- **Equidistant from two lines**

All the points on the line bisecting an angle are **equidistant** from the two arms of the angle.
This means that they are always the same distance from the two lines. Both the blue lines are the same length. So are both the red ones.

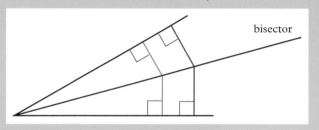

- **Bisecting a line**

Bisecting a line means cutting it exactly in half.

Perpendicular bisector

Two lines which are at right angles are called perpendicular.
On this diagram, CD is perpendicular to AB and CD bisects AB.
CD is called the **perpendicular bisector** of AB.

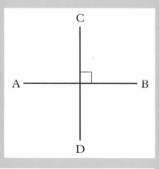

- **Equidistant from two points**

All the points on the perpendicular bisector of a line are **equidistant from the two points** at the ends of the original line

Every point on CD is the same distance from A and B.

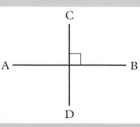

You can describe CD as the locus of the points that are equidistant from A and B.

1 Pat's house is 4 km from the school
   and 3 km from the motorway.
   a Copy the diagram.
   b Find the two possible positions
      of Pat's house.

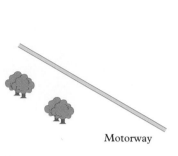

School

Motorway

Scale: 1 cm to 1 km

2 Don is watering his lawn.
   He has two sprinklers, A and B.
   They both spray areas up to 4 m
   away. The diagram shows Don's
   lawn and the sprinklers.
   a Make a sketch of Don's lawn.
   b Show the area of lawn that is
      watered by both sprinklers.

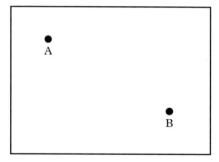

Scale: 1 cm to 2 m

3 Janine wants to put a path across this field.
   She wants the footpath to cross the field
   so that it is the same distance from both
   sides of the field.
   a Make a copy of the diagram using
      an angle of 70° between the two sides.
   b Use a construction to show where
      the path should go.

4 a Draw points P and S which are 8 cm apart.
   b Join the points with a straight line.
   c Draw the locus of the points which are equidistant from P and S.

16 Get in shape

You can make a Möbius strip with a piece of card or paper.

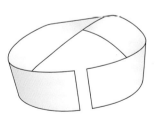

Make a half twist (180°) before sticking the two ends together.

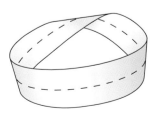

What happens if you draw a line down the centre of the strip and cut along it?

1 Symmetry

This building consists of two houses.
One house is the reflection of the other.

Where the houses join inside there is a vertical wall. This wall is the plane of symmetry of the houses.

◀◀**REPLAY**▶

Line of symmetry	A **line of symmetry** divides a shape into two equal parts. Each part is a reflection of the other.

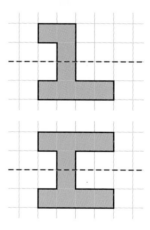

Example   Look at this pattern of shaded squares. Louise has to complete the pattern so that the dotted line is a line of symmetry.

Louise has shaded two more squares. The pattern is now complete.

Exercise 16:1

1   Copy these shapes on to squared paper.
Shade in one more square on each shape so that the dotted line is a line of symmetry.

a

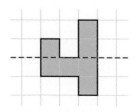

b

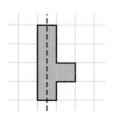

2 Copy these shapes on to squared paper.
Shade in two more squares on each shape
so that the dotted line is a line of symmetry.

a

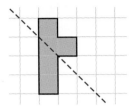

b

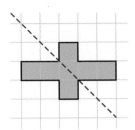

| Rotational symmetry | A shape has **rotational symmetry** if it fits on top of itself more than once as it makes a complete turn. |

| Order of rotational symmetry | The **order of rotational symmetry** is the number of times that the shape fits on top of itself. This must be 2 or more. |

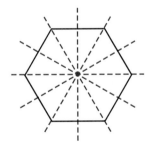

C marks the centre of rotation

A regular hexagon has 6 axes of symmetry.
It has rotational symmetry of order 6.

For each of the regular polygons in questions **3**, **4** and **5**:
a Draw a sketch.
b Draw the axes of symmetry on your sketch.
c Mark the centre of symmetry on your sketch.
d Write down the order of rotational symmetry.

3 Equilateral triangle   **4** Square   **5** Regular pentagon

6 **a** Write down the number of axes of symmetry of a regular octagon.
    b Write down the order of rotational symmetry of a regular octagon.

7 Copy these sketches of regular polygons.

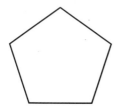

a Add a line to the regular pentagon so that it has exactly one axis of symmetry.
b Add a line to the regular hexagon so that it has rotational symmetry of order 2 about its centre.

Example Complete this shape so that it is symmetrical about the mirror.

The completed shape looks like this.

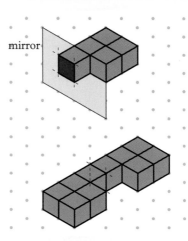

Exercise 16:2

1 Make each of these shapes with cubes.
Complete each shape so that it is symmetrical about the mirror.
Draw the completed shape on dotty isometric paper.

a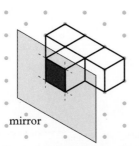

b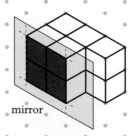

c

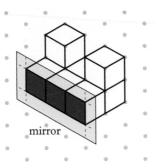

mirror

d

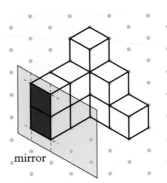

mirror

· ·

Plane	A **plane** is a flat surface.
Plane of symmetry	A **plane of symmetry** divides a *solid* into two equal parts. Each part is a reflection of the other.

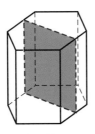 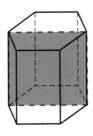 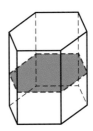

The sketches show three different planes of symmetry for a hexagonal prism.

2 The base of a prism is a regular hexagon.
   a How many vertical planes of symmetry does the prism have?
   b How many horizontal planes of symmetry does it have?
   c How many planes of symmetry does the prism have altogether?
   d Write down the order of rotational symmetry of the prism about the red line.

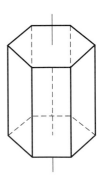

3 The bases of these prisms are regular polygons.
  a Write down the total number of planes of symmetry of each prism.
  b Write down the order of rotational symmetry of each prism about the red line.

(1) 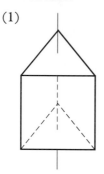　　(2) 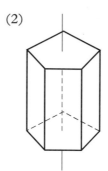　　(3)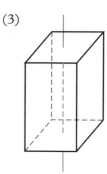

4 Each of these pyramids has a regular polygon for its base.
  a Write down the number of planes of symmetry for each pyramid.
  b Write down the order of rotational symmetry for each pyramid about the red line.

(1) 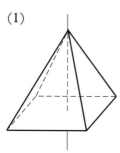　　(2) 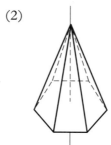　　(3)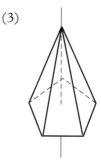

5 **a** Write down the number of planes of symmetry of each of these objects.
  b List the objects that have rotational symmetry.

2 Nets of solids

Katie has a chocolate bar. The box for the bar is in the shape of a triangular prism.
Katie wants to see how the box was made. She has opened out the card.

◀◀**REPLAY**▶

| Net |

A **net** is a pattern of shapes on a piece of paper or card. The shapes are arranged so that the net can be folded to make a hollow solid. Notice that a net does not have flaps.

A cuboid has six faces but they are not all the same size.

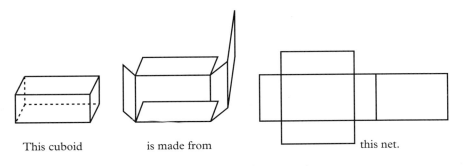

This cuboid   is made from   this net.

Exercise 16:3

1 Which of these patterns are nets of cubes?

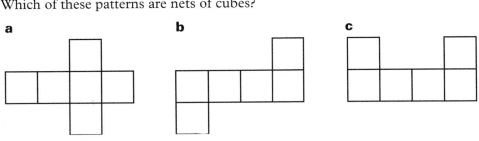

a   b   c

2 Look at this pattern of squares.
It is a net that can be folded to make a cuboid.
Each square represents 1 cm².
  a (1) What is the length of the cuboid in centimetres?
   (2) What is the width of the cuboid
     in centimetres?
   (3) What is the height of the cuboid
     in centimetres?

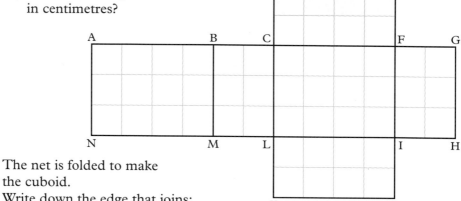

The net is folded to make
the cuboid.
  b Write down the edge that joins:
   (1) edge DC   (2) edge DE
  c What other two points meet at J?

· ·

To make a solid you need to add flaps to the net.

Half the edges of these nets have flaps. The flaps are on alternate edges.

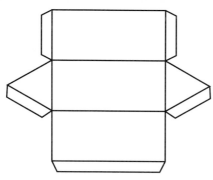

Net of a triangular prism
with flaps

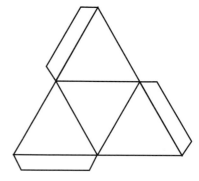

Net of a tetrahedron
(triangular based pyramid)
with flaps

3 **a** Make a copy of the net of the cuboid in question **2**.
Use squared paper.

b Add flaps to your net.
Put them on alternate edges.
Make the flaps just less than 1 cm wide.
If the flaps are too narrow they will be difficult to stick.

c Cut out the net and fold it to make a cuboid.
Check that the flaps are on the correct edges.

d Check your answers to question **2**.

4 **a** Use paper to draw an accurate net of each of these solids.
Use compasses to construct the triangles accurately.

b Add flaps to each of your nets. Put them on alternate edges.

c Cut out each net and fold it to make a solid.
Check that the flaps are on the correct edges.

(1)

(2)

(3)

(4)

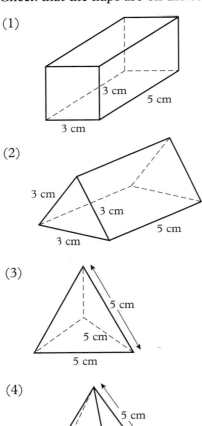

5 Here is a sketch of the net of a prism.
The shape at the ends of the prism is a regular polygon.
  a Write down the name of the polygon.
  b How many rectangular faces does the prism have?
  c How many faces does the polygon have altogether?

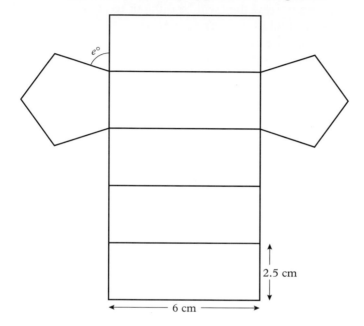

2.5 cm

6 cm

6 The angle marked *e* on the net in
question **5** is an exterior angle of
the polygon.
  a What do the exterior angles of
    a polygon add up to?
  b How many exterior angles are
    there for this polygon?
  c Work out the size of angle *e*.

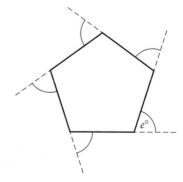

7 **a** Make an accurate copy of the net in question **5** on paper.
    Use the exterior angles to help you draw the polygons.
  b Add flaps to your net.
    Put them on alternate edges.
  c Cut out the net and fold it to make a solid.

8 The polygons at the ends of these prisms are coloured red.
The faces at the sides of the prisms are yellow.
Each solid has two red faces.
Write down the number of yellow faces that each solid has.

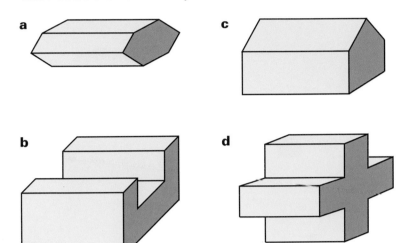

9 Choose one of the shapes in question **8** and sketch its net.

10 Look at this net.
Which one of the
cubes does it make?

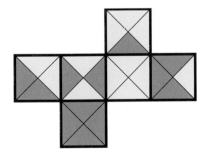

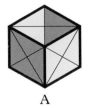

A   B   C   D   E

3 Building a shape sorter

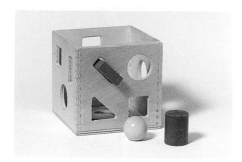

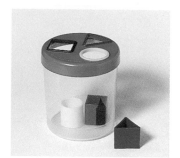

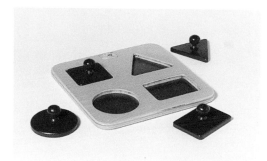

Look at these children's toys. They are shape sorters.

They are used to improve children's motor skills and co-ordination.

They also help to teach children about shape and colour.

It is very important that each shape will only fit through its own hole. If it fits through another hole, the child will not learn to match the shape of the piece with the shape of the hole.

Most shape sorters have at least six shapes in them.

The holes are often regular polygons or symmetrical shapes.

This makes it easier for the child as there are more ways that a shape will fit through the right hole.

Most of the shapes are prisms.
They have the same cross section along their whole length.

Building a shape sorter

Build a child's shape sorter using card.
Use the work you have done in this chapter to help you.

Your project needs careful planning before you start.
Here are some of the things you should consider.

- How many shapes are there going to be?

- How big should each shape be?

- What shapes are you going to have?

- Can you construct the nets of your shapes?

- How are you going to make sure that each shape will only fit through one hole? You can make one shape bigger so that it will not fit through a small hole. One of the smaller shapes may then fit through the hole that you make for the bigger one!

- Are all the shapes going to be symmetrical?

- You do not need to make a whole posting box.
  You can just make the lid with the posting holes.
  If you decide to make a box, make sure it is big enough to contain all the shapes.

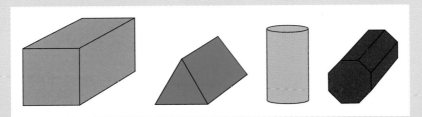

1 This regular polygon has 10 sides.
   a How many lines of symmetry does the polygon have?
   b What is the order of rotational symmetry of the polygon?

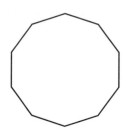

2 Copy each of these diagrams.
   Complete them so that:
   a the dotted line is a line of symmetry,
   b C is the centre of rotational symmetry for a shape that has rotational symmetry of order 3.

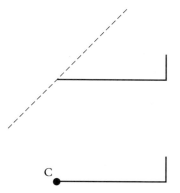

3 Write down the number of planes of symmetry of each of these objects. List the objects that have rotational symmetry.

a

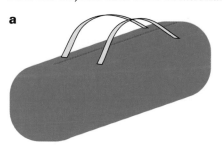

c

b

d

4 Sian has started to draw a net of this cuboid.

   a (1) How many faces does the cuboid have?
      (2) How many faces has Sian drawn on her net?
      (3) How many faces are missing from Sian's net?

   b Copy Sian's unfinished net on to paper. Leave room to put in the missing faces.

   c Complete the net. Add flaps on alternate edges.

   d Cut out the net and fold it to make the cuboid.

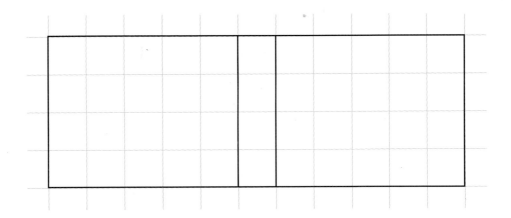

5 Val has drawn this net of a cube. Val folds up the net.
   a The tab on edge LK will stick to edge JK. Write down the letters of the edge that the tab on edge AB will stick to.
   b What other two letters will meet point E?
   c Make a copy of Val's net. Make the sides of each square 2 cm long. Cut out the net and fold it up. Use your net to check your answers to parts **a** and **b**.

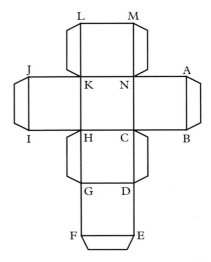

1 Make **two** copies of the diagram on squared paper. Shade one extra square on each copy so that your new shape has:
  a just one line of symmetry but no rotational symmetry,
  b no lines of symmetry but rotational symmetry of order 2.

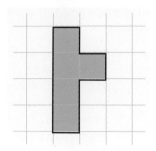

2 Two identical square based pyramids are stuck together to make this octahedron.
Write down the number of planes of symmetry of the octahedron.

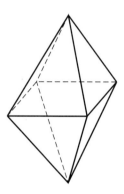

3 Write down the names of the solids that can be made from these nets.

a

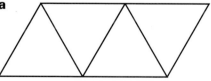

b

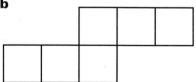

c

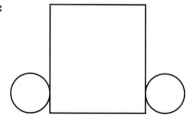

d

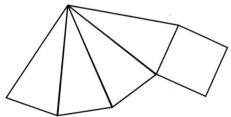

- **Line of symmetry**

A **line of symmetry** divides a shape into two equal parts.
Each part is a reflection of the other.
A line of symmetry is also called an **axis** of symmetry.

Rotational symmetry

A shape has **rotational symmetry** if it fits on top of itself more than once as it makes a complete turn.

Order of rotational symmetry

The **order of rotational symmetry** is the number of times that the shape fits on top of itself. This must be 2 or more.

- **Plane of symmetry**

A **plane of symmetry** divides a *solid* into two equal parts.
Each part is a reflection of the other.

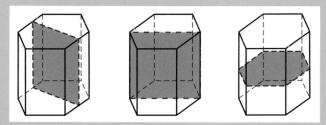

The sketches show three different planes of symmetry for a hexagonal prism.

- **Net**

A **net** is a pattern of shapes on a piece of paper or card.
The shapes are arranged so that the net can be folded to make a hollow solid.

Half the edges of these nets have flaps. The flaps are on alternate edges.

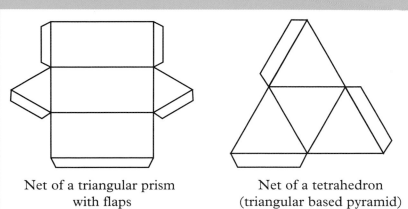

Net of a triangular prism
with flaps

Net of a tetrahedron
(triangular based pyramid)
with flaps

1 **a** Make a sketch of this rhombus.
   b Draw the axes of symmetry of the rhombus on your sketch.
   c Write down the order of rotational symmetry of the rhombus.
   d Mark the centre of rotation of the rhombus and label it C.

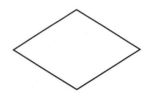

2 The cross section of this prism is the rhombus from question **1**.
   a Write down the number of vertical planes of symmetry of the prism.
   b Write down the number of horizontal planes of symmetry of the prism.
   c How many planes of symmetry are there altogether?
   d Write down the order of rotational symmetry of the prism about the red line.

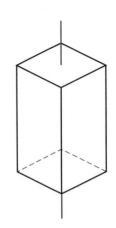

3 The rule for putting spots on the faces of dice is that opposite faces add up to seven.
This is the net of a dice.
How many spots would go on faces A, B and C?

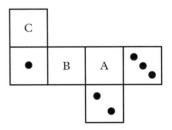

4 Write down the names of the solids that can be made from these nets.
   a

   b

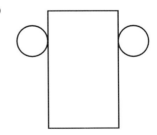

5 Sketch a net of this solid.

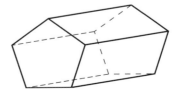

Help yourself

1 Multiplying

When you are adding lots of the same number it is quicker to multiply.

Example

```
  31                    31
  31  is the same as  ×  5
  31                  ̅1̅5̅5̅
  31
+ 31
 ̅1̅5̅5̅
```

```
To do      31    first do      31
         ×  5    5 × 1       ×  5
         ̅ ̅ ̅ ̅ ̅              ̅ ̅ ̅5̅
```

```
then do 5 × 3       31
                  ×  5
                  ̅1̅5̅5̅
```

Remember to keep your numbers in columns.

Here are some more examples:

```
    62              51
  ×  4            ×  9
  ̅2̅4̅8̅            ̅4̅5̅9̅
```

Exercise 1

1
```
    33
  ×  2
  ̅ ̅ ̅ ̅ ̅
```

2
```
    132
  ×   3
  ̅ ̅ ̅ ̅ ̅ ̅
```

3 31 × 4

4 133 × 3

Sometimes you need to carry.

Example

```
    26              26
  ×  3     →      ×  3
  ̅ ̅ ̅8̅            ̅7̅8̅
    ₁               ₁
```

3 × 2 = 6
Then add the 1 to give 7

Exercise 2

1
```
    45
  ×  2
  ̅ ̅ ̅ ̅ ̅
```

2
```
    35
  ×  2
  ̅ ̅ ̅ ̅ ̅
```

3 54 × 4

7 157 × 9

4 125 × 3

8 634 × 9

5 349 × 2

9 555 × 5

6 428 × 5

10 901 × 4

Other words

These words can also mean **multiply**.

times   **product**   **of**

Examples

Find 24 **times** 16
Find the **product** of 24 and 16
Find one half **of** 24

2 Multiplying by 10

When you multiply by 10, all the digits move across **one** column to the **left**. This makes the number 10 times bigger.
You can use the headings **Th H T U** to help.
They mean **T**housands, **H**undreds, **T**ens and **U**nits. Units is another way of saying 'ones'.

Example

23 × 10 = 230

```
H   T   U
    2   3
      ×10   ×10
2   3   0
```

Here are some more examples:

Th H T U

4   6   46 × 10 = 460

4   6   0

2   5   3   253 × 10 = 2530

2   5   3   0

Exercise 3

Multiply each of these numbers by 10

1 48   **3** 842   **5** 7000

2 54   **4** 777   **6** 9003

---

3 Multiplying by 100, 1000, ...

When you multiply by 100, all the digits move across **two** columns to the **left**.
This makes the number 100 times bigger.
This is because 100 = 10 × 10
So multiplying by 100 is like multiplying by 10 twice.

Example

74 × 100 = 7400

Th H T U

7   4

7   4   0   0

When you multiply by 1000 all the numbers move across three columns to the left.

This is because 1000 = 10 × 10 × 10
This means that multiplying by 1000 is like multiplying by 10 three times.

Example

74 × 1000 = 74 000

TTh Th H T U

7   4

7   4   0   0   0

Exercise 4

Write down the answers to these.

1 27 × 100   **7** 4153 × 100

2 91 × 100   **8** 900 × 1000

3 74 × 1000   **9** 4004 × 1000

4 291 × 100   **10** 924 × 10 000

5 4270 × 100   **11** 301 × 10 000

6 840 × 1000   **12** 737 × 100 000

---

4 Multiplying by 20, 30, ...

When you multiply by 20 it is like multiplying by 2 then by 10. This is because 20 = 2 × 10

Example

To do 18 × 20:
first do
```
    18
×    2
    36
     1
```

Then do   36 × 10 = 360

So   18 × 20 = 360

In the same way multiplying by 30 is the same as multiplying by 3 and then multiplying by 10

Example

To do 26×30:
first do

$$\begin{array}{r} 2\,6 \\ \times\ \ 3 \\ \hline 7\,8 \\ \scriptstyle 1 \end{array}$$

Then do $\qquad 78 \times 10 = 780$

So $\qquad 26 \times 30 = 780$

Exercise 5

Work these out.

1	39×20	**7**	92×40
2	42×20	**8**	25×50
3	26×30	**9**	71×50
4	23×30	**10**	304×20
5	65×30	**11**	291×30
6	34×40	**12**	525×70

5 Multiplying decimals by 10

You can multiply decimals by 10 in the same way.

Examples

1 41.5×10

H   T   U . $\frac{1}{10}$

$$\begin{array}{ccc} 4 & 1 & . 5 \\ 4 & 1 & 5 . 0 \end{array}$$ $41.5 \times 10 = 415$

2 56.87×10

H   T   U . $\frac{1}{10}$ $\frac{1}{100}$

$$\begin{array}{cccc} 5 & 6 & . 8 & 7 \\ 5 & 6 & 8 . 7 & \end{array}$$ 56.87×10
$= 568.7$

Exercise 6

Multiply these decimals by 10

1	7.4	**4**	72.34
2	32.5	**5**	20.8
3	18.91	**6**	0.4

6 Multiplying decimals by 100

When you multiply by 100, all the digits move across **two** columns to the **left**.

Examples

1 27.65×100

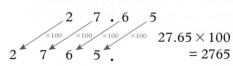

Th   H   T   U . $\frac{1}{10}$ $\frac{1}{100}$

27.65×100
$= 2765$

2 96.5×100

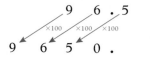

Th   H   T   U . $\frac{1}{10}$

96.5×100
$= 9650$

Exercise 7

Multiply these decimals by 100

1	65.86	**4**	721.8
2	22.94	**5**	70.39
3	16.4	**6**	4.01

7 Long multiplication

When you want to multiply two quite large numbers you have to do it in stages. Here are two methods. You only have to know one of them.

Method 1

Example
146×24

First do 146×4

```
   146
×    4
   584
   1 2
```

Then do 146×20

```
   146
×    2
   292
     1
```

$292 \times 10 = 2920$

Now add the two answers together.

```
    584
+  2920
   3504
```

Usually the working out looks like this:

```
    146
×    24
    584
   2920
   3504
```

Here is another example.

```
    223
×    36
   1338  ← (223 × 6)
   6690  ← (223 × 30)
   8028
   1  1
```

Method 2

Example
125×23

First set out the numbers with boxes, like this:

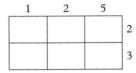

Now draw in the diagonals like this:

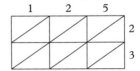

Fill in like a table square then add along the diagonals like this:

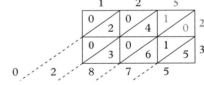

$1 \times 3 = 3$

Notice the 0 in the top box when the answer is a single digit.

So $125 \times 23 = \mathbf{2875}$

Here is another example.
When the diagonal adds up to more than 10, you carry into the next one.

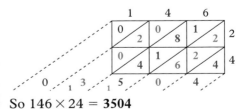

So $146 \times 24 = \mathbf{3504}$

Exercise 8

Use the method you prefer to work these out.

1 27×25 **7** 391×45

2 76×24 **8** 317×84

3 123×53 **9** 545×22

4 404×26 **10** 821×65

5 382×25 **11** 754×71

6 271×54 **12** 989×89

8 Dividing

Example

$68 \div 2$

$2 \overline{)68}$

First work out $6 \div 2 = 3$. Put the 3 above the 6:

$$\overset{3}{2 \overline{)68}}$$

Now work out $8 \div 2 = 4$. Put the 4 above the 8:

$$\overset{3\,4}{2 \overline{)68}}$$

So $68 \div 2 = 34$

Here is another example: $84 \div 4$

$$\overset{2\,1}{4 \overline{)84}}$$

So $84 \div 4 = 21$

Exercise 9

Work these out.

1 $2 \overline{)66}$ **4** $66 \div 3$

2 $3 \overline{)39}$ **5** $82 \div 2$

3 $8 \overline{)88}$ **6** $484 \div 4$

Sometimes you need to 'carry'. This happens when a number does not divide exactly.

Example

$72 \div 4$

$4 \overline{)72}$

First do $7 \div 4$. This is 1 with 3 left over.
Put the 1 above the 7 and carry the 3 like this:

$$\overset{1}{4 \overline{)7^{3}2}}$$

Now do $32 \div 4$. This is 8. Put the 8 above the $^{3}2$ like this:

$$\overset{1\,8}{4 \overline{)7^{3}2}}$$

So $72 \div 4 = 18$

Here is another example: $75 \div 5$

$$\overset{1\,5}{5 \overline{)7^{2}5}}$$

So $75 \div 5 = 15$

Exercise 10

Work these out.

1	$2 \overline{)54}$	**7**	$90 \div 6$
2	$3 \overline{)51}$	**8**	$144 \div 8$
3	$64 \div 4$	**9**	$432 \div 4$
4	$52 \div 4$	**10**	$284 \div 2$
5	$91 \div 7$	**11**	$531 \div 3$
6	$68 \div 4$	**12**	$378 \div 7$

Sometimes there is a remainder left at the end.

Example

$58 \div 4$

$$\begin{array}{r} 1\,4 \\ 4\overline{)5^{1}8} \end{array} \quad \text{remainder } 2$$

You carry the 2 by putting in the decimal point and extra zeros.

$$\begin{array}{r} 1\,4 \\ 4\overline{)5^{1}8\,.\,0} \end{array}$$

Now you can finish it off.

$$\begin{array}{r} 1\,4\,.\,5 \\ 4\overline{)5^{1}8\,.\,^{2}0} \end{array}$$

So $58 \div 4 = 14.5$

Exercise 11

Work these out.

1	$63 \div 6$	**5**	$442 \div 5$
2	$178 \div 4$	**6**	$604 \div 5$
3	$157 \div 4$	**7**	$357 \div 8$
4	$242 \div 8$	**8**	$964 \div 8$

9 Long Division

Sometimes you need to do long division. This is usually when you are dividing by a number bigger than 10

Example

$468 \div 12$

$$12\overline{)468}$$

12 will not go into 4 so

first do $46 \div 12$

You need to find out how many times 12 goes into 46

$$\begin{array}{l} 12 \times 2 = 24 \\ 12 \times 3 = 36 \quad \leftarrow \\ 12 \times 4 = 48 \end{array}$$

12 will go in 3 times.
Put the 3 above the 6

$$\begin{array}{r} 3 \\ 12\overline{)468} \end{array}$$

Work out 3×12 and put the answer under the 46

$$\begin{array}{r} 3 \\ 12\overline{)468} \\ 36 \end{array}$$

Now subtract the 36 from the 46

$$\begin{array}{r} 3 \\ 12\overline{)468} \\ 36 \\ \hline 10 \end{array}$$

The 10 is the carry.
You don't put it with the 8
Instead you bring the 8 down to the 10

$$\begin{array}{r} 3 \\ 12\overline{)468} \\ 36\downarrow \\ \hline 108 \end{array}$$

Now do $108 \div 12$

$$12 \times 8 = 96$$
$$12 \times 9 = 108 \ \leftarrow$$

12 will go in 9 times exactly.
Put the 9 after the 3

$$\begin{array}{r} 3\,9 \\ 12\overline{)468} \\ 3\,6 \\ \hline 1\,0\,8 \end{array}$$

Work out 9×12 and put the answer under the 108

When you subtract this time there is no remainder.

You have finished!

$$\begin{array}{r} 3\,9 \\ 12\overline{)468} \\ 3\,6 \\ \hline 1\,0\,8 \\ 1\,0\,8 \\ \hline - \end{array}$$

So $468 \div 12 = 39$

Sometimes there is a remainder left at the end.

Example

$383 \div 14$

$$\begin{array}{r} 2\,7 \\ 14\overline{)383} \\ 2\,8 \\ \hline 1\,0\,3 \\ 9\,8 \\ \hline 5 \end{array}$$

You could carry on and divide the 5 by the 14 to get a decimal.

It is easier to leave it as a fraction.

$5 \div 14$ is the fraction $\frac{5}{14}$

So $383 \div 14 = 27\frac{5}{14}$

Exercise 13

Work these out.

1	$698 \div 12$	**7**	$212 \div 14$
2	$664 \div 13$	**8**	$517 \div 17$
3	$818 \div 16$	**9**	$209 \div 13$
4	$925 \div 22$	**10**	$310 \div 18$
5	$550 \div 24$	**11**	$2834 \div 14$
6	$872 \div 32$	**12**	$8721 \div 15$

Exercise 12

Work these out.

1	$540 \div 12$	**7**	$805 \div 23$
2	$806 \div 13$	**8**	$754 \div 26$
3	$938 \div 14$	**9**	$928 \div 32$
4	$690 \div 15$	**10**	$648 \div 27$
5	$600 \div 12$	**11**	$1056 \div 16$
6	$540 \div 18$	**12**	$1656 \div 18$

10 Dividing by 10

When you divide by 10, all the digits move across **one** column to the **right**. This makes the number smaller.

Example

230 ÷ 10 = 23

Here are some more examples.

580 ÷ 10 = 58

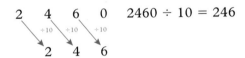

2460 ÷ 10 = 246

Exercise 14

Divide these numbers by 10

1 820   **5** 8160

2 60   **6** 9400

3 4820   **7** 7000

4 930   **8** 500 000

11 Dividing by 100, 1000, ...

When you divide by 100, all the digits move across **two** columns to the **right**. This is because 100 = 10 × 10 So dividing by 100 is like dividing by 10 twice.

Example

7400 ÷ 100 = 74

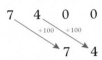

When you divide by 1000, all the numbers move across **three** columns to the **right**.

Example

74 000 ÷ 1000 = 74

TTh Th H T U

7 4 0 0 0

÷1000 ÷1000

7 4

Exercise 15

Work these out.

1 5400 ÷ 100   **5** 84 000 ÷ 100

2 7100 ÷ 100   **6** 84 000 ÷ 1000

3 8200 ÷ 100   **7** 400 000 ÷ 1000

4 64 000 ÷ 1000   **8** 400 000 ÷ 10 000

12 Dividing by 20, 30, ...

When you divide by 20, it is like dividing by 2 then by 10. This is because 20 = 2 × 10

Example

To do 360 ÷ 20

first do
$$\begin{array}{r} 1\,8\,0 \\ 2\,\overline{)3\,{}^16\,0} \end{array}$$

Then do   180 ÷ 10 = 18

So   360 ÷ 20 = 18

In the same way dividing by 30 is the same as dividing by 3 then by 10

Example

To do $780 \div 30$

first do

$$\begin{array}{r} 2\,6\,0 \\ 3\overline{)7\,{}^{1}8\,0} \end{array}$$

Then do $260 \div 10 = 26$

So $780 \div 30 = 26$

Exercise 16

Work these out.

1	$820 \div 20$	**5**	$7520 \div 20$
2	$480 \div 30$	**6**	$4620 \div 30$
3	$3720 \div 40$	**7**	$1980 \div 90$
4	$5250 \div 50$	**8**	$24\,480 \div 80$

13 Dividing decimals by 10

You can divide decimals by 10 in the same way.

Examples

1 $47.1 \div 10$

T U . $\frac{1}{10}$ $\frac{1}{100}$

$$4 \quad 7 \quad . \quad 1$$

$$4 \quad . \quad 7 \quad 1$$

$47.1 \div 10 = 4.71$

2 $2.9 \div 10$

U . $\frac{1}{10}$ $\frac{1}{100}$

$$2 \quad . \quad 9$$

$$0 \quad . \quad 2 \quad 9$$

$2.9 \div 10 = 0.29$

Exercise 17

Divide these decimals by 10

1	32.7	**3**	3.4	**5**	3.01
2	96.4	**4**	8.79	**6**	10.3

14 Dividing decimals by 100

When you divide by 100, all the digits move across **two** columns to the **right**.

Examples

1 $257.1 \div 100$

H T U . $\frac{1}{10}$ $\frac{1}{100}$ $\frac{1}{1000}$

$$2 \quad 5 \quad 7 \quad . \quad 1$$

$$2 \quad . \quad 5 \quad 7 \quad 1$$

$257.1 \div 100 = 2.571$

2 $52.3 \div 100$

T U . $\frac{1}{10}$ $\frac{1}{100}$ $\frac{1}{1000}$

$$5 \quad 2 \quad . \quad 3$$

$$0 \quad . \quad 5 \quad 2 \quad 3$$

$52.3 \div 100 = 0.523$

Exercise 18

Divide these decimals by 100

1	182.5	**3**	23.4	**5**	10.2
2	479.1	**4**	17.6	**6**	31.02

Other words

These words can also mean **divide**.

share   **quotient**

Examples

Share 240 by 12
Find the **quotient** of 240 and 12 } both mean $240 \div 12$

15 Multiplying and dividing by 0.1, 0.01, ...

Multiplying by 0.1 is the same as dividing by 10.
Multiplying by 0.01 is the same as dividing by 100 and so on.

Dividing by 0.1 is the same as multiplying by 10.
Dividing by 0.01 is the same as multiplying by 100 and so on.

Exercise 19

Work these out.

1 28×0.1	**9** 81.4×0.01
2 65×0.1	**10** 9.6×0.01
3 3.9×0.1	**11** 3.17×0.001
4 2.3×0.1	**12** 6.9×0.001
5 $29 \div 0.1$	**13** $89.4 \div 0.01$
6 $74 \div 0.1$	**14** $34.8 \div 0.01$
7 $263 \div 0.1$	**15** $8 \div 0.001$
8 $7.8 \div 0.1$	**16** $1.32 \div 0.001$

16 Adding fractions

To add fractions, the bottom numbers (denominators) **must** be the same.

Examples

$\frac{2}{7} + \frac{3}{7} = \frac{5}{7}$

two sevenths + three sevenths = five sevenths

$\frac{3}{5} + \frac{3}{5} = \frac{6}{5} = 1\frac{1}{5}$

three fifths + three fifths = six fifths = One and one fifth

Exercise 20

Work these out.

1 $\frac{3}{9} + \frac{4}{9}$	**3** $\frac{9}{12} + \frac{2}{12}$	**5** $\frac{6}{8} + \frac{7}{8}$
2 $\frac{6}{12} + \frac{5}{12}$	**4** $\frac{4}{5} + \frac{4}{5}$	**6** $\frac{9}{11} + \frac{8}{11}$

Sometimes the two bottom numbers are different. Before you can add the fractions you **must** make them the same.

Example

$\frac{2}{3} + \frac{1}{6}$

You need to find a number that 3 and 6 both divide into exactly.

Numbers that 3 goes into:
3 ⑥ 9 12 ...
Numbers that 6 goes into:
⑥ 12 18 ...

The first number that is in both lists is 6. The 6 is called the common denominator.

Now write the fractions with 6 as the bottom number:

$\frac{2}{3} = \frac{?}{6}$ so $\frac{2}{3} = \frac{4}{6}$ so $\frac{2}{3} = \frac{4}{6}$.

You can see this in a diagram.

The $\frac{1}{6}$ does not need changing.

So $\frac{2}{3} + \frac{1}{6} = \frac{4}{6} + \frac{1}{6} = \frac{5}{6}$

Here is another example

$\frac{2}{3} + \frac{1}{4}$

Numbers that 3 goes into:
3 6 9 ⑫ 15 ...

Numbers that 4 goes into:
4 8 ⑫ 16 ...

349

You need to change both fractions to twelfths. 12 is the common denominator.

$\frac{2}{3} = \frac{?}{12}$ $\quad$ $\frac{2}{3} \xrightarrow{\times 4} \frac{8}{12}$
$\xrightarrow{\times 4}$

$\frac{1}{4} = \frac{?}{12}$ $\quad$ $\frac{1}{4} \xrightarrow{\times 3} \frac{3}{12}$
$\xrightarrow{\times 3}$

So $\frac{2}{3} + \frac{1}{4} = \frac{8}{12} + \frac{3}{12} = \frac{11}{12}$

Exercise 21

Work these out.

1 $\frac{1}{4} + \frac{1}{8}$ $\qquad$ **5** $\frac{5}{9} + \frac{1}{18}$ $\qquad$ **9** $\frac{2}{5} + \frac{1}{6}$

2 $\frac{1}{5} + \frac{1}{15}$ $\qquad$ **6** $\frac{1}{3} + \frac{1}{6}$ $\qquad$ **10** $\frac{1}{7} + \frac{4}{8}$

3 $\frac{2}{7} + \frac{3}{14}$ $\qquad$ **7** $\frac{1}{3} + \frac{1}{4}$ $\qquad$ **11** $\frac{1}{8} + \frac{3}{5}$

4 $\frac{5}{9} + \frac{1}{3}$ $\qquad$ **8** $\frac{2}{7} + \frac{1}{3}$ $\qquad$ **12** $\frac{1}{2} + \frac{1}{3} + \frac{1}{4}$

17 Subtracting fractions

This works just like adding fractions.

Example

$\frac{3}{5} - \frac{2}{5} = \frac{1}{5}$

The two bottom numbers must still be the same.

Example

$\frac{3}{8} - \frac{1}{4}$

Numbers that 8 goes into:
⑧ 16 24 …
Numbers that 4 goes into:
4 ⑧ 12 16 …

$\frac{1}{4} = \frac{?}{8}$ $\quad$ $\frac{1}{4} \xrightarrow{\times 2} \frac{2}{8}$
$\xrightarrow{\times 2}$

The $\frac{3}{8}$ does not need changing.

So $\frac{3}{8} - \frac{1}{4} = \frac{3}{8} - \frac{2}{8} = \frac{1}{8}$

Exercise 22

Work these out.

1 $\frac{5}{8} - \frac{2}{8}$ $\qquad$ **5** $\frac{6}{8} - \frac{1}{4}$ $\qquad$ **9** $\frac{7}{8} - \frac{2}{3}$

2 $\frac{3}{5} - \frac{2}{5}$ $\qquad$ **6** $\frac{11}{12} - \frac{1}{3}$ $\qquad$ **10** $\frac{3}{4} - \frac{1}{3}$

3 $\frac{6}{11} - \frac{2}{11}$ $\qquad$ **7** $\frac{1}{4} - \frac{1}{6}$ $\qquad$ **11** $\frac{5}{8} - \frac{2}{6}$

4 $\frac{2}{5} - \frac{1}{10}$ $\qquad$ **8** $\frac{2}{4} - \frac{1}{3}$ $\qquad$ **12** $\frac{10}{11} - \frac{6}{8}$

18 Simplifying fractions

This is also known as **cancelling**.
You look for a number that divides exactly into both the top and bottom numbers.

Examples

1 Simplify $\frac{6}{15}$

3 goes into both 6 and 15 exactly

$\frac{6}{15} \xrightarrow{\div 3} \frac{2}{5}$
$\xleftarrow{\div 3}$

You can divide by more than one number.

2 Simplify $\frac{18}{24}$

$\frac{18}{24} \xrightarrow{\div 2} \frac{9}{12} \xrightarrow{\div 3} \frac{3}{4}$
$\xleftarrow{\div 2} \qquad \xleftarrow{\div 3}$

Exercise 23

Simplify these.

1 $\frac{2}{6}$ $\qquad$ **5** $\frac{8}{12}$ $\qquad$ **9** $\frac{25}{35}$

2 $\frac{4}{12}$ $\qquad$ **6** $\frac{30}{50}$ $\qquad$ **10** $\frac{8}{40}$

3 $\frac{5}{15}$ $\qquad$ **7** $\frac{24}{36}$ $\qquad$ **11** $\frac{30}{60}$

4 $\frac{6}{9}$ $\qquad$ **8** $\frac{18}{27}$ $\qquad$ **12** $\frac{38}{80}$

19 Converting units

Common metric units of length

10 millimetres (mm) = 1 centimetre (cm)
100 centimetres = 1 metre (m)
1000 metres = 1 kilometre (km)

Examples

1 Convert 6.9 cm to mm.
6.9 cm = 6.9 × 10 mm
= 69 mm

2 Convert 5.34 m to cm.
5.34 m = 5.34 × 100 cm
= 5.34 cm

3 Convert 7.3 km to m.
7.3 km = 7.3 × 1000 m
= 7300 m

Exercise 24

1 Convert these lengths to mm.
  a 3.4 cm   **c** 131 cm
  b 12.8 cm   **d** 113.7 cm

2 Convert these lengths to cm.
  a 4.1 m   **c** 12.1 m
  b 2.8 m   **d** 324 m

3 Convert these lengths to m.
  a 8.8 km   **c** 15 km
  b 9.7 km   **d** 100 km

Common metric units of mass

Units of mass have similar names to units of length.

1000 milligrams (mg) = 1 gram (g)
1000 grams = 1 kilogram (kg)
1000 kg = 1 tonne (t)

Examples

1 Convert 2.5 kg to g.
2.5 kg = 2.5 × 1000 g
= 2500 g

2 Convert 5000 g to kg.
5000 g = 5000 ÷ 1000 kg
= 5 kg

Exercise 25

Convert the units in each of these. Think carefully whether you need to multiply or divide.

1 **a** 3 kg to g   **d** 3000 g to kg
    b 7 kg to g   **e** 6000 g to kg
    c 21 kg to g   **f** 800 g to kg

2 **a** 3.5 kg to g   **d** 6500 g to kg
    b 7.2 kg to g   **e** 3200 g to kg
    c 3.84 kg to g   **f** 2800 g to kg

3 **a** 5 g to mg   **d** 3000 kg to t
    b 8000 mg to g   **e** 4 t to kg
    c 1640 mg to g   **f** 2.5 t to kg

CHAPTER 1

1   **a** $s^2 = 4^2 + 5^2$
           $s^2 = 41$
           $s = \sqrt{41}$
           $s = 6.4$ cm correct to 1 dp

   b $18^2 = 14^2 + n^2$
      $n^2 + 196 = 324$
           $n^2 = 128$
            $n = 11.3$ cm correct to 1 dp

   c $56^2 = y^2 + 45^2$
     $y^2 + 2025 = 3136$
          $y^2 = 1111$
           $y = 33.3$ mm correct to 1 dp

   d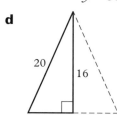
$$20^2 = a^2 + 16^2$$
$$a^2 + 256 = 400$$
$$a^2 = 144$$
$$a = 12 \text{ mm}$$
$$q = 2 \times 12 = 24 \text{ mm}$$

2 $8.5^2 = 72.25$ (This is the longest side)
     $4^2 + 7.5^2 = 16 + 56.25 = 72.25$
     The triangle has a right angle.

3 $3.5^2 = h^2 + 1.2^2$
    $h^2 + 1.2^2 = 3.5^2$
          $h^2 = 12.25 - 1.44$
           $h = 3.3$ correct to 1 dp

CHAPTER 2

1   **a** $t = s + c$
   b $t = £1.50 + £0.70 = £2.20$

2   **a** $T = 2 \times n + 70 = 2n + 70$
   b $T = 2 \times 54 + 70 = £178$

3   **a**

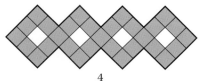

4

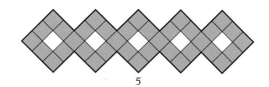

5

b

Number of pattern	1	2	3	4	5
Number of tiles	8	15	22	29	36

c Number of tiles = 7 × number of pattern.

d

Number of pattern	1	2	3	4	5
	7 + 1	14 + 1	21 + 1	28 + 1	35 + 1
Number of tiles	8	15	22	29	36

e $t = 7n + 1$

f $t = 7 \times 20 + 1 = 141$

4 **a** The sequence goes up in 4's starting from 6.
$t = 4n + 2$

b The sequence goes up in 7's starting from 1.
$t = 7n - 6$

CHAPTER 3

1 **a** Circumference = $\pi \times$ diameter
$C = \pi \times 18$
$C = 56.5$ cm to 1 dp.

b Diameter = 2 × radius
$d = 2 \times 4.1$
$d = 8.2$ cm
Circumference = $\pi \times$ diameter
$C = \pi \times 8.2$
$C = 25.8$ cm to 1 dp.

2 Circumference = $\pi \times$ diameter
Diameter = circumference ÷ π
$$d = \frac{82}{\pi}$$
$d = 26.1$ cm to 1 dp.

3 **a** Area = $\pi \times$ radius × radius
$A = \pi \times 2.9 \times 2.9$
$A = 26.4$ cm^2 to 1 dp.

b Radius = diameter ÷ 2
$r = 30 \div 2$
$r = 15$ cm

Area = $\pi \times$ radius × radius
$A = \pi \times 15 \times 15$
$A = 706.9$ cm^2 to 1 dp.

4 a This shape is one quarter of a circle.

Area of whole circle
$= \pi \times$ radius $\times$ radius
$= \pi \times 7 \times 7$

Area of this shape
$= \pi \times 7 \times 7 \div 4$
$= 38.5$ cm^2 to 1 dp.

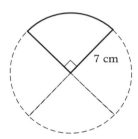

7 cm

b Area of shape
$=$ Area A $+$ Area B

Area A $= 12 \times 6$
$= 72$ cm^2

B is a semicircle. The radius is 6 cm.

Area B $= \pi \times 6 \times 6 \div 2$
$= 56.5$ cm^2 to 1 dp.

Area of shape
$= 72 + 56.5$
$= 128.5$ cm^2 to 1 dp.

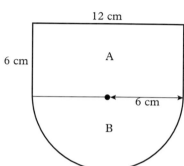

12 cm

6 cm

A

6 cm

B

CHAPTER 4

1 a Mean amount

$$= \frac{3.20 + 3.70 + 2.40 + 2.40 + 3.50 + 2.80 + 2.40 + 2.60 + 2.40 + 2.40 + 3.40 + 2.90}{12}$$

$$= \frac{34.10}{12}$$

$= £2.84$ to nearest penny (2 dp)

b Put the values in order:

2.40   2.40   2.40   2.40   2.40 $\boxed{2.60}$ $\boxed{2.80}$ 2.90   3.20   3.40   3.50   3.70

Median $= \dfrac{2.60 + 2.80}{2} = £2.70$

c Mode $= £2.40$
d Range $= £3.70 - £2.40 = £1.30$

2 **a**

Amount of rain (mm)	Tally	Number of days
0–5	JHI JHI	10
5–10	JHI III	8
10–15	JHI I	6
15–20	JHI	5
20–25	I	1
	Total	30

b

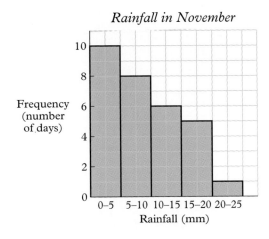

Rainfall in November

c 30 (10 + 8 + 6 + 5 + 1 = 30)

d April is wetter. The bar-chart for April has the taller bars on the right, ie there are more days with higher rainfall than November, where the tall bars are on the left for small amounts of rain.

e November:

Rainfall (midpoint)	Number of days	Amount of rain	
2.5	10	25	(10 × 2.5)
7.5	8	60	(8 × 7.5)
12.5	6	75	(6 × 12.5)
17.5	5	87.5	(5 × 17.5)
22.5	1	22.5	(1 × 22.5)
	Total 30	Total 270	

$$\text{Estimate of mean rainfall} = \frac{270}{30}$$

$$= 9 \text{ mm}$$

April:

Rainfall (midpoint)	Number of days	Amount of rain
2.5	3	7.5
7.5	4	30
12.5	5	62.5
17.5	8	140
22.5	10	225
	Total 30	Total 465

$$\text{Estimate of mean rainfall} = \frac{465}{30}$$

$$= 15.5 \text{ mm}$$

CHAPTER 5

1 **a** 24 **c** 35.6 **e** 39.473 **g** 0.038
b 350 **d** 75 **f** 27.5 **h** 0.007 01

2 **a** 5.65 m **b** 0.378 kg

3 **a** Peter
b When you multiply by a number less than 1 the answer is less than you started with.

4 **a** $3.67 \times 10^3 = 3670$
b $6.293 \times 10^6 = 6\,293\,000$

5 **a** 164.7 **b** 732 000

6 Lower limit is 15.65
Upper limit is 15.75

7 **a** Length: lower limit is 129.5
upper limit is 130.5
Width: lower limit is 51.5
upper limit is 52.5
b Minimum perimeter = 129.5 + 51.5 + 129.5 + 51.5
= 362 cm
Maximum perimeter = 130.5 + 52.5 + 130.5 + 52.5
= 366 cm
c Minimum area = $129.5 \times 51.5 = 6669.25 \text{ cm}^2$
Maximum area = $130.5 \times 52.5 = 6851.25 \text{ cm}^2$

8 **a** $80 \times 40 = 3200 \text{ cm}^2$ **b** $78.5 \times 44.5 = 3493.25 \text{ cm}^2$

CHAPTER 6

1 Volume $= 42 \times 5 = 210 \text{ cm}^3$

2

Area of cross section $= 16 + 9 + 8 = 33 \text{ cm}^2$
Volume $= 33 \times 10 = 330 \text{ cm}^3$

3 Area of cross section $= \dfrac{9 + 15}{2} \times 8 = 12 \times 8 = 96 \text{ cm}^2$
Volume $= 96 \times 20 = 1920 \text{ cm}^3$

4 Area of cross section $= 3.14 \times 12 \times 12 = 452.16 \text{ cm}^2$
Volume $= 452.16 \times 30 = 13\,564.8 \text{ cm}^3$

5 Height $= 1287 \div 33 = 39 \text{ cm}$

6 **a** Area of circular base $= 3.14 \times 13 \times 13 = 530.66 \text{ cm}^2$
   b 5 litres $= 5000 \text{ ml} = 5000 \text{ cm}^3$
      Volume $=$ area of cross section $\times$ depth
      $5000 = 530.66 \times$ depth
      depth $= 5000 \div 530.66$
      depth $= 9.4 \text{ cm}$ to 1 dp.

7 Area of cross section $=$ area of circle $\div 2$
                                $= (3.14 \times 4 \times 4) \div 2$
                                $= 25.12 \text{ m}^2$
   Volume of earth removed $= 25.12 \times 250$
                                    $= 6280 \text{ m}^3$.

8 Nostrum: 25 ml costs £2.10 $\div$ 6 = £0.35
   Hair clean: 25 ml costs £1.80 $\div$ 5 = £0.36
   Nostrum is cheaper and so is the better value for money.

CHAPTER 7

1 $100 - 46 = 54\%$

2 $\frac{35}{250} \times 100 = 35 \div 250 \times 100 = 14\%$

3 **a** $\frac{4}{5} \times 100 = 4 \div 5 \times 100 = 80\%$

   b $0.39 \times 100 = 39\%$

4 **a** $16\% = 16 \div 100 = 0.16$

   b $\frac{16}{100} = \frac{4}{25}$

5 5% of £240 $= \frac{5}{100} \times 240 = £12$
   His new salary is £240 + £12 = £252

6 $5 + 3 + 1 = 9$ shares are needed
   One share is £360 ÷ 9   = £40
   1st prize is £40 × 5   = £200
   2nd prize is £40 × 3   = £120
   3rd prize is £40 × 1   = £40
   Check: £200 + £120 + £40 = £360

7 One car costs £2.61 ÷ 3 = £0.87
   7 cars cost £0.87 × 7 = £6.09

8 **a** Density = 67.7 ÷ 5 g/cm³
               = 13.54 g/cm³

   b Mass of 12 cm³ = 13.54 × 12 = 162.48 g

9 Time, $T = \dfrac{D}{S} = 2320 \div 580 = 4$ hours

10 Distance D = S × T = 300 000 × 6 km
                       = 1 800 000 km.

CHAPTER 8

1 **a** $4e$ **b** f^3 **c** $6g$ **d** q^3 **e** h^5 **f** $2k$

2 **a** $7f + 4g$ **c** $9u + 2v$ **e** $7x + y$
   b $11r$ **d** $g + 2$ **f** $3r + 6$

3 **a** $12a$ **b** $10r^2$ **c** $3cd$ **d** $3y \times 3y = 9y^2$

4 **a** $6r - 15$ **b** $t^2 + 4t$ **c** $2ed - 5d$ **d** $6rs + 12r^2$

5 **a** $7(f + 3) + 2(5f - 4) = 7f + 21 + 10f - 8$
$$= 17f + 13$$
   b $4(p + 2q) + 3(p - 2q) = 4p + 8q + 3p - 6q$
$$= 7p + 2q$$

6 **a** $x + 5 = 17$
$$x + 5 - 5 = 17 - 5$$
$$x = 12$$

   b $5x = 35$
$$\frac{5x}{5} = \frac{35}{5}$$
$$x = 7$$

   c $\dfrac{x}{3} = 11$
$$3 \times \frac{x}{3} = 3 \times 11$$
$$x = 33$$

   d $x - 5 = 22$
$$x - 5 + 5 = 22 + 5$$
$$x = 27$$

7 **a** $3x + 15 = 8x$
$$3x - \mathbf{3x} + 15 = 8x - \mathbf{3x}$$
$$15 = 5x$$
$$\frac{15}{5} = \frac{5x}{5}$$
$$3 = x$$
or $x = 3$

   b $5x - 7 = 18$
$$5x - 7 + 7 = 18 + 7$$
$$5x = 25$$
$$\frac{5x}{5} = \frac{25}{5}$$
$$x = 5$$

8 **a** $6x - 3 = 4x + 5$
$$6x - \mathbf{4x} - 3 = 4x - \mathbf{4x} + 5$$
$$2x - 3 = 5$$
$$2x - 3 + \mathbf{3} = 5 + \mathbf{3}$$
$$2x = 8$$
$$\frac{x}{2} = \frac{8}{2}$$
$$x = 4$$

   b $4x + 6 = 21 - x$
$$4x + \mathbf{x} + 6 = 21 - x + \mathbf{x}$$
$$5x + 6 = 21$$
$$5x + 6 - \mathbf{6} = 21 - \mathbf{6}$$
$$5x = 15$$
$$\frac{5x}{5} = \frac{15}{5}$$
$$x = 3$$

9 **a** $5(x + 4) = 35$
$$5x + 20 = 35$$
$$5x + 20 - \mathbf{20} = 35 - \mathbf{20}$$
$$5x = 15$$
$$\frac{5x}{5} = \frac{15}{5}$$
$$x = 3$$

   b $3(x - 2) = 18$
$$3x - 6 = 18$$
$$3x - 6 + \mathbf{6} = 18 + \mathbf{6}$$
$$3x = 24$$
$$\frac{3x}{3} = \frac{24}{3}$$
$$x = 8$$

CHAPTER 9

1 a

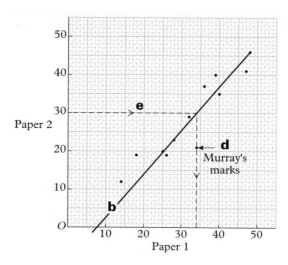

c Paper 1 because the marks are higher.
d 21 (see mark on graph)
e 34 (see dotted line on graph)

2 a $\frac{1}{4}$

b The section for Europe is a bit less than 50%.
An estimate for the percentage is 40%.
(You can give any answer in the range 35% to 45%.)

c $\frac{1}{4}$ of the form chose America
$\frac{1}{4}$ of 28 = $\frac{1}{4} \times 28$ = 7 pupils

d Total number of pupils = 30
Each person gets 360° ÷ 30 = 12°

Where my form want to go on holiday

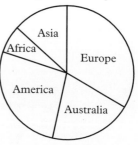

Holiday choice	Number of pupils	Angle
Europe	10	120°
Australia	6	72°
America	8	96°
Africa	2	24°
Asia	4	48°

3 The bars are not the same width so the Spring term looks a lot more than 3 times the Autumn term.

CHAPTER 10

1 There are 6 beads altogether.
  a (1) Probability of red bead $= \frac{2}{6}$ since there are 2 red beads
    (2) Probability of green bead $= \frac{3}{6}$ since there are 3 green beads
      Probability of black bead $= \frac{1}{6}$ since there is 1 black bead
  b Debbie needs equal numbers of each colour bead, so add 1 red bead and 2 black beads.

2 **a** False. There may be more pupils taking one language than the other.
  b True

3 $1 - 0.8 = 0.2$

4 **a** (1) $\frac{31}{100}$ (2) 0.31   (3) 31%
  b Chicken and chips because it has the highest frequency.

5 **a**

		Dice					
		1	2	3	4	5	6
Spinner	W	W, 1	W, 2	W, 3	W, 4	W, 5	W, 6
	B	B, 1	B, 2	B, 3	B, 4	B, 5	B, 6
	R	R, 1	R, 2	R, 3	R, 4	R, 5	R, 6
	G	G, 1	G, 2	G, 3	G, 4	G, 5	G, 6

  b There are 24 possible outcomes altogether.
    (1) Probability of a red and a 6 $= \frac{1}{24}$
    (2) Probability of a green and a 1 $= \frac{1}{24}$

CHAPTER 11

1 **a**

Value of x	Value of x^2	Value of $x^2 + x$	
6	36	42	too small
6.5	42.25	48.75	too big
6.3	39.69	45.99	too small
6.4	40.96	47.36	too big
			x is between 6.3 and 6.4
6.35	40.3225	46.6725	too big
			x is between 6.3 and 6.35

    $x = 6.3$ correct to 1 dp.
  b $x = 3.3$ correct to 1 dp.

2

Value of x	Value of $x + 5$	Value of $x(x + 5)$	
3	8	24	too small
4	9	36	too big
3.8	8.8	33.44	too small
3.9	8.9	34.71	too big
3.85	8.85	34.0725	too big
3.84	8.84	33.9456	too small

x lies between 3.84 and 3.85

3 a 4.35 is the most sensible number to try next.
It is halfway between 4.3 and 4.4.
$4.35 \times 4.35 = 18.9225$ too small.
$4.36 \times 4.36 = 19.0096$ too big.
4.355 is halfway between 4.35 and 4.36
$4.355 \times 4.355 = 18.966$ too small
$4.356 \times 4.356 = 18.974$ too small.
You can try other numbers.
The answer is 4.359 correct to 3 dp.

b $x^2 + 4 = 23$

Subtract 4 from both sides $x^2 + 4 - 4 = 23 - 4$
$$x^2 = 19$$
so $x = \sqrt{19}$

Use the answer you got in part **a** for x.

4 a $-7, -6, -5, -4, -3$ **c** $-6, -5, -4, -3, -2$
b $-6, -7, -8, -9, -10$ **d** 7, 6, 5, 4, 3

5 a $-2, -1, 0, 1, 2, 3, 4, 5$ **c** 0, 1, 2, 3, 4
b $-3, -2, -1, 0, 1$

6 a

b

c

d

7 a
$$x + 1 > 7$$
$$x + 1 - 1 > 7 - 1$$
$$x > 6$$

b
$$\frac{x}{7} > 4$$
$$7 \times \frac{x}{7} > 7 \times 4$$
$$x > 28$$

c
$$3x < 21$$
$$\frac{3x}{3} < \frac{21}{3}$$
$$x < 7$$

d
$$4x < 16$$
$$\frac{4x}{4} < \frac{16}{4}$$
$$x < 4$$

e
$$2x + 5 \leqslant 17$$
$$2x + 5 - 5 \leqslant 17 - 5$$
$$2x \leqslant 12$$
$$\frac{2x}{2} < \frac{12}{2}$$
$$x \leqslant 6$$

f
$$4x - 12 \geqslant 20$$
$$4x - 12 + 12 \geqslant 20 + 12$$
$$4x \geqslant 32$$
$$\frac{4x}{4} \geqslant \frac{32}{4}$$
$$x \geqslant 8$$

CHAPTER 12

1 a $\dfrac{(3.4 + 5.5)}{3.7} = 2.405\,405\,4$
$$= 2.41 \text{ to 3 sf.}$$

b $\dfrac{5.6}{(1.4 \times 8)} = 0.5$

c $\dfrac{(67 - 14.6)}{(4.3 + 5.9)} = 5.137\,254\,9$
$$= 5.14 \text{ to 3 sf.}$$

d $4\sqrt{(4.5^2 + 6^2)} = 30$

2 $p = \dfrac{q^2 + r^2}{q - r}$

$\quad = \dfrac{(14.8^2 + 12.3^2)}{(14.8 - 12.3)}$

$\quad = 148.132$

3 a 9.7   **c** 3.12   **e** 0.4
  b 0.65   **d** 8.7   **f** 6.3

4 a 2.1   **c** 6.0   **e** 0.5
  b 0.24   **d** 0.33   **f** 0.08

5 a 8.019, 8.109, 8.19   **b** 1.002, 1.02, 1.2

6 a
$$\begin{array}{r} 7.62 \\ \times\ \ \ \ 5 \\ \hline 38.10 \\ \scriptstyle 3\ \ 1 \end{array}$$

b
$$\begin{array}{r} 34.8 \\ \times\ \ \ \ 6 \\ \hline 208.8 \\ \scriptstyle 2\ 4 \end{array}$$

7 a
$$\begin{array}{r} 6.74 \\ \times\ 36 \\ \hline 40.44 \\ \scriptstyle 4\ \ 2 \\ 202.20 \\ \scriptstyle 2\ 1 \\ \hline 242.64 \end{array}$$
6.74×6
6.74×30

b
$$\begin{array}{r} 74.8 \\ \times\ 27 \\ \hline 523.6 \\ \scriptstyle 3\ 5 \\ 1496.0 \\ \scriptstyle 1 \\ \hline 2019.6 \\ \scriptstyle 1\ 1 \end{array}$$
74.8×7
74.8×20

8 a
$$8)\overline{4.^{4}5^{5}6}^{\ 0.\ 5\ 7}$$

b
$$7)\overline{7.5^{5}9^{3}0^{2}0}^{\ 1.0\ 8\ 4\ 2}$$
1.084 correct to 3 dp

9 a
$$\begin{array}{r} 3.7 \\ 16)\overline{59.2} \\ 48\ \downarrow \\ \hline 11\ 2 \\ 11\ 2 \\ \hline - \end{array}$$

b
$$\begin{array}{r} 3.4 \\ 26)\overline{88.4} \\ 78\ \downarrow \\ \hline 10\ 4 \\ 10\ 4 \\ \hline - \end{array}$$

CHAPTER 13

1 $a + 60 = 180$ $\qquad a = 120°$
$40 + b = 360$ $\qquad b = 320°$
$c + 90 + 40 = 180$ $\qquad c = 180 - 130 = 50°$
$d = 125°$ $\quad$ (vertically opposite angles)
$e = 55°$ $\quad$ (vertically opposite angles)
$f + 110 + 125 + 55 = 360°$ $\qquad f = 360 - 290 = 70°$

2 a $360 \div 6 = 60°$ $\qquad\qquad$ **c** $360 \div 10 = 36°$
$\ \ $ **b** $360 \div 9 = 40°$ $\qquad\qquad$ **d** $360 \div 7 = 52°$

3

Number of sides	Name of polygon	Exterior angle	Interior angle
3	equilateral triangle	120°	60°
5	regular pentagon	72°	108°
8	regular octagon	45°	135°
12	regular dodecagon	30°	150°

4 To find the number of triangles, divide by 180°
$1620 \div 180 = 9$.
The polygon has been cut into 9 triangles. It has 11 sides.

5 **a**
b

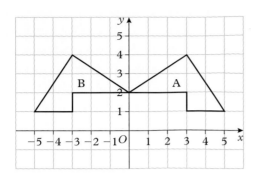

6

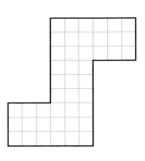

CHAPTER 14

1 **a** $y = 5x - 2$ The largest number in front of the x is 5.
b $y = 2x + 5$ The smallest number in front of the x is 2.
c $y = 2x + 5$ The number after the x is 5.

2 $y = 2x - 4$ $(3, 2)$ $2 \times 3 - 4 = 2$
  $y = x - 4$ $(9, 5)$ $9 - 4 = 5$
  $y = 3x - 2$ $(3, 7)$ $3 \times 3 - 2 = 7$

3 **a** $y = 2x$ The line is parallel to $y = 2x + 6$ so must have $y = 2x$.
    It passes through O so the equation is just $y = 2x$.
b $y = \frac{1}{2}x - 1$ The line is parallel to $y = \frac{1}{2}x + 5$ so must have $y = \frac{1}{2}x$.
    It passes through -1 so its equation is $y = \frac{1}{2}x - 1$.

4 2 apples + 1 pear = 20 p $2a + p = 20$
  1 apple + 2 pears = 22 p $a + 2p = 22$
  You need to draw the lines for
  $2a + p = 20$ and $a + 2p = 22$
  When $a = 0$ $p = 20$ When $a = 0$ $2p = 22$
  When $p = 0$ $2a = 20$ $p = 11$
             $a = 10$ When $p = 0$ $a = 22$
  So $(10, 0)$ and $(0, 20)$ So $(22, 0)$ and $(0, 11)$
  lie on the line.   lie on the line.

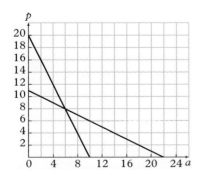

The lines cross at $(6, 8)$
so an apple costs 6 p and
a pear costs 8 p.

5 a (1) $\qquad 2x + y = 11$
(2) $\qquad\qquad\underline{5x - y = 17}$
Add (1) and (2) $\quad 7x \qquad = 28$
$\qquad\qquad\qquad\qquad x = 4$
Put $x = 4$ in (1) $\quad 8 + y = 11$
$\qquad\qquad\qquad\qquad y = 3$
So $x = 4$, $y = 3$
Check in (2) $\quad 5 \times 4 - 3 = 20 - 3 = 17$ ✓

b (1) $\qquad\qquad 7x + y = 44$
(2) $\qquad\qquad\underline{3x + y = 20}$
Subtract (2) from (1) $\quad 4x \qquad = 24$
$\qquad\qquad\qquad\qquad x = 6$
Put $x = 6$ in (1) $\qquad 42 + y = 44$
$\qquad\qquad\qquad\qquad\quad y = 2$
So $x = 6$, $y = 2$
Check in (2) $\quad 3 \times 6 + 2 = 18 + 2 = 20$ ✓

CHAPTER 15

1

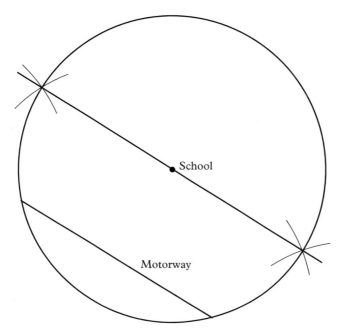

Scale: 1 cm to 1 km
✕'s show two
possible positions.

2

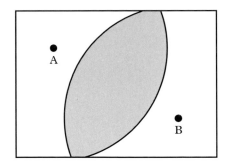

Scale: 1 cm to 2 m
Shaded area is covered by both sprinklers.

3

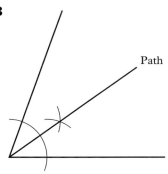

Path

4

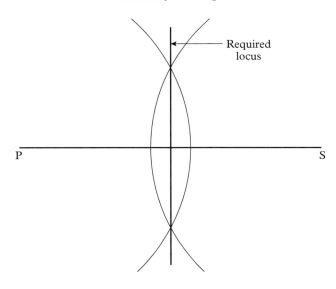

Required
locus

P   S

CHAPTER 16

1   **a, b, d**
     c 2

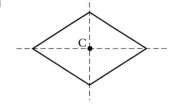

5

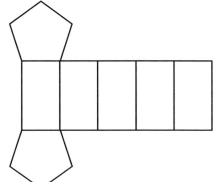

2   **a** 2   **c** 3
     b 1   **d** 2

3   A has 6 spots, B has 4 spots, C has 5 spots

4   **a** Pentagonal pyramid   **b** Cylinder

Exercise 1

1	66	**3**	124
2	396	**4**	399

Exercise 2

1	90	**6**	2140
2	70	**7**	1413
3	216	**8**	5706
4	375	**9**	2775
5	698	**10**	3604

Exercise 3

1	480	**3**	8420	**5**	70 000
2	540	**4**	7770	**6**	90 030

Exercise 4

1	2700	**7**	415 300
2	9100	**8**	900 000
3	74 000	**9**	4 004 000
4	29 100	**10**	9 240 000
5	427 000	**11**	3 010 000
6	840 000	**12**	73 700 000

Exercise 5

1	780	**5**	1950	**9**	3550
2	840	**6**	1360	**10**	6080
3	780	**7**	3680	**11**	8730
4	690	**8**	1250	**12**	36 750

Exercise 6

1	74	**3**	189.1	**5**	208
2	325	**4**	723.4	**6**	4

Exercise 7

1	6586	**3**	1640	**5**	7039
2	2294	**4**	72 180	**6**	401

Exercise 8

1	675	**5**	9550	**9**	11 990
2	1824	**6**	14 634	**10**	53 365
3	6519	**7**	17 595	**11**	53 534
4	10 504	**8**	26 628	**12**	88 021

Exercise 9

1	33	**3**	11	**5**	41
2	13	**4**	22	**6**	121

Exercise 10

1	27	**5**	13	**9**	108
2	17	**6**	17	**10**	142
3	16	**7**	15	**11**	177
4	13	**8**	18	**12**	54

Exercise 11

1	10.5		**5**	88.4
2	44.5		**6**	120.8
3	39.25		**7**	44.625
4	30.25		**8**	120.5

Exercise 12

1	45	**5**	50	**9**	29
2	62	**6**	30	**10**	24
3	67	**7**	35	**11**	66
4	46	**8**	29	**12**	92

Exercise 13

1	$58\frac{1}{6}$	**7**	$15\frac{1}{7}$
2	$51\frac{1}{13}$	**8**	$30\frac{7}{17}$
3	$51\frac{1}{8}$	**9**	$16\frac{1}{13}$
4	$42\frac{1}{22}$	**10**	$17\frac{2}{9}$
5	$22\frac{11}{12}$	**11**	$202\frac{3}{7}$
6	$27\frac{1}{4}$	**12**	$581\frac{2}{5}$

Exercise 14

1	82	**5**	816
2	6	**6**	940
3	482	**7**	700
4	93	**8**	50 000

Exercise 15

1	54	**5**	840
2	71	**6**	84
3	82	**7**	400
4	64	**8**	40

Exercise 16

1	41	**5**	376
2	16	**6**	154
3	93	**7**	22
4	105	**8**	306

Exercise 17

1	3.27	**4**	0.879
2	9.64	**5**	0.301
3	0.34	**6**	1.03

Exercise 18

1	1.825	**4**	0.176
2	4.791	**5**	0.102
3	0.234	**6**	0.3102

Exercise 19

1	2.8	**9**	0.814
2	6.5	**10**	0.096
3	0.39	**11**	0.00317
4	0.23	**12**	0.0069
5	290	**13**	8940
6	740	**14**	3480
7	2630	**15**	8000
8	78	**16**	1320

Exercise 20

1	$\frac{7}{9}$	**4**	$\frac{8}{5} = 1\frac{3}{5}$
2	$\frac{11}{12}$	**5**	$\frac{13}{8} = 1\frac{5}{8}$
3	$\frac{11}{12}$	**6**	$\frac{17}{11} = 1\frac{6}{11}$

Exercise 21

1	$\frac{3}{8}$	**5**	$\frac{11}{18}$	**9**	$\frac{17}{30}$
2	$\frac{4}{15}$	**6**	$\frac{1}{2}$	**10**	$\frac{9}{14}$
3	$\frac{1}{2}$	**7**	$\frac{7}{12}$	**11**	$\frac{29}{40}$
4	$\frac{8}{9}$	**8**	$\frac{13}{21}$	**12**	$1\frac{1}{12}$

Exercise 22

1   $\frac{3}{8}$

2   $\frac{1}{5}$

3   $\frac{4}{11}$

4   $\frac{3}{10}$

5   $\frac{1}{2}$

6   $\frac{7}{12}$

7   $\frac{1}{12}$

8   $\frac{1}{6}$

9   $\frac{5}{24}$

10   $\frac{5}{12}$

11   $\frac{7}{24}$

12   $\frac{7}{44}$

Exercise 23

1   $\frac{1}{3}$

2   $\frac{1}{3}$

3   $\frac{1}{3}$

4   $\frac{2}{3}$

5   $\frac{2}{3}$

6   $\frac{3}{5}$

7   $\frac{2}{3}$

8   $\frac{2}{3}$

9   $\frac{5}{7}$

10   $\frac{1}{5}$

11   $\frac{1}{2}$

12   $\frac{19}{40}$

Exercise 24

1   **a** 34 mm   **c** 1310 mm
   b 128 mm   **d** 1137 mm

2   **a** 410 cm   **c** 1210 cm
   b 280 cm   **d** 32 400 cm

3   **a** 8800 m   **c** 15 000 m
   b 9700 m   **d** 100 000 m

Exercise 25

1   **a** 3000 g   **d** 3 kg
   b 7000 g   **e** 6 kg
   c 21 000 g   **f** 0.8 kg

2   **a** 3500 g   **d** 6.5 kg
   b 7200 g   **e** 3.2 kg
   c 3840 g   **f** 2.8 kg

3   **a** 5000 mg   **d** 3 t
   b 8 g   **e** 4000 kg
   c 1.64 g   **f** 2500 kg

FREDA LIGHTFOOT

Fools Fall in Love

CANELO

First published in the United Kingdom in 2006 by Hodder & Stoughton

This edition published in the United Kingdom in 2021 by

Canelo
31 Helen Road
Oxford OX2 0DF
United Kingdom

Copyright © Freda Lightfoot, 2006

A CIP catalogue record for this book is available from the British Library.

Print ISBN 978 1 80032 490 9
Ebook ISBN 978 1 78863 669 8

This book is a work of fiction. Names, characters, businesses, organizations, places and events are either the product of the author's imagination or are used fictitiously. Any resemblance to actual persons, living or dead, events or locales is entirely coincidental.

Look for more great books at www.canelo.co

Printed and bound in Great Britain by Clays Ltd, Elcograf S.p.A.

I

Chapter One

1956

It was even noisier than usual on Champion Street Market: the stallholders calling out their wares, the Salvation Army band performing their normal Saturday morning routine, buses roaring by, splashing through puddles and soaking traders and customers alike. A brisk October wind slapping the wet canvas over the market stalls, making them sound like ships in full sail.

So much noise and bustle that no one paid any attention as a young woman walked by, glancing longingly at the fish stalls with their colourful array of pink salmon, glistening white cod and plaice, yellow-smoked haddock, the slate blue of cockles, and glistening heaps of whelks and oysters.

'Pair of kippers for threepence, love. Buy your pippins here. Best Cox's orange pippins in all of Manchester.'

The girl showed little interest in a stall decked out in witches' hats and capes, red feather boas and masks, obviously in preparation for Hallowe'en at the end of the month. She lifted her, elfin face to smell the tantalising aroma of the sea, so far away from her now, mingling with hot baked potatoes, fried onions, freshly baked bread, and chocolate from Pringle's Chocolate Cabin. Her stomach growled.

But on reaching Barry Holmes's fruit and veg stall she lingered for a long, telling moment over the bright globes of fresh oranges, the bloom of cauliflowers, red cabbage, luscious pears and plums, and rosy tomatoes, her cornflower blue gaze resting hungrily upon the shining red apples.

'Go on, you can have one, chuck. I'm in a generous mood today,' Barry said.

She glanced up at him, surprised and embarrassed that he should catch her looking, holding one clenched fist against the hollow of her empty stomach as if willing it to resist. Then she cocked him a cheeky grin and swiftly slid an apple into her pocket. She might be hungrier still later, if she didn't find what she was looking for.

'Know of any jobs going, mister?' she asked, since he'd proved to be friendly.

'On this market, in this weather? You'll be lucky.'

She laughed again. 'You sound like Al Read.'

Her long blonde hair, held back from her face by a wide Alice band, fell to her shoulders as straight as the rain that had been coming down in torrents all morning, and every bit as wet. It had thankfully stopped now, much to the market traders' relief and a rare glint of sunlight illuminated the girl's translucent complexion, making the elfin features appear all the more delicate. Barry thought she seemed a bit sad and pinched looking, in sore need of a good meal, with the faintest blue shadows beneath her lower lashes. Yet there was something in the blue eyes as they looked about with such lively curiosity that appeared to be piquant and challenging in their sparkling depths. A radiance that had he been twenty years younger, he'd have fallen in love with her on the spot.

'You could try Belle's cafe, there's rarely a week goes by when one of her waitresses hasn't upped and left. But then that's because she's the very devil to work for.'

A voice rose above the general din, loud as a foghorn. 'Fran! Amy! Where the hell are you? I'll batter your brains in when I get my hands on you, you great lummocks.'

Barry snorted with laughter. 'That's Big Molly. Take no notice, her bark is worse than her bite. You could always try her pie stall. She's got two daughters of her own who are supposed to help out, mind, but she might be glad of the change. They give her a lot of grief one way or another. Nice enough girls at heart, but at each other's throats the whole time. Like all sisters, I suppose.'

The girl smiled. 'Thanks, I'll maybe give it a try.' She half-turned away, and then seeming to come to a decision returned to Barry's stall. 'I heard there was another pair of sisters here, Higginson, I believe the name is.'

'Oh, aye, they have the milliner's stall. That's a pair of spinsters on the inside market, in the market hall. Do you know them?'

She was shaking her head and backing away at the same time. 'Thanks for your help. I might give them a try.'

'Good idea, if you're fond of hats.'

Barry watched her go, his gaze on the soft tresses of her hair, drying to a silvery fairness in the sun. It crossed his mind that it would be a pity to hide such beauty under a hat.

–

Big fat Molly Poulson slid a warm meat and potato pie into a brown paper bag, and, bag in hand she took a step back to yell down a flight of stone steps. These led to a storeroom below the market hall, to which her daughter Fran had disappeared a good half hour since. 'Get up here this minute, girl, if you know what's good for you.'

Close to dinnertime, the stall was busy. Smiling sweetly at her customer, Molly smoothly changed gear to a softer tone. 'There y'are, get that down yer neck and it'll warm the cockles, all right? Aye, we do have more steak puddings, and no love, I haven't the faintest idea what the hangment is taking that girl so long fetching them. Anyone would think she was making them from scratch. That I didn't get up at four to bake them meself.'

Sadly, Fran was paying not the slightest attention to her mother, even when she heard her full-throated shout. At that precise moment she was too busy savouring the pleasure of having Eddie Davidson's tongue down her throat and his long, sensitive fingers squeezing her plump breast. She gave a low moan, rubbing her hips provocatively against his so she could feel the satisfactory hardness of the bulge in his trousers.

He paused long enough to curse softly beneath his breath. 'You're a tease, Fran Poulson, that's what you are? A right little floozy.'

Fran ran the tip of her pink tongue over lips rosy from his kisses, laughing when she saw his eyes glaze over her with desire. 'I can't imagine what on earth you're talking about. I'm nothing but an innocent lass enjoying a bit of a kiss and cuddle. No harm in that, now is there?' She lifted a pair of fine eyebrows, widening her amber eyes in pretend outrage. 'Are you saying you want more than kisses and a quick feel? Well, strike me down with a feather. What could you have in mind?'

'I'll show you what I have in mind.' He pushed her back against the rough brick of the wall, trapping softly rounded arms above her head with a neat flick of one hand, while the other pushed up her skirt. He stopped her squeals with his mouth as he homed in on his target.

Out in the market, Molly was beginning to lose patience. Not so the customer, who knew that she'd find no better steak and kidney puddings, not in a ten-mile radius, than she could buy here at Poulson's. 'I'm sure they'll be worth waiting for,' she said with a smile, attempting to pacify Big Molly.

Hands on hips and raising her voice several decibels so that she could easily have been mistaken for a sergeant major yelling at recruits on parade, her large frame affording her excellent lung capacity, Molly let rip one more time. Calling first for one daughter, and then the other, she lifted up her several chins, cocked her head to one side and waited, as if expecting them to materialise up through the cobbles beneath her feet.

This was her usual way of dealing with recalcitrant family members, assuming she wasn't near enough to take actual physical reprisals against whoever was disobeying her; a state of affairs her two daughters and one son preferred to avoid, if at all possible. They were more than ready to cross their mother, and did so on a regular basis at the least opportunity, but never when they were within grabbing distance.

'That lass should be here,' Molly informed her customer, outrage in her deep booming voice. 'Right beside me at this pie stall when there's work to be done. But then, when was that little madam ever where she was supposed to be? Bane of my life, daughters. If it's not one, it's the other.'

The woman took one look at Molly's fierce glare and began to go off the whole idea of steak and kidney puddings. 'Look, I'll come back tomorrow, shall I? We can have something else for us supper tonight.'

But Molly was having none of that. She wasn't prepared to allow the customer to escape, nor lose the business from the queue lining up behind her. Didn't the appetising aromas from her stall bring them from miles around? 'Don't you fret, love, she'll come this time if I have to drag her up by her hair. *Fran!* Are you making your last will and testament or what? 'Cause you'll need one when I get me hands on you. How long are you going to be down there fetching them puddings? I've customers waiting.'

Her mother's voice buzzed in her ears like an angry bee as Fran's excitement mounted, the weight of her lover's body leaving her breathless, although, disappointingly, he'd stopped kissing her now. He had both hands on her buttocks and was trying to lift her on to him, which wouldn't be easy since she was no lightweight.

A part of Fran knew it was in her interest to obey Big Molly, not the kind of mother who was easy to ignore. Oh, but didn't she fancy Eddie like crazy? And he seemed to like her, so to hell with her mother.

'Get on with it, Eddie, we've just time for a quick one.'

And it wouldn't be the first time. She was no shrinking virgin, and at twenty-one why should she be? It wouldn't take Fran more than a minute to reach satisfaction. Eddie was nothing if not skilled, so flexible he could take his time and linger over their lovemaking, or be as swift and efficient as the situation required.

Fran had every intention of escaping Molly, and the ties of home life, and finding a place of her own now that she was of age.

Just as soon as she could get a bit of cash saved up. She had plans for her future, and they didn't include spending her days slaving away on a market stall. She'd happen have a business of her own one day, where she could make other folk do the running round for her while she sat back and pocketed the cash.

What's more, she had absolutely no intention of tying herself down with one man; of donning the chains of matrimony and sinking into the oblivion of domesticity. Fran shuddered at the prospect.

So it hadn't come as too great a shock when she'd learned that Eddie was already married. Fran believed that she'd taken it really well, considering he'd lied to her for some weeks on the subject. But in all honesty she hadn't been in the slightest bit disappointed, or concerned, and if people saw her as a trollop for that, then let them. The old fuddy-duddies could think what they liked. Mam, Dad, and her stupid sister, Amy, too.

Fran's thoughts were interrupted by the heavy tread of her mother's feet on the stone step, and she instantly decided that this was neither the place nor the time, after all. Besides, best not to let Eddie think her too easy, however willing she might be for a bit of the other.

'Gerroff!' she said, as if he were about to violate her against her wishes. 'Get your hands out of me knickers, you bad boy. Who do you think I am, some cheap tart?'

Pushing him firmly away, Fran tossed back her bleached blonde curls, straightened the short tight skirt that had crept up her plump thighs in the excitement of the tussle, and pinged her bra straps back into place. Then reaching up, just to show she wasn't really cross with him, she grabbed him by the chin and gently bit his lower lip. 'See you later, alligator.'

'Christ, Fran, you can't leave me like this!'

Laughing delightedly, she snatched up the tray of steak puddings and skipped up the steps while Eddie flopped against the wall with a low, agonised groan, knowing he'd have to stay there until parts of his anatomy had returned to normal. He was beginning to wonder why he'd ever got himself involved with the stupid cow in the first place. There were plenty of other women just as willing, and much less likely to blow hot and cold on him. Even Josie, his sad neglected wife, was less trouble than this, and didn't require feeding in posh restaurants or tanking up on brandy and Babycham before she agreed to open her legs.

Molly, in no mood to wait a moment longer, met Fran on the stairs. Snatching the tray from her daughter's hands, she dropped it on to the stall with a hiss. 'I'll speak to you later, madam.' Then catching sight of a girl with a tousled head of blonde hair, held in place by an Alice band, bent over her pies, she snapped, 'Can I help you? Only, there's a queue back there, if you haven't noticed.'

'I was only looking.'

'If you've touched one of them pies, that'll cost you a tanner.'

'I haven't got a tanner.'

'Well, take your nose away then.'

The girl in the Alice band backed off a pace, but the moment Molly moved away to serve the next customer, she snatched up a pie, turned tail and set off at a run across the cobbled setts, Molly Poulson's screech of outrage resounding in her ears.

Chapter Two

Patsy couldn't believe how stupid she'd been. Hadn't she sworn to herself never to do such a thing ever again, not after what happened the last time? Oh, fudge, why hadn't she simply asked about a job as she'd intended? Because she didn't want to work on a pie stall, that's why.

She ran headlong through the market, tripping over dogs, colliding with prams, falling over orange boxes, and sending their contents rolling all over the cobbles, heedless of women and old men shouting obscenities after her. And all the time she could hear the heavy footsteps of her pursuer gaining on her.

Gasping for breath, sides splitting in agony, Patsy knew she should have stopped dallying and putting the moment off and gone straight to the hat stall and the Higginson sisters. She should have gathered her courage and stuck to her original plan. She didn't have to tell them anything, not right now. In any case, she needed the money. Didn't they owe her that much at least? So why steal the damn pie? Why be so stupid, just because she was hungry? Oh, but how could she resist? The smell of those delicious pies had utterly defeated her.

Patsy could feel the greasy warmth of the stolen pie clutched tight against her pounding heart, which itself competed with the sound of the heavy footsteps behind her, growing louder by the second. A half glance back over her shoulder told her that this woman wasn't for giving up. She might have the girth of an all-in wrestler but she also had the stamina of an athlete, and her age didn't appear to be any sort of handicap.

Looking around, Patsy realised that she'd run into the market hall, her heels ringing on the mosaic-tiled floors, echoing in the high chamber of the vaulted, iron-framed building.

'Stop, thief! Stop, thief! Catch the little bleeder, someone! She pinched one of my pies.' Big Molly was gaining on her. People were turning and staring.

And then, to her horror, Patsy saw the hat stall ahead of her. A middle-aged woman standing beside it paused in reaching for a hat to see how the chase turned out. Without thinking, Patsy ran towards her and flung herself into the woman's arms, just missing by seconds being snatched by Big Molly's fat fingers. Patsy heard the woman's cry of surprise, felt her thin, wiry frame jerk, but, amazingly, she held on, sheltering Patsy with the warmth of an instinctive embrace. Then she put the girl gently behind her, at a safe distance from her pursuer.

Patsy began to gabble, her one thought being to save her own skin. 'I didn't mean to do it. I swear. I don't know what came over me.'

Big Molly had skidded to a halt and was standing, hands on hips, breathing so hard Patsy wouldn't have been in the least surprised had flames roared from her nostrils.

'Don't let her take me, please! I don't want to go to jail.' If the police were called, it wouldn't just be a year's probation this time; they'd lock her up for good and throw away the key.

'She should be hanged, drawn and quartered,' said Big Molly, her voice a low growl.

'What is this all about?' Clara Higginson disentangled herself from the girl's clinging fingers and addressed her question directly to her. 'Did you really steal this pie from Molly's stall? If so, then you are a thief and should be punished.'

For the first time in her life or at least a long while, since she didn't hold with tears, Patsy began to cry. Not so much for the fact she might end up before the beak, or dangling from the end of a rope, but for all the trouble she'd taken to find this place and to get here, only to cock it all up when she was within sight of her goal. 'I only borrowed it, I was hungry,' she retaliated, her voice an angry wail.

'Huh, I'd like to know how you can borrow a pie?' said Molly, in a reasonably matter-of-fact tone. She was struggling to keep her temper on a short leash, since Clara had got herself involved.

'I'd have paid you back, once I had some money. You didn't have to chase me, you miserable old...'

Big Molly opened her mouth to retaliate but Clara shushed them both with a slight lift of one hand. 'That is no excuse at all. Do you know what people usually do when they need food? Answer me, child. Do you know?'

Hating herself for being put in the wrong, and her accusers even more for being right, Patsy answered in her most truculent voice, 'They work.'

'And why do they do that?'

'To earn money.' She turned pleading eyes up to Clara. 'I did want a job, honest. That's why I came here to Champion Street Market. But not on a pie stall, begging your pardon, I'm fair starved. I wanted to work here, on this fine hat stall.'

'Flattery will get you nowhere,' said Clara, a hint of wry amusement warming her voice.

'But it's true, cross me heart and hope to die. I heard about your famous millinery stall and knew I'd love to work here. Give me a job, missus, you won't be sorry.' Oh, drat and damnation, Patsy thought. She could see by the expression of disbelief on this woman's face that she'd screwed up her chances. Patsy could kick herself, she could really, and swallowing her pride decided to give it another try. 'It's only a pie, for God's sake. I'm ready to work and pay for it. Don't put me in the clink, missus. Give me another chance, I'm begging you.'

There was a pause during which all Patsy could hear was Big Molly's heavy breathing, and the crack of straw as Clara Higginson picked up a hat and started to smooth out its brim with her fingers, as if it might help her consider the options.

'We seem to have a problem here, Molly. What do you reckon we should do with our miscreant? Should we give her a second chance or call the police?' Another pause, longer this time.

'You know my opinion of girls, Clara. They're nothing but trouble. I've certainly enough with me own two, I'm not taking responsibility for anybody else's.'

Clara frowned. 'I couldn't possibly consider hiring her myself. That's my sister's job and she isn't here. She'll be back shortly when she's completed her business.'

Molly folded her ham-like arms. 'Annie wouldn't take kindly to having a thief on her stall in any case. I'd think carefully before I took any undue risks, if I were you. You know your Annie.'

'I do indeed.' Clara looked at the girl who had run to her for help, little more than sixteen or seventeen at most, and something inside her wrenched, a twist of the heart with which she was all too painfully familiar. How many times had she watched girls over the years and thought Marianne would be about this age now. If only... before pushing the thought away and ruthlessly getting on with her life. Where was the point in looking back? As Annie frequently and caustically reminded her?

Except that no daughter of hers would ever have behaved like this, so audacious and brazen. Was that the word? Not a pleasant description. But then what product of a respectable home would look like this? The girl was dressed in a scruffy red circular skirt that dipped at the hem, a cardigan worn fashionably back-to-front though it had seen better days, judging by its matted wool in a faded turquoise, plus a pair of white dangly earrings in her pierced ears. Clara thought it was at least a point in the girl's favour that her face wasn't plastered with pancake make-up and scarlet lipstick, although nor was it particularly clean. It certainly didn't glow with health like it should, as Marianne's would surely have done. But her hair seemed clean, washed by the morning's rain, and held neatly in place by an Alice band in the same turquoise as the cardigan.

Nevertheless, despite her unprepossessing appearance, Clara recognised a thinly disguised vulnerability behind the girl's fierce bravado. A deep anger against someone or other buried beneath the insolence: this was a troubled child in need of a little tender loving care. Clara set the straw boater back on its stand, feeling her heart constrict and then start to soften. 'Maybe I should take a chance.'

The girl stopped snivelling upon the instant, as if a switch had been flicked, and glancing from one to the other of the two women, hope dawning in her bright blue gaze.

Clara turned again to Molly. 'I would be happy to pay for the pie, to see that you suffer no loss, if you agree to take the matter no further. For my part, I will undertake to speak to my sister about the possibility of procuring honest employment for this girl. If we cannot provide it, I'll find someone who can.'

'You're a generous woman, Clara Higginson.'

Clara smiled. 'Annie would say I'm easily taken advantage of.'

Big Molly put one of her plate-sized hands on the other woman's shoulder and smiled, all the anger seeming to drain out of her. 'No, you've a soft heart, that's all. Something your Annie lacks.'

Clara hid a smile as she reached for her purse and, handing over a few pennies, said, 'We have an agreement then?'

Molly weighed the pennies in her fat fist and scowled at Patsy. 'You don't know how lucky you are, lass. Personally, I'd as soon see you boiled alive in my meat pan as see you get off scot-free.'

Patsy gulped but judged it wise to say nothing further. Her fate seemed to have been taken out of her own hands.

Clara was chuckling. 'Oh, I wouldn't say she's entirely off the hook. As you rightly say, Annie doesn't hold with thieving. She stands no nonsense from anyone doesn't my sister.'

Big Molly smiled. 'Eeh, that's true. You might long for a quiet prison cell before you're done, girl, you might indeed.' Whereupon she strolled off, jingling the pennies in her apron pocket, still chuckling.

'Oh, bugger!'

Clara was startled. 'We'll have no swearing here, girl. That's an absolute rule.'

Patsy cast a wary glance at her new employer and felt deep regret that she wasn't experiencing the excitement she should have been feeling at this moment, or any sense of relief or comfort. She'd spoiled everything, yet again, as she so often had in the past. And if the other sister was even worse than this one, heaven help her.

—

Amy Poulson had heard the rumpus, and chosen to stay well hidden until it was over. It was always best to keep out of the way when her mother was on the rampage, particularly where her elder sister was concerned. Once Mam had disappeared inside the market hall, Amy slipped seamlessly into place behind the pie stall and carried on serving so that customers craning their necks to watch the unfolding drama were reminded of their real purpose for being there, and gave precedence to their hungry stomachs.

Her sister was already flashing smiles and acting as if nothing untoward had occurred. Amy was under no illusions as to what exactly Fran had been up to, turning into a right little fast piece, no bones about it. She'd end up with a reputation if she carried on like this, which could scupper Amy's own chances of persuading Mam to view her love life in a kindly light.

'I suppose you were with that Eddie. I do wish you'd show a bit more sense,' Amy muttered under her breath as they met at the cash till at the same moment. 'It'll end in tears, mark my words.'

'I'd be obliged if you'd keep your nose out of my affairs. When I want your opinion, I'll ask for it,' Fran said, slamming the till drawer shut with a loud clang, very nearly trapping her sister's fingers in it. Not that Fran cared, being nagged by her mother was bad enough, but she drew the line at being lectured by her little sister.

'I'm only warning you what might happen if you carry on like this.' Amy cast her a furious glance before turning self-righteously to serve a customer. 'There you are, Mrs Dawson, three pork pies. Will there be anything else?'

'And who are you to offer advice?' returned Fran through gritted teeth, smiling at a customer nonetheless as she handed over two sausage rolls and a pasty. 'You love to see yourself as Mam's favourite, taking her side in everything.'

'That's because I've inherited her good sense.'

'So what does she say about you seeing that Romeo then?'

Amy had the grace to look uncomfortable but quickly masked her emotions as she pretended to be fully occupied serving customers.

'Ah, just as I suspected. You haven't plucked up the courage to tell her yet, have you? Huh! Some favourite you'll be once Mam finds out who her darling younger daughter is knocking around with. None other than Christopher George, son of her arch rival.'

'Shut up! Leave Chris out of this.'

'Maybe I should let drop a few hints.'

Amy's fierce glare might have skewered her sister to the spot, but the very evident fear behind her eyes only made Fran laugh, which infuriated Amy all the more. 'If you say one word, you'll live to regret it, I swear.'

'Ooh, I'm shaking in me shoes.'

'Trouble with you is you can't think beyond the end of next week, the end of your painted finger-nails or a good...'

'Go on, say it, why don't you? I'd like to hear the word come out of your prissy little mouth.'

'Don't you dare call me prissy! My Chris respects me, but you wouldn't understand anything about respect, would you? All you care about is having a good time.'

'Better than sitting at home every night with me legs crossed.'

The next customer, patiently waiting in line to be served while the two girls snarled and snapped at each other, had finally had enough. 'Which one of you two lasses is going to find time to sell me a steak and kidney pie before I collapse with starvation?'

They both reached for one simultaneously, glaring at each other for a furious second before Amy had the wit to put it into a paper bag and take the customer's money. As if by mutual accord, the girls moved to opposite ends of the counter.

And as each served a long queue of hungry people anxious for their dinners, Fran continued to nurse her discontent that she hadn't reached the pie first, and fumed over her sister's cheek in lecturing her. Wouldn't she give her soul not to have to work here, on the family pie stall. She'd love to find a more exciting way of earning her living. Chance would be a fine thing.

Chapter Three

Amy arrived back later than expected because Chris had walked her home and they'd nipped up a back street so they could share a few kisses and a bit of a cuddle. Sadly, though, it hadn't turned out to be the happy encounter she'd hoped for because, as they so often did these days, they fell to quarrelling instead.

'We've been out twice already this week,' she explained, 'and I've been forced to lie on both occasions. I told Mam I was round at me friend Eileen's, but even she's getting fed up of covering for me. Says I should come right out and tell Mam, easy for her to say. And Mam would be sure to get suspicious if I went out again tonight.'

He'd wanted to pick her up later in the evening and take her to the pictures but Amy had said no. He wasn't pleased. Chris hated the fact they were forced to meet in secret, that he wasn't welcome at Amy's house. Not a sign of the wide smile she so loved, or the usual bright twinkle in his green-grey eyes. No kisses were forthcoming, and he kept his hands thrust deep in his trouser pockets as he frowned and scowled, arguing with her, doing his utmost to persuade her to change her mind.

'I reckon your friend is right, Amy. We can't go on like this. I love you, and if you love me then you'd agree to stand firm.'

'How can I, knowing how Mam feels about your family? And she has enough on her plate right now with Dad being ill, not able to work, and now our Fran acting daft with that Eddie Davidson.' She cast him a most coquettish glance. 'Aren't you even going to kiss me?'

It seemed not. Amy had remained adamant that she wasn't coming out. Consequently they hadn't parted on the best of terms, Chris strode off home with his shoulders hunched and his face set tight. It was only a little quarrel and they'd be friends again tomorrow, she was sure of it, both regretting the harsh words they'd exchanged, but it upset Amy because it was all so unnecessary. Now, as she hastily dabbed away her tears, Amy could hear her mother and father arguing in the kitchen, voices raised in temper as was so often the case in this house. Whenever she heard them like this she felt sick, as if she were the cause of it.

Yet Amy knew that once she'd told them she was in love with Chris George, as Fran had rightly said, the son of their fiercest rival, all conflict between her parents would cease. They'd join forces against her and make a formidable double act.

The wireless was on full blast, some show or other from the London Palladium. Slipping off her shoes so as not to disturb them, although they probably wouldn't hear her above the sound of Victor Sylvester's orchestra, not to mention the din they were making themselves, Amy crept upstairs to the room she shared with her sister. Fran too would be in a bad mood, following their earlier scrap.

She let out a weary sigh. Why did there have to be so much conflict and dispute in her life?

Amy thought that one of the main reasons she and Fran were constantly at each other's throats was because they were in such close proximity to each other the whole time. Their bedroom, like the rest of the house, was small and untidy, since her sister never thought it necessary to put away anything, which might be needed the following day. She took after her mother in that respect.

Right now it smelled of the fried onions Mam must have made for their tea, and the sickly-stale aroma of cheap powder and scent that her sister used in vast quantities.

They would get on so much better if they weren't compelled to sleep under the same roof, and work on the same pie stall together. Every moment of every day and night her sister was there, omnipresent. Forever prying into Amy's life, commenting on what she was doing, or not doing, and endlessly mocking her for what Fran termed her 'goody-goody ways'.

Now, the minute she walked through the bedroom door, Fran swung herself off Amy's bed and jumped to her feet, her round cheeks suffused a guilty pink. Had she been prying into Amy's diary? She kept it well hidden under her mattress, but wouldn't put it past her nosy sister to root it out. Amy decided not to give Fran the satisfaction of commenting upon it. She put her coat and shoes neatly away in the wardrobe and made a mental note to find another hiding place for her very private diary. Then picking up her sister's grubby bra from the rug at her feet, she held it up in front of Fran's nose.

'Does this have a home? Or was it on the way to the wash tub?'

Fran snatched it from her and stuffed it under her pillow. The guilt, if that's what it had been, was swiftly set aside and her face came alive with curiosity. She was clearly itching to know why Amy was late and what she'd been up to. It took mere seconds for her to ask. 'So, where've you been till now?'

'Nowhere.'

'Seeing lover boy?'

'Put a sock in it, Fran. It's you they're rowing about downstairs, not me. You're the one in the mire.'

Fran's full lips drooped in a sulk. Didn't she know it? She'd been listening to the argument hammering away beneath the floorboards for what seemed like hours. She'd very nearly gone down and joined in, but had thought better of it. Just as well. There'd be blue murder done if she showed her face down there. She was about to tell her sister all of this, and seek her sympathy, when she saw that Amy was crying. 'Oh, for pity's sake, not tears again? Look, why don't you go down and tell them, own up to the fact that you love him? Be brave for once in your life.'

'I was going to,' Amy shouted back. 'This secrecy is making us so unhappy we can't go on much longer. But how can I, now they're so furious with you? It's not the right time. I daren't take the risk of antagonising them further.'

'What have I done? Only skived off work for an hour, that's all. Hardly a hanging offence.' Fran gave a little pouting shrug. 'Well, so far as Mam knows that's all I'm guilty of.'

Amy really saw red. 'You think she's stupid, that she can't guess what's going on behind her back? You reckon she doesn't know you're behaving like a right little tart? How can I tell her about Chris and me when she's in such a bad temper the whole time because of you!'

Fran looked shame-faced.

'Eddie's no good for you, Fran. You should give him up.'

'I can't.'

'Why not, for heavens sake? It's not like it'll be going anywhere, will it?'

Fran sat down with a bump on her own bed, clasping her hands between her knees, her face a picture of anguish. 'I don't care, and can't give him up, not yet. I just need him. He makes me laugh.'

How could Amy admit that she envied her younger sister for being slimmer and prettier than she, the favourite daughter, always being the centre of attention for the bevy of boys forever hanging around, and eagerly competing to take her out? At least that had been the case until she'd fallen in love with Chris George. He adored her, and would do anything for her. Fran envied that.

No matter how much effort she put into her own appearance, she despaired of ever looking other than fat, untidy and dishevelled. Crumpled must be her middle name. She was a freak. Admittedly she had good legs, which were rounded or slender in the right places, and neat, delicate feet. The rest of her, however, looked like an apple dumpling with the round solid apple still inside. She'd end up as big and fat as her mother one day, and Fran hated the thought.

True, boys seemed to like her dimpled smile, claimed to adore her peachy skin. Some were ready enough to flatter her by saying she had a pretty face with lovely rosy cheeks, but Fran knew in her heart what they were really after. She believed that no bloke would look her way unless she was prepared to give him what he wanted, in Eddie's case what he clearly wasn't getting from his frigid wife.

It had all started the night she'd gone to the Ritz ballroom with her friend Sal, one of the endlessly changing stream of part-time waitresses at the market cafe. Mam had believed her to be locked in her bedroom as punishment for something or other, Fran couldn't remember what. She did recall being thoroughly affronted that she should still be treated as a child when she was only weeks away from turning twenty-one at the time.

But she hadn't remained confined to the room for long. Fran had slid down the drainpipe, clutching a bag containing her best frock and dancing slippers, climbed over the wash-house roof, then run off to her friend's house. There they'd dolled themselves up, twisting their hair into curls with pipe cleaners, added a dab of Goya face powder and poppy-red lipstick they'd bought at Woolworth's, and were soon ready to take the town by storm.

And didn't they just?

That evening was to prove a turning point in Fran's life. The heady mix of sweaty bodies and loud music in the ballroom excited her as it always did, bopping away to 'Rock Around The Clock' or smooching to 'Love Me Tender'.

She and Sal were regulars at the dancing, although Fran never bagged so many partners as Sal, more often than not being lumbered with the 'friend'. But once Eddie Davidson strolled casually over, everything changed for her. One glance at his sexy smile and she'd been instantly lost. Fran thought him absolutely gorgeous. His fair hair, cut in the latest style, flopped disarmingly over his brow and those charcoal grey eyes had set her whole body quivering with emotion just by the way they looked at her.

That was nearly six months ago and they'd been inseparable ever since. Fran had instantly gone on a crash diet, anxious to make herself more attractive, but he'd insisted he liked her exactly the way she was. Compared her to a full-blown rose, ready for the picking. Fran's stomach had turned somersaults over that. She'd even bleached her mousy, blonde-brown hair to please him, causing no end of bother with her mam.

At first Amy had teased her, saying they'd be hearing wedding bells soon but Fran had swiftly put paid to such speculation by admitting that Eddie was already married. Her prissy sister had been shocked and deeply disapproving but Fran insisted that it was nobody's business but theirs and Amy should keep her nose out. Even so, whenever the two sisters quarrelled, the question always came up, as it had now.

'Don't fret about me, I'm happy as Larry. You won't find me ending up like Mam, looking after a husband and kids from dawn to dusk. Me, slaving away baking pies and puddings, and serving on a market stall all day then coming home to wait on a lazy husband? Not on your nelly.'

'Mam likes looking after us, and Dad can't help being out of work.'

'He could try to do something about it. He never lifts his backside out of that chair, while she waits on him hand, foot and finger like some sort of skivvy. I wouldn't be so stupid! I want a man to look after me, not the other way round.'

Amy sighed, having heard it all before. 'You know that Dad's not been well, and Mam's standing by him till he gets on his feet again.'

'Huh, which will be sometime never! The only time he gets on his feet is when they're taking him down to the pub for a swift half, or to put on an illegal bet. Why would he bother to do anything else with them, when he's got her to run around for him?'

Fran had little time for her father. Mam was always saying she should be more understanding because he'd had a tough war and come back wounded, with a bad hip. He told a fanciful yarn about being shot down in his aircraft, making himself out to be some sort of Second World War hero. Fran didn't believe a word of it. Ozzy Poulson was, in her opinion a layabout, a lazy weakling who was forever ailing. Some hero! She rarely bothered to acknowledge his presence in the house, and since nowadays she was more often than not at daggers drawn with her mother too, home was not the pleasant place it used to be. Fran snorted her derision and said a rude word, which would have had Molly reaching for a bar of Lifebuoy toilet soap to wash her mouth out.

Amy's lovely face took on its familiar pitying expression. 'I feel sorry for you, Fran, I do really. Don't you want to marry and have children? It's what I want most in all the world.'

'That's the kind of daft remark you would make. There's much more to life than a dish cloth and nappies, believe me.' The only exciting things in her life, Fran thought wryly, were the clandestine meetings she enjoyed with Eddie Davidson. But that was half the fun, the fact that they were secret and forbidden, so that his soft little wife didn't find out, and because her mam would do her nut if she ever discovered what her elder daughter was up to.

Fran smiled to herself. Where was the harm in that? Secrets could be such fun.

Chapter Four

If asked, this would not have been the opinion of Molly's next-door neighbours, Clara and Annie Higginson. They might have said that the possession of a secret had blighted rather than enhanced their lives. The tension of it lay between them, like a scab that must never be picked in case it might bleed. Yet they had muddled on, making the best of things, earning an honest living and keeping to themselves, as Annie liked to do.

Annie Higginson had a reputation for being unapproachable and severe. There were many on the market that said she was a bully and had bossed her sister about something shocking. Clara would have laughed at the very idea, although she was deferential towards her sister. Annie's cold grey eyes set close together beneath lowering dark brows, seemed to demand respect before she issued one of her fierce orders or sharply worded criticisms in her deep, husky voice. And she had no facility for enjoyment. The smallest pleasure would be denied on the ground that it was unnecessary.

On a dull Sunday afternoon Clara might suggest they bake a cake for tea. 'You like my pound cake.'

'I do. But as flour makes me sneeze, you should make it while I'm not around and at the stall.'

If Clara suggested a trip to the pictures she'd get another poor response: 'Why would you want to, when you've no idea who would be sitting next to us? We'd be sure to catch their cold, or worse.'

If sometimes Clara chafed at the tightness with which her sister held the reins, and longed for something more out of life, she tried to remain philosophical and stoically cheerful, considering disappointment to be her just punishment. Sins had to be paid for, after all, as Patsy must pay for hers. Unfortunately, exactly as Molly had predicted, Annie was not pleased at the prospect of taking a thief into their employ.

'What were you thinking of to make such an offer? No, don't tell me, I can guess. She looked at you out of milk-soft blue eyes and your tender heart crumbled.'

'Something of the sort, Annie, I will confess.'

The long day was now over and they were at home, cosy by a roaring fire in their tiny house on Champion Street. It might be only a two-up and two-down but it was neat and tidy, kept so by Clara herself, and handy for the market. A few treasures rescued from the larger family home in Southport where they'd been brought up leavened its sparseness, and which they'd been forced to sell on the death of their parents.

Having enjoyed a sheltered childhood, and a good education, they'd always assumed they'd be comfortably off after their parents died. Sadly, that had proved not to be the case. Yet they'd stuck together through thick and thin, and had remained surprisingly close, despite the difference in their temperament. But then appearances could be deceptive, especially where Annie was concerned.

Even so, Clara took the utmost care not to cross her sister. Today there had been a simmering tension between them ever since Annie had returned from her errands and discovered what Clara had dared do in her absence. Now, at last, the question of the girl's future could be properly discussed and debated in private. Clara had been hesitant over her explanation, and aware as was generally the case, Annie would undoubtedly have the final word on what was to be done with Patsy.

She'd enjoyed one small victory. In spite of Annie's initial shock and furious insistence that the girl should be sent packing, Patsy was now safely ensconced upstairs in the spare room, tucked up and fast asleep, her belly full of lamb hot pot. Neither of the

Higginson sisters had managed to prise a word out of her with regard to her circumstances, despite her clearly being homeless, friendless and in possession of no luggage, not even a toothbrush. She wore neither coat nor hat, as if she'd simply walked out of somewhere on a whim. Consequently, she'd been practically soaked to the skin and greatly in need of the hot bath Clara had run for her.

It was to Annie's credit, Clara decided, that she hadn't instantly called out Police Constable Nuttall. But then the girl's outwardly battle-scarred appearance hid her fragility, like a plant that had grown without proper nourishment or sunshine. Her choice of costume might not have been to Clara's taste, the earrings probably acquired in the same way as the pie, since a teenager always liked to experiment a little. Yet the style was in keeping with her age, the dirt on her skin no more than superficial, and her underwear of good quality and perfectly clean. She was most puzzling.

'If we get to know her a little better we may discover where she has come from and be better placed to make up our own minds as to whether she is honest or not. Between us we can surely keep a close eye on her.'

'That won't be easy,' Annie protested, rubbing her brow with her fingertips, as if she had a headache coming on.

'She speaks reasonably well, don't you think? She doesn't sound as if she comes from the slums, maybe from a broken home?'

Annie looked sceptical. The flat planes of her long face, cheeks, brow and chin all deeply angled, with a high-bridged nose upon which were perched her spectacles, seemed sharper even than normal and tense with anxiety. 'Manufacturing a background for her won't help in the slightest. Someone may be missing her badly and looking for her, even calling out the police to search for her. Have you considered that?'

'But she isn't missing them, is she? And she's not a child, a young woman, albeit a confused one. What if she's run away from an abusive father or cruel stepmother?'

'Now you're sounding like the very worst kind of cheap novelette.' Annie made an impatient clicking sound in her throat, as if her false teeth had come loose. 'What if she's a liar as well as a thief? Ask yourself, Clara, how would we recognise the truth, even if she gave her version of it?'

It was a sound Clara was deeply familiar with, and at times she came close to disliking her sister because of her attitude. Her tension rising she felt pain to plead the girl's case and sat, clasping her hands hard in her lap. 'She needs help not condemnation, and surely as good Christians, we are in a position to provide that and assess her situation more fully before handing her over to the authorities. We've never turned our backs on those needing help in the past, have we?'

There was silence.

Clara let it spin out between them, knowing that just because Annie may not be good at showing emotion, did not mean she didn't feel it. But Clara had to make her see how vital it was for her to agree.

After a moment Annie came out of her frowning thoughts and patted her sister's hand, as if Clara were a fretting child who needed to be placated. 'I could not bear it if she hurt you, dear. You know how you too easily allow your heart to rule your head.'

The words may sound understanding and caring, but as always Clara found her tone gently scolding. 'But she's a young, homeless girl.' A long uncomfortable silence again stretched out between them, seemingly forever, broken only by the fall of hot coals in the fire. Clara then shifted forward in her seat. 'What if she were Marianne?'

'Now you're being ridiculous.'

'I mean, what if Marianne were in this situation, equally bereft and homeless? Wouldn't we want someone to take her in and look after her?'

Again a silence, which not even Annie attempted to find an argument to refute this statement.

Clara flopped back in her chair, exasperated. 'I sometimes feel that you don't want me to be happy.'

The irritating clicking sound came again. 'Stop this at once. You're growing positively maudlin. Let us not open up old wounds, Clara, for pity's sake.'

If this remark was meant to close the discussion, it had the opposite effect. It was really daring of Clara to continue to argue so passionately, not being in the habit of standing up to her more forceful sibling, yet she persisted. The two sisters continued to talk long into the night until gradually, little by little, Clara wore down Annie's resistance with the argument that it was indeed their Christian duty to assist the girl. Only hunger had driven her to take that pie, not malice. And surely everyone deserved a second chance.

Clara made no mention of the swear word Patsy had used. Annie would never tolerate profanity.

–

By the time Patsy lumbered downstairs the next morning at around eight o'clock, having been called at seven on the dot, Clara could announce that her future had been settled. She was safe from the police, for now. There would be no arrest. 'But it really is up to you, Patsy, to be expected to work hard, as I have already made clear. If you show promise you might even learn a useful craft. Right now, you can begin by getting yourself off to the stall.'

'But I haven't had my breakfast yet.'

'That is your problem. You were called in good time but chose to stay in bed.' Annie had been all for going up and dragging her out of it, but Clara had insisted she must be allowed to make her own mistakes and learn reality.

Annie had given her that old-fashioned look, the kind that shrivelled Clara's confidence to shreds. 'We will both be responsible for that little madam or the deal is off, and I hope and pray we won't live to regret it. I shall know who to blame if we are both robbed and murdered in our beds.'

Now remembering the conversation they'd had, Clara continued, 'You'll be less inclined to be lazy tomorrow and choose to make a better impression. Now, put on this old coat of mine and you can start by helping Annie with the morning's chores, while I finish tidying up here. Hurry up, my sister doesn't care to be kept waiting.'

Right on cue Annie appeared at the kitchen door, buttoned from throat to ankle into a grey worsted coat. She'd wound a long woollen scarf around her short neck as protection against the cold wind, and pinned her everyday felt hat of the same drab colour firmly in place over her neatly cropped hair. A pair of kid gloves and a black handbag completed the picture, which never varied. She'd been wearing this same outfit every single day for the last ten years to Clara's knowledge. But then, Annie was careful with her money.

'Is she ready?' Annie was ignoring the girl completely and addressing her question to Clara. 'I've a great deal to do this morning. I can't hang about waiting much longer.'

'Get off with you,' Clara said, giving Patsy a gentle push of encouragement as she still hung back. 'What are you waiting for?'

Then, to Clara's great surprise, the girl lifted her chin, transforming her appearance from skinny waif to haughty young miss. 'I'd like to make it clear that I'll not be put upon in the smallest degree. I'm prepared to work for you, for as long as it pleases me to do so, but nothing has been said yet about wages. I insist on being paid at the proper going rate. I will pay you back for the pie, which is fair since I shouldn't have stolen it, but after that, my wages will be mine to keep.'

Clara straightened her spine and considered the girl with closer attention, half admiring her spirit, and half amused by it. She was back in the droopy red skirt and faded cardigan, which Clara had quickly washed and ironed for her overnight, making a mental note that the purchase of alternative attire must be a high priority. 'You'll need to pay for bed and board.'

Irritated, Patsy shrugged this fact aside, as if it were incidental. 'I understand that, but I'll not be used as a skivvy for scrubbing, washing and such like.'

'You must do your share of the chores, Patsy, as we all must.'

'But I'll not have you two telling me what to do all the time, even if I am living under your roof, glad as I am of the work.'

'I should hope you are,' Annie snapped, glaring at Patsy over the tortoiseshell rim of her spectacles. 'I've heard enough of this nonsense. You should be more than glad, girl, to have been spared incarceration in a prison cell, or at best a hefty fine and a criminal record. You should show proper gratitude and be appreciative of our generosity.'

Patsy rolled her eyes, and her lovely young face twisted with cynicism. 'Now where have I heard that before? Gratitude! That's the only reason folk do anything for you these days, so they can feel good themselves.'

'You should learn to watch that impudent tongue of yours or you'll find yourself back out on the streets in a trice. Do you understand? And make no mistake, miss, there will be rules if you are to live under our roof. Most certainly! You won't find me as easy to manipulate as my sister.'

'So long as it's understood,' Patsy persisted, undaunted by the tightening of Annie's lips, 'I'm not to be put upon. I'm a woman now, not a child.'

'That is still open to conjecture.'

Clara watched the incongruous pair leave, Annie's manner stiff-backed and starched, the young girl with a strange mix of restrained excitement and a kind of nervous agitation. But what was she afraid of? Why did she feel it necessary to make such a spirited stand when she had nothing in the entire world to fight against? Did it have something to do with this strong objection she had to feeling gratitude? If so, who had she been forced to show gratitude to, and for what reason? The girl clearly wasn't going to be an easy lodger to accommodate.

'Oh dear, what have I done?' Clara murmured, hand pressed tight against her beating heart. 'What have I let myself in for?'

Chapter Five

Amy was wrapped tight in Chris's embrace, as they lay together beneath the protective arms of an old chestnut tree in the autumn sunshine, as lovers do. They'd enjoyed a trip on the pleasure steamer *Little Eastern*, on the large boating lake at Belle Vue. Found themselves a quiet corner away from the crowds, eaten the meat paste sandwiches they'd brought with them, and kissed till they were all hot and breathless and aching with frustration. It was just as well they were in a public place or they might well have been tempted to go further. Now they were overcome with despair, and swamped with frustration and misery.

'It's right what you said the other day,' Amy conceded. 'We are going to have to tell them soon. We can't go on like this for much longer.'

'I know, love, but you're right too. Let's not kid ourselves that it's going to be easy. Your mam doesn't like me and that's a fact.'

A child skipped past, chasing a ball, his mother calling to him that if he didn't hurry, the steamer would leave without him.

'She's never really met you. It's your family she hates, though I don't know why, save for the obvious – that they're in competition with each other, them both being bakers. But there must be more to it than that. Do you know what it can be?'

Amy had asked this question a million times before, and always his answer was the same, nothing but a shake of the head. 'I did once ask my mother why she wouldn't speak to yours, but she clammed up tight. Said it was past history and none of my business.'

'Maybe they can't even remember,' Amy offered hopefully. 'I do wonder sometimes if that's the case.'

'No, it's far more serious than that. And it's not just because your mam has decided to make cakes as well, instead of concentrating on pies and steak puddings, though I'll admit that doesn't help.'

Amy said, 'I don't know about making cakes, not just yet, but our Robert is setting up proper kitchens so that we can expand. Mam can't make enough pies and puddings in our own kitchen, not now we're so busy. He has big ideas though, my brother, so who knows what he might do with the business in the future? Anyway, your dad's bakery makes pies too.'

'I know, but Mum nearly threw a fit when she heard. Dad had a right job calming her down.'

'Oh, Chris, how will we ever get together? It's so awful!'

'I feel the same love, and I'm at my wits' end. I am really.'

A slight pause, during which the pair clung to each other in their distress, kissing and stroking cheek or mouth, each delicious fingertip, hair, eyes and throat, as if by way of comfort, till they became dazed by emotion, giddy with their love.

Having him touch her so tenderly made Amy's chest go all tight, and there was a sick feeling in the pit of her stomach. She really didn't know how much longer she could resist him when they wanted each other so badly. Chris had been the light of her life for over a year now. She adored his gentle, green-grey eyes, his long, brown curling lashes, and he only had to smile at her for her insides to melt.

He was neither particularly handsome nor tall, just lean and skinny, not padded with muscle like some, though she knew he would like to be and regularly attended Barry Holmes's boxing club in an effort to improve his physique. But since she was only five foot two herself, Amy didn't mind in the least. He was perfect for her. They were perfect for each other, in every way.

They both liked music and dancing, and riding out of a Sunday together on their bicycles as they were doing today. They were neither of them overly ambitious, Chris happy being a milkman, but seemed to share the same simple dreams for the future, and if only things were different they'd be planning their wedding by this time.

Amy knew in her heart that Chris longed to ask her to marry him, but couldn't pluck up the courage to do so because of this insoluble, mysterious problem, which separated their two families. She wished she was twenty-one, old enough to please herself as Fran was, instead of three years younger. Always bitter rivals, right now Amy almost hated her sister for having that freedom.

'Have you told your family yet? Have you told your dad about me?'

Chris shook his head, 'Though I reckon he might've guessed I've got a girlfriend. He hasn't said anything but he doesn't miss much, my dad. Probably waiting for me to confess to whatever it is he knows I'm up to.'

He rubbed his cheek against the smooth sheen of Amy's hair, looped her auburn curls around his fingers to pull her close while he kissed her again. A kiss that swiftly changed from soft and gentle to fierce and demanding, that had him pulling her blouse out of her skirt so that he could slip his hand inside and savour the softness of her. He kneaded her flesh with a reverent gentleness, his hunger for her growing to a painful ache in his loins. He needed her so badly, so desperately. He wanted to make her a part of him, so that they could never be separated again, not by anyone. He reached for her bra fastening, but then thought better of it and broke away, breathing hard.

Chris sat up, put his head in his hands. 'I need you so much, Amy, but I want us to come together in a way that's right, not a hole in the corner like this. I'll tell them tonight, I promise.'

Amy wrapped her arms about him, resting her cheek against his shoulder, her eyelids squeezed tightly shut to stop the tears from falling. There had been so many occasions in recent months when she would have been more than willing to surrender to him, even run the risk of getting pregnant. Maybe if she were, her parents would be keen then to see her march down the aisle. Yet Chris was always the one to call a halt, respecting her too much to take advantage, and sufficiently mature at twenty-two to understand that an unwelcome pregnancy wouldn't solve anything. Might even make things worse.

But telling her parents, her mother in particular, wouldn't be easy. It would be like dropping a bomb in their midst.

'Right, I will too,' she said, wiping away a betraying tear. 'I'll tell Mam and Dad tonight. Then once it's all out in the open, they can do their worst eh?'

'Don't worry, love,' he said, cupping her rosy cheeks between his hands, his voice low and fierce. 'I'll come over about eight, once I've told mine, and we'll tell yours together. I won't let any of them hurt you, I swear it.'

Sometimes Amy felt as if Chris was the only person in the world who really cared about her.

–

It was a quarter to eight and Amy breathed a sigh of relief that at least all was quiet below. No loud voices raised in argument permeated the floorboards this evening, at least so far.

She glanced across at her sister, painting her nails a bright crimson, and drew a steadying breath, Amy said, 'Chris is coming over later to talk to Dad.'

'What?' Fran paused in the painstaking process, small brush dripping spots of red nail polish like blood on to the carpet, as her eyes grew wide with shock. 'You and Chris? Is he going to say…?'

'That we mean to marry? Yes, he is.' Amy nodded, unable to keep the happiness out of her face.

Fran seemed momentarily lost for words, as she rubbed frantically with the sole of her shoe at the red blobs, hoping the smears would blend in with the floral pattern. They didn't.

'He's coming to ask for your hand? Oh, how romantic. Tonight? Oh, my God! He has more guts than I gave him credit for. This I must not miss. What time is he coming?'

Amy's face turned crimson. 'I don't want you anywhere near. We're going to tackle Mam and Dad together face to face. We intend to make it very clear how much we love each other. That we mean to get married and nothing anybody can say will stop us.'

'Well, bully for you, girl.' Fran dropped the brush on to the dressing table top, stretched out her arms and gathered her younger sister into a swift bear hug. It was so unexpected, so unlike her, that Amy burst into tears.

Drying her sister's face with the flat of her hand, Fran said, 'I hope it works out for you. And at least if you marry Chris I'll get the bedroom to myself.'

Amy laughed. 'You do like him, don't you?' Much as Fran brought out all her worst instincts, her sister's good opinion was still important to her.

'You do, and that's all that counts. You stick by him, girl, and don't let anyone persuade you otherwise. But don't expect it to be a double confession. The less they know about my Eddie, the better. Mainly because he isn't mine at all,' she added, half to herself, picking up the brush again. 'You keep your trap shut about him and me, right?'

'As if I'd say anything! What do you take me for?'

So far as Fran was concerned, she was answerable to no one. Free to have fun and enjoy herself if she'd a mind, without anyone controlling her and telling her what to do. It was a good feeling, and in her opinion did no harm to anyone. Except Eddie's wife, but then if the daft cow was so stupid that she couldn't hold on to her husband that was her lookout.

If only her sister would show something of the same spirit, she might find happiness with her lovely Chris, after all. It was the nearest Fran would ever come to a generous thought.

—

'And who might this be when he's at home? Not the rent man, is it?'

This was one of Mam's droll little jokes. Trouble was, Amy wasn't in the mood for laughing. She was far too nervous. They were both standing fidgeting on the mat and there wasn't a word of welcome on it. They stood there long enough wiping their feet for Amy to look around and see her own home as a stranger might, as Chris was seeing it now for the first time.

She hadn't warned her mother of the impending visit so the living room looked as it always did, messy and far from clean with clothes and newspapers strewn everywhere. The milk bottle still stood on the table along with the remains of a half-eaten meal; the blue and white checked cloth was spotted with grease. One of her mother's old cardigans hung from the doorknob, the stockings she'd peeled off when she came home from work were half tucked under a cushion. Amy made an instant decision not to ask Chris to sit down.

Molly's kitchen was the only room where cleanliness and order ruled, just as well since that was where the pies were made, but she showed little interest in the rest of the house, which struck Amy. Her father was sitting in his grubby vest and trousers, feet up on a stool making notes on his newspaper as he listened to the sports' results on the wireless. Beside him, amongst the ash on the smeared brown tiles of the hearth, stood a glass of Guinness. The dog lay at his feet, patiently waiting for the odd crust from the bread he was eating.

And through the dirty lace curtains could be seen a grim view of a long backyard split in two by a line of none-too-clean washing with little hope of drying in the steady drizzle; the old tin bath in which the two sisters had been bathed every Friday night when they were small, before they'd had the bathroom put in upstairs, hung in full view on the wash-house wall.

Amy was overwhelmingly ashamed. Why on earth had she brought Chris here? What would he think of them?

Molly herself stood before him, her large frame swathed in a wrap-around pinny, fat bare legs scarred with knobbly blue veins, flabby arms folded and pursed lips well-nigh invisible above her several chins.

Chris stretched out his hand politely. 'I expect you've seen me around. Chris is the name,' he offered. 'Christopher...' and for a split second Amy thought he was going to come out with it and bluntly announce that he was Christopher George, son of her mam's arch rival. Oh, no, that wouldn't do at all. Swiftly she intervened, eyes wild, her voice sounding panicky and high-pitched.

'He's a friend of mine. We went to the same school. Only, we weren't in the same class.'

'That's right, I'm four years older.'

'Three and a half to be exact, only a bit older than me, since I'm nearly nineteen.' Amy knew she was gabbling, felt as if she were dying inside.

Her father chuckled in his chair in the corner. 'You're a sly one. Getting round to boyfriends now, eh? We'll have to watch you, lass. They grow up too quickly these days, eh Molly?'

'Actually...' Amy took a deep breath, anxious for them to get the whole thing over and done with, and make their escape. Once she'd told them she was in love, however much they might dislike the idea of an alliance between the two families, what else could they do but accept the inevitable? 'Chris and me have been seeing each other for a while now.'

'Over a year,' he added, taking firm hold of her hand.

'That's right, and there's something we'd like to talk to you about – to tell you.'

'You're not up the creek, are you, lass?' her father asked, putting down his newspaper long enough to study his daughter, instead of form for the next race. 'Not in the pudding club, eh?' And Amy found herself blushing.

'No, how can you suggest such a thing? The fact is...'

Her father interrupted again. 'Did you know anything about these goings-on, Molly?'

She didn't answer, too busy staring at the young lovers, her shrewd eyes narrowed in thought, looking very like hard black currants in the large round bun of her face. 'You were about to tell us your name, young man. There's something familiar about you. Why is that?'

This time Amy did get in first, though even to her own ears her voice sounded shaky. 'That's what we want to tell you. This is Chris George. His father is Thomas George, the baker, as you know.'

Somewhere a clock whirred and began to strike. Not a soul in the room spoke a word, or even seemed to breathe, and the heat from the fire became stifling. Her parents sat as if turned to stone, not revealing their thoughts by the slightest flicker or twitch of eyebrow, nerve or muscle. Even her father's pencil had stopped making marks on his newspaper.

Amy's pounding heart began to compete with the clock, hammering into her brain the words she longed to shout out loud – I love him! But she didn't dare. She cleared her throat. 'Did you hear me, Mam? Chris is…'

'I heard.' Swifter than you would expect from a woman her size, Molly moved to the door and flung it open so ferociously that it banged back against the living-room wall. There was already a dent in the plaster from similar occurrences in the past. 'Out!'

'But, Mam…'

'Out, I say, this minute!'

'If he goes, then so do I.'

Chris demurred, 'No, Amy, don't say such a thing. I'll go. Don't worry. I was hoping we could talk things over rationally, in a mature and adult way. I love your daughter, Mrs Poulson, and I mean…'

'Don't say another word, if you know what's good for you. I want you out of my house this minute or…'

'I'll throw you out,' said Ozzy Poulson, rising to his feet and reaching for his stick, as if he meant to break it over Chris's head.

'Okay, I'm going.' Chris held up the palms of both hands placatingly. 'But I don't want you to take this out on Amy. It's not her fault either that we fell in love.'

Amy was feeling frantic by this time. She'd never seen her invalid father move so quickly, nor her mother look so white and angry. 'I'll be all right. You go, Chris. We'll talk later.'

Chris went, though not before kissing her swiftly and gently full on the lips. She loved him for that.

Chapter Six

Patsy Bowman didn't know what she'd let herself in for. Annie was even now explaining to her the mysteries of the cash register which were bewildering, to say the least. Patsy did her best to look alert and interested, but her mind was elsewhere, replaying the events of the last few days in a desperate attempt to come to terms with it all.

Patsy didn't care to admit, even to herself, that she was bitterly disappointed. That would be foolish. Had she imagined the Higginson sisters might welcome her with open arms? Why would they do such a thing after abandoning her in such a callous way? In any case, she wouldn't want them to. They weren't what she'd expected either, or hoped for.

They were old, for one thing, or at least they seemed so to her, particularly Annie.

Clara wasn't so rigid and didn't peer at you over those dreadful horn-rimmed spectacles. Admittedly she was far more malleable than her crochety sister, if a little awkward and reserved. But however well meaning Clara Higginson might appear superficially, the woman must be cold and unfeeling inside. Patsy only had to consider what she'd done in the past, to know that. She was also dull and rather ordinary. Even her clothes were faded and well worn, so money must be a problem.

But then, what had she expected? She'd been looking for answers to a puzzle but was intelligent enough to realise these wouldn't be easy to find, so where was the point in fretting?

When did a dream ever match reality? Never, in Patsy's experience.

All her life people had accused her of being a dreamer. It could be the case. Her probation officer had used the word 'fantasist', accusing her of not being able to tell the difference between reality and fancy.

Patsy had openly scorned the notion, laughed in his face. She understood reality all right, none better. She just didn't care for it, that's all, and sought any opportunity to escape from its fierce grip. Where was the crime in that?

All her life Patsy had dreamed of finding her mother. Sometimes she'd seen her as beautiful and fragile, always intending to return for her daughter one day. But for some reason because she was sick and confined to a wheelchair, or desperately short of money and struggling to better herself, she wasn't able to manage it. Patsy had spent hours watching for her arrival out of classroom and dormitory windows. But she'd never come. That was the fantasy Patsy had spun for herself. At other times, when she was feeling particularly at odds with the universe, or at least her small part of it, she had viewed her absent mother far more realistically.

On those bitter, lonely days, of which there'd been plenty, she'd seen her as wicked and selfish, caring only for parties and a good time, sleeping with men presumably and not interested in bringing up a child. That was the reality. Patsy knew in her heart it was more likely to be the truth. In the end it had been easier to make up her mind that her mother was probably dead.

Never, in her wildest moments, had Patsy considered she might turn out to be a dull mouse of a woman named Clara Higginson. Not that it had been proved absolutely that Clara was her mother. Not yet. That too might be pure fantasy.

'Are you listening to me, girl? Are you taking any of this in?'

Patsy looked up, her expression studiously bland. 'Yes, Miss Higginson,' she lied.

'I very much doubt it. Well, we shall see. Can you add up and subtract? Do you know your times tables?'

The corners of the girl's lips seemed to be compressed together as if she were repressing a giggle, and her eyebrows twitched. Annie did not care for the expression one bit. 'Well?'

A quick nod, followed by a half-choked gurgle. Patsy was thinking, If only she knew how many times I'd been made to write out those blasted tables, as punishment for my impudence or some prank or other.

Annie said, 'I assume you've had an education. Where did you go to school? Was it local?'

Patsy remained silent but her impish smile faded, her pale, delicate features resuming their look of watchful caution, becoming once more politely uncooperative. Why should she open up old sores to tell this old cow that she'd been sent away to board at a school in Harrogate by her foster parents? And how thereafter they'd largely ignored her.

Watching this metamorphosis, Annie stifled a sigh. It was clearly going to be a long process to get anything out of the girl at all, and she really didn't think she had the energy for it.

'Very well, you can begin by brushing all the felts. Do it carefully, always in the direction of the nap. Do you even know what that is? I shall show you.'

Patsy looked on in helpless bemusement as Annie demonstrated, wondering how she would ever learn to live with these two old maids! She would surely die of boredom and claustrophobia.

Their home was small and cramped and the lavender furniture polish they used did not entirely mask the smell of bad drains and rotting vegetables from the market. Patsy shuddered inwardly at the prospect of staying there for any length of time. Why had she come? Why had she imagined she would find anything good here? Anyone who cared!

–

Surprisingly, as the days slipped by, things did begin to improve, albeit slowly. Patsy got used to using the till, and to brushing the felt hats. She even came to enjoy helping people choose a suitable hat to buy for a wedding or social function, although they couldn't claim to get many of that kind of customer since the hats on display were so dull and boring. Or many customers of any sort, come to that. Trade was desperately quiet.

By employing her on the stall, Clara was apparently able to spend more time at home to deal with the housework, which, strangely, she actually seemed to enjoy. Incredible! It seemed to Patsy that the woman was never happier than when she had her arms elbow deep in washing water, or was pounding dough to make bread, or crocheting endless covers for the backs of chairs.

So Victorian!

Clara did, however, buy her a new outfit, if not necessarily the kind Patsy would have chosen for herself, being a sensible pleated skirt and jersey to wear every day when working on the stall. It reminded Patsy of her old school uniform, although she tried not to think about that.

She was at least free to buy whatever clothes she really wanted with her own money. With her very first wage packet she bought herself a pair of tight black toreador pants, and the following week a bright red and wonderfully baggy, sloppy joe sweater. Admittedly, both second-hand from Abel's stall, but utterly cool. She practically lived in these, much to the sisters' surprise and dismay.

The first time they saw her wearing them, they were horrified. 'What on earth are those?'

'The latest fashion,' Patsy said, tying a scarf cowboy-style about her neck. 'I like them.'

'But those trousers are so tight – disgracefully so – you are showing every curve.'

Patsy grinned. 'Sexy, huh?'

Annie had walked away practically bristling with disapproval, like an offended cat. Clara attempted to reason and cajole, to persuade Patsy to return them and choose a nice pair of capris instead, which she'd heard were equally fashionable. 'And isn't that a man's jumper? It's huge!'

'It's supposed to be big. It's a sloppy joe.'

'A sloppy…?'

'Joe. Don't you know anything?'

Then she'd started on about '…those silly earrings…'. Patsy ignored her.

Another time Clara gently suggested that it might be a good idea if she bought a more sensible pair of shoes instead of those dreadful high stilettos which would surely deform her feet if she wore them for too long, and were in danger of ruining the polished wooden floor of the fitting room where customers came to try on the hats.

Reluctantly, Patsy had to concede this probably to be true. She'd bought the shoes off Abel's stall too and they were killing her. Clara very kindly loaned her the money for a pair of black ballerina flatties, which she wore every day at work, but she still loved to wear the stilettos on her days off. Later she teamed them with a pencil skirt, worn long and elegant with a kick pleat at the back. She would strut around the market, hips swinging, striving to look glamorous and grown-up; knowing all eyes were upon her.

Oh, things were definitely improving.

Yet at the back of her mind was a growing worry.

When should she broach the subject? Was it too soon? If she was too impatient they might think she was only after their money. Not that they seemed to have much, though Patsy suspected they were more prudent than poor. Even so, whatever funds they had were of no interest to her. She had another goal in mind entirely.

On one occasion in the first week Clara had suggested that her parents might be worried about her, and that she should write to them or telephone. Patsy responded by saying that such 'parents' as she had wouldn't care in the least where she was, and had refused to be drawn further.

She could tell Clara was longing to pursue the issue, and would, eventually. What she would say then, Patsy hadn't the first idea. All her carefully devised plans seemed to have flown out the window.

The sad fact was she hadn't made a good first impression.

–

Nothing had gone according to plan, but then, when had it ever? Wasn't that the story of her life? Ever since she could remember Patsy had felt obliged to do battle and fight, every concession grudgingly given.

No, that wasn't right. There had been a time when all had been sunshine and play, happiness and undivided attention. She had felt herself to be the centre of the universe. Emily and Arthur Bowman had been her dearly beloved parents, and she their adored child. A safe, ordered world.

And then Emily had got pregnant, produced a baby of her own, and the stars had fallen out of the sky. Nothing had been the same after that. They'd constantly neglected to provide basic essentials such as clothes, hockey sticks and boots for school, money for spends and for school trips. Sometimes they scarcely remembered even to feed her.

The reason for this, Patsy soon learned, was that they weren't really her parents after all. She wasn't even adopted, only fostered. Her own mother had presumably abandoned her as a baby and they'd taken her in out of the goodness of their hearts, because they were childless.

Once that was no longer the case, and when a second baby followed the first, Patsy felt herself becoming more and more isolated. She was the odd one out. Neglected. Rejected. Unwanted. Like a parcel that they'd return to sender only they couldn't locate the forwarding address.

Was it any wonder if she became disruptive and attention seeking, and difficult, to use Emily's own word?

It was just as well they packed her off to boarding school at eight. Patsy had rarely been allowed back since, even during holidays. More often than not she would remain at school, rattling around with the other neglected waifs and strays whose families for some reason or another couldn't have them home.

These were her only friends. Like Mary, whose people worked in Africa, and believed it to be too dangerous for her to travel there all on her own. Or Julia, whose father was in the forces and moved around a lot.

In Patsy's case, however, she knew it was simply because her parents – foster parents, as she was now expected to call them – didn't care for her enough to be bothered. Having her around the place was a nuisance. They had their own daughter now, and a son to carry on Mr Bowmans' business in the fullness of time. Far better she be left at school, with the experts, who understood difficult young girls.

Look on the bright side, Patsy would say to herself. If I'd gone home, I might well have faded away altogether and nobody would even have noticed. That was the reality, which Patsy understood very well, with nothing in the least fantastic about it.

It was reality too that she knew nothing about herself, not even her own name. The Bowmans had bestowed their own upon her as a baby 'for the sake of appearances'. Generously, they allowed her to keep it since she had no other.

So if Patsy made the rest up, who could blame her? Indulging in flights of fantasy and imagining where she might have come from, who her real family might be, kept her amused in dull moments, and helped her fall asleep at night.

Was it any wonder if she got into trouble? Her teachers accused her of being disruptive, of getting in with the wrong crowd: a gang of local youths who were more fun than most of her classroom companions. All right, so she'd truanted, stayed out late, pinched a few sweets and cheap jewellery from Woolies. What of it? Was that any reason to shop her to the police?

Her own father – foster father – did that to her. His excuse was that such behaviour was unacceptable, that it upset his wife and brought disgrace upon his family.

His family, not hers! But then I no longer have a family, Patsy would think. I have no one.

Since she'd left school in June and been forced to return to the Bowmans' home, life had become a living nightmare. As if being

45

put on probation for a year wasn't bad enough, she'd compounded her sins by not passing the right number of exams. But then, Patsy had rarely bothered to turn up to lessons. Where was the point? Who cared?

Arthur Bowman said this meant she'd flung their generosity and sacrifice back in their faces.

It was made abundantly clear that she was no longer welcome in their home, and Patsy almost began to regret not getting those scholarships. If she had, then she might have found herself a good job and made something of her life. Instead, in Arthur's own words, she was 'hoist on her own petard'. No respectable company would employ a girl with a criminal record and no qualifications, so she would simply have to make the best of things.

This apparently meant being used as unpaid help. So long as she acted as skivvy in their kitchen, she would be fed and clothed, after a fashion.

It proved to be a long summer, one filled with fear and depression. But what else could she do? What would happen to her? Would she be confined forever in the Bowmans' basement, to die there an old maid?

And then, out of the blue, they announced one morning that they'd had news her grandmother had died. This had come as a huge shock to Patsy, who didn't even know she had a grandmother, or even that she possessed a single relative in the entire world.

'Unfortunately you are not mentioned in her will. She left you nothing, not a penny,' Emily had coldly informed her, as if Patsy were to blame for this oversight.

That was the moment she fully understood, when everything became crystal clear to her. It wasn't the Bowmans' who had paid for her schooling or her clothes and food all these years. It had been this elusive grandmother, who apparently hadn't wanted her either. And sometimes when she was ill, the cheque would be late, or insufficient for her needs, and Patsy would be obliged to wear clothes she'd outgrown for months on end, or have less to eat than the Bowmans' own offspring. The cruelty of it struck her afresh. She hadn't left it at that. Patsy had demanded to know the full details. Who was this grandmother, and where did she live?

All they knew was her address in Southport, and her name, the one she had refused to allow her granddaughter to use, for fear of scandal.

That was the day Patsy had walked out of the house. There hadn't been any heated words, no accusations, no argument of any sort. They were over long since. She'd been too choked with emotion to consider any kind of confrontation at that particular moment. The Bowmans had bluntly told her the facts, and made some bitter comment about how on earth they were going to afford to keep her in the future. Patsy had responded by saying she could look after herself, thanks very much, and walked away.

It had seemed the best thing to do at the time.

Chapter Seven

Ever since the night Chris was thrown out of the house, relations between Amy and her parents had been strained. She hated any dispute, above everything hating to be at odds with the mother whom she adored. Amy was a sensitive, caring girl who believed everyone should be happy and kind to one other, and would take almost any course rather than provoke an argument. On the other hand, she would be the first at your side if you were in trouble, and seeing the man she loved being so ruthlessly rejected by her own parents was more than she could bear. She had to fight for him, and for the love they felt for each other.

Amy tried on several occasions to reopen the discussion about Chris only to be met every time by a blank wall of hostility. It was so frustrating, and utterly heartbreaking.

'What have you got against him... against his family anyway?'

'You might well ask,' Molly would irritatingly and unhelpfully remark.

'Did you have an affair with his dad or something?' Amy recklessly suggested in desperation. Her mother was incensed.

'Wash your mouth out! As if I would, with that pig.'

'Then what?'

'Never you mind. You're too young to understand, but take it from me that all relations with that young man must stop, as from now, before they go any further. Do you understand? Do you hear me?'

'Loud and clear, but it's too late, Mam, I love him. And Chris loves me. We're going to get wed and there's not a thing you can do about it.'

There was a long, drawn-out silence in which Amy half feared for her mother's health. Molly went purple in the face, fists clenched fiercely by her side as she drew breath so deeply Amy thought she might be about to explode. But she merely turned on her heel and stalked off from the stall without another word.

For a while Amy thought that she'd won, and made her point. But before the day was out her mother confronted her carrying a packed suitcase. A taxi, of all things, appeared at the front door and before Amy knew what was happening she'd been bundled into it, the suitcase placed at her feet, and a ticket to Penrith pressed into her hand.

Worse, her mother climbed in beside her, just to make sure she didn't escape, and accompanied Amy personally right on to the train at London Road Station.

'Get on it, and stop shilly-shallying. You're staying at your Aunt Jessie's for a few weeks, till you get this nonsense out of your system. And don't think you can get off at the next station. This isn't a stopping train and our Jess will be waiting for you at the other end. Don't try telling lover boy where you are either because the farm is in the middle of nowhere and Jess will make sure you aren't disturbed.'

Amy was in tears as the train drew out of the station, fearing she might never see Chris again.

–

Fran was jubilant. Her dear, darling sister had drawn all the flak away from herself, leaving her freer than ever. Unfortunately that meant she had to work a lot harder too, helping Mam with the chores as well as doing longer hours on the stall, but at least she got the bedroom to herself. Definitely a bonus.

She could nip in and out at will, scrambling over the wash-house roof without fear of her sister asking awkward questions, or the risk of Amy inadvertently blurting out what she was up to.

Fran could also indulge her love of experimenting with cosmetics without her efforts being commented on or criticised by her more conventional sister. She tried out different shades of eye shadow, blues and browns and greens, with pencil liner and mascara; devil's horn kiss curls to adorn her forehead, and even put up her hair into a sophisticated French pleat. She'd bought a hairpiece to pad out her bleached blonde locks.

She tried out any number of creams, lotions, facemasks, and lipsticks in a dazzling range of shades from cherry red to strawberry pink. She rifled through her sister's wardrobe, intending to borrow some of Amy's clothes, which had been left behind. Trouble was, few of them would fit her as, infuriatingly, her sister was so much thinner.

Fran bought herself a girdle, making a vow to go on a diet which lasted at least until she'd got it home. Even as she struggled into the tight elasticised garment she was nibbling on a cream horn. Admiring herself in the mirror, Fran found she looked inches thinner. The girdle had done the trick. She'd start the diet tomorrow, or next week. Anyway, Eddie liked a woman who was cuddly, he'd told her so countless times.

He called her his lovely, giggling girl, and couldn't keep his hands off her ripe, plump breasts.

'And these love handles of yours turn me on something shocking,' he'd say, kneading the excess flesh around her middle, and Fran would feel faint with desire. Ooh, he was lovely was Eddie. Always knew the right thing to say to please a girl.

--

Molly too was feeling mighty pleased with herself. In her eyes she'd put paid to whatever nonsense young Amy was up to. See how long romance would continue to bloom with a hundred or so miles between them. Not very long, if she was any judge. Men, young ones in particular, didn't have the staying power. She constantly wailed that she missed Amy, but loved her girls too much to have them fall into the wrong hands.

It was Ozzy who was the one most distressed by his younger daughter's sudden departure. He adored Amy, and loved having her around. Didn't she fetch his slippers for him, buy him his paper each day and make him a cuppa whenever he felt the need? He didn't wish to imagine how he would manage without her. 'You can be a hard woman at times, Molly Poulson. Where's your heart? Sending our lovely Amy away isn't going to solve anything.'

'It's worth a try. If I know young men, he'll soon get bored with her, and find himself another girl to mend his broken heart. And since we know he comes from a family notorious for their selfishness and fickleness, that will happen before the month is out.'

Ozzy was consoled. 'I suppose you're right.'

Neither of them expected to be coping without Amy for more than a month, two at most. Just as well. She was too handy to have around, particularly with the business expanding. The girl was a hard worker, unlike her empty-headed, selfish sister. And Molly missed having a camp with her over a cuppa when the day's work was done.

Even Buster the dog missed her. She'd sat moping and whimpering at the bottom of the stairs most of the time since Amy had left. A small, black and white terrier bitch, she was devoted to Amy and followed her everywhere when she was at home.

'Gerroff with you,' Molly told her, but Buster simply gazed sadly at her with pleading dark eyes and started barking in indignation. 'Oh, don't start, you stupid animal. You'll wake Ozzy up.'

It was only nine o'clock but she was fair worn out. Her husband was already asleep and, knowing she had to be up at the crack to do the baking, Molly liked to retire early too. She'd already undressed, leaving her clothes handily spread out on a chair by the fire so they'd be warm when she came to slip them on again in the morning.

Now the dog was being a pain, and how could Molly take him out when she was already in her old dressing gown and slippers?

Fran was the perfect solution. Her lazy daughter could do the honours tonight. Molly herself had walked the animal round the block for the last week since Amy had gone. Let Fran take on the duty for a change. She might be less malleable than good-natured Amy, but was considerably younger and had far more energy than Molly herself, particularly at this time of night.

'Fran, come and take this animal out, it's driving me round the bend.'

No response.

'Fran?' Surely the lass wasn't asleep already? Molly started up the stairs. The dog became increasingly agitated, barking like a mad thing, and Molly was complaining bitterly by the time she'd puffed her way to the top. 'Fran, for God's sake, this silly animal is yapping it's head off. Take it out this minute, will you? It must be busting to go.'

Whereupon she opened the bedroom door and found the room empty. In that moment Molly realised that she didn't just have one recalcitrant daughter, she had two.

–

She was still there, seated on Amy's bed, when Fran climbed back through the window at past midnight.

'Oh, my giddy aunt, you nearly gave me a heart attack,' the girl cried out as a light snapped on.

'Pity it didn't, that'd save your father having one instead. He'll go off his chump when he hears about this. Are you going to tell me what you're up to, madam, or shall I make a wild guess?'

'How did you find out?' was Fran's first, if predictable, response. It couldn't be her sister who'd told on her, so who had blown her cover?

'It was the dog.'

'What? Learned to tell tales now, has it?'

By the time Molly had explained, Fran was near ready to strangle the creature, and her sister for having left it behind.

'Are you going to come clean or what? Who is it you're seeing? Not another of the George family, I hope.'

'Nobody you know,' Fran said, and unscrewing a small white jar began to slap Pond's cold cream over her face. She had no intention of becoming involved in an argument, not at this time of night. 'Now can I get to bed? We can talk about this some other time.'

'When you've come up with some fanciful excuse, you mean? By your reluctance to explain, I assume I wouldn't approve of him any more than I do our Amy's chap. Why is that, then?'

Fran was wiping off her make-up with a face cloth when she saw understanding dawn in her mother's eyes. Molly always was sharp, but her expression now made Fran's stomach clench into knots.

'He's married, isn't he? Dear heaven, you're having an affair with a married man. Your dad'll kill you – that's if I don't do the job first. What have I done to deserve this? As if I haven't enough to contend with keeping our Amy away from that dreadful family, now you're at it an' all. Haven't I been a good mother to you both? Why would the pair of you deliberately set out to hurt me?'

'This isn't about you, Mam, it's about me. And what our Amy does has nothing to do with me neither.'

'Who is he? Go on, tell me the worst. What's his name?'

Fran sighed, feeling deeply weary. It seemed such a shame. Her mother was ruining what had been a perfectly wonderful evening. She and Eddie had been dancing together at the Ritz and could hardly keep their hands off each other. So much so they'd had to sneak out during the interval and slip up a back street for a quick one.

Eddie had slammed her up against a wall and practically devoured her. His urgency had excited her so much, she'd even forgotten to ask him to use a rubber johnny, as she usually did. Which was a bit worrying, come to think of it. The last thing Fran wanted was trouble landing at her door. Still, once wouldn't hurt, surely. Fran was sure her luck would hold.

There really didn't seem any point in pretending innocence, not any longer. Once her mam had her teeth into you, or rather her dentures, Fran thought irreverently, you might as well lie down and confess. She didn't want to be banished from Champion Street as daft Amy had been. Best to make a clean breast of it, own up, swear to stay away from Eddie in future, and then in a day or two, when Mam had forgotten all about it, they could carry on where they'd left off.

Fran told her mother everything, bragging about the passion they felt for each other as if he was Mark Anthony and she Cleopatra. She gave Molly not only Eddie's name, and the fact that he worked for the gas board, but also inadvertently mentioned where he lived and even what his stupid wife was called.

It proved to be a bad mistake.

–

During the rest of that sleepless night, Molly made up her mind on two points. One, that she wouldn't make any mention of Fran's transgression to Ozzy, not at this stage. The two of them didn't get on, were more often than not at daggers drawn, constantly sniping at each other, Fran having no sympathy whatsoever for her father's situation. So what would be gained by making a difficult situation worse?

Secondly, Molly intended not to be beaten by her daughters' foolishness. If they were daft enough to fall in love with the wrong men, then they must suffer the consequences. Molly was determined to make them both see the error of their ways. She'd put a spoke in the wheel of their respective romantic adventures, or her name wasn't Big Molly Poulson.

She'd already sorted Amy, so all she had to do now was think of a way to stifle their Fran's amorous gallivanting.

Molly was rolling out suet pastry for the last batch of her steak puddings the following morning when she heard a knock at the back door. It was still early, a little past seven o'clock.

She glanced about her with a sigh of irritation. She'd intended to put this last dozen puddings on to steam, then wake the rest of the household and make them all a nice cuppa. A visitor was an unexpected nuisance but she assumed it would be Robert. Who else would call so early?

Life would be so much easier once he'd got the new premises up and running. Her son constantly moaned about the state of his mother's house where Poulson's pies and puddings were made. The kitchen was cramped, although reasonably clean and tidy in comparison with the rest of the house anyway. The untidiness of the living area didn't trouble Molly in the slightest. That was Ozzy's province. Besides, she didn't have the time to be bothered with it. When she wasn't confined to this kitchen, baking, she spent her entire day at the market.

In any case, Molly was of the school of thought that a bit of muck never hurt anyone. Her son, however, did not agree, and kept nagging her about food hygiene or some such nonsense.

Robert had become very particular since he married that fancy wife of his. Mind you, he always had been the picky sort, ever since he was a lad, putting his clothes in the wash long before they really needed it. And since he'd taken up with that Margaret from down Cheshire way, he'd gone even worse. Posh new front door on their terraced house, fancy new car, fresh flowers on the windowsill. The pair of them had big ideas.

Not that Molly was averse to the idea of improvement and expansion. Plans were progressing, although as always, money and time were the problem. So until he had it all set up, she kept on with the old routine, trying to cope with the baking side herself. If only she could persuade Ozzy to get off his backside and help. She'd then get it done twice as fast, but he was too wrapped up in his own pain and depression, and the *Sporting Chronicle*, poor man. Maybe Robert had a bit of good news. She could do with some right now. 'Don't stand on ceremony, chuck, t'door's on the latch,' she shouted, hands still covered in flour.

And there he was, standing on her clean doorstep. Chris George, large as life, his young face such a picture of misery Molly almost felt sorry for him. Almost. Then she recalled who his father was and which family he came from, and her heart armoured itself afresh in its hard shell.

'What do you want? I'm busy.'

'Is Amy here? I haven't seen her in days and I'm worried. Where is she? Why hasn't she met me at our usual spot?'

'Oh, so you have a secret trysting place, do you? Well, not any more, you don't. Our Amy has gone, and she won't be back until she's got you out of her system, which I'm sure won't take long.'

'Gone where?'

'That's my business.'

'Mine too, I love her.'

'Then you'll just have to get over her.'

He looked so shocked and hurt by the very suggestion, it almost made Molly laugh out loud.

'How can I do that? Love isn't like chicken pox, something that you can treat and it will get better.'

Molly snorted her derision, wiped her hands on the back of her stained apron. 'Find yourself another girl, there's plenty around, and leave my lass alone.' With that she started to close the door but, quick as a flash, Chris inserted his foot in the crack to prevent her from doing so.

'Here, don't you start no trouble or I'll call the polis.'

'Just tell me where she's gone.'

'Not on your sweet life! Get over her, it's finished.' And kicking his foot out of the way, Molly slammed the door shut.

Chapter Eight

Patsy became increasingly intrigued and entertained by the comings and goings on Champion Street, by solemn-faced women in drab coats and headscarves rooting through racks of second-hand clothes. They might choose a jumper for young Johnny to wear to school, a skirt for themselves, or a new apron from several pegged up on a clothes line strung over a stall stacked high with towels. And despite the large price tag, which adorned each garment, they would still argue over the price.

She was fascinated by the lines of market stalls with their intricate displays of tablecloths and lace doilies, strings of bags, and ropes of beads and knitted scarves creating a kaleidoscope of colour. The colours and smells were what had struck her most about the market on that very first morning, the hearty Lancashire voices calling out their wares, and the stallholders' droll sense of humour.

Such as Barry Holmes getting his own back on a fussy customer. 'Don't look down your nose at these King Edward tatties. You could fit five pounds in your hat, yer head is that big.'

Amazingly the man concerned thought this so funny he happily bought ten pounds, saying he'd have to borrow Barry's bowler as well to carry them all home.

Patsy remained grateful for his gift of a rosy red apple, but saw Barry himself as a strange little gnome of a man with his sloping forehead and upper lip that was well-nigh invisible. He had large bony hands with long fingers, and straight black hair slicked down with Brylcreem. Yet he was friendly enough, giving her a cheery wave most mornings, although he showed no inclination to repeat his generosity.

And there was Molly Poulson, always striving to draw a crowd. 'Never try flicking mushy peas at your old man, love, they might get stuck in his ears and then he won't be able to hear the foul names you're calling him. Throw a black pudding at him instead.'

As well as pies, puddings, and the essential mushy peas, Poulson's also sold cheese and butter. Patsy loved to watch the stack of yellow cheeses dwindle as they were cut into wedges, weighed and wrapped and slipped into waiting shopping baskets. Huge links of Jimmy Ramsay's prize-winning pork sausages were strung up for all to admire. Baskets of flowers and buckets of roses, crates of lettuces and barrels heaped with rosy apples nestling in sawdust littered the cobbles. Home-made rock cakes as big as doorstops, and perfect eggs, all brown and speckled were sold by farmer's wives on their little clutch of stalls.

Pringle's Chocolate Cabin was a favourite stop whenever she had money to spend. Patsy could choose from slabs of toffee in a range of delicious flavours from raspberry to banana cream, peanut brittle to sticky treacle. Lizzie Pringle would break it into pieces with a little silver hammer. Or Patsy might buy a triangular paper bag filled with pear drops, or milk chocolate buttons covered all over with hundreds and thousands.

Pringle's were famous for their rich chocolate, truffles and coffee creams, montelimar and caramel, none of which Patsy could afford, but she would linger in the cabin simply to breathe in the glorious aroma before treating herself to a bag of dark mint chocolate chips.

Not such a bad place to live, after all.

-

After a few weeks at the market, Patsy decided it was time to test the security of her position. If the test failed, she could walk out and move on before she started to feel settled, got too attached to the place and to everyone in it. Annie was in charge of the purse strings so she was the one to tackle first. Patsy knew she could always appeal for help from Clara later, if necessary.

One of her favourite places was Alec Hall's music stall. Patsy was a member of the Frankie Vaughan Fan Club and back home in Yorkshire she'd left her collection of records, together with all her other stuff. Not that it mattered. There was nothing particularly precious and personal that she missed, but she would like to replace some of those records, and buy Frankie's new one, 'The Green Door'.

Unfortunately, she didn't have anything to play them on, having left her record player behind too.

'I need a record player,' she bluntly announced to Annie one evening. Patsy had waited until she'd set aside her Bible, as it was risky to interrupt her when she was reading it, which she did every evening. Although any time could be a bad time where Annie was concerned.

'I beg your pardon?'

Patsy sighed. 'I'd like a record player, please.'

Annie frowned at her as if a record player were something she'd never heard of in her life before. The sisters still used a wind-up gramophone to play their scratchy, ancient dance music. It sounded excruciatingly bad, like cats screeching in an alley. Every time they put it on, Patsy would stop up her ears.

Annie's response was predictable. 'Why would you want one of those? Whatever it is.'

'To play records.'

'Do you have any?'

'No, I don't. At least, not any more, but I could buy some from Alec Hall's music stall. I'm in the Frankie Vaughan Fan Club.'

It was clear from Annie's expression that she hadn't heard of him either. 'But why would you want to buy records when you don't have anything to play them on?'

Patsy sighed. This was getting silly. It was perfectly clear, however, that there would be no record player. Did that mean the test had failed, that it was a waste of time her staying here because she really wasn't wanted? But Annie was not done yet, never being one to miss the opportunity to give a lecture.

'You've only been here five minutes and already you're making demands. You could always save up and buy your own record player.'

'On what you pay me? You must be joking.'

'My sister, in her generosity, has decided not to charge you very much at all for bed and board, not until you get on your feet, so that needs to be taken into account. When you have proved your worth, which could take some time the way you're going on, I may consider a small rise.'

'Don't I work hard enough for you?' Patsy was still unwilling to admit that the test had failed. After all, Annie was at least offering her hope for the future and the prospect of leaving made her feel ill.

'I am prepared to review the situation in, say, a month.'

With that she had to be content. By way of compensation, all Patsy could hope to do was to go round to Hall's music stall and play records in the music booths, finding little point in buying any, since she had no means of playing them.

But she did secretly retune the wireless and listen to Radio Luxembourg, very quietly, once the Higginson sisters were safely tucked up in their beds.

–

Patsy decided that wearing an Alice band was more childish than cool. She pulled her hair up into an elastic band to form a ponytail, hoping that the new style would make her look more grown-up and glamorous, which in turn helped her to feel happy and upbeat. She would enviously watch Fran Poulson, who always looked so sexy, voluptuous and curvy, swinging her bottom outrageously as she walked along, and try to do the same.

She'd stick out her bust as far as it would go, not happy about her lack of curves. Patsy liked to behave like a tomboy, but had no wish to look like one. She tried stuffing socks down her bra but the result just looked weird and lop-sided.

Once or twice she attempted to strike up a conversation with Fran, although the other girl was a few years older and not overly friendly. She tried asking after her sister Amy, whom she hadn't seen around for a week or two, and was told she was staying with relatives in the Lakes. Fran's expression said much more, that Patsy should mind her own business for a start. Which only confirmed her belief that you never knew where you were with people. If you tried to be open and friendly, it didn't always work.

But her best intentions were to remain aloof and detached from everyone. Patsy grew increasingly content living on Champion Street, and the market folk were such characters. Molly Poulson, for instance, would scowl at her as she passed by. They were just about on speaking terms now, Patsy having paid Clara back for the pie she'd 'borrowed'.

'Let that be a lesson to you,' Molly said, rather mysteriously. Although since she'd got a job as a result of her thieving, Patsy wasn't complaining as crime did pay, rather irreverently.

There were many others.

Sam Beckett, who sold all manner of puzzling items on his ironmongery stall, looked pretty tough to Patsy, although good-looking for a man of his age, unlike his ugly bulldog. Patsy had been terrified the first time she came across the animal. The second time even more so as it bounded towards her and leaped right up, placing its big paws on her shoulders, although fortunately only to lick her face.

'He likes you,' Sam had said, pleased. 'You're his friend for life now.'

Patsy liked Jimmy Ramsay, the jolly butcher, though she wasn't so sure about Winnie Watkins who only nodded to her through the drapery of fabric that trimmed her stall.

'It's none of my business, lass, but are you new around here?' she asked one day.

'Clever of you to spot that,' Patsy insolently responded, and earned herself a boxed ear the next time she passed that way.

Every morning, watching from her bedroom window, Patsy would see the Bertalones pour down the steps of their house opposite and out on to the street, a tide of colour and noisy exuberance, all talking at once so that it seemed a miracle anyone would hear a word anyone else said. Papa Bertalone would always lead the way, marching proudly to his ice cream parlour, expecting his family to follow, while Mama stood on the steps to see them off, waving her handkerchief as if they were travelling miles and not simply to the local school, or to the market to work.

The boys, being Italian, were all dark and good-looking. Patsy would draw in her breath and marvel at their beauty. Sometimes she would spot one of them out and about on the market, but, wracked by shyness, she never dared risk speaking to any of these demi-gods, her efforts to appear tough and in control.

She'd learned that the youngest was called Giovanni and was about eight or nine, then there was Alessandro. The eldest was called Marc, and was the most handsome of the three. But whenever she met them, Patsy would always carefully avoid making eye contact and hurry away.

It was the little girls who delighted her the most.

Their dresses were a rainbow of reds, blues, yellows, mauves and greens, with mismatched sleeves, frilly skirts and collars, polka dots, checks and stripes, all stitched together in a riot of disharmony. It was as if Mama Bertalone was in possession of a huge bag of patchwork pieces from which she would make a random selection. From these she would sew a dress for one of her girls, and when its wearer had outgrown it or become tired of the design, each part would be unpicked and put back into the bag, so that what had once been a skirt could later become a bodice, and in time take its turn as a sleeve or a collar.

Patsy was almost sorry when the sunny October days passed and they all started wearing navy gabardines against the cold and wet of coming winter.

But when she saw them smile and laugh, kiss each other goodbye, her heart would ache. Why could she not be part of a big loving family? For Patsy, watching this daily parade was never anything less than fascinating, for all it reminded her of what she herself lacked.

And as she watched the folk of Champion Street, so they in turn watched her, trying to make up their minds what they thought of this newcomer who had come into their midst.

Belle Garside, who ran the Market Hall cafe and considered herself queen of the market, or would be, folk said, given half a chance, naturally found it necessary to introduce herself when Patsy went in one morning for a bacon butty. She was particularly keen to make her own credentials clear.

'I shall be on the committee once I've won the next election. In the meantime, I have the ear of the market superintendent so you'd best mind your Ps and Qs with me. I heard what happened about that pie you stole from Molly Poulson. I shall be keeping a close eye on you in future.'

'Along with everyone else, so far as I can see,' said Patsy, taking a huge bite of her bacon sandwich. 'Nosy old beggars, the lot of 'em.'

A short stunned silence, and then, 'How long do you expect to be with us, I wonder?'

Patsy lifted her nose in the air and said she hadn't decided yet, but when she did, Belle would be the first to know.

'I can see you've been in the knife drawer. Take care you don't cut yourself, girl. And remember,' Belle continued, tapping Patsy in the chest with one lethally sharp, scarlet fingernail, 'it doesn't pay to make enemies round here. So put a guard on that clever tongue of yours, if you know what's good for you.'

Patsy stood up, saying, 'And next time you take a cigarette from that packet, remember the rest of us poor sods have to put up with the stink of it on your breath.' Whereupon she picked up her sandwich and walked out, without paying.

Annie very nearly suffered a heart attack when Belle came round later to complain. 'Why didn't you pay for it?' she asked Patsy.

'I forgot.'

'Forgot? You'll be out on your ear next time, that's what will happen to you, girl, if you don't mind your manners. Packed off to the police station to make your excuses there.'

Patsy shivered over that threat later, once she was safely in her own room where no one could witness her fear. Would she ever be anything but an outsider, an unwanted outcast living on the edge of the law?

Chapter Nine

Having dealt with one daughter's lover to her own satisfaction, Molly set about ridding herself of the second. She discovered the section of the gas board Eddie worked in, which proved to be remarkably easy. All she had to do was hang around outside first thing in the morning when the staff were arriving.

Once she'd spotted him drive up in his Vauxhall Cresta all she had to do was wait until he was safely inside and the coast was clear. She crept quietly up to his car, keeping a sharp look out to make sure no one spotted her and unscrewed the valves to let the air out of his tyres.

Pity she couldn't do the same to his lungs, or other parts of his anatomy, but this was a start anyway. Eddie Davidson would find life far less comfortable in future. He'd soon be wishing he'd never set eyes on their Fran.

But as the weeks went by Molly knew in her heart that, despite her claims to the contrary, Fran was still seeing him. Letting down his tyres had achieved nothing at all, as he'd assumed it was a bunch of kids playing tricks on him. Molly decided that much more radical action was called for.

She would stand guard outside his smart little semi-detached till she knew he'd spotted her. He'd come to the door and they'd glare at each other across the road. Then he'd go inside, close the door and draw the curtains in the room he called the lounge. But for all his fancy modern ways, he was, in Molly's estimation, nothing but a dirty-minded cheat. He had no right at all to touch her lovely lass.

At least he knew she was on to him.

One day Molly sauntered over, took a key from her pocket and scratched the wing of his nice new car. She tied tin cans to the bumper, and broke all the plant pots in his pretty little garden. Then she dropped an envelope through his door containing a dead mouse. The note with it said, 'This is only a mouse. You're the rat!'

And still Fran kept dolling herself up every Wednesday and Friday evening, to go swaggering off to meet her married lover, defiance in every bright-eyed glance of triumph she shot in her mother's direction.

–

Molly was in despair. No wonder the once rich tones of her brown hair were fading to a dull grey, and she wasn't even fifty yet. It seemed that the more she tried to stop Fran, the more determined the stupid mare was to stick by this Eddie Davidson. Big Molly clipped her offending tresses back with an old tortoise-shell hair slide and sat deep in thought, all alone in the sanctuary of her kitchen as she waited for the kettle on the gas to boil for her morning cuppa. Here she was, up and about at four in the morning, with not even any baking to do.

Robert was now in charge of the production side of the business, in the new kitchens he'd had fitted out with the very latest equipment.

'All you have to do, Mam, is run the stall,' he'd told her as he'd emptied her cupboards of the tins she used for steaming the individual steak and kidney puddings. She'd objected to him taking them, because he'd bought all new ones, together with huge steamers and industrial-style ovens. But Robert said that if he left them there, he didn't trust her not to use them and interfere, as she so loved to do. 'And if anything went wrong, I'd lose my licence.'

'What could go wrong?'

'This isn't a hygienic kitchen, Mam. Somebody might catch something.'

Molly had been outraged. 'I've not poisoned anyone yet, not in all the years I've been catering.'

'Who cared, with a war on and food in short supply? But this is the fifties now. We're in the modern world. We need to be more efficient and adventurous. I might try lamb hot pot, chunky beef stew and dumplings, or maybe a new line altogether, like pâté, once I've got the routine running smoothly.'

'What's pâté when it's at home?'

Robert had explained, in careful detail.

'Oh, like potted meat? Why didn't you say so? Stick to the old favourites, they're the best.' But he was another who didn't listen to her advice.

'No, Mam, I can't do that. Life is changing and competition is fierce. I mean to get on, make something of Poulsons. Leave the cooking to me now and you stick to running the stall, then you can put up your feet of an evening and sleep in of a morning. Take life easy for once.'

That's all she ever heard from him these days, like a stuck record. Day after day he'd tell her that she should leave the worrying to him, as if she'd become decrepit. 'So you're putting me out to grass, are you?'

'I want you to relax and enjoy life. And stop worrying about our Fran and Amy. They're grown women. Leave them to sort out their own lives while you take things easy and lie in bed.'

Molly had never had a lie-in in her life, and she certainly wasn't going to start now.

As she sat and drank her tea at the empty table, she felt oddly bereft. She massaged the swollen joints of her fingers. Her hands were red and sore from all the kneading of dough and pastry that she'd done over the years, a task they would be spared in future. She tried to tell herself that it was a good thing Robert was playing a proper role in the business, making it his own. Didn't he want only the best for her? She'd been only eighteen when she'd had him twenty-five years ago, so was hardly in her dotage now. Still, Molly was not against taking things a bit easier, so long as she could still play a role in the business. And wasn't she proud of her fine son?

It worried her slightly though that she wasn't made particularly welcome at his house by that toffee-nosed wife of his, Margaret as she liked to be called. She wasn't a Maggie, and she was clearly even more ambitious than Robert. If Molly ever tried visiting the new kitchens, she'd be equally unwelcome there as well.

'Eeh, what is the world coming to? It's not what it was, that's for sure,' she told the small black and white terrier who lifted her head to listen, and when Molly said nothing further, sighed and propped her chin back on her paws.

Molly echoed the sigh as she sipped her tea.

Robert was probably right, though. She should be looking forward to a more relaxing life, to grandchildren and time to have a bit of a laugh with her mates.

But how could she when she had all this trouble on her hands? How could she sit back and do nothing when her beloved girls were about to destroy their lives? He was wrong on that score at least.

The annoying thing was, Fran could have any lad she fancied. She had but to cast them a sideways glance from those warm, come-hither amber eyes of hers, and they fell at her feet with the eagerness of a thirsty man in the desert heading for water. Yet she'd no confidence in herself and had instead chosen this loser, got herself embroiled in an affair that was going nowhere.

Both her daughters, fools that they were, had allowed themselves to fall in love with the wrong man, absolutely refusing to heed a mother's sound advice.

Molly sipped her tea, wishing she had some dough to thump about, instead of sitting here stewing in self-pity. She felt cheated. She'd done her best for her two girls. All right, they might never have had much money but she'd fed and cared for them with precious little help from Ozzy, and, more importantly, loved them to bits.

They both had good jobs in the family business, and she'd dreamed of them finding nice young men to marry. She'd hoped to see them settled by now, producing a clutch of grandchildren for her to enjoy. Instead, they'd brought nothing but trouble to her door.

Life was so unfair.

The tea had gone cold. Molly got wearily to her feet to brew herself some fresh, her anger mounting, souring her mood. If neither girl was able to stand up for herself, then she must be the one to do it for them. Wasn't it her responsibility, as their mother, to protect them? Something she'd been denied during her own sadly neglected childhood. So she'd do everything possible for her two lasses, and tackle anyone who threatened to hurt them.

Molly mentally rolled up her sleeves just thinking about it.

Two cups of tea later, she had her plan all worked out. She would send a letter; a carefully worded anonymous missive addressed personally to Eddie Davidson's wife. This she did later that same day, delivering it by hand to his house so that there would be no betraying postmark, choosing a time when he was safely at work and unable to intercept the delivery.

There was no one, Molly thought, better skilled at controlling a cheating husband than his adoring wife. Once the poor woman had read that letter, she'd tighten the reins and keep him safely at home. That would soon cool his ardour. And if that didn't work either, then Molly had one or two more ideas up her sleeve. Eddie Davidson would rue the day he'd ever laid a finger on her daughter.

Pleased with her enterprise, Big Molly Poulson sat back to wait on events.

–

It was only a day or two after Molly's secret delivery that the daughter in question was rolling in long grass, giggling and gasping and begging her lover for more. There was a faint hint of spring in the air on this cold February day, not that Fran cared about the weather. She only had to look at the sexy little smile playing at one corner of Eddie's mouth and she went all funny inside.

They'd taken a drive out into the Yorkshire Dales, enjoying a picnic by a gushing stream, now she happily spread her legs and encouraged him to get on with it.

Eddie wasted no time in obeying.

He peeled off her clothes, one by one, her batwing sweater and cotton skirt with its layers of flounced petticoats, which might be pretty but was a nuisance as it got in the way. Next he stripped off the pink satin knickers and black suspender belt, which excited him. Eddie had objected to the girdle and Fran had never worn it again. He had very fixed ideas on how he liked his women to look.

Finally, he rolled down each stocking, smoothing her shapely legs and pretty feet, desire rising in him as he did so, making him instantly hard, so that by the time they were bare and she was stroking his chest with her toes, the agony in his groin was almost unbearable. He longed to slam her down and drive into her with all he'd got but valiantly managed to hold back, wanting it to be good for her too, which was generally to his advantage. And they had all afternoon, after all, since Josie was at her mother's.

He stroked the soft cushiony flesh of her inner thighs, parted her legs and touched the secret cleft, caressing and tantalising, hearing her soft moans, and as he slipped his fingers inside he heard her breath quicken, saw her eyelids flicker closed in ecstasy. He paused, to fumble with his flies.

'Ooh, don't stop now, do it some more. Please, please. Put your fingers here, no, further down. Oh, God, Eddie, you're so clever with your hands.'

'All engineers are good with their hands, sweetheart. Part of the tools of our trade.'

'Go on, show me what other tools you've got handy,' she urged, letting her mouth fall slack as she ran the tip of her pink tongue over her lips.

That's what Eddie liked most about Fran, her eager passion. So unlike his wife, who never refused him but was only really keen to have sex at the time of the month, which she believed offered the best chance for her to get pregnant. That was all she ever thought about these days. Babies! Eddie was sick of the whole subject.

It wasn't that he didn't adore Josie, and she was a good wife to him in a lot of ways. Never made any demands or the slightest fuss, no matter what time he came in at night. But she'd got this bee in her bonnet about having a kid, and nothing would shake it. Eddie didn't even know if he wanted one, but he didn't want the getting of one to stand in the way of pleasure. Seemed odd somehow that it should. Most of all he hated seeing her in tears every month when she'd failed all his best efforts. It was frustrating and humiliating.

Fran knew nothing about any of this. She believed his marriage to be chaste, that he'd lost interest in his boring little wife.

'Go on, don't stop!' She brought his straying attention back to the task in hand and Eddie obligingly applied himself, kissing every tiny part of her, devouring all those secret places and bringing her to a pitch of near madness.

Fran flung back her arms in apparent surrender, although Eddie knew that the moment he entered her, as he was doing now, she'd grip him like a tiger, clench him tight, and nothing on God's earth would separate them until he was thoroughly spent. God, she was one of the best he'd had, and he'd enjoyed quite a few. Afterwards, as he lay exhausted beside her, she licked his ear and whispered, 'I want that all over again.'

Eddie laughed, a coarse, smoky sound. 'You'll have to wait a minute till I get my breath back then I'll be only too happy to oblige. Though I'm not sure I've brought enough johnnies with me, not if we go on at this rate.'

'You don't have to worry,' Fran told him. 'I've a little treat for you today. I've had myself fitted with a Dutch cap. It will be so much better, so good not to have them rubbers in the way.' She nibbled his ear lobe. 'Why don't we try it? I'm sure you'll spot the difference.'

Some innate sense of caution made Eddie uneasy. He didn't care for the idea of losing control of this most intimate situation.

He never had been one to court danger, not even when he was serving his time with the Royal Navy. He'd happily seen out the war working in stores, though he could tell a good tale and embroider reality with a bit of adventurous fiction, should anyone ask. Making out he'd been bombarded with shells and suffered a near death experience was always a turn-on for women. Which, in his view, was what life was all about. Sex. Pleasure. Why else would women have been invented, if not to please men?

But he said none of this to Fran. And he knew that she liked things just as they were between them. She had no greater wish than he to court trouble, nor did she expect commitment from him. That had been agreed between them from the start, so if she said she'd taken care of it, he'd no reason not to believe her. Fran was a canny lass. And so sexy! Oh, God, and he definitely wanted it again.

'You'll be the death of me, woman, you will really. You're the sort of crumpet who drives a man demented.'

'Ooh, Eddie, what a thing to say!' And as Fran pushed his trousers down to his ankles with her agile toes, then wrapped her plump thighs around his waist, she was telling him, between gasps, how she would, in fact, be the making of him.

'Ooh, what power you have, what zest and energy. I'm the one who can't keep up with you. A real man you are.' And she let out a great squeal, sobbing as he thrust into her over and over again, tuning her rhythm perfectly to his. 'Oh, yes, yes! You're wonderful, Eddie. Absolutely incredible!'

This time it was Fran who slept, or appeared to, her mind busy with delightful plans, wondering if she could ever manage to sneak Eddie into her bedroom via the wash-house roof without waking her mam. Think of it, a whole night alone with him in her bed! No, she'd never get away with it, not with Gaumont British News, the eyes and ears of the world, for a mother.

The frustration of having to live at home under Molly's gimlet gaze, made her want to weep with despair. The sooner she left home, the better.

It was only later, when Fran was getting ready for bed that she realised she'd forgotten to take the Dutch cap with her. It was still in its blue box in her knicker drawer.

Chapter Ten

One Friday afternoon, when Annie handed over two one-pound notes and one ten-shilling note as her wages, a pitiful sum in Patsy's opinion for yet another boring week, she went straight over to the music stall to rifle through the records and see if she could spot 'Too Many Heartbreaks', or 'Istanbul, Not Constantinople', which were two of her favourites. She'd already bought 'The Green Door', and still had no way of playing it.

'Don't much care for Frankie Vaughan myself. Obviously, all you girls think he's a dreamboat.'

The masculine voice speaking in her ear made Patsy jump as if she'd been stung. Spinning round, she found herself facing the most beautiful pair of brown eyes she'd ever encountered, rich as chocolate and alive with merry laughter. They belonged to a tall, strong, good-looking young man whom she recognised in an instant. One of the Bertalones, the demi-gods she watched in secret from behind her bedroom window's lace curtains. Her heart started to race, and since she couldn't think of one sensible thing to say, Patsy was glad that he kept on talking.

'I like Johnnie Ray. "Broken-hearted" is a good one, and "Cry", of course. My favourite though is "Rock Island Line" by Lonnie Donegan. *I got pig iron, I got pig iron, I got all pig iron,*' he crooned.

When still she didn't speak, he laughed. 'I'm Marc Bertalone, by the way. I reckon I shall be broken-hearted if you don't at least say hello. So, which are you going to buy?'

His dark hair was neatly cut and slicked back, a crinkled sea of waves, although some curls sprang stubbornly forward on to a brow framing the kind of classically oval face you would expect an Italian to have, lean and with high cheekbones, completed with a perfectly straight Roman nose.

Patsy loosened her dry tongue from the roof of her mouth. 'I – I don't have a record player.' Now why had she said that? How stupid! She sounded like an idiot, one of those boring people everyone called square.

'You don't have a record player? I don't believe it! Why ever not?'

She cleared her throat, striving to sound casual and unconcerned. 'Matter of fact I do have a record player, course I do, only not with me. I've only been here a short time and, um – haven't sent for my stuff yet.'

'You're staying with the Higginson sisters, right? Are they your aunts or something?' He leaned back against the counter, hands in the pockets of his blue jeans, smiling at her. 'I see you come and go when I catch the bus to the art college in the city. It is good to have a new pretty face around.'

Patsy felt the ground start to slip away from beneath her feet. He was an art student, sophisticated and worldly, and he thought her pretty! Oh, if only she didn't feel so tongue-tied.

'And you've certainly livened things up around here,' he continued. 'You seem to have caused a stir.'

She blinked. As always, Patsy's damaged self-esteem was quickly on the alert, her ears pricked for any signs of criticism or put-down. Was he trying to score some sort of point? Make out it wasn't her actual presence that interested him, or her looks, so much as the gossip attached to her, the things she'd said and done, like that flaming pie, the outlandish clothes she liked to wear, or not paying for a bacon butty. 'Meaning what exactly?' she snapped.

He shook his head, put up his hands in a defensive gesture. 'Don't blame me if the older generation are a bit set in their ways. They're square, right? Love the pants by the way.'

Patsy relaxed a little, almost giggled. 'Toreadors.'

'Yeah, cool! Sweater looks good too.' His eyes flickered briefly over her, as if he'd like to study more closely what was under the sweater. He edged nearer and Patsy held her breath.

'Thought I'd introduce myself. Considered you might be in need of someone on your side, someone batting in your wicket, as it were. Why don't we go for a coffee? I'll tell you all about how I plan to spend my free time getting to know the prettiest girl on the street, and you can tell me how you came to be here, and if you're really going to go on working at that dreadful hat stall. Oh, and you can explain why you have been avoiding me all these weeks, when I know you're just dying to get better acquainted.'

'I haven't!' Patsy was outraged as her cheeks fired up.

'It feels that way. Every time you see me, you hurry away in the opposite direction.'

Most normal people, those with safe, secure backgrounds, would take this show of natural curiosity in the spirit in which it was offered. Nothing more than mild flirtation, but merely a way of making friends. Sadly, Patsy had been hurt too often in the past to take anything or anyone at face value. In addition, she'd never had much to do with boys, having attended an all girl school, or had a boyfriend. Nor did she have any intention of looking for one. Love and marriage, and all of that stuff, seemed too fraught with problems and pain for her to take the risk. It clearly hadn't worked for her mother, so why would it work for her?

Patsy was determined to trust no one and to keep her private life just that: private.

Besides, now that she came to look at him, Marc was nothing special, just a boy with a big mouth and full lips, wide and smiling. She half closed her eyes in an attempt to blot out his handsome features, and, heart still pounding in her ears, lifted her chin in a characteristic gesture of defiance and said, 'Why would you want to?' unconsciously imitating Annie's tone as well as the words she so frequently used. 'Can't you find any other girls willing to go out with you?'

That was clever, she thought, instantly regretting her vow of eternal chastity. As soon as I get to meet a boy I fancy, I alienate him from the start. Why did she always have to say the wrong thing? Patsy stared miserably at the record in her hands, wishing for the floor to open and swallow her up.

But he seemed to think her comments highly amusing and laughed out loud. 'I thought maybe we could be friends. Isn't that good enough reason?'

She knew from bitter experience that friends needed to be made with caution. They always got too nosy, just as he was being now, pestering her with questions she really had no wish to answer. Then when you weren't forthcoming, they got fed up and dropped you.

On the few occasions she had owned up to having no family, not even an adopted one, except foster parents who didn't want her, the tentative friendships had quickly fizzled out. One of her so-called friends' mothers had actually told her she really didn't want her beloved daughter to mix with 'people of your sort'. As if Patsy had an infectious disease.

'And I know you're interested in me,' Marc continued, 'because I've seen you watching me from up in your room. Don't think I haven't noticed. You're there most mornings, peeping from behind your lace curtains.' He laughed again, as if he'd said something amusing.

Shame and embarrassment seared through Patsy like a flame, scalding her cheeks to crimson, scorching her pride. 'I have not! Why would I watch you, for God's sake? Who do you think you are that I should be interested in a twerp like you? And if you think I need your pity, you couldn't be more wrong. As a matter of fact I don't need anyone on my side... batting in my wicket, as you call it. I can manage perfectly well looking after myself.'

'I'm sure you can. I just thought...'

'That's the trouble with you men. So damned full of yourselves! Think you only have to flatter a girl and she'll roll over and think you're adorable.'

'Hey, I just wanted to buy you a cup of frothy coffee.'

'And really, I don't think I could be friends with someone who doesn't like Frankie Vaughan. I doubt we'd have anything in common.' Patsy half turned ready to flounce away, then bounced back to say something more, in case she hadn't made her point clearly enough. 'I expect you thought I'd be easy, one of those sort of girls who'll open her legs for anyone. Well, even if I were, I wouldn't be looking in your direction.'

His eyes darkened and there was no smile on his face now. 'Don't flatter yourself. I wouldn't touch you if you were the last girl on earth and I was gasping for it, which I am not. I've no trouble finding birds ready and eager to go out with me.'

'There's a fool born every minute.'

'And from what I've heard, you're nothing but a cheap little thief.'

At which point she smashed the record over his head. As Patsy stormed out through the door she heard Alec Hall shout: 'Hey, you'll have to pay for that.'

–

Living with the Higginson sisters was not proving to be easy. If Patsy stepped one inch out of line they were on to her, lecturing and hectoring and ordering her to behave. They were so well mannered, so correct. They would ask her to join them for supper but Patsy would more often than not make some excuse, preferring to take a tray upstairs to her room where she could eat in private without being under constant scrutiny or bombarded with a litany of questions.

She only had to be alone with one of them for five minutes, five seconds, and they'd start. 'Where did you say you were born?'

'Under a gooseberry bush.'

'And your parents, have you written and told them where you are living now? I could provide a stamp, or post the letter for you.' And when Patsy didn't respond they'd start on about her school, asking if it was in Manchester, or Cumbria, or Yorkshire; if it was a private school.

'No, anyone could go, so long as they could afford the fees.'

'So your parents were well off then?'

'They'd pay anything to get me out of the house.'

Light laughter. 'I'm sure that's not true.'

Patsy didn't answer because she didn't need their pity. She could cope perfectly well on her own, without help from anyone. Hadn't she done so all her life? Which was why she'd walked out on the Bowmans, and how she'd come to find the sisters in the first place.

Patsy thought now that the day she'd walked out on her foster parents she must have been in shock. She hadn't even stopped to collect her things, pitifully few though they were.

Fortunately, she'd had enough money in her pocket to pay the bus fare to Southport, where this unknown grandmother had apparently lived, although not enough to pay for accommodation. She'd spent the last of it on fish and chips that first night, then slept on the cold, clean sands, a brisk sea breeze chilling her to the bone.

Finding the house had taken most of the next day. Patsy had walked for hours up and down wide streets, all of which looked exactly alike, lined with fine houses and tall trees.

Her grandmother's old house, once she'd finally located it, was a tall Edwardian villa, locked and bolted, the windows shuttered. It looked surprisingly shabby and uncared for, the garden overgrown. Patsy had stood gazing up at those blank rectangles, at the closed door, unaware of the tears streaming down her cheeks, feeling close to exhaustion after her long search.

A woman appeared from the house next door. 'Excuse me, but were you looking for Mrs Matthews? I'm afraid she recently passed away.'

'I – I know. I'm her granddaughter.' The words had popped out of her mouth before she could stop them, sounding strange and awkward, even to her own ears. They produced a startling effect upon the neighbour.

The woman's hand flew to her mouth. 'Oh, my goodness! You must be Rolf's daughter.'

'Rolf?' Patsy tried out the name. Rolled it on her tongue. Was that her father's name then? Rolf Matthews. So what about her mother?

The neighbour invited her in for tea and cake, for which Patsy was deeply grateful. She'd had no breakfast, no lunch, nothing to eat since supper the night before.

'Call me Shirley, dear, I don't hold with formality. Unfortunately there's not much I can tell you. I only learned the story second-hand,' the woman sadly informed her, having listened to Patsy's entire life story and wiped away a few sympathetic tears. 'My husband and I retired here only a couple of years ago so I hadn't known Mrs Matthews very long. She was a lovely old lady, but sad. Kept herself very much to herself, looked after by a dragon of a housekeeper. Goodness knows where she's gone now. Pity we don't know, or we could have asked her for a few details.

'All I know is that Mrs Matthews had a son, though whether he's still alive I really couldn't say. Apparently his wife walked out on him and their young baby before the war. Mrs Matthews told me he went to America. How strange though that he should leave you behind. So you were adopted, you say? How very odd.'

'Fostered,' Patsy corrected her. 'If I am that child, that's what I'm trying to discover.' Inside she was shaking. This was the place she might have lived, gone to school, been brought up by her parents, or her grandmother anyway, if she'd not been sent away. Why hadn't her grandmother wanted her, and why had her mother left, not taking her child with her? Her father too had apparently abandoned her. Why had no one wanted her? Patsy wondered, feeling the rejection more keenly than ever in this moment of revelation.

The neighbour, busybody though she undoubtedly was, couldn't seem to leave the subject alone and kept on going over and over it, while Patsy sank deeper into depression.

What did it matter? Her grandmother was dead. She was too late. And what on earth did she do now? Where should she go? She was homeless.

Shirley was still chattering away, explaining when and how she'd come to Southport, how she and her husband had bought this house from a doctor. 'Before that it was owned by the Higginson family... Oh! I've just remembered something.'

'What? Something important?'

'Stay there, dear, pour yourself another cup of tea. Have another cake. I'll just nip down the road to speak to my friend Betty. There's not much goes on round here that she doesn't hear about.'

Heavens, Patsy thought, two nosy neighbours. Maybe she'd struck lucky after all.

When Shirley had returned, nearly an hour later, she'd proudly announced that her research among various older residents in the avenue had paid off. 'I've learned a bit more about the Higginsons.'

Patsy experienced a spurt of disappointment. She wasn't interested in the Higginsons, only in Mrs Matthews, her grandmother.

But Shirley was in full flow and continued undaunted by Patsy's gloom. 'The Higginson parents are long dead apparently but, according to my friend, they had two daughters and the younger one did have a child, although it's not certain whether or not she was ever married. And very friendly with Rolf Matthews.'

'Are you suggesting that she, this Higginson person, might be my mother?'

'It's a strong possibility, dear. You must bear in mind there was gossip at the time that perhaps she wasn't married, so if they were lovers, as seems likely, you might be illegitimate.' The woman looked sympathetic, but when Patsy didn't react, went on with her tale. 'No one ever saw the baby or learned the child's name as the sisters were living abroad around the time it must have been born. Very common to go away, dear, rather than risk scandal. Nor was Mrs Matthew's son around then either, so we can only surmise that either they did marry because she fell pregnant, or else he abandoned her and ran off to America to avoid his responsibilities, the cad.'

Patsy couldn't think of a thing to say in response to this startling observation. Her head was beginning to ache and her heart was racing with emotion, a sick feeling creeping through her stomach, and spreading into her limbs, so that it felt like she had pins and needles in her feet and hands.

'The sisters came home sometime during the war. And when their parents died, they sold up and went to live in Manchester, apparently to run a hat stall on one of the markets, though no one could remember which. Quite a come down for them, I should think. But they might have moved on somewhere else by now.'

Could this Higginson woman really be her mother? Patsy had wondered. Could she herself be that child? She'd been almost too excited to breathe. It all fitted perfectly. Her parents must have simply dumped her on old Mrs Matthews, then gone their separate ways to continue with their lives as if she'd never been born. They'd been so wrapped up in their own quarrel they'd no love left for her. Not a pleasant thought. Patsy shuddered.

But at least she had a clue to follow up, somewhere to go next in her quest.

The nosy neighbour generously offered Patsy a bed for the night, a substantial supper and breakfast the following morning. Patsy had thanked her most sincerely for this and also for the packet of sandwiches and train ticket Shirley had provided for the onward journey. The woman had proved to be the kindest person she'd met in a long time. But when Patsy had thanked her, she'd dismissed her gratitude as unnecessary.

'Every child deserves to find their mother. It's shaming that you weren't told about your grandmother, or allowed even to visit her.'

'Obviously she didn't want me,' Patsy said, feeling the raw pain of this knowledge scald her heart. So that's how she came to be here, still feeling that, yet stubbornly seeking out the truth. More than anything Patsy needed to know who she was, and who her mother was. As if anybody in the entire world cared. But in order to do so, like it or not, the sisters' curiosity had to be faced at some point, so that she could ask some questions of her own.

Chapter Eleven

Amy had been condemned to live in obscurity for the entire winter, largely because her mother wouldn't allow her back home until Chris gave up calling. Not a week went by without him coming knocking on their kitchen door. Over and over again he obstinately demanded to know where Amy was, to be given her address or telephone number.

Fran knew he was driving her mother demented by his persistence.

If it weren't for Molly's vow not to speak to the George family she would have gone across there, sleeves rolled up, the battle light in her eyes, and played holy hell. Poor Mam had expected Chris to crawl away into some sort of black hole, or fix himself up with a replacement girlfriend in double quick time, but it simply hadn't happened.

Recently, she'd even started talking about bringing Amy home again, since it was hard for them to cope without her. Robert had the new kitchens up and running and Poulson's Pies was going from strength to strength, but costs had to be kept down and an extra pair of hands would come in useful.

Not for a moment would Mam see this as an admission of defeat on her part. Fran had written to her sister to tell her as much, and in spite of the warning had received a heart-wrenching letter back, begging her to put in a plea for her return.

Amy had complained more than once over Fran's refusal to slip a letter to Chris, but Fran was adamant that she'd no wish to get involved. Didn't she have enough on her own plate? And, poor Amy couldn't risk writing to him, because his mum and dad would be sure to see the envelope.

If she wasn't so concerned for her own situation, Fran might even have found the time to feel sorry for her younger sister. As it was, Mam was creating problems for her too.

First there'd been the episode of the tyres, which Fran was certain had nothing to do with the neighbourhood youths. Eddie, bitterly complaining that Molly had ruined his life, their precious moments together were now ruined, as she'd damaged his new motorcar, smashed up his garden and even sent him a dead mouse.

He seemed more annoyed that Josie, his silly wife, might have opened the envelope and been upset by it. Fran had been hard put not to laugh at that. As if she cared what his wife thought? But she did see that it wasn't in the least amusing to have her mother sticking her oar in where it wasn't wanted, the interfering old bat.

Now there'd been an anonymous letter, which fortunately his wife had torn up and thrown away, treating it as lies told by some mischief maker, according to Eddie. He'd been pretty good about that really, although they were both convinced who had caused this particular piece of mischief.

Fran had had enough. It was getting beyond a joke. She went straight to her mother and they rowed about it for days. 'You've got to stop this, Mam. I'm twenty-one, nearly twenty-two, old enough to please myself. Stop interfering in what doesn't concern you. You'll only make things worse.'

'Then give him up, stay away from him.'

'I'll please myself what I do. Keep your interfering nose out of my business, all right?'

Fran was so desperate she felt driven to call upon her father for assistance. 'Don't just sit there, picking your nose and doing nothing, can't you stop this daft cow from interfering in other people's marriages?' She took care not to use the word affair, since it would be less likely to invoke his sympathy.

'Don't call your mother names,' he chided her, but, to her immense surprise, Ozzy was indeed on her side for once. 'The lass is right though, you can't be sending anonymous letters to a woman you don't know, Molly love. You'll get yourself arrested. It's a criminal offence.'

'Rubbish!' Big Molly huffed and puffed, as she generally did when she knew she was in the wrong, hacking slices off a loaf she held clasped to her bosom as if she wished it were Fran's head. 'Anyway, who are you to accuse me of being a criminal? You've been no saint in your time.' And then recalling the flapping ears of her daughter, she turned on Fran with increased venom, wagging the bread knife in her face. 'You'd be glad enough of my help if you ever found yourself in trouble.'

'You're not in trouble, are you, lass?' Ozzy asked, less certain of his ground now.

'No, I'm not! I've more sense.'

Molly said, 'Watch your lip, girl. Let me tell you here and now, if you do get yourselves up the duff, you'll be out on your ear, make no mistake about it.'

Thank goodness she'd gone to the clinic, Fran thought, though she must try to remember always to put the damn thing in. Being determined to live life on your own terms was one thing; acting stupid, as she had recklessly and foolishly done a few weeks back, that was another – she'd got away with it twice now. She might not be so lucky next time.

–

Amy was brought home in time for Easter and instantly locked in her room; not with any hope that she would stay there indefinitely, but mainly because Molly couldn't think what else to do with her. She believed that it would be necessary only for a few days at most, just long enough to make her point. She wasn't prepared to put up with any more nonsense – Amy being back from exile.

'Okay, I get the message loud and clear,' Amy conceded in a tired voice. A long, cold winter spent being watched like a hawk the entire time had nearly driven her to the brink of insanity. Nobody could class her home on Champion Street as either commodious or comfortable but living conditions at the farm had been like something out of the dark ages, cold and cheerless;

her Aunt Jess no more sympathetic to her lot than her mother was.

A tough, hard woman, widowed and childless, Jess had little patience with romance. She showed no sign of grieving for her own loss, and since her opinion of men was even lower than her sister-in-law Molly's, Amy didn't care to think what Jess's late husband might have been like. Aunt Jess was also very set in her ways, managing the farm with only a couple of labourers to help with the heavy work. And she too hated the George family.

'We don't talk to that lot, or about them.' That had been her blunt response to Amy's first efforts at seeking an explanation.

But over the long winter, by dint of sheer persistence and with little else for them to do but brave the bitter winds by day to feed cows and sheep, and sit night after night in the farm kitchen, huddled round the stove for warmth with only each other for company, Amy had finally dragged out of her aunt the story behind the feud. It proved to be even more terrible than she'd feared, and she couldn't wait to tell Chris what she'd discovered. They had some big decisions to make.

Not that she had any intention of allowing her mother to guess that she knew. Aunt Jess had been adamant that this must remain a secret between them.

'If she ever found out that I'd told you, my life wouldn't be worth living. I'm very fond of my dear sister-in-law, she can be a good laugh can Molly. But she's had a hard time of it over the years, a tough life one way or another. She's a very private sort of person, your mam, and once someone has let her down, she's not strong on forgiveness. She ruthlessly cuts them out of her life – that's if she hasn't cut their throats.' The laughter following this attempt at a joke, didn't sound genuine, being far too much truth in the jest. 'As for our Ozzy, he's useless, bless him. As we all realise.'

Amy had every intention of complying with her aunt's terms, since she felt a great deal of sympathy for her mother's situation. How could she fail to, after what she'd learned? If only Mam would show the same compassion for her own situation. Tragic as her mother's life had been in many ways, a person couldn't live in the past. Everyone knew that it was totally unfair to blame one generation for the sins of its forbears.

Amy had little hope that life would be any better now that she was back home. Yet somehow, against all odds, she managed to hold on to her faith that Chris would find a way for them to be together, otherwise what was there left for her to live for?

She'd missed him so desperately. All these weeks and months apart, with not even a letter or a postcard to cheer her. And deep inside her as the cold winter had progressed, the fear had grown that he might give up on her.

Fran had allayed that fear to some extent by assuring her that Chris kept on pestering her mother week after week for her address, but not until he was holding her in his arms would Amy feel entirely happy. She loved him so much, she needed to be with him every single day. Nothing less would do.

'You're going to keep me locked up here until when? Till I agree to give up the man I love? That could be a life sentence.'

Molly looked into her daughter's steady and determined gaze and almost quailed, very nearly backed down. Amy was an awkward little madam, every bit as stubborn as that young man had proved to be, drat it. Oh, but didn't she love the bones of her? Why couldn't the daft cow see how foolish and obstinate she was being?

But then Molly remembered the reasons why she'd put her there, and tightened her resolve. Failure was out of the question, must not, could not, be tolerated. The pair had to be kept apart until it finally sank in that no son of the George family would ever be allowed to marry any daughter of hers. The lad was selfish and stubborn, that's all it was, wanting to have his own way. There were plenty of other young men, after all, who would be glad of the opportunity to have Amy on their arm.

It was essential that Molly remain tough. 'The choice is yours. You can stay in there for a few days, or forever, depending on how much sense you show.' And she walked from the room, turning the key in the lock.

—

'Where am I supposed to sleep while all this is going on?' Fran demanded to know, when she heard of this new arrangement.

'With your sister, where you've always slept.'

'Behind locked doors? Never!'

'That way I get to control both of you, with one key.'

'Don't talk daft. You can't keep our Amy locked up indefinitely. In any case, we need her on the stall, or else in the new kitchens. Our Robert is stretched, he's said as much. And I'm fair worn out doing her shift as well as me own. This can't go on, Mam, you have to bow to the inevitable. We're both women now, and can do as we please.'

'Not under my roof you can't. Anyroad, you lasses today don't know the meaning of hard work. You've never had to suffer as we suffered.'

'Oh, don't start going on about the war again. I know you had to bake pies largely from vegetables, how we'd no sugar to make cakes, or petrol for deliveries. How the family business was in danger of going under.' Fran rolled her eyes in exasperation. 'Well, things are different now. The war's over, in case you haven't noticed, and we've moved on.'

Molly sat warming her legs before the fire, skirt drawn up to reveal a pair of none-too-clean Directoire knickers which she'd bought cheap on the market, her large hands resting on knees flattened from too many years of kneeling and scrubbing. One good reason, in Molly's opinion, was not to do any more. Dashing a mop or a vacuum cleaner around was good enough these days, and not too often at that.

'You'll do as you're told, the pair of you, or you'll learn what it means to suffer. Mark my words.'

Ozzy cleared his throat, wanting to put in his two pennyworth but his back and hip had been giving him gyp all day, he'd lost a packet on the three-thirty which he still hadn't told his wife about, and he'd really prefer to remain invisible. But then he thought of his lovely Amy, locked upstairs in her room, and how if she was around, she'd run down to the pub for him and help him win the cash back. The dog was good company, but it couldn't put a bet on for him.

'Our Fran might have a point, Molly love,' he quietly ventured, only to be immediately shouted down.

'Never! She'll do as I say. They both will. Not that you care. You're only interested in yourself, like all men. But I'm not beaten yet, not by a long chalk.'

–

Molly knew all about selfish men. As a child she'd been brought up, if that was the phrase, by her father, her mother having died giving birth to her. For all she had an elder sister, it had been a lonely childhood since much of the time her father rarely bothered even to speak to his two daughters, finding solace for his bereavement in the bottom of a bottle.

He never laid a finger on them, neither by way of chastisement nor in any show of affection. Either would have done, just an acknowledgement that he cared, but he rarely seemed aware of their presence in the house. Young Molly was the one expected to put food on the table for him to eat, keep his clothes and home clean and tidy, though since she had no one to teach her how to do that, it very rarely happened.

Lena certainly couldn't have shown her, for all she was two years older, because she was a bit simple in the head. Molly had to take care of her too, protect her from the bullies in the playground who thought it fun to taunt her for her ignorance, just because she wasn't as bright as them.

Her father never thanked her for that either.

Molly knew that he blamed her entirely for the death of her mother, for causing her death simply by being born. That was what was wrong with all men: they were entirely self-obsessed.

He never gave a thought to his children's loss, to the fact they'd been forced to grow up without a mother.

And if the young Molly had thought that was bad, there'd been worse to come.

Was it any wonder that she'd married a weak, useless man like Oswald Poulson? She'd married him for his family business, not his winning charm, so what did it matter? They largely went their separate ways and he didn't trouble her, doing exactly what he was told, the daft ha'p'orth, which was just as well since he couldn't think of anything beyond the next sure fire winner, or pint of Guinness.

Her two girls were another matter. She might not be good at showing it, but they were the light of her life, and Big Molly would allow no one to quench their brightness or take advantage of them. Like a lioness protecting her cubs, she'd get the best for them or die in the attempt.

The trouble was that they were daft young lasses who didn't know what was good for them. They imagined that now they were grown-up, they no longer needed to march to her tune. Even Robert, her precious son had no further use for her, discarding her like an old paper bag after he'd emptied it of everything of value.

Well, the whole bang lot of them would soon learn different. She was no spent force, no decrepit old soul ready for the knacker's yard. Wasn't she Big Molly? Hadn't she always been in charge and wouldn't she remain so?

No matter what the cost, Molly meant to win.

–

The following day the gas board received a letter to say that one of their employees, Edward Davidson, had taken advantage of a young girl who must remain anonymous for the sake of her reputation. That she'd been well-nigh ruined by his bad behaviour. It went on to complain of the immense distress caused to her family.

The unsigned letter was begging the board to administer justice by dispensing with his services.

'Where have you been dipping your wick?' Eddie's boss wanted to know when he called him into the office to discuss the letter, amusement ripe in his voice. 'Sort it out, lad, will you? We don't want this sort of carry-on, not at the gas board.'

Chapter Twelve

Patsy remained steadfast in her desire for independence. If there was a dispute, she would give as good as she got, hotly defending herself against any criticism, no matter if the sisters accused her of being impertinent, or said, 'Less of your sauce, girl.' Their threatening to throw her out of hearth and home proved to be a regular occurrence during those first few months. It happened every time Annie told her to be in by ten, and she wasn't, which would generally lead to a row.

Patsy paid her bed and board regular as clockwork nowadays, and therefore considered herself free to come and go as she pleased. Most of the time she was only taking a walk, or thinking things through down by the canal. She never did anything outrageous, like going to a pub, or dancing even, because she had no one to go with. But she liked watching others go out and enjoy themselves, seeing them stroll home again in a happy group, imagining she was part of it.

In the end, the sisters' insistence that danger lurked on every street corner once darkness fell, won through. Patsy knew they simply didn't want to be held responsible if she was found murdered up a dark alley, her body chucked into some coal heap, so had to be content with keeping herself amused reading second-hand magazines she bought from Abel's stall. She was still saving up for a record player. Trouble was, she kept being tempted to buy other things, too, like clothes and nail varnish. She'd come down to breakfast one morning with a rainbow of colours on her nails, from pink and poppy red through to a violent purple, but Annie had been appalled, demanding she wash it off that instant.

'Don't be daft, you can't wash nail polish off, you have to use a special remover.' In any case, Patsy refused point-blank. Old-fuddy-duddies, the pair of them. 'I might put some colour tints on my hair too. It's all the rage now you can do it without splitting the ends. That'd be fun, don't you reckon?'

'Not unless you were planning to seek alternative accommodation,' Annie told her sourly.

'What makes you think I was planning on stopping long anyway?' Patsy hit right back, determined to keep up her defiance.

Annie proved to be deadly serious, and stood over her while she cleaned the painted nails with nail polish remover. Such a fuss over nothing! Even Clara objected if she had the radio on too loud, or found her bopping in the living room to Radio Luxembourg at midnight, using the chair as a partner. The next morning Annie would launch into yet another lecture, quoting from the good book, or sharply remind Patsy that using other people's belongings without permission was tantamount to theft.

'Theft? I didn't run off with the flipping radio, or even try to pawn it,' Patsy protested.

'You stole the electricity needed to power the instrument, if nothing else,' Annie insisted, and went on to make it clear that she wasn't even permitted to alter the dial on the wireless without her say so.

'Or blow my flipping nose either, by the sound of it, in case you have to use soap and hot water to wash my hanky. I'd hate to be a drain on your purse.'

'Don't say such things, Patsy,' Clara begged, clearly shocked by her rebellion. 'It has nothing to do with the cost of your keep. Annie is concerned about you, that's all.'

'She has a funny way of showing it.'

Annie scowled at her more fiercely than ever, as if she were a stray cat. 'We are the ones responsible for you, child, until someone claims you.'

'We want only what is best for you,' Clara hastily intervened, seeing how the sparks flew between these two. 'Have you written to your parents yet? Have you told them that you are safe?'

Patsy had heard enough of this. 'Not another interrogation! I've told you before I'm not a child, and I haven't got any parents, none that matter anyway. They were only my foster parents, and they threw me out too, so why should they care where I am?' She hadn't meant to say any of that, and was rewarded by a stunned silence as both sisters sat staring at her, shock registering on each startled face.

After a moment, Clara said, 'Would you like to talk about it?'

'Would the pair of you like to keep your long noses out of my business?' And Patsy had slammed out of the room, only to find herself in tears down on the towpath. She should have used their concern as a way to ask some questions of her own. Why hadn't she? Oh, and why couldn't she bring herself to ask, because she was afraid of the answer? Whenever they'd had one of these spats, Patsy would sit huddled on the wall down by the canal, or by the lock, breathing in the smell of tar and coal dust, of cold damp water, mud and grass, hating her life, hating herself. She would tell herself to forget all this nonsense about mothers and move on, to make a fresh start some place else.

Patsy would start off resenting the sight of a patch of blue sky, or a ray of sunshine lighting a prettily painted passing barge, bringing a startling new resonance to the industrial scene. In the end, though, she would find herself helping the barge owner to work the lock, or laughing as a mother duck took her young offspring for a walk in the spring sunshine. These moments would remind her that, if nothing else, she too possessed the power and vigour of youth. Only when the anger had died down, and she felt calm once more, would she return to number twenty-two Champion Street.

No more would be said about their quarrel. Supper would be served as if nothing untoward had occurred, the conversation keeping to safe topics such as the weather and trade.

But irritating as these incidents were, Patsy came to accept that the sisters at least provided her with employment and a roof over her head. They fed her regularly, didn't ask her to do any chores that they weren't equally prepared to do themselves, and as time went by complained about her less and less. That could simply be because they realised how pointless that was, but Patsy kept hoping it might be because they did like having her around, although they would never admit as much.

The tattoo on her ankle proved to be a step too far though. She'd found an old sailor who did them, down by the docks. Patsy watched him scald the needles and took the chance that it was safe enough. The sisters, unfortunately, were aghast, absolutely hit the roof, and hovered over her anxiously for days in case she came down with some dreadful disease. Which, in an odd sort of way was strangely comforting.

Nobody had ever cared before what happened to her.

Now if she could just raise the courage to ask a few questions of her own? What did she have to lose besides everything?

—

'Is this Cheddar cheese mature?' Patsy wanted to know. 'Perhaps I should take the Double Gloucester instead. Clara and Annie like plenty of flavour in their cheese.'

'Try it.' Fran held a piece out on the end of a knife. She wasn't paying much attention to Patsy, her expression showing complete disinterest, seeming far more engrossed in the comings and goings in the market around them.

Patsy had only been shopping for half an hour, carefully following Clara's list, and already her stomach was full to bursting. She'd tried pickles and prawns, gingersnaps and gooseberries, black pudding and a chocolate cupcake. A strange mixture, and she was beginning to feel slightly ill.

Patsy agreed that she would take the cheese but Fran made no move to cut it for her. She was standing on tip toe, looking as if she were about to call out to someone, and then subsided, disappointment keen on her face.

'Are you looking for someone?'

Fran shrugged. 'No one you'd know. How much were you wanting?' and then weighed a piece that was a good ounce over. By the time Patsy had decided to complain, the cheese had been wrapped and she felt obliged to pay for it.

Money continued to be a major cause for concern in the Higginson household. It troubled Patsy, as it seemed to threaten her own situation.

At least the hat stall had been busier in the last week or two, with ladies buying their hats in readiness for the Whit Walks, and Patsy couldn't rightly recall how many straw bonnets she'd sold to small girls. They'd run out of rosebuds and pink ribbon.

Even so, Annie had instructed her, only this morning, to always ask for 'a little bit of something on the side'. Rather like the baker's dozen, where you in fact received thirteen bread rolls instead of twelve, Annie always expected something extra by way of goodwill. Not that this happened very often these days, as Clara had gently pointed out. Nevertheless, Annie insisted that she ask, which Patsy found acutely embarrassing.

Sometimes she'd be lucky. Barry Holmes had given her a whole bunch of soup greens, Jimmy Ramsay had slipped a sprig of sage in with the chicken she'd bought, and it had been the smallest bird he had available on his stall. Patsy knew that Annie would be disappointed. She would have preferred a few sausages instead.

Patsy was on her way back to the hat stall with her purchases when she caught sight of Marc Bertalone, and her heart contracted.

Ever since they'd had their argument at Hall's music stall and she'd broken the record over his head, she'd managed to neatly avoid him. Even so, she was always acutely aware of him whenever he was around, indicated by a little prickling sensation at the base of her scalp.

Patsy had resolutely made up her mind never to speak to him again. No matter how often she saw him smiling or winking at her as he watched her go by, the vision from the corner of her eye being surprisingly good, Patsy refused to weaken. Let him wink as much as he liked. She'd seen him tease Fran and Amy Poulson in exactly the same way. Marc Bertalone was an incorrigible flirt. She had no intention of allowing him to break her heart.

The other day he'd actually had the effrontery to speak to her. It had only been a cheery hello but Patsy had tossed her head and walked on without giving him the satisfaction of responding. His laughter had filled her with fury, which made her all the more determined to ignore him.

Now here he was again, constantly turning up like a bad penny wherever she went. Champion Street Market was a small place. Too small.

'Hiya, Patsy, and how are you this fine morning?'

He sounded cheerful, and so full of himself. Patsy would have carried on walking this morning, a basket on her arm, but he deliberately stepped in front of her. 'I was hoping that you and I could get together. It could be fun, don't you think?'

'I very much doubt it.' Damn, now she'd allowed him to trick her into speaking.

'I paid for that broken record by the way, but you could at least tell me what I did to deserve it.'

'If you don't know, then there's no point in my wasting time explaining.' She really didn't want him poking his nose into her business, or feeling sorry for her, let alone accusing her of drooling over him. She didn't need anyone, least of all this arrogant Italian. And Patsy just knew he'd been talking about her to all and sundry, laughing at her for watching him from behind her lace curtains, and for cracking his head with that record. Some friend he would be.

But he didn't seem to be getting the message. 'How about you and me going to the pictures, but for a dance if you prefer? There's a new skiffle group playing at the co-op rooms tonight. Fancy going along to listen?'

She would have loved to go and her heart did that funny little skipping sensation at the very thought, but Patsy pressed her lips together and lifted her chin in the air. 'I'm busy, thanks,' she said before brushing past him and walking away.

He gave a heavy sigh. 'I'm heartbroken. We'd be so good together, you and me. When will you give me a chance, Patsy?'

As she turned the corner of the market hall, she glanced quickly back over her shoulder. To her horror he was still standing there, one hand pressed to his heart, watching her. When he saw her looking he lifted the hand and waved, and that gorgeous mouth of his twisted into a wide smile, the straight dark brows giving a little up and down jerk of amusement, as if he were mocking her. Feeling her cheeks flare with fresh embarrassment, Patsy fled indoors.

—

She'd barely unpacked the basket and set the items out on the kitchen table when Annie pounced. 'What do you call this? A twig?' She was twirling the sprig of sage round in her fingers.

Patsy took it off her with an impatient sigh. 'Don't you know anything? It's sage to make the stuffing with.'

'Less cheek from you, girl! I am well aware that it is sage, what I'm wondering is why Jimmy Ramsay imagines this is going to make us want to shop at his stall in future, seeing as how his generosity seems to be on the slide. A few strips of fatty bacon would have been more use.'

'He knows we've no choice, since it's the cheapest place around, and we don't buy a lot of meat anyway, do we?' Patsy put the bread rolls in the white enamelled bread bin. They'd be stale before they ate all thirteen, in her opinion.

Annie's face went white, then a deep shade of crimson. 'Are you implying that I'm not feeding you properly? I'll have you know that things haven't been easy for us recently. Trade isn't exactly as buoyant as it might be, and we do have other problems to deal with.'

'Having to accommodate me, you mean, and endure an extra mouth to feed,' Patsy said, brushing the crumbs from her fingers.

'The money for your food, and your wages too for that matter, have to be found from somewhere. We're not made of brass.'

'So you're telling me it's time I moved on, is that it? You mean to turn me out, to save a bob or two.'

'That's not what I was going to say, and you know it.'

'I'm sure it wasn't anything pleasant. I can sense bad news when it's coming, like a foul smell in the air.' The light of defiance in Patsy's eyes caused Annie to avoid meeting her gaze. It made Patsy's heart sink, as she realised she must have struck dangerously close to the truth. Annie looked as if she was going to give her a push, and the thought filled her with dismay. It was all very well for her to consider leaving of her own free will, but had no wish to do so.

As if she sensed it, Clara set down her crocheting, and pressed her sister's arm with the gentle touch of one hand, as she so often did when she couldn't pluck up the courage to say the right words.

Folding her lips into their accustomed thinness, Annie marched out of the room. Whatever Annie had been about to say, Clara had saved her from it, but Patsy could sense the prospect of banishment hanging over her like an unspoken threat. Blast the woman, let her do her worst! She'd no intention of begging for a roof over her head, not one that should have been hers by right in the first place. And Patsy flounced out of the house, determined to enjoy herself while she could.

Chapter Thirteen

Chris was waiting for her on the corner of the street after she'd finished her first day back at work, as Amy had known in her heart that he would be. Anticipation of seeing him again after all this time had made her stomach churn for days beforehand. She'd spent a week locked in her room before finally being allowed out, not to work on the stall in the market, but with her brother Robert in the new kitchens a few streets away, part of an old warehouse down by the Brunswick Basin. It was better than nothing.

Even so, she had been forced to promise faithfully that she wouldn't go looking for Chris. Amy didn't see her agreement to this as telling lies exactly, it was just that her loyalty now must be directed primarily towards him, and not her mother. The past was the past, and her concern was with the future.

Amy wasn't worried about not being allowed back on to the market. Chris would be sure to hear she was out and about and come looking for her. Then they must decide what they were going to do about this impossible situation. She was almost nineteen, old enough surely to plan her own life?

Now here they were, cuddled up on a bench in Heaton Park with the sound of birds in the trees, a soft spring breeze and the sun warming their faces, hardly able to believe they were together again, reunited at last.

'I really don't know how I've survived the winter without you. It's been an absolute agony,' Amy sighed.

'For me too.' Chris was kissing her nose, her eyes, a kind of wonder in his gaze as he stroked her hair and cradled her close in his arms, as if imprinting the image of her anew on to his soul. 'You're safe with me. I won't let them take you from me again. I'd die first. If they can't recognise true love when they see it, that's their problem.'

Amy cast him a sad glance. 'It's our problem, and you know that I've found out what the feud was all about? Bullied it out of Aunt Jess.'

'Tell me.'

'It isn't pleasant, Chris. Really nasty, in fact! So awful that I can see why Mam would never agree for us to be together. Never in a million years!'

'Whatever it is, however bad, we can overcome it,' Chris insisted, blindly resolute in his love.

Amy let out a tremulous sigh. 'I wish I could believe that.'

'Go on, love. I'm listening.'

She grasped his hands, glad of the feel of his strong fingers beneath her own, and took a deep breath. 'Mam and Jess were friends long before she married Jess's brother. They went to school together, and that's when it all started – when it happened. Mam was about fifteen at the time. You see, she had a sister called Lena, two years older than herself, and not particularly bright. Aunt Jess said she was a lovely girl, very affectionate and friendly, but a bit simple. She was still a child in her head even when her body had grown into that of a young woman of seventeen. And that was the problem. Thomas George, your father, had a younger brother. I think Jess said his name was Howard.'

'I don't have an Uncle Howard. At least, I've never heard of one.'

Amy pressed a silencing finger to his lips. 'You said you'd listen. The story goes that this Howard interfered with Lena and got her pregnant. Jess thinks she might have had a bit of a crush on him. She used to follow him everywhere like an adoring puppy. It wasn't rape or anything, but he knew how it was with her, that she wasn't up to the mark, and took advantage.'

'Oh, God!'

'Anyway, once this was discovered, it was agreed that she couldn't possibly keep the baby. A doctor advised that she shouldn't even be allowed to give birth to it, which was so sad, don't you think? She was forced to have an abortion, and, tragically, caught an infection and died days later. Mam has never forgiven your uncle – your family – for what happened. Had it not been for this Howard doing what he shouldn't, Lena would still have been alive to this day.'

Chris looked stricken. 'That's terrible! Tragic. And what happened to him?'

'He vanished, disappeared off the face of the earth. It's thought your grandparents paid for him to go to America or Australia, somewhere far away from my family's wrath. According to Aunt Jess, Mam looks upon your uncle as little short of a murderer, and the rest of your family as conspirators in his escape from justice.'

'But it wasn't his fault that she caught that infection.'

'I know, but if he hadn't touched her, she wouldn't have needed the abortion in the first place, would she?'

'I shall ask Dad. See what he has to say.'

'No, no, you mustn't do that.'

Chris grasped her hands firmly between his own. 'I have to, don't you see? I have to know what their attitude is to all of this. Don't worry, I'll try to ask in such a way that I don't implicate you. I'll say I've heard a bit of gossip, and want to know if it's true. Not that I hold out much hope of a good response. When I finally told my parents about you and me, they were not happy about the situation any more than your family were, and they wouldn't tell me the reason for the feud. They made no mention of Dad even having a brother called Howard, let alone this terrible story.'

'It must have happened nearly thirty years ago now, yet still neither family can let it go.'

'I suppose it's easier for us to be distanced from it, since we didn't have to live through it.'

'And Lena was Mam's sister, whom she'd loved and protected all her life. Aunt Jess said, that to make matters worse, Mam's father blamed her for what happened. Said she should have looked after Lena better, and hardly ever spoke to her again after the death. And since he'd already lost his wife, he was a broken man and died shortly afterwards himself. Isn't that dreadful? Mam's carried that guilt all her life, unfairly in my opinion. No wonder she's filled with bitterness. That's the reason they'll never let us be together. Never! No matter what we say, and how much we claim to be in love. It's over, Chris. We don't have a hope in hell of ever getting married.' And she fell into his arms and began to weep.

—

Fran was also feeling desperately sorry for herself. She hadn't seen Eddie in over two weeks. She'd hung around outside his offices at the gas board, watched for his car every morning, even waited at their favourite coffee bar every chance she got, but not a sign of him anywhere. Anyone would think he was avoiding her.

And serving pies to yet another queue of hungry customers did not inspire her. Robert might be excited about the new pâtés, hot pots and apple turnovers he was introducing, but they did nothing to fire Fran with any great enthusiasm. She wanted only to be with Eddie.

She could hear her mother talking to Winnie Watkins round the back of the stall. Right pair of old gossips they were. Their cheerful chatter only reminded her how bored she was, how anxious to leave this place.

'I never got to vote in the first place,' Winnie was saying, 'because of my accident, if you can call it that. But I shall register it this time, and it won't be for a Garside, I'll tell you that for nothing.'

All the stallholders could talk about these days was the coming election. Belle Garside, who'd finally been elected market superintendent, had been accused of gaining votes through the bullying tactics of her son Kenny. The whole thing had been declared void, and had to be gone through again.

'What, vote for Joe Southworth again?' Molly was saying. 'What a prat! Ruled by women, he is. Don't forget Belle has influence over Joe, very much so.'

'No better than she should be, that madam,' Winnie said, with a loud sniff of disapproval.

'Aye, lowest of the low,' Molly agreed. 'As is any woman who steals another woman's husband.'

Fran was riveted, taking in every word. Surely her mam wouldn't tell that old gossip Winnie Watkins what she'd been up to.

'So we can't entirely escape her, no matter who we vote for.'

'I'm afraid not.'

They turned then to the new market regulations Belle was wanting to impose and Fran stopped listening. The call for a second election was connected in some way with a protection racket run by Belle's son, Kenny, now thankfully stopped and nothing at all to do with her.

Fran was far more interested in her own problems.

Good Lord, now Winnie was talking about her own coming wedding to Barry. Something about her young friend Dena being busy making her dress, and how Winnie was trying to decide where she and her new husband should live. 'Not that we're in a hurry, mind! I like long engagements, myself.' Fran was astonished. Why on earth would the old goat bother to get married at all? It wasn't as if she was capable of any actual sexual activity, surely? Fran shuddered at the thought.

But Winnie's obvious happiness depressed her, making Fran wish her own life could be half so rosy, when really it wasn't looking good at all. What hope did she have of ever having a home of her own? She'd probably still be suffering from her nagging mother when she was in her dotage. Even marriage was beginning to sound attractive to her now, compared to the alternative.

Fran was late. She couldn't believe it had happened but she was nearly three weeks overdue. Which must be bad news because her monthlies were usually regular as clockwork. Besides, she'd nearly passed out the other morning when she'd walked past Belle's cafe and smelled the coffee. It had made her want to throw up.

So she needed to find Eddie and talk to him. Fast! They had to decide what they were going to do about this.

But, oh, lord, what would her mam have to say about it?

—

Big Molly watched her younger daughter as she stood before the hall mirror applying a delicate slick of pink lipstick. Fran tended to plaster on a thick coat of crimson or vibrant orange. Not their Amy. Such a little lady. Then as she pulled on a pale blue duster coat and picked up her clutch bag, Molly placed her substantial bulk between Amy and the front door. 'Where you off to then, all dolled up?'

'I'm not dolled up, as you call it. Just trying to look respectable. I'm going to the pictures with a friend. Is that a problem?'

'Depends who this friend is.'

Amy rarely lost her temper. That was the thing people liked most about her, her air of dignity and serenity, her ability to remain calm and not overreact. But she was fast coming to the end of her patience, so far as her mother was concerned.

Amy's nerves were in shreds, her misery so deep and ingrained that it felt as if she were going mad. She couldn't think, couldn't concentrate on anything, not the baking of pies and puddings, nor her brother dreaming of buying himself a flat in one of the new skyscrapers they were building all over Manchester, which were supposed to provide the answer to the housing problems. Why would she care when she couldn't ever get married, so would never buy a new home?

And morning, noon, and night, her mother would warn her not to go anywhere near the George family, as if their very presence would contaminate her in some way.

Amy felt trapped, forced to choose between the two people she loved most in all the world.

'For goodness' sake, Mam, I can't live like this, with you breathing down my neck the whole time. This isn't a jail. I'm surely allowed some freedom. Tell her, Dad.'

Ozzy didn't hear. He was engrossed in watching Mr Pastry acting daft on the new telly while listening to a football match on the wireless at the same time. He'd splashed out and bought himself a Bush television set, following a lucky win he'd had on the horses. All the family were gripped by it, except for Amy. She couldn't bring herself to watch, not even managing to laugh at *The Clitheroe Kid*. She just felt too depressed.

'I'm going out, right?' And with tears standing proud in her eyes Amy marched out of the house, closing the door behind her with meticulous care.

Molly flung it open again and yelled after her daughter, her foghorn voice carrying the length of Champion Street so that heads turned and wry smiles were exchanged as folk acknowledged that Big Molly was on the rampage again.

'Be back by ten, madam, or I'll fetch that key out of storage. Ball and chain an' all, if necessary.' Then Molly slammed the door so hard the whole house shook, before turning to vent her fury on her ineffectual husband. 'And if you weren't such a useless lump of seaweed, you'd get out of that chair and follow her.'

'With my bad hip?'

'I notice your bad hip didn't stop you getting down the pub this afternoon. Billy have a good tip for you, did he?'

Ozzy didn't take his eyes off the screen. Mr Pastry was in a right mess, as usual. Everything was going wrong for him, just like in Ozzy's own life. 'Leave our Amy alone. She'll come to no harm. Happen it's time you let bygones be bygones, Molly. Let the past stay buried.'

Molly slammed a huge fist down on the table, making the teapot jump a good three inches in the air, and the milk bottle topple over and spill its contents all over the dog-chewed rug. 'I will bury her before I'm done! You too, you great useless pudding! Nobody defies Big Molly Poulson, do you hear?'

'I hear,' Ozzy said, his voice thrumming with emotion, finally removing his attention from the screen. 'As can half the street, so shut it. Just for once in your life, Molly Poulson, shut your gob and leave that lass alone!'

It was the first time Molly could remember he'd ever stood up to her and it shocked her to the core. She watched in amazed silence as her usually weak, pliant husband hobbled out of the door, leaning heavily on his stick.

'Don't you dare walk out on me!'

But he did. He walked out of the door without even a backward glance. He would be back with a skinful, but Molly didn't like this show of resistance. Not one little bit. She couldn't abide insubordination. The whole family were out of control. Even the dog had gone.

Chapter Fourteen

'Have you owned this stall long?' Patsy risked asking Clara one afternoon as she sorted and tidied hat trimmings. Annie had gone to visit a supplier in the centre of Manchester while Clara was happily fashioning lengths of ribbon into bows, making them curl with the ends of her scissors.

It was a quiet day on the market. In fact, business was growing ever quieter so far as the hat stall was concerned. At least, it seemed so to Patsy. Fewer and fewer people wore hats these days, preferring to show off their new hairstyles instead.

Patsy had tidied all the glove drawers, brushed all the felt hats, remembering to brush correctly in the direction of the nap; now she was sorting trimmings. There were daisies and forget-me-nots, pearl buckles and jet beads, bows of every hue, bunches of cherries, and feathers ranging from pheasant to ostrich, all needing to be properly sorted and stowed safely in their allotted places. She enjoyed playing with them.

'Heavens, yes,' Clara said, in answer to her question. 'It feels like we've been here forever.'

'Since before the war?'

Clara paused, thoughtfully smoothing a satin ribbon as she stared off into the middle distance. 'We came here towards the end of the war, I believe, after our parents died. It sounds so long ago now, and yet it feels like only yesterday. Strange!'

'Where did you live before? With your parents, I mean.'

Clara smiled. 'Southport. Do you know it's a delightful town? The golden sands stretch forever, and there are flower gardens and fun fairs. Oh, I used to adore shopping on Lord Street with those delightful verandas and arcades, so continental. That is probably where I developed my love of shops. Bon Marché being a particular favourite. We were very spoiled, my sister and I. Had rather an Edwardian childhood in many ways, although we aren't that old, you understand. But our parents were set in their ways so it was a sheltered upbringing. Rather privileged, I'd say. Smart girls' school, panama hats, afternoon tea on the lawn. What about you, dear? What sort of an upbringing did you have? Far more difficult than mine, I take it? Oh, dear, I forgot. I really must stop prying.'

'I was born at the start of the war,' Patsy volunteered, steeling herself to accept the apology and not run away this time. 'In 1940.'

Clara gave a little jerk, turning curiously intent eyes upon her. 'Were you really? How extraordinary.'

'Why?'

'Er – no reason.' She seemed to shake herself mentally, and gave a distant sort of smile. 'I'm being reminded of how young you are, and to be born at the start of the war is unfortunate. It was a lovely summer, I seem to remember.' She seemed to lose track of what she was saying for a moment, then collected herself and made another attempt at a smile. 'Put all the fruit into the lower drawer, dear, and the flowers in the top one. They're all in such a dreadful muddle.'

'Right.' Patsy set about untangling the wire stems of a bunch of violets from what looked like miniature oranges and lemons. Who on earth would choose to have fruit on a hat?

But her mind was not on the task in hand. Patsy was obsessed by the thought that Clara might actually be her mother, and this was the closest she'd come to approaching the subject. What should she ask next? She'd at least confirmed that Clara was a member of the very same Higginson family who came from Southport, who had once owned Shirley's house.

Dare she come right out with it and bluntly ask if they could possibly be related? If Clara was her mother, she'd no doubt deny it, even if it were true? But if she said yes, what then? She had only Shirley's theories to go on, Patsy realised, which were nothing more than gossip and suspicion. But could they be right?

Clara had seemed disturbed by the mention of Patsy's year of birth. Was that significant?

And if she was indeed her mother, why had Clara abandoned her as a child? Why had she walked away? Had she been married to this Rolf Matthews and reverted to her Christian name, or should Patsy assume that they'd never married and she herself was in fact illegitimate?

Yet much as she longed to know the answers to these questions, Patsy felt her mouth go bone dry, her tongue stick to the roof of it and her heart quicken it's beat as it always did when faced with the reality of her quest.

She was ashamed to admit, even to herself, that she was afraid. Why was that?

Was it because she didn't know if she could ever forgive Clara for the callous act of abandoning her? What kind of mother would do such a thing? Or because the course of her entire life might be decided in the next few moments, and Patsy didn't even know if she was ready to cope with that? She couldn't find the words to describe the turmoil she felt inside. Far easier to brazen things out and pretend it didn't matter. Oh, but she would like to know, and to understand.

'Did you ever marry or have a child?' The words came out in a rush, of their own volition, and Patsy counted the beats of her heart as she waited for the answer.

Clara was gazing right through her, as if she were seeing something else, someone else entirely. Patsy felt a chill between her shoulder blades. What would she say? What was she about to learn?

But all she did was give a small, tired smile. 'Marriage wasn't exactly my thing,' was her enigmatic reply, which wasn't an answer at all.

More firmly, Clara continued, 'But we were talking about you, Patsy. I really do want to know more about you so that I can understand you better. Where were you born? Do you recall anything of your early life, dear, before you were taken in by your foster parents?'

Patsy bit back her disappointment, could think of nothing more to say as this was a question she couldn't answer, even if she wanted to, because she really had no idea. Had she been born in Southport, or somewhere else entirely? And even if she and the Higginson sisters did come from the same place, what did that prove? Nevertheless, Patsy made an instinctive decision not to mention her own tenuous connection with the town, not at this juncture. Not until she could cope with all that might follow such a revelation.

'I must have been born somewhere, I suppose,' she said, attempting to appear unconcerned, and managing only to sound flippant.

'Don't you know?'

'I'd need to check my birth certificate.'

'Ah, and you don't have one,' Clara accurately guessed. 'That's the war for you. Papers going missing all over the place. Is that what happened?'

'I wouldn't know, would I, being too young at the time?' A sharp retort accompanied by a sidelong glance of pure insolence. Patsy was rapidly backing off from the whole idea of taking this interrogation any further. She'd got absolutely nowhere, only useless stuff about Paris, and was no nearer to knowing whether Clara was ever married.

Clara was frowning. 'You should pursue it, though. There must surely be a record somewhere, in a church register. I could find an address for you to write to, if you like? Or have you done that already? What about your parents, or your foster parents? Have they tried?'

There was a painful silence as Patsy desperately sought escape. She wouldn't mind having such an address, being able to check official records, but surely had that been possible the Bowmans would have done it already and packed her back off to wherever it was she came from.

She closed the drawers on the fruits, flowers and bows, snap, snap, snap. 'Why don't I rewind those reels of ribbons you've used? They're in a proper tangle now.'

'I suppose they are.' Clara looked down at them bemused, knowing when she was beaten. The girl had clammed up tight, as always. 'And I shall put on the kettle and make us a nice cup of tea.'

As Patsy listened to Clara humming softly to herself while she rattled tea cups and brought out the tin of biscuits, she decided that patience was not really her forte, being more the impulsive, jump in with both feet kind of person herself. But, oddly echoing Annie's thoughts, she recognised that she was going to have to acquire some. She really didn't feel ready to confront Clara with what she suspected, to lay bare her hopes and dreams and risk seeing them demolished by the wrong answer to her probing questions.

The trouble was that Patsy had discovered she loved living here on Champion Street. She was growing used to market life and the people involved in its day-to-day running, for all she was careful to keep herself at a safe distance from them all. She really had no wish to leave, but would have to do so if she asked that important question and received a negative response.

–

One morning while Patsy was listening to 'At the Hop' by Danny and the Juniors on Hall's music stall, the door of the booth opened and Fran Poulson slipped in beside her. 'What are you listening to, that jolly one? I've asked Alec to put "Great Balls of Fire" on for us, bit more snaz to Jerry Lee Lewis, don't you think?'

Patsy was startled by the older girl's sudden appearance but secretly pleased by it all the same. She said, 'I like Little Richard too. Bit of a wild card though.'

Fran grinned. 'Like us, eh? That's what I am, a wild child. You too, in a different way. Oh, listen, I just love the way he says "Great Balls of Fire" with that little hiccup in his voice.'

They listened to a couple more songs then the door of the booth opened again. This time Alec's head appeared, a wry grin on his face. 'I hope you're behaving yourself today, Patsy. No more broken records?'

She felt warm colour suffuse her cheeks. 'I'm short of an arrogant head to break them on.'

Alec chuckled. 'Anything else I can get you two girls?'

Fran said, 'I'll take the Jerry Lee Lewis, what about you Patsy?'

'Sure, I'll have one too.' Not wishing to feel left out.

As Alec slipped the *78* into a bag and passed it over, he said in a friendly fashion, 'Got yourself fixed up with a record player then, Patsy?'

'Yeah, sure,' she lied, wanting the ground to open in case Fran started asking awkward questions. But she should have known better. Fran wasn't interested in her. Her attention seemed to be entirely elsewhere.

'Spit it out,' Patsy said, as they strolled out of the shop back into the side aisle of the market hall. 'I can see you've got a problem. I'm an expert, I can recognise the signs.'

Fran considered. 'Let's have a coffee.'

The two girls went to Belle's cafe and had a large Nescafé each with half an inch of froth on top. They chatted easily enough, mainly about music and clothes. Patsy admired Fran's nails, saying she wished hers could grow as long. 'Not that Annie approves of nail varnish,' she laughed.

'Take no notice. Do as you please, I always do.' Fran looked at her more closely for a second. 'You could look pretty, if you tried.'

'Do you really think so?'

'I like the ponytail. But don't ditch the Alice band completely, it's kinda cute and boys love that. You're lucky to be a natural blonde. I have to give my hair a bit of help. You should wash it every day in a lemon shampoo then it'd stay that way.'

Patsy purred to herself, feeling older and more sophisticated for being engaged in girl talk with sexy Fran Poulson.

No mention was made of any problem, and Patsy didn't like to ask again. Something was definitely eating Fran, and she seemed vague and distracted. Maybe something to do with that married chap rumour had it she was running around with.

After about half an hour, Fran looked at her watch and stood up. 'I'd best get back to the stall or Mam'll kill me. Nice talking to you, Patsy. See you around.'

'Yeah, right.' Feeling a warmth inside, Patsy watched her go. She felt cheered by the encounter, as if she'd taken the first steps in a new friendship. But then she remembered she wasn't supposed to be making friends, since Annie might be about to ask her to leave.

Which brought her right back to her own problem.

–

What had she learned so far? That Clara had never married, but had neatly avoided the question about a child, which Patsy saw as significant. She drew in a deep breath, knowing that she needed to think it all through very carefully before taking her quest any further.

Instinctively, Patsy felt the need to discover more evidence from the elusive housekeeper, if she could be found. Or from her grandmother's private papers! It might help give her courage to ask that ultimate question, if she was sure of her facts.

The helpful Shirley had offered to investigate the matter through Mrs Matthews's solicitors. They'd agreed that Patsy would send her a forwarding address, once she was settled, which she'd done early on. She'd written twice more during the last few weeks. Patsy had hoped to hear something by this time but all she'd received from the neighbour so far was a short note bearing a few cautious sentences, naming no names, presumably in case anyone else, the sisters for instance, should open the envelope and chance to read it.

'My source is not being particularly cooperative, but I haven't given up hope yet of finding the information we need. I'm seeking advice regarding how best to tackle the problem. Try to be patient.'

There it was again, that word, patient. The note wasn't even signed, which seemed to show excessive caution on Shirley's part but Patsy appreciated her efforts.

Every morning she would watch for the post. Sometimes she'd wonder if she should telephone and try to find out that way what was happening back in Southport. But she couldn't pluck up the courage to do so.

She'd give Shirley a few more weeks, Patsy decided, and then if there was nothing further, she would indeed telephone. There'd be no harm in that, surely, so long as she chose a moment when the Higginson sisters were out of the house, otherwise they'd be curious about who she was ringing.

Nothing could be achieved in a hurry, Patsy reminded herself. Were Shirley to find something, the housekeeper for instance, visits would need to be arranged, documents or letters studied. It would take time to ascertain the facts, to prove the case one way or the other, and it must be done carefully, without raising alarm or suspicion.

And if it should all turn out to be a false trail, nothing more than coincidence and gossip, and Clara was not in fact her mother, then far better to move on, however painful, rather than have everyone know she'd considered a crazy notion.

In view of all this uncertainty, Patsy decided that lovely as it was talking to Fran, and much as she might fancy Marc Bertalone, she must take care not to become too involved in case she did have to leave. That way she could at least keep her pride intact.

What Patsy dreaded most of all was rejection!

Sighing, she tucked her new record under her arm and set off back to the hat stall to finish her shift, swamped yet again by a sense of deep loneliness and insecurity.

But there really was no alternative. She must simply be patient and wait for news. In any case, right at this moment, she couldn't even say what she hoped the outcome would be.

Chapter Fifteen

Patience never had been one of Molly's strong points, and she'd really had a bellyful with those two obstreperous daughters of hers. If it wasn't one, it was the other. Now, even Ozzy had turned awkward. Nobody listened to her any more. And as if she didn't have trouble enough at home, now there were problems with the market. The re-election had taken place and Belle Garside was firmly established as the new market superintendent, holding meetings and throwing her weight about left, right and centre. She planned to put all the rents up for a start, which was bad news so far as Molly was concerned. And for others, such as the Higginson sisters, for whom she knew money was tight.

Molly had learned all of this from her friend Winnie Watkins. Not that Winnie was on the market committee, but little escaped her notice.

'What's more,' Winnie was saying to her now, 'traders will be expected to pay for a full fifty-two week year, irrespective of whether they choose to trade in every one of those weeks, and every stallholder must personally attend at least one week in every month. It's the farmers' wives I feel most sorry for, who come only when they have produce to sell. They'll have to pay whether they attend or not.'

'Well, we don't want a half empty market,' Sam Beckett reasonably pointed out. 'And those with the best positions pay the most, which is surely fair enough.'

Undeterred in her condemnation of her enemy, Winnie went on, 'I suppose you've heard that if regulations aren't followed, suspensions or fines will be imposed?'

'I heard that too,' Sam acknowledged with a sigh. He'd been friendly with Belle in the past so was cautious in his condemnation of her now.

'Nay!' Molly said, aghast and far less reticent. 'That's not right. I don't like the idea of fines. That's not right at all.'

'It's right enough. She's a powerful lady now, is our Belle.'

Big Molly grudgingly envied her that fact. She couldn't even control her own family, let alone a whole bleeding market. 'Course, Belle got away with it because she had charisma and sex appeal. All the men wanted to sleep with her, though they might claim only to be interested in her ideas.

'At least she's planning to build a proper solid row of stalls for the fish and meat market, which can only be a good thing,' Jimmy Ramsay put in, smoothing down his blue and white striped butcher's apron. 'She's even approached the council for a grant to help pay for it.'

'Aye, and we're all waiting with bated breath for the result of their deliberations,' Winnie drily remarked. 'I mean, when has the council ever given us owt for nowt?'

Big Molly wouldn't trust the council so far as she could throw them, but she agreed with Jimmy that new stalls with proper solid roofs over the food would be a good thing. Robert and her dear daughter-in-law would approve. But she could understand her friends feeling unsettled and worried. Change was in the air, costs were rising and all the stallholders were feeling anxious about the future.

Papa Bertalone wandered over during this conversation, standing quietly at the back of the group as he listened. Now he elbowed his way into the centre of the little group and lowered his voice, as if about to impart a dire secret. 'Have you heard the latest?'

Heads lifted, glances shifted, checking they were not overheard as they waited for Marco to go on.

'The market, it *ees* going to be sold!'

'What?'

'Sold?'

'Don't talk daft, Marco. How can you sell a market?'

'It *ees* very simple, my friend. You sell the land to a developer, to build*a* more of these big high rise flats they are putting up all over the city. You no see them?'

Jimmy Ramsay rubbed his ruddy face with the flat of his hand. 'By heck, that's a shaker. Where did you get this from? It's surely nobbut gossip.'

Marco Bertalone shrugged his shoulders and lifted his hands in that expressive Italian way he had, and which his son Marc seemed to have inherited. 'I know nothing, nothing, only what Joe Southworth say. He tell me, on the QT, as you call it.' He tapped the side of his nose. 'And there will be a rake for Belle if she pulls it off.'

'Rake?'

Sam Beckett cleared his throat. 'I think he means rake-off. Are you saying that Belle will get a backhander if she lets it go through?'

Again the expressive shrug. 'I no understand thees backhanders and rake-offs but Belle, she sell the market she makea de big money in her pocket, *sì*?'

The talk now became anxious, increasing in volume with everyone talking at once, until Jimmy Ramsay hushed them by offering to speak to Belle herself. 'It's no good us getting all aerated till we know the proper facts.'

There was general agreement that Jimmy should ascertain from her what, exactly, was going on, and then they'd meet up again and discuss the matter further. One by one they all drifted back to their stalls, frowns and anxious expressions still very much in evidence. They'd voted her on because they were tired of Joe Southworth, fussy and ineffectual as he was. Now they seemed to have opened up a whole new Pandora's box of trouble.

The news didn't help Molly's temper on this particular morning.

Raised rents, possible fines and a power-hungry superintendent who might well sell off their livelihood without a by-your-leave; all on top of recalcitrant daughters intent on getting themselves mixed up with the wrong sort of chap: husbands who no longer did as they were told, and sons who stole your pie-making business from under your very nose and treated you like a decrepit has-been. It was enough to make a body run mad.

So when she spotted Thomas George, the baker, striding through the market as if he owned the bleeding place, Molly knew just what to do about it.

–

'Thomas George, the leper of Champion Street, as I live and breathe.'

Thomas sighed. 'Don't start, Molly. I don't like the way things are any more than you do, but there's not a lot we can do about it. My wife and I have tried, as I'm sure you have, to keep the pair of them apart, but to no avail.'

Molly propped her hands on her substantial hips and stood four square before him. 'Aye, you would say that, useless lump that you are. Your family always did believe in taking the easy way out. With that brother of yours, for instance, who should have stood trial for what he did to our Lena.'

Thomas George's face flushed a dark red. 'That's nonsense, and you know it. It's tragic what happened to your sister but Howard wasn't entirely to blame. He too has been lost to his family for years because of what happened. Now get out of my way and let me go about my lawful business.'

Molly screeched with laughter. 'Lawful? You Georges don't know the meaning of the word. How many innocent girls has that no-good brother of yours interfered with since then, eh? Free to do as he pleases for all these years in some foreign land.'

'I'm not going to stand here defending my brother.'

'No, because you can't, he's indefensible.'

A tug at her sleeve and Winnie's voice came in her ear. 'Don't take on so, Molly. You'll get yourself all worked up for nothing. Leave it be.'

Molly snatched her arm away. 'It isn't nowt to me. As for that son of yours, if you aren't man enough to control him better, then I'll do it for you. He leaves my girl alone, understand, or I'll have somebody fix his wedding tackle so's it won't be any further use to him. Pity that brother of yours didn't suffer the same fate.'

Thomas made a low growling sound deep in his throat, but making no reply, he brushed right past her and headed for his cake stall.

'Here, don't you walk away from me when I'm talking to you. I asked you a question, are you going to control that son of yours or not?'

Still Thomas George ignored her. As he reached his stall, he meticulously fastened back a loose canvas flap, murmured a few quiet words to his anxious-looking wife then turned with a smile to his first customer. 'Your usual granary, is it, Mrs Marsh? And a couple of custard tarts, right you are.'

If there was one thing Molly couldn't abide above all else, it was being ignored. 'Here, you, listen when I'm speaking to you! You get that son of yours off my back, right? Stop him keep coming round to mine moaning about wanting to wed our Amy. It isn't going to happen. I'll lock her up till doomsday sooner.'

'Aye, you do that,' Thomas George shouted right back, leaning over his cakes and wagging a furious finger at her, oblivious to his wife murmuring something about his blood pressure and doing her best to calm him. 'The last thing I want is for my lad to be associated with any cheap little tart you might have produced.'

That was all Molly needed. Grabbing the nearest thing to hand, which happened to be a lemon meringue pie, she flung it in Thomas George's face. It splattered most satisfactorily down his large bulbous nose, all over his prattling mouth and right down the front of his clean white overall. Molly punched one fat fist in the air and cheered. But her triumph didn't last long. Thomas George struck back with a strawberry pavlova.

In seconds, custard tarts, vanilla slices and apple crumbles were flying everywhere. Customers ran for their lives while the stall-holders abandoned their pitches and gathered round to watch Molly Poulson enter into armed combat with the Georges, her sworn enemies. She hadn't entertained them half so well in years, not since she'd chased Ozzy home with a frying pan after he'd been seen chatting up that floozy in the Crown.

'Eeh, if Ozzy were watching this, he'd be taking bets on his missus winning,' said one wag.

It ended, predictably enough, with Big Molly grabbing hold of the front of the Georges' bakery stall. With one heave from those massive shoulders of hers, she flipped it over, demolishing any remaining stock in a glorious puddle of custard, cream, and pastry.

Then she walked away with a wide grin on her face, feeling utterly perked up.

–

Amy cuddled close in Chris's arms on the park bench, weeping softly into his shoulder. The golden warmth of a May evening bathed them in its soft light, gilding the fire in her auburn curls. There was the sound of children's voices, as they played on the swings and roundabout close by. An old man strolled by happily whistling on his way to the pub, a courting couple wrapped in each other's arms, a family laughing and joking together as they took the dog for its evening walk. Ordinary people going happily about their ordinary, everyday lives.

How Amy envied them. Everyone, but Chris and herself, seemed to be happy.

'That's it then, our last hope, the end of all our dreams of being together. What a fracas! Brawling in the street like that, like a – like a – oh, I can't even find a word to describe it, it was so awful. I can't believe Mam would do that.'

'Can't you? I can.'

Amy bridled. 'It takes two to make a fight. If your father hadn't provoked her...'

Chris smoothed a hand over her cheek, his eyes gently pleading. 'Let's not get involved in this. It's their quarrel, not ours.'

'Oh, Chris, yes, you're right. This is what they've reduced us too. Making us take sides in their stupid feud. And if your family won't even discuss it with you, there's absolutely nothing more we can do. Did they even admit that he existed, this Uncle Howard? Did he go to Australia?'

Chris's expression was grim, his pallor answering her question even as he shook his head. 'I asked them that. My mother took refuge in tears, as always, my father said he thought he'd already made it clear that the subject was closed, then ordered me to my room as if I were still a schoolboy.'

They were both silent for a moment, digesting this.

Amy said, in a small voice, 'But you aren't – a schoolboy, I mean.'

'No, I'm damn well not! I can please myself what I do.'

The anger in his tone frightened her and she began to weep again. 'But I can't please myself. I'm not of age yet.'

'Don't cry, Amy, please don't cry. I love you. I can't bear to see you so upset. I'm sorry I shouted. It's just that it's all turned out so – so awful!'

'You weren't shouting. Mam's the one who shouts, not you. It's a wonder I didn't hear that fight from our Robert's kitchens. I wish I had seen it in a way, the battle of the custard tarts.' Amy almost giggled, though it was more from nerves than amusement. 'Everyone's talking about it. It's so embarrassing. I can't look people in the face.'

He held her close, kissed away her tears. 'There has to be something we can do, and I've been giving the matter a great deal of thought. Do you love me?'

Her mouth curved into a shy smile that seemed to soften and blur her features. It brought a naked vulnerability into eyes still red from weeping, revealing the depth of her emotion, her fear of losing him, and making him want her all the more. 'I was thinking that maybe I do.'

'And you still want to marry me?' He tenderly tucked a curl behind her ear.

'I'm trying to think of a good reason why I shouldn't.' Amy rolled her eyes upwards, her rosy lips pouting in a delightful mockery of deep thought. Unable to resist, Chris captured her mouth with his and kissed her fiercely.

'Stop teasing me, woman, this is serious. We have to concentrate.'

'I know, I know, and I can't bear it.' All pretence gone she flung her arms about his neck and for several long moments neither of them spoke, being far too busily engaged in exchanging more kisses, and fresh avowals of love and devotion.

After a while Chris disentangled himself. 'I want you to listen to me very carefully, Amy. But first you must answer one more question. Do you trust me?'

'I trust you with my life, as I love you.'

'Then this is how I see it. You're absolutely right, they're never going to agree to us getting married. My father says this so-called feud has nothing to do with me and yet it clearly does because when he'd calmed down today – after he'd cleaned off all the custard and cream, and remembered I was twenty-two and not twelve – I asked if I could bring you round to meet him, so that he could judge for himself. And he was off again. Absolutely hit the roof! He's barely spoken to me since and Mum has that look in her eye, as if I've let her down in some way.

'Don't get me wrong, as I have every sympathy with your mam's grief, Amy. It must have been terrible losing her sister like that, but clearly my family have suffered too. Dad must have lost a brother, in a way. Now he refuses even to mention his name, maybe looks on him as some sort of black sheep. Or Dad thinks he was hard done by. I don't know. Since it's never to be discussed, how can I ever know? And why should it matter now? The important thing is, that it all happened nearly thirty years ago, and has nothing at all to do with us!'

Amy had wiped away her tears; listening avidly to every word of this assessment, which she knew already in her heart. 'So where does that leave us? What can we do?'

'We can elope. In Scotland you're old enough to marry at sixteen so we wouldn't have a problem there.'

'Oh, Chris!' Her eyes were shining now with hope. 'Would you do that for me?'

'It won't be easy. They might come after us. Could contact the newspapers or the police. Say I've kidnapped you.'

'I don't care!'

'Even when we get there, to Gretna Green, we'd need to lie low for two or three weeks before we could marry in front of the anvil. Would you mind sleeping rough, beneath the stars?'

'Oh, Chris, no, not if I was in your arms.' She was in them now, clinging tight to him, determined never to let him go. 'When do we leave?'

'I thought tomorrow night, after dark. I'll be waiting for you at the end of Champion Street. Once everyone is asleep, I want you to sneak out, but don't bring much with you, just pack a few things in a bag. I'll see to the rest, food and stuff.'

Amy shook her head. 'No, I can't do that, Mam watches me like a hawk. And our Fran sleeps in the same room, so I'd never manage to get away. Can you meet me after work, as you did the other day? I could take a bag with me in the morning, with just the barest essentials.'

'I'll be there on the dot.'

And so it was arranged. Amy could only hope and pray that she'd get through the next day without giving anything away, or arousing her mother's suspicions.

Chapter Sixteen

Taking Fran's advice, Patsy started to pay more attention to her hair and nails, this time painting them all one colour in an attempt to look elegant and sophisticated. She also bought some lemon shampoo, and Annie was heard at times to complain that Patsy was never out of the bathroom, constantly washing her hair, not to mention that her nails were growing into talons.

Clara would laugh and say, 'She's a young girl, having fun. Leave her be.'

Patsy reminded herself of this fact the very next time Marc Bertalone sauntered by as she walked through the market, and had the gall to wink at her. Especially when her heart did that little acrobatic flip, leaving her short of breath for a moment.

'Have you succumbed to my Latin charms yet?' he teased.

'Has hell frozen over already?' Patsy said, glancing up into the bright blue heavens. But then it was far safer to study the puffy white clouds than the muscles on his bare arms, or the way he stood, legs astride, like a great colossus. So vain, she thought, so proud of himself. How could a man be so beautiful? It shouldn't be allowed.

'*Tammy and the Bachelor* is on at the Gaumont. Cool song. In the hit parade. Do you like Debbie Reynolds?'

'I'm sure you do, since you're woman mad.' His melting brown eyes came alive with merry laughter; the long curling lashes sweeping upwards as he chuckled.

Marc shook his head in despair, wishing he could learn to ignore her, but for all her put-downs, her obstinate refusal to speak to him in a civil fashion, he nonetheless found Patsy utterly irresistible. She was the most infuriating girl he'd ever met yet he had to keep trying. Why couldn't she see that he only wanted to get to know her better? 'Can't bear for me to look at another woman, huh? I knew it.'

'Don't flatter yourself.'

'So that's a no, is it?'

'You're so bright.' Patsy turned to walk away.

'Hey, you ask me next time, all right?'

'Keep watching for that freeze.'

Following her advice about not becoming involved with the market folk, was proving to be harder than Patsy had anticipated. For all she'd made a few enemies at the outset, people seemed more accepting of her now.

'Hiya, Patsy!' they would call, or 'like your outfit', if they saw her in something new and daring. She bought a pair of canary yellow capris which turned heads whenever she passed by.

Winnie Watkins said, 'I may be interfering but I must say that with your colouring, you really suit yellow. It makes you look like a little ray of sunshine.'

Patsy beamed her thanks, as this was high praise indeed, coming from Winnie. With summer approaching she bought a couple of circular skirts from Dena's rack that stood by Winnie's stall. She absolutely loved them, one was patchwork, and the other had a pair of cherries appliquéd just above the hem. Even Annie approved, which must be a miracle.

'That's a pretty skirt,' Clara said one day as Patsy helped her with the washing up. 'Much nicer than those dreadful toreador pants.'

Patsy bristled. 'I love my toreadors, and my sloppy joe sweater. Didn't you wear crazy clothes when you were young?'

'Oh, I expect I did. I can't really remember. It was different in those days with a war on. There weren't so many exciting things around to wear.'

'I suppose not.' Patsy took the next plate and began to wipe it, wondering if this might be an opportunity to do a bit more digging. 'So what did you do during the war? Were you in the ATS or something?'

'No, nothing so sensible, as Annie and I were in Paris when war broke out.'

'Paris!' Imagining dull, mousy Clara in Paris was beyond her, not to mention tight-lipped disapproving Annie. 'What were you doing there, for goodness sake?'

'My sister was a teacher of English, at the university. I stayed with her for a while, to keep her company, you know.'

Patsy frowned at the plate, slowly went on wiping it. Did this fit in with what she'd learned? The gossipy neighbours had mentioned that Clara might have gone abroad to have the baby, so possibly it did. 'Were you a teacher too?'

Clara laughed. 'Goodness, no, I'm not clever enough. I think that plate is dry now.'

'Oh, sorry.' Patsy set it in the rack, picked up another. 'So when did you come back to England?'

'It wasn't easy getting out. Any hope of escape became increasingly difficult as the enemy advanced. Once Germany invaded France in June, 1940, many anti-Nazi refugees were in danger of being arrested by the Gestapo. They were the German secret police, in case you didn't know.'

Patsy said that she did know, and showed proper concern. 'So you were in danger of becoming trapped?'

Clara paused, soapsuds popping on her stilled hands in the washing-up water, a faraway expression in her grey eyes, seeing again some remembered horror. 'We were in very grave danger at times. You had to have the right papers, reach the Belgian coast without being spotted, then find a ship to take you, all extremely difficult to achieve. We were not the only ones, you understand. The Jews, they suffered the worst... and the children. Some of our friends we... we never saw again.'

Patsy's eyes opened wide. She knew that Clara was referring to the death camps, to the holocaust, but didn't dare ask about that. Who would wish to speak of such horror?

'Sometimes you had to resort to forged papers, and secret routes with the help of what became known as the Underground. It was expensive – we had to sell our possessions to pay for the necessary help and required documents. We got out in the end on the back of a pig lorry. The animals were supposedly being taken to market. Annie and I hid under a tarpaulin right in their midst, terrified of being trampled underfoot, but the lorry driver did the best he could by getting us about halfway to the coast. After that, we walked for miles, but I can't remember how far or how long it took, maybe days and days. We were young then, and reasonably fit, but bone weary nonetheless, dirty and bedraggled, and stinking of pigs.'

'Weren't you stopped by the Germans?'

'There were one or two close shaves. We had to lie low for a while and... well... anyway... we got back to England eventually. I can't recall when exactly. We were lucky.'

Patsy would like to have heard the bits of the story she'd left out, but it seemed rude to ask, since remembering was clearly painful for Clara. 'You must have been scared.'

'Terrified! They were difficult times.'

Her hands jerked into action once more, scrubbing a pan with renewed vigour. 'Enough about me,' Clara said. 'Now it's your turn to tell me something about yourself.'

'There's nothing to tell.' Patsy felt ashamed. Her problems seemed insignificant after hearing what the sisters had gone through during the war. And she suspected there was much more, that Clara had no wish to recall.

'You're sixteen years old and...'

'Seventeen now.'

Clara looked at her in surprise. 'You've had a birthday and not told us?'

Patsy shrugged. 'It's not important. I have never celebrated my birthday. Who would care?'

There was a slight pause while Clara digested this piece of information, feeling sad deep in her heart that someone so young could be so cynical, and sorry that she hadn't thought to ascertain this simple fact before. 'You were born in 1940, though you aren't sure where. Can you at least tell me where you slept the night before you came here?'

'Why? What does it matter?'

'I'm interested. Where did you live? You must have had a home, a school, a family some place. These foster parents of yours, tell me a little about them.'

This was far too intrusive so far as Patsy was concerned. If the sisters found out about the Bowmans, their address and so forth, wouldn't they send her right back?

She put the plate in the rack and set down the dishtowel. 'There are only two things you need to know about me. One, I don't answer questions. Two, I don't do housework.' And with this, she walked out of the kitchen.

'Oh, dear,' Clara said to herself. 'It really isn't getting any easier.'

Later, Clara told Annie how badly she'd failed. 'I thought if I confessed some of the traumas we'd suffered, she might open up and tell me about hers. It didn't work.'

Annie said, 'How much did you tell her?'

'Just about our leaving Paris, how difficult it was for us to get out.'

'That's all?'

Clara nodded. 'I thought it was enough.'

'But not enough to coax her own story out of her?'

Clara shook her head. 'I'm afraid not. Would it help, do you think, if I told her more, and about Marianne? About why we want to help her?'

Annie put a gentle hand on her sister's arm. 'No, and it would only bring you pain. Let us simply have patience and wait. Patsy may come to trust us in time.'

Coffee with Fran Poulson became a regular occurrence and the two girls were increasingly friendly, although Fran remained oddly jumpy and distracted. Whatever her problem was, she clearly wasn't about to share it, which was disappointing in a way. Patsy felt that since she'd suffered so badly herself, she had a great deal to offer, if anyone was interested in asking her advice.

Though why should she care? What did it have to do with her if Fran had a problem with her love life? Any day now the sisters would say they could no longer afford to keep her, and ask her to leave. Patsy lived in hope that they might get to like having her around too much to do that, but then she'd screw things up by being awkward or difficult, as she had done today. She couldn't seem to help herself.

And then something happened which confirmed, all too clearly, that she was right not to imagine she was anything more than a stranger in this place.

When Annie's birthday came round in the first week of June, Patsy bought her a pretty silk scarf in a box. She was pleased with her choice, and took a great deal of trouble wrapping it in silver paper and tying it with crimson ribbon, complete with a curly bow.

From the startled surprise in the woman's eyes, and the flush on her cheeks, anyone would think she'd never received a gift before. Clara gushed about how kind it was of Patsy to have remembered her sister's birthday, but Annie's reaction, pleasure being something completely alien to her, was less forthcoming.

Her cool response was insulting. All she said was that she hoped the scarf hadn't cost Patsy too much money, and was adamant that it must be returned. 'I do hope you kept the receipt.'

Patsy felt as if she'd been struck. 'Don't you like it? I chose it most carefully. You like blue, I know you do, it's your favourite colour.'

'I wear navy a good deal, that is true, but not this bright cobalt – azure – this brilliant blue. Navy is far more serviceable.'

'I know, but I thought this scarf might brighten up that navy suit you wear, and you can wear it with your grey coat too.'

The scarf had to be returned, and Patsy was deeply hurt. She made a point of not speaking to Annie for days afterwards. Clara tried to ease things between them by explaining how tight money was, trade being so slack, and how her sister could never abide waste, but Patsy was unmoved by the excuses.

'It was my money, so why shouldn't I spend it as I like?' Miserable old bag could do without a present, and see if she cares. In her heart Patsy knew they didn't want her here, no matter how they might pretend otherwise. Nobody did. To add to her deep sense of insecurity the very next evening when Patsy went for a walk down by the canal, she became aware that someone was following her. It turned out to be Marc.

Patsy swung round on him, hands on hips. 'Were you wanting something?'

His grin was very nearly her undoing, tripping her heart and melting her insides. 'Now that's a question I'd better not answer. What is it that you want, Patsy Bowman, that's more to the point? If I could only find that out, I might discover the key to your soul. To your heart at least.'

'It's not for sale.'

'Is that because you don't have a heart, or because you've simply mislaid the key?'

If she smiled at him, instead of arguing all the time, he'd probably fall into step beside her and they could talk, even become friends. He might hold her hand, laugh with her. Kiss her. Her gaze drifted to his mouth, trying to imagine what it might feel like. Patsy was seventeen years old, a rebel at heart, yet had never been kissed, not properly. Nothing more than a few clumsy fumbles which she'd quickly put a stop to. She'd made sure to keep boys always at a safe distance, as she was doing now. But this one was different from all the rest. This one she actually liked. Patsy considered.

And what if she did let him do any of those things? She'd fall for him, that's what. And when Annie gave her the old heave-ho, which might happen any day now, money being as tight as it was, where would she be then? Heartbroken, that's where.

She tossed back her hair, free from both Alice band and pony-tail on this occasion, so that the fine silver fronds floated about her face in the evening breeze. 'I'm sure there are any number of hearts for sale. All you have to do is take your pick. I'm keeping mine in cold store for now, just to be safe.' Patsy turned to walk away but Marc followed her, keeping just one step behind. Turning on him, she shouted: 'Don't do that.'

He stopped, held up his hands, palm outwards. 'What are you afraid of, Patsy? Why can't you unbend just a little? You might find you actually like me if you took the trouble to get to know me. If you went out on a date with me.'

'I'm sure there are plenty of girls simply aching for a date with you. I'm not one of them, so leave me alone and go and pester them, why don't you?'

There was a sadness in those chocolate brown eyes of his as they roved over her face, as if determined to memorise every detail. 'Oh, I agree, I am the big catch. It's Alessandro who wants to go into the ice cream business with Papa, not me. They think I am rich, that I will inherit my father's business. It can't be my simple, country-boy looks, after all, can it?'

Patsy said nothing. Just gazed at the square jaw, the perfect oval of his handsome face, the crisp dark curls falling so enticingly over his brow; she dug her hands deep in her pockets in case they should betray her by reaching out and touching them.

'So the girls, they queue round the block just in the hope of my noticing them.'

'How wonderful for you.'

'But they don't interest me because you're the one I want, little one, not them.'

She wanted to say 'stuff and nonsense', but her breath caught in her throat at his words, at the dangerous intensity of his gaze. What was he saying? What did he mean? This was all getting far too intimate. 'When I'm ready to start dating arrogant show-offs, I'll let you know. Till then, stay off my patch, Marc Bertalone. Leave me alone!'

He shook his head in sad resignation, allowed a beat before giving a half shrug with those powerful shoulders of his. 'Okay, have it your way.'

He didn't follow her this time as she walked away, but the quiet smile that lifted the corners of his wide mouth should have warned her that he wasn't done yet, not by a long way.

—

Patsy arrived home from work the next day to find a large cardboard box in her room. Filled with curiosity, wondering if it had come from Shirley, it reminded her that she still hadn't plucked up the courage to ring her and ask after any further news, she cut off the string with her nail scissors and opened it. Inside was a record player. Not any cheap sort of record player either, but a Ferguson with twin speakers and autoplay, so you could put on more than one record at a time.

There was a card with it. It read, 'Happy Birthday, whenever it was, Annie and Clara'.

Unable to contain her excitement, Patsy galloped downstairs and flung herself first at Annie and then at Clara, kissing them both soundly on each cheek.

'You are the most wonderful people in the world, and I love you!'

Clara said, 'Oh my,' and sat down abruptly.

Annie, crimson cheeked, mumbled something about Clara having scolded her for behaving badly over the returned birthday gift.

'We've both been a bit hard on you recently,' Clara added, as if unwilling to allow her sister to take all the blame.

Annie pursed her lips against the hint of a smile. 'Besides, we wanted our old wireless back. We're more *Third Programme* people ourselves than Radio Luxembourg, and we thought it might take too long for you to raise the money. By which time our nerves will be in shreds and our hearing ruined. But, yes, I suppose we have grown surprisingly fond of you.'

And then, just in case Patsy should interpret this as weakness on her part, she quickly added: 'But it mustn't be on too loud and distress the neighbours. I will have respect and good manners in my home, at all times.'

'Of course, Annie, would I do anything else? Shall I show you how to bop?' and grabbing the older woman around the waist, Patsy flung herself into a demonstration, twirling her into a dizzying spin. Flustered, Annie put a stop to such nonsense at once, her cheeks flushed and her mouth very nearly twitching into a smile.

'Really, Patsy, you are incorrigible, far too much of a live wire.'

'Oh, I do hope so. I want to be happy, don't you? It makes life so much more fun. And thanks so much for the record player. Now I can start buying more records. Thank you, thank you, thank you.' And running back upstairs, Patsy spent a happy evening setting it all up and playing the only two records she owned so far: Frankie Vaughan's 'The Green Door' and Jerry Lee Lewis's 'Great Balls of Fire', over and over again.

Maybe they did like her a little, after all.

Chapter Seventeen

It wasn't going to be easy. It seemed to Amy's agitated mind that her mother had eyes everywhere that morning. Amy tried to sneak some basic essentials such as a hunk of cheese and a few slices of bread from the kitchen cupboards into her overall pocket while she was making herself a slice of toast for breakfast. But Buster kept sniffing and nosing at her pocket, taking obvious interest in food being put in strange places, so she had to give up on that one, and hope that Chris would have better luck, as he had promised.

Her mother was constantly walking in and out of the kitchen, hovering around, watching with her narrow-eyed shrewd gaze as if she guessed what was going on. But how could she? Amy would reassure herself, smiling serenely as she spread butter and jam on her toast, her heart beating pitter-pat.

Getting out of the house was another problem. Amy had to dash back upstairs to her room to snatch up her bag into which she'd packed pyjamas and toothbrush, clean underwear and a change of blouse and skirt. She'd done this while Fran was snoring away in the middle of the night, and could only hope her sister hadn't found it tucked under her bed.

No, it was still there. She snatched it up, turned to leave and bumped straight into her mother. 'What've you got there?' Big Molly wanted to know.

'Nothing!'

'Don't look like nothing to me.'

Amy told herself to stay calm, act natural, and smile. 'I meant, nothing important. Excuse me, Mam, but I must dash. Our Robert will be furious if I'm late.'

135

'No need to worry about him! I thought you could happen help me on the stall today. I'm fair sick of our Fran's moans and groans.'

Amy was mortified. Oh, no, this would never do. This wasn't the plan at all. Chris was meeting her at Brunswick Basin, near to the kitchens, not here on Champion Street. If she wasn't there he'd think she'd deserted him. Stood him up. 'Sorry, Mam, I can't do that. Wouldn't be fair on Robert.' She tried to make a joke of it. 'Can you see our Fran with her hands covered in flour?'

'She doesn't need to. Hasn't he got mixers now to make the pastry?'

'Well, yes, but you still have to roll it out, cut out the circles. He hasn't bought that sort of machinery, not yet, and Fran wouldn't enjoy all of that. She'd be bored. I know she moans, but she likes chatting to the customers on the market. It's much quieter in the kitchens.'

'Well, she'll have to get used to it. She's already gone. I sent her off an hour ago. You're stopping here today, with me.'

It was the longest day Amy could ever remember. It was hot and sticky in early June, and trade was poor. Such customers who did venture into the market seemed to take forever to decide what they wanted to buy. It sadly wasn't the weather for pies and puddings, or the delicious home-made crumpets Poulson's were also famous for. But cheese was popular, Robert's new pâté, and various cooked meats.

'Eeh, you only want a bit of ham salad, don't you chuck? Too hot to eat,' said one old lady. 'Go on, slip an extra slice on, and it'll do me a nice sandwich tomorrow.'

Amy wondered if it would still be hot in Scotland. She hadn't brought a blanket, couldn't carry one. So if it was cold at night, how would they manage? The day wore on and she kept thinking of all the things she should have packed, a lipstick and perfume she hadn't thought to bring. A pretty nightie rather than boring pyjamas. What would Chris think of her? This was her wedding after all.

She didn't really regret not having a white dress, bridesmaids and all that eating and drinking at a crowded reception. Amy wasn't the sort of person who liked a fuss. And since their respective families weren't speaking to each other, what would be the point? But she had dreamed of what her honeymoon might be like. She'd pictured a hotel, crisp white sheets, a meal together first and a glass of wine, just to get in the mood. Amy guessed they might both be a bit nervous, since it would be their first time, and your wedding night was so important, wasn't it? It had to be just right. She was going to spend hers in a field, without even a blanket.

'Are you daydreaming again?' Molly asked, giving her a hefty nudge. 'You've got your head in the clouds today. I've asked you three times if you want to take your tea break. Happen you'd better, before you fall asleep on the job.'

'Oh, yes please, that'd be great. Can I get off early, Mam, I am a bit tired.'

'No, you can stay till six, as you always do.'

'Dad's right, you are a hard taskmaster. But I'm taking half an hour for me tea, right? I'm shattered.' That might give her time to find Chris and explain the change of plan. Amy went to pick up her bag.

'You don't need to take that with you, not just for a cup of tea,' Molly said.

Amy floundered for an excuse, couldn't find one and shrugged, giving a vague sort of smile. 'You never know,' then fled as quickly as she could, the bag tucked firmly under her arm, in case her mother decided to intervene physically and deprive her of it, which she was perfectly capable of doing. And Amy was convinced that if she left it there, under the counter, she was nosy enough to open it and go through her things.

Running through the market, Amy desperately tried to think where Chris might be. He often spent his afternoons sleeping, since he had to be at the dairy at the crack of dawn to deliver milk, but sometimes he would go for a walk first, or do a few jobs for his mother. And if she didn't find him in the next half hour, and Mam wouldn't let her off early, what on earth would she do?

–

Amy hadn't gone more than ten steps when she was halted by Winnie Watkins who was deep in conversation with Alec Hall, Sam Beckett, Abel and several other stallholders. If Belle Garside was queen of the market, Winnie was its eyes and ears.

'Hey up, chuck, what do you think of this latest carry-on?' She was drawing Amy into their group whether she liked it or not.

'What carry-on?' Amy glanced about her, hoping for a glimpse of Chris.

It seemed that the rumour was true. A developer was indeed keen to flatten all of Champion Street and put a block of flats on it. 'To help solve the housing problems of Manchester, apparently, and since there'll probably be a kickback for our Belle, she's seriously considering accepting the offer.'

'She can't do that,' Barry Holmes protested. 'Not without our agreement, surely?'

'If she believes it's in her interests to agree with the plan, she'll certainly try. Anyway, there'd be compensation for us all,' Sam put in. 'Not just Belle. Trouble is, would it be enough to justify losing our livelihoods?'

Alec Hall agreed. 'We'd have to find another market prepared to let us in, or open a shop somewhere. Not easy.'

'Aye, and far more expensive,' Abel put in. 'My second-hand stuff wouldn't run to paying shop rent.'

'Don't forget, many of us would be losing our homes too, if all of Champion Street goes,' Alec reminded them. 'That would be a sorry situation in my eyes, and I for one would miss the camaraderie of the market.'

There were murmurs of assent all round. Amy was intrigued, concerned by this news, and yet fidgety and anxious to be away.

She had only half an hour to find Chris and warn him of the change in arrangements. Surreptitiously she glanced at her watch.

Unfortunately, Barry Holmes spotted the movement. 'Are we keeping you from somewhere?'

'No, no – well, I did have an appointment but it doesn't matter.'

Winnie frowned at her. 'I would've thought you'd be more interested in the prospect of being homeless. Your mam will be.'

'We can't let it happen,' Lizzie Pringle said, handing round a bag of caramels to try to cheer them all up.

Barry nodded as he sucked the delicious sweet. 'No, we have to fight it. Someone has to speak to Belle, make our feelings on the issue clear. Didn't Jimmy say he'd do that? Have we heard yet how he's got on?'

Winnie shook her head. 'Not yet, but word has it that some of the newer stallholders are saying they'd be glad of the compensation, content to fill their pockets with a bit of brass and leave. Which means we have to speak to everybody to put the other side, happen get a petition going.'

Jimmy Ramsay, guessing he was being talked about, strolled over. 'Hey up, if this is what I think it is, rebel committee members stirring up mischief, I'd like to be included.'

He explained how he'd spoken to Belle, putting forward the reservations of the other stallholders, and got absolutely nowhere. 'She's saying nothing. Keeping schtum, so I've put out some feelers with one or two council members that I know.'

Sam suggested they call a proper meeting and Jimmy agreed.

'Aye, not some hole in the corner gossip like we're doing now. This is serious stuff. We need a public meeting, one that every stallholder must attend. We'll hold it in the market hall on Friday night.'

'That's the ticket,' Winnie said, always pleased to have an excuse to set herself up against Belle Garside, whether it was a serious issue or not. They never had got on and after her son Kenny had caused the death of Dena's young brother, and attacked Winnie herself while Belle stood back and did nothing, she'd no time for her whatsoever.

Arrangements were soon made and Winnie turned again to Amy. 'Think on, you tell your mam that we're having this meeting on Friday. It's important everyone comes. Spread the word, right?'

Amy nodded and quickly made her escape. But her mind was still on finding Chris and their intended elopement, and she instantly forgot all about the meeting, the moment she left the group.

–

Fran finally found Eddie skulking in the bar of the Pack Horse, a pub far enough from Champion Street for them to use as an occasional meeting place. He must have known she was looking for him for he'd been deliberately avoiding her. She wasted no time dancing around the issue but bluntly announced that she believed herself to be pregnant, and watched the horror dawn on his face.

'Bleeding hell, what did you go and do a thing like that for?'

'Er, I think you had something to do with it too.'

'Yeah, but I thought you were taking care of things.'

'Oh, and it's not your responsibility too then?'

Eddie sulked. 'You told me you'd got one of them Dutch thingies.'

Fran felt her cheeks grow warm as she recalled she had indeed told him to stop using condoms. Except she'd forgotten to put the Dutch cap in on more than one occasion. It was so difficult to remember. She'd have her bath and everything, experiment with make-up and fuss over what she was going to wear, trying on different blouses, skirts and frocks, never sure what he'd like best. Then she'd be in such a rush not to be late, that at the last minute she'd dash off and forget to put the damn thing in. Sometimes she'd remember, sometimes she wouldn't, never having got into the habit. But that didn't mean Fran would let him off the hook entirely.

'Don't put all the blame on me. It takes two to tango. So, lover boy, what are we going to do about it, eh? I'm making a babby and it's going to pop out before too long. Like it or not, chum, you're going to be a dad.'

Eddie's face went deathly pale. This was the last thing he needed, a disaster in his eyes. What the hell Josie would have to say, he didn't dare to contemplate. 'No, I can't be a dad, not with you. This isn't how it's meant to be. It was all supposed to be just a bit of slap and tickle, a laugh. Nothing serious, right?'

Fran looked into his panic-stricken eyes and realised in that moment what a complete and utter fool she'd been, what a mess she'd made of everything. Amy had been right all along: Eddie was a loser, a selfish pig who thought only of himself, of having a bit of a leg-over without any of the responsibility.

And worse even than that, Fran realised in one blinding flash that nearly knocked her for six, that no matter what he was, she loved him. She actually loved the stupid bastard.

–

Chris was at home and Amy woke him by throwing gravel at his window. Within minutes, it seemed, he was beside her and she was explaining about her mother upsetting their plans.

'So I can't meet you after work. I'll have to go straight home with Mam. Ooh, and I've a message for her. I mustn't forget.'

Chris looked dismayed by this news. 'But if you can't sneak out at night, when can we get away?'

'I don't know,' Amy said, deeply distressed and near to tears.

'Let's leave now.'

'What?'

'Why wait? You've got your bag with you, I see. Let's go.' The next moment he was hurrying her down the back street to his car, which he'd already packed with blankets, cushions, a suitcase full of clothes and a huge box of food. 'I hope I've thought of everything,' he said with a grin.

'Oh, Chris, I hope we're doing the right thing,' said Amy, filled with doubts.

He stood stock-still! 'If you've changed your mind, now is the moment to say so.'

She looked up at him and her heart filled with love. She couldn't imagine life without him. No matter where he was, she wanted to be at his side. It was as simple as that. 'No, I haven't changed my mind. I'm just a bit nervous, that's all.'

He smiled at her and kissed her nose. 'Me too! Come on, love, we'll be fine, so long as we're together.'

—

'Have you seen our Amy?' Molly demanded of anyone who came near the pie stall. 'Little monkey went off for a tea break and I haven't seen her since. That must be more than an hour since. I'll give her what for when I get my hands on her.'

'I saw her earlier, when we were holding our impromptu meeting,' Winnie said.

'What impromptu meeting?'

'Didn't Amy tell you? She was supposed to.'

Big Molly heaved a sigh. 'I've just said, haven't I? I've not seen our Amy for over an hour.'

Swiftly, Winnie filled her in on the details but Molly was more concerned about her own affairs. 'It'll not happen. Nobody would dare to flatten my house without my say so. What I want to know is, where is our Amy?'

'Eeh, Moll, them girls of yours give you a lot of hassle.' Barry chuckled as he happily polished his apples. 'You should try giving them a longer leash.'

'Oh, aye,' Molly agreed. 'Any longer and they'd choke themselves with it.'

'If you're going to start another rumpus, can I have tickets for the front row?'

'You'll get a clip round the lug-hole, you, if you don't shut up. You and our Amy both.'

Barry laughed as if she'd made a joke. 'You've got to find her first, and if I were your Amy I'd be a million miles from Champion

Street right now. Running as fast as me little legs could carry me. Have you thought of that possibility?'

'Nay,' Molly said, her face a picture. 'She wouldn't dare, the daft little cow.'

'I'm not so sure. When fools fall in love they dare do all sorts of daft things. She could be heading north even as we speak.'

Chapter Eighteen

'Do you sell Davy Crockett hats?'

Patsy looked up at Marc in disbelief. 'Davy Crockett?'

'You know the guy, hero of the Alamo, owned a gun called Betsy, as seen on TV played by Fess Parker. My little brother is desperate for one of those coonskin hats.' And when she still looked blank, he continued with a sigh, 'Made of fur with a long bushy tail, looks like a racoon, only I expect it's rabbit. Surely you've seen them around. All the kids are wearing them.'

Patsy was wishing with all her heart that she was dressed in something more stylish than her plain pleated skirt and jersey. She wished she hadn't chosen to wear her Alice band this morning either. It was so childish, or cute as Fran termed it. And she had no wish to look cute for Marc Bertalone. She wished his presence, so close beside her, wasn't making her feel all wobbly inside.

She tilted up her pert little nose so that she could try to look down it, not easy since Marc was so much taller than she was. 'This is a ladies' hat shop, so why would we sell Davy Crockett hats?'

'Maybe because people are making a lot of money out of selling them, which sounds a good enough reason to me. Anyway, girls would like to wear them too. Why not?'

'You think you're so clever.'

Clara's voice floated over from the fitting area where she was stitching green leaves into a corsage. 'Now don't be rude to customers, Patsy, particularly to handsome young men.'

Marc grinned at her. 'You should listen to Miss Clara. She is a kind and clever woman.'

'We still don't have any Davy Crockett hats.'

'When will you be getting some? Soon, I hope. Giovanni is driving us all mad. He has the Davy Crockett pyjamas but it isn't enough. He must have the genuine Injun fighter hat.'

'I really don't think…' And then to her horror, Marc brushed past her and popped his head around the door of the fitting room. She was still yelling at him that he couldn't possibly go in there when Clara glanced up from her sewing and smiled.

'Hello, Marc, how's your mama?'

'She's good. And yourself, Miss Clara?'

She pulled a wry face. 'As well as can be expected, considering my great age.'

Then he walked right over to her and to Patsy's complete surprise, kissed her on both cheeks. 'You know, in Italy, the older a woman gets, the more beautiful she becomes. That is true for you too.'

Cheeks flushed a becoming pink, Clara said, 'You grow more incorrigible every day.'

'Naw, only more handsome.'

She laughed. 'And modest with it. We'll see what we can do about finding a Davy Crockett hat for Giovanni. Maybe getting a few in stock would be no bad thing, if I can persuade my sister to agree.'

Marc's expression was carefully non-committal at this refer-ence to Annie, known for a judgement in hats as stern as that she exercised on people. Anything remotely frivolous would never be seen on the sisters' hat stall, or not without Clara's intervention. 'I would be grateful,' he said with a little bow.

'You can go now that you've got what you want,' Patsy said, striding over and looking fairly stern herself. 'Men aren't allowed in the fitting room.'

He looked down at her, a strangely pitying expression in his chocolate brown eyes, then turned back to Clara. 'There is one other favour you can do for me.'

'And what is that, Marc?'

He rested a hand lightly on Patsy's shoulder. It felt fragile beneath his touch, too fragile, but at least she didn't flinch away. He took encouragement from that. 'You can persuade your lovely assistant here to come out with me one evening. She has hardened her heart against me, for no reason I can understand.'

'Well,' said Clara, grey eyes alight with amusement, 'and where was it you were wanting to take her?'

He spread his hands, in that inimitably Italian way, as if he were at a loss to understand why life was so impossibly difficult. 'I have offered her the dancing, the pictures, the walk in the park, none of which appeals. So next Sunday, we have the big family wedding. So many Bertalones. Too many. I need a girl to dance with, you understand, to rescue me from dancing with all my sisters. Will you ask her if she will do that small thing for me? I will not keep her out late, Miss Clara. And you know you can trust me to look after her.'

'I do trust you, Marc, and I really see no reason why Patsy shouldn't go with you. It sounds fun.'

'Ah, Bertalone weddings are always that. Noisy, but fun.'

Clara laughed, at which point Patsy spoke in her coldest tones. 'Excuse me, but do I have any say in this? I mean, I am still standing here, in case you haven't noticed, while you two make arrangements about my social life.'

Clara smiled. 'I've thought for some time, Patsy, that you really aren't getting out enough. It isn't right for you to spend all your time with two middle-aged ladies. You should mix more with people your own age.'

'I should at least be allowed to choose my own friends.'

Again Marc held his hands, palm upwards, in an expression of disbelief and despair. 'You see how cruel she is to me. What have I ever done to deserve it?'

Clara stood up and patted his broad shoulder. 'I shall speak to her. But Patsy is right, our tiny fitting room is no place for a gentleman, even a handsome young fellow such as yourself. Go home, Marc. Leave it with me.'

'I won't go. Why should I?'

'Because it will do you good as you're young, Patsy, and, as I said, you should spend more time with people of your own age. Go and enjoy yourself. He's a good lad, is Marc Bertalone. You won't have any problems with him. His family teach their children to show respect.'

Patsy desperately wanted to dance with Marc, the answer to her secret dreams. But after the way she had so clearly rebuffed him, how could she swallow her pride? And what dangers lay in store for her if she did go? 'I'll think about it,' she said, tossing back her hair so it floated like silver skeins across her lovely face. In a show of defiance, she pulled an elastic band from her pocket and gathered the wilful hair firmly into a ponytail.

Annie arrived at that moment, so the conversation was thankfully dropped while the sisters embarked upon their usual analysis of the purchases she'd made at the wholesalers. Clara bravely put forward her suggestion that they might try a few Davy Crockett hats.

'We could sell at least one to Marc Bertalone, as he wishes to buy a present for Giovanni. But as all the kids are wanting them, it might prove worth our while to get a few in stock.'

'Stuff and nonsense!' Annie said. 'We are not turning ourselves into a souvenir stall.'

'But, Annie, don't you think we should at least consider it?'

'No, I don't. I think you should leave such decisions to those who can think beyond what happens to be merely fashionable. You know I am far better suited to choosing the right stock for the stall than you, Clara, as I am not so easily influenced and duped by the whim of the moment.'

'But you must admit, Annie dear, there have been times when even you have been glad you conceded to my suggestions on fashion. The velvet petal range, for instance. And we did so well with the pillbox, which I persuaded you to buy, remember? It's turning into a classic.'

'Lucky guesses,' Annie said dismissively, clicking her false teeth in that irritating manner she had. 'I cannot allow myself to follow every fad and fancy, since I'm the one who has to pay the bills. Only this morning I have spent an uncomfortable half hour with the bank manager, discussing our lack of profitability.'

'But that's my point exactly,' Clara insisted. 'The Davy Crockett hats might well increase our profitability.'

Annie went red in the face, almost purple, her prim mouth trembling. 'How much plainer can I make it, Clara? We cannot afford to buy any more stock.'

Patsy was on the point of completely changing her own viewpoint by agreeing with Clara that they should at least give them a try, since she simply couldn't bear to see her bullied, when Annie startled her by swinging round upon her, eyes gimlet hard.

'As a consequence of that discussion, I'm going to be forced to let you go.'

Patsy looked bemused for a moment. 'Let me go where?'

'I can no longer afford to employ you, and before you say anything, let me assure you we've been perfectly satisfied with your work, haven't we, Clara?'

Her sister, looking equally dumbstruck, merely nodded.

'You're sacking me?' Patsy felt sick, could hardly get the words out. She'd seen it coming ages ago, but not like this. This news had come so unexpectedly, in the middle of a conversation about Davy Crockett hats, for goodness' sake. It was like a bolt from the blue and hurt so badly. It wasn't long since they'd given her the record player and made her feel as if they were used to having her around, might even be getting to like her. Now she was out on her ear.

She should have known it was all a trick, nothing more than a sop to their own guilt. Didn't folk always want to get rid of her, just as soon as they could?

Annie was still talking. 'The fact of the matter is that we simply can't afford the extra wages. The stall isn't doing as good a business as it used to, not now that hats are going out of fashion, more's the pity. Shocking, how modern standards are slipping. At one time no one would dream of setting foot outside their house without a hat. Now they're only being worn for weddings and such. Utterly appalling!'

Clara gently touched her arm, as if to say something, but couldn't seem to pluck up the courage to do so.

'All right, Clara, I'll get off my hobby horse,' Annie said, irritation strong in her tone. 'Anyway, you've no need to fret. I've made enquiries and found you a position in the ice cream parlour. Part-time to begin with, to see how you go on. You'll enjoy that, I'm sure. Much more fun than hats.' She even attempted a smile as she said it.

Clara picked up a bundle of the corsages she'd been making, then as if not knowing what to do with them, she set them down again, looking deeply distressed.

Patsy was still struggling to come to terms with this sudden change. 'You mean – I'm to work for the Bertalones – in their ice cream parlour?'

'Starting from tomorrow.'

Panic hit her. Patsy didn't know whether to laugh or cry, whether to jump for joy or run a mile. The bolt of excitement that shot though her was utterly shaming. Firmly, she stamped it down. How could she work beside someone and still refuse to speak to them? She would be forced to endure Marc Bertalone chatting her up day after day, endlessly showing off and preening himself before her like some sort of gladiator. She'd be working with him the whole time, particularly during the summer holidays while he was home from the art school. Clara had first of all embarrassed her by forcing her to agree to accompany him to this stupid family wedding. Now she was being put in an even more impossible position. She really couldn't do it.

'I don't think that's such a good idea,' Patsy protested. 'I really have no wish to work for the Bertalones. Maybe it's time I moved on. I don't want to stay where I'm not wanted.'

Clara jumped as if she'd been scalded. 'But you are wanted. Very much so! You must stay, Patsy. I won't hear of your leaving.

You don't know what it's meant to me, having you here. It's very important to us – to me.'

Annie put out a hand. 'Clara, please. This isn't the time and...'

'No, I want to explain. A monstrous thing happened to me once and I need you to see the effect it has had upon our lives, like a ripple through time. Patsy, sit down, please. Let me open my heart to you so that you can understand why I want you to stay.'

Patsy found she was holding her breath, certain that Clara was about to confess at last that she was her mother, that she couldn't bear to part with her a second time. The pain in her chest was crippling, yet she could do nothing to release the tension pounding within. She could hear customers moving up and down the aisles of the market hall. The sound of their laughter, their comments to each other as they browsed among the hats, intruded upon her concentration as she breathlessly waited for Clara to begin. Patsy wanted to shout at them to go away as she sat and waited, hot with impatience, hands clasped tightly together. Then just when she thought Clara was about to start, Annie interceded yet again.

'This is neither the time nor the place, Clara, for personal discussion. We can continue it later, somewhere more private. In the meantime, have you remembered to tell Patsy about her letter?'

'Oh, goodness, I forgot, how remiss of me. Now where did I put it?' Clara began searching through her pockets and her sewing bag.

'Letter?' Patsy too was instantly distracted and her eyes lit up. She'd stopped watching for the post ages ago, had half forgotten Shirley's promise to make investigations through her grandmother's solicitors. Now she felt tension bite as Annie walked over to a little side table to pick up the letter.

'Here it is, where I left it this morning for you to give it to her. It's postmarked Liverpool. Do you know someone there, Patsy, or is that where you came from originally? We still know surprisingly little about you.'

Patsy said nothing. The envelope was long. Was that good or bad?

Clara said. 'Give her the letter, Annie. I'm sure if Patsy wishes us to know what it contains, she will tell us.'

Annie turned the envelope over in her hands, again studied the postmark, and finally, she reluctantly handed it over. Patsy snatched it up and thrust it straight into her pocket. She knew it would burn a hole there till she had a chance to read it. But it was essential that she be alone when she did.

Chapter Nineteen

The ancient village of Gretna had been welcoming young lovers for centuries, drawn north by the power of their love. They would spur their horses over the border into Scotland where couples as young as sixteen could rush to plight their troth before two witnesses, with no clergy necessary. Nor was there any need to post banns or use a registrar. It was the blacksmith – one of the most important persons in the community before the age of the car – who officiated, using his anvil as the altar. Here, in his smithy shop, right in the centre of the village, he shaped young lives as easily as he moulded metal.

In more recent times it had become a requirement for the couple to spend three weeks together in the area. This was viewed as a cooling-off period, a time for them to reflect about what they were doing.

Aware of the strength of their love, to Amy and Chris three weeks sounded a long time they could ill afford. Time enough for them to be found and brought home. So caught up were they in their fear of being discovered that they didn't think to declare their presence to anyone, not even to the smithy who was supposed to marry them. Their aim was to stay well out of the village itself, just in case someone should come after them.

They also knew there were no shortage of villagers willing to take advantage of the 'trade' in weddings, either by acting as witness to the handfasting ceremony, or supplying accommodation to the hopeful young couple.

Chris carefully explained to Amy that they really couldn't afford the luxury of bed and breakfast in one of the many hotels and boarding houses in the area that had sprung up for that purpose. He'd sold the watch his parents had given him for his twenty-first birthday in order to pay for petrol for his old Ford Prefect. From this he'd set aside a sum to pay for three nights' bed and breakfast for their honeymoon.

Other than that, his savings were limited, and since Amy had even less money she happily agreed they must be careful. 'It would be too risky anyway. The hotels and boarding houses would be the first place Mam would look, and at least we can sleep in the car.'

It was so exciting to be together at last, free from family restrictions. It felt like being on holiday and seemed a shame not to enjoy themselves so they drove around Dumfries and Galloway along quiet country lanes, admiring its craggy mountains, ancient castles and fine lochs, or exploring its enchanting gardens. They took a trip out to the Mull of Galloway and were entranced by the number of wild birds, and by the way the light changed over the shimmering sea.

Next, they took the opportunity to soak up some history by visiting Dundrennan Abbey, and listened to the stirring tale of how Mary Queen of Scots had spent her last night in Scotland there, before setting forth for England to face the dangerous ire of her cousin.

'I wouldn't much care to face Mam's ire, if she ever caught up with us.' Amy shivered to think of it.

They saw no one for those first few days but didn't mind in the least, were content simply to be together, walking and swimming, lazing about in the sun, resting after their long journey and the trauma of their escape.

But the cost of petrol and oil alarmed Chris. He decided there must be something wrong with the car for it to use so much, and decided they'd best stop touring and park the vehicle up a country road, by a small patch of woodland.

The days grew hotter, too hot for them to sleep at night. Besides, it wasn't very comfortable in the car. Whichever of them was taking a turn sleeping in the front had to wrestle with gear lever and steering wheel. Sometimes they would cuddle up together on the back seat which was lovely, kissing and making plans for a long and happy future, although not entirely conducive to a good night's sleep.

Three days later they ran out of food. After ten days money became a problem. Chris still had the sum he'd set aside for the honeymoon but it was important they didn't waste that on ordinary living expenses, which he'd gravely underestimated.

He decided that the car had become a liability and must be sold. He was disappointed with the price he got for it, and couldn't help suspecting he'd been done, but was in no position to argue. If they carried on like this, they would run out of money completely and be unable to afford even food for the whole three weeks, let alone a honeymoon.

So the car, as well as his birthday watch, were gone and they were both aware that they had nothing else left to sell.

Chris used the money he got from the car to buy food, lemonade, and two train tickets home. After that, they made themselves a little nest in the woods with the blanket and cushions, and prayed it would stay fine. It was at least cool beneath the trees, they could stretch out on the soft bracken and breathe in the sweet scent of bluebells and new grass.

Amy wrapped her arms about his neck and pressed her body to his. It felt so hard and strong, so powerful. She adored the way his green-grey eyes seemed to smile with great tenderness at her, even when he was being serious. She loved to smooth the hairs at the nape of his neck, kiss his wide brow, his nose, his chin, and tease his mouth till he opened it to snatch greedily at hers, unable to resist her kisses.

Even the smell of the sun on his skin excited her. Amy needed Chris to know how very much she loved him, and that she was more than willing for him to make love to her. 'I don't care about waiting. I want to love you now.'

But Chris was adamant that they wait. 'What if something should go wrong and you accidentally got pregnant? How would we cope?'

'What could go wrong?' she said, unbuttoning his shirt. 'I love you, and you love me. We're to be married in less than three weeks, just over two in fact. What is there to wait for?'

The road to Gretna was paved with heartbreak. Many a young woman had hurried north to a promised marriage with her beloved, seduced in one of the inns along the way, and then been abandoned before the ceremony ever took place. Even if the young man's intentions were honourable, as Chris's were, and the marriage did take place, on their return home family members would claim that the marriage wasn't truly legal, since it hadn't been blessed, and the scandal of what they'd done would haunt them for the rest of their lives.

Amy knew all about those other unfortunate women but her own story would turn out differently. She had no fears that Chris would abandon her, or leave her pregnant and alone. He wasn't that sort of man, and he loved her.

Chris, however, being older than Amy and striving to be sensible, remained cautious. He was desperate for nothing to go wrong.

'Let me prove to you how much I love you. How much I want you,' she said, climbing astride him. She tugged off her sweater, unhooked her bra, smiling at his dazed expression as he smoothed his hands in awed wonder over her bare breasts. Inside she felt shy, her throat tight and her heart racing, but she wanted him so much; longed for them to be happy. She pushed open his shirt and lay upon him as she kissed him, allowing them both the seductive pleasure of flesh upon flesh.

He gave a low groan. 'I want you too, Amy. So very much.' He gathered her in his arms, rolled her beneath him and began to kiss her in earnest with mouth and tongue, sucking her, devouring her as if he couldn't ever get enough of her, and Amy's heart soared with happiness. They'd had a difficult time this last week or so, but everything was going to be fine.

He captured her breasts, felt the soft weight of them in his hands, kissed the hardening nipples as she spread out her arms above her head in willing surrender.

And as she lay half naked beneath him Chris was overwhelmed by a wave of love for her, a tender urge to protect her. He loved the softness of her, the vulnerability, her tiny waist that he could span with his two hands, and the round curve of her small buttocks as he lifted and pressed her against himself. He stroked the mass of tumbling auburn curls back from her angelic face as he kissed her again and again. That's what she was to him, an angel, one he mustn't spoil however much he might long for that sweet release. Oh, but he needed something. Every instinct cried out for him to make love to her.

He slid his hand between her legs, cupped the soft mound of her, gently awakening her to the knowledge of love, revelling in her soft moans of pleasure. He wanted to do so much more but desperately strove to curb his excitement, his need. Chris took her hand, showed her how and where to rub him, first outside his trousers, and then inside. Saw how her eyes widened with shock at the size of his erection.

This was the first time Amy had seen a man in the flesh and she was truly startled. 'Heaven help me, how will it fit?'

He was filled with shame, believing he'd gone too far and alarmed her. It was as if he had no right to be doing these things to her, since they weren't even married, and out in the open in a damp wood. This wasn't proper respectful behaviour, no way at all to treat the girl he loved. Abruptly, he let her go, jumped to his feet and walked away. It was the hardest thing he'd ever done.

Amy sat up, shivering in the soft June air, cold now in her nakedness, and called after him in a tiny, heartrending voice. 'Chris?'

By the time he returned she was dressed, huddled in her thin sweater and weeping silently, feeling unloved and rejected.

He came and put his arms about her, held her tight as he kissed the top of her head. 'I love you more than you can possibly imagine, more than life itself. But I want you to be my wife first, before I make you mine. I want us both to be free to enjoy our lovemaking properly, not as a hole in the corner affair. I don't want you to feel I'm taking advantage of these peculiar circumstances, or to be afraid of any possible consequences. It has to be special between us, Amy, because our love is special.'

He kissed away each tear, warmed her ice-cold cheeks with his hands, and filled her heart with fresh wonder and love for him.

'All will be well once we are married, I swear it.'

—

They filled the days with talking and planning their future. But even walking hand in hand through the woods became fraught with emotion, the longing to touch, to kiss and to caress almost overwhelming. When the slightest glance could spark a desire to make love, which must at all cost be resisted, they were forced to draw apart a little.

Without lovemaking to distract her, Amy began to worry about practicalities. 'What about your job? Will they keep that open for you?'

Chris brushed her fears aside. 'If I can't get my old job back, I'll find another. I don't mind what I do, so long as we're together.'

And then the weather changed.

It rained for five solid days by the end of which Amy was sneezing and shivering, showing every signs of starting with flu. Their elopement wasn't turning out to be half so romantic as she had hoped. Very much the reverse! All Amy's worst fears were coming true. Water dripped from the trees above their heads, the blankets were soaked, and the ground was damp and cold beneath them. Amy longed for a hot bath, and for a plate of her mother's steak and kidney pudding and peas.

She was tired of sleeping on the hard ground, of eating stale bread and cheese and having nowhere to wash herself except in a cold running stream.

'They'll have a fit if we turn up to get married covered in mud and sneezing our heads off,' she giggled, trying to see the funny side although not really feeling much like laughter.

'You'll get pneumonia if we don't do something to get you warm soon,' Chris said, anxiety ripe in his voice. 'What happened to all that lovely June sunshine? And why the hell did I sell the car?'

'We had to eat, and we didn't have any money left for petrol anyway. Don't worry, Chris, I'll be fine.'

But she grew worse as the day wore on, and their funds being limited, Chris decided that a night's bed and breakfast was essential for Amy.

'I'm not going on my own. Only if we're together.'

'I shall sleep on the floor then.'

'Or on top of the covers, to start with anyway,' she teased. Amy was beginning to think that a bit of romance would be no bad thing, and then sneezed loudly and realised she must look an absolute sight. Eyes streaming, nose all red, and hair like a bird's nest from sleeping rough. Who'd want to make love to such a creature?

They found a tiny, typically Scottish single storey house on the outskirts of the village where a shrewd landlady, experienced in the ways of the heart, recognised them for what they were and took pity on them. She provided them with hot baths, fed them Scotch broth and apple dumpling, then packed Amy off to bed with an aspirin and a hot water bottle.

Although it proved to be even less romantic than their nights in the woods, with Chris stoically sticking by his insistence that he sleep on the floor with only a pillow and blanket for comfort, Amy was asleep in seconds. She woke in the morning feeling much better, almost human and with optimism reborn.

The landlady stoked them up with a double egg fried breakfast, and only then, when they were well fortified with food, warm and rested, did she deliver the crushing blow.

Chapter Twenty

Patsy set the envelope on her dressing table then climbed on to her bed, wrapped her arms about her knees, and looked at it. Actually bringing herself to slit it open seemed beyond her. What might the friendly neighbour have discovered? It was all nonsense that old Mrs Matthews was not her grandmother after all? That Clara Higginson was not, in fact, her long-lost mother? And as she had always known, she had no family, belonged to no one and was completely unwanted. A bleak prospect she didn't care to consider.

Patsy stared hard at the envelope, willing her eyes to remain wide open and dry. So what if it did say that? She'd known all of this already, so wouldn't be any worse off if she saw the facts in print, would she? In her heart she knew that she would be considerably worse off. All hope would then be dead. Patsy already understood that she was a burden upon the sisters' generosity. Hadn't Annie made their straitened circumstances only too clear today in her decision to sack her? They couldn't afford to pay her wages any longer, maybe didn't even want her in the house, and why should they? She was nothing to them but a petty thief they'd taken pity on. Not their responsibility.

If she proved that she was Clara's daughter, they would decide to keep her, and she could stay here, on Champion Street Market, for always. They might actually come to love her, but maybe that was all a foolish dream. Another fantasy, and did she really want to spend her life with two drab spinsters?

What of working alongside Marc Bertalone, who might liven things up considerably if she could bring herself to agree to go out with him? But that would mean letting down her defences, and Patsy wasn't sure she was ready for that either. She glared again at the envelope.

Perhaps Shirley had failed to discover anything at all, and the letter was nothing to do with her grandmother but simply the Bowmans wanting to know where she was. No, she dismissed that idea almost the instant it came into her head. It couldn't possibly be from them. Why would they care where she was or what she was doing? But she'd never know the answer to any of these questions unless she opened the flipping envelope.

She slipped out of bed and picked it up, turning it round in her fingers, studying the postmark as Annie had done. It told her nothing except that it was blue, and came from the Liverpool area. Back on the bed, she slit it open with her finger and swiftly read the contents. It was a very short will, evidently written after the end of the war by her grandmother, Felicity Matthews, duly signed and witnessed.

Patsy frowned over the legal jargon but then came to a sentence, which Shirley had underlined for her. 'That my son Rolf Matthews be sole beneficiary to my estate. In return I ask him to make provision for all my grandchildren as I have done for him over the years.'

And there was nothing after that, but more legal jargon. Not a mention of her by name, nor of Mrs Matthews's daughter-in-law, Patsy's mother. Patsy read the will with more care a second time. How could she be certain of anything if she didn't even know her own name? How could she hope to belong anywhere? The humiliation of this fact cut deep, pouring salt into the raw wound.

Was her grandmother entirely without heart? She'd given Patsy away without a second thought, handed her over to foster parents. Did the woman take no responsibility for that? Apart from sending a little money from time to time, she'd never once contacted Patsy or allowed her to visit. Why? And even in her will she'd made no special provision but left all her grandchildren's future care in the hands of Rolf, the father who'd abandoned Patsy as cruelly as her mother had, by going off to live in America.

It all seemed unbearably cruel.

And who were these other grandchildren? Had her father remarried? Did Patsy have sisters and brothers she didn't even know about, or had they been fortunate enough to be taken to America with him? So many unanswered questions!

There was a letter from Shirley tucked inside the document. Patsy unfolded it and began to read, her brow creased with anxiety and puzzlement. 'I do hope you aren't too disappointed with this, Patsy. The solicitors weren't prepared to help, client confidentiality I'm afraid, so I had to wait till the will went through probate before I could get a copy. That's why it's taken so long. I realise it gets us no further. A clerk at the solicitor's office was more sympathetic when I went back to try for any further information, but he admitted that your grandmother's will was a pointless exercise. She died penniless, the house mortgaged to the hilt, most of her worldly goods having already been sold. She did indeed have a granddaughter but the clerk has no information about her, nor anything about the other grandchildren mentioned either, which is unfortunate to say the least. The partner who dealt with her affairs died in 1949, and the young solicitor who handled probate knows very little about her. According to the clerk, she was considered to be a very kind woman, well liked, had been a widow for years, was heavily involved in charity work. The son wasn't particularly well thought of, so far as he was aware, and is assumed to still be in America. Generally, all most unsatisfactory.'

Patsy felt overwhelmed, her mind still buzzing with questions. There was a PS.

'I suppose if you were to present yourself to them in person they might be more forthcoming, but I believed the clerk when he said they knew nothing further. He was also of the opinion that Mrs Matthews's housekeeper was old, even at the end of the war, and is probably dead by now. Sorry I couldn't be of more help, and that it's taken so long. Remember that you're always welcome to visit any time, Patsy, and don't forget to write and let me know how you're getting on. And don't worry, I'll keep on digging.'

This long awaited reply was still no nearer the facts. Patsy looked again at the letter with its signature, 'Your friend, Shirley'. At least she had tried, being the only real friend Patsy had in the world; she put her head in her hands and sobbed as if her heart might break.

—

Clara fussed around her the next morning at breakfast, Annie casting long quizzical glances in her direction. Patsy could tell by the open curiosity on both their faces that the Higginson sisters were aching to know the contents of the letter. She had no intention of satisfying their nosiness.

What could she say? Unfortunately the will had provoked more questions than answers. Why hadn't her grandmother made proper provision for her? Didn't she owe Patsy that much at least, after the way she'd been treated? Since Patsy knew that both her mother and her father had abandoned her, so why hadn't her grandmother taken her in? Why give her away to the Bowmans? And why had the old woman formally left all her money to a son who had neglected her too, when in fact she had nothing left but debts? Had she gone crazy in her dotage, as people sometimes did?

Patsy still didn't know if Clara Higginson was Felicity Matthews's daughter-in-law, or even the ex-mistress, of this Rolf, her son. And most vital of all, the will offered no proof as to whether or not Patsy herself was Clara's daughter. It was all so frustrating.

Patsy had written back to Shirley, a short letter of thanks for her effort, making no mention of her dissatisfaction with the result. Shirley had promised to keep in touch, but she wouldn't. Patsy knew the woman had only said that out of politeness. In reality they were little more than strangers, not friends at all. She didn't have any real friends, and where was the point in making any if she was going to have to leave the market?

Clara placed a boiled egg before her, not even glancing at Patsy, as she seemed more concerned about Annie. She was lecturing her sister about needing a proper breakfast inside her, but Annie refused, saying her tummy was playing up this morning.

'At least have some porridge, dear.'

'Don't you listen to a word I say, Clara? Porridge would be far too heavy. I have stomach-ache and pains in my chest. Is it any wonder, with all the worry I have? Why can't you accept that I don't wish to eat anything this morning?'

'Why not a boiled egg, as I'll have one ready in one minute?'

'Clara, I shall lose my temper shortly, and where will that get us?'

Patsy stopped listening to their squabbles, too wrapped up in her own problems to care about Clara's concern for her sister's health. She cracked open her egg and began to eat, although her appetite had utterly deserted her. If only Clara had not been interrupted by Annie yesterday. Patsy felt she'd been close to a revelation that Clara had been about to divulge the truth about their relationship, and about this monstrous thing that had happened to her. Could she bring her back to that moment now?

A few moments later, Annie went upstairs to the bathroom and Patsy decided to take advantage of her absence. 'Um, yesterday, before Annie gave me the old heave-ho, you said you wanted to tell me something.'

'Did I?' Clara looked deliberately vague. She buttered a slice of toast for herself then left it untouched as she took the second egg off the stove, cooled it under the tap then began to chop it up and make it into a sandwich, in the hope Annie might eat it later.

Patsy knew she had only a few moments alone with Clara before Annie returned. 'Something monstrous, you said, once happened to you.'

After a pause, she said, 'I can't think what that might have been.'

'You said it had badly affected you, like a ripple through time.'
Patsy dipped a finger of toast into the yolk, watching as it ran over
the sides of her egg.

'Dear me!' Clara went pale, and then with an embarrassed
little laugh, she cut the sandwich in half and began to wrap it
in greaseproof paper. 'I never meant to sound melodramatic. It
was about our fleeing from Paris, and I'd forgotten I'd already
told you. But I wanted you to know, Patsy, that you are welcome
to continue lodging here, even if you are no longer going to be
employed by us.'

Patsy's disappointment was keen. She liked working on the hat
stall, had started taking an interest in the catalogues and magazines
that were kept behind the counter. The stall may be dowdy and
old-fashioned, and its stock far from up-to-date, but it did still
have a regular clientele. However, more often than not, they didn't
find what they were looking for. Annie didn't hold with veils and
flowers and pretty hats for weddings, and kept very few in stock.
Besides all of that, working on the stall with the sisters made Patsy
feel useful, almost as if she did belong and was part of a family.

She glared at her half-eaten egg, knowing she must eat it or
Clara would guess there was something bad in the letter, and try
to make her say what it was. Life for her seemed to be filled with
pain. Why couldn't it be simple, and happy? Why couldn't her life
be normal, like that of other girls? Patsy so wanted to be happy,
to find a place for herself and build a new life.

Clara said, 'We'll talk later, dear, when I have more time. Now
you mustn't be late on your first day at the ice cream parlour, so
eat up your breakfast quickly. You'll like Papa Bertalone. He's a
lovely man.'

'Pity we can't say the same for his son,' Patsy grumbled,
nibbling on her toast as she went to fetch her coat.

Clara chuckled. 'Marc isn't half the braggart he pretends to be,
but he does love to tease. See that you accept his invitation to the
wedding. It will do you good.'

Patsy's first day at the ice cream parlour was tiring and confusing but good fun, she supposed. There were many new things to learn, not only how to operate a different cash register, but also how to make up the various ice creams: the Raspberry Dash, the Strawberry Ripple, the Peach Sundae and the Knickerbocker Glory. Then there were the chocolate and coffee varieties, the various sauces, nuts and different toppings, all a little bewildering!

Marco Bertalone, Marc's father, gave her a small sample of all the different flavours, heaped into one glass dish. 'You eata every scrap, as much as you like, but don'ta make yourself sick. I always tell my new girls they can eat as mucha icea creama as they want. And at first they are greedy, but soon they stop, yes? They can face no more icea creama. Too much of a good thing, yes?'

Patsy thought if she ate one of these every day, she might very well feel the same. But right now, she gobbled it all up and licked the spoon clean. It was delicious. She was sorely tempted to lick the dish too but fortunately stopped herself in time.

Just as well she hadn't, as a voice in her ear said, 'I understand we are to have the pleasure of your company in our ice cream parlour in future? Does that mean you've had second thoughts about me?'

Patsy turned to glare at Marc, her expression as haughty as she could make it. 'Why would you imagine that my working here has anything at all to do with you? This may come as a great shock to you, but you were the last thing I considered. In fact, your presence very nearly put me off, but I need employment and your father kindly offered me a job, so it would have been churlish to refuse.'

Marc grinned at her. 'Churlish! You use long words for a girl who came out of nowhere.'

'I had an education like anyone else, a good one actually.'

He shrugged, as if it were of no account, but inwardly he smiled to himself. Every scrap of information he acquired about her was like a nugget of pure gold to Marc. 'I think you've decided that you might get to like me better if you saw me more often. You want to come to the wedding, that's it, isn't it? You like me enough after all, yes?'

'No, I think you're insufferable! There, is that a long enough word for you? Too long, I should think.' She spun on her heel, chin in the air, and hurried away to serve a young woman and her child.

By the end of the day, hectic though it was, Patsy decided she had enjoyed herself. It didn't feel like work at all.

'You likea your new job, yes?' Mr Bertalone asked her. 'You do well, for a first day. You forget the nuts on the Chocolate Nut Sundae. You put the scoop back in the wrong ice cream once or twice, and you are hopeless on the till. But you will learn, no?'

Patsy gave a sheepish smile. 'I will try.'

'And my Marc, he tell me you come to the wedding next Sunday, always the lucky day for a wedding. That ees good! You will likea my family and they will likea you. My wife, my children, my sons, and I likea you, young lady. We get on good, *sì*?' And he kissed her on both cheeks before striding away, humming happily to himself.

He'd gone without allowing Patsy the opportunity to explain that she had no intention of going to the wedding with his son. Yet how could she refuse now that Papa Bertalone himself expected her to be there? He might be insulted by such a refusal and sack her. She couldn't afford to lose two jobs in one week, though everyone seemed to be conspiring against her. Biting her lip, she sauntered over to where Marc was washing the ice cream scoops in a special solution. Patsy felt smitten by an attack of nerves. How could she tell him that she'd changed her mind, after insulting him the way she had earlier? How could she find the courage to swallow her pride? She needn't have worried as he turned to her with a wide grin.

'I'll pick you up at a quarter to two on Sunday, okay? We don't want the celebration to start without us.'

Chapter Twenty-One

The landlady told Chris and Amy, with sorrow in her voice and pity in her heart, that if they'd come to Gretna to get married, they were too late. It was no longer possible for them to marry before the anvil. 'The law put a stop to all of that back at the start of the war.'

Chris went white. 'I don't believe you.'

'It's right enough. Ask at the smithy, if you don't believe me. We still get plenty of tourists, and even weddings, but not irregular weddings. No marriage here unless it's all done legal and proper with a registrar present. Och, I'm sorry, but there it is. Poor wee bairns, don't look so sad.'

Chris was devastated. Amy looked dazed, not able to take it in.

But sadly, when they checked later with the smithy, something they should have done when they first arrived they found that their landlady was absolutely correct.

But there was still hope, of a sort. They could indeed be married, if they signed the proper forms and found a local priest or vicar willing to marry them. Notice should preferably be lodged with the registrar about four to six weeks before the date of the proposed marriage. Which, naturally, necessitated much more expenditure than Chris had bargained for, and yet more time spent waiting. But the easy route to a quick marriage had been stopped.

Consequently they were back in the woods, mulling over the problem and their bad luck, worrying over what was best for them to do.

Amy was the first to break the silence, her spirit and determination undiminished. 'I still want to marry you. I'm nineteen, old enough to know my own mind, and considered to be so here in Scotland. I wouldn't have to wait here till I'm twenty-one before I can marry you, even if the quick, handfasting weddings are gone. That fact is still true, so we'll just have to fill in the necessary forms and stay a bit longer, that's all.'

'But it won't be easy, love.'

Amy could read the worry in his eyes. More quietly, she asked, 'How much money, exactly, have we got left from the sale of the car?'

Chris sat on a fallen tree and counted it out, making separate piles of notes, shillings, sixpences and half crowns. 'I reckon we'd have just about enough to survive another couple of weeks, but we'd have to forego the honeymoon, and no more bed and breakfast. We'd have to carry on sleeping here in the woods and it's going to get much hotter in August. Then it could be well into September before we get a date for the wedding, when it will start to feel cold.'

Amy's eyes were gleaming. 'Two weeks, that's ages? We might have found a way to earn some money by then, and when we find a priest we could ask him to try and hurry things up a bit, couldn't we?'

'I suppose.' Chris couldn't help but respond to her eagerness, her face alight with hope, and she was so dear to him, how could he refuse? 'We must keep our train tickets safe, or how will we ever get home?'

She put her arms about his neck and kissed him soundly. 'Then we can still do it?'

Chris remained cautious. 'It might be worth a try. I suppose I could get a job, here in Scotland, for the summer.'

Amy jumped to her feet. ''Course you could. Me too. I could wait at tables, work in a shop, turn my hand to anything so long as I have you as my husband at the end of it. And we can go on living here, like babes in the wood.'

He was smiling at her now, won over by her enthusiasm. 'But no canoodling, right? We have to be careful for a bit longer, Amy. We can't start a baby till we have that ring on your finger, even if it is one of me mam's curtain rings.'

They looked at each other for a long moment of poignant sadness, knowing this would not be easy for either of them.

'I can cope if you can.'

'I can do it for you, love.'

And then they were hugging each other, all happy smiles again, eager that they could triumph over their misfortune, and that their love would see them through any adversity.

–

Fran could hear her mother ranting on at some unfortunate woman, claiming she had only one pair of hands, which was fairly immaterial since they were at least twice the size of everyone else's. Of course, she knew why Mam was carrying on. She was desperately worried about Amy. Her period of working with her brother in the kitchens hadn't lasted beyond a day. Once Amy had vanished, she'd been sent back to the pie stall to take her sister's place. Fran was not in the least bit happy with the way things had turned out. Having the bedroom all to herself was one thing, but being the one Molly could call on to do all the chores, and extra jobs around the house, as well as working all day on the stall right beside her, it was driving Fran up the wall. She never seemed to be free from her mother, not for a second.

In addition, Robert had insisted she go round to the kitchens several evenings a week to help out there too, since they were so short staffed. To her great surprise, Fran actually found herself missing her little sister, irritating and sanctimonious though Amy may be at times. Fran had no one to talk to, no one to listen to her woes, of which she had plenty right now.

But however unhappy and hard done by Fran might feel, Molly was complaining the loudest. 'If I carry on working as hard as this, I'll be wearing a wooden overcoat before long.' By which she meant a coffin.

The woman customer seemed to find this amusing. 'Eeh, Molly, you're allus good for a laugh, chuck. They'll need an extra large size when it gets to be your turn, but I doubt it'll be soon. You're a right live wire, full of beans. Outlive us all, you will.'

'Not the way them girls of mine are carrying on. They'll be the death of me, for sure. Have you seen how grey I've gone lately? And I'm a mere shadow of me former self.'

'Aye, I can see you are love, by the size of you,' laughed the woman, running an amused glance over Molly's substantial figure.

Fran was heartily sick of her mother's moans and groans, and when she spotted Patsy hovering near, she called her over. 'Do me a favour, girl, and take me mam for a frothy coffee. She's driving me doo-lally this morning going on about our Amy doing a flit.'

'What? Where's she gone?'

'She disappeared weeks ago. Mam'll tell you all about it. At length.'

It took some persuasion, but eventually the efforts of both girls paid off and Big Molly conceded that a coffee break might do her the world of good.

—

Patsy was agog to learn what had happened to Amy but it took two cups of tea, Molly not being fond of frothy coffee, and a couple of chocolate éclairs in Belle's cafe to calm her sufficiently to prise the tale out of her. Even then, they first of all had to listen to Belle's grumbles. 'They're all out to get me, the whole bleeding market up in arms just because Billy Quinn wants to build a block of flats here. He's prepared to pay good compensation so I'm only thinking of everyone's welfare.'

'And whose would that be, Belle?' Big Molly dryly enquired. 'Yours or theirs?'

Belle blinked her long mascara-coated lashes and pouted crimson lips. 'Don't you start, Molly. I'd like to think someone was on my side.'

Big Molly gave a harsh laugh. 'Oh, aye, you can see I'd be dead chuffed to have some bulldozer come and knock down my house. Have a heart, Belle love. We like it here on the market as it is, and we don't like change.'

'Well, I call that a very selfish attitude, I do really. People are desperate for houses. You could still have a home here, a modern flat in a high-rise block, and you could live on the rest of the compensation for life. You'd never have to work again.'

Big Molly considered this enticing proposition for a full thirty seconds, and then an image of herself sitting in her empty kitchen every morning, wondering what to do with herself now their Robert did all the baking, came into her mind. 'It don't do for me, being idle. I'm not the retiring sort. Think again, Belle love. You tell the developer, this Billy Quinn, to go sling his hook. It won't wash, we're not selling.'

'Tell me about Amy,' Patsy reminded her, as soon as Belle had flounced off in high dudgeon.

Molly loaded three spoons of sugar into her third cup of tea before starting on her tale. 'She vanished from the stall one day. She went for a cuppa and never came back. He abducted her, that's what's happened. She's run off with that lad, that Chris George. He hasn't been seen around for ages either. Mrs Crawshaw, one of my customers, who's on his milk round, was furious when her milk delivery was late. Had to send her husband off to work without his porridge, poor man. It shows very little consideration, don't you think, leaving folk without their breakfast? Never gave so much as a day's notice to the dairy, just upped and left, along with our Amy. Now she's sent us a postcard from Carlisle, though what the hecky-thump she's doing in that neck of the woods, I've no idea. Says I'm not to worry me head about her, she's fine. How can I not worry? Oh, God, where is the silly cow?'

Big Molly took out a large handkerchief and blew loudly into it, wiping her eyes on it too before tucking it back into her overall pocket. It was upsetting enough to be facing the possibility of losing her home and livelihood, without all this extra worry about Amy. She'd worked herself up into a fine lather, telling her tale, kept sweeping a hand over her eyes, and brushing away a few stray tears.

'Mind you, I told Mrs Crawshaw, fat lot you have to worry about if you're only missing a dish of porridge. It's my flipping daughter he's run off with. How am I supposed to feel about that? I'm not a bad mother, am I? I have feelings too, you know.' Whereupon she burst into tears.

Patsy was shocked. She'd never seen Big Molly in such a state. She chewed on her lip for a moment then said, 'I can make a guess why she's in Carlisle, Molly.'

The tears dried instantly. 'You can?'

'You aren't going to like this but I think she and Chris might be on their way to Scotland.'

'Barry Holmes said as how they'd be heading north. But why the hangment would they be doing that? It'll be cold in Scotland, and full of midges,' Molly said, still not getting the picture Patsy was drawing for her.

'They could be eloping, to Gretna Green.'

Molly slapped a hand over her mouth, and looked to be on the point of collapse. 'Oh, my giddy aunt! Oh, put me daft head in a bucket and batter me brains, I never thought. We have to stop them. Where's our Ozzy? Ozzy, where are you? Get out here this minute.' She was on her feet, rushing out of the cafe and through the market hall, causing startled customers and stallholders alike to leap out of her way.

Big Molly pushed her way through the market stalls, knocking baskets and boxes everywhere as she hurtled across the street in record time, considering the girth she was carrying, flinging open her front door and charging down the hall. Patsy wasn't far behind, having managed to keep pace with her remarkably well, eager not to miss a moment of this drama.

Surprisingly, considering he was incapacitated by a bad hip and knee, Ozzy was not at home.

'He's down at the pub again, flipping lives there. Never around when he's needed.' Then Molly collapsed on to the battered old sofa among the detritus of newspapers and old cardigans and sobbed as if her heart might break.

Patsy's own heart filled with compassion. 'Don't take on so, Molly. She'll be all right. They've probably, you know – done it by now – so it's maybe best if he does marry her, don't you reckon?'

Evidently this did not offer the consolation Patsy had aimed for.

Molly looked at her out of bloodshot eyes as if she must have run mad. 'What're you saying? Done what? Oh, blimey, no, not that!' She let out a great wail that must have been heard the length of Champion Street. 'No, I'd rather be put in that wooden coffin than have any lass of mine marry one of them Georges, even if she is up the duff!'

'Why, for goodness' sake? I'm sorry, Molly, but I have to ask. What have you got against them? You make pies, they are best at making cakes. Their pies and pasties aren't a patch on yours, so you aren't really in competition, and they seem nice enough people to me.'

'That's all you know.' And then Molly told her the tale of the feud, how Chris's uncle, his father's elder brother, got Molly's sister Lena pregnant, and because she wasn't fit to bring up a child, being simple-minded, she had been forced to have an abortion. As a result she'd contracted an infection and died. 'And he got off scot-free. Beggared off to live in Canada, or Australia or some such fancy place. I'd kill him with me own bare hands if I ever got chance.'

Patsy tried to sound sympathetic but was still feeling slightly bemused and more than a little concerned for Molly's state of health. 'I can appreciate how dreadful it must have been, Molly, but that was years ago, surely, and nothing at all to do with Chris. What can you have against him?'

'He's a George, that's reason enough. And as if I haven't enough trouble with our Amy running off to Scotland, there's that other little madam, our Fran. I'm going to fettle her though, see if I don't. I'll clip her wings good and proper, first chance I get.'

—

When Ozzy returned, Molly gave him a good earwigging for not being there when she needed him, which he thought unfair.

'What can I do? I can't chase after them to Scotland, can I? Not with my hip.'

'How would I know? You claim you can't get out of that chair half the time, but you can toddle off down the pub fast enough, or the chippy if you're hungry. Do you ever win anything in these bets of yours? Because I never see any of it.'

'It's a mug's game,' Ozzy sadly remarked.

'That explains everything,' Molly agreed, slapping a plate of sausage and mash in front of him. 'You're well suited to it then.' She piled a plate for herself but by the time she was seated before it with knife and fork at the ready, her appetite had deserted her. 'Eeh, I'm that worried about her, lad. What'll we do?'

Ozzy loved his younger daughter dearly but now he shook his head in despair. 'I don't know. It's a bad business and no mistake.'

'Aye, and if it's not one, it's the other. Where's our Fran tonight? She hasn't even come in for her tea.'

They sat and ate in silence, eating not so much out of hunger as of necessity. Molly was a great believer in keeping body and soul together with a plate of good food. 'What we need,' she said at last, as she washed and stacked dishes and Ozzy made an effort to dry, 'is to put the frighteners on him.'

'On Chris George? How can we do that when we don't know for sure where they are, and don't have a car to chase after them? And nobody would give us a lift, not all the way to Scotland.'

'I'm not talking about our Amy now. I'm talking about that other little madam,' Molly said, as if she were addressing a child, which was how she saw Ozzy. 'Fran still hasn't turned up for her tea, you'll notice. Been in a right pet for days, and we know who to blame for that. She'll be with her fancy man, that Eddie Davidson. I've been thinking there must be some way we can put a stop to that young man's philandering... What we need is a bit of help from the right quarter, and listening to you just now, it came to me where we might find it. Who is it what runs the betting from that pub of yours? Hasn't he a reputation for being tough?'

'What, Billy Quinn?'

'Aye, that's the chap. By heck, is he the same Billy Quinn who's trying to buy Champion Street from under our feet?'

Ozzy's eyes opened wide in fear. 'Aye, that's him. You mustn't mess with the likes of Billy Quinn. He's dangerous. Trouble with a capital T. Stay well clear of him, lass. You have to handle Quinn with kid gloves, and show proper respect. Betting may not be legal but that doesn't stop him. He's been doing it for years, has the polis in his pocket. Nothing and nobody gets in the way of Billy Quinn.'

Molly snorted her derision. 'I notice it doesn't stop you going down t'pub most days, whether betting is legal or illegal, this so-called proper respect you have to show for him. Well, I might just pop down myself and have a word. I can tell him where to put his offer for Champion Street at the same time. He sounds like the sort of chap who doesn't mind getting his fingers dirty. It can do no harm to ask him for a bit of help with what I have in mind.'

Had he been capable of it, Ozzy would have been jumping up and down on the spot, as he was getting agitated. He was in such danger of dropping the plate he was supposedly wiping, that Molly snatched it from him with a sigh. But even that didn't silence him.

'It can do a great deal of harm. Leave well alone, Molly love, I beg you. Don't get involved. Let Jimmy Ramsay sort Belle out. She can't get anywhere without our support. As for our Fran, she'll come round in time, mark my words. It's a phase she's going through, that's all. The more we set us-selves against it, the more she'll go for him. Just ignore it, that's the best way.'

'Ignore it? We don't have time to ignore it. We can't afford to take the risk, you daft fool. She'll be up the duff if we don't watch out, then what will we do? We couldn't make him marry her, could we, since he's already married? Oh, for goodness sake get off your backside and do something for once in your useless life.'

Ozzy was shaking his head with extraordinary vigour. 'Not if it means tackling Billy Quinn.'

'Then I will. I'm not afraid of anyone, certainly not some jumped up Irishman who runs a bit of betting on the side. If he can sort out that Eddie Davidson for me, it'd be one less worry on my mind. And when he's put an end to that daughter's romance, we can send him after the other one.'

Chapter Twenty-Two

On Friday evening Annie and Clara announced they were off to listen to the Hallé Orchestra. 'The Free Trade Hall was badly damaged during the war and it's the first time we've attended a concert there since it was reopened a few years ago,' Clara told Patsy. 'It's a little treat for us. I do hope you don't mind being left on your own for once.'

Patsy was delighted. 'No, course I don't mind. Why should I?'

She'd been waiting and hoping for just such a chance ever since she'd received Shirley's letter, little enough though it had told her. Patsy intended to take advantage of the sisters' absence to do a bit of digging on her own account. If she could discover a few more facts then she might feel able to pluck up the courage to confront Clara, demand to know the truth, one way or the other.

Even if she didn't find the answer she was looking for, it might put an end to her agonising, and her sleepless nights. She could then start to make some proper decisions about her future.

Clara said, 'We should have got you a ticket, too. It's Sir John Barbirolli, a wonderful conductor. He's Italian, you know. We've been fortunate enough to have him here with us in Manchester for many years.'

'I don't suppose it's Patsy's sort of music,' Annie dryly remarked, and as 'Hound Dog' was even now blasting away on the new record player up in her room, they couldn't help but laugh. Even Annie gave a droll little smile. Unheard of! Poor Annie, having a teenager in the house was not easy for her.

'You're absolutely right, not my cup of tea at all. Sorry! Anyway, I reckon I'll have enough of Italians on Sunday,' Patsy commented, glaring meaningfully at Clara who had pushed her into accepting the invitation. Not that she saw it as a date exactly, merely a duty. 'Have a nice evening.'

I fully intend to, Patsy thought. Once she'd given the place a thorough search, she'd put up her feet and relax with the hit parade on Radio Luxembourg and enjoy some precious privacy for a change, without Annie breathing down her neck.

After they left, Patsy immediately switched her record player off and stood for several long minutes, listening, making sure that they truly had gone. Clara had a nasty habit of forgetting things, like keys or her hanky, and would frequently come dashing back.

When she was finally convinced that it was safe, Patsy made her way to Clara's room.

She began with the dressing table, searching meticulously through every drawer. She wasn't entirely sure what she was looking for. A birth or marriage certificate would be perfect, but too much to hope for. A letter, a photo, anything at all that would give a clue to her past, but she found nothing.

Patsy searched the wardrobe next, then the small chest of drawers by the bed. Again she drew a blank. Her disappointment was keen. How could a person not have anything to show for all the years she'd lived on this earth?

The loft! Clara was a remarkably well-organised, tidy sort of person. Perhaps she'd stored away all her documents in the attic, where they wouldn't remind her of earlier pain.

It was a struggle to get the ladder from the backyard in through the kitchen and up the stairs. Patsy was terrified of knocking it against the flocked wallpaper and making a dent, and very nearly did so. With another precious twenty minutes wasted, she quickly climbed up it and pushed at the square loft door with all her might. It opened easily. Moments later she was inside, the flick of a switch illuminating a bewildering assortment of boxes, most were, by the shape of them, hat boxes. Was this where they put old stock, surely not?

It turned out that the hat boxes were an ideal repository for all the detritus that cluttered the sisters' lives but which they couldn't bear to part with. Silver photo frames, cracked vases, chipped figurines and ornaments, piles of cheap saucers, although why they had kept these, Patsy couldn't imagine. Books by the score, and stacks of pictures ranged against the walls. A collection of Victorian hat pins, a rusty tobacco tin containing a clay pipe, and any number of old gas mantles.

And finally, when Patsy was jumpy with nerves, only too aware of the clock ticking and precious time passing, she eventually found what she was looking for, a bulky brown envelope of what must be family papers. She sat on an old tin trunk to go quickly through them. The envelope contained numerous marriage and birth certificates of various members of the Higginson clan, and featured several other strange names and places that she didn't recognise at all. But, infuriatingly, none of them mentioned Clara, let alone Patsy's own name. It was so frustrating.

She stuffed everything back in the envelope and put it where she'd found it in a flurry of despair. She was getting absolutely nowhere! Patsy was just about to close the trunk when she caught sight of something pink. She moved one or two things gently out of the way before reaching for it.

It was a baby's slipper. Patsy cradled it in her hands in wonder. Made of pink and white silk, it seemed impossibly tiny, so very fragile.

Had this been her slipper once? Had she worn it as a baby before Clara had left her husband or lover, whatever Rolf Matthews was to her; before she had walked out and abandoned her child?

Patsy found tears blurring her vision, one slid down her nose and plopped on to the slipper. Quickly, she wiped it off. It really wouldn't do to spoil it. It had been wrapped in tissue paper and smelled of lavender. Carefully, she rewrapped the slipper and slid it back beneath the large brown envelope, then closed the trunk.

–

Patsy was so moved and upset by this discovery that she scrambled back down the ladder and ran straight out of the house, desperate for a breath of fresh air. Collapsing on the doorstep, she buried her head in her hands and wept. She'd no idea why, except that she was filled with an overwhelming sadness for what might have been.

She hadn't been there more than a minute when a hand touched her shoulder. 'Why do you cry, Patsy? Can I help?'

She looked up into a pair of gentle brown eyes. Instantly she scrubbed at her tears with the flat of her hands. 'Oh, Marc, I didn't see you there.'

He hunkered down beside her, tucked a stray curl behind her ear, and when she didn't protest or yell at him, risked sitting next to her on the step. 'I shall wait quietly here, till you tell me.'

Patsy covered her face with her hands. 'I c-can't. No one can help. No one. Leave me alone, you don't understand.'

'How can I understand if you won't tell me what is wrong? You won't ever speak to me. But I make a good listener. Look at me, Patsy. Look at me.'

'I must look a mess.'

'Not to me.' He held her face between his hands, smoothed away the tears with the heel of his thumbs and looked deep into her eyes. 'You are in great pain, I think. Tell me what it is, little one. Let me share your burden. I can do that, at least.'

The next second he put his arms about her and Patsy buried her face into the warm hollow of his neck, and while she sobbed into his shirt, he held her close, murmuring soothing little noises against her ear. After a moment, the tears gradually subsided and she glanced shyly up at him, her small face pinched with pain, then out it all came, as if she was incapable of keeping the poignant discovery to herself any longer.

'I found a slipper, a baby's slipper. Pink and white silk that I think was mine when I was a baby. I believe that Clara is my mother but I can't prove it. Oh, and I don't know what to do about that.'

Marc was stunned by this revelation, as well he might be. He'd expected some silly feminine worry, a squabble with the sisters. Yet Patsy had confided in him something real and vitally important. His heart sang. After a moment, and still holding her in his arms, he softly asked, 'Have you spoken to Clara about these suspicions of yours?'

Patsy shook her head. 'Heavens no, I couldn't possibly. I daren't. I don't want to be a nuisance to them, a burden. I mustn't push my nose in where I'm not wanted. They might send me away altogether then.'

'How do you know that you're not wanted?'

'Annie has just given me the push from my job so it's pretty clear I'm only here on sufferance.'

'That's because of money, I should think, not because she doesn't like you.'

'You don't know that, not for sure. She's been against me from the start. I really should leave, but where would I go? I have no one. It's right what you said the other day. I come from nowhere and I have nowhere to go.'

'But I think you cannot go on like this, not knowing. Everyone has a right to be told who their mother is. Why would Clara keep such a secret? Are you sure you are right? Because if so, no wonder you feel neglected and depressed, a little bit sorry for yourself.'

Patsy was already beginning to regret having told him and this last comment instantly unsettled her. 'I'm not feeling sorry for myself, and not absolutely certain, but almost! I have a problem I can't solve, that's all. I don't know why Clara doesn't tell me. I have any number of questions, but no answers.'

'Then you must be brave and ask them. You have all my heartfelt pity, Patsy. I am fortunate to have the love of my family, you have not. I cannot imagine what it must feel like to be alone in the world.'

She jerked away from him and jumped to her feet. 'I don't want your pity, heartfelt or not! It's all right for you to hand out advice, since you do have a family: a mama and papa, brothers and sisters. What do you know about not belonging?'

'That is what I am trying to say, Patsy, I cannot imagine how it must feel to be alone in the world.' Marc felt helpless in the face of her distress. Why could he never find the right words to say to her? He was always so clumsy, so stupid. He stood beside her, trying to take her back into his arms but she resisted, pushing him away even as he told her again that he wanted only to help.

'You can help best by leaving me alone. Go on, go back to your lovely family and take your heartfelt pity with you. I don't need your sympathy, ta very much.' Then she went back inside number twenty-two and slammed the door behind her.

Marc let out a heavy sigh of exasperation. Whatever he did was wrong.

Patsy had just about managed to stow the ladder away in the backyard and put the kettle on the gas when the front door opened and the two sisters walked in.

'I do hope you haven't been too bored on your own, Patsy?' Clara said, glancing about her.

'N–no, not all.' Patsy was slightly breathless and doing her best to smile. 'Fancy a cuppa? I've got the kettle on.'

—

It was midday on Saturday when Patsy came home for her dinner, that she found Clara waiting for her, a grim expression on her face looking unlike her usual cheerful self. She wasted no time in revealing the reason for her anger.

'Have you been looking through my things, Patsy?'

'What?'

'Don't play games with me. How did you occupy yourself while we were out last night? Did you take the opportunity to go through my things? Because somebody has! I can tell that some of my personal possessions have been moved. Why did you do that?'

Patsy was filled with fear. Yet what else could she do but continue to deny she'd be lying? 'I never touched your things. Why would I?'

'I don't know, that's why I'm asking. And there's a mark on the wall at the top of the stairs. Did you go up into the loft? Why on earth would you do such a thing? Tell me, Patsy. I'm not a fool. Tell me the truth.'

But she couldn't. How could she possibly own up to seeking evidence to prove that Clara was her mother? It was beyond her. The very prospect of asking that question made Patsy go all sick and funny inside. Not just yet. Oh drat, why hadn't Shirley found some genuinely useful evidence, then she might have found the courage to confront Clara with it? But how could she take the risk with nothing more than gossip and suspicion to go on?

It would be too easy for Clara to avoid answering, simply to dismiss the whole notion as pure fantasy on Shirley's part, accuse Patsy of interfering and throw her out of the house. Come to think of it, why didn't she save her the trouble?

Patsy began to shout: 'You only ever see the worst in me. Right, well I'm off. I'll pack my flipping bags this minute, and leave. I'm not staying where I'm not wanted, where people don't believe a word I say.' And she stormed upstairs to her room, slamming the bedroom door with a satisfying crash behind her. Then she sat down on her bed, struggling not to cry, hoping and praying that Clara would come upstairs and beg her to stay.

It didn't take long. A tiny knock on the door, then a small voice saying, 'Can I come in?'

Patsy leaped to her feet and quickly pulled open a drawer. She was tossing clothes on to the floor as Clara came in, trying to hide a small smile of relief.

Clara sat on the edge of the bed. 'I do hope you don't mean it, Patsy, about leaving. That's the last thing I want.'

Patsy shrugged her shoulders. 'What do I care? I can live anywhere.'

'You can, but I hope you'll continue to live with us. Haven't I said it's important to me, because I...' Clara hesitated, as if wanting to say more, but not knowing how in the ensuing silence. Patsy feared, hoped or prayed that Clara might be about to reveal the truth, at last.

But the next second she was on her feet and heading for the door. 'I was wrong about you snooping through my things, but we'll say no more on the matter. I think you understand how I feel about my privacy now. I would also like you to remember that Annie has enough worries at the moment without your adding to them. I shall go and finish making dinner. Be down in two minutes, please.'

And she was gone.

Patsy felt a small spurt of triumph. She'd won, probably because she'd made Clara feel guilty. It wouldn't do the sisters' reputation any good at all if they turned a poor homeless orphan out on to the streets.

Yet in her heart of hearts, Patsy hated herself for what she'd done, both for snooping through Clara's things and for manipulating her into letting her stay. The sisters had been kind to her, even grumpy Annie, even if it was out of their sense of Christian duty. If only it didn't have to be this way. If only they truly liked her instead of just being charitable, then she could be rid of this constant fear that they might at any moment ask her to leave. If only she belonged.

Chapter Twenty-Three

Fran called in at the ice cream parlour the next day for a Chocolate Nut Sundae, and a quick word with Patsy. 'Will you be free later? Only I've got a bit of a problem and I could do with talking things through, with a sympathetic friend like.'

Patsy was flattered to be considered both sympathetic and a friend of the more sophisticated, gregarious Fran. 'Okay, when and where?'

Fran's glance shifted over Patsy's shoulder as she saw Eddie walk into the market hall. He didn't often come near but there he was, large as life standing by the main door, clearly looking round for her. Fran was thrilled and instantly forgot all about Patsy. 'I'll let you know later. I've got to run.' And she was gone.

'Charming!' That friendship didn't last long, Patsy thought.

Fran practically flung herself into Eddie's arms, would have done so had he not grasped her by the shoulders. 'Not here you stupid girl! What are you thinking of? I can only spare a few minutes but we have to talk.' Grabbing her wrist, he marched her out of the market hall, through the stalls and out on to Hardman Street where he'd parked his car.

She thought he might be about to drive her somewhere, out into the country, or to the park where they used to go, instead he drove through a mire of streets then parked up a back alley close by the docks. She could smell tar and wood shavings, the skyline nothing but brick walls and cranes. 'My goodness, this is romantic!'

'I've not brought you here for romance. We need to talk about this problem of yours, Fran.'

She looked at him. 'It's your problem too, Eddie. It's your kid.'

He gulped. His face seemed pinched, she noticed, and his usual cockiness had deserted him. 'The point is, what're we going to do about it?'

Fran settled down in the front passenger seat, hitched up her skirt and crossed her legs so that they were displayed in all their glory. Then folding her arms across the fullness of her bosom, she stared up into the mesh of ironwork that girded the cranes, pretending to give deep consideration to the question.

'Let's see... we could pretend it doesn't exist. But babies have a way of making their presence felt in the end, no matter how hard you might try to ignore them. I could rush to the altar with someone else, but I don't know anyone willing to sacrifice themselves to protect my honour. So I guess we have no choice. You'll have to be the one to make an honest woman of me.'

'Don't talk daft!'

'Daft, is it, to want a father for our child?'

When he didn't respond, Fran giggled and tickled him under his chin as if he were Buster the dog. 'Go on, give us a smile, you know you still fancy me rotten.' She swivelled about in her seat, and, curling herself up as best she could in the confined space, lay across his lap, pressing her breasts close against his chest. 'We're good together, you and me.'

'I'm already married, Fran. You knew that from the start.'

'So what? Marriages can be ended. Divorce her and marry me. Why not? You no longer love the silly cow anyway. You do nothing but complain about her.'

She flashed him a teasing, sideways glance from beneath mascara-darkened lashes, trying to judge his reaction. In all the months they'd been together, never once had the word marriage been mentioned. It just wasn't on the agenda. Now it was, so far as Fran was concerned at least. But how would Eddie feel about this change of plan?

He didn't move, didn't touch her; simply sat staring at those blasted cranes as if he were in some sort of stupor. Just when she thought he never would speak, he said, 'Josie is pregnant too, Fran. She told me last night.'

'What?' Fran sat up quickly, cursing when she banged her ribs on the steering wheel. 'What do you mean she's pregnant? She can't be. You told me that you and she weren't even – doing it!'

'I lied. I didn't want to upset you. She's my wife, and she's been desperate for a kid for years. Had two miscarriages already but wouldn't give up trying. She's over the moon, can't believe how lucky she is.'

'Lucky?' Fran, struggling to right herself, pulled her skirt down over her knees, making it plain that if that was how things stood, he was no longer entitled to view the goods on offer.

'I'm in an impossible situation, can't you see that Fran love? Josie wants this kid – desperately. I can't let her down or risk upsetting her, not right now, or she'll lose it, like she lost the others. You'll have to get rid of yours, there's no other answer. I can probably find you the money. I don't know how or where from, but I'll manage it somehow.'

He looked like a man sleepwalking but Fran had no sympathy for him. She was feeling too sorry for herself. Anger was rising in her, hot and strong. 'I don't want your money. This is your kid we're talking about here.'

His expression was colder than she'd ever seen it. 'No, Fran, it's your kid. Not my problem. I'm going to be the father of my wife's child, not yours.'

'So I can just disappear off the face of the earth, can I?' Fran had never been so angry, so upset, in all her life.

Eddie turned the ignition key, kicked the engine into life. 'I'll take you back to the market. Soon as I've got my hands on a bit of cash, I'll be in touch.'

Fran was flabbergasted. This wasn't how it was meant to be. This wasn't the way the story was supposed to end. 'And that's it, is it? That's the end. You're chucking me.'

He smiled at her then, ran a hand up the length of her leg and fondled her. ''Course I'm not chucking you. I shall need you more than ever, with our Josie wrapped up in babies and nappies and stuff. It's her that wants the kid, not me. You and me don't need any of that baggage. Get rid of it, Fran, then we carry on as if nothing has happened, the way we like it, just you and me. God, you're gorgeous.'

He turned off the engine then, pulled her towards him and began to kiss her hard. Fran found herself whimpering with need, and couldn't seem to deny him.

Eddie very efficiently slid back the seat, and relieved her of her panties. Seconds later he was doing what he knew he did best, the easiest way in the world to keep a woman happy.

–

Finding employment in Gretna Green was proving less easy than Chris and Amy had imagined. It was a surprisingly busy little town, and they soon discovered that they weren't the only couple hanging around waiting to get married. There were any number of young hopefuls looking for temporary employment.

Amy went back to their landlady to ask if she was in need of a chambermaid, or if she knew of anyone who might be. She named one or two possibilities but the only response Amy got to her enquiries were shaken heads and regretful refusals.

They'd found themselves a priest willing to marry them, filled in the right forms and served the proper notice. There was nothing more to be done now but wait. Every morning they counted their money to check how much they had left, discussed priorities, often forced to choose between soap powder and another small meal. Sometimes, when they were out shopping they'd smell fish and chips, or roast lamb being served at the corner cafe, and would stand at the window breathing it in like the Bisto kids. There had been the odd occasion when hunger had driven them inside.

'Hang the expense,' Chris would say, taking in the pallor of Amy's complexion, feeling the frailness of her over thin body pressed close against his side in the curve of his arm. 'You need feeding up.'

Living in the woods, as they were, it became increasingly difficult to keep clean. They washed themselves carefully in the cold water of the stream every morning, laughing and splashing each other, but once or twice the water play had got a bit out of hand. Seeing each other like that, even if it were only partially naked, was too enticing, too tempting. One morning they'd fallen upon each other and very nearly broken their pledge not to make love.

Chris had pushed her down in the long grass on the bank and kissed her as he never had before, unable to resist. Then he'd got up and stormed off, as was his wont when he thought he'd gone too far, only to return hours later, silent and moody.

After that, Amy would creep down to the stream while he was still asleep, or pretending to be, to wash and dress herself quickly before he stirred. Somehow, being so secretive, yet wanting him so much, made her feel even more unclean.

Once a week she would take their clothes to the launderette, but it was expensive and when it rained, as it seemed to do a great deal, the clothes took ages to dry. Amy thought she must have spent most of that summer sneezing and coughing.

And cooking, particularly on wet days, was well-nigh impossible. At first it had seemed fun to light a fire in the woods and cook sausages at the end of a stick, or make bread dampers out of flour and water, wrap them around a green twig and bake them over the heat as Amy used to do in the Girl Guides. It seemed romantic, in a way. They would laugh if the dampers were smoked, the baked potato turned into charcoal or a sausage dropped into the flames and burned to a cinder.

But after a while it ceased to be either fun or a novelty. If they were wet and hungry and they couldn't get the fire going, or couldn't afford to buy any more flour or sausages that week to replace the food they'd lost, they became tense and upset.

They learned to keep some dry kindling in a bag, a stack of wood covered by bracken under the tree, but it was frightening how quickly it got used up, then they'd be scouring the woodlands again for more dead wood dry enough to burn, an endless and soul destroying pursuit. Tried to fashion themselves a shelter out of sticks and bracken, but no matter how carefully they wove reeds and leaves into it, rain would pour through and soak them anyway, and if the wind blew, it fell down.

And since they didn't sleep well, because it was either too hot, too cold, too light at night, too quiet, too wet, the ground was too hard or else they were simply lying there worrying about how long they could afford to go on like this, they became tired and tetchy with each other.

'Why don't you try for a job at the petrol station?' Amy suggested one morning. 'I told you about that notice I saw stuck up on the office wall when we walked past the other day.'

'Because I don't know anything about cars.'

'You know enough to put petrol in a tank, surely.'

'Amy, the job was for a car mechanic. I'm a milkman.'

Another time, she suggested he apply to the council to be a street cleaner, and this just because she saw one paper bag blowing in the street.

'Gretna has a street cleaner. I've seen him.'

'They might need another. He's old, and maybe can't manage the job by himself.'

'He's not old and he can manage perfectly well. The streets here are clean. This isn't Castlefield or Champion Street Market.'

'Have you even tried at the local dairy?'

'It was the first place I visited. It's no good, love, I've been everywhere, asked everyone.'

Amy was near to tears. 'Then go round and ask them all over again. It's not as if we can give anyone a telephone number to ring us if a job becomes available, is it? I'll go round again too. Maybe that cafe on the corner has lost one of its waitresses by now, or is busier with the summer trade and needs extra help.' She got to her feet, as if she were about to go that minute, although it was past nine o'clock at night.

'All right, love. We'll give it another go tomorrow, if you want to. Now try to get some sleep. You're tired out.' Chris pulled her gently down again. He was very patient with her, wishing he could put everything right.

She sat huddled in misery. Tears filled her eyes and Amy knuckled them away, like a child. She felt exhausted, bone weary, though she didn't understand why. It wasn't as if they had any real work to do, often having hours on end with nothing to fill the time at all. It must be something to do with the strain of not daring to touch or even look at each other, of how hungry she was, and truly frightened. Eloping was no fun at all.

Chapter Twenty-Four

Sunday morning dawned bright and clear, a perfect day for a wedding. Patsy was nervous but looking forward to it. The market was closed on Sundays so she was able to take her time getting ready, enjoy a relaxing bath, wash her hair, apply make-up with a little more discretion than normal. She'd spent all her carefully hoarded savings on a new dress: ice blue polished cotton with string straps and a knee length skirt that swirled delightfully over layers of crisp lace and net petticoats. She cinched in her waist with a broad white belt, put on high-heeled strappy white sandals, and felt ready for anything.

Not that she was trying to look attractive for Marc Bertalone, she told herself. She'd only taken all this trouble for the sake of her own self-esteem, which needed a bit of boosting right now. Patsy had never felt so low as she had since reading her grandmother's will. It had made her realise what little consideration had ever been given to her future care. What kind of a family could be so heartless? And she'd made a bad situation worse by losing Clara's trust. Patsy had known all along that it was wrong to go through her things, so was it any wonder she'd been accused of snooping? If only she could explain.

But she must try not to think of all that today.

Annie was even now giving her a lecture on social graces and how she must be pleasant and polite to people. 'It wouldn't do for you to offend the Bertalones. Apart from being well respected in Champion Street, Mr Bertalone has been good enough to give you a job, so do try not to be... how shall I put it...?'

'Difficult?' Patsy supplied.

'I couldn't have put it better myself,' Annie said tightly. Patsy thought she looked even more condemnatory and miserable this morning, her lips so tightly pressed together they seemed robbed of all colour, almost blue.

Clara, ever the peacemaker, smiled and kissed Patsy on both cheeks. 'I know you hate to be fussed over but you'll get a great deal of that today, so accept it. The Italians love kissing. And don't look so anxious, dear, your new dress looks delightful. Very pretty. I'm sure Marc will think so too. Ah, here he is now.'

Marc had arrived on the dot and Patsy could tell by the widening of his eyes at the first sight of her, and the low whistle he gave under his breath, that he was impressed. 'You look beautiful,' he told her, handing her a corsage of pink and cream orchids.

Patsy was struck speechless by this touch of kindness, didn't know how to thank him.

Clara busied herself pinning the flowers into place. 'Thank Marc for his generosity,' she whispered in the girl's ear.

Patsy pouted. 'I thought it was usually carnations for a wedding?'

'Only the best for my date,' he said.

'I'm not your date.' Clara and Marc exchanged speaking glances, which infuriated Patsy all the more. Oh, but she was pleased he thought her beautiful.

'Have a good time,' Clara called after them as they left, Marc extending his arm for Patsy to take with old-fashioned courtesy. She studiously ignored it.

The two sisters stood side by side, watching them walk down the street, several chilly inches separating them, and Clara shook her head in despair. 'If that girl manages to keep that sharp tongue of hers under control for the entire afternoon, it will be a miracle.'

–

The wedding ceremony passed in a whirl. The groom stood patiently waiting at the church door for his bride, ready to present her with her bouquet. And she arrived late, as tradition dictated, looking incredibly beautiful.

When the service was over the bride and groom disappeared for a short time to catch their breath and decide how they felt about being married to each other. Meanwhile, the guests were served refreshments: delicious little ham pasties and cubes of cheese and pineapple on sticks. Patsy had never seen the like. The women, herself included, were given a sweet liqueur to accompany them, the men something stronger.

It was all very relaxed with lots of jokes being cracked about how everyone was looking forward to free ice cream later. And there were any number of toasts including *per cento anni*, for a hundred years.

'Heavens, I can't imagine being married to someone for ten months, let alone a hundred years,' Patsy said.

Marc gave her a quizzical look. 'You don't want to marry? To have babies? But you would make the beautiful mama.'

'I – I'm too young to think about such things, but I can't see myself as a – a mother.' She was startled by the unexpected compliment, if that's what it was. But how could she imagine herself in that role when she had no proper example to base her ideas on? Mrs Bowman had never demonstrated the kind of affection and care one would expect from a mother.

'Why not? Are you afraid you won't find the right man? Or that some other girl will snap me up first?'

'Very funny! Let's say, not everyone is as fortunate as your own parents when it comes to finding wedded bliss.'

He put back his head and laughed, revealing strong white teeth. 'That shows how little you understand Italians. If my parents are displeased with each other, everyone knows about it. But the next day, or the next hour, it is all forgotten. They kiss and make love. That is the Italian way. Latin fire stokes a good marriage.' He reached forward and tentatively touched her cheek. 'But I forgot that you don't know who your mother is. Who brought you up, *mia carina*?'

'You'll grow a long nose like Pinocchio if you keep asking questions.'

Marc laughed. 'He got the long nose for telling lies, not for being curious. Do you tell lies, little one?'

'Yeah, I'm really the daughter of a millionaire. Didn't you guess?'

He immediately adopted an expression of mock sadness. 'Oh, that is a great pity. If that is true, then you would never look at a humble Italian boy. My heart is broken.' And he dramatically held the flat of his hand to his left side. Patsy began to giggle. She really couldn't help herself.

After the cocktails, the guests gathered in the hotel dining room, ready to be introduced to the bridal party. Patsy had never seen so many people at a wedding, not that she'd ever been to one in her life before, so how was she to judge?

Everyone lined up opposite a partner, forming a pathway for the bride and groom. There was a great fanfare of music and then the newlywed couple progressed along the path, nodding and smiling and kissing people as they went along.

The bride carried a small satin bag on her arm, and sometimes an envelope would be slipped inside it as she passed by. Patsy asked Marc what it was and he told her that many people preferred to give money as a wedding gift, and that was the accepted way to present it.

'I've brought them a present.' And she showed him a small parcel. 'Should I slip that in too? Not having much money I bought them a silver jam spoon, second-hand, but I've cleaned and polished it to make it shine.'

'They will love it,' Marc said. 'That was kind of you, Patsy. But then, you are a kind girl at heart, not at all the rough diamond you pretend to be.'

She wasn't given the opportunity to argue with him on that one, as it was her turn to kiss the bride and groom. As she did so, she slipped her gift into the little satin bag and wished them many congratulations and a hundred years of happiness, which seemed to be the right thing to say.

Next came the speeches by friends and family, and seemingly endless champagne toasts to the newly wedded couple. Patsy began to feel giddy from the wine and Marc teased her about getting 'squiffy'.

Papa Bertalone was on top form, boasting how Italians always provided the best food. 'No one will go hungry at a Bertalone wedding,' he roared.

And he wasn't wrong. First came the antipasti and the salad, followed by chicken in a delicious sauce with a variety of vegetables and several assorted pastas. Fortunately, time was allowed between courses for people to relax and make room for the next one.

In one such interval Marc whispered in her ear 'And now, at last, I get to dance with you.'

'I'm not sure that's such a good idea…' Patsy began, but he was dragging her to her feet and across the floor to join a crowd of people, all of whom seemed to be jumping up and down to rousing music in dances such as mazurkas and tarantellas, which involved a great deal of circling and clapping, waltzing and twirling, and any amount of helpless laughter. Never had Patsy laughed so much at her own ineptitude.

Marc gave his famous wide grin. 'You're having the good time. Don't pretend you're not, I can tell.'

She laughed up at him, too happy for once to argue.

Next came the cake cutting, and an array of desserts that made her mouth water just to look at them: a delectable selection of pastries, fruits, cakes, and ice cream were presented on what Marc called a Viennese Table.

'Or it is often called the Vienna Hour,' he told her. 'You have a spot of cream on your mouth, and I most desperately want to lick it off.'

She licked her lips quickly before he could carry out the threat but, laughing, he must have taken that for assent anyway for he bent his head and captured her mouth with his. The moment his lips touched hers she was lost, the room seeming to spin about her. It would only be the champagne having that effect on her, not his kiss. It lasted only a moment before he was once again grinning down at her, stroking her flushed cheeks.

More dancing followed, while the matrons sat and gossiped, and children slid and skated on the slippery floor or pretended to ape the dancing of the adults. The bride and groom circled the floor, speaking to everyone and handing out small gifts to their guests, in this case a few sugared almonds wrapped in net the same colour as the bride's cream dress.

'My sister Maria, she is beautiful, yes?'

'Oh, she is indeed,' Patsy breathed.

'Amazing when she was once such a skinny, ugly kid.'

Patsy giggled, thinking that she might well have been transported to another world, a paradise of warmth, and love, and happiness. It felt wonderful to have Marc's arms about her, holding her close in a waltz or quickstep. Patsy wasn't used to this style of dancing, being more accustomed to rock 'n' roll. Marc felt the same because he trod on her toe for the second time, making her yelp.

'I am not the good dancer,' he excused himself, eyes mournful, begging for her forgiveness.

'That is clear, but the trouble is I'm not much better.'

He grinned down at her. 'But that doesn't mean I don't enjoy it. I like to hold you. You feel so good in my arms, as if you belong there. Do I hold you right? Ees like this... or this? I no good with girls.' Each time he spoke, he snuggled her ever closer, holding her tightly in his arms, his cheek pressed against hers. 'You tell me what I do wrong. Where I put my hand. Here? Is good for you, yes?'

Patsy burst out laughing, and brushed his wandering hand away from where it had settled on her bottom. 'Don't play the innocent with me, Marc Bertalone. And don't play the dumb Italian either. You've lived in England all your life, so don'ta speaka the pigeon English to me.'

'You mock us?' said an outraged voice in her ear, and, mortified, Patsy turned to find Papa Bertalone scowling down at her.

'Oh, goodness, it was merely a joke. Marc and I... we... I mean, I was teasing him. He was pretending to...'

'He was being the naughty boy, yes?'

Patsy gave a rueful smile. 'Maybe just a little, but his charming tricks don't work on me. I wasn't born yesterday.'

Papa Bertalone put back his head and laughed loud and long, slapping his son on the back with great vigour. 'I thinka you have met your match in this little princess. She have you taped, as they say here in Lancashire. Come, little one, come and see the rest of the family.'

And so Patsy at last got to meet Mama Bertalone, and all the little girls who had acted as bridesmaids for their elder sister, resplendent in a pastel rainbow of dresses. She already knew Alessandro and Giovanni, but it was good to talk with them too.

Patsy was sorry when the time came for the bride and groom to leave for their honeymoon, and for all the guests to go home, back to their mundane lives. For one afternoon she had forgotten her troubles, had laughed and danced as a young girl should, a handsome and attentive young man by her side.

Marc walked her home, stopping only when they came to the Higginsons' doorstep. And it seemed the most natural thing in the world that she should kiss him. His mouth tasted so good against hers, the smell of his skin intoxicating: of wine and garlic and sweet pastry, of heat and desire.

'That's by way of saying thank you for a lovely day,' she murmured. 'I know I didn't want to come but I'm glad that I did. Your family are wonderful. You are so lucky to have them.' And to her horror Patsy felt a tear spill over and start to roll down her cheek. She brushed it away with a laugh. 'Weddings always make people cry, don't they?'

'Let me kiss you again, to keep that light shining in your eyes for a little longer.' And when he took her in his arms and kissed her this time, Patsy thought she might like to stay there forever.

They kissed for some time, Patsy matching his passion with her own till she burned with need inside, yearning for more and more.

Marc seemed almost startled by her response, but how could she resist when she'd dreamed of this moment night after night? He was the one to break away first.

'This is not the place *mia carina*, and it is late. I promised Miss Clara I would bring you home safe and on time.' He stroked the fall of her silver hair, treasuring its silky quality. 'You will see me again, I think. We will have the second date.'

'And what makes you so sure?'

'I know you will. How could you resist?'

Patsy pursed her lips, striving to appear cross and unimpressed by his charms when inside her heart was racing. Unaccountable happiness flowed through her veins, bubbling through her blood like the champagne she'd been drinking. Was that what made her feel so joyous and light headed, or something else entirely? She'd never felt so wonderful in all her life. It was as if every part of her were on fire, alight with emotion. 'And you are as full of yourself as ever, I see.'

He tapped her nose in a gesture of affection. 'For once, little one, do not argue. You will see me again, tomorrow, when we can continue where we left off. *Buonanotte*.' Popping a kiss on her brow, he gave her a smile and a wink, then opened the door and ushered her into the house. 'Till tomorrow,' he whispered. 'Be careful not to wake the sisters. Sweet dreams.' And closed the door softly after her.

But there was little hope of sweet dreams at number twenty-two that night. The moment Patsy walked into the living room, she saw at once that something was terribly wrong. Clara was wringing her hands and crying, and Annie was stretched out unconscious on the floor. She'd suffered a heart attack.

Chapter Twenty-Five

Fran stood outside the semi-detached house. She had noted its neat front garden, pretty lace curtains and the gravelled drive leading to an adjoining garage. Eddie Davidson was doing well for himself, and his wife must be living in the lap of luxury, while Fran herself had nothing but his leftovers. She was supposed to be walking Buster, but hadn't been able to resist taking a detour round to Eddie's place, to see if she could catch a glimpse of the woman who stood between herself and true happiness.

Her mam must have stood here when she came that time to deliver her anonymous note, scratch his car and break the wonderful Josie's plant pots. Fran began to feel some sympathy for her mother's actions. Maybe she should try something similar. Eddie deserved to be punished, mean, selfish pig that he was, but how? What could she do? How could she hurt him the most? Even as she tried to think of a way, her heart melted with love for him. Oh, but she didn't want to hurt him. Why would she hurt the man she loved?

The door opened and Josie emerged. Purse in hand, she carried a basket on her arm, clearly on her way down to the shops to buy something to make for Eddie's tea.

As Fran watched her carefully lock the door, rage boiled within her. That was something she would never have the chance to do. She couldn't make his tea, sit on the sofa with him in his fancy lounge to watch his brand new TV. She couldn't sleep with him in his bed, or wake up beside him of a morning. She was the bit on the side, who must be grateful for any crumbs he could spare after he'd spent every day and night with this woman.

Josie began to walk away and Fran couldn't help noticing her jaunty step, the swing of her hips and the unmistakeable bump, which indicated she was pregnant. Now her own rage changed to hatred.

Josie was the one she ought to be concentrating her attention on, not Eddie. She needed to find a way to eject her from his life, some way to rid both herself and him of this woman's presence, then they would be free to be together. It was her, Fran, he really loved, she was sure of it. He was stuck in this situation, this loveless marriage. He was too soft-hearted to leave because of the stupid child his wife was carrying. Yet why should Josie's child be more important than Fran's own?

Why should his wife be more important than her?

As Josie turned the corner of the avenue and disappeared from view, Fran made the decision that if Eddie couldn't bring himself to leave, then she would think of some way to make that cow of a wife leave him instead. She meant to have him all to herself, else make his life an absolute misery. One way or the other, she'd win.

Though for the life of her she couldn't think of a way to achieve that, not offhand. And then Fran noticed that while she'd been standing there contemplating the situation, the dog had made a mess on the pavement.

Smiling to herself, she found a piece of newspaper, scooped it up and plopped it through Josie's letterbox on to her new fitted carpet. That would do nicely, for a start.

'Has your mother been round to my house again?'

Fran gazed at Eddie out of wide, innocent eyes. 'How would I know?'

Since it was a beautiful summer's day, they were on the Liverpool ferryboat, the *Royal Daffodil*, taking a trip down the Manchester Ship Canal from Salford Docks to New Brighton. To give them time to talk and sort out their problem, Josie was at her mother's. They'd left the docks, the cranes, and Irlam railway bridge behind them, gone through Mode Wheel and Barton Locks, and were now cruising through some of the most spectacular scenery the north could offer; past farms and woodland, and on towards the Irish Sea. Fran wished they could keep on sailing, to Ireland or across the Atlantic to America. Far away from Champion Street and the annoying Josie.

Eddie rested his elbows on the ship's rail. Fran stood beside him, leaning her head against his shoulder, watching the countryside slide serenely by, trying to pretend she was happy. She had six hours to win him round to her way of thinking, and meant to make the best of every one of them.

'Somebody put dog shit through our letterbox, and it isn't hard to guess who. Josie nearly had a fit. Can you imagine having to clean that up, on a new carpet too? That's why she's gone to her mother's, to get away from the smell.'

'Oh, that's awful. Poor Josie.' Fran struggled to keep the amusement out of her voice but Eddie must have detected it.

'It isn't funny. You wouldn't believe the stink it made! We can't seem to get rid of it. You've got to speak to that blasted mother of yours. She's out of control. That carpet cost me a fortune.'

'I will speak to her.' Fran tugged him round to face her, pushing her cushiony breasts against the hardness of his chest. She was wearing the lowest cut dress she could find and plump flesh spilled out enticingly above the square neckline. His gaze was riveted upon the delicious sight and Fran smiled when she heard his low moan.

''Course, if you and your lovely wifey were to split up, you could let her have all the carpets, so long as we get the bed...'

'Fran, I've told you already, I can't possibly leave Josie, not yet, not while she's pregnant. I'm terrified of her finding out about us. I daren't risk telling her. Far too dangerous.'

Her amber eyes widened still further. 'You really think she might lose the baby, if you did?'

'Yes, I do, from shock.'

'That would be dreadful,' Fran said, falsely sympathetic. 'But what if someone else tells her – not me!' She rested her hand on her cleavage in a show of sincerity. 'You know I'd never let you down in that way, Eddie. But what if Mam opened her gob and spilled the beans, as it were? Or gossip from the market reached her. What then?'

Eddie frowned, dragging his gaze from her breasts to study her face with narrowed eyes. 'You don't think that's likely, do you? Is there gossip about us? I haven't heard any. If there's any danger of that, then we'd best stop meeting like this. We should maybe lie low for a bit, at least until the baby is safely born.'

'I'd lie anywhere with you, Eddie love.' Fran half glanced over her shoulder. An old man seated on the slatted wood bench was reading a newspaper, but apart from a few school kids there was no one else around. 'But which baby would that be, Eddie, hers or mine? Both of them?' Looking mildly perplexed, she began to unbutton his flies and slipped her hand inside his trousers. She believed no one could see, but the threat of discovery added a spice of danger to the game.

Eddie was more cautious. 'Not here, you daft mare!' Pushing her hand away, he marched her to a more secluded corner tucked behind a lifeboat where, after a few kisses to warm her up, Fran happily obliged him again.

He put back his head on a low groan as she grasped his penis, stroking it rhythmically up and down. 'H–haven't you made arrangements yet, to get yourself sorted?' He was finding it diffi-cult to breathe, to think even, as his excitement mounted. 'I'm c-counting on you, Fran. D–don't make trouble. Oh, Christ…'

He reached for her then, and ten minutes later, when he could speak again, said, 'You have to get rid of it. You promised you would. Anyway, you don't want a kid any more than I do.'

'That's true,' Fran murmured, cuddling close against him, purring with pleasure. Pouting rosebud pink lips, she ran her hands under his shirt over his bare chest at mid-ships, then back below decks once more. 'Are you all done, or is there life in the old engine yet?'

'Christ, Fran, give me a minute to catch me breath. Are you listening to what I'm saying? I daren't think what effect it might have on Josie if she were ever to find out.'

'Ooh, we mustn't let that happen,' Fran agreed. 'We could get in the lifeboat? There's nobody looking, and it could be a right life-saver for you, judging by the pained expression on your face.'

They quickly scrambled inside, and the lifeboat's rocking motion in the next half hour or so wasn't entirely due to the tidal waters.

–

Days later Fran was back outside Eddie's house. This time she boldly marched up to the front door of the new semi-detached and rapped on the knocker. She could hear Buddy Holly singing 'Peggy Sue' on the radio inside, and someone singing along with it.

Josie opened the door the next moment. She was dressed in a bright pink floral maternity smock over black drainpipe trousers, feather duster in hand, just as if she'd stepped out of one of those adverts for Mansion polish in a glossy magazine. For a moment, Fran couldn't speak. She was much prettier close to, more fragile, and younger than Fran had expected.

Josie smiled at her. 'Yes, can I help you?'

'I – I... Is Eddie in?'

'Sorry, you've just missed him. He's already left for work.'

Fran knew this already, since she'd watched him go. The woman – little more than a girl as she couldn't be a day over twenty-two, about the same age as Fran herself – was still smiling helpfully at her, asking if she was a work colleague in need of a lift?

Still Fran said nothing. What was she doing standing here like a lemon? She had to speak, to say something. She'd made her plan, she should stick with it. But how could she tell this pretty innocent what she and her selfish, philandering husband got up to in the back seat of his car, let alone in a lifeboat for God's sake? The girl must be at least four or five months pregnant, if not more, further gone than she was herself. Fran found herself smiling back, almost feeling sorry for her, experiencing a sudden and unexpected shaft of pity for Eddie's wife of all people!

'Er, yes, that's it, it was about work, never mind. I'll catch him another time, bye.' And before she knew what she was doing, or why, Fran was walking back down the garden path away from the house. She must be turning soft.

Later, in her dinner break from serving on the pie stall, filled with self-loathing for her own cowardice, Fran wrote an anonymous note. Without giving herself time to think, she sealed the envelope and dropped it into the letterbox. That was the best way to tell Josie about her philandering husband, and it couldn't be traced back to Fran. Dear God, she was turning into her own mother.

–

Eddie's anger was incandescent. The moment Fran clapped eyes on him, she knew at once that she'd gone too far. He hadn't come to see her today for a kiss and cuddle in the car, or a bit of slap and tickle up a back alley, and he wasn't about to suggest another romantic cruise up the Ship Canal. But then she saw that it wasn't her he'd come to see at all.

He marched right up to the pie stall, bold as brass, and shouted at her mother, for heaven's sake, roared at Molly in front of everyone.

'If you think you've done something clever, Molly Poulson, then you're mistaken.'

'What the hangment…? And which smelly rat hole did you crawl out of?'

Red-faced, Fran was beside herself with embarrassment. The stall was as busy as ever, and the entire queue of customers stood watching, goggle-eyed, ready to enjoy the entertainment. There always seemed to be some fun around where Big Molly was concerned. 'I'll see to this, Mam. Not here, Eddie, for God's sake! Come on, let's go somewhere more private.'

'Like thump we'll go somewhere more private. Let's have it out here and now, in the open. Why not? Since my wife has been told by some "well-wisher" what you and me have been up to, why not tell the whole blasted world?'

As the queue willingly parted for him, only too ready to hear what it was exactly the pair of them had been up to, Eddie stepped to the front so that he could address Big Molly directly.

'First you put dog's mess through my letterbox, now you've sent my poor pregnant wife an anonymous letter. Don't try and deny it, I'm not stupid. I know it's from you because it's not the first time, is it? You've already scratched my new car, ruined my garden and sent nasty letters, but this is too much. You've gone too far this time, Molly Poulson.'

'Eeh, have I really?' Big Molly said, smiling benignly. 'Now how did I manage all of that, I wonder, when I haven't been up your way in months?'

'You don't deny you've been there before then?'

'I don't poke about in rat holes. I leave that to vermin like you. Fran, will you serve Mrs Dawson before her jaw drops off?'

'In a minute, Mam.' Fran was scrabbling at his arm, pushing and pulling at Eddie to make him move. 'Not here, Eddie, in front of half the market!'

He shook her off, pushing his face to within inches of hers, so that he could spit his words at her with vicious contempt. 'I don't know which of you sent that letter. I don't even care! But she's in hospital now, my Josie. She could lose it, this baby she's wanted for so long. Because of you! So I hope you're satisfied!'

Fran stood as if turned to stone as he stormed away. Her mother was shouting something about it being all his fault for not keeping his trousers buttoned up, but all Fran could hear were those two poignant words: my Josie.

Chapter Twenty-Six

Patsy set the last hat on its stand, a sensible navy straw with matching ribbon, and tilted her head on one side to admire her handiwork. She had left her job at the ice cream parlour and was back working at the hat stall. She'd been there ever since Annie had suffered her heart attack. After a couple of weeks in hospital she'd been allowed home with strict instructions to take things easy for a while, at least until she had made a full recovery. The heart attack could have been much worse, but it was a warning she must heed.

Consequently, Clara was run off her feet looking after her sister and Patsy found she was left more or less to her own devices running the stall.

On one occasion she'd even been allowed to visit a supplier, and in addition to buying the school felts and boaters she'd been sent for, also purchased a few Davy Crockett hats. Marc had been delighted and instantly bought one for Giovanni, the rest had gone by the end of the day.

'We must buy more,' Patsy told Clara, who looked alarmed at the prospect.

'I suppose it may be profitable to do so, but you mustn't tell Annie, it might upset her. It's essential she be kept calm.'

Patsy gave a wicked little grin. 'I won't tell if you don't. Can I close early then and nip back to the wholesaler?'

'No, I'll come and take over for the last hour so that you can go. But don't buy too many or spend too much. We mustn't take any risks while Annie is ill. Oh, dear, it's such a worry.'

Marc offered to go with her this time, and they went together on the bus. Patsy protested, telling him she could cope very well on her own, ta very much, but in fact she was glad of his help carrying the boxes.

Ever since the Bertalone wedding when he'd kissed her so thoroughly, their relationship had changed. It was less easy to pretend that she didn't like him, although she tried her best to remain aloof. The last thing Patsy wanted was to appear soft, or easy. If she should weaken whenever she looked at him, or caught him smiling at her, which always made her heart do a little skip, she would remind herself to remain cautious. She mustn't become too attached.

Just because she was back in favour during Annie's illness, didn't mean the situation was permanent.

Once Annie was on her feet again, Patsy would be out of work, and asked to leave the market altogether. There was talk the place might not survive, that a developer was planning to move in and flatten it. Nothing was certain in life, and Patsy knew she must protect herself.

'Could you at least try to smile and look pleased that I've decided to come along,' Marc cajoled her as they sat on the top deck of the bus.

She glanced at him disdainfully. 'What, sit here grinning like an idiot at nothing in particular? I don't think so.'

'What if I kissed you, would that make you smile?'

'Oh, that would be a good laugh, because then I'd have to slap your cheeky face. This is a public place, Marc Bertalone. What are you thinking of?'

'I think only of you, *mia carina*.' He slipped his arm along the back of the seat, studiously concentrating on the passing view of London Road fire station with its Accrington brick façade, trolleybuses, a delivery van for Bear Brand nylons on its way to Lewis's. In Piccadilly Gardens, a group of little boys in short grey trousers were paddling in the fountain to cool off in the August heat. They hadn't, as Marc had promised, carried on the next day where they'd left off. Thank goodness! But then there hadn't been the opportunity with all the rushing to and fro to the hospital, and fears and worries over Annie. He was convinced that Patsy would be delighted to let him kiss her, if they could find a place where they could be alone and private. A heady prospect!

–

The next morning Patsy put up a large poster, announcing the arrival of new stock, and the Davy Crockett hats continued to sell steadily throughout the rest of that week. Annie would surely be glad of the profit, even if it did turn her stall into a souvenir stand.

Patsy began secretly to imagine that the hat stall was hers. As she sat waiting for customers, or played at rearranging the displays, she would pretend that Annie had retired and then she would ask herself what she could do to brighten up the image of the stall. It seemed to be full of sensible, everyday hats in boring brown and grey and navy. The kind of hat that, as Annie herself had said, a woman used to automatically put on before she ever left her house.

Unfortunately, that wasn't the case any longer. Most women now spent more money at the hairdresser's, and liked to show off their perms or their kiss curls. They all wanted to look as though they'd had their hair done by Mr Teasy-Weasy, even if it was in fact Joyce's Hair Stylist on the corner of Champion Street. Joyce was doing well as a result, and had taken over neighbouring premises in order to expand. But hats were suffering by comparison, nowhere near as popular now as they once were.

The older woman still wore a hat to church on a Sunday, and little girls were still bought an Easter bonnet, which they would often wear for the Whit Walks too. And people still wore them for special occasions, like weddings, christenings and funerals. Unfortunately, Annie never had enough of these dressier, showy sort of hats to meet demand.

Patsy found herself staring at the dull navy straw hat she'd put on display only yesterday. High-crowned, with a narrow, insignificant brim, and circled by a ribbed-silk ribbon in the same colour, she saw nothing in the least appealing about it. That hat had sat on its stand for all the months she'd been here, and nobody had even tried it on. Patsy put her head on one side to study it more closely. It needed livening up, a touch of colour and frivolity.

For want of something better to do in the boring wait between customers, she began to study the catalogues Annie had left under the counter. The brightly coloured pictures inside showed only too clearly what could be achieved with just a little artistry and imagination. Next, she set about searching through the trimmings' drawers. Fruit, or maybe a bunch of violets? Better, but not right either. She tried one or two more possible solutions and then right at the back of the drawer found what she was looking for: several beautiful butterflies in palest lemon gauze.

Patsy stitched each one neatly on to the front of the navy straw so that it looked as though a flight of butterflies had settled upon it. The hat was instantly transformed. It suddenly became distinctive and eye-catching. What's more, she sold it the very next day.

Thrilled by her own success, Patsy next trimmed a dull green felt hat with a pink satin ribbon, forming a bow with curly ends, as she'd seen Clara do on occasions, and added a few pink rosebuds. It made all the difference, and that sold too.

She remembered what Clara had told her: that a hat must flatter the face, and set off the whole ensemble. It should make a woman more attractive, and lend her grace and poise. Few of the hats Annie had chosen were capable of doing any such thing. It was clear that many of these trimmings had lain in their drawers for years untouched, save for when Patsy had been asked to tidy them out and put them all back again. Now she had great fun bringing them out into the light, stitching them on to the hats on display and then watching with interest as more people paused to study the results of her labours, and frequently tempted to buy.

It might be more fun serving, and eating, Strawberry Sundaes in the ice cream parlour, Patsy thought, particularly in this drowsy summer heat, but making hats attractive enough to sell was a more interesting challenge.

Patsy was seeing Marc that evening. He'd finally persuaded her to go out with him on a proper date but she was already regretting it. She fancied him like crazy, but what good would that do her if she had to leave? Patsy could sense, in her heart, that he was already becoming far too important to her, which was surely a bad thing. Better to end it now before they got any more involved.

He was taking her dancing at St John's Sunday School, and was holding what they called 'a hop' to raise money for the starving babies in Africa. Even so, there was a large notice on the door saying, 'No jiving or bopping'.

'How can you have a dance without bopping?' Patsy scornfully remarked.

Marc chuckled. 'See those big guys? They're here to make sure we obey. Just wait till the quickstep starts, though, and you'll see they'll have their work cut out trying to stop kids from rocking and rolling.'

And so it proved. The band weren't exactly wonderful, comprising a piano, a double bass and a violin that sounded like a tomcat having a bad night on the tiles. But every now and then the three musicians would retire outside for a smoke and be replaced by a man putting records on a gramophone.

The more sedate adults stayed in one half of the dance floor doing the quickstep as it should be done, while in the other half the teenagers rock 'n' rolled. Patsy had never been to an actual dance before, other than the wedding where the dancing had been lively and mainly Italian, but she'd practised all the steps in the privacy of her own bedroom to the records she played on her new record player, using the door handle or a chair as a partner. Here at last was the opportunity to try them out.

Oh, and it was wonderful! Marc might not be brilliant at the foxtrot but he could rock 'n' roll. He had a real sense of rhythm, knew all the steps, and could spin and catch her without missing a beat. They went wild to a Jerry Lee Lewis number, 'Whole Lotta

Shakin Going On', and laughed till they cried to 'Giddy-Up-A-Ding-Dong'. Patsy couldn't ever remember having such a good time.

There were egg sandwiches and yellow sponge cake for supper, and after that came more dancing, including a smoochy number to end the evening with The Platters singing 'Only You'. Patsy's heart just melted as Marc held her close in his arms, his cheek against hers, his breath stirring wisps of her hair. She felt as if she could spend her life in his arms, threading her fingers through the dark curls at his nape, gazing into those chocolate brown eyes.

Later, though, as he walked her home, Patsy remembered her earlier vow to finish with him this evening before she got to like him any more than she did already. Not that she intended to tell him the real reason, but when he asked if he could see her again, she simply shrugged her shoulders in a dismissive gesture and said, 'No, I don't think so. Why would I want to?' That well-worn phrase of Annie's came in so useful.

'Because you find me irresistible?'

'And utterly arrogant.' Patsy tried not to look into his face as she said this, aware of the hurt dawning in those big brown eyes. 'I went to your family wedding. You persuaded me to go out with you on a proper date, and I've enjoyed it. It was good fun. But let's leave it at that, shall we?'

Now she did look at him, curious to know his reaction to her misgivings. His eyes were hooded so that Patsy couldn't see his expression, but by the way the muscles tightened around his jaw, she could tell he wasn't happy with her decision.

'Why do you drop me? You have problems, Patsy? Is Annie ill again?'

'No, nothing like that! I just don't think it would be a good idea for us to see each other any more.'

He gave a harsh little laugh, as if she had said something amusing. 'And why would you make this crazy decision, little one?'

'Don't call me that, I'm not little.'

'You seem so to me. You are the elf, the pretty fairy with your long silky silver hair, *mia carina*. You are slender and fragile, not the big, strong creature you imagine yourself to be. And since you know how good we are together, that I am the man for you, why do you turn away from me?'

Patsy cast him the fiercest glare she could summon up, furious at his description of her. 'I'm not in the least bit fragile! I've had to be strong, believe me, to get through what I've had to deal with in life. And no, I don't want to talk about it, and I don't want your pity either. Just don't you dare say such a thing.'

But when he reached out and gently touched her cheek she didn't feel strong. Her knees went all weak, something melted inside her and Patsy recognised her own vulnerability. She ached for him to hold her, to tell her that he could make all the bad things go away, that he would love her and care for her. Panic hit her. If she didn't put a stop to this dangerous emotion right now, she'd be doing more than kissing him, and what good would that do?

It was but a short walk up Gartside Street, along Grove Street and then they turned into Champion Street. Patsy didn't say a word throughout the short journey but resolutely kept her gaze fixed on the glimmer of moonlight on the cobbles, determined not even to look at him again. Marc walked silently beside her, hands in pockets, not attempting to touch her.

When they reached the door of number twenty-two, they stopped. 'You could at least tell me why. Don't I deserve that much, Patsy?' His voice was gentle, coaxing. How could she resist?

Patsy swallowed. 'The fact is, I can't stay here. Even if the stallholders manage to save the market, the sisters don't want me to stay. Why would they? I cost too much. I'm nothing but a nuisance, an irritating, noisy teenager in their quiet house. A little thief who steals pies. No wonder nobody likes me or wants me around.'

He took her by the shoulders, turned her to face him and gave her a little shake. 'I like you. I want you around. I think you know how much I like you, so maybe you're simply fishing for compliments, denying me so that I'll want you all the more.'

Patsy was appalled that he should consider her to be so devious. 'I'm not! That's not how it is at all.'

'Then how is it? Do you like me, or are you playing cruel games?'

'No, I don't play cruel games!' Patsy said, in as firm a voice as she could muster, wishing he would let her go, that she couldn't smell the enticing warmth of his skin, trace every dark curl. She pushed him away, whipped off her Alice band, shook back her hair and slipped the band back in place again, tucking and tidying each strand. Anything rather than meet the intensity of that gaze.

'The whole problem with men like you is that you don't listen to a word a girl says. It's over, right? Got that clear now, have you? I'm chucking you.' And tilting up her chin, Patsy walked away. It was the hardest thing she'd ever done.

But still he wouldn't let her go. 'I don't believe you, Patsy. I know that you like me really because your nose is growing long, like Pinocchio's.' Then he caught her to him and kissed her hard.

Oh, and Patsy was eager for his kisses, couldn't seem to help herself. The feel of his mouth against hers, their tongues dancing together, was utter bliss. She tasted his need, his power, his sorrow; even though she dealt with him so heartlessly. The kiss deepened and she arched her back, instinctively pressing herself closer.

Encouraged by her response, his hands fell to the buttons of her blouse and he unfastened one, then another, without breaking the kiss. She felt his cool fingers graze the warmth of her breast, slip beneath her bra to stroke the tautness of her nipple. It was like a bolt of electricity racing through her and Patsy knew she wanted him to make love to her.

But she also knew that she really couldn't take the risk of loving him and it was all going badly wrong, as it surely would. When had anyone ever stayed in her life longer than five minutes? And once she'd given herself to him, all the cards would be in his hand then, instead of hers.

To give in now, like this, would mean Marc Bertalone was getting her on his terms, and Patsy was having none of that. If – when – she came to him, it would need to be very much on hers, and so much could go wrong before that dream ever had a chance to come true.

Chapter Twenty-Seven

Fran had been avoiding her mother for what felt like weeks but was in fact only a matter of days. She couldn't go on like this indefinitely but right now it was the best defence she could devise. Her mother would be bound to realise in the end that she was the one who had done the dirty on Eddie's wife, and want to know why. Fran had no wish to tell her. The less her mother knew about her problem, the better. If she could somehow find a way to put things right, then Mam need never know.

The solution, however, was becoming only too clear. Eddie was in no mood now for sweet talk or to be fooled by clever manipulation. He was beyond all of that. My Josie! That's how he'd spoken of her, that wife of his, his pregnant wife, who he wasn't supposed to be sleeping with any longer.

Fran shivered, feeling sick deep in the pit of her stomach. She'd been made a fool of, in more ways than one. He'd used her for a bit of fun on the side because he was fed up with Josie's constant nagging about wanting a kid. At first, Fran had been content with those terms, believing his marriage to be a bad one anyway. But he'd lied. He clearly still adored the silly cow, and that hurt. Very badly.

And now that he'd got them both up the spout, he couldn't believe his ill fortune. Nor could Fran. Falling in love with the daft beggar hadn't been part of the plan at all. This wasn't supposed to happen, not to her.

She could think of only one way out of this mess. He was right about that, at least. When Fran spotted Patsy at dinnertime sitting in Belle's cafe, she went over to join her.

Patsy looked at the cup of tea and plain biscuit Fran set on the table as she sat down and said, 'No frothy coffee?'

'Don't feel like it.'

'Only a Marie biscuit, no chocolate éclair – you'll fade away. Or have you been nibbling your mam's pies all morning?'

Fran shook her head. 'Even the smell of them makes me feel sick. Coffee is even worse, and anything fried just makes me throw up.'

The smile slid from Patsy's face. 'Oh, no, so that's the way it is?'

Fran edged closer. 'I have to do something about it, Patsy, pretty damn quick.'

Patsy gasped. 'What, you mean…?'

'Shush! Don't say the word, not here.' Fran glanced around to check they weren't overheard. 'It's illegal, you know it is, so I shall need your help, and I haven't much time. I must be well over two months now, nearly three happen.'

'Hell, what can I do? I don't know anything about…'

'Don't worry, I know where to go to get it fixed, and I believe the money can be found. But I can't go alone, too scared. Will you be a friend and come with me? Hold my hand, at least. You're the only one I can trust to keep my secret.'

Even as Patsy agreed that she would, flattered at being selected for this important and intimate task, she knew in her heart that she would live to regret it. And she really didn't need any more secrets.

–

Unaware of her daughter's situation when Eddie Davidson had appeared the other morning, shouting vile accusations at her, Molly had assumed the culprit who'd left the dog mess to be not Fran, but Billy Quinn. She'd gone from pub to pub looking for him, all over Castlefield, from the Donkey to the Crown, from the Pack Horse to the Globe, finally finding him in the Dog and Duck on her own doorstep. Making the arrangements, as she'd vowed to do, had not been a pleasant experience. It hadn't helped when Ozzy point-blank refused to go with her.

'On your own head be it', was his attitude.

But then, Quinn wasn't the sort of person anyone could warm to.

He had a lean, hard face with high cheekbones, a long straight nose and wide mouth. His brown hair was turning grey and starting to thin on top and he was obviously much broader of girth than he'd been as a young man, though the extra weight suited him. It seemed to add to his aura of power. He was really good-looking, for a man in his late fifties. But it was the eyes that got to you the most, being a deep, piercing blue that could smile softly at a woman, or freeze her to the spot. He still wore the trademark slouch cap at a rakish angle, a cigarette permanently attached to his lower lip.

Legend had it Billy Quinn had come over from County Mayo as a lad of fifteen to seek his fortune, with nothing more than a bag of clothes slung over his broad shoulders, a bit of luck money in his pocket and the devil in his eyes. He'd slept in ditches and under haystacks, common lodging houses, or kip houses as they were called then, and clawed his way, tooth and nail, to the top.

Merely the sight of him chilled Molly. Violence seemed to be latent in him, like a coiled viper waiting to strike.

But then nobody took the risk of crossing Billy Quinn. Even Big Molly knew that wouldn't be wise. Stories abounded about those who had lived to rue the day they'd ever thought to try. She almost felt sorry for Belle. No wonder she was considering Quinn's offer of compensation for developing Champion Street Market. It wouldn't be easy to refuse. Big Molly shelved the notion of tackling that subject with him herself. She had enough to deal with right now. No point in alienating him unnecessarily.

So when he'd agreed to do what she'd asked and named his price, she'd quickly stifled her gasp of outrage and agreed. It was more than she'd expected but if it got Eddie Davidson off her back and out of Fran's life for good, it would be cheap at the price.

Molly hated the thought of her lovely young girl being interfered with by a man a good ten or twelve years older than herself, and married at that, the dirty beggar. If the worst happened and Fran fell pregnant, they'd be the talk of Champion Street. The scandal would kill her. After all, Big Molly had her own reputation to think of. She'd tried broaching the subject with Fran once or twice more in an effort to persuade her to give him up, only to get the brush off or for the lass to turn near hysterical so that they almost came to blows on one occasion. Molly had given up, realising that wasn't the way.

Eddie must be the one to pay for his sins. And serve him bleeding right.

So it was that the morning he'd turned up at her stall, Molly's first reaction on seeing him standing there, waving his arms about and slagging her off, had been one of keen disappointment. She'd asked Quinn to do him over. Not exactly break his legs, but make it painful for him to walk for a while. But there he'd stood, fit as a fiddle, bold as brass, and bristling with pride and self-opinionated anger.

If Quinn had done nothing more than post a bit of dog mess and a poisonous letter through his letterbox, she wasn't getting value for money, not good news. Molly had only made the first payment so far. Later that afternoon, around the time she knew Quinn called into the Dog and Duck to pick up another round of bets, she took him the second payment. 'Haven't seen much for me money yet,' she casually remarked, as she handed the envelope over.

He stared at her, his blue eyes hard as chipped ice, his expression unfathomable. Transactions such as this were carried out in a private room at the back of the pub. Molly attempted to soften her words with a smile, knowing she was on unfamiliar territory. But somehow the smile came out a bit shaky and her jocular tone sounded forced.

Quinn sat, perfectly relaxed, in a wing chair, eyes half closed against the spiral of smoke rising from his cigarette, his slouch cap draped over the arm. 'Is it a complaint you're wanting to make?' His spoke in that soft Irish accent which entirely belied the ruthlessness of his nature.

She swallowed. There wasn't much Big Molly was afraid of, but she was keenly aware that she'd met her match in Quinn. She felt entirely out of her league. 'No, 'course not. I were just wondering when you were going to do the deed, that's all. I want that rat to regret taking up with my girl. He needs a good seeing to.'

Quinn counted the notes she had given him with punctilious care, before sliding them into a tin box, which rested on a small table beside him.

When he had carefully locked the box and slid the key into his waistcoat pocket, he raised his head to smile at Molly, a smile that transformed his grim features, making him look almost benign. It clearly revealed how handsome he must have been when he was young; still was in a way. She very nearly gasped, and could see why he'd always been considered one for the ladies.

'He will be dealt with, Molly, all in good time. Don't worry. Have I ever let a client down? I shall keep my side of the bargain, so long as you keep yours. I shall expect the final payment by the end of the month. Is that convenient?'

Molly swallowed, wondering how the hangment she could put her hands on so much money so quickly. Hell, worry about that tomorrow. Now she beamed at him, feeling happier for having discovered there was more punishment to come for that arrogant, philandering, no-good piece of work, Davidson. 'Aye, perfectly convenient. No problem. I look forward to hearing from you when the job's done, then.'

Quinn's penetrating blue eyes were expressionless as she smiled and nodded and hastily backed out of the room. Once outside, Molly leaned against a wall and drew in great gulps of cold night air, the sour taste of the canal in her mouth seeming infinitely more pleasant than the one she'd experienced in Quinn's office.

Now all she had to do was find the rest of the bleeding money and the job was as good as done.

'This must be the one,' Fran said, stopping at the front door of an end-terrace house just beyond the railway arches.

'Are you sure you want to go through with this?' Patsy asked, struggling to disguise an involuntary shudder. 'It's not too late to change your mind.' The house looked blank, as if nobody lived within, or whoever did had no wish to be disturbed, with dark green curtains drawn across grubby windows.

'I'm sure.' In Fran's mind she really didn't see any alternative. If she couldn't have Eddie, and it seemed he'd turned against her completely, she didn't want his child – his leavings – as he would show no interest. What was it about society's obsession with marriage that made it necessary for her to go through with this barbaric practice? Why was it so shameful to be an unmarried mother? It took two to make a baby, so why was it only the girl who was considered immoral? It wasn't fair.

Except that she didn't want the kid anyway.

Even so, a back-street abortionist had not been her first choice. Fran had braved possible scandal and gone first to her own doctor who had been utterly shocked at the very idea of agreeing to what he termed a 'therapeutic abortion', as if she had deliberately got herself into this mess in order to enjoy the benefit of one. He'd then gone on to lecture her on her morals till she felt like screaming; telling her that marriage was created specifically for the purpose of procreation. This, he explained, was woman's true role in life, and no other, as if she were nothing more than a womb without a brain attached, didn't have any wishes and aspirations other than to marry and have children.

By the time he was done with her, Fran had felt dirty and sordid. He made it only too clear that abortion was immoral, unnecessary and illegal unless she could get written agreement from two doctors, which, in her case, was out of the question. 'It's not as if having a child would damage your health, so you must pay for your foolishness. You should have thought of the consequences before.'

Quite, Fran thought, with pragmatic honesty. The sad truth was that he was right. What she was about to do was dreadful, cruel, wicked. Nevertheless, she stepped forward and rapped loudly on the door with the backs of her knuckles, knowing that if she hesitated she'd be lost, and might never find the courage to go through with her plan.

–

Fran and Patsy sat awkwardly together on an old sofa, its worn chintz once a swirl of leaves and roses that had long since faded, due to the restless shifting of many other callers such as themselves on exactly the same mission.

They'd been led along a grim hall, its walls painted a shiny dark brown, which didn't help to lighten their mood. Fran had duly handed over a sum of money to the girl who'd let them in, and now they were patiently waiting to be called.

The furniture in the small, cluttered room comprised a table covered by a chenille fringed cloth, four velvet-backed chairs, and an old-fashioned sideboard stacked with a miscellany of plates and cups. An armchair stood by the hearth, empty on this warm summer night, and beside it stood a small side table and lamp featuring a crinolined lady base. The rosy glow from the latter served to disguise the squalor of the room but could do nothing to mask the pervasive smell.

Patsy and Fran glanced at each other, noses curling in distaste as they each tried to identify the cause. In amongst the more obvious sweet-and-sour odour of poverty and decay was something more, something that set Patsy's teeth on edge as it reminded her of the rusty taste in her mouth after a trip to the dentist to have a tooth pulled.

Fran sat with her hands clenched between her knees. Had she been able to, this would have been the moment she prayed, though for what she didn't know. Divine deliverance from this mess?

A part of her longed to turn tail and run, yet if she didn't go through with it she would be vilified and spat at, the child labelled a bastard for its entire life. She'd seen the way other girls had been treated. That Dena Dobson, for instance, when she had her baby daughter. Nobody would speak to her, yet to her credit Dena had stubbornly hung on to her child.

Fran was honest enough to realise that she didn't have what it took to do the same. Mainly, she supposed, because she didn't possess the right sort of maternal instincts. She longed only to be rid of her problem, to be free to get on with her life.

When she heard the door of the front parlour open and the whispered order to the young girl to say all was ready, she cursed the day she'd ever met Eddie Davidson. He should be the one suffering, not her.

She grasped Patsy's hand. 'You'll come in with me, won't you?'

'It's not allowed,' said the girl, in the kind of bored tone used by one who has seen and heard this scene enacted too many times and simply wants to get it over and done with as quickly as possible. 'Your friend can wait here, so's she can see you safely home afterwards. You don't want her keeling over at the sight of a bit of blood, now do you? Then we'd have two patients on us hands.'

Patsy, relieved that she was to be spared from stepping into what she viewed as the jaws of hell, promised faithfully to wait.

Fran didn't say a word, instinctively shying away from the images these words had created in her terrified mind. She shot Patsy one last anguished glance, then on a great shuddering breath, got to her feet and obediently followed the young girl into the other room.

She obediently stripped off her panties behind a screen then lay down on the table. She could feel herself shaking.

'Don't worry, girl,' the woman named Maureen told her. 'I've done this scores of times. You'll be fine and dandy in a trice. Everything's scrubbed down and clean as we can make it. You'll get no infection here if I can help it. Now, are you ready?'

Fran intended to say she was as ready as she'd ever be, but her throat closed up and all she managed was a brief nod. Looking about her, wild-eyed, she struggled to focus on the woman's face, which seemed to swim and blur before her eyes. She focused on the room, the green curtains, anywhere but on the frightening-looking instrument Maureen held in her hand.

It was only when Fran felt the piercing pain and then everything being sucked out of her that she thought, No. She wanted to scream at the woman to put everything back. But it was far too late.

–

Eddie was not having a particularly good day either. He'd come home from the gas board at his usual time of five o'clock, parked his car in the drive then gone into the garage to find a chamois leather to wipe it down, which he always did before putting it away. He didn't want his pride and joy to go rusty.

He never saw who hit him. Afterwards, he remembered being extraordinarily surprised that someone should be in his garage at all, apparently waiting for him. He didn't have time to see who it was. One minute he was startled by the dark shape of a man emerging from the shadows as he opened the double doors, the next he was aware of a huge explosion of light in his head. Then he was lying on the ground with ample time to pray for unconsciousness, as steel-capped boots kicked him in the sides and back, but it was a long wait before it came.

Chapter Twenty-Eight

Patsy took Fran straight to her own room at number twenty-two, where the poor girl spent the afternoon bleeding into towels and worrying that she might be about to peg out. She stayed there all night, alternately groaning in pain or weeping, though more from fury at her situation than shame. Patsy explained to Clara, who already had enough on her plate looking after Annie, that Fran was too ill to move. She only lived next door at number twenty-four, and Patsy would look after her. Clara was naturally concerned and offered to send for a doctor, and Patsy hastily assured her that wouldn't be necessary.

'But if she's too ill even to walk next door, she must be bad. What exactly is wrong with her, Patsy?'

'Nothing more than a bad stomach upset, but she's had some violent cramps and vomiting, and now she's asleep at last. Surely you don't object to her staying over? I don't mind looking after her.'

Nothing more was said as Clara had no wish to be seen as uncharitable, although she did insist on popping next door to explain all of this to Big Molly. Patsy was thankful Clara hadn't asked her to do that. There were only so many times she could repeat this lie.

Fran was half afraid her mother would come tearing round at once, demanding to know what was going on, but, strangely, she didn't.

The bleeding and the fierce cramps began to ease a little during the night, and dawn found Patsy stuffing the spoiled towels into a neighbouring dustbin, so that they wouldn't ever be found by

Annie or Clara. How she would explain the missing items she had no idea, but nor did she have any clue how to get them properly clean again either, so she'd just have to think of some excuse or other. Yet another lie! Her nose really would be growing as long as Pinocchio's soon.

Patsy instructed Fran to stay in bed until she felt well enough to get up, all day if necessary. 'You can stay here as long as you like, as long as you need to, but I have to get off to work since I'm in charge of the stall while Annie is ill. Clara pops back and forth, dividing her time between looking after Annie and helping me on the stall, so she doesn't have much time either. Will you be okay on your own?'

Fran gave a weak smile and assured Patsy that she would. She was certain that if the cramps started up again, she'd be dead by teatime. Drat Eddie Davidson.

–

Fran received the very best of care, there already being one invalid in the house. Clara would pop upstairs after she'd washed the breakfast things, tap lightly on the bedroom door and bring in a cup of tea on a tray.

At first she would say, 'I didn't prepare you any food, Fran dear, since it's a stomach bug you've got, and we should starve it out. Fasting is generally the most effective method. But I thought you might appreciate a cuppa. Do you think you could keep one down?'

'That's very kind of you, Miss Clara. I could murder a cup of tea.' Fran was ravenous but had no choice but to keep up the fiction of the stomach bug.

'You look very pale still. Stay right where you are, dear, then when you feel up to it, help yourself to a bath. There's plenty of hot water. Annie has hers first thing so leave yours till later, which should suit you. Give you the chance to get a bit more sleep.'

Fran thanked her and some time in the late morning when the house seemed quiet, decided to do just that. The hot water felt wonderful against her skin and the more sore parts of her anatomy, and she lay back on a blissful sigh.

Everything was going to be all right. Apart from being half starved with hunger, Fran was beginning to feel decidedly better. Maybe she wasn't going to die, after all.

Rightly or wrongly she was a free woman again. Her problem had been solved, but she'd take more care in future, and she'd get her own back on that Eddie Davidson, see if she didn't. He'd learn soon enough the meaning of the time-honoured phrase, 'Hell hath no fury like a woman scorned'. He'd be sorry he'd ever used and then spurned her. In the meantime, she still had her mother to face.

–

'Is it difficult to make hats?' Patsy asked Clara a day or two later, when she once more felt free to concentrate on her own future.

Clara laughed. 'Not in the least! You need the right equipment – blocks, straw cones and capelines – those are the shapes you can buy ready formed to start off your hat. Or you can buy the fabric, linen, raffia and sinamay, or synthetic straw, which is popular at the moment, and form the shapes yourself over a block. Then you will need such items as glue, millinery braid and wire, even dye if you wish, in any shade you choose. You can wrap the crown and brim in chiffon or tulle, add a veil or dress the hat with an appropriate piece of trimming. The only limit is your imagination, and I can see you've already explored yours.'

Patsy pulled a face. 'It's boring just sitting here doing nothing. And some of the hats I trimmed have sold.'

Clara picked up an emerald green felt hat decked out with purple feathers and chuckled. 'I'm not too sure about this one, but it might well be to somebody's taste. Would you care to learn hat-making, Patsy? I could start you off by teaching you the little I know. And if you're still interested after that, you could take a course at the local night school.'

Patsy was filled with uncertainty, as if she'd been caught out doing something sinful simply because it gave her pleasure. Where would be the point in her doing such a course? She wasn't staying. The market might not even be here a year from now, and it was unlikely she'd still be living at number twenty-two if it was. This was only a temporary job and she'd be unemployed again just as soon as Annie came back to work. Probably forced to move out of Champion Street Market altogether.

'Naw,' she said, scoffing at the idea with a forced laugh, as if it were really of no consequence. 'Don't really think it's my thing.' And then she ripped off the purple feathers and tossed them to one side.

Don't get involved, she told herself. The success of the hat stall was not her problem.

–

Marc came round at lunchtime, as he so often did, casually asking if she'd like to come and have a coffee with him, or listen to the latest hits in Hall's music booths. 'Do you like Paul Anka? He's got a new single out, "Diana".' She'd told him it was over between them, and Marc knew he should take no for answer, but somehow he couldn't seem to accept it. He was convinced that if he could just persuade Patsy to talk about whatever was bothering her, he'd breach this wall she'd built around herself.

'Do you know a Diana then? Is that why you like it?' Patsy sharply retorted, not even pausing as he spoke to her but keeping right on walking, nose in the air, aware he was striding after her. It was her lunch break and she liked to take a turn about the market. She paused idly to study a jigsaw on Leo's toy stall, smiling sweetly at him.

'Hiya, Leo. Busy?'

'Can't complain. I'm selling yo-yos like nobody's business. Do you want one?'

'Why not?' Patsy handed over a few pennies and started practising with the yo-yo, rolling it up and down the string, throwing and tossing it in the air, much to Marc's annoyance.

He felt a burst of frustration, a feeling that was growing all too familiar. Never had he known a girl more perverse, more difficult; part aggravating wild child, part fascinating woman. 'Where you have got this idea from that I flirt with all the girls, I cannot think. Have you seen me with anyone other than you?'

'You'd make sure that I don't see you. In any case, you don't belong to me, so why should I care?' Oh, but she did care, very much. She half glanced at him, and wished at once that she hadn't. His eyes were devouring her, robbing her of the ability to think straight. Why wouldn't he leave her alone? Why did he keep pestering her? Hadn't she made it very clear that they were finished? She flung herself back into showing off her yo-yo skills, so vigorously that it flew from her hand, skidding under a market stall and she had to scrabble after it to get it back. Most undignified!

By the time she'd straightened her slim pencil skirt, tugged off her Alice band and tidied her flyaway hair, she felt all pink-cheeked and flustered. 'You can do as you please,' Patsy snapped.

'Then why are so cross with me the whole time? Why is it that I always seem to say the wrong thing with you?' He caught her arm, forcing her to stop, giving her a little shake when she obstinately refused to meet his gaze. 'What is it you want from me? Tell me, then I can be whatever it is you need. I care about you, Patsy. Can't you see that? Don't you believe me?'

She looked at him then and he saw her mouth tremble, as if she were moved by his words, but then they firmed into rigid tightness and his heart sank once more. Her next words only deepened his despair.

'I believe,' she said, 'that you would say whatever it took to get your own way. Isn't that how boys always are?'

'Is that your problem, then? Has some boy let you down in the past, and I'm getting the fallout from that?'

Patsy shook her head, half-turned away but he held on to her, wouldn't let her go. 'No, tell me. Explain to me, Patsy, what it is I've done to hurt you? Or what someone else has done?'

'I've got to go. I'm due back at the stall.'

She wrenched herself free and, as she strode away, Marc dropped his arms to his side in a gesture of despair. He felt more like tearing his hair out, but where would that get him? He would abandon all hope of winning her; if only deep in her troubled heart she secretly cared for him as much as he cared for her.

It was with this thought in mind that Marc called out to her, in a firm, strong voice, sounding far more confident than he felt. Loud enough for heads to turn and Patsy to pause, in her helter-skelter dash, to listen to his words over her shoulder.

'I can't keep on waiting and hoping forever for you to change your mind about me, Patsy. I like you, I think I could get to like you, and I want to see more of you. Will you give me a chance, or at least think about it?'

She didn't answer, but as she lifted her chin and carried on walking, one or two customers, men and women alike, were intrigued by what they saw as a lovers' tiff, and called after her: 'Aw, go on, love. Give him a chance.'

–

Patsy couldn't get this little scene out of her head. She kept on replaying it constantly, like a stuck record. She began to wonder if she was being hard on Marc, although he'd sounded genuine. She guessed there was absolutely no reason to think he was two-timing her. That was just an excuse she'd made up, and not at all the reason she'd refused to see him again.

She had tried to tell him the truth, but he hadn't listened.

No matter how much she might like him, she didn't dare agree to go out with him because she liked him too much. And when she had to leave the market, which was bound to come sooner than later, she'd be badly hurt. Where was the fun in that?

Yet there was another deeper reason.

She was also afraid that once he got to know her better, learned something of her past – not only her lack of a family but that she had done rather more than steal a pie; that she was well known to the police, with a criminal record – he would turn away from her and reject her, as all the other people in her life had done before him. Hadn't she watched her friends drop her, one by one, pretending they hadn't been involved in that first childhood prank and leaving her to carry all the blame? She still carried the scars her foster father had inflicted, and they ran deep. Her anger and sense of injustice stirred her to commit greater mischief, not less.

Having Marc see her the way she really was would be unbearable.

Live for the day: that was the answer.

–

Desperate to keep her mind from constantly thinking about Marc, and bored with sitting doing nothing as she waited for customers who were finding it far too hot to try on hats in the August heat, Patsy changed her mind about learning hat-making.

It was Dena Dobson's fault. She'd been buying one of Dena's summery daisy skirts and they had got chatting about clothes, hats in particular. Patsy happened to mention how she'd trimmed one or two of Annie's more drab choices and sold them as a result, and that Clara had offered to teach her something of the craft. Dena had bluntly told her to have a go.

'How do you know what you can do if you don't try?'

Patsy was careful how she responded to this. She couldn't be too dismissive as she and Dena had much in common, in a way. They'd both suffered from a difficult background, and uncaring mothers. Patsy knew a little of Dena's history: how she'd been put into care after her brother had drowned and now was making a real success of her life, having an illegitimate baby. She was building up a business of her own making really beautiful, fashionable clothes.

Not that Patsy had told Dena anything of her own background. That was something she kept entirely to herself. 'But what if I start on a course and then have to leave?'

'Why would you have to do that?'

'When Annie is better, she won't need me any more.'

'She will if you're making fantastic hats that sell,' Dena had said.

And so Patsy had been tempted to try. She'd started lessons with Clara, but after two whole hours of battling with wire and blocks that afternoon, she was already regretting the decision.

Patsy felt all fingers and thumbs and just couldn't get the hang of it. The fabric seemed to have a life of its own, bending and flicking off in all directions, and the hat just wouldn't stay in shape, as the blocking pins kept popping out. Now her fingers were sore, her back was aching and she was in a fury of frustration.

'It won't go where it's told,' she cried, flinging the half finished hat to the ground.

'Given up already?' The sound of the familiar Italian drawl had Patsy glowering across at Marc.

Every single day he stuck his head round the door of the fitting room to chat to her, or to try and persuade her to come out with him. He absolutely refused to give up, she having dumped him and told him to stay away. Marc would shrug his shoulders in that characteristic Italian way and hope that she would change her mind about him in the end. All he needed was patience, yet he was trying hers to the limits.

'Go away!' she shouted. 'I don't need you to see my humiliation. I can't do it, and that's that.'

Clara put a gentle hand on her arm. 'Manners, Patsy! Marc is only showing interest. Now, dear, let's try this again, shall we? I do think you should go though, Marc. She needs to concentrate.'

'Thank you,' Patsy said with deep gratitude when they were alone again. But she'd seen the glint of pain in his eyes and struggled to curb the urge to run after him.

Chapter Twenty-Nine

While Fran was still at number twenty-two, Molly received word from Quinn that the job had been done. The moment she saw him approach the stall with his characteristic swagger, feet flung out, hands in pockets, slouch cap in place and a cigarette hanging from his lips, her heart gave an uncomfortable jerk.

'Hiya, Billy. Your usual, is it?' She was reaching for two steak and kidney pies as casually as she could, giving no indication of the turmoil she felt within.

Big Molly handed them over. When he made no move to pay she very nearly sharply reminded him that they weren't free, but fortunately stopped herself in time. She still owed him the last payment on the favour he'd just done for her, so was in no position to argue about a few pennies.

He glowered at her from beneath the brim of his slouch cap. 'I'll be expecting a visit from you shortly, Molly, regarding our bit of business.'

She looked up at him, curiosity in her keen-eyed gaze. 'It's been done then?'

'Done and dusted, as they say. Our friend will not be doing the quickstep for some time.'

The folds of Molly's several chins shook softly as she gave a broad grin. 'Eeh, that's best bit o' news I've heard in a long while.'

She glanced about her, relieved the day's rush was largely over and there was no one around. Even so, she took the precaution of dropping her voice as she leaned over the counter. 'I'll have the rest for you by the end of the month, as we agreed. I'd get some of it for you now only I'm on me own today, our Fran is off sick.'

'I'll be waiting.' He nodded curtly and turned to go, but then raised one finger in the air as if a thought had just struck him. 'Ah, she is and doesn't that remind me what it was I came for, besides two of your delicious pies. While I was carrying out that little task for ye the other day, I came across a bit of information that might interest ye.'

'And what would that be?' Instinctively, Big Molly didn't want to hear any more bad news, yet she was intrigued.

'That daughter of yours… Fran is it? Well, didn't I see her going into Mo's house, just under the arches, near the Bridge-water viaduct? I mentioned this to our friend, not that he was in much of a mood for conversation, you understand, but he did admit that getting the business done had cost him a packet.'

'What bit o' business?'

'Don't tell me you didn't know? Well, would you believe it, and you the wee girl's mammy. There y'are then, a bit of free info on the side regarding your daughter's state of health. All part of the service. Ah, and did I mention the extra fee?'

'Extra fee? What extra fee?' Molly continued to look blank. She was still striving to take in what exactly he'd just told her and couldn't focus on this sudden change in direction. What bit of business could he be referring to? And why should Quinn concern himself about their Fran's health?

True, Molly had heard her being sick the other morning. She'd said she must have eaten something that didn't agree with her. And so it had turned out. Hadn't Clara explained how she was round at number twenty-two where young Patsy was looking after her because she was suffering from some stomach bug or other? She still wasn't back, in point of fact.

But who was this Mo, and what would Fran be seeing her about?

Quinn's mention of the extra fee threw her completely. Here was something else to worry about. It had been difficult enough finding the fifty quid he had demanded to deal with Eddie, the thought of an extra charge made Molly's heart quail. She'd paid him twenty-five so far: fifteen up front and another ten later. But she still had another twenty-five to find from somewhere. A fortune to Molly.

'Shall we call it a mummer's fee?' he was saying, and chuckled, seeming to find his own wit amusing. 'If you're wanting me to keep me gabbing mouth shut about our little arrangement, not to mention the scandal of what your Fran has been up to, I'll be needing a bit extra, if you catch my drift. Hush money, and, to be sure, silence always has to be paid for. I'm thinking you'll not be wanting the rozzers to get wind of this private arrangement of ours, now will you?'

Molly near exploded with outrage. 'But that's blackmail!'

Quinn's piercing blue eyes narrowed, and he went so far as to remove the cigarette from his lower lip while he adopted a pained expression. 'I'm thinking that's a nasty word to be using between friends, is it not, Molly girl? Wouldn't you agree that a service rendered ought to be paid for? And silence is a service too, so far as I'm aware.'

'Yes, Billy. Sorry Billy. You're right, Billy.'

He smiled at her then, and handsome though he still was, it was not a smile intended to warm her heart. 'The name's Quinn, by the way. That's what I prefer, Molly girl. Quinn. Only me old mam used to call me Billy, and that's a long time ago now, back in Ireland when I was a boy. Don't forget again.'

Molly would like to have returned the favour by telling him not to call her 'girl', but once again common sense prevailed. 'Right, em – er Quinn. And what would this extra fee amount to?'

The sinister smile softened a little and he looked almost perky as he stuck the cigarette again between his lips. It bobbed up and down as he talked. 'Just add ten per cent to our agreed sum.'

'Ten per cent!' Molly was horrified and had to swallow hard to bite back the sharp retort that sprang to mind.

'Would that be a problem for you, Molly girl?'

'N-no, I'll find it from somewhere – somehow, B— Quinn.'

'Same time as you made the last payment, if you don't mind.'

Molly swallowed. 'End of the month it is then.' Not for the world would she admit it, but deep down Big Molly was frightened. Hadn't Ozzy warned her from the start that you didn't mess with the likes of Billy Quinn. Now she saw why.

Dear heaven above, where was she going to find another five quid? She hadn't even found the last twenty-five yet. She hoped she'd had good value for money. It would be worth it to know that Eddie had suffered. As she watched Quinn swagger away she kept saying that strangely familiar name he'd mentioned, over and over in her head.

Which Mo lived down by the arches? Must be short for Maureen. What bit of business could our Fran have with a woman down by the Bridgewater? And why would it be important for Quinn to keep quiet about it? When it came to her, she keeled over from shock.

–

It took two more days before Fran felt brave enough to go home, by which time she'd been allowed scrambled egg and dry toast, and even a bit of fish. She was pounds lighter, in more ways than one, and still fairly sore, but otherwise almost her old self again. Fran knew that she couldn't avoid facing the music any longer, and could but hope she'd bluff it out. The moment she walked through the door, one glance at her mother's angry face brought a sinking feeling to the pit of her stomach. There was no possibility of bluffing her way out of this mess. She could see that Mam already knew everything.

Big Molly hoisted her full bosom on to her folded arms and glared at her elder daughter. 'And where have you been all this time, might I ask?'

Fran repeated the story of the stomach bug, knowing her words were falling on deaf ears. Molly didn't even trouble to let her finish.

'Try another yarn, that one won't wash. So what were you doing going into that Mo's house then? Borrowing a bottle of Milk of Magnesia?'

Fran could actually feel the blood drain from her face. Her suspicions were correct then, her mother did indeed know. How? Who could possibly have told on her? Nobody else knew except Eddie, and it was unlikely he'd want to blab to anyone about her 'little problem'.

Fran turned and deliberately walked away, deciding she really had no wish to get into a shouting match with her mother.

Molly yelled at her in her loudest, sergeant-major voice. 'Don't you turn your back on me, madam, when I'm talking to you. Answer me! Where've you been this last couple of days?'

Cradling her stomach in a protective gesture, Fran sank into a chair with a grateful sigh. 'You know damn well where I've been. Miss Clara brought you a message that I wasn't well.'

'Pull the other one and see if that's got bells on it. Come on, I want to know. Were you with him? You've been up to no good, I know it.'

Fran jumped to her feet again in a fury, instantly forgetting her vow not to get involved in a row. Sticking her face up close to her mother's, she shouted right back. 'No, I wasn't with him, and yes, you're right, I did go to see Maureen. I had a problem, as somebody has clearly told you, and she sorted it out for me. So what? What are you going to do about it? Send me to bed early for being a naughty girl?'

'So what? *So what?*' And Big Molly flung out one ham-like hand and struck Fran across the face, sending her flying.

As luck would have it, Ozzy chose that precise moment to walk in. He was sorry he had, the instant he saw what was going on. Ozzy was not a man for confrontations. Big Molly was fond of saying he'd hide behind a stick insect rather than face a row. But he could hardly ignore the sight of his own daughter lying crumpled on the floor, sobbing her heart out.

'What have you done to our Fran? Why can't you two try to get on a bit better?'

'Because she's a trollop, that's why. A whore, and a tart, because she got herself knocked up, then got rid of it.'

'Got rid of what?' Ozzy asked, eyes blinking in puzzled confusion behind his spectacles. Ask him the odds on the outsider in the two-thirty and he was your man. But anything that smacked of 'women's troubles' and he was lost. A state of affairs he intended to keep that way. 'Don't tell me. I'm sure I don't want to know.'

'Well, you should.' Molly wagged a finger at Fran who had dragged herself up off the floor to huddle back in her chair. 'That little trollop has had an abortion! Is that clear enough for you? She went round to that prossy Maureen's house, seeing her what does little jobs on the side, and got herself sorted.'

Ozzy looked at his lovely young daughter with a sad expression as understanding dawned. 'Is this true, love?'

Fran could do no more than give a hiccupping sob as she nodded miserably.

'Aw, lovey, what pickles you do get yourself in.' Going over to her, Ozzy gathered her in his arms for a cuddle.

'Don't you mollycoddle her. She's no better than she should be, the little whore. Never would listen to good advice.'

'Nay, lass, we all make mistakes. Why should she go through life saddled with hers? She's the right to choose, surely. It's none of your business.'

Fran could hardly believe that her daft, useless father was the one taking her side. She turned her face into his old tweed jacket that smelled of dogs and beer, and sobbed. It felt almost as if she were a child again, and he was protecting her from the bullies in the playground who called her Fatty Arbuckle.

Big Molly's face had gone purple with rage. 'Is it not then? Well, I'll tell you what is my business, and that's whether or not I'm prepared to have her in my house after her shaming me like this. And I'll tell you for nothing, I'm not.'

Picking up a bag she'd previously packed, Molly dropped it at her daughter's feet. 'There's your stuff. Now pick it up and start walking.'

Fran stared up at her mother in startled disbelief. 'Are you throwing me out?'

'Got it in one. What you did was a criminal act, not to mention immoral and disgusting. You ought to hang your head in shame. If that's the way you want to behave, having affairs with married men then disposing of the inconvenient consequences, you can go and do it some place else.'

Obviously distressed by the tension and loud voices, Buster started to bark in sympathy.

Ozzy put out a hand as if he wanted to say something, but whatever it might have been he didn't get the chance. Fran leaped to her feet, snatched up the bag and screamed at her mother: 'All right, you win! I'll go, and don't expect me ever to come back! I hate you, do you hear me? Some bleeding mother you are!'

The sound of the front door slamming behind her echoed through the house for endless moments after she'd gone, followed by a dreadful, deafening silence before Ozzy said, 'There was no call to do that. No call at all.'

But for once in her life Big Molly didn't have an answer. She just stood in the middle of her untidy, grubby living room and wept.

–

Fran went straight back next door to Patsy. 'Can I stay here for another night or two, just till I find somewhere more permanent?'

Patsy looked worried. 'I'm not sure. It's not my house, you see. Annie makes all the decisions here. You'd have to ask her.'

'You ask her,' Fran begged, feeling weary of facing further conflict. 'I know she isn't well and I don't want to upset her, but I've had a row with Mam. She's found out about – you know – what I've been doing, so she's chucked me out. I've nowhere else to go.'

Patsy frowned with concern, then glanced back down the lobby. She could hear the strains of a violin as the two sisters listened to an orchestral recital on the *Third Programme*. Annie was making good progress and some time in the next week or two would be reclaiming her stall, a fact that filled Patsy with trepidation and regret. She'd really enjoyed having it all to herself for a while, was even becoming interested in hat-making.

But interrupting the two sisters would not be easy, and she knew in her heart that Annie would be against becoming involved in what she termed the 'domestic disputes' of the Poulson family. Nevertheless, Patsy felt sorry for Fran, who had to sleep somewhere tonight. She came to a swift decision.

'Come on. If we can get you upstairs without making a sound and disturbing them, you'll be safe till morning in my room. After that, you're on your own, right? You'll have to leave first thing, before anyone's up.'

Fran breathed a sigh of relief. 'Thanks, Patsy, you're a pal.'

–

She left at first light, without the sisters even being aware she'd been in the house. Her intention was to find employment on one of the other market stalls, and accommodation with a friend, if she was lucky. Patsy wished her every success.

'If necessary, Eddie could always let me kip down on his sofa.'

'Oh, I'm sure his wife would love that.'

'He owes me a roof over my head. It's his fault I got in this mess, after all.'

Patsy thought this was stretching the truth, but it was something she didn't even want to attempt to argue. Fran was clearly upset and still hurting from her treatment at the hands of the back-street abortionist, let alone the row with her mother. Privately, Patsy thought she'd got off lightly not to suffer any serious infection as a result. At least Maureen seemed to know what she was doing.

She breathed a sigh of relief when Fran had finally gone. The girl wasn't an easy person to have around and Patsy found that she secretly disapproved of what she'd done, knowing she herself could never have disposed of a child so callously. What if someone had done that to her just because she was an inconvenience? As she clearly had been. Better to have no mother than no life at all.

Chapter Thirty

It took the better part of three days but by the end of it Patsy had made what might be recognised as a hat, albeit lop-sided, but at least all her own work. She was secretly delighted and really proud of her first effort.

Clara was too. 'You have the touch. I could teach you so much more. Annie was never particularly interested in our going into custom-made hats, but I've always thought it an interesting possibility.'

Over the following week Clara showed her how to dye the sinamay to exactly the right shade, how to make flowers out of silk, and how to mount feathers so that they were suitable for fixing to a hat or head band.

Patsy enjoyed working with Clara. She was kind and patient, taking time and trouble over the task, almost as you would expect a mother would when teaching her daughter a new skill. This was something she'd never before experienced and Patsy felt herself growing closer to the older woman.

Yet she understood that Clara was also engaged in nursing her sister with loving care. Annie was demanding and had been really hard work, needing her meals taken upstairs, things fetched and carried for her, and was still not able to work at the stall. She wasn't even permitted to do the accounts or correspondence, and required a daily report of what was going on. Clara would give her a carefully edited version and then distract her by asking what she would like for her tea.

Patsy secretly hoped her convalescence would last a long, long time; although she doubted it would. Annie was as tough as old boots.

Most difficult of all, at least for Patsy, was learning how to cut the sinamay correctly, sometimes on the cross, sometimes in interesting shapes of leaves, petals or coils which could be dyed, twisted, wired or stitched into all manner of designs. There was a lot to learn, but Clara was an excellent teacher.

'I shan't need to go on a course, after all you've taught me,' Patsy said, feeling a warm burst of satisfaction. She had never expected it to be such fun.

Best of all, she loved working with net and feathers. So exciting! If Clara ever gave her the opportunity, Patsy could design the wildest, craziest hats; however, whether they would sell or not was another matter. She was still a long way from daring to put one of her own efforts out on sale, but felt confident that her skills were gradually improving.

Clara was at constant pains to keep her mind on the tightness of their means. Reminding Patsy from time to time how everything they made must eventually be saleable, even if Clara had to remake every one of Patsy's failed attempts herself. Not a penny could be wasted in this experiment.

'Where did you learn hat-making? Did you go on a course?' Patsy wanted to know.

'Yes, I attended a course in Paris. It was very exciting at first, but then the war came and spoiled everything.'

'Tell me about Paris. What was it like? Where did you live? Did you fall in love with a sexy Parisian?'

Clara paused in her cutting and that familiar, faraway look came into her eyes, a smile playing at the corners of her mouth. In these moments she didn't look middle-aged at all, but rather girlish.

'We lived close to the university, handy for Annie's teaching, and it was fun, yes. We were young and idealistic, spent a good deal of time sitting in cafes, discussing Hitler and the wrongs of the world; how we could make everything come right. And, yes, you've guessed correctly, I did fall in love. But I'm afraid I made the same mistake that Fran has made. Don't look so surprised.

'I've heard the rumours about her, and did wonder about this so-called tummy bug she apparently suffered from. However, I have no wish to hear the details. Who am I to judge? I too fell in love with a man who already had a wife. A bad mistake.'

'Oh!' Patsy was startled. This possibility had never occurred to her. But then, Clara seemed to be a woman full of surprises. Just when Patsy thought she had a possible scenario all worked out in her mind, Clara would let fall some unexpected new snippet of information.

When did Clara have this affair? When, and why, did she hand over her child to her mother-in-law? Was that why Rolf left her, because of this affair, or had he already gone off to America, leaving Clara pregnant and alone? If so, why would he do such a thing? Was that the real reason she went to Paris? And if he did leave her, no wonder she fell in love with someone else.

But if she, Patsy, was that child – and she wasn't born until 1940 – the affair must have been after that, unless...

Oh, heavens! What if Rolf Matthews wasn't her father after all? What if it was this Frenchman, whoever he was? Patsy felt a tightness in her chest, couldn't think what to say in response.

She furiously stitched the hat and tried to think.

Clara had still not confirmed that she'd ever been married. In fact, she remained vague about most things, such as when exactly the sisters had left France. They didn't come here to Champion Street until after the death of their parents, towards the end of hostilities. So what had happened in between? Did the sisters spend that time nursing their elderly parents, or doing something else entirely?

Patsy was growing increasingly confused. The dates didn't fit, as nothing made sense. Dare she ask for more details? She cleared her throat, trying to steady her nerves. 'Who was this man? Was he handsome?'

'A lecturer at the university! Oh, indeed, yes. Très handsome! All the students were in love with him. Me too, fool that I was.'

'You never married him then?'

'Marry my lover? No, I never married him. He went back to his wife, as they generally do.'

'Did you ever marry anyone?'

But Clara was no longer listening. There was a bleakness to her gaze now, a desperate aching sadness, as if she really had no wish to remember but couldn't seem to help herself. It didn't surprise Patsy when she called a halt to the conversation.

'That's enough chatter for one day. Finish stitching that spotted veil in place then we'll shut up shop and go home. Grilled plaice for tea, I think. Fish will be good for my dear sister's fragile health.'

And Clara gave Patsy what she could only describe as an arch look. She didn't dare ask any further questions.

–

'May I experiment on my own for a little while?' Patsy asked, and explained how she wanted to try her hand at making some little flirty numbers with the scraps they had left over. Cocktail hats, she called them, which could equally well be worn at a wedding or any other social event. Patsy had seen pictures of them in the catalogues under the counter; the ones that Annie largely ignored.

'I feel we need to appeal to a wider clientele, not just teenagers and old ladies. We have to attract women with money.'

'On this market?' But seeing Patsy's eyes flicker with disappointment, Clara recognised that she had given the subject serious thought, so didn't press the point. The girl had been far less disruptive and argumentative since she'd become absorbed in this new craft. It would do no harm to give her some space for a while longer.

And Clara too was aware that once Annie was back in power, she would not be allowed such leeway.

She smiled indulgently. 'If you wish. We are now selling some of the hats you've made, so I have every faith in you, Patsy. But don't make too many. Annie doesn't care much for frivolity. She will not approve of silly hats.'

'Did you wear frivolous hats in Paris?' Patsy tentatively enquired, hoping to draw the conversation back to Clara's past, but she only laughed.

'Not at all, as I've told you we were far too bohemian. We didn't wear hats at all. I suppose it's hard for you to imagine us ever being young, but we were once. Annie was always conservative, but I was a little more radical.'

'It's hard to imagine Annie as anything but critical and disapproving. Didn't she ever do anything silly, even in Paris? Was she always so prim and boring?'

'Now you are being impudent, child. Annie is a talented, strong woman, with many attributes, which are not always visible on the surface. A woman to admire.'

'Why, what has she ever done that was so wonderful, besides a bit of teaching?'

Clara looked at her for a moment then sadly shook her head. 'Spoken with the innocence and ignorance of youth. Believe it or not, there was a time when I was a little too radical, too bohemian, but she didn't criticise me then. She stood by me, even when it all went terribly wrong.'

Patsy's fingers stilled and she leaned closer. 'You mean, when you had your affair with the professor?'

'He wasn't a professor, only a humble lecturer, a teacher like my sister, but yes, that is what I mean. She didn't preach to me then. At least, not when she saw how pointless it was. And later when the monstrous thing happened, she was the greatest support in the world.'

Patsy could hardly breathe. This was the closest she'd come to hearing the whole tale. 'What was it, this monstrous thing that happened to you? You were going to tell me once before.'

Clara looked at her, eyes blank, and Patsy knew that she didn't hear the everyday sounds of the market, didn't see that child fingering the straw bonnet or her mother slap her prying fingers away.

'It wasn't something that happened to me, not directly. It happened to Louis. That was his name, my lover, Louis Simons.

When the Germans came he tried to get his wife and children out of France, but they were caught and killed. All of them. Louis included.'

Patsy sat as if turned to stone, in complete shock. After a long moment, she managed to find her voice. 'I don't know what to say.'

Clara gave a half smile with no hint of humour in it. 'There is nothing to say.'

'Do you know how it happened?'

She drew in a breath, clasped her hands tightly together in her lap. 'I know very little. Louis decided not to risk the Gare du Nord as the Germans were searching every train, so they packed a few essentials, a change of clothes and a little food, and rode out on their bicycles one bright May morning as if they were going on a family picnic. The roads were packed with refugees: women pushing prams or handcarts heaped with household goods, dragging their children along beside them, or sitting them on top of the pile. Some families drove their cars with all their life's possessions strapped to the roof. They were constantly dive-bombed by German planes, forced to run and hide in ditches.

'There were military personnel everywhere, German officers with yellow lapels who could stop anyone and ask to see your papers. You didn't argue, you put up your hands and let them search you... feel you...'

In that moment Patsy saw that Clara was not simply relating a story, she was speaking from experience. She did not interrupt.

'You could bribe railway officials, buy yourself transport some-times, but you would never attempt to try such tricks on the Gestapo.'

Only by the tightness of her laced fingers could her tension be seen. Patsy kept her gaze fixed on those hands, wanting to hold them but not daring to.

'As for Louis and his family, they were never seen again.' After a moment Clara's gaze came back into focus and she gave a helpless little shrug. 'I heard from other students who had word from survivors that they'd joined up with a group of refugees heading for the Belgian coast. They were stopped and searched, bundled into trucks and taken away, the men in one, women and children in the other. Possibly to Dachau or one of the other death camps, I don't know. Some of the escapees resisted arrest and were shot on the spot. Louis was one of those who died trying to protect his family, and he had such a brave heart. I only know that he promised to telephone or write to me when he reached safety, but he never did.'

'He was Jewish then?' Patsy softly asked, not wishing to sound intrusive.

'He was a delightful, sweet man. He had two beautiful little girls, seven and five years old. They were the reason for my guilt. That I, young and foolish as I was, should dare to draw their papa's attention and love away from them. I never meant to harm them, and he always put them first, so when the time came for them to leave, he did not hesitate to choose them before me.'

'It must have hurt a little though, when you loved him so much,' Patsy ventured.

'A little, yes, but I was a grown woman. I could look after myself. They were children.'

'Yet he chose his wife too.'

Clara looked up at her, clear eyed. 'She was the mother of his children. It makes a difference. But, like many others, they did not make it.' After a moment she seemed mentally to shake herself. 'I survived, though whether I deserved to is another matter.'

'It wasn't your fault that this terrible thing happened to them.'

'It was my fault that Louis neglected his wife in the last year of her life. She might have found more happiness if I hadn't been around. She deserved that, don't you think, dying so young? And her children too! The guilt of my youthful selfishness will haunt me for as long as I live.'

The silence between them now was sad and reflective, the hat-making lying forgotten.

Patsy saw her own problems in a different perspective, and realised in that instant that many terrible things happen in life, over which she had no control. Even Clara, who had enjoyed the advantage of a loving family: a mother and father, a sister who cared for her, a sheltered upbringing, couldn't help herself from falling in love with the wrong man. She couldn't stop this monstrous thing happening to Louis, and to his family, and to all those other refugees helpless at the hands of fate.

So what right did Patsy have to complain?

Clara said, 'I'm sorry to burden you with all of this, but the ripples of that event still affect me, still colour my judgements.'

'That's why you were willing to help me, isn't it? You wanted me to have a second chance, because you didn't. Because Louis and his little daughters didn't.'

Clara smiled, and there was warmth as well as sadness in it this time. 'You really are a remarkably perceptive as well as sensitive girl, Patsy. Not nearly so tough and unfeeling as you make out.'

When Patsy said nothing to this Clara continued on a brisker note, as if needing to put away all this sadness and move on, 'I should mention that Annie will be coming back to work on the stall soon, probably by the first week of September.'

'Oh!' Patsy tried to think of something pleasant to say. She was aware, naturally, that Annie had been making good progress, but had secretly hoped for a little bit longer on her own at the stall. She'd been making such good progress herself, really getting into this hat-making lark.

'It does not mean we will no longer need your help,' Clara continued. 'We shall continue to require your assistance for some considerable time, and I hope you'll feel able to give it. Everything has changed now.'

Patsy felt a huge sense of relief, elated and fearful all at the same time. She was delighted that the sisters wanted her to stay, and yet, in the face of Clara's sad tale, her own particular quest seemed somehow much less significant. Did that mean she was growing up, coming to accept her own fate at last?

Clara was saying, 'I've made it very clear to Annie that she may do mornings only. I thought you could look after the stall in the afternoons, and in the mornings, once I have done my chores in the house, you and I could continue with our hat-making. There's not a lot more I can teach you though. You should go on a course if you wish to learn more.'

Patsy didn't answer. Where was the point?

It was perfectly clear that with Annie coming back to the stall, she wasn't ever going to get the chance to create her own designs. Annie had already been delving into the accounts and making criticisms. If she was insisting on returning to work so soon, then Patsy's freedom was almost at an end. Actually a great pity, as there was so much more she longed to learn, and not just about hat-making.

Clara's next words seemed to echo this thought. 'As well as the obvious improvement in your skills, I believe this time together has given us the opportunity to get to know each other a little better, which is a good thing, don't you think?'

Patsy nodded, giving a shy sort of smile.

Clara gave her a wry look. 'Though it goes without saying I would welcome your feeling able to trust me with your confidences, as I have trusted you with mine.'

Had the time come to tell Clara how she came to be here, on Champion Street Market? How she longed to solve the puzzle of her birth?

Yet Patsy still nursed a lingering fear that when she did finally speak of it, all her hopes and dreams would be shattered. The only way of keeping them alive was not to ask the question until she was absolutely certain she would receive the right answer. And that might never be possible.

Chapter Thirty-One

Summer had gone and September was upon them, but with still over two weeks to the date of their wedding, Amy and Chris were on the brink of starvation. Neither had managed to find employment, having tried everywhere they could think of, even walking out of town to neighbouring villages. They couldn't reach bigger places such as Dalbeattie or Castle Douglas, not without transport, and so had no alternative but to stay close to Gretna. They daren't even risk spending money on bus fares to check out jobs in those more distant places.

This morning Amy was warming a can of soup on a pitiful fire by their shelter. Chris had gone out at first light, job hunting as usual, and she'd promised to have a meal ready for him on his return. She had been reduced to tears by the difficulty she'd found in getting the fire going in the damp Scotch mist that had lain low over the entire woodland all morning. And then having finally got it going, she carried a can of water from the stream to boil up for a cup of tea and accidentally spilt it on the fire. She'd had to start all over again.

Amy was ashamed of the way she kept on weeping. She'd never expected this to be easy, but neither had she expected it to be so difficult. Much as she loved Chris and wanted to stay and see it through so that they could become man and wife, as they so longed to be, there were times when she would have given anything to go home. She missed her mam and dad, longed to see her friends on the market. Even missed the silly scraps she used to have with Fran.

She wondered if her sister ever missed her, though doubted it, not if she was still seeing that selfish twerp, Eddie Davidson.

And what she wouldn't give for some of her mam's home cooking: a piping hot steak pie running with gravy; Lancashire hot pot with lamb chops and kidneys; a creamy rice pudding or treacle sponge and custard. Amy's mouth watered at the thought. She couldn't stop dreaming about food.

Gone were the days when she and Chris could afford to treat themselves to cod and chips, or sausage and mash. They felt themselves fortunate now if they had a heel of bread and a dish of soup to help get them through the day, which was what they were having today.

It was nearly three o'clock and Amy had been waiting hours for his return, her stomach was aching with hunger and all she could think of was a bowl of hot and tasty tomato soup. She would put the pan on the fire to warm it, then take it off again when he didn't show up. An hour later she'd build up the fire and try again.

By four o'clock she was utterly exhausted and close to despair when she heard him crashing through the undergrowth. Chris came galloping towards her, leaping over fallen trees to reach her as fast as he could.

'Where have you been till this time?' she cried, an uncharacteristic sharpness in her tone.

He knelt beside her, stroked her auburn curls back from her face. 'I've got a job!'

'Oh, Chris, where?'

He grinned at her. 'You'll never believe this. I'm going to be milking cows.'

She stared at him for a whole ten seconds and then burst out laughing. 'I don't believe it!'

Chris was laughing too, holding her tight and rocking her in his arms. 'No one can say I don't know about milk. First I sell it, now I'm going to be at the production end for a change. How about that?'

He explained how he'd met a farmer while he was out and about exploring that morning. 'I'd walked a couple of miles down the lane out of town and spotted this farmer having a bit of bother with his cows. One had taken it into her head to go walkabout and the others followed her, and in trying to get them back he'd lost control of the rest of the herd and they were all over the place. His dog was going in one direction, him in another and the cows were everywhere. I helped him get the wanderers back to the herd and he was so grateful, he invited me in to share his breakfast. Before I knew it, he'd offered me a job.'

'Oh, Chris, that's wonderful!'

'It's only temporary, for a couple of weeks while his son is away on holiday but I said that was all I needed. His wife was lovely too, and she seemed pleased by the arrangement. Said she had enough to do, thanks very much, with the house, the hens, the vegetable garden, the pigs and calves, without helping with the milking as well.

'And Mrs Duncan, that's what she's called, the farmer's wife, insisted that I bring you with me every morning. She says it's not safe for you to be left on your own in the woods, and anyway, she'd be glad of an extra pair of hands in the house while her daughter-in-law's away. How about that? We both have a job.'

'Oh, Chris, that's wonderful! How clever you are. I can't believe it. We're saved!'

'It'll see us through, love, don't you think? We can survive, and you won't run out on me before the big day, will you?'

She could see anxiety in his eyes, and hear it in his tone of voice. 'You've asked me that a score of times these last few weeks and my answer is always the same, Chris George. I love you, and while I've breath in my body I'll hang on, half starved though I may be.'

'Hey, I was forgetting.' He handed her a brown paper bag he'd been carrying. 'Look at this, Mrs Duncan gave it me for our supper.'

Amy looked inside and found two freshly baked scones, thickly buttered and rich with fruit. She stared at them in open disbelief, breathed in the intoxicating aroma then lifted moist eyes to Chris.

'I can't believe what I'm seeing. Real food! Such bounty, and look at me, I'm happy now instead of sad, but I'm crying again.'

As always, he smiled and kissed her tears away.

–

Fran had gone round the market time and time again, asking every stallholder if they could give her work, and without exception they had all said no. Only blunt talking Winnie Watkins had been willing to give her a reason.

'Your reputation on Champion Street Market isn't good, lass. Even if I needed an assistant, which thankfully I don't, I wouldn't give you the time of day. I'd listen to your mam, if I were you. Go home and eat humble pie, that's your best bet.'

'It's for Mam to apologise to me, not me to her. It's my life, and I'll live it how I choose. I suppose she's told you what happened, but she was the one who asked me to leave. And she'll have to go down on her bended knees and beg if she wants me back.'

'The pair of you are as stubborn as mules, bad as each other. But don't expect any help round here. If Big Molly doesn't trust you, why should we?'

This attitude, Fran soon discovered, was reflected throughout the market. She considered leaving Champion Street altogether, but where would she go? At least while she stayed in her home territory she could find a roof over her head at one or other of her friends' houses, although none of them was keen for her to stay very long. She was constantly packing up her stuff and moving on to the next.

Fran did find herself a job in the end, packing and sorting goods in a warehouse down by the docks, but it wasn't what she wanted. She still craved excitement, not monotony, a bit of fun rather than filling out boring shipping dockets. The job wasn't particularly well paid and it was only part-time, which left the afternoons free for her to look for something better, or more likely wander around like a lost soul.

Fran would often see Dena Dobson strolling around with her baby, still unmarried, though walking out apparently, and happily building a new life for herself, having an illegitimate child.

'I'm sorry, Fran, that we don't need anybody,' Dena told her. 'I've got Joan Chapman and her sister working for me.'

'That's okay, I've got myself fixed up with something. I'm no good at sewing anyway.'

Watching Dena jiggle the pram and chat away to her little girl as she walked away, Fran felt an unexpected shaft of envy. For the first time the reality of what she'd done finally registered. She couldn't bear even to look at the kid, pretty little thing though she was. Or into Dena's happy face.

It was as if Fran was seeing herself with new clarity and didn't much care for it. In that moment she hated herself, but most of all she hated Eddie for getting her into this mess.

One afternoon she went round to his house, hoping to see him. He owed her, and Fran's intention was to blackmail him into slipping her a few quid to help tide her over. She'd give him a piece of her mind if nothing else. But there was no sign of either him or his precious wife. A neighbour saw her hovering in the garden and came out to tell her that they'd gone away.

'They've had such bad luck, bless them. First Josie very nearly lost the baby, had to spend the better part of a week in hospital before she got the all clear, then poor Eddie startled some burglars and ended up in hospital himself with cracked ribs and a broken foot. I think they've gone to stay with Josie's mother for a bit, till she's safely delivered, I expect. Such a shame. I really don't know what the world is coming to.'

Fran mumbled some sympathetic remark and escaped. So she hadn't lost the baby after all? Drat the woman. What right did she have to be so lucky?

Back at the market, Fran wandered about in a lost sort of daze, in and out of the market hall, up and down the rows of the outside stalls, all the time worrying about where to go, what to do, how to fill her time. She'd been banking on Eddie, and as usual he'd let her down.

It started to rain and since she didn't have an umbrella Fran huddled under the dripping awning of Abel's stall, minding it for him while he went for a warming cuppa. She could do with one herself. And with the heat of August long gone, how she would face the coming winter with no place to call her own, Fran didn't dare to consider.

She was staying with Sal again for a night or two, but daren't go to her house till after her mam and dad were safely watching television, as they didn't approve. Sal would choose her moment to open the door and let Fran slip quietly upstairs, as Patsy had done at the Higginson's house.

It didn't surprise her that there was gossip, but Fran hated the high moral tone everyone was adopting. They'd turn their backs as she approached, or pretend they hadn't heard if she spoke to them.

'I bet their lives aren't so perfect as they make out.' It was all so sordid, so gut-wrenching being turned into an outcast. And she didn't for a moment imagine Eddie would be suffering the same sort of treatment.

A part of her hoped she would never clap eyes on Eddie Davidson again, but the rest ached to have his arms about her, to have him make love to her with the passion she'd come to need. Love and hate were all mixed up in Fran's head, adding to her general misery. Maybe she should give up men altogether, since she couldn't seem to find a decent one.

As the rain beat down she wished Abel would hurry up, then she could go back into the market hall where at least she'd be warm and dry, even if folk did talk behind their hands about her. If things didn't improve soon, she'd be on the next bus out of here. Fran was turning over various possibilities in her mind when Marc Bertalone came around the corner. He was carrying a pile of boxes, clearly in a hurry to get somewhere, but with a deep frown on his handsome face and his gaze fixed on the ground as he strode along.

Fran shook back her damp hair and stepped out from under the awning to greet him with a smile. 'You look a bit down in the mouth. I'm feeling low, not to mention wet. Care for a coffee so's we can cheer each other up?'

Marc came out of his reverie to look at her in surprise. As usual he'd been worrying about Patsy, trying to work out a way to win her round, how to melt the frozen shell she'd built around herself. Now here was a pretty face smiling up at him. An attractive, friendly girl, if a bit brash for his taste, with soft round breasts filling her sweater, and an old friend. One might almost call Fran an old flame, since they'd enjoyed one or two dates in their youth.

It was true what she said, that he was feeling low. It wasn't as if he could look forward to seeing Patsy later today, more's the pity. Not unless he went looking for her, and even then she'd probably bite his head off. Patsy Bowman didn't want to know. She just kept on pushing him away, had pretty well shut him out completely.

So why the hell not? What harm could it do? It was only coffee, after all.

'Okay,' he agreed. 'I'll just deliver these to Papa then meet you later at Belle's cafe.'

—

It was the end of September and Molly could see no possibility of paying her debts. When she hadn't found the money by the end of August, she'd gone to see Quinn and begged for more time. He'd been surprisingly understanding and given her another month till the end of September, but still she couldn't pay him more than a tenner, and as interest had been added, this hardly made a dent in the debt.

People laughed in her face when she asked if they could lend her thirty quid. Even Ozzy admitted to owing Quinn money for gambling debts, and Molly knew she was in deep trouble.

It was brought forcibly home to her just how much when she returned home one afternoon after a hard day on her stall to find a message attached to her door knob. It was a piece of rope, the attached noose swinging in the breeze. There was no note with it, but she knew what it meant. If he gave her enough rope, she'd hang herself.

'Lord above, I'm in dead lumber now.'

When there came a knock at the door the very next day, Molly began to shake. He'd come for her. What now? Panic struck her and she looked about in desperation, seeking a place to run. There was nowhere.

The tapping came again, following by a whispered, 'Hello! Mam, are you in there?'

Molly allowed herself the luxury of a smile of triumph. So madam had come crawling back, had she, begging to be allowed home?

Didn't she love her daughters to bits and want only the best for them? Clearly Fran had at last realised this fact and seen the error of her ways. The little floozy had discovered that she couldn't possibly manage on her own. If she'd come back ready to kiss and make up, Molly was willing enough to do that; on her terms, naturally.

She rolled up her sleeves and went to open the door. But it wasn't a contrite and humble Fran standing on her nice clean doorstep, it was Amy. And standing right beside her, bold as brass, was Chris George. They were even holding hands.

And as if that weren't shock enough, Amy held up her left hand to show off the glint of a ring on her third finger. If Big Molly had been a weakling, she would have fainted clean away on her own doorstep. As it was, her scream of outrage could be heard the length of Champion Street. It went down in history as one of the loudest ever recorded.

Chapter Thirty-Two

Annie was back with a vengeance, bossing and ordering them about something shocking, complaining that the accounts weren't in order, that the stall was untidy, which was patently untrue, and objecting to the flibbertigibbet hats on sale. All Clara's plans for herself and Patsy to spend their time quietly making hats, once the morning chores were done, went out of the window. Annie considered this to be a complete waste of time.

'We'll have no more of this nonsense, far better if Patsy helps me. She can climb ladders, fetch and carry, keep things clean and shipshape while I concentrate on serving customers.'

'No,' Patsy said.

'I beg your pardon, young lady?'

'I said no. I'm going to continue to make hats whether you like it or not.'

Annie gasped, clearly unused to being challenged. 'I think not! Certainly not using my money and materials, you won't. Far too much has been wasted on this foolish enterprise already.'

Clara ventured to put in a word. 'I believe you are being hard on the girl, Annie. We have actually sold a good many of Patsy's efforts. A fact you wouldn't be aware of, since you were ill and never saw them.'

'If those silly little cocktail numbers are anything to go by I'm glad I didn't see them. I'm sure it would have worsened my health considerably. Those are not the kind of hats normally sold on my stall.'

'I intend to do a course at the local college,' Patsy said, perversely coming out with the very opposite of what she had decided, in her determination to stand her ground. 'And I shall pay for my own materials.'

Annie flounced off, greatly annoyed and clearly agitated, while Clara rested a staying hand on Patsy's arm, a typical gesture. 'Remember, her health is not what it might be.'

'Her temper's as sharp as ever though.'

Clara's lips twitched into a smile. 'I'm afraid so, but we must not tax it too far, Patsy. She is my sister. We must take care not to vex her and cause another attack.'

Patsy nodded. 'I know, I'll try and behave, only I said from the start that I wouldn't be used as a skivvy, either in the house or on the stall.'

'Of course you did, and quite right too. Give Annie time, and she'll come round to the idea of your hats, once she sees how fine they are. In the meantime, signing yourself up for a course is a good idea. Why don't you go and make enquiries today?'

–

Patsy's emotions seemed to swing between complete optimism and total despair. She was delighted that the sisters wanted her to stay, for now at least, even if it was only out of necessity until Annie grew stronger. On the other hand, she was no nearer solving the mystery of her own background and was beginning to wonder if she ever would.

Patsy didn't know where to begin to find a course on hat-making, so started by walking over to the university buildings.

'Good heavens, we don't dabble in such trivia at the university,' said a frosty-faced receptionist. 'You'll have to look elsewhere for such amusement.'

'It's not for my amusement,' Patsy smartly responded. 'It's to help me earn a living, make a career for myself. I reckoned that's what universities were all about.'

'Then you reckoned wrong, girl. Universities are about education, something it's obvious you know little about. And we don't offer a degree in hat-making. Ask at the town hall, dear, or your local technical college.' And the woman slammed shut the window that separated her from the rest of humanity.

'Well, there should be a degree in hat-making! People still need hats!' Patsy shouted through the glass, before marching out of the building.

She stood out on the pavement, breathing deeply. Why get herself in a lather over a stuck-up receptionist, and a course she'd never intended to do in the first place? It was a stupid idea, one she'd only agreed to in order to get up Annie's nose, and to please Clara. She was learning all she needed from her, with the added benefit that they were growing increasingly friendly as they worked on the hats together. She'd just have to use her charm on Annie a bit more, persuade her to let them carry on as before.

In any case, she should put her mind to solving the puzzle of her birth, not fussing over some silly course. But once she'd geared herself up to ask the right questions, she might not receive the right answers. So even if Annie didn't actually give her the push, Patsy knew she would feel obliged to move on anyway.

She wished she could talk her problems over with someone, but who? Who cared about her enough even to listen?

Marc. The one person she most definitely couldn't ask.

–

She was sitting in the fitting room with Clara the following afternoon, in defiance of Annie's instructions, attaching black velvet petals to a smooth satin cap so that it framed the face beautifully. 'I think a small veil too, don't you, Clara?'

'That might give it a little extra interest, yes. Try this one with the tiny French knots. Oh, yes, that is delightful, Patsy. Hello Marc, look what Patsy has made. Isn't she clever?'

Inwardly shrinking from facing him, Patsy shot a quick glance in his direction, brief enough to protect herself from his compelling gaze, but sufficient to register the dark crinkled hair, the wide smile, and the casual way he leaned his lithe body against the door frame, hands in pockets, as if he had all the time in the world. The very confidence of his stance infuriated her.

'I would've thought you'd be back at your art school by now,' Patsy sharply remarked.

'I have the results of my examinations. I have passed with flying colours.'

Clara jumped up and kissed him on both cheeks. 'Oh, well done, Marc. I'm so pleased for you. And what now?'

'Now I seek employment. And who knows where that might be?'

A sick feeling settled in the pit of Patsy's stomach before she could do anything to stop it. The possibility of Marc leaving the market before her, was not something she'd considered. She'd always thought she would be the one to leave, not him.

'Patsy is trying to find herself a course too, in hat-making.'

'Have you found one?' His gaze upon her was keen and interested.

Patsy shrugged, as if it were of no concern. 'Not yet, but Clara can teach me all I need to know. So I might as well learn what I can, while I'm here.'

'But you aren't leaving, are you? You do intend to stay on the market?'

'Where else would she go?' Clara said. 'If you will excuse me, Patsy, while you have Marc here to chat to, I'd like to nip home and check on Annie. She's had a tiring morning. Her first one back at work, Marc, and I need to check that it wasn't too much for her.'

'Don't worry, you go and see to Annie. I shall stay and keep Patsy company.'

'Bless you!'

Patsy was annoyed, and after Clara had gone turned on Marc, her eyes flashing fire. 'There's no need for you to do any such thing. I'm perfectly fine on my own.'

Ignoring her completely, Marc casually took the seat that Clara had vacated, resting his arms on his knees and leaning so close to her that she could see her own reflection in those bewitching brown eyes, framed by softly curled lashes. 'You must stay. You cannot think of leaving. Clara, she wants you to stay too. She needs you, as do I.'

Patsy felt her cheeks grow warm. Somehow she found the breath to speak. 'Annie is the one who makes the big decisions round here. If she decides to sack me again, I'm on the next bus out of here.'

'It doesn't have to be that way. You can always come back to the ice cream parlour. Papa likes you too. He says you have spunk.'

'I prefer hats.'

'And being with anyone but me, apparently. Why will you not give us a chance, Patsy? What are you afraid of, or are you finding that you do like me a little, after all? I am wondering if there is any hope for me.'

In that moment Patsy admitted to herself that she didn't want Marc to give up hope. The ache of longing, deep in the pit of her stomach, swelled and grew at his words, seeming to fill her entire being. No matter how many times she might tell him to stay away, perversely she wanted him to still be there. 'What about you? Now that you've finished your art course, you might be the one to leave first, not me.'

There was a gleam of triumph in the smile he gave her. 'I am thinking you would miss me.'

'I didn't say that.'

'You didn't need to. I may leave, or find a job here in Manchester. It all depends on whether it is worth my while to stay. Do you think it is, Patsy?'

She pouted a little, kept her eyes on the hat in her hands, though her fingers didn't seem to be working as they should, and the velvet petals were falling all over the place. 'How would I know?'

'How can I convince you that I am not the big bad wolf of the horrid fairytale?'

She giggled, unable to help herself because she had a sudden insight into how foolish and childish she was. But there was something to do with the way he took the hat from her to gather her hand in his and stroke each finger in a delicate caress.

'I came today with an invitation. My papa and mama send to you their best regards and wish to know when they are to see you again.'

Patsy stared at him in stunned surprise. This was the last thing she'd expected. 'Why would they wish to?'

He shook his head in despair. 'You sound more like Annie every day. Are you sure she isn't your mother, and not Clara at all?'

Patsy had momentarily forgotten that she had confessed the nature of her quest to Marc. Now her heart nearly stopped in shock at being reminded of this indiscretion. How stupid of her! And the very idea of Annie being her mother was too dreadful to contemplate. Patsy had always been convinced that it was Clara. Hadn't Shirley discovered it was the younger daughter who was believed to be pregnant, the one who was particularly friendly with Felicity Matthews's son?

Marc was still waiting for an answer, wondering if once again he'd said the wrong thing. What had he done this time? 'I'm sorry I shouldn't have said that about your mother. I haven't mentioned what you told me to a living soul, Patsy. I swear your secret is safe with me.'

She was glaring at him with no sign of forgiveness in her expression, which meant there would be no simple acceptance of his invitation. When was anything straightforward where Patsy was concerned? He had great sympathy for her problems, and admiration for the way she had coped with rejection by her foster parents, but sometimes he wondered if she appreciated that other people had problems too. It was a lesson she needed to take on board, then she might find the courage to confront her own personal demons. If only she would let him help.

He tried again. 'Papa was sorry when you left the ice cream parlour. He had been happy to give you a job and would have been equally happy for you to stay.'

Patsy bent her head, hiding her face in the fall of her hair as she returned her full attention to stitching velvet petals. 'I'm sorry, I do feel a bit guilty over letting him down, but Clara needs me here.'

'I can see that. You must help your mother and your aunt.'

Patsy jerked, pricking herself inadvertently with the needle. 'I've told you not to call them that. Don't ever use those words.'

Marc's expression softened as he considered her. 'I won't say anything in front of them, I promise, but it's time that you did. Long past time, in fact, that you came right out with it and asked Clara to tell you the whole truth.'

'I know, I only wish...' Patsy's fingers stilled as she hesitated, desperate to talk to someone, her voice dropping to little more than a whisper. 'She has told me more about her past, about something that happened to her when she and Annie were in Paris.'

'And did you ask if she had a child?' When Patsy shook her head he drew back the curtain of fair hair to peep at her. 'You are not so brave as you pretend, little one. Shall I ask for you?'

'No, that would be wrong. Please don't do that, Marc. This is my problem. I must be the one to solve it. I suppose I have been behaving a bit foolishly.'

He put back his head and laughed out loud. 'What is this? Not an apology. You have strength, and the heart of a lion. There is no shame in being afraid, but how can I encourage you when you will not even let me see you?'

Patsy couldn't help but respond to it. She was affronted. 'Why would I need to apologise?' She stared at him, astonished by what he'd just said and mesmerised by his nearness. When he bridged the distance between them to place his mouth gently over hers, Patsy couldn't have prevented that kiss, not for the world.

'Why indeed? When a man says he cannot sleep for thinking of you, cannot get you out of his head, why would you care?' He lifted his head and looked deeply into her eyes, ran one finger down her cheek. 'Be brave, Patsy. Stop hiding from yourself. Stop running away. There are people ready to help you, me included, but you have to be prepared to let them into your life. You have learned to trust folk, and not everyone will let you down as your foster parents did.'

She was silent, not attempting to answer, or able to take in the full import of what he was trying to say. Patsy was once again thinking of Clara's story; of her lover's attempted escape and his death. She'd had no choice but to face up to that reality and go on. Life was like that.

Patsy knew, in her heart, that what Marc was telling her made sense. She had a great desire to feel settled, to make far-reaching decisions about her life, to form real friendships and lasting relationships, but many unanswered questions needed to be addressed. She must somehow find the courage, as Marc said, to finish her quest, no matter what the outcome.

He got to his feet. 'I've told Papa that you will come to tea on Sunday. We eat at six o'clock. I shall expect you to do that for him, and for my mother and sisters who also like you, even if you don't care about my feelings. They are good people, and they too have had their problems. Italians were not popular round here during the war. Yet Papa survived, against the odds, through years interned in a camp on the Isle of Man. We all survived those difficult years, as you will get through yours, believe me. Please don't be late.' Then he dropped a kiss on top of her head, and left.

After he'd gone, Patsy put her head in her hands and wept for shame at her own selfishness. It really was time she stopped worrying so much about herself, and started to put others first.

Chapter Thirty-Three

Amy was in despair. She supposed she should be grateful that at least Chris's parents had allowed them the use of their back bedroom, the one which he had occupied since he was a boy. But the situation was far from ideal, extremely difficult in fact. Mr George had rarely remained in the house longer than half an hour since they'd arrived, always seeming to have work needing attention at the bakery, and Mrs George hadn't yet spoken a word to her.

Amy would go into the kitchen and as politely as she could offer to help prepare the tea. Unfortunately, this would be met either by stony silence or an irritable flick of the hand.

'Shall I set the table?'

Filled with panic and aching with misery, Amy felt desperate to make things right between them, for Chris's sake if nothing else. She noticed the sink stacked with used cooking utensils. 'I'll wash up, shall I, while you cook?'

But as she approached, Mrs George set down the skillet she was using and stood with her hands gripping the edge of the sink, forming a physical barrier so that, short of pushing her out of the way, Amy could do nothing. And her mouth was still pressed into that hard, tight line, clearly determined not to exchange one civil word with her daughter-in-law.

Amy gave up and crept away, painfully aware that her assistance wasn't welcome. Even her presence in the house was clearly a trial to them. At first Chris had insisted they all sit together in the living room, doing his best to start up a conversation with his parents, but the pervading silence had done for him too in the end.

'Look, if there's something you want to say, why don't you come right out and say it? Let's clear the air then we can all get on with our lives.'

No response.

'Go on, speak to me, and to Amy, as she's done nothing wrong to deserve being cold-shouldered in this way.'

When still they said nothing, simply kept their eyes glued to the flickering television screen in the corner, Chris leaped to his feet and switched the set off. Then he yelled at them both about their bad manners. 'She's my wife, damn it, and I'll not have her ignored, or sent to Coventry, or whatever childish game it is that you're playing.'

'We're not going to argue with you, son,' his father quietly remarked. 'We aren't that sort of family.' Casting a meaningful glance in Amy's direction, as if silently adding, Unlike some.

Since then they'd preferred to spend every moment they possibly could either out of the house or, as the nights drew in and grew colder, in their own room. But even that was difficult. It was so cramped and tiny. Worse even than the room Amy had shared with Fran. And there was nothing to do in it but play cards or read library books, or sit cuddled up on the bed dreaming of a better future.

'It's only temporary,' Chris would reassure Amy, stroking away her tears, kissing her flushed cheeks. 'Till we find a place of our own.'

Easy to say, but such dreams took money.

Chris was still looking for work, though thankfully Amy's brother had welcomed her back with open arms, putting her straight into the new kitchens and telling her not to fret about Mam.

'Leave her be. She'll come round in the end.'

Amy wasn't so sure. Knowing her mother, not for a moment did she imagine Big Molly would gracefully accept defeat. But at least she and Chris were married now, husband and wife at last. Nobody could alter that simple fact.

The ceremony had gone off smoothly enough with both Mr and Mrs Duncan, the farmer and his wife, and their kindly landlady attending and wishing them well.

Knowing they hardly had a penny between them, Mrs Duncan had insisted they all go back to her farm kitchen for a slap-up tea. And what a feast that had been. Ham and pork, bowls of green salad, rosy ripe tomatoes, fresh fruit salad, and a lovely iced sponge cake with a basket of rosebuds made out of marzipan on top. Amy had cried, overwhelmed by such kindness.

Afterwards the Duncans had driven them straight to the station, standing on the platform to wave to them as the train drew out. And their lovely landlady, still suffering from guilt for having been the one to spoil their dreams of a quick handfast wedding in the first place, presented them with a hamper of food for the journey.

A perfect, wonderful wedding day, one that Amy would forever remember.

Now she sat on Chris's old bed and stared at her face reflected in the dark of the window against the night sky. It was pale and sad, not the sort of face one would expect to see on a new bride. It would help if she put on a spot of lipstick, but Amy didn't have a mirror, or a lipstick for that matter. She had few possessions of any kind. Chris had access to his own clothes again, still hanging in the narrow mahogany wardrobe where he'd left them all those weeks ago, but Amy's own were still at number twenty-four. They might as well have been a million miles away.

There was no dressing table, simply a chest of drawers, since it was a boy's room. Apart from a few school photographs and sporting trophies, a cricket bat propped in one corner and a plaid dressing gown hanging behind the door, it was remarkably tidy. One might almost say bare. But then Mrs George was not like Big Molly, content to scatter her belongings all over the place. The living room and kitchen downstairs were equally stark. A place for everything, and the bed was a narrow single, not a double.

Amy didn't mind the squash, she liked to cuddle close to Chris at night, but married life had not turned out as she'd expected.

They'd been man and wife sleeping in this bed for almost a week, and still they hadn't done it. Chris said the reason was that there hadn't been the opportunity, and the right moment hadn't come. The first night they'd been too upset, both by Molly's reaction and by the cool reception from his parents. Since then, whenever they started a bit of a cuddle it would take only the creak of a floorboard out on the landing to make them both freeze. The very idea of making love with his mother and father listening in, was too painful for either of them to contemplate.

'We'll have to wait a bit longer,' Chris decided. 'Till we can find a place of our own.'

But houses, like romance, Amy discovered, were not as easy to find as one might expect.

–

'Hey up,' said Winnie Watkins, in her mildest tones. 'It might not be any of my business, Molly, but there's no pleasing some folk. You're angry with one daughter for not being married, and with the other because she is.'

'You're right, Winnie, it is none of your business.'

'You chose to tell me, so what now?'

'I don't know, and that's a fact. And you keep all of this under your hat, right?'

'Oh, I can keep a secret all right,' Winnie dryly remarked, inaccurately.

'By heck there were fair ructions last night when our Amy got back. She shed that many tears when I refused to let that chap of hers stay, it's a wonder we weren't all washed away.' Molly sat with her head in her hands behind her friend's fabric stall, feeling ridiculously close to tears herself.

Why was her life in such a mess? Why had everything gone wrong? Why wouldn't her girls pay attention to what she told them any more? It had been so much easier when they were small. She'd known what they were up to all the time then, and they'd been good little girls, doing as their mam said. Most of the time, anyroad, but it was a whole different kettle of fish now. It had cost her a small fortune trying to put matters right, yet so far she'd got nowhere beyond putting lover boy Eddie Davidson's foot in plaster and cracking a few of his ribs. Nothing like enough, but how could she ask Quinn for more help when she owed him all this money?

'I don't suppose you could lend me a few quid, could you?'

'What, to pay that piece of low life? Not on your nelly. I'm not getting involved with the likes of Quinn, even if I had that amount of spare cash, which I don't. And you must have a screw loose to get yourself tied up with him, an' all. If you don't watch out he'll come and collect that rope he left and wrap it round your neck.'

'I know.' Molly felt the blood seep from her every limb at the thought, leaving her weak and trembling.

Winnie shook her head in despair. 'You've bitten off more than you can chew this time, Moll, and I can't help you. You should've left well alone, let your lasses sort their own lives out. You aren't responsible for their mistakes any more.'

Big Molly scowled, hating to be put in the wrong, to hear her old friend repeat what Ozzy had already told her.

'What does your Ozzy say about all this?' asked Winnie, as if picking up on the thought.

Molly snorted. 'You know our Ozzy, won't bat a fly in case it hits him back.'

'Find the money somehow. Can't you borrow it from the bank, or your Robert?'

Molly too shook her head. 'He's up to his neck paying off the bank loan for the new kitchens.'

'Well, you have to find some way to pay Quinn, and fast. Then you need to make up with your two girls and be glad you've still got them. That's my advice, for what it's worth.'

'It's easy for you to talk, not having a family dragging you in the mire, and you don't remember how it was when our Lena died, all because of them Georges. Since our Amy has chosen to join them by marrying into the family, she can go and live with them, see how she likes that.'

'Hecky-thump, you're a hard woman, Molly Poulson. You'll rue the day you chucked them lovely lasses out on the street. You will really. You'll rue the day.'

–

'This is nice,' Fran said, pouting her lips as seductively as she could, then giggling enticingly. 'I can't remember the last time you and I shared an ice cream, Marc. Too long ago. Must have been when we were young, but we aren't kids any more, are we? Still, I always did fancy you rotten.'

She scooped up a spoonful of Marc's strawberry ice cream and licked it slowly with the tip of her tongue, never taking her eyes from his as she did so.

Marc frowned as he watched the unmistakeable sensuality of the gesture, wondering what had possessed him to agree to this meeting, yet fascinated nonetheless by her full ruby lips, by the challenge in those amber eyes. Although it was true that they'd known each other for a long time, he'd no wish to be reminded of their youth, about how they'd once been more than friends.

He could see his father out of the corner of his eye, watching them from behind the counter. Gossip was rife over Fran Poulson and Papa did not approve. Marc wasn't feeling particularly proud of himself either, so what the hell did he think he was doing sitting here with her like this?

It was something to do with Fran's woebegone expression, with her plea that she was being treated as an outcast, nobody else prepared to speak to her. In any event, Marc found it hard to refuse a plea from a helpless female, particularly one who was pretty and sexy. Fran always had a charm, an earthy appeal that no red-blooded male could entirely resist; all the more beguiling because it was one she didn't always recognise in herself. He was aware that she'd been teased and bullied as a child, that she saw herself as fat not voluptuous, plain rather than pretty, constantly comparing herself unfavourably with her more slender sister. She crossed her legs at the knee and Marc inwardly groaned, for no one could deny that she had stunning legs.

He'd wanted to help, for old times' sake, but Fran, he realised, had other ideas on her mind. She'd made it very clear she was still interested in him. But was he interested in her? Marc asked himself if he wished to risk compromising the progress he'd made with Patsy, if you could call it that. She'd agreed to come to tea on Sunday, which was something, although there was no guarantee it would lead anywhere. Come Monday, she could just as easily slam the door in his face.

How many times he could keep on putting his head over the parapet only to be rejected and knocked down again, he really didn't know.

Marc glanced at his watch. 'I don't have time for this, Fran. You can finish mine too, if you like. I have a job interview this afternoon at Lewis's.'

'Good for you,' Fran said, panic shooting through her as she saw she was losing his attention. 'Did you hear about Paulden's fire? Wasn't that dreadful? The whole store destroyed in just a few hours. You wouldn't catch me working in one of those places. I'd get claustrophobia. Are you sure it's wise to want to work in one? I mean, what's wrong with staying on the market, working for your papa?'

'I'm not interested in spending my life selling ice cream, thanks. Anyway, Papa has other sons and daughters who can do that, once they are old enough. The Paulden's fire was unfortunate, but generally speaking a department store is pretty safe. Anyway, I need the job. It might be only the first step on the ladder but it would suit me perfectly, so I'll leave you to your strawberry ice and dash off, if you don't mind.'

She reached out to grab him, curling long, slender fingers around his wrist. 'Oh, but I do mind. I always used to think you and me had something going for us. We were mates once, if you remember.'

Marc laughed. 'That was when we were at school, and both young and foolish.'

'I'm still young and ready to be foolish with you any time, Marc. Why don't we take in a movie or something? And I seem to remember you were pretty cool on the dance floor.' She gave him that crooked smile that had once had him melting at the knees. The promise in it was undeniable.

His father appeared at the table. 'Marc, are you forgetting your appointment? You must not be late.'

He was on his feet in a second. 'No, Papa, I hadn't forgotten. I'm going now. Bye, Fran. See you.'

'When?' she cried, jumping up to chase after him.

'Um... I'll call you.'

Fran giggled. 'Don't be silly, why would you need to call me when I live just across the road? How about Friday?'

Papa Bertalone had followed them to the door, had heard her suggestion, and his frown deepened. 'Um, sorry no can do.'

'The weekend then?'

'I'm busy all this week. Sorry, Fran, got to go.' Marc cast an anguished look at his father and fled.

Chapter Thirty-Four

Sunday afternoon came and Patsy felt as if she truly were part of the family. They ate a delicious meal of macaroni and cheese, sausages and home-baked bread, everyone talking at once, with much laughter and joking as they teased and jostled each other.

The four little girls were even prettier, and since the days were cool now they no longer wore their multi-coloured dresses. Instead they all had brown skirts, and sweaters, knitted, predictably, out of rainbow-coloured wool. Patsy could see Mama Bertalone's knitting bag set beside her chair, brimming over with balls of wool in every colour of the rainbow.

The older woman saw her looking and smiled, then whispered something to her husband who translated for her.

'My wife say in our country, in Italy, we havea the sun to bringa light and colour into our lives. Here, in this grey land, you have to make it yourself.'

Patsy thought this was the loveliest idea imaginable, to knit yourself a rainbow or sew a scrap of sunshine.

As the remains of the meal were tidied away, many hands making light work of it, Patsy offered to help Mama Bertalone with the washing up. Papa Bertalone wouldn't hear of it.

'No, you are the guest. We will do that later when you young people have gone off to be alone. Now we sit by the fire and we talk. Italians, they likea to talk with their friends. It ees good, yes?'

He asked after Annie's health, and the hat stall. He showed Patsy his prize possessions: a miniature figure of the Madonna which had once belonged to his own mother, the bell from his father's horse-drawn ice cream cart, and a pressed flower taken from the bouquets carried by his small daughters at their first Whit Walk. His pride in his family was evident.

'And here are the boxing trophies of my sons Giovanni, Alessandro and Marc.' He slapped him on the back, laughing at Marc's embarrassment as he went on to praise his newly acquired artistic skills, and boasting of how easily he'd passed his examinations. 'He is clever, my boy, yes?'

The crimson tide of embarrassment spread right up Marc's neck into his cheeks. 'Papa!'

'Now he looka for the big job in the city.'

Smiling even as Marc cringed, Patsy was curious. 'What would you like to do, Marc?'

'Window displays! There are many big stores in Manchester. I'd like a job doing their displays. It's hard work, and very important.'

'It is *molto importante*,' Papa Bertalone declared. 'Very important! How will people know what you are selling if you don'ta show it off properly in the store window? Today my son will be the dresser of windows, tomorrow, who knows? The big artistic director, the man of business, *si*?'

Marc groaned. 'Don't start on that now, Papa.'

'And all my little princesses they will marry rich, wonderful husbands who will adore them.'

'Yeeesss,' chorused the little girls in question, climbing all over him for kisses and hugs, pulling his nose and ears as they fought to reclaim his attention. Patsy watched them in delight, laughing at the fun.

Later, once the little ones were in bed, she learned that Clara and her lover were not the only ones to suffer during the war. It was Patsy herself who asked to hear the Bertalone's story. She wanted to understand, thinking that it might help her to come to terms with her own past. Which, in turn, might assist her in sorting out her confused feelings about Marc, and making decisions about the future.

At first Mr Bertalone refused. 'We do not speaka of those sad times.'

'I wish you would. I'd like to hear your story. Isn't it important that we young ones understand what went before? Marc tells me you spent three years interned in the Isle of Man. And Clara has told me her story, how she had to escape from Paris, and from France.'

'Ah, yes, the sisters.' Marco Bertalone paused, seeming to sink into deep thought for a long moment, his kindly face solemn. '*Sì*, they were very brave, I think. All right, I will tell you quickly, then we speaka of other things, yes?'

Patsy smiled her thanks.

He spoke of a banging on his front door at midnight, of a military vehicle taking him away, leaving his wife and children to cope alone as best they could in their fear and horror. Yet he claimed he was lucky.

'I did not have to fight in the war as so many of our boys did, though I would have been glad to do so, had I been accepted on the side of the British. I did not drown in a sinking ship, like the Arandora Star, which carried hundreds of Italian internees and was sunk by a U-boat off the west coast of Ireland. I was the lucky one, *sì*?

'My wife, she suffered the curfew. The missing of my wages was a problem for her and for my children. She couldn't even makea the ice creama. Manufacture was banned because of the shortage of food. Marc was only four or five, and his elder sister Maria, whose wedding you attended, was only seven or eight, and there were two other bambini. Mucha worka for their mama. *Molti problemi!*'

Marc said, 'I remember being disappointed that we weren't allowed to take part in the Whit Walks, nor even permitted to have radios. Presumably we weren't trusted not to make reports to the enemy. Huh, as if we knew what was going on, or would have told if we did. It was insulting.'

'That is war,' his father remarked with a philosophical shrug, hands waving dismissively. 'The military, they have to do these things, to be safe. But we survived. The war ended and our British friends they welcome us all home, and we are happy again, *sì*? So enough of this solemn talk. You walka with my boy now. It is dusk, but young ones do not mind the dark, I think. Have this precious time together. Enjoy your youth. It will not come again.'

Patsy glanced shyly across at Marc to find he was smiling at her. Embarrassed now, but unable to refuse to go out for a walk with him since that would seem rude, she allowed Papa Bertalone to fetch her coat.

As he helped her put it on, he said, 'You mention the sisters, your dear aunts...'

'They aren't exactly my aunts.' Had Marc been telling his father about her? She cast him a fierce glance but he gave a little shake of his head, telling her otherwise.

Papa Bertalone shrugged. 'Whatever. They tell you how they escape Paris? What they were doing there? When they leave?'

'Yes. Annie was a teacher at the university, and they left early in the war, 1940, I think, when the Germans invaded. They escaped in a pig truck, of all things.'

'No, no. The truck of the pigs, that may be true, but it was much later that they leave. Paris was occupied and they did not get out until 1942 or 3. And they were very busy in that time. They show much bravery. *Molto coraggio*. You aska them whata they do in the war. Maybe they tell you.'

Patsy had believed she'd heard all there was to learn about Clara's life, except her own particular role in it. Now she saw that she had learned only half the story, that there was another intriguing insight into the sisters' lives in Paris to be gained. Yet another puzzle to be solved.

–

Having Marc walk her home in the dark was the last thing Patsy wanted. It only reminded her of how much she liked him, and she really didn't dare to think about that too much.

Yet there had been something different between them today. She'd felt far more relaxed than previously. They'd chatted and

laughed together, exchanged glances and smiles, as if they understood each other. He'd treated her with great courtesy and respect,
welcoming her into his home and the heart of his family almost
as if she belonged there. It had given her a warm glow inside.

But Patsy warned herself to be careful. It would do her no
good at all to get carried away and read more into this than there
actually was, just because she'd enjoyed being with the Bertalones
today.

'I think you enjoyed yourself,' Marc said, taking her hand as
they walked along.

Patsy couldn't help but smile. 'How can I deny it? You have
a lovely family. Your sisters are so bright and pretty. No wonder
their papa adores them. Thank you for inviting me. I hope I didn't
upset him by asking too many questions.'

'Always you are so curious, little one.' He tucked her hand into
the crook of his arm, stroking her fingers as he liked to do. Marc
was thinking that today had gone better than he could ever have
hoped, and wondering how much further he could chance his
arm. 'Have you asked Clara the big one yet?'

Patsy shook her head. 'Don't let's talk about it.'

'Have courage, my little lion-heart.'

'I will, I will. When the right moment comes, I will ask her
straight out – Are you my mother?' Patsy spoke in a mock-
dramatic tone to disguise the importance to her of the question.
'But first I need to prepare myself for the answer to be no. She
might laugh at the very idea.'

'It is not easy, I know, but I have every faith that you can deal
with it, whatever happens.'

She glanced up at his face then, saw not a trace of pity in it,
only a belief in her. It warmed her heart to see it. They seemed
to have reached a new understanding, one where Marc avoided
showing sympathy because he knew how very much she disliked
it.

'What did your father mean by saying how brave the sisters
were in the war, I wonder? What do you think they did?'

Marc slipped his arm about her waist and kissed her ear. 'Another question for you to ask.' And Patsy giggled. It felt good to be so at ease with him, to have someone who understood her uncertainties. 'May I ask you one?'

'What?' She looked up at him through her lashes, feeling strangely shy all of a sudden, deeply aware of the warm comfort of his arm about her, the intimate way he pressed her to his side.

'Will you come out with me again? Will you be my girl?'

She waited a beat before answering, her smile teasing. 'That's two questions.'

'Answer one of them then.' His eyes were on her mouth and she could feel it slackening in expectation of his kiss.

In the event she really didn't need to answer either question. The kiss said everything. When it was over, she lightly scolded him for taking advantage, although not really meaning it.

'A man has to take what advantage he can, where you are concerned, Patsy Bowman. You are so fierce, you make me shiver with fear!'

She laughed out loud at that, the very idea of Marc Bertalone being afraid of anything, let alone herself, seemed utterly ludicrous.

He gave the familiar Italian shrug. 'It is true. You are always scolding me.'

'And I shall scold you again. You shouldn't have told your papa that the sisters were my aunts.'

'I didn't, I swear. Cross my heart. Papa makes assumptions. You can trust me on this, Patsy. I've talked to no one about what you told me. I wouldn't wish to hurt you. You are the only girl for me. You can trust me on that too, because I think I am falling just a little bit in love with you.'

Patsy stood stock-still, heart beating loudly in her chest. She didn't ask herself how she felt about him as she studied his expression. She wanted only to read his mind, to judge if he was speaking from the heart or simply throwing her a line. He looked entirely serious, seemed so fervent, so genuine. Could she believe him? Could she truly trust him? Patsy's own expression was filled with doubt. 'I think you're spinning me a tale, a fanciful yarn.'

'Why? Why would I say such a thing if it isn't true? Why will you never believe what I say? Don't you trust my word, Patsy?'

And then, as he started to kiss her again, she began to think that it really didn't matter whether she did or not.

–

The autumn days were turning colder as winter approached so as a change of activity from the hat block, and aware of the need to bring in some profits, Patsy got out Clara's Singer sewing machine and fashioned a hat out of a remnant of striped fabric. She'd bought it from Winnie Watkins stall because it was not only cheap but beautiful, hand-woven in a rich palette of colours. It reminded her of the Bertalone girls. She would make a rainbow hat, bring a little sunshine into their lives. Patsy folded back the brim and caught it in place with a stitch here and there, then cut out a scarf in the same fabric to match.

'Should I add a tassel to the hat, do you think?'

'No, leave it just as it is. It looks almost Russian. I love it,' Clara said, full of enthusiasm. 'So will all the young girls who see it. I believe we have a winner here, Patsy.'

And she was right. Ignoring Patsy's modest reservations, she put the set out on display and it sold to a bright and pretty fifteen-year-old girl that very day. Patsy made two more and those sold too.

Clara was excited. 'Should we make more, do you think? Or is that it?'

Patsy said, 'We could buy different coloured fabric.'

'Yes, vary the design a little.'

'So long as it is warm for winter and suitably bright and cheerful.'

'I'm sure they'll sell.'

Clara offered to make some too. They were so close, such good friends on the same wave-length. 'Clara, there's something I wish to say...'

'Oh, I can see Winnie putting out a length of green and mauve. It looks like heather. Pop over and buy some, Patsy. It would be perfect.'

By the time she had done so, the hat stall had a sudden rush of customers and yet another opportunity was lost.

Chapter Thirty-Five

Molly stood in the back room of the Dog and Duck, managing to hold her ground as she met the gaze from Quinn's piercing blue eyes, although as always her instinct was to turn tail and run. She could feel the sweat under her armpits and it crossed Big Molly's mind that Quinn might be able to smell her fear, as she could scent the hostility emanating from him.

'I just want her scared out of that house, that's all. I want her to wake up to what she's let herself in for,' Molly said doggedly.

'And you think this is the way?'

'It might work.'

'It's not my normal way of doing business, Molly girl.'

'I know it's a bit beneath you, B... er, Quinn, but you could put one of your lads on the job, surely.'

He smoothed a hand over his chin, as if considering the matter, and rocked himself back in his chair. At that moment they were interrupted by a knock at the door and a pause was called in the proceedings while a young girl bustled in with a loaded tray, placed a heaped plate of roast beef and Yorkshire pudding before him, a pint of Guinness and a shot of Irish whiskey beside it.

When she had gone, Quinn swallowed the whiskey in one, tucked a napkin into the neck of his checked waistcoat, loaded his fork and began to eat. Molly stood silently watching, praying her stomach wouldn't rumble with hunger. She'd come here straight after closing the stall, hadn't even been home yet. Ozzy would be doing his nut. He did like his meals on time.

At length, Quinn quietly remarked, 'It'll cost extra, and so far as I'm aware you're still owing me from the last time. Is that not so, Molly girl?'

'I've fetched what I can.' She slid two ten pound notes across the table towards him. Quinn carefully folded each one and slipped them into his waistcoat pocket before considering her again, one eyebrow raised in mute enquiry. 'Aye, I know there's still another tenner owing. I'll have that by next week, end of October at the latest.' She would if she nicked it out of the takings as she'd done this month, hoping and praying Robert didn't notice.

'Plus another for this extra job.' He speared a piece of beef and wagged it in the air, inches from her face. 'Sure and I can see that you're a very determined woman, Molly Poulson. I'm glad you're not my mother.'

Molly panicked, wondering if it was hunger that was causing the tight feeling in her chest or whether she was about to suffer a heart attack. 'You don't touch my lass, right? Just scare the shit out of the Georges. I want her back home, without him. Is that clear?'

Quinn smiled. 'Crystal. Whether this will achieve your ends is open to speculation, but the choice is yours. The task will be carried out, forthwith, according to your instructions.' Pushing the loaded fork into his mouth he chewed on the beef, dabbed meticulously at a trail of gravy that ran over his full lower lip.

Molly cleared her throat. 'There's just one other small task. That lad my lass married...'

'You mean, your son-in-law?'

'He's no relation of mine.' Molly said, outraged. 'I hear he's looking for work, asking all over the shop. I want you to put out the word that he's not to be taken on, not by anyone who wants to stay friendly with us Poulsons.'

Quinn raised both eyebrows in wry amusement, speaking through another mouthful of food. 'And it's my clout you'll be using to get this message across, is it?'

'Aye.'

'Very clever. You mean them to listen, eh?'

'I do.'

'And you've money to pay for this little job too?'

'I'll find it.'

'Money to burn, apparently.'

Molly swallowed, a momentary doubt nudging at her. Was she making a big mistake? She was getting in deeper than she'd ever intended, but this feud wasn't over yet, not by a long chalk. If her daft daughters wouldn't listen to common sense, then she had to find some other way to make them understand. Wasn't that a mother's duty? She had to make Amy see what a mess she was embroiled in, what a mistake she'd made, getting herself involved with that stupid lad.

'Just make them Georges sorry they ever got took the Poulsons on, that's all I ask. I want my lass back home.'

'It will be done, Molly. All of it. It will be done.'

–

Amy was in the kitchen with Mrs George when it happened. She'd come to offer her help with making tea, as usual, and with her mother-in-law's resolve not to speak to her, or even acknowledge her presence, she had picked up a knife and begun to slice bread. Amy did her best to be friendly. It felt as if she were talking to a brick wall, but she was determined to keep trying.

'Hasn't it been a lovely day? The weather is just perfect, even if it is a bit cold. I love these golden autumn days, don't you?'

Mrs George reached for a colander and began to peel potatoes, saying nothing.

Amy gazed bleakly at the pile of neatly folded shirts on the kitchen dresser. 'Good drying weather too. Thank you for ironing Chris's shirts. There was really no need to trouble yourself though, I'd have done it for him this evening.'

Still no answer, nothing but the blank wall of her mother-in-law's silence.

'Something smells good. I must say you're an excellent cook, Mrs George. I'm sure we're very fortunate, Chris and I, to be so well looked after.'

The woman levelled her chin and ignored this compliment.

Amy felt close to despair. The fact that she and Chris were now married had changed nothing. It didn't seem to have made the slightest difference to relations between their families. The feud continued to bubble away in the background of their lives. The great barrier of animosity and anger was firmly wedged between the two families. No matter how hard they tried not to allow it to affect them, it was doing so.

The table was already laid with its lace edged cloth and pretty blue and white crockery. When the tea was ready they would all sit around it to eat in silence, as they always did. It was a wonder the tension in the room didn't give them indigestion. She wished the Georges would say something, anything. Maybe if they had a good ding-dong argument as her mam and dad were inclined to do, it might clear the air.

But the young couple's resolve to be happy in spite of the feud was gradually being worn down. Not only was there no physical contact between Amy and Chris, but they too would often sit in silent misery for hours on end, unable to find a single good thing to say to each other.

It frightened Amy to see her beloved husband so depressed, but she really didn't know how to put matters right.

Sighing, she reached for the butter, which was hard and would need softening. Mrs George wouldn't entertain margarine, and the bread had to be cut very thin, not in great doorsteps like Mam would cut. 'I do love your son, you know. All we want is to be together, and be happy. Chris is trying so hard to find himself a job. I can't understand why he's having such difficulties, can you? He's such a lovely bloke, and you'd think anyone would be pleased to employ him.'

It was then that it happened.

The brick smashed through the dining room window, landing amidst a shower of glass right in the centre of the pretty lace table-cloth, sending plates and cups flying everywhere. Mrs George let out a frightened gasp, and Amy stood frozen to the spot. They could hear other windows being smashed in the front of the house too.

For the first time Mrs George spoke to her. 'What is it? What's happening?'

Then another brick struck. This one came through the kitchen window right over the sink where her mother-in-law was standing. Amy never saw it hit her but it must have done, because one minute Mrs George was standing with the potato peeler in her hand, her face full of fear, the next she was lying on the floor in a pool of blood.

—

Chris's mother had to undergo nineteen stitches in her head, the windows had to be boarded up until a glazier could be found to put in new glass. Amy was left in no doubt that her own family were the ones responsible for this act of vandalism. For once, she lost her temper with her mother. She was shaking as she marched across the street to confront Big Molly. Never had her home looked more squalid by comparison with the stark tidiness of the George's, even with a great brick in the middle of their dining room table. 'What do you think you're doing?' Amy shouted. 'You could have killed someone back there.'

Molly kept her expression carefully blank. 'I haven't the first notion what you're talking about.'

'Oh, yes, you have. Don't play the innocent with me. Just leave me and Chris alone, and his parents. How will it help us to make a good start in life if you keep on attacking them?'

Molly adopted her most pitying tone. 'Come home, chuck, why don't you? It's not safe for you to be living with that lot. They've no heart, that's their trouble. They're evil. You've said yourself how hard it is, with them having sent you to Coventry an' all. That lad can't even support you, his own wife. Leave the bastard, and come home.'

'How do you know he can't support me?'

'I know he can't find work and nor will he, not in this market.'

Amy glared at her mother in cold fury. 'And how would you know about that? Is that your doing as well? I wouldn't put it past you. Why can't you just keep your interfering nose out of our business? You won't split us up, not if I've any say in the matter. If you starve Chris, or drive him out of Champion Street, I'll starve with him. I'll go with him to the ends of the earth. Got that?'

'You don't mean it,' Big Molly whined.

'I mean it right enough. Just you watch me.'

—

Amy and Chris found a place of their own, a tiny bedsit overlooking the fish market, which Dena Dobson told them about, but that didn't help as much as Amy had hoped. It was poky and damp, with barely room for anything beyond a bed and one chair, and it smelled strongly of smoked haddock.

Mr George put an advert in the local paper accusing an unnamed rival of trying to drive him out of business, but saying he was determined to withstand this cowardly attack and stay put. He also stuck up posters to the same effect all over the market.

As a consequence, since Champion Street folk were perfectly able to put two and two together as well as witness the devastation to the Georges' house: Big Molly's trade fell off and the Georges' soared. Her efforts had not had the desired effect. And now she was even more in Quinn's debt with nothing to show for it.

Neither Big Molly, nor Chris's parents, came near the bedsit, and when Chris and Amy called round to see how his mother was, Mr George stood on the front doorstep and refused to let them in. He said that she was still in bed with a terrible headache and didn't wish to see anyone.

'Not even me, her own son?'

'Not anyone,' he said, casting a sour glance in Amy's direction.

Chris continued to argue that he surely had the right to see his own mother, but to no avail. His father simply closed the door in his face. There'd been no contact between them since. It seemed the young couple were on their own, outcasts from both their respective families.

This, more than anything, deeply affected Chris. 'It might have helped if you'd tried to get on better with my mother,' he said reproachfully one day.

Amy gasped. 'But I did try. I used to offer to help make tea but she always shooed me away.'

'You should've persisted, peeled the potatoes at least.'

'How could I? It's her kitchen, not mine. I couldn't snatch the potato peeler out of her hand, could I? I would offer to set the table or wash up but she absolutely refused any assistance, didn't want me in the room. She wouldn't even let me do your washing and ironing. Any jobs I insisted on doing, such as buttering the bread, she put up with under sufferance. And she never spoke to me, not once, in all the time we lived under her roof. How was I supposed to deal with that?'

'She said you were difficult, constantly trying to take over and interfere.'

Tears filled Amy's eyes. 'That's so unfair. I'm damned if I do offer to help, and damned if I don't.'

Chris looked at her ashen face and was instantly filled with remorse. 'Oh, love, I'm so sorry. What are we doing, quarrelling over this awful business? Didn't we once promise ourselves that we wouldn't?'

Then they would kiss and make up, curl up together in their misery; yet still they didn't make love. All the fire and passion seemed to have gone out of them, replaced by a curious restraint, as if Chris were still holding back. Amy could only think that the long difficult months of not daring to touch each other, coupled with the antagonistic reaction to their marriage of their respective families, had in some way built a barrier between them too.

Somehow the feeling of being natural and happy together had dissipated. A strange awkwardness was growing between them, even a cool politeness, almost as if they were strangers and not a young married couple deeply in love.

There were occasions when all would seem to be well between them. Over breakfast when they were at their most relaxed, or if they met up in the afternoons, they would laugh over something that had happened during the day; still good friends like they had always been. Content simply to be together, ready to sit and chat or enjoy a bicycle ride.

But in the evening, when the door of the tiny bedsit was closed against the outside world, instead of feeling cocooned in their own private space, free at last from the simmering anger and resentment of their parents, an awkwardness would fall upon them, a pressure build-up between them. Amy had fallen into the habit of dressing and undressing quickly and furtively, in private, as she had done every morning back in the wood when they were striving to be sensible and not inflame each other's passion, which at that time had been so alive, so vibrant.

The fact was that although they at last had a double bed, the distance between them was now so great, neither was willing to make the first move, afraid of rejection, or too beaten down by family warfare.

Chris would climb into bed and read the newspaper while Amy lay silently beside him. After about half an hour, he would stroke her back a little or kiss the top of her head, switch out the light then turn on to his side, away from her. And the pair of them would lie, back to back, not speaking, not touching, overwhelmed by circumstance and their misery, as if they'd once been shown a fleeting glimpse of paradise but somehow the moment to savour it had been lost to them forever.

They'd lived together for over three months, had been married for almost one, and still they had not made love. Their love had not been consummated, and secretly each of them wondered if it ever would be.

Chapter Thirty-Six

Patsy couldn't stop thinking about Papa Bertalone's remark on how brave the sisters had been during the war. She longed to know more. She was also deeply troubled by Marc's casual comment that Annie may actually be her mother, and not Clara at all. The thought haunted her and eventually drove her, for the first time, to approach Annie on the subject.

She chose the moment when she was up a ladder tidying the hat boxes off the top shelves, handing them down to Annie for her to dust, and check out the contents before putting them back again, probably for another twenty years. A total waste of time in Patsy's opinion. But it seemed an ideal opportunity to engage in a little gentle quizzing.

Patsy so longed to be accepted, to feel secure. And Marc was right. One way or another, the only way to achieve any sense of security was to face her gremlins and deal with them. She had to discover the truth, no matter if it turned out to be the exact opposite of what she wished to hear. If she and Annie talked together a little more, she might persuade her to open up and warm to her, as Clara had done these last weeks. The only way to do that, Patsy decided, was to open up a little herself.

'I remember doing this sort of thing for Mrs Bowman, my foster mother. She was a great one for organising and tidying. Drove me mad, it did.' Patsy laughed, trying to sound relaxed and casual.

It was a moment before Annie answered, and then came a question, just as Patsy had expected.

'I trust she wasn't a cruel foster mother?'

'Not intentionally, only neglectful! Once she had children of her own she lost interest in me.'

'I see. That must have been difficult, hard for a young girl to understand and deal with.'

'Oh, I understood well enough. The reason was perfectly clear, but yes, dealing with it was hard. Mr and Mrs Bowman dealt with it by sending me away to school.'

'How old were you then?'

'Eight.'

'And where was this school?'

'Harrogate. That was the nearest town, about twenty miles from the village where the Bowmans lived.'

'So they were able to visit you often?'

Patsy shook her head. 'I don't remember them ever coming except on speech days and parents' meetings, when the teachers practically ordered them to attend.' The moment to change the subject had come, she decided. 'Your own family must have been so different. You were very lucky to have such adoring parents. Do you remember, Annie, telling me that your family home was in Southport? I was wondering why you decided to leave. I mean, it's such a lovely place, why would you want to leave the seaside to come to the heart of a city?'

She could see Annie frowning as she considered this, but the answer came, frank and open as her own had been. 'I had no reason to stay. It was my childhood home but I grew out of it. I was ready to stand on my own feet. You can understand that, surely? Such friends and good neighbours as we had were of my parents' generation, not mine.'

'What about Clara? Didn't she have any friends? Did neither of you have a boyfriend, for instance?'

'We led a very sheltered life.'

'Even so, did none of your neighbours have sons?'

When Annie said nothing to this, Patsy stumbled on. 'I ask only because if either of you did have a beau, as I expect you would call them, it must have been hard to leave. And Manchester is so different from Southport, so big and noisy, and it suffered badly during the war. Was there some sort of problem, did you feel compelled to move for some reason?'

Aware that the question was rambling on for far too long, she added to it out of sheer nervousness; Patsy couldn't seem to stop herself from talking. Yet Annie had now fallen stubbornly silent.

'You weren't involved in a wicked scandal or anything, were you?'

Patsy knew she'd gone too far almost the instant the flippant comment was out of her mouth. She could feel Annie almost physically withdraw. Cold fury emanated from her in waves as she gripped the sides of the ladder. Then with a sharp crack of her knuckles she rapped on a rung and ordered her to come down at once. The tone was such that not even Patsy considered defying it.

Standing before the older woman, she felt very much as she used to feel when standing before her housemistress at school. Patsy knew she was going to be punished but couldn't for the life of her think what she'd done to deserve it.

'I dislike this fondness you have for asking questions. I've been aware of you pestering my sister, winkling out of her all manner of indiscretions while I've been laid up.'

'She wasn't indiscreet, and Clara volunteered, so...'

'Do not interrupt when I am speaking. Now I learn that you have been pestering the Bertalones, which is unforgivable.'

'I haven't. I mean, they asked me to tea and...'

'And you interrogated them on what they were forced to endure during the war.'

'How did you know?'

'It may surprise you to learn that I hear a great deal of what goes on in this market. I am not the bumbling old fool you take me for. Mr Bertalone himself told me that you had been showing an interest.'

'He called you very brave and suggested I ask you to tell me what you did in France after 1940?' Patsy was holding her breath as she waited for Annie's reaction. It wasn't long in coming, and ferocious in its tone.

'Impudent child! How dare you presume to ask such a question? You are far too inquisitive for your own good.'

'Don't call me a child.'

'I shall call you whatsoever I choose. You have far too much to say for yourself, in my opinion, which shows lack of breeding and not a vestige of good manners. Perfectly vulgar! These endless questions must stop at once, do you hear? Nor will I have Clara upset. After she spoke to you the other week, many painful memories far better left in the past where they belong, were stirred in her by your obstinate persistence.'

Patsy was distressed. The last thing she'd wanted was to upset Clara, and she hurried to say as much. 'I'm sorry, I didn't mean to upset anyone, but I did have a reason for asking. A very good reason actually. I wanted to know because… well, because I think about my own past sometimes, and I thought that if Clara told me she'd ever been married, for instance, ever had a child…' There, she'd got it out at last. 'Then I might come to understand the reason—'

'Enough, I say! Aren't you even listening to me?' Annie clicked and whistled through her false teeth in a fury of impatience. 'We will have no more of these interrogations. You will leave Clara alone. She has endured enough of your poking and probing. Not another question, it stops right now, or you will indeed be out on the next bus. Is that clear enough for you?'

'Yes, Annie,' Patsy said, deeply contrite.

–

Patsy was looking for Marc. She was anxious to tell him of the utter futility of her latest efforts, to gossip a little over the scandal of the Georges' broken windows and speculate over the culprit, and eager to learn how he'd got on with his interview.

Since it was a Saturday, she went straight round to the ice cream stall and found him talking to Fran Poulson. Marc saw her and instantly jumped to his feet, hurrying over with a broad smile on his face.

'*Mia cara*, great to see you, do you fancy a Nut Sundae?'

'Don't call me that,' Patsy grumbled, as she always did without knowing why, then stared past him, right into Fran's eyes, and saw the triumph written bright in those amber depths. It was this expression, this purring gleam of satisfied superiority, which made her think that something was going on. 'I can see what it is *you* fancy!' And turning smartly on her heel, Patsy made to walk away but wasn't quick enough.

Marc grasped her by the wrist and pulled her up short. 'Hey, don't just walk away like that. What's biting you now? I thought you'd come looking for me. I hoped you had. Okay, you don't have to say it, I can see it written in your eyes – you wouldn't come looking for me if I were the last man in the world.'

'Got it in one.'

'Then why are you here?' He frowned and looked around in puzzlement, his gaze finally settling on Fran who still sat at the table. Until just a moment ago, she'd been pouring out her troubles, telling him how Big Molly must have lost her mind completely, how she'd get herself arrested if she carried on this fashion. 'Ah, I do understand that now. You thought that Fran and I were...' He put back his head and began to laugh.

Patsy didn't join in, and Marc's laughter quickly faded. Even Fran was looking less than pleased by his reaction. This clearly wasn't a joking matter for either girl. Yet again he'd said the wrong thing. He pulled Patsy close, his voice tender and concerned. 'It's you I want to go out with, Patsy, not Fran Poulson. Haven't I made my feelings plain enough? Just say the word and I'm yours.'

Fran appeared at his elbow and reaching up, cupped his face in her hands to kiss him full on the mouth. 'Thanks for the coffee and our little chat. See you later, alligator. Seven o'clock suit you? Oh, hi, Patsy. Byee.' And swinging her hips with blatant sexuality, she sauntered away.

Marc met Patsy's furious gaze, his own filled with panic. 'I can explain. This isn't what you think...'

'Get knotted!'

–

It didn't take long before word was spreading round the market that Fran Poulson was setting her cap at Marc Bertalone, and he was falling for it, hook, line and sinker. Which must mean that poor Patsy Bowman had very firmly had her nose put out of joint. Some took satisfaction from this, never having taken to the cheeky newcomer, while it gave others the opportunity to murmur fresh complaints against the Poulsons.

Without exception though, everyone had something to say on the matter. The goings-on of the Poulsons and the Georges was an entertaining diversion from their general worry over the future of the market.

'By heck, if anyone asked my opinion,' said Winnie Watkins to Lizzie Pringle as she bought her daily bag of Everton Mints, 'I'd say they could make a film out of this.' She pronounced the word 'filum' and Lizzie had to agree. Barry Holmes was for ringing up Paramount and offering to sell the story to them. 'Aye, well, that young madam needs her bottom smacking, and I might be the one to oblige.'

Lizzie giggled. 'Which one, Fran or Patsy?'

'Happen both, but no, I was thinking of that little Poulson tart.'

'We'd sell more tickets for folk to come and see you having a go at Fran than any picture house could to see Elizabeth Taylor. But I'd recommend you stay out of this, Winnie. There's big trouble brewing between the Poulsons and the Georges, and you don't want to get involved.'

'You're probably right. I have an awful feeling it'll end in tears, and it'll be them what's shedding them. How that poor young couple are coping with all of these carryings on, I daren't think. They have my deepest sympathy.'

At that moment Alec Hall sauntered over to inform them that he'd just spoken to Belle Garside who'd told him the development company had upped their offer, and she was seriously considering accepting it.

'No, she can't do that! Drat Fran Poulson and a pox on her daft mother, this is far more serious. Our livelihoods are hanging in the balance here. What do we do now?'

'Good question, Winnie,' Alec said. 'What indeed? The Extraordinary General Meeting we called did no good at all. Belle is steaming ahead regardless, transfixed by Billy Quinn's offer like a rabbit in the headlights of a car.'

'I'll go and bend her ear with my views on the matter, shall I?' Winnie suggested.

'Take care,' warned her friends, but Winnie was off, hot footing to confront her worst enemy.

–

Marc's pleas for Patsy to believe in his innocence seemed to be falling on deaf ears. 'Look, okay, so Fran was trying it on, that doesn't mean I was interested.'

'Oh, you were interested all right. I saw the way you were leaning over the table as close as you could get, looking right down her blouse.'

Marc responded to this taunt with exemplary patience. 'It wasn't like that at all. She was speaking in a quiet voice. I had to lean close to hear her properly. Things are in a mess in that family right now.'

'Huh, and they think they're the only ones with problems?'

'What's this? I never thought to hear Patsy Bowman wallowing in self-pity.'

'Damn it, I'm not!'

Nevertheless, the accusation hit home and Patsy winced. The pair of them were huddled in a music booth, Fats Domino singing 'Ain't That A Shame?' Utter misery was etched on both their faces.

You made me cry, when you said goodbye. Ain't that a shame?

Patsy let the music waft over her, hoping it would calm her down, trying to get a grip on the sick feeling that had settled in the pit of her stomach. Following Sunday tea with the Bertalones, and the walk home in the dark when Marc had confessed he might be falling in love with her, she'd felt a bit more disposed to trust him. She should have known better. It'd all been a lie, an absolute porky. But just the thought of Marc fancying Fran made her want to throw up. Why did nothing ever go her way? Why did she even allow herself to care? If he preferred the likes of Fran Poulson, then he wasn't the man she'd thought he was.

The music was beginning to annoy her, and Patsy reached for the door handle. 'I really don't know why I agreed to come in here with you. I'm off.'

Marc grabbed her by the shoulders, pulling her round to face him. 'Not yet, Patsy, please. Give me a chance, will you? You know you want to. Fran has a lot of problems right now, and we've known each other a long time, since our schooldays. She's also, for once in her life, concerned about Amy, usually at odds with her sister. I was just listening, being sympathetic, that's all.'

You broke my heart when you said we'll part. Ain't that a shame?

Patsy regarded him with a cool, appraising glance. 'Oh, is that so? You were just listening and being sympathetic, were you?'

Marc gritted his teeth. He wanted to laugh this off, tell her she was being stupid, kiss her and have done with it, prove to her here and now how much he cared for her. But that wasn't the way, not with Patsy. She was too sensitive to have her feelings ridden over roughshod, too raw and sore inside. 'Yes, I was. What is so wrong in that?'

Patsy shrugged her shoulders. 'Nothing, so what's happening at seven o'clock tonight? What was all that about?'

Infuriatingly, Marc gave his most dazzling smile, the one that made her go weak at the knees. It almost made her fall into his arms.

'I never expected you to be jealous, Patsy, never thought you cared enough. Maybe I should've talked to Fran, or some other girl, before now. But for your information, nothing is going to happen at seven o'clock, not tonight or any other night. She only said that to annoy you and it seems she's succeeded. Though maybe she's done me a favour. I like it when you're jealous, *mia carina*. When you are mad with me for talking to someone else.' He kissed the tips of her fingers.

Patsy's cheeks fired to a bright crimson and she snatched her hand away. 'I really couldn't care less which girls you talk to, or whether you're going out with Fran this evening, or not. Haven't I said all along that you are an incorrigible flirt, Marc Bertalone, and totally insincere? Now I have absolute proof.' And she whipped open the door of the music booth and stormed away. 'Farewell, goodbye, although I'll cry. Ain't that a shame?' she muttered largely to herself.

Alec Hall watched her go, saw how Marc slammed the heel of his hand into the doorframe and uttered a few furious words to himself. Alec shook his head in sympathy. 'Maybe I chose the wrong record for you today, huh? Still, take comfort from the fact that at least she didn't break it over your head this time.'

Chapter Thirty-Seven

Amy stared miserably at the calendar. It was an anniversary, of sorts. They'd been married more than a month and she was still a virgin. She couldn't go on like this any longer and thought that maybe she should see a doctor. There must be something wrong with her. She'd heard of women who were frigid. Was she one of them? Or maybe there was something wrong with Chris. She'd asked him if he would come with her but he'd dismissed the idea out of hand.

'You're not getting me to go to no doctor. There's nothing wrong, Amy. You're worrying unnecessarily.'

'Then why haven't we – you know?'

Chris avoided the agony in her gaze. 'Need you ask, with the way your family has treated mine these last weeks?'

'And what about the way your mother, and your father for that matter, have treated me? Doesn't that count?'

'My mother is ill in bed suffering the after-effects of concussion because of what your mother did. And it'll cost Dad a small fortune having all those windows renewed.'

'You've no proof Mam broke them, that's pure speculation.'

'It's a fair assumption. And if you'd just relax instead of weeping and wailing about things all the time, we might start to get somewhere.' He was very nearly shouting at her, and raising his voice. Amy's eyes filled with tears yet again, and she dashed them swiftly away, hating him to be proved right.

'Look at us,' she sobbed. 'We do nothing but fall out all the time, that's assuming we're speaking at all. Is it any wonder if I cry?'

'And whose fault is that? Where's the point of talking when we only end up with you blaming my parents for everything?'

'Or you blaming mine?'

'It was your mother who started it!'

'No! Your father's brother started it years ago when he caused the death of Mam's sister.' At this point, Chris slammed out of the flat, and Amy sank to the floor in floods of tears. It was their worst quarrel yet.

—

Attention may have been temporarily diverted from Fran's situation but hours later, when she returned to her friend's house, weary from a long day stacking boxes in the warehouse, Sal too had heard the gossip about her chatting up Marc, and bluntly asked her to leave.

'You know very well Marc is potty over Patsy. Why do you always have to prove your pulling power with men? Why do you have to interfere? You're just like your mother, always poking your nose in, trying to make other folk do what you want, determined to be in control.'

Fran saw that her bag was packed, standing ready and waiting at the front door. She was appalled. 'You're not throwing me out now, this minute, Sal? I've nowhere to go.'

'You should've thought of that before you got yourself into this mess. You should learn to show respect for other people. Pinching another girl's fella isn't the answer to filling the gaps in your own loveless life. You'll be after my Bill next.'

Sal opened the door. It was that time of day when goods were being stowed away, stacked into boxes and hauled off to lock-ups for the night. Stallholders were calling out to each other, enjoying a few jokes or making plans for the evening ahead. Fog was drifting in from the canal and dusk was already starting to fall. Fran was swamped with loneliness.

'Where the bleeding hell am I supposed to go at this time of night?'

'That's your problem, not mine. You could always try making it up with your mam.'

As luck would have it, Big Molly was standing at her own front door as Fran stepped outside. She was leaning on the doorjamb, arms folded as she watched the goings-on in the street. A couple of glaziers were fixing the glass in the Georges' windows opposite. She saw that Winnie was haranguing Belle Garside, which was always entertaining, waving her arms about and shouting that the market was more important than any stupid development, even if there was a housing shortage and a lot of money being offered. There'd be a punch up at any minute, the way they were going hammer and tongs at each other, all part of the rich texture of life on Champion Street. Molly considered stepping in to add her own two pennyworth, when she spotted Fran and her suitcase.

'By heck, what's dragged you out of hibernation? Don't tell me you've seen the light of day and come to beg for my forgiveness?'

Fran stared at her mother for a long moment, her gaze shifting to the Georges' broken windows then back to Big Molly again. 'Have you any idea of the trouble you've caused? Not satisfied with ruining Eddie and throwing me out into the street, now you're after Chris and our Amy.'

'I'm not after our Amy. I just want her to leave that lot and come home.'

'And you think this is the way to achieve it, by breaking all their windows? Why I should care I really don't know, only for once I'm on our Amy's side in this, not yours. You're turning yourself into a laughing stock, Mother, and what good will it do? They're married. Even you can do nothing about that, you stupid mare.'

'Don't you call me names!' Big Molly was out in the street immediately, the pair of them facing each other like two gunslingers at the O.K. Corral. Faces turned in their direction, work stopped, even Winnie and Belle paused in their heated argument to listen.

In her desperation and misery over the way her life had gone so badly wrong, Fran needed someone to blame other than herself.

Her voice rose several notches. 'You're an embarrassment to me, Mother, and to our Amy. Can't you see what you're doing? You ought to be ashamed of yourself, throwing bricks through windows at your age. Grow up, will you! More important, let us grow up. Leave us alone.'

'I didn't throw bricks.'

'Who did then? No one hates the Georges more than you do, so who else could it have been?' Fran looked into her mother's face and something inside her went cold, and her voice dropped to a whisper. 'Oh, no, tell me it's not true? Tell me you didn't involve that Billy Quinn in our Amy's problems too? Dear God, do you have a brain in that fat head of yours?'

'It was worth every penny.'

'And have you managed to pay off every penny?' Fran shouted, knowing full well how hard up her mother was.

'Not yet, but I will.'

Fran shook her head in disbelief. 'Whatever possessed you to get involved with the likes of Quinn? Once he's got his claws into you, he'll never let go.'

Molly had heard this remark during the last weeks more times than she cared to recall. Ozzy never stopped bleating on about it, morning, noon and night, jumping at shadows half the time. He'd even taken to staying in, not going half so often down to the pub, complaining that she'd ruined what little pleasure was left in his miserable life. Molly had stopped listening to him long since, and she had no intention of heeding a warning when it was issued by her own daughter.

'Right,' Fran said. 'That's it. You're on your own this time, Mam, and may the angels protect you, because I can't.'

For once in her life, she didn't have the appetite for a shouting match with her mother. She felt at her wits' end. Big Molly had ruined her cosy little affair with Eddie, now she was interfering in Amy's marriage and she'd ruin that too. So if somebody had her on the run, and Quinn could do that if he'd a mind to, maybe she deserved to suffer too.

Picking up her bag, Fran walked right past, nose in the air. Enraged, Molly shouted after her, 'I did it for you… for you and our Amy! You're my girls. I need to look out for you.'

Fran whirled about to scream at her mother, making heads turn once more. 'Not like this, you don't! This isn't the way. Just leave us alone, will you?' Then she carried on walking.

'Where are you going? Stop right there! Don't you walk away from me when I'm talking to you…'

'I'm done listening. You don't have any control over me now, you daft cow, so shut your face!'

'Don't speak to your mother like that?'

A soggy tomato hit Fran in the back of the head. 'What the…?' Now her own temper flared too and she turned furiously on Big Molly. 'All right, if you want a row, you've got one coming!' And scrabbling in the gutter she picked up several more pieces of rotten fruit that Barry Holmes hadn't yet swept away, and began to pelt her mother with them. Big Molly yelled like a banshee and began to throw equally vile stuff back.

Nobody made a move to stop them. Being entertained by the wild Poulsons was turning into a way of life, rather like the shorts before the big picture, though the way they'd been going on lately, it was more like a gala performance.

A door banged and Amy came running across the street towards them. 'What do you two think you're doing? Mam, stop it! Fran, give over and leave off, will you? You're making a spectacle of yourselves.'

She stepped between them her hands outstretched, and caught a heavy clod of earth right in the chest. She staggered for a moment then sank to her knees and collapsed in the filthy detritus left by a typical day on the market.

–

Amy was brought round by Winnie, who had come running with a mug of water, shouting at folk to stand back and give the lass air. Barry rushed to find Chris, believing that the poor lass would be in need of her husband after being knocked for six by her own stupid mother.

Once Winnie managed to get Amy sitting up, some colour was coming back into her cheeks, and she turned on the two warring women, venom in her voice. 'It might be none of my business but you ought to be ashamed of yourselves, the pair of you. What do you reckon you're doing to this little lass? I'll tell you you're destroying her. You sure as hell have nearly destroyed her marriage, so go home, and get out of my sight before I clock you both.'

'But—' Fran was about to say that she'd nowhere to go, but Winnie wasn't listening.

'Go *now*!'

Big Molly was visibly shaking. 'Is she going to be all right?'

Amy managed to find her voice. 'No thanks to you, but yes, I'll live. Now do as Winnie says, Mam. We've entertained the neighbours enough for one day.'

Molly turned on them all in her fury. 'Stop your gawping, the lot of you! As for you, Belle Garside, I'll speak to you later. I'm not done with you yet.' Then she marched into her own house, slamming the door after her.

Fran hunkered down to hug her sister and kiss her on the cheek. 'I'm sorry, love. I never meant to involve you in this stupid row. Don't let the daft cow bully you. Could I stay at yours tonight?'

'Oh, Fran, we only have one bed in our tiny room, how can you?'

'Never mind, it was just a thought.' She stood up to face the assembled company, her so-called friends and neighbours: Sal, Lizzie Pringle, Alec Hall and Sam Beckett, Jimmy Ramsay, not forgetting Patsy and the two Higginson sisters. 'Is anybody prepared to offer me a bed for the night?'

Her request was met by complete silence, no one willing to meet her gaze. Even Patsy didn't show a jot of sympathy. But then why should she, after the way Fran had tried to steal her chap?

Fran picked up her bag and walked away, straight out of Champion Street, although she hadn't the first idea where she was heading. As dusk fell, with various other friends' hospitality seemingly worn to shreds, Fran bedded down under the railway arches, furious with her mother and fiercely jealous of her sister's wedded bliss.

The ground was wet, hard and bitterly cold, but there didn't seem anywhere left for her to go, until Maureen found her there some time in the early hours and took Fran back to her place. The crinolined lady lamp was beaming rosily, the kettle was on the hob, and, after a bite of food and a sip of a hot toddy to warm her chilled bones, Fran fell into bed with relief, the smell of cheap perfume, excitement, and stale sex strong in her nostrils amidst the jumble of bedclothes. It felt very like coming home.

–

Amy could feel Chris's restlessness. He'd hardly slept a wink all week. Night after night he would toss and turn beside her, tangling himself in the sheets and muttering to himself if he did sleep, as if he were having some sort of bad dream. She wasn't feeling too good herself tonight, after this latest performance by her family. She hadn't suffered any lasting ill effects from being knocked off her feet, but shame over the very public brawl was eating into her. Amy wondered when her problems would ever end.

Chris had shown little interest in the tale, making the comment that nothing her family did would surprise him. What was happening to them all, and to her lovely husband in particular? He couldn't seem to find work anywhere, and if it weren't for Robert they wouldn't even be able to afford to pay the rent on this awful bedsit. Not that this fact pleased Chris. He was racked by guilt, hating to take money off his wife, which he saw as demeaning.

'But it's money I'm earning by working hard in Poulson's kitchens,' she'd told him. 'Not charity at all.'

'That's the point, Amy. It's money you are earning, not me.'

If they weren't falling out over their parents, it was about jobs, or money; Chris constantly complaining because he couldn't afford to take her out of an evening, not even for a drink or a bag of chips. He had no job, no car, no decent home to offer her. He called himself a useless husband, not worthy of the word. She hated to hear him talk this way, sounding so defeated, but no matter how often Amy assured him that it really didn't matter which of them earned the money, that she loved him anyway, nothing would convince him. He'd sunk into depression, overwhelmed by his own feelings of inadequacy and failure, and nothing she said could bring him out of it.

This evening, he'd come home late, clearly having had several pints of beer. Amy had made the mistake of asking him where he'd got the money from and he'd been angry with her all over again, shouting at her that his mates had bought the rounds, out of pity. She'd felt his own shame that, jobless, he couldn't afford to buy them one in return.

Amy was keenly aware that time was running out for them. If Chris couldn't find a job soon, if they didn't overcome this barrier between them, whatever it was, they'd have to leave Champion Street or their marriage would be over when it had hardly begun.

Now, aware of him tossing and turning beside her, Amy stroked his back. 'Can't you sleep, love?'

'I'm too uncomfortable. It's this awful bed. I can feel every spring sticking into me.'

Amy reached for him. 'Come here, and let me give you a cuddle. I'm sorry about what I said earlier, about you going to the pub. We really shouldn't quarrel like that. It only upsets us both when we argue about money and get involved in this blasted feud.'

'I know.' He stroked her cheek, kissed her gently on the lips and something shot through her. It was the first response to his kisses she'd experienced in a long time, and it thrilled her. Chris felt it. He kissed her again.

'I love you, Amy.'

'Oh, and I love you, Chris. So very much!'

He was stroking her breast and Amy could feel herself start to relax. It felt so good, just as it had all those months ago in the quiet of the wood. Then he pulled up her nightie, and, half dazed with sleep, smelling strongly of beer, lay on top of her. She was alarmed by the weight of him and the speed with which things were progressing. He'd stripped off his pyjama trousers and Amy could feel something large pressing between her legs. She had a sudden memory of her first sight of his erection and instinctively knew that she wasn't ready, wasn't moist enough to accept it. He'd kissed her only once, touched her breast only a little. It was too soon, too quick.

She felt him trying to penetrate her, pushing as hard as he could to get inside, grunting a little, and the harder he pushed the more she shrank and closed up. She felt dry and tight. 'No!' she cried. 'Not yet, give me time...'

'Damn it, Amy, I need you!'

'I'm sorry, I don't feel ready.'

'When will you ever be?' He jerked away, flung back the blankets and flounced out of bed, pulled on his trousers, and, as he did so often these days, snatched up his shirt and jacket and slammed out of the flat.

Amy sat bolt upright and called after him, her eyes wide with fright. 'Chris, don't go! Please don't leave me like this.' Everyone in the entire block must have heard his footsteps clattering down the stairs.

He crept back into bed around dawn, put his arms about her and whispered an apology for his impatience. 'I'm sorry, Amy, for being so clumsy. I wasn't thinking properly. I do love you, and I so want it to be good between us.'

'I know you do, it's all right, love.' He lay in her arms while she cuddled him and soothed him into sleep, but neither of them made a move to try again. By then her tears had dried but any urge to make love had gone.

Chapter Thirty-Eight

Patsy felt desperate for good news, for something pleasant to happen to her. She hadn't seen Marc in a couple of weeks, not since they'd had words in Alec Hall's music booth over that business with Fran. She hadn't seen Fran either, for that matter. Nor did she care. The girl had turned out not to be a friend at all, her behaviour serving only to renew Patsy's inherent distrust of people who tried, or at least pretended, to get close to her.

Why had she expected Marc to be any different? He might profess to like her, had even claimed at one point to be falling in love with her. What a tale! It had been nothing more than pity and a self-serving desire to get what boys always wanted: sex. And when she didn't come up with the goods, he'd turned back to his old flame, Fran Poulson.

The pair of them deserved each other. Patsy sincerely hoped they'd rot in hell. She wasn't going to give Marc Bertalone another thought.

But if that were the case, why did she spend so much time looking out of her bedroom window, watching the Bertalones as they filed out of a morning, as she had always done, aching to see one particular figure come striding down those steps? She longed for a glimpse of his dark curls, his wide smile, his strong athletic figure. Morning after morning she would watch for him, breathless with anticipation, and if he should appear, she drank in the sight of him, desperate for him to glance up at her window and smile at her, or give that famous wink of his. He never did, and disappointment would be a raw ache in her side all day.

By way of consolation and comfort Patsy concentrated on her hat-making. Keeping her fingers busy helped to keep her mind off what might have been. It prevented her from dwelling too much on the memory of Marc's delicious kisses, the ones that still turned her insides to water whenever she thought of them.

Today, Patsy was forming a hat from a swirl of pink georgette, while Clara was busily stitching flowers on to a cap of lime green tulle, to create a fun hat for a wedding. Customers were coming to them with specific requests now, asking Patsy to design a hat especially for them. She loved doing this, matching the colour and shape to their chosen outfit, creating a glamorous, chic and elegant look.

They'd also done well recently with a line in baker's berets in a range of jewel colours, which looked splendid all set out on display and were particularly popular with young girls. Clara had taken to selling the corsages she was so good at making. One of autumn fruits and berries could freshen last season's costume and make it look new and different.

Not that any of this was making Annie happy. There was a healthier bank balance and a slight improvement in her health, but she insisted on worrying and working too hard; claiming custom-made hats were an expense and a responsibility; that sales of a few berets weren't going to save them from penury.

'It's the way you're always so cheerful, Annie, that keeps us all going,' Patsy teased, making Clara giggle. Annie didn't even smile, but declared she was off to the wholesaler to buy some *proper* hats.

'Don't buy any more drab felts,' Patsy warned. 'They aren't selling.'

She could tell by the way Annie's mouth tightened that she disliked being told what to buy by the hired help, but a touch from her sister's hand silenced whatever riposte she'd been about to make, and she left without further argument.

–

Over in Belle Garside's cafe, Big Molly and her friend and comrade-in-arms Winnie Watkins were laying down the law over the threatened demolition of Champion Street Market.

'Over my dead body,' Winnie was saying. 'And don't take that as some sort of challenge, Belle. I mean, we won't let it happen, not at any price. We've had a meeting, several in fact, and all the stallholders are agreed. We don't want our livelihoods destroyed, not even for a wad of notes by way of compensation. We don't want no block of flats to replace Champion Street. For all its faults, its draughty old houses, mucky backyards and bent chimneys, we like it as it is, warts an' all, all right?'

'Aye, we do,' Big Molly agreed. 'So keep your mitts off it. And tell that Billy Quinn to do the same. He's not getting it, no matter how hard he pushes, or how much money he offers. He can look elsewhere for his so-called development.'

Belle Garside, with her pointed chin, heart-shaped face and skin like the hide of a rhinoceros, merely smiled at them with lips plastered in fuchsia pink lipstick. 'I heard you and Quinn were getting cosy, Moll, so I'm surprised you aren't more on his side. I should've thought it would be in your interests to get your hands on a wad of money just now. Isn't he pulling your purse strings a bit too tight for comfort?'

'By heck,' Big Molly said, 'you can't sneeze round here without somebody sending round word you've got pneumonia.'

Belle smiled, her violet eyes sparkling with mischief. 'Now don't take offence, Moll. You know you have my complete sympathy. Your Fran's not the first to find herself up the spout, and your Amy is a sweetie. It's just a pity that husband of hers can't get it up.'

Big Molly went puce in the face. 'How would you know?'

Belle gave an elaborate moue with her mouth, revealing a beguiling dimple at one corner. 'I was standing under their window, minding my own business, you understand, and I heard them arguing. It was perfectly plain what the problem was, I'm afraid.'

'Walls are that thin in this row, you can hear folk stirring their tea,' Winnie Watkins put in.

'Maybe he doesn't fancy her as much as he thought he did, or else he's been put off his stroke by his mother-in-law expecting him to be a real stud, just like his Uncle Howard.'

Before Big Molly could catch her breath to answer that one, Winnie hastily chipped in once more. 'That's a bit near the knuckle, Belle. It was a tragedy what happened to that poor lass. Moll has suffered enough over it, so leave off.'

'Oh, right! Okay, sorry, Moll.' Looking chastened, Belle tried and failed to get a smile out of Big Molly. The woman's fat cheeks were quivering with emotion. It looked as if she'd either commit blue murder or burst into tears at any moment but hadn't made up her mind. Belle quickly changed the subject. 'As for the market, am I to take it that you two are here as a deputation?'

'Whatever that is when it's at home, aye we are,' Winnie agreed.

'They're scraping the barrel this time, then?'

'Don't sharpen your wit on us, Belle. We're here to give you the opinion of all the stallholders, not simply our own. We won't agree to sell. We won't sign any form proposing to hand over our market plots, or our houses, to Billy Quinn, or any other developer for that matter.'

'He won't like that.'

'He can lump it.'

Belle's mouth pursed into a hard line of annoyance! She'd already planned what she would do with her own cut of the compensation, not to mention the little back-hander Quinn had promised her for pulling off the deal. She'd been considering a nice little property in the South of France, and an early retirement. Now she saw these dreams fade into the distance like a puff of smoke from one of Manchester's many mill chimneys. 'And this is the opinion of you all?'

'It is Jimmy, Alec, Sam, Lizzie, Abel, Barry, even the Higginson sisters who haven't two halfpennies to rub together. Everyone, in fact, and we've signed a petition.' Winnie handed over several sheets of paper filled with names. 'So don't try none of your tricks. The answer is no.'

'Right,' Belle murmured, stunned by the level of opposition. 'I'll pass your decision on, inform Quinn of your decision.'

'Light the touch paper and retire to a safe distance,' Big Molly warned.

Belle attempted a smile. 'I'll let you know how I get on.' And as the other two turned to go, she tried to have the last word at least. 'Maybe he'll agree to put it on the back burner for a while, allowing you all more time to consider your options.'

'We don't need more time,' Winnie said, incensed that they still didn't seem to have settled the matter.

And now Belle did smile, a sunny, sexy, crooked little number that would have had the men eating out of her hand, which was why Big Molly and Winnie had elected to be the ones to act as representatives. 'All I would say is that it isn't simply the stall-holders who have any say on this matter. You don't all own your own houses, do you? Some of you only rent, and the landlords too will be given their say.'

It wasn't till they were back behind Winnie's stall that the pair expressed their disquiet over this. Big Molly drew in a great breath and blew it out again as if her lungs were a pair of giant bellows. 'We never thought of that, did we, chuck?'

Winnie shook her head, looking troubled. 'No, this problem might come back to haunt us one day, if we don't watch out.'

–

Patsy apologised for being rude to Annie. 'But she's always against everything I say, and she lives in the past.'

'There will always be ladies who prefer what you term "drab felts", although I admit we shouldn't buy too many.' There was a short silence while they concentrated on their stitching before Clara continued. 'I understand that Annie warned you off talking to me, or at least asking any more questions.'

'I only asked if she was sorry to leave Southport, if either of you missed your friends.' Patsy did not feel it necessary to mention her own tenuous connection with that town, or her grandmother,

Felicity Matthews. It seemed more important at this juncture to ease Clara's concerns, and to reopen a channel of enquiry. 'I told her I was sent to school in Harrogate by the Bowmans, and how thankful they were to be rid of me.'

Clara looked stricken. 'That is so sad for you not to have enjoyed a loving home life. I can see, my dear, this may well be the source of your insecurity, and I'm not pitying you or even attempting to offer sympathy. I can well understand how that could grate. But there was really no necessity for Annie to take such a stand. She can be a bit too protective of me at times, which makes her sound fiercer than she means to be.'

Patsy was sceptical about this since she'd rarely seen Annie any other way, but made no comment and kept her attention on her work. Criticising one sister to the other, she'd discovered, was never productive. Clara could be equally as protective of Annie, for all they might often appear to be at odds.

Clara continued, 'I want you to know that I haven't once found your questions intrusive, Patsy. There have been times when I've wondered what you were driving at, when you'd get to what all this interrogation must be leading up to.'

Patsy looked up from her stitching, startled by this remark, cheeks flushed and feeling embarrassment ripe in her expression. 'Was it so obvious?'

Clara smiled. 'Why don't you ask it now, whatever it is?'

Patsy drew in a steadying breath. The moment seemed to have come out of the blue. She'd lived with the Higginson sisters for almost an entire year, and in all that time she'd never plucked up the courage. But this was the day, the hour, the moment, and she cleared her throat. 'Well, it's true that there is a question I've been longing to ask. I know you told me about your affair with Louis, but I asked you once if you'd been married, but you didn't properly answer. More importantly, what I really want to ask is, did you once have a daughter?'

'Oh, my goodness!' Clara dropped the scissors from her lap with a clatter.

Patsy spent several moments scrabbling about looking for them, heart racing, almost thankful for the diversion, as she felt unable to face Clara while she waited for her answer.

'Whatever makes you ask such a thing?' Clara gently asked, when order was once again restored.

'Well, I wondered if that was why you took me under your wing in the first place, not just because you felt sorry for me but because you missed your own daughter.'

Clara drew in a deep breath, which sounded remarkably shaky. 'You are a surprisingly perceptive young woman.'

'I'm not in the least bit perceptive. It was just a thought I had, and then I found a baby's shoe, among your things. You were right as I did go through your stuff, Clara. I was looking for a birth or marriage certificate, anything, which might provide an answer, and all I found of any interest was a pink and white silk shoe. Did it belong to your child?'

Clara was silent for so long that Patsy thought she might never answer and all this agonising would be for naught. There was on her face that same faraway expression she assumed whenever she was deep in thought, as if she'd been transported to another place, another time. At last she spoke. 'I did once have a daughter, though as you must realise by now, I was never married.'

To Patsy, in that moment, it felt as if the world had stopped spinning. She could hardly breathe for the tension clamping her chest. 'When was she born, was it in 1940?' The hat in her lap forgotten, Patsy laced her fingers tightly together as she waited for Clara to look at her and tell her that was indeed the year, and Patsy was that daughter.

Clara said, with a slight nod. 'It was January the fifth, 1940. We named her Marianne and she died of whooping cough before she was five months old. She was the child of my lover, and I – we – were both devastated by her death. I blamed myself because I was ashamed of my fall from grace. And Louis already had a family, as I told you.' She lifted her eyes to Patsy, half expecting to find sympathy and understanding, but what she saw in the young girl's face was utter shock and bewilderment, and something so terrible, she didn't even wish to put a name to it. 'What is it? What have I said?'

The girl seemed to be in a state of near paralysis, her face ashen, her whole body shaking.

'What is the significance of what I've just said? I don't understand… Oh, my God, that's the year you were born too.' Clara put a hand to her mouth. 'Oh no, is that why you've been asking me all these questions about where I lived, when I came back from Paris, whether or not I was married and if I ever had a child? You thought that child might be you, didn't you?'

Patsy couldn't have found her voice in that moment, even if she'd tried.

'Oh, my dear girl, what can I say?'

Patsy was on her feet, scattering half-stitched georgette, scissors, silk and pins everywhere. 'Don't say anything, not another word. I – I think I'll just go to my room for a bit, if you don't mind. I need to think things through.'

And before Clara could stop her, she was gone.

–

She was not Clara's daughter then, after all. This whole story had been nothing more than speculation on Shirley's part. Patsy was filled with unreasonable anger, not only towards the busybody neighbour who had first sown the seed of this idea, but also towards Clara herself.

Why had she not owned up to it before now? Why had she strung Patsy along like this for the better part of twelve months? In her heart, Patsy knew this to be unfair, since how could Clara have known she'd even imagined such a thing?

It was truly herself she was angry at, for being too afraid to ask the question sooner. Oh, but it hurt so much. The knowledge that she still belonged to no one, had no family of any kind was once again a deep, open wound in her heart. The pain was spreading across her chest, stopping her from breathing, even from crying.

Patsy had lived with this idea for so long that she had come to believe it to be true. Asking the question had seemed almost unnecessary, as if it were merely academic. Clara was her mother, she must be because Shirley had guessed as much; gossip and circumstance had made the idea so feasible that it must indeed be true. And Patsy had wanted, needed, to believe in this dream. All she'd required from Clara was confirmation of that fact.

But that confirmation hadn't come.

Instead, Patsy had received a very firm negative. She was not Clara's daughter, no relation at all. That was the deep-seated reason why she had been afraid to ask the question, because Patsy had known all along it was really only a dream, a fantasy, a product of her own desperation.

She had been in need of a mother so she had invented one, exactly as she had done when she was a child, lonely and afraid at school.

Now anger was replaced by shame. She'd made a complete fool of herself, not only with Clara and Annie, but also with Marc. She'd trusted and hoped, dreamed and believed, that her future might lie here, with them on Champion Street Market, but it had been nothing more than a foolish daydream.

And this was the moment when the dream ended.

Solemn-faced, she got to her feet. Still reeling from shock and without shedding a single tear, Patsy began to pack. She couldn't stay, not now that she knew the truth. The dream was over, finished, and she must move on.

Chapter Thirty-Nine

The doctor sat and contemplated Amy over the rim of his spectacles. 'Can't have sex, you say? And how long have you been married?'

Amy told him again. She couldn't remember ever having felt so embarrassed or humiliated in all her life. But much worse was to come.

The doctor told her to hop up on to his couch and he'd take a look at her.

Amy felt herself freeze inside. 'Is that really necessary? I mean we – we haven't got anywhere yet.' Most girls had a mother they could turn to in times of trouble. Amy's mother was the one who had caused her problem. She wished now that she'd asked Fran to come with her, but she hadn't seen sight nor sound of her sister in ages, not since the confrontation with their mother in the street.

'I need to examine you before I can help. Isn't that the reason you came?'

The doctor brought out a small black box and from it took out various pieces of plastic. Amy was bemused as to their purpose, but then he told her to slip out of her undies and her heart skipped a beat. What on earth was he going to do to her? She glanced across at the nurse standing nearby. The woman gave a brisk nod, indicating that she should get on with it, and stop wasting the doctor's time.

What he did was to test the opening of her vagina with various plastic penises, after having asked Amy to choose one, which was roughly the size of her husband's. Blushing furiously, Amy scarcely glanced at the one she chose. She wanted to cross her legs and slap his hands away, but the nurse had a firm hold of her knees.

'Now try to relax.'

Amy thought she would never be able to relax, not in a million years. However, he didn't just push the awful thing into her without thought, he put some jelly substance all over her, stroked her with it, then very gently began to insert it. But every time it got partway, she would feel herself grow tense and it would slip out again. He went back to the stroking. Just as she was beginning to think the sensation was not too unpleasant after all, he stopped.

'You're very tense, your muscles are seizing up every time. Vaginismus, if I'm not mistaken.'

Amy was appalled. If she had something wrong with her, which demanded such a long word to describe it, no wonder Chris had never wanted to make love to her. 'Is that very serious?'

When she was dressed again and seated once more before him, a miserable sensation of failure creeping through her, he gave her a kindly smile. 'Is your husband not very patient with you?'

Amy said, 'Oh, yes, he is indeed. It's just that he never wants to try. Neither do I. We've waited so long, months and months, and we've been living with his parents and—'

'Ah, then I should think the problem is guilt, and fear of failure. Anxiety is usually the cause of the vaginal muscles tensing. He is probably afraid of disappointing you, and you are worried about it hurting. And if you are both working hard, and you're tired or your parents are nearby, that will make the situation worse. Didn't you have a honeymoon?'

Amy shook her head.

'Well, couldn't you go away on holiday alone together somewhere?'

Amy thought of the months at Gretna, which had felt very like a holiday, at least at first, and anything but by the end. 'Not really! We can't afford one.'

'Then you'll have to take up walking or cycling. Get as far away from these parents you mention as you possibly can, then catch your husband unawares. Vamp him. You can do that, surely, a pretty girl like you?'

Amy smiled shyly at him. He was being so kind. She really didn't know what to say. How could she explain about the family feud, the terrible things her mother and Chris's father were doing to each other? It was unthinkable. 'I'm not sure—'

'A good sex life is essential for a strong and healthy marriage so you must put your mind to making more of an effort. You must, as I say, seduce your own husband. Kiss him and encourage him to kiss you. Undress in front of him, allow him to see you naked, or better still half dressed. Nothing arouses a man more than a half-dressed woman. And there are things you can do to yourself, to relax your own muscles.'

By the time he'd finished explaining, Amy was hot with embarrassment, itching to get out of the room and escape, if only from the open disapproval of the nurse. But the doctor was still talking.

'Try to make time for regular lovemaking, two or three times a week, or he might start looking elsewhere, and you wouldn't like that, would you?'

As she sat on the bus going home, Amy thought about the doctor's words. He had been very kind and gentle with her, had given her a book in a plain brown paper cover, which was supposed to help her. A mere glance inside at the diagrams made her feel utterly inadequate.

And she simply couldn't imagine herself deliberately undressing in front of Chris. Those happy, golden days of blissful, passionate ignorance when she'd peeled off her sweater and put his hands to her bare breasts seemed long gone. Going to see the doctor had done no good at all, only reminded her of what she had lost.

—

Fran was staying with Maureen, occupying her back room in her house just by the railway arches. At first no board or rent had been required, but then one day her landlady gently pointed out that she usually accommodated only working girls.

'I do have a job,' Fran said, anxious not to lose the only accommodation she could find right at this moment. 'I work part-time in a warehouse on the docks.'

Maureen chuckled. 'That's not exactly the kind of work I was thinking of. But if you're set on going straight, this isn't the place for you, chuck.'

She had known: Fran wasn't that stupid. She'd heard the muffled laughter, the snorts and gasps, the heavy tread of men's feet up and downstairs and the pounding of the bed head. She'd tried to imagine what it might feel like to have sex with a stranger, and, to her shame, the thought brought a flame of excitement to the pit of her stomach. They were just men, after all, like Eddie, most of them sad and lonely in need of a bit of tender loving care. Where was the harm in giving them a bit of pleasure?

Fran thought she could do with a bit of pleasure herself right now. She wouldn't object to a pair of loving arms and a randy young man. She regretted trying it on with Marc, since it had resulted in the loss of Patsy's friendship. Fran had really liked her. She had spunk, that girl, and had an interesting character, not like other namby-pamby wimps she could mention, her own sister included, Fran was sorry to say. Why Amy didn't stand up to the whole blame lot of them, she couldn't imagine. She was going to lose that lovely husband of hers if she didn't watch out.

Keeping hold of a man wasn't easy, there being plenty of predatory females on the look out. Patsy had over-reacted though, seeing her in that role, making a lot of fuss over very little. Nothing had happened, after all. It wasn't as if she'd been to bed with Marc, just shared a couple of ice creams, tried, and failed, to get a kiss out of him. Fran had only given it a whirl because she was bored and lonely, had felt in need of the challenge and a bit of a laugh.

And there was no denying that Marc was good-looking and worth the effort. Only she hadn't succeeded. She'd underestimated how besotted he was with Patsy.

What good was Fran now to any decent bloke, having had an affair with a married man and an illegal abortion? Spoiled goods, wasn't that what her mother had called her? Tarnished, damaged, ruined. Fran pulled the covers over her head to blank out the sound of Maureen's happy cries and whimpers. What of it? She'd never been one for half measures.

Anyway, there was money to be made in this game. Maureen said as much the following morning, when Fran asked her about it, and made no secret of the fact that she enjoyed her work.

'There's few men haven't woken in a strange bed, a whore's bed, at least once in their lives. The poor chaps have a hard time of it, trying to please their wives while still bringing home the bacon. It's a tough world. Don't they deserve a bit of fun? Where's the harm in a bit of slap and tickle? And a girl has to find some way to keep the wolf from the door, eh? If you'll pardon my pun. Want to give it a go, girl?'

Fran hesitated. 'Don't people look down on you? Aren't you an outcast? Couldn't you get arrested?'

'Yes, yes and yes, in answer to your questions, but who cares what other folk think? I've coppers for clients so I'm safe enough. And with your looks and youth, you could make yourself a tidy sum. I'd be sitting pretty if I hadn't been robbed of what was rightfully mine.'

Fran was agog. 'Robbed? How? Who robbed you?'

'It was my own fault, I should've known better. If you do decide to go on the game, girl, watch who you take on for clients. Don't go for them with shifty eyes, or the odd ones who don't talk.'

By the time Maureen had finished describing all the strange men a working girl might encounter, how to avoid the violent ones and to stay clear of pimps because they were the ones who robbed you blind, Fran began to think that maybe it wasn't such a good idea after all.

But Maureen only laughed. 'It doesn't have to be that way. Mostly you get young lads out for a bit of a laugh or eager to lose their virginity, and sad old farts who can hardly get it up. I've a sailor and his mate coming to see me later. Let me know if you'd like a taster, without obligation. Help yourself if you're interested. Be my guest.'

She made it sound like a bite of cherry pie.

–

When the two sailors in question did turn up later that evening, one patiently waiting in the living room while the other was taken upstairs, Fran crept down the stairs to take a peep at him through the crack in the door. He was young with fair hair, little more than nineteen or twenty, and clearly nervous. She could tell that by the way he turned his sailor hat round and round in his hand, and kept glancing about him. It reminded her of her own first visit here, on less pleasant business.

Fortunately, Maureen had also educated her on how to avoid such a predicament happening in future. Given her a right talking to in fact. Never again would Fran forget to use proper protection, for any number of reasons. When the young sailor turned his head and she saw how good-looking he was, Fran pushed open the door and strolled into the room.

He jumped to his feet, his handsome young face flushing crimson, and Fran's heart went out to him. If this wasn't his first time, she'd eat that flipping hat of his. She took it from him and tossed it on to the cluttered table. He watched it settle on the milk bottle and then his eyes met hers.

'Sorry if I startled you, love, I was just looking for Maureen.'

'She's upstairs, with m–my m–mate.'

''Course she is.' Fran considered the young man, treating him to her most dazzling smile. 'And poor you has to play second fiddle, eh?'

'I – I d–don't mind waiting.' He paused, then as his gaze roved over her plump breasts and long, shapely legs, went on in awed tones, 'I wouldn't mind waiting a bit longer, if I could have you instead. I've nothing against Maureen but she's...'

Fran laughed. 'A bit old?'

The flush deepened, sliding the length of his throat right along his strong square jaw. His mouth was good too, wide and generous, the lips full and slightly parted. With excitement, she assumed. My God, the poor beggar was panting for it.

Fran could never have said afterwards, what made her do it, but one minute he was gazing entranced into her eyes, the next she had him by the hand and was gently leading him upstairs. The first time he came so quickly he very nearly missed his shot altogether, but Fran soothed his disappointment and told him that since it was his first time, he could have another go for free.

'Any more for the roundabout?' she said, wrapping her shapely legs about his skinny waist. 'Ooh, that's better. Good lad, push hard. Yep, there we go! Steady as she goes, m'boy.'

Before his allotted time was over he was growing adventurous. Fran taught him how to explore her with his tongue, and carried out a similar service for him, which seemed only fair. And for his third and final effort she demonstrated a little trick using a chair arm, which proved to be both inspiring, challenging and good fun. Fran hadn't had such a good time in months, not since her last encounter with Eddie, and even that had been a bit below his usual standard. This was far more exciting than stacking boxes in that flipping warehouse, or serving steak and kidney pies on her mother's stall.

Chapter Forty

Clara wouldn't hear of Patsy leaving, not until she had found other accommodation and suitable employment, at least. 'Just because things haven't worked out as you'd hoped, is no reason to throw away all you've achieved this last twelve months. What about the hat-making, and the customers who have come to rely on your skill and care? And we still need help on the stall. We still need you, Patsy. We're very fond of you, you know.'

Patsy blinked, feeling the sting of tears at the backs of her eyes. 'Why would you care about me?'

Clara smiled. 'Because you're you, so what better reason could there be? You put yourself down too much, dear. Let's leave things as they are for a while, shall we? See how we get on. Annie and I have talked about this and we wouldn't be able to rest in our beds at night if we thought you were out in the cold, without a place to lay your head. I'm still riddled with guilt that we did nothing to help Fran Poulson.'

So that was why they wanted her to stay: out of a sense of guilt, not because they liked her at all.

Carefully watching Patsy's reaction to her words, Clara seemed to recognise her mistake and tried to put it right. 'Not that we feel guilt that you're different, Patsy? You're almost family, even if you're not.'

There it was again, that word. Almost. Never just 'a part of', never 'belong'. But then, how could she expect that? The sisters were just being kind, and, thankful as Patsy was for the respite, to have this time to collect herself and to make proper plans for her future, yet she'd really no wish to discuss her own situation right now. It was too raw, too painful.

She gladly turned her attention to Fran's problems, for all Patsy felt little compassion for her. 'Fran Poulson doesn't deserve any help.'

Surprisingly, it was Annie who disagreed with her. 'She's a fellow human being, a neighbour, and it was our Christian duty to offer help and succour in her time of need. I believe she's living with harlots, rogues and vagabonds now, from whom we could have saved her.'

Patsy couldn't help smiling at this picturesque language. 'I very much doubt anyone could make Fran do anything she'd no wish to, but I'll go and have a word with her, if you like? See if I can straighten her out.'

Clara said, 'Goodness, are you prepared to do that, Patsy, after the way she chased after Marc?'

Patsy shrugged, not feeling half so generous or confident as she might sound. 'Why not? It takes two to tango, as they say. If they did get up to something, which they surely must have judging by the triumphant glances she was sending me, then he was to blame too. Anyway, word has it she's staying with that Maureen. I know the house, I've been there before.'

'Indeed?'

'Er, that time when Fran came down with a stomach bug!'

'Ah yes, I remember. Well, do take care,' Clara warned. 'We wouldn't want you catching such dreadful ailments.'

Patsy gave a wry smile. 'I intend to avoid any possible likelihood of that.'

Annie said, 'I shall come with you, just in case.'

'Oh, no! There's really no need. Besides, she'd never talk to me with you present.'

'Then I shall wait at the end of the street until you are done. Do not argue, Patsy. I insist, it's my—'

'Christian duty, I know.' And she smiled fondly at the older woman. 'You're quite a card, do you know that, Annie Higginson? Nobody can say you haven't got spunk too.'

They made unlikely companions, the pair of them, and Annie an incongruous protector. Nevertheless, Patsy found herself glad of her no-nonsense presence as they made their way through this particularly disreputable neighbourhood.

The sight of Annie's rigid, statuesque figure marching along in an ankle-length grey coat and hat, walking stick in hand, with Patsy doing her best to keep pace with her long strides, would be sure to keep the vultures at bay. Even the most notorious youths would think twice before tackling this familiar figure. Wasn't she the one who used to whack them over the head with her hymnbook if they sang out of tune, when they'd been young enough to be bullied by their mothers into attending Sunday school?

Fifty yards from Maureen's door, Annie stopped. 'I shall wait here. If you're not back in fifteen minutes, I'll come looking for you.'

'I think half an hour is more realistic. Fran isn't going to be easy to convince, and she and I were hardly the best of mates.'

'Very well then, thirty minutes, not a second more.' Annie tapped her walking stick on the pavement, to show that she meant business.

Patsy glanced about her at the grim, impoverished maze of streets huddled together under a confusing canopy of railway arches; at the overcrowded back-to-back houses, half of them still lying derelict, bombed-out shells not yet cleared away following the war. Kids played amongst the rubble, using old air-raid shelters as hideaways, taking their lives in their hands as they explored broken down factory buildings with treacherously unsafe floors. Fog from the canal roiled around the old-fashioned lamplights, making the street look like something out of a Dickens novel Patsy had once been made to read at school.

She shivered. 'Will you be all right here on your own, Annie?'

'I've been in worse danger than this in my lifetime, Patsy. Be back in thirty minutes. I'm counting down from now.'

And as Patsy was ushered into that familiar living room with its well-remembered, nauseating smell, she felt grateful for Annie's support.

'If you were looking for Fran, she's not here.'

Patsy stared at the woman called Maureen in surprise. 'Not here, then where is she?'

'Ah, that's a good question. Cup of tea or cigarette?' Maureen moved to set the kettle on the stove but Patsy shook her head. The thought of eating or drinking anything in this house made her come over all queer.

'No thanks! I have someone waiting for me at the end of the street. A friend, you understand.' Making it sound as if she had a strong male in tow, not an old woman.

Maureen tossed aside a heap of dirty underwear and slumped down in a chair, darkly muttering something about not knowing why she stayed in this business. Patsy propped herself on the edge of a kitchen chair, waiting impatiently while Maureen lit a cigarette, took a long drag on it, letting the smoke drift out through her nostrils.

'You were going to tell me about Fran?'

The woman focused upon Patsy with difficulty. Was she even sober? Patsy could see a half empty bottle of gin on the table next to a stinking milk bottle. At last she began to talk, to explain how Fran had wanted to give the life a try and had taken to it, apparently, like the proverbial duck to water.

'But then, she'd had a good taster, a young sailor lad. No kissing, I says to her. Owt else you do is up to you. I think she fancied him, silly cow. Then she went out on the street last night, which didn't turn out so well. She complained the bloke smelled and refused to deliver, if you take my meaning. It must have been Dell the Pong, who works for the council on the rubbish carts.'

Patsy hid a smile. 'Fran is surprisingly fastidious, considering she lived with Big Molly.' Not that Patsy blamed her for that. The very thought of doing *it* with a perfect stranger, whether he ponged or not, turned her stomach.

'Aye well, she'd already told me she'd no intention of stopping here, in this hole. How she had big plans and intended to move up in the world to better paying clients. Fast!'

Maureen took a quick slug of gin then explained how she'd given her some advice, to which Fran clearly hadn't listened because the next time she ventured out, she'd got herself mixed up with Billy Quinn.

'I believe he came looking for her. I warned Fran not to have anything to do with him. He's evil is Quinn, but according to the other "girls" he was flashing money around like a man with ten arms and Fran fell for it. She was having a bit of a run in with Elsie at the time and then Quinn happened along. She's a liability, that woman. Most of the "girls" stand by each other, but not Elsie. She's one on her own. Anyway, they had this set to, then Fran went off with Quinn. According to my mate Rita, Quinn offered to install her in his Pleasure Palace, as he calls it. Some bleeding palace! She'll be pandering to the dregs of society in there, and nothing and no one will get her out of Quinn's clutches now.'

Patsy was struggling to take this all in, horrified by what she was hearing. 'But why would she go? Fran isn't stupid. She doesn't even like Quinn. And when did this happen? You haven't seen her since when exactly?'

'Yesterday, when she chucked out Dell the Pong. Like I say, my mate Rita saw her this morning, out on the street. She kept out of sight while all this was going on, but Rita heard everything. Apparently her mam owes Quinn money, and he's decided that Fran, or at least the value of her services, will be in lieu of payment. Rita says Fran didn't look too happy about it, but went with him anyway.'

'Oh, my God! I don't suppose she had much choice. Does Big Molly know?'

Maureen drew hard on her cigarette. 'I'm not going to be the one to tell her. Are you?'

Patsy considered. 'I reckon I must, and just have to hope she doesn't decide to crack the pavement with my head when I do.'

Big Molly looked at Patsy as if she'd run mad. 'You dare to stand there and tell me that my lass is on the game? My Fran?'

Patsy had sent Annie off home, so that Clara wasn't worried about them any longer than necessary, while she spoke to Big Molly alone. But one look at the woman's furious expression and Patsy began to doubt the wisdom of that move. Big Molly was more frightening than any gang of youths down by the canal. 'That is what I've been led to believe.' Best not to be too definite, she decided.

Big Molly's great fat cheeks seemed to expand with fury, turning an odd shade of purple, and her eyes popped. 'It's that Maureen character, isn't it? The one who sorted her when she fell pregnant to that Eddie Davidson.'

Patsy had no choice then but to tell Molly what Maureen had told her, how Fran must now be under Quinn's control, how he must have lured her into one of his 'palaces' in lieu of Big Molly's debts. 'It's very much a strong possibility.'

All Molly's anger at once evaporated, and the older woman appeared to shrink in size like a punctured balloon. They were standing in her kitchen. Neat as a new pin, and with not a sign of baking equipment in sight it seemed to have lost its soul, rather like its owner. Patsy thought Big Molly might be about to keel over, as the colour drained from her face, and she actually swayed on her feet, the size of meat plates though they may be. 'He wouldn't do that to me. I promised I'd pay by the end of the month.'

'Yes, but which one?' Patsy dryly asked.

'He wouldn't hurt my lass, just because him and me have a bit of outstanding business to clear up.'

'It seems he would. He has.'

The big woman's knees gave way under her and she sank into a kitchen chair, her head in her hands. Patsy couldn't help but feel sorry for her as she'd got herself, and her daughters, into a right pickle, one way or another.

'Oh, my giddy aunt, what have I done? Oh, Lord, what have I done?' She grabbed hold of Patsy and almost shook her. 'What will it take to get her out of there?'

'Leave off, Molly. How should I know?' Managing to extricate herself from the woman's frantic grip, Patsy took a chair at the opposite side of the table. There was only so much she was prepared to do in the name of friendship. Tackling Quinn was way beyond that. 'This really has nothing to do with me. It's your problem. Yours and Fran's, and Billy Quinn's.'

Big Molly leaned across the table, fat fingers clasped tightly together as if she were praying. 'You must go and ask him for me. Now, before he does something to her. I can't go. He'd not agree to see me. What with the interest and the extra charges for another little favour he's done for me recently, I daren't go near him without a wad of notes in me hand. Our Ozzy won't do owt, and who else is there, if you won't? No one on this market will give me the time of day right now. Even trade on the pie stall is dropping off something shocking. Just ask him how much it'll take to get my lass out of his clutches. You can do that for me, can't you?'

Patsy was shaking her head. 'Not if I want to live, I can't. Why the hell should I? Like I say, this is your problem, not mine.'

'I love my girls to bits. You must make him see that. I only wanted the best for them.'

'You've a funny way of showing it. I'm glad I haven't got a mother, if you're an example of the breed.'

It came to Patsy then, in a moment of startling revelation, that just because a person had a mother didn't mean their life was simple or easy, that the streets were paved with gold for them, their path through life smoothed and the relationship everything they could wish for. Mothers made mistakes too, even if they did love their children. Patsy had no reason to doubt that Big Molly loved hers, for all her misguided attempts to control them and make them do what she thought best. And Fran and Amy loved her too, amazingly enough, which was why they were all in this mess, she supposed. Relationships could be complicated, however close the blood tie.

Patsy gave a weary sigh. 'I suppose there may be times when outside help, from someone not so emotionally involved, comes in useful.'

They were interrupted at this delicate stage in negotiations by a furious hammering at the front door. They heard Ozzy curse loudly. He'd been watching television in the living room, studiously avoiding the issue of recalcitrant daughters, but they heard him shuffle along in his slippers to answer it.

Big Molly went on talking. 'Are you prepared to sit back and do nothing while Quinn helps himself to my girl?'

'Are you?'

The kitchen door burst open and there stood Chris, wild-eyed and ashen-faced. 'Tell me Amy is here. For God's sake tell me she's here, and safe.'

'What?'

'Amy has disappeared.'

–

Once they'd calmed Chris down sufficiently to speak, he told them the tale, still in such frantic anxiety they could hardly take it in. 'I haven't seen her since I came home for a bite of dinner about one o'clock. I went to the kitchens looking for her but your Robert says she didn't go back to work this afternoon. I've been looking for her everywhere, asking everyone. She was last seen talking to Billy Quinn. Nobody's seen her since. Tell me it's not true and he hasn't got her? That she's here with you.'

Big Molly groaned, wrapped her arms about her plump bosom and rocked herself, making little keening sounds like a woman in the throes of grief. 'Oh, Jesus, Mary and Joseph, I never expected it to come to this. Oh, hecky-thump, what have I done?'

'What have you done?' Chris roared.

Patsy jumped to her feet, fearing there might be blue murder done any minute. 'Not now, Chris. This isn't the moment for a row. We have to find Amy.'

They searched everywhere, even Ozzy too, who was desperate to find his little princess, hammering on doors, calling on other stallholders, friends and neighbours, but Amy had apparently vanished off the face of the earth.

Patsy heard a shout, and, looking up, saw Maureen hurrying towards them, emerging from the fog like a spectre. The market folk were accustomed to her presence in and around Champion Street, and largely ignored her, few were prepared to speak to her, nor did anybody approach her. Thankfully Maureen came straight over to Patsy and drew her to one side, away from the curious stares of onlookers.

Flushed from running, her hair standing on end like a bird's nest, she was clad only in a tatty old dressing gown and slippers. But even as she struggled to catch her breath, she was scrabbling in her pocket for a cigarette. 'I've dashed over here to tell you something, girl. I've heard a bit of news from a punter. It's right, what I suspected. Quinn has got Fran, but worse than that, he's got her sister too.'

Patsy went cold. So it was confirmed that Quinn had them both. As she looked over to Molly, she saw the big woman crumble to her knees on the cobbles. She'd read the awful truth in Patsy's face and collapsed.

Chapter Forty-One

Their worst fears had been realised. They were back in Big Molly's kitchen, Chris too, and no one was objecting to his presence. Patsy was saying, 'I'm prepared to give it a go and act as intermediary, but not without taking Quinn a sweetener. You have to find some money, Molly, to prove you're serious, even if you have to sell every stick of furniture in your house to find it, right?'

'There isn't time for that!' Chris shouted.

Patsy put a hand on his arm, as Clara did with Annie. 'No matter what, you aren't coming. You'd lose your rag and then we'd be in a worse mess.'

'Don't ask me for any money,' Ozzy said, his eyes wild with fear. 'I'd give me right arm for our Amy and Fran, and might have to if Quinn turns nasty, but I haven't got a bean. I haven't dared place a bet in weeks, thanks to you,' he shouted at his wife.

'And what about your gambling debts with Quinn? They haven't helped either,' Big Molly shouted.

Patsy tried to calm them both down, saying that falling out between themselves wouldn't solve anything. Looking shame-faced, Ozzy suggested they borrow the money from the pie stall takings, until Molly reminded him that Robert had already been to collect it.

'Ask for it back then,' he said. 'These are our girls, and that's as much our money as his. We can't stand back and do nothing.'

Big Molly was on her feet, needing to be doing something, anything, rather than sit here moaning. 'Aye, you're right, lad. Stay here, the lot of you, you included,' she instructed the hapless Ozzy, 'while I pop round to our Robert's.'

It didn't take her more than a few moments, since her son only lived on Hardman Street, but he point-blank refused to help. 'If any sister of mine wants to go on the game, she deserves all she gets, but I'm not bailing her out.'

Molly kept tight hold of her patience, knowing that losing her temper wouldn't help, acutely aware that if she started a row her prissy daughter-in-law would order her out of the house. Nevertheless, she was at pains to emphasise that Amy had not chosen to do any such thing, and the cash was meant to save his sisters from this fate worse than death. Robert wasn't listening, and his sour-faced wife wasn't either. The prim and proper Margaret stood right beside Robert, looking very much as if she'd been sucking lemons, muttering prophecies of doom for those who chose not to exhibit proper moral standards.

'I'll have you know that our Amy has very high moral standards, and our Fran, well, she has a big heart, I'll say that for her,' Big Molly stated, a comment received with a snort of derision. 'If you and Robert don't help your own family, for God's sake, Quinn will have them girls shut up in that rat hole he calls his Pleasure Palace, quicker than a cat catches a mouse, and then what? Have you considered what he's going to use them for? Have a heart Robbie lad, these are your sisters we're talking about.'

'You got the cat bit right, anyroad. I'll not help no toms, no matter what the excuse, even if they are related to me.'

Big Molly was outraged. 'Amy isn't a prossie! Don't even suggest such a thing.'

Robert looked troubled, but Margaret was unmoved. 'Happen not, but my husband is not going to be the one to tackle him. Billy Quinn is the vengeful type and could make all our lives a misery. Anyway, I doubt even Quinn would have the nerve to touch Amy. He'll see she's an innocent and let her go. As for Fran, she'll just have to take her chances.'

'Chances?' Ignoring Margaret, Big Molly glared at Robert. 'You're so afraid of getting your hands dirty, you're willing to take a chance on your little sister's virtue?'

'You'll not find much virtue left in our Fran! Let her look after our Amy for a change. She got her into this mess.'

'Absolutely,' chimed in Margaret. 'Let Fran take her punishment and reap what she has sown.'

'By heck,' Big Molly said, struck dumb by their selfish attitude. 'If you ever make a mistake, girl, and set yourself alight by accident, don't expect me to blow the fire out. I'll make sure you suffer for your sins in exactly the same way.'

Faced with the brick wall of Robert's refusal, Big Molly had no choice but to return to her kitchen empty-handed. Oh, but things would change in future. Once they were out of this mess, she'd put her pie stall back on a different footing altogether. Robert wouldn't get away with ignoring his own kith and kin, and depriving his own mother of her hard-won profits.

With no one else to attack, Big Molly railed at Ozzy, banged a few kitchen cupboard doors, then sat down and sobbed her heart out into her mucky pinny.

She'd done this to her own girls. She was the one who'd got Amy into this, without any help from anyone. It was all her fault. Oh, God, but she was sorry. Whatever the daft cows had done, they didn't deserve this, not to be used as playthings by Quinn and his mob. Big Molly's heart nearly gave out at the thought. Oh, Christ, what had she done? And how the hangment was she to put it right?

–

Chris was the one to save Molly's skin. He borrowed the money from his father, although he had a *royal* battle getting it out of him, with Thomas George at first shouting that he'd do nothing to save the skin of a Poulson.

'Amy is my wife for God's sake! If you don't help, Lord knows what he'll do to her. I'll never forgive you for that. Never! I'm convinced Quinn is the one who put word out and stopped me getting work. Now he's taken my wife! Do you seriously expect me to sit back and do nothing?'

Grumbling vociferously, Thomas George finally dipped into his retirement fund and loaned his son the necessary sum. Big Molly was forced to swallow her pride and accept it, since the risk to both her girls was desperately serious. She knew that although she was the one who'd involved Quinn in the first place, the one who had got them into this mess, there was no way she could get them out of it without assistance. She didn't have two halfpennies to rub together. The worst of it was that Thomas George, her hated enemy, had been told her part in all of this. Now shame licked through her like a forest fire.

'I'll pay him back,' she cried. 'I'll not be in debt to the George family.' This seemed to Molly almost more terrible, more humiliating in her eyes than owing money to Quinn, though admittedly less of a danger to her nearest and dearest.

She turned to Patsy. 'It's all up to you now, lass. You're my lucky charm.'

–

Patsy didn't feel like someone's good luck charm facing this awesome responsibility. Realising the Higginson sisters would be worrying and waiting for her, tense and anxious, Patsy quickly slipped next door to let them know what was happening. Once she'd outlined the plan, they were far from happy. She point-blank refused Annie's offer to accompany her on this occasion, knowing that she'd be more likely to alienate rather than placate Quinn. And Clara was simply too nervous to be of any use at all.

'Don't worry, I'm expecting to be in and out in no time, and Chris is going to hang around outside, as Annie did when I visited Maureen, while I go inside to talk to Quinn.'

Clara was wringing her hands with anxiety. 'Chris should go in with you. What use is he down some back alley?'

Patsy disagreed, telling them Chris wasn't himself at the moment: when she'd said they all needed to keep their heads and not go charging in with guns blazing, he'd muttered something about wishing he did have a gun.

Clara nodded, still looking deeply worried. 'I can see that Chris losing his temper wouldn't help in the slightest. But you'll be so vulnerable, Patsy dear, and it's getting late.'

As one they glanced out of the window. Dusk was falling for all it wasn't yet seven o'clock, the fog growing thicker. Although it felt like twenty-four hours since Maureen had brought them the news, it was in fact less than one. Quinn usually called in at the Dog and Duck for his supper between eight and nine. Patsy intended to catch him earlier, before he left his so-called Pleasure Palace.

'Leave it till morning,' Clara was urging her. 'It will be much safer in daylight.'

'And what about tonight? Who knows what could happen to those poor girls before morning?' A point the sisters silently conceded.

Annie suggested they call the police but Patsy pointed out that this might get Big Molly into trouble too. 'She's been no innocent in all of this, but we've agreed that Chris will call them if I'm not back out again within thirty minutes.'

'I shall call them myself in that event,' Annie firmly stated.

Patsy smiled at her. What a trouper she was. 'Give me a bit of leeway, Annie. It's a fair walk there and back.'

Clara quietly asked, 'What makes you think you are the right person for this task, Patsy? You say Big Molly has interfered in her two daughters' lives, what gives you the right to do the same? Why do you imagine you are the one to help?'

Patsy looked at her for a moment, unspeaking. It was a question she'd already asked herself many times. 'I don't honestly know. Maybe I can't help. But I feel I have to try because I've made mistakes. And I know what it feels like to be stuck in an impossible situation and have no one to turn to. I always thought that having a mother must be the answer to all of life's problems. Now I see that it isn't. We make our own luck here, and whether we have a blood tie with a person or not, we are still responsible for them. We're all part of one big family, in a way, here on

Champion Street Market. I'm not sure if any of that makes sense, if I'm explaining myself correctly.'

Clara smiled. 'No, you're explaining yourself perfectly, very clearly indeed. We are each responsible for our neighbours, our friends, the people we love. I hope, when this is all over, you and I can sit down and talk again, Patsy. Carry on where we left off the other day.'

Patsy nodded. 'I'd like that.'

Annie said, 'And we'll hear no more talk of you leaving, not until everything that is worrying you has been thoroughly discussed and aired. Is that clear, girl?'

She smiled, although Annie's face was oddly glimmering, almost as if Patsy were looking at her through a veil of tears.

'As for this business tonight, don't worry,' Patsy assured them. 'I'm neutral in this and acting only as intermediary, nothing more. Quinn has nothing against me personally. I mean simply to ask him what he wants to settle the matter, and be out of there in double quick time.'

Clara, however, remained adamant that proper provision be made for Patsy's protection. 'I can see that Chris might be the wrong person to go inside the place with you, being far too closely involved, but nor should you go in on your own. You need someone with you, someone at your side who is not directly involved but a steadying influence, to show Quinn that you are not alone but have friends too. I shan't allow you to go otherwise,' Clara cried in desperation. 'Someone has to look after you, and since you don't have a mother, who else is there but me? Anyway, I feel I'd like to apply for the role, if it's vacant?'

Patsy blinked, could find no response to this startling remark. Clara merely smiled, then instructed her to stay right where she was and not move an inch until she got back. 'I believe I have the answer, the very person.'

The person she had in mind was none other than Marc Bertalone. He came willingly, ready to help even before he'd heard the whole story, agreeing with Clara that Patsy should not tackle Quinn alone.

As he walked through the door of the little house, the blood rushed to Patsy's cheeks, her whole being glowing that he should come so quickly in answer to her need. Even so she pretended to object, not wishing him to see how pleased she was. And she refused point-blank to allow him to accompany her.

'Oh, yeah, this will look good, me going to speak to Billy Quinn with a protector in tow. Though what you would hope to do if he did turn nasty, I really can't think.'

'Thanks for the vote of confidence.' Marc folded his arms, standing before her with his legs astride, making it abundantly clear he had no intention of leaving.

Patsy frowned. 'Go home. If I ever do need help, I'll be sure not to call on you.'

He merely smiled at her droll wit, but Clara had turned awkward for once. 'Please humour me on this one, Patsy. You would be far too vulnerable on your own. I doubt my nerves could stand it.'

Patsy stared at the older woman in bemusement, saw tears standing proud in the grey eyes. Even Annie had taken out her handkerchief and was busily blowing her nose. Could Patsy's safety possibly matter so much to them? The thought caught her off balance, made her uncertain how to proceed.

She began with a loss for words, then fixing Marc with a fierce glare she briskly rallied. 'Don't think this means you're forgiven because you're not, or that I care a jot about your stupid friendship with Fran Poulson. I'm doing this for Amy, and for Big Molly, oh, and I don't know why. Maybe because I'm a bloody fool.'

'No profane language,' Annie put in, quick as a flash.

'Right, Annie! I'll make sure I remember that when Quinn is hanging me up by my thumbs.'

A small silence fell before each of them realised this was Patsy's attempt at a joke. Whether she'd still be laughing when she came face-to-face with the man himself in the house they called Quinn's Pleasure Palace, was another matter entirely.

–

The walk from Champion Street to the least salubrious part of the docks was scary. Patsy was used to her own company, to walking out of an evening, and watching other people stepping out for a night on the town, but not round these parts. With the fog rolling in off the Manchester Ship Canal, the squeaking of rats in the drains and under the bridges, and the inevitable darkness of the narrow streets and alleyways around the canal basin, she was glad enough of Marc's company.

They walked quickly and in silence between smoke-blackened warehouses and tumble-down sheds, stepping over the criss-crossing railway lines that linked the various wharfs, anxious to get the job done. As they paused by a stack of timber to catch their breath, Marc asked in his soft, gentle tones, 'Are we still speaking?'

'I haven't lost my voice, have you?'

'You know what I mean, Patsy.'

There was awkwardness between them that hadn't been there before. But then she'd made it very clear, during the last conversation they'd had in Alec Hall's music booth, that she'd have nothing to do with a man who two-timed her, a man she couldn't trust. Patsy knew that there was something going on between Marc and Fran. Why else would he even be here? Didn't this prove it? She said as much now. 'I know why you've come, because you want to help Fran.'

'I told you Fran is an old friend, but that doesn't mean there's anything more to it than that, or that I'm not here for another reason entirely. Because I care about you.'

She saw the glimmer of moonlight on the wide black expanse of water, could smell the damp of it on the night air, and lowered her voice to a whisper. 'No more lies Marc as I don't want to hear them.'

'They're not lies. I've missed you, and hope you've missed me.'

There was urgency in his tone now as he pulled her to a halt, and although she couldn't see the expression in his eyes in the half-light, she sensed he wasn't smiling. Anger pulsated from him, as if he were exasperated with her. 'Well, haven't you?'

A slight hesitation before she answered, time enough for Patsy to recall the times she had missed him, ached for him, longed to feel his mouth on hers, to smell the intoxicating warmth of his skin. 'Why would I? I've been too busy with my hat-making.'

He drew an angry intake of breath. 'You've looked out for me though, every morning. Don't think I haven't noticed. I understand your reluctance to get involved with me, until you feel more secure about staying here, but it's been nearly twelve months now. The sisters would have asked you to leave long since if they'd wanted to. Besides, isn't it up to you? There are others jobs you could do here, even if they did sack you. And I've got a good job too now, the one in Lewis's that I went for, remember? I've more money in my pocket, a good future before me. Couldn't we start again? Won't you give me another chance? I swear I'll never so much as glance in Fran Poulson's direction, let alone share an ice cream with her, however innocently.'

Patsy found herself swaying towards him, wanting desperately to believe him as her heart raced with renewed hope. And then Chris emerged from the shadows, and grim reality struck anew.

She said, 'This isn't the time. Let's concentrate on the job in hand shall we? Getting a stupid girl out of a fix.'

Chapter Forty-Two

Fran was seriously frightened, her usual cocky self-assurance slipping away fast. Some palace this was! Although it was big, with heaven knows how many rooms leading off its endless corridors, and high ceilings and plaster cornices reminiscent of a grander past, it had been somewhat neglected in recent years. It smelled of cheap scent, bad drains and fear; this made her wonder what the former Victorian shipping magnate or mill owner, a stern Methodist who'd once owned this place, would think of its current role.

Fran didn't know whether she approved of it herself.

Amy was huddled beside her, weeping, silently frightened; she didn't have the first idea what sort of place this was, or what fate awaited them.

Fran did. If only she hadn't met up with daft Elsie. The old slag had threatened to take her face off, if she didn't move off her patch. Fran had denied wanting her patch. It was cold and wet, a freezing wind blowing a gale under the arches and she'd almost made up her mind to jack it in and go home. Eating a bit of humble pie with her mam would surely be preferable to life out on the streets, if this was representative of it. Before she could move, the old cow had gone for her, screaming and wailing like a banshee. Then Quinn had appeared out of nowhere, like magic.

Fran realised now that he must have been following her. Elsie had been taken away by one of his henchmen, poor cow, while Quinn had spelled out the facts of life to Fran.

Oh, they were in a terrible mess all right, and Fran knew who to blame for that: their mother. Quinn had taken great pleasure in explaining how he'd beaten Eddie Davidson to a bloody pulp, at Big Molly's request, and blackmailed her into paying hush money. And later, when he'd picked up Amy too in lieu of those same debts, he'd laughed like a drain as he revealed how he'd been asked to break all the windows in the Georges' house, as well as putting out the word not to employ Chris George, in a vain attempt to persuade Amy to leave him and go home.

Not that any of this came as any great surprise to either of them, but hearing it spelled out that their own mother had deliberately set out to harm the men in their lives filled them with cold fear. As always, Big Molly had made a mess of it by not having the money to pay Quinn off.

Therefore he'd collared her two daughters instead.

'Don't I deserve some compensation?' he said, pinching Fran's chubby cheeks with nicotine-stained fingers. 'You're not my taste, sweetheart. I prefer my girls skinny, like your little sister here, but I know plenty who relish a handful of female flesh, to be sure.'

Fran had felt sick, longing to slap his hand away but unable to summon the courage. She was evidently to be handed around among his mates like some sort of apple dumpling after the main course, and these were not handsome young sailors, these were hard-faced villains, men with twisted minds and no soul. Meanwhile, Quinn himself would slake his lust on Amy as and when he chose.

They'd spent most of the day locked in an upper room with three other girls in a similar situation. Fran couldn't believe this was happening. It was one thing to decide to seek out a bit of excitement on her own account, but quite another to be used by Billy Quinn and his cronies for theirs. Fran knew she wouldn't see a penny for the work she'd be asked to do for them.

As for Amy, Fran could see that she wasn't really taking it in. Her eyes were glazed with shock. Far better if she didn't, but reality would kick in and she might never recover from this. Fran found herself unexpectedly overcome with a rare compassion for her sister, and putting an arm about her, pulled her close.

'Don't worry, chuck. I'll get you out of this see if I don't. I'll not let the bastards touch you.'

'How, Fran love? How will we get out?'

'I don't know. I'll have to give that a bit of thought.'

Oh, God, why hadn't she listened to Maureen and gone back home? Why hadn't she listened to Amy and not got herself involved with Eddie Davidson in the first place? She'd kill him with her own bare hands when she got out of here.

'When do you reckon he'll come for us?' one young girl sobbed. She couldn't be a day over fifteen but her da owed Quinn a bundle, and until he paid up, in full, the poor lass would be his play thing. And she too was skinny, just like Amy.

Fran tried to reassure her. 'Happen not tonight. But by tomorrow I'm sure your da will have settled up, eh, and you can go home. Our mam will have too, then we all can.'

The sound of weeping came from the corner of the room where two other girls sat, obviously less comforted by her words. 'You don't reckon he'll sell us to the white slave market, do you?'

'Naw, that don't exist no more,' Fran scoffed, doing her best to sound confident, though the idea brought a fresh chill to her heart. She made a private vow to kill Quinn first, if she got half a chance, before she started on Eddie Davidson. After those two, she'd start on the rest of mankind.

The girls became aware of a commotion downstairs, a loud hammering on the front door. They heard someone curse and trundle along the hall to answer the knock. Fran pressed her ear against the locked door, hoping to hear what was going on. 'It might be my da,' said the skinny girl.

'Or Mam?' Amy suggested, her eyes bright.

Fran could only hope so.

–

So here she was, in the lion's den, face-to-face with the man himself. Marc's parting words that she should approach Quinn with caution were still ringing in Patsy's ears.

Chris was stationed just outside at the corner of the building with a view to front and side. Patsy had persuaded Marc to stay round the back, on the grounds that he'd be more use to her there to call to for help. He'd break in the back door to rescue them if something went wrong. The two young men were to be her cavalry. They'd come riding to her rescue if things turned nasty, although she sincerely hoped it wouldn't be necessary to call on them. Patsy was keenly aware that even the three of them together possessed precious little power set against Quinn's bully boys.

But Marc had not recommended that she marched right in, casually duck under the arm of the heavy set character who'd opened the door to her, and push past two others who were far too surprised to stop her.

Quinn was regarding her sudden appearance with a startled expression on his face, as well he might. It was almost as if a house mouse had leaped up through a crack in the floorboards and bitten him.

'And who might you be, to come knocking on my door at this hour? Wasn't I just on me way out for a jar and a bit of supper?'

'I'll not take more than a minute of your time.' Patsy cleared her throat and tried to smile, hoping and praying Quinn couldn't hear the way her heart hammered in her chest. And that Marc and Chris were well within calling distance. Squaring her shoulders, she stoutly continued: 'I've come to ask you one question, that's all. It's from Big Molly, as you might have guessed. She wants to know what it'll cost to get her girls out of this place and back home.'

Quinn regarded her from beneath dark, lowering brows for one long, frightening moment, blue eyes glinting like chips of ice, then he put back his head and roared with laughter. He laughed so much that he had to hold his sides, aching from the effort. His heavies also relaxed and began to laugh with him as if he'd made some sort of joke, although Patsy guessed it was because they were privately every bit as scared of their boss as she was.

'And why would you care what happens to them?'

Patsy was still wondering very much the same thing. Had she completely lost control of her common sense, to put herself in this seriously risky situation? One big family indeed! She might feel sorry for Amy, but she didn't owe Fran a thing. 'You do have them both, right?'

'I do.'

'It's Amy I'm concerned about, if not... at least... and I'm friendly with their mam, sort of. Big Molly did me a favour once, let me off after I nicked one of her pies.' Damnation, now her tongue was running away with her. Pure nerves! Why the hell had she mentioned that?

Quinn's expression sharpened. 'So you're not the young innocent you appear?'

'Leave the Poulson girls alone. Let me take them home, that's all I ask.'

'I'd advise you not to interfere.'

'If I see something wrong I try to put it right, so don't think you can bully me.' Patsy set a bundle of dirty notes on a small round polished table. 'Molly says she's lost track of what she owes you, and guesses there'll be a bit extra to pay anyway, for a recent favour you've done her apparently, but this is the best she can manage right now. You've only to name your price, if more is required, and she'll find it.'

'Will she indeed? And will she go on finding it, month after month, to save her little darlings?'

Patsy paled, startled by the prospect of long-term blackmail, the possibility of which had never occurred to her. 'I – I wouldn't know about that. I expect she was thinking more of a fixed sum than a regular payment.'

'Indeed. Yet it's my neck on the line, I'm thinking, should the rozzers come round asking awkward questions? Doesn't that cost a deal of money, if a body wants to be safe?'

Quinn picked up the dirty, crumpled notes and began to count them. When he was done, he folded the wad in half and shoved it into an already bulging waistcoat pocket. There were three other pockets in the dandified, checked waistcoat, Patsy couldn't help noticing, equally well stuffed with cash. 'I make that thirty quid, which just about covers what she owed me from our first bit o' business, not counting interest for the extra three months she's taken to pay it. Fetch me the same again tomorrow, and the two wee colleens can go home to their mammy.'

Patsy gasped. 'Thirty pounds is a lot of money! How could Molly find that all over again within twenty-four hours? She's not bleeding Rockefeller.'

'That's the deal. Take it or leave it.' Quinn's smile had turned cold as he ran an assessing eye over her, from the top of her silvery fair hair tied up in a ponytail, lingering over the pert line of her breasts in the red sloppy joe sweater, and down the slender line of her black toreadors to the tips of her toes in their flat ballerina pumps. 'Unless you were thinking of changing places with the wee lass yourself? I could offer a discount if that's the case.'

Patsy's temper fired up. Nobody looked at her as if she were a piece of meat on a slab. 'I'll tell you what the deal is, mister. You take the thirty pounds, and here's ten more for that extra favour you did Molly, including any interest she might owe. An over-inflated price for breaking a few windows, I'd say.' Patsy had been holding the last few notes back, just in case she needed a bit more bargaining power. Now she slapped them down, one at a time on the table.

'Make it twenty and they're yours.'

She counted out five more one-pound notes. 'That makes fifteen, on top of the original thirty. My final offer! I take Fran and Amy home with me this minute, and there's an end of the matter. You've had your pound of flesh. This comes to an end, right now, or it'll be the police coming knocking on your door next time.'

The silence that followed this rash remark was terrifying. Patsy wondered what on earth had possessed her to speak so forcibly. She must have run mad after all. She'd lost her marbles, gone completely doolally to be issuing such dangerous threats to the likes of Billy Quinn. She could hear the heavy breathing of his bouncers as they drew closer, almost feel the brutality emanating from them. They could squash her like a fly with one tap of their weighty fists, the merest pressure of the heel of one thumb. Should she call out for Marc? He'd come running fast enough, but could he get here in time? Could Chris? Would they arrive before she was mincemeat on the floor?

The silence dragged on, giving her ample time to notice how those chilling blue eyes glinted menacingly at her from beneath beetled brows. Quinn was known as a man short on patience, and as he stood before her, thumbs hooked in his bulging waistcoat pockets, rocking slightly on his booted heels like a tightly coiled spring, Patsy prayed she hadn't stretched it too far.

'Did nobody warn you not to cross me?'

Patsy nodded.

'Did they tell you how dangerous I was when roused?'

'They did, but I didn't come alone,' she said. 'I have friends outside.'

The words were barely out of her mouth when the door creaked open and there stood Marc, arms folded over his broad chest, an expression on his face, which surely meant business. Chris was right beside him.

Quinn regarded them both in silence for a moment then slid his amused gaze back to Patsy. 'Is this the best you can do?'

Patsy didn't flinch. She kept her gaze steady, a directness to it that many found appealing, and others disquieting.

Quinn began to laugh. 'Jesus, Mary and Joseph, but I like you. Have we ever seen spunk like this, lads? Not in a mere slip of a girl like you. I wouldn't mind having you on my team, the administrative side, not the chalk face,' he said, indicating the rooms above with a lift of his fine brows. 'Though you'd be a powerful attraction there too, if'n you ever change your mind, girl. Make a small fortune you could, at the top of them apples and pears.'

Patsy swallowed, silently resolving to hold her nerve, no matter how he might try to goad her. 'You've got the money

Molly owed you, with interest. If you're a man of your word, as I've heard that you are, then you'll have her girls brought down, right now.'

Quinn jerked his chin in Marc's direction, his eyes cold again. 'Those two go back outside first.'

'No!' Marc said. 'We stay right here.'

Patsy intervened. 'It's all right, Marc. I'll be fine. We've made our point. I think Mr Quinn is aware that I've not come unprepared.'

The two young men reluctantly withdrew. Quinn made some sort of gesture to one of the heavies who slipped quietly out of a side door. Patsy heard the man's weighty tread on the stairs, held her breath until a lighter one came running down, and there Fran was, standing in the doorway, looking around with wide, frightened eyes. She ran into Patsy's arms on a gasp of relief, just as if they were bosom pals. Seconds later, Amy appeared behind her.

'Fran? Amy? Are you all right?'

It was as they were heading towards the door, relief making Patsy almost run those last few yards to freedom that Amy spoke up. 'What about the others? We weren't the only girls in that room upstairs.'

Patsy stopped. 'Is that so?'

'They're nothing to do with us,' Fran countered, desperate to get out while the going was good.

Amy protested. 'But they shouldn't be held against their will, just because of something their parents have done wrong.'

Patsy swallowed. She'd come here under pressure to free the Poulson sisters, not the whole bleeding universe. 'That's a fair point,' she said, sounding braver than she felt. 'Maybe Quinn will consider allowing them to come home with us too, if he doesn't want visits from the local constabulary in the morning.'

She heard Fran's gasp, and felt a desperate tug at her elbow, but Amy was standing firm by her side, not a tear in sight. 'I do think that would be sensible, Mr Quinn,' Amy said, her hazel eyes lovely enough to melt the hardest heart.

Their three companions were thankfully released, and Patsy stood watching with relief as they all crept, disbelieving, out of the door.

–

Patsy was shaking by the time she got outside, with the uncomfortable feeling that she'd only postponed trouble and not solved anything. She'd thought it had all seemed too easy, and Quinn wasn't acting like a defeated man. Patsy had been about to follow the girls out into the street when he caught her by the elbow, to whisper in her ear, 'Let's hope you don't regret tonight's bit of business. You may think you've wrapped Big Molly's little matter up, but I'll leave it to you to talk to these other young ladies' parents. I'm sure they'll see fit to speedily settle their debts, or else we're back at square one,' he said, then vanished.

Now what in damnation had he meant by that? Surely he wouldn't hold her responsible for their debts? The three unknown girls had taken to their heels and run. Patsy felt a strong urge to do likewise. The sight of Fran in Marc's arms distracted her. He was patting her back, soothing her near hysterical sobs, the whites of his eyes gleaming in the moonlight as he held Patsy's gaze over Fran's shoulder.

'Why didn't you call out for us? And why did you make us leave?'

'A third party would only have made things worse at that delicate stage in the proceedings. There really was no need for you to come in at all. Anyway, he didn't lay a finger on me. I handed over the money, and he agreed to let them all go. It's over. They're safe.'

Chris said, 'You're shaking.'

'I'm not surprised. Mice and lions don't generally make good housemates.'

But Chris was getting agitated, looking frantically about him. 'So where is Amy?'

That was the moment they realised they hadn't won at all.

Chapter Forty-Three

They heard the scream, spotted a group of figures running away across the docks: Quinn, his two bully boys, and Amy. The scream was cut off in mid-cry, as if someone had stifled it. Then Chris was running after them, and Patsy wasn't far behind. Marc shouted at Fran to stay exactly where she was and set off in hot pursuit too.

Patsy jumped over railway lines, tripped over fallen masonry, raced in and out of stacks of timber, bags of grain, crates and containers, ran till her sides split with pain and her chest felt as if it might explode. Yet still she kept on going, desperately trying to keep up with the two boys' more powerful legs. They all three came to a halt, breathing heavily.

'Where the hell are they?'

'Over here!' Marc yelled. 'I think they went this way.'

They stepped cautiously through deserted warehouses, eased open creakily swinging doors. No sign of them.

'My God, no, look up. That's where they are!' Just the sound of the fear in Chris's voice chilled her, even before Patsy looked skyward at the mesh of girders that formed the sixty-ton floating crane. This huge monstrosity could lift a railway carriage as easily as a pack of butter. But climbing up its frame of metal slats were Quinn and Amy. The outline of their two figures stood out black and stark against the moonlit sky.

Quinn was laughing as he called down to them. 'What is this little colleen's life worth now, would you say, my friends? Surely another thirty quid? Fifty or a hundred? Cheap at the price, wouldn't you say?' He was holding her by the neck and giving her a shake. Amy screamed again, clearly terrified he would let her fall down to the docks below.

Chris shouted: 'Hold tight, Amy! I'm coming to get you.'

'No!' Patsy grabbed Chris, struggling to hold on to him. 'Let me. I'm lighter, can climb like a monkey. And we need to talk Quinn round, not fight him up there.'

'You've already tried talking to him, Patsy, and it didn't work. You can't reason with a monster like that.'

Patsy glanced up, her mind frantic, knowing he was making a valid point yet undecided over what was the right thing to do. Then she heard a great roar. It came from Marc as he charged at one of Quinn's heavies. He ran into him head first, catching him off guard, and shoved him backwards into the canal, only just saving himself from falling in with him. Chris didn't hesitate. He instantly flung himself on to the second man, and between them Marc and Chris punched, kicked and chucked him too into the canal, along with the first. The two bully boys were much less agile in the water than on land, screaming about not being good swimmers, not able to climb the smooth sheer wall of the dockside.

Marc and Chris left them to struggle, and turned back to the problem of Quinn. Chris shouted again to him. 'You're on your own now, Quinn. Let her go. Send her back down, nice and easy, or we'll come up and fetch her and you'll be coming down head first to join your two mates here.'

Patsy ran to stand beneath the towering crane, her head spinning dizzily just from looking up. Heaven knows what poor Amy was going through. 'We should call the police, Marc. Find the dock office and ring them.' Then she shinned up the cab of the crane and began to climb. Within seconds she seemed to be half a mile off the ground, though it was probably no more than a few feet. Amy was screaming at her to get down, the wind whistling through the metal spars, whipping her hair across her face.

'Don't look down!' Marc called. But she did and came over all giddy. Patsy had never felt so afraid, almost too petrified to move as her knees began to shake, and she became paralysed by fear, positive she was about to fall.

Hands grabbed her. 'You stupid girl! What the blazes are you doing? You think I'd let you do such a daft thing? I'd rather die than see you hurt.'

Patsy stared into Marc's eyes, shock and something she couldn't name, pulsing through her. Nobody had ever said such a thing to her before. Who else would wish to die for her? Nobody. He must care for her. She swallowed, tried to concentrate her mind on what was happening. This wasn't the moment for any show of weakness. 'I have to save Amy. I must.'

'I know, but this isn't the way. Maybe you're right and we do need help.'

'No, we can't wait for that. Let me go to her. Let me try.'

'Then Quinn will have two hostages, instead of just one.'

Marc was trying to make her go down but Patsy struggled in his arms, attempting to free herself, slapping his hands away and begging him to let her go. Even as they hung perilously above the ground, they felt the crane quiver, and became aware of Chris climbing the girders at the opposite side. He was talking to Quinn in a calming voice, begging him to let Amy go free.

They saw Quinn lean over one of the lower spars and say something to Chris, laughed mockingly, and taunted him. It was then they saw Amy balance herself by holding tight to a metal spar, lift one foot and kick Quinn right in the middle of his back with her booted foot. There was a loud cry as he lost his footing and slithered down between the slats.

'Oh, my God, he's falling! He'll be killed.'

He fell awkwardly on to a lower girder and catching hold of it he wrapped his legs around it, hanging on tight just above their heads. He was clearly injured. Nobody moved, except for Amy. She was frantically edging herself closer to a main spar. Grabbing hold of it, she half slid and half climbed down it to where Chris was waiting to capture her in his arms.

Marc and Patsy carefully climbed down too and ran to hug her. They were jubilant, hugging and laughing together in a joyous bunch. Then Chris said, 'What about Quinn?'

Marc gave a harsher sounding laugh. 'He's good at hanging around. Leave him to it.'

Patsy said, 'His mates are out of the water, and further down the docks there. I reckon this is the moment we should make ourselves scarce.'

As they ran back across the docks, out of nowhere Fran appeared. She flung herself at Marc, fastening her arms tightly around his neck as tears flowed and hysteria threatened yet again. Anyone would think it had been her at the top of that sixty-ton crane.

'I thought you'd left me, Marc! I thought you were never coming back. Take me home, please. I'd've been done for in that place if it weren't for you. Thank you so much for saving me. What would I have done without you?'

Patsy gasped. No mention of her own gallant efforts, nor even a word about poor Amy who had suffered far more. It was all me, me, me! Patsy suspected that Fran had been hovering around, hiding behind one of the containers, watching their efforts to rescue Amy, but not wanting to risk getting involved. What kind of a sister, or friend, for that matter, was she?

And as Fran clung tighter to Marc, sobbing hysterically, Patsy lost patience. 'Oh, take her home, Sir Galahad, why don't you?'

'We'll all go home together,' he snapped. 'Do stop your whining, Fran, for God's sake. It's Patsy you have to thank, not me.'

But it was too late for him to scold her as the damage was done. They all walked home, shocked and distressed by what they'd been through, in complete silence, save for the sound of Fran's self-pitying sobs as she clung tenaciously to Marc's arm.

–

After Chris's brave intervention, Molly was forced to conclude that the lad couldn't be that bad, despite his family name. Maybe he wasn't the black sheep his Uncle Howard had been.

'Will you accept then,' Amy asked, gazing into his eyes, 'that Chris is not responsible for his family's past misdeeds, and is in fact a good man? Not only that, but has proved beyond doubt his love for me?'

After a beat Molly said, 'Aye, I will say that for him. I can see he loves you petal, and he helped to get us all out of a big hole. Though it's not too comfortable eating my hat.'

'Right then,' Amy said, grinning with pleasure over this concession on her mother's part, 'I think this deserves a celebration, don't you? We've seen off Quinn, and we're all safe home. You've admitted that my husband is a decent chap, and even accepted help from your worst enemy, Mr George.'

Big Molly wagged a finger furiously. 'That's only temporary. I'll pay him back soon as maybe, if I have to sell every stick of furniture I possess.'

She fully intended prising the money out of her greedy son, and in future would keep the market stall takings separate from the kitchens, even if she was no longer allowed actually to bake the pies. Didn't she deserve it for building up this fine business? She saw no reason why she should simply hand it over, free and gratis, without some benefit to herself.

Amy was excitedly making plans. 'We'll have a bit of a knees-up this Friday night after the market closes. You can knock up a few buns and biscuits, Mam. Dad can go down the Dog and Duck for a jug or two of ale while Fran and me will make a few sandwiches and things on sticks, just like Fanny Craddock on the telly. How about it, Fran?'

Fran shrugged, feeling strangely detached from this celebrating lark. All right, so she'd escaped Quinn and his mob, but where did that leave her? Back in her mother's clutches, and on the stall by morning – where was the excitement in that?

She was filled with resentment for her sister's wedded bliss; hated the fact that Amy was getting all the glory and attention, just because Quinn saw her as a weak link and ran off with her. Why did everything turn out right for her sister and wrong for her?

Amy was too thrilled with this surprising turn of events to notice Fran's sulks; too busy organising her belated wedding reception, believing that if she could only gather their respective families together under one roof for a bit of a do, then all their troubles would be over. And with Quinn off their backs, Chris would surely find himself a job. They could both relax and, hey presto, sex on demand would be the order of the day.

She beamed around at them all. 'Chris and I have never celebrated our wedding with you. It's long past time we did.'

Chapter Forty-Four

Many believed it to be the best party Champion Street had seen in a long while. All the neighbours and stallholders came round to join in the fun and everyone got very drunk. There were far too many people to fit into Big Molly's little house, so they all spilled out into the street. Alec Hall's son provided the music by playing his guitar, stalls were cleared out of the way, and in no time all the lads and young girls were dancing. The oldies sat sipping their Guinness or milk stout, joining in with a bit of rowdy singing now and then. Buster the dog howled along with gusto and made everyone laugh.

Winnie Watkins and Sam Beckett did a knees-up to 'All The Nice Girls Love A Sailor', and everybody joined in, laughing and clapping at their antics. The Bertalone girls danced too, looking a picture in their rainbow of dresses, their mama and papa looking on with proud smiles.

The food was excellent: ham sandwiches, sausage rolls and huge stacks of Big Molly's home-made pork pies, even some fancy vol-au-vents filled with shrimps in a pink sauce, tiny cocktail sausages and cubes of cheese and pineapple on cocktail sticks. Fanny Craddock would have been proud of them. Champion Street had never seen the like.

Best of all, the bride and groom were clearly in love and happy together, hardly out of each other's arms all evening, smooching away to 'It's All In The Game', and the Everly Brothers', 'Dream Lover'. Rocking and bopping, and generally having fun.

And nobody could miss the interest Marc Bertalone was showing in Patsy Bowman either. He kept asking her to dance and she kept on refusing, till in the end Barry Holmes called out, 'Go on, lass, give the lad a chance, as he only wants to hold you in his arms. Don't be mean.'

Blushing furiously, and to stop the chorus of agreement which this remark provoked, Patsy was forced to give in. 'You can take that grin off your face,' she hissed at him, slipping easily into his arms, just as if she were meant to be there.

'Oh, no, it's staying right where everyone can see it. And why shouldn't I look happy? Haven't I got the prettiest girl in the street in my arms at last?'

Patsy felt a powerful urge to talk to him, for things to be as they had once been between them, yet couldn't think of a thing to say. Was it really her that he liked, or Fran Poulson? Patsy remembered his fear when she'd been set on climbing that great crane, and finally thanked him, stiffly and awkwardly, for helping to tackle Quinn.

'For God's sake, Patsy, you don't need to thank me. I wouldn't have let you face him on your own. I thought you were so brave, still my little lion-heart. And how is it with the sisters?'

Patsy almost smiled. 'Even Annie has mellowed.'

They both glanced across to where the Higginson sisters were sitting on stools talking to Winnie. They were drinking nothing stronger than best Yorkshire tea but they looked happy enough. Patsy waved to them, and Clara waved back. Annie gave what might pass for a smile, and Patsy giggled. 'See what I mean?'

'If you can't win her round and make that frozen heart of hers melt, nobody can.'

Patsy cast him a sideways glance, struggling to read what he meant by this remark, but his eyes were hooded, and their expression unfathomable. They had two dances together, both slow waltzes. Patsy was just starting to relax and allow Marc to rest his cheek against hers while she happily breathed in the familiar scent of his skin, the vanilla of his father's ice cream, the incense from his mother's parlour, the fresh tang of his soap.

Fran appeared at his elbow. 'This is a ladies' excuse-me please, so it's my turn now.'

'We're not done yet,' Marc told her. He'd been hoping to take Patsy for a bit of a stroll later so that they could be alone to talk, and maybe she'd let him kiss her again.

Fran elbowed Patsy to one side and wriggled herself into his arms. "Course you're not done yet, not by a long chalk. The night is young. Move over, Patsy, love, and let a real woman show him what's what.'

Patsy stalked away, head high, not even listening to Marc begging her not to go far. Alec Hall noticed her obvious distress and quickly asked her to dance with him instead. 'Come on, Patsy, love. Nobody sits out tonight.'

Patsy was glad of his offer, which made her feel so much less conspicuous, but her heart was aching. Why hadn't Marc refused to allow Fran to separate them? Why didn't he care enough to do that?

Alec answered her unspoken concern. 'He's only being polite, and it really is an excuse-me. You can always go and get him back in a minute.'

'Over my dead body!'

'Aw, come on, Patsy, I've seen you two together often enough. Don't let pride spoil things for you.' After a few moments, Alec said, 'Go on, Fran has had him long enough. You go and excuse them now.'

Patsy decided it might be worth a try. Why let Fran win so easily?

–

Peeved with the way her life had turned out, that she was in fact no better off, Fran felt filled with a determination to do something radical to put things right. It was long past time she took her revenge on Eddie Davidson. She'd lost her child, lost her lover, almost been attacked and abused by Quinn's heavy mob. Somebody, she decided, needed to pay for all that, still not recognising her own role in this litany of misfortunes. What was worse, she'd seen an announcement in the paper that the awful Josie had given birth to a healthy son, and she still had her husband. It just didn't seem fair.

Why couldn't she find herself a decent chap? Fran asked herself. Marc Bertalone would do nicely. Good-looking, with steady employment, and she always had fancied him. Patsy Bowman must be wetting herself, having wanted him so much. But in order to work her charms, Fran needed to get him on his own, up a dark alley.

'I need to post a letter,' she told him now, gazing at him with huge, amber eyes. 'I forgot to do it earlier and it's important, but I daren't walk down the street on my own in the dark. What if Quinn's bully boys are lurking up a dark alley, just waiting to grab me again, like they did our Amy?'

Marc considered this unlikely, and said as much as he glanced about, seeking Patsy. She was dancing with Alec Hall, laughing at something he'd said, obviously enjoying herself. She wouldn't miss him for a few minutes, and the post box was only a few yards down the street. Out of politeness, and just in case Fran had a point about Quinn, he agreed.

They walked together down the darkened street, Fran popped the letter in the box, and then jumped as if startled. 'Did you hear that? Someone's following us.' And she flung herself into his arms.

'I didn't hear a thing.' Marc tried to extricate himself from her grip, longing to get back to the dancing, and to Patsy.

And then Fran burst into tears. She put her head on his shoulder and sobbed. 'Oh, I'm sorry, Marc, I just can't help it. I keep on crying like this, all the time. My nerves are in shreds. How will I cope? No decent bloke will ever want to know me now. They'll think Quinn had his wicked way with me, that I've been ruined. You think that too, don't you?' She gazed up at him out of liquid eyes.

'No, course I don't,' Marc stammered, awkwardly patting her shoulder and wishing he was anywhere but here, alone in the dark with Fran Poulson. Patsy would never believe in his innocence after this. He was done for. He thought he heard her coming and glanced up hopefully, saw what he imagined to be a fleeting shadow, heard the tinkle of breaking glass. 'I heard something then, did you?'

Fran lifted her ruby lips to his, so thick with lipstick, he noticed, that they glistened in the lamplight. 'It was only a cat.' As if to confirm her words, there came a loud howling and cater-wauling, like tomcats fighting. Marc half-turned away, listening carefully.

'You're repulsed by me, aren't you?'

'Why would I be repulsed?'

She wriggled closer in his arms, pressing her plump breasts against his hard chest, managing to undo a couple of buttons on her blouse as she did so as to reveal a fine cleavage. 'Show me then, prove to me that you've not been turned off by Quinn's attentions. You came to save me, and I can never thank you enough for that. Never! Though I wouldn't mind giving it a try. What do you say, Marc love? One for old time's sake, eh?'

Marc saw the pit opening up before him. One more tentative, polite step on his part and he'd be in it. Taking a firm grasp on both Fran's wrists, he unclasped her hands from around his neck and set her a little distance away from him.

'Stop this right now. It's time you got a grip on yourself. We don't have that kind of relationship, Fran, not any more, though there are plenty of blokes who'd be happy to be seen out with you. You were saved from Quinn's unwelcome attentions, thanks to Patsy. It's her you should be grateful to, not me. Now stop putting on this silly helpless act and behave yourself.'

He looked into her eyes and saw the flash of anger in those amber depths, watched as her expression hardened from seductive and sensual to something he could only describe as ice-cold rage.

Then she pulled her hands free and slapped him across the face. 'Wait till I tell dear, darling Patsy what you just did to me, Marc Bertalone!'

'I did nothing.'

'Ah, but she doesn't know that. I'll make sure that I screw up any last chances you might have had with her.'

Patsy was intercepted on her way over by Jimmy Ramsay offering her a hamburger. He was frying them on a griddle, he said, '…American style, would you like to try one?'

Patsy politely declined, but by the time she reached the spot where Marc and Fran had been dancing, there wasn't a sign of them. They'd vanished.

Winnie saw her looking helplessly around. From her chair set next to Jimmy Ramsay's stall where she could enjoy the smell of frying onions, she shouted across, 'He's just nipped to the post box with a letter. He'll be back in a jiffy.'

So that was the tale he was telling, was it? Yet Patsy could see that Fran too had disappeared, and it didn't take a genius to work out why. She spotted a couple of figures disappearing into the shadows of the side alley that led round to the back of Marc's house, and her heart plummeted. She'd been right all along about Marc Bertalone. Flirt with anything in a skirt and didn't mean a word he said. Girl mad!

Winnie Watkins saw her expression and followed the direction of her gaze, a puzzled frown on her face.

Convinced she must be the only one not having a good time, Patsy could bear it no longer and walked away from the market, the sounds of the music and laughter fading as she strode along Champion Street, turned left on to Hardman Street and kept on walking. How long she walked, she'd really no idea, but having done a complete circle she came back up Champion Street from the direction of Lower Byrom Street. The first person she met was Big Molly.

The bride's mother was sitting glum and silent on a kitchen chair just by her own front door, an untouched plate of food in front of her, Ozzy with a full pint of stout he clearly hadn't even tasted was seated at her side. Unheard of for Big Molly and Ozzy not to eat and drink, let alone sit in such close proximity to each other.

Mr and Mrs George, the groom's parents, hadn't turned up at all.

Patsy went and sat with them for a while, then Clara came over to say that she and Annie were ready to retire for the night, and Patsy went home with them. She was in bed by ten-thirty, worn out and drained of all emotion.

Back at the party, Marc looked everywhere for her but found no sign. Winnie told him she'd walked off down the street, and later, when he couldn't find her there either, that she'd gone home with the sisters. He was filled with regret for the lost opportunity, angry for stupidly allowing himself to be put into such a vulnerable position by Fran. How would he ever get out of this one?

–

Afterwards, no one could deny that the party to celebrate the young couple's unconventional, romantic wedding at Gretna Green had been great fun. A happy evening with plenty of laughter, good food and booze, singing and dancing. A night to remember.

But as an attempt to breach the chasm between the two families, it had failed miserably. The feud wasn't over, not by a long chalk.

And following this failure, Chris and Amy had their worst row yet. Amy was desperately disappointed and upset that his family hadn't even bothered to turn up.

'We went to all that trouble. It was a special party to celebrate our wedding, and they didn't even send their apologies. At least my mother baked cakes and pies for us, and she's accepted you.'

'Amy stop kidding yourself. Molly has not accepted me, not for a minute. She sat in a corner all night in a sulk. Ozzy too. I'm still the son of Thomas George, her sworn enemy. She hates me.'

'That's not true!' Tears were rolling down Amy's cheeks, but Chris was angry. He hated to see his young wife treated so badly, by his own family as much as her own. First their wedding wasn't exactly as he'd planned it with no money left to pay for a honeymoon, then she'd nearly been killed as a result of her mother's meddling, and now even their party had been ruined too.

'She doesn't give a shit about me, nor you neither. If Big Molly cared half as much as she claims to, she wouldn't go on hurting you like this.'

'Don't say such things about my mother.'

'Why not? It's true! I'm not saying she doesn't love you, in her own idiosyncratic way she probably does, but she doesn't care a jot about your happiness. She's too wrapped up in her own feelings even to consider yours. She doesn't give a thought to your safety.'

'How dare you say that?'

Amy gazed frantically about their tiny bedsit, the cramped living conditions overlaid by the smell of the fish market, a bitter reminder of their lack of money, of decent employment or hope for the future. And then her gaze fell upon the double bed, the symbol of their failed marriage.

'I've had enough, Chris. It's over! I can't go on like this any longer. This feud is never going to end. The whole thing is tearing us apart and I can't bear it.'

Amy snatched up her coat and bag, and marched to the door. She could hardly see for tears, the pain in her chest cutting through her like a hot knife. 'I'll come back for the rest of my things tomorrow.'

'Where the hell do you think you're going?'

'Home.'

'This is your home, dammit, with me. I'm your husband.' In two strides he reached her, knocked the bag out of her hands and, grabbing her shoulders, gave her a little shake, just to make her cease her crying long enough to listen. 'We have to stop worrying about our parents, Amy, and this damn feud of theirs! We need to get on with our lives in our own way. We have to stop trying to please your mam, or my father, and concentrate on our own happiness. If my parents choose never to speak to us, so be it. To hell with them because I have you!'

'How can you say that?' Amy was almost screaming now, beside herself with misery and disappointment and frustration. And a terrible, yawning fear that had her in its grip.

'Because I love you! You're the first person I think of when I wake in the morning, my last thought at night. All day I look forward to the moment I'll come home to you, even here, in this awful flat, even when I know I shall disappoint you by once again admitting that I still haven't found a job. You are the only reason my heart is still beating. Why else would I care whether it did or not? Amy, you are my very soul.'

'Oh, Chris!' She felt herself melt at his words, and an aching void opened within her. 'I love you so much.'

'And I love you.'

Then she was in his arms and he was kissing her with a passion she'd forgotten through all the trauma of the last months. His hands were in her hair, cupping her face, peeling off her clothes, and her own hands were tearing at his shirt, popping buttons in her anxiety to match flesh to flesh.

There was a roaring in her ears, as if the great barrier of ice that had separated them for so long had snapped apart deep inside her, cracked and shattered, leaving her overwhelmed by emotion. It flooded into her, searing every nerve ending, threatening to tear her apart.

She was clutching at him, grabbing his hair, opening her mouth for him to devour as he crushed her to him. She wanted, needed, him so much. Never had she felt such a powerful compulsion, as if she must somehow meld herself into him, make herself a part of his very being. She could feel his bare flesh burning beneath her hands, the pounding of his heart against hers. He lifted her, carried her over to the bed and together they fell on to the tousled sheets.

'I love you, Amy. Oh, God, how I love you.'

He snapped open her bra and where her panties went she had no idea and really didn't care. When he entered her, the fullness of him delighted her, making her his at last. Amy wrapped her legs about his waist, rocking, matching her rhythm to his, and as he pushed harder, turning her bones to liquid fire, she thought she must be the luckiest, happiest woman alive.

Chapter Forty-Five

There were many thick heads the next morning but the market was crowded, as always on a Saturday. Women picking over Barry Holmes's vegetables, arguing over apples or pears they were prepared to buy; little girls with pigtails handing over their Saturday pennies for a dressing-up doll book; young boys getting yelled at for kicking a ball under the canvas of Jimmy Ramsay's stall. One urchin eating chestnuts out of a paper cone, another licking an ice cream.

The stalls themselves were piled high with all manner of goods: pots and pans, bundles of firewood, second-hand clothing, cure-all medicines, sarsaparilla and warm winter woollies, stacks of books and *Beano* comics, military medals, stamp collections, and old sheet music of songs by Gilbert and Sullivan, and Kathleen Ferrier.

Marc, oblivious to it all, strode through the outdoor market without a glance to right or left. He had but one thought on his mind, to make it up with Patsy.

He neatly avoided a barrow loaded high with flowers being wheeled into position by the big double doors of the market hall, paid no attention to Big Molly's bellow to another of her long-suffering customers.

'Make your mind up, do you want tasty Lancashire or mild? It's all the same to me, I'm not eating it.'

He pushed open the doors and headed for the hat stall. It was lucky that Saturday was his day off. The sooner he set things right between them, the better. He found Patsy busily stitching a figured veil on to a blue velvet Juliet cap. She didn't even glance

up as he entered. Clara, who'd been sitting beside her, excused
herself and hurried off to Belle's cafe in search of a cup of tea.

Marc waited a moment, hoping Patsy would look up and smile,
show that she'd forgiven him for disappearing like that. She went
on stitching. 'We seemed to lose track of each other last night,' he
said, a false brightness in his tone. He was anxious not to make it
seem important, not to give the impression it was deliberate on
his part.

'Indeed. I expect you had bigger fish to fry.'

'I'm sorry I missed you. Fran needed to post a letter and was
afraid of the dark, in case Quinn or his heavies were around.'

'I see.'

Patsy too had received a letter, only this morning. More of a
note, really, delivered by hand and pushed through the Higginsons' letterbox. It was from Billy Quinn, warning her to keep
her nose out of his business in future, or she'd be sorry. Patsy
had showed it to no one, not even to the sisters. She'd felt a
momentary chill between her shoulder blades then screwed the
note into a ball and thrown it on the fire. So far as she was
concerned, the whole nasty business was done and dusted.

Marc stifled a sigh. He was getting nowhere. Her voice, her
entire manner were ice cold and she wasn't even looking at him.
He edged closer, hands in pockets, trying to sound unconcerned.
'I was back within minutes, hoping for the last waltz, but I
couldn't find you.'

'I went home with Clara and Annie. I was tired.'

'Winnie told me.' Another awkward pause when he watched
her pale hands skilfully stitching the veil. Marc cleared his throat,
tried again. 'I wondered if you felt like going to the pictures
tonight? There's a *St Trinian's* film on. Give us a laugh. We could
do with one, don't you think—'

'I don't think so,' Patsy interrupted. 'I don't reckon there's
much point, do you?' She risked a glance up at him and almost
quailed before the agony in his eyes. She went quickly back to
her stitching. 'You're still with Fran, right?'

'No, no I'm not! Whatever gave you that idea?' He hunkered down beside her. 'I'm going to ask you only once more, Patsy, because there are only so many rejections a guy can take, but as I said the other day, I'd like us to try again. Please, come to the flicks with me this evening? It will give us a chance to talk. I can tell you about my new job, and you can tell me about your plans for taking a hat-making course, and how things are between you and the sisters. What do you say? Isn't it worth giving it one more shot?' He rested one hand on hers, preventing her from moving the needle. 'Isn't it?'

She looked at him then, met his steady gaze and almost drowned in it. Oh, how she wanted to say yes, how she needed him, ached for him. He must have read her answer in that look because he responded with a smile. 'I'll pick you up at seven.'

-

Fran was still nursing her grievances: the rejection by Marc, and the sorry state her life seemed to be in. Her sister's face, by contrast, had seemed alight with happiness this morning, her eyes shining: a rare glow about her as she hummed merrily to herself. Fran had seen her when she'd delivered a tray of pies to the stall.

'I thought I'd pop over with these in my coffee break,' Amy told her. 'I wanted to see how you were after that dreadful business with Quinn, and if you had a good time at the party last night?'

Fran muttered something unintelligible.

'Oh, we did. Absolutely fabulous, and Chris and me have made a decision. I wanted to tell you before you heard it from anyone else. We're thinking of leaving Champion Street. If Chris still hasn't found work by the end of this week, we're off to pastures new. It's 1957, and there must be jobs everywhere. We aren't going to let Quinn hinder us and spoil our future any longer, nor our parents either with this stupid, outdated feud. Much as we might sympathise with their feelings, we have our own lives to lead, and we mean to concentrate on ourselves from now on.'

Fran found herself listening carefully to all of this, and couldn't help but feel admiration for her sister. 'Good for you, girl.' Overcome by an unexpected burst of affection, she put her arms around Amy and hugged her. That was twice in one week. She must be going soft in the head. 'Don't let anyone stop you two from being happy.'

Amy laughed. 'Don't worry, we don't intend to.'

But watching Amy walk jauntily away made Fran's heart ache. Her own problems seemed huge by comparison, her life even more of a miserable mess. Marc had been avoiding her all morning, and she'd pretty well accepted that there was no hope for her in that quarter, not any more.

Worse, she'd be stuck on this dratted pie stall for the rest of her life, if she didn't watch out. As the day wore on, Fran's feelings of discontent grew and she turned her mind back to the source of all her troubles: Eddie Davidson.

Spotting her mother's discarded copy of the *Manchester Guardian*, Fran scanned quickly through it till she reached the personal column. Seconds later she was smiling once more. She'd got her revenge. Last week she'd placed a small ad in the newspaper, claiming to be from friends and family offering deepest condolences to Mr and Mrs Eddie Davidson over the recent loss of their beloved son. It was a pity she hadn't known the child's name, but never mind, this would make him sit up and take notice, the bastard. Oh, sweet revenge!

–

Patsy had a second visitor to the stall that morning: Eddie Davidson, looking half demented with worry and begging for her help. He showed her his copy of the *Guardian*, gabbling out some story about Fran not only having placed this unforgivable ad in the paper, but also sent his wife an anonymous letter. 'She received it just this morning. It threatens to kidnap our baby boy who is alive and well, as Fran well knows.' Eddie was clearly fearful that he may not be for much longer, that Fran may just be mad enough to make the ad come true. 'I know it was from her. I recognise her writing.'

Patsy was appalled. 'I'm sure Fran would never actually hurt the child. She's probably just trying to be difficult and frighten you.'

'Well, she's succeeded. And since she used to speak about you as a friend, and I heard how you saved Fran and her sister Amy from that evil shit, Quinn, I thought you might help. Tell her she's wasting her time. I'm sorry if I hurt her. It was agreed between us from the start, that it wouldn't be anything more than a fling. Nevertheless, I'm sorry, do tell her that.'

Patsy listened in silence, wondering why the hell everyone came to her for help in dealing with Fran; why she'd allowed herself to get mixed up in her affairs.

Eddie was still talking. 'We're making a fresh start, Josie and me, and our little lad. He's a right bobby-dazzler, a real little treasure. I never thought I'd take to kids, but I have, and I don't want anything to spoil it for us. So, can you also tell her that we're moving on? We're leaving Manchester and emigrating to Australia to start a new life as a family. We're happy, Josie and me, and I hope Fran will be too, one day.'

'I wonder if Fran Poulson knows how to be happy. She won't want to hear that you are,' Patsy said with foreboding.

–

Patsy related to Fran, word for word, what Eddie had told her. Fran had no wish to hear how happy he was, delighted with his son, or his wonderful plans for a new life down under. She was furious, swearing she would follow him to the ends of the earth to get her revenge one way or another.

'Don't talk daft. You've got to stop this at once. Be thankful he doesn't sue you over those dreadful condolences you put in the paper, not to mention the anonymous threat to kidnap his son that you sent to his wife.'

'He deserved it. *She* deserved it. Her son is alive, and mine is dead. What's wrong with offering my condolences to Eddie for the loss of our son?'

'Stop that. You weren't thinking of your own child. You wanted to hurt him and his wife, but it's not her fault. And she very nearly did lose her child, thanks to you. Face it, Fran, you are the one responsible for your own misfortunes, as I am mine. We can't blame anyone but ourselves for the choices we make. You chose to have an affair with a married man. You knew what you were letting yourself in for, so why be surprised that it all went wrong, and Eddie rightly decided to stay with his wife? Revenge is not the answer for making a big mistake and suffering for it? Nor will it do you any good beating yourself over the head because of that abortion. You made that decision of your own free will, so live with it.'

Fran stared at her, distraught.

'Look at Amy, she's faced up to her problems and is getting on with life. You should do the same. It's long past time you made a fresh start.' As Patsy turned to go, she let drop one final comment. 'Oh, and keep your thieving little mitts off my man, right?'

Fran swept a stack of pork pies on to the ground with one clenched fist then walked smartly away, fury burning her up like a ball of fire. She didn't care where she was walking, chose to ignore her mother's raucous voice yelling and shouting after her. She stormed out of Champion Street, down Gartside Street and headed for Quay Street. Nothing had changed for her. She was right back where she'd started, chained to a boring routine serving meat and potato pies day after boring day, jumping to attention whenever her mother called.

Fran walked for a good ten minutes her mind in a whirl, rage eating her up inside, and then a voice spoke in her ear.

'Hey, up, are you working today, Fran?'

She whirled about, ready to give an earful to whoever was daring to suggest she should go back to the pie stall, when she saw a grinning face that she recognised all too well. 'Well, strike me down with a feather, it's you.'

'My ship's just come in,' the young sailor said, beaming happily at her.

'I could just do with a bit of cheering up? Hey, this is the life, eh?' she said, taking his arm with a dazzling smile.

This was the excitement Fran craved, the fun she so longed for. She could stay with Maureen tonight, but tomorrow she'd rent herself a little nest and feather it exactly as she chose, entertain lots of sailors and never again come running in answer to Big Molly's call. Never mind Champion Street and the pie stall. This was the life for her.

–

Patsy had one more visitor that day. Around dinnertime, just as she was about to sit down to a dish of tomato soup, the police came knocking. Not to Quinn's Pleasure Palace, as she had threatened, but to number twenty-two, Champion Street. They wished to take her in for questioning over a burglary. It seemed the Madonna statuette, which the Bertalones kept in their display cabinet had gone missing, and the police had evidence to show that Patsy was the culprit.

'That doesn't mean a thing,' Clara vigorously protested. 'How can you prove it was Patsy who stole it? Who says so?'

The police constable avoided Clara's fierce glare, but nonetheless remained firm. 'We had an anonymous tip-off.'

'And we can guess where that came from,' Patsy said. 'Quinn taking his revenge by implicating me for something he set up himself. Maybe the parents of those other girls didn't pay up. How can we find out? I don't even know who they are.'

'They have absolutely nothing to do with you,' Clara stoutly assured her. 'Quinn won't get away with this.'

The policeman was saying, 'We don't know nothing about any revenge but the lass will have to come along with me to answer a few questions down at the nick. Meanwhile, begging your pardon, ma'am, my colleagues will need to search the premises. Would you mind showing them to this young lady's room?'

'We will do no such thing,' Annie stoutly responded, stepping forward as if she might be about to embark upon fisticuffs with the young policeman. 'Do you possess a warrant, officer?'

Patsy cringed and gently touched her arm. 'Don't argue with them, Annie. It's all right, I didn't do it, so let them search as much as they like. They won't find anything.'

Unfortunately, they did. The police found the Madonna tucked right at the back on the top shelf of her wardrobe. The window of the downstairs back kitchen was found to have a broken latch, but neither sister could prove that it had been forced, or that someone had sneaked into the house while they were all out enjoying the party and hidden the statue in Patsy's room.

Patsy was taken off to the police station in a large black car. It was her worst nightmare come true.

Chapter Forty-Six

Patsy sat in the police station, answering the same questions over and over again. They'd called in a local solicitor: a large, red-faced individual with a bald head, shiny suit, and a school tie spotted with the remains of his breakfast. Jonathan Fairbrother, as he introduced himself, sat beside her throughout the interrogation, saying little except now and then warning her: 'Don't answer that.'

He'd been at pains to explain the seriousness of the charge. Were they to charge her with the offence of burglary, she would be brought before the magistrates without delay and remanded in custody.

'It means what exactly?' Patsy had tentatively enquired.

'You will go straight to prison and stay there until the case comes before the quarter sessions. So do please take care how you answer the officer's questions.'

Patsy was desperate to answer everything, to be as clear and honest and upfront as she could possibly be with the police, in a desperate bid to prove her innocence. What else could she do? She'd no wish to have all her past offences brought before the public gaze; for Clara and Annie, and most of all Marc, to hear just how badly she had behaved over the years.

Patsy knew she'd lost Marc for good this time. He wouldn't be picking her up to take her to the pictures tonight, or any other night, once he heard she'd been arrested. He'd never want to see or speak to her ever again. The Bertalones had welcomed her into their home, trusted her, made a friend of her and shown her their most private and valuable possessions. Now they would think she'd rewarded that trust by stealing from them. How could she hope to convince Marc otherwise?

And her stomach quailed at the prospect of serving a jail sentence.

'I didn't do it. I'm innocent, I swear it.'

'Now where have I heard that before?' the policeman sarcastically responded.

'I was set up, framed.'

His face was a picture. 'Oh, aye, who by? King of Siam?'

'By Billy Quinn, I got one over on him and he wants his own back. It all started when Big Molly—'

The police sergeant put back his head and roared. 'A little sprat like you got one over on Quinn, biggest villain in the manor? Don't make me laugh.'

'It's true. It was all because I saved Fran and Amy from the nasty scheme he had planned for them. Then he ran off with Amy and we had to chase after him, climb a crane to get her back. He was furious and sent me a threatening letter.'

The policeman's eyes were merry with laughter. 'I doubt our Billy can write, and where is it, this alleged letter?'

She didn't have it, if only she hadn't burned it. 'I threw it in the fire.'

'How convenient. So you have no proof of this far-fetched tale.'

Patsy shook her head, mute with misery.

'Let's get back to business then, shall we? And I'd advise you not to mess me about any more, girl, I've not got all day.' He pulled out a sheet of paper, and it didn't take a genius to guess what it was: a long list of her previous misdemeanours. 'Isn't it true that you stole a pie from Molly Poulson on the very first day you arrived on Champion Street Market?'

Someone else has been telling tales, Patsy thought. Or had Quinn himself told the police this fact when he'd made his anonymous call? She remembered foolishly admitting this to him, during their bargaining. 'I was starving hungry, but it was paid for later.'

'Yet on the day in question, you took it without permission. You stole a pie from Mrs Molly Poulson?'

'Yes.'

'Speak up.'

'Yes!'

'And on the fourth March, 1952, you stole a pair of earrings and a copper bracelet from Woolworths?'

'I was twelve years old,' Patsy muttered. 'It was a dare.'

The policeman ignored her. Instead he began to read out a list of other offences from this period of her life which ranged from sweets taken from the corner shop, to five pounds stolen from her own father.

'Foster father,' Patsy said, interrupting his flow. 'I needed money to pay for sports kit at school, and he wouldn't give it to me.'

Mr Fairbrother at her elbow made a growling sound in his throat. Patsy ignored him. She remembered the occasion only too well. Mr Bowman had called her a scheming little thief who had shown him up in front of the head teacher, then locked her in the understairs cupboard for two hours with the spiders. She supposed she deserved it. Stealing, from so-called family members was wrong, but it seemed a harsh way to discipline a child. It was a life-changing moment for Patsy, one in which she learned not only that he was neglectful, but that he really didn't care for her at all. Nobody did. This simple, soul destroying fact left deep scars on her, fuelling her hatred of the world from that day forward.

The sergeant scowled at her. 'I'm sure your foster father had his reason for so doing. Presumably these foster parents of yours never saw fit to adopt you?'

'No!' Patsy almost screamed at him. 'Why would they, when I'm obviously the child from hell!'

'We might have a short recess?' suggested Mr Fairbrother. 'My client is not surprisingly upset at finding herself in this predicament.'

The policeman, however, was determined to press on. Time, he said, was of the essence.

It was awful. The questions went on interminably, repeated over and over again until her head ached and Patsy could no longer think clearly. What had she told them? Was there some-thing else, something nudging the back of her mind? Something significant that she should tell them about? Her mind was buzzing, failing to focus properly.

'Didn't you break into the Bertalone's house via the back window?'

'No!'

'Didn't you break their display case and steal the Madonna statuette?'

'No, I never touched it. I wouldn't do such a thing.'

'Yet you are a thief. Doesn't your record, your list of previous convictions and misdemeanours, prove this simple fact? You apparently even stole from a fellow pupil. Isn't it true you once took another girl's coat, and your parents were called to the school by the local constabulary?'

'My coat no longer fitted me and I was cold, so I borrowed it, that's all, for a school outing. I meant to put it back but I forgot. The teacher spotted it in my locker before I got the chance.'

The policeman snorted. 'Your reputation was evidently well known by then. It seems to me that you consider everyone to be at fault, but yourself. And I cannot believe that your parents could afford to send you away to a fancy boarding school and not buy you a decent coat.'

'Well, that just shows how much you know.'

Mr Fairbrother tut-tutted, once more begging for a short respite, so that his client might calm herself. A mug of tea was brought for Patsy, although her stomach heaved at the mere sight of it, and as she attempted to sip the sludgy brown liquid, the solicitor whispered further warnings in her ear.

'This attitude of yours isn't helping. Try to remain calm and cooperative at all times. That is absolutely essential if we are to successfully avoid your being charged.'

Moments later, the questioning began again.

–

Patsy was close to despair. Mr Fairbrother had finally gained the recess he'd been asking for, but only because the police were anxious to make further enquiries before proceeding with the case. In the meantime Patsy was banged up in a police cell, seated on a hard slab of wood they laughingly called a bed, with nothing but a tiny barred window breaking the monotonous yellow walls set far too high for her to see out. Beside her lay a folded grey blanket that smelled of stale urine, a tin tray on which stood a plate of beans on toast, and yet another mug of dark brown, over-brewed tea.

Patsy put her face in her hands and wept, the tears sliding down between her fingers and dripping off the end of her chin. She was done for. This was what she'd always dreaded; that one day she'd go too far with her difficult, obstreperous behaviour, exactly as her foster parents had predicted. The annoying thing was that she hadn't! She'd been behaving herself magnificently lately, was innocent of this blasted crime, and hadn't touched the flipping statuette. Where was the fairness in being charged for something you didn't do? It was a wicked lie, dreamed up by that Quinn. But those final telling questions replayed themselves now in her mind, and Patsy had to admit she'd messed up there.

'Can you account for your movements at this party, Miss Bowman? Where were you, say, at around nine o'clock?'

'At the party.'

'Flippancy will not assist you.'

Mr Fairbrother jabbed her in the ribs as the police constable calmly suggested she do her best to remember.

'I danced with Marc.'

'That would be Marc Bertalone, the son of the household you robbed?'

The solicitor interrupted. 'Allegedly robbed.'

'My mistake.' Patsy gave a thin smile. 'Fran Poulson butted in, so I danced with Alec Hall instead.'

'And you were annoyed at having your nose pushed out of joint?'

'No, I couldn't give a—'

'It was only a ladies' excuse-me,' the solicitor interposed. 'Hardly motivation to burgle his family dwelling.'

'Who knows what these teenagers might take into their heads to do?' The police sergeant scribbled something on his pad before instructing Patsy to continue. 'What happened next?'

'Nothing. I didn't see Marc again,' Patsy said.

'Why not? What time did you leave?'

'I left with Clara and Annie around ten. I was in bed by half past.'

'So what were you doing in the intervening period, between the excuse-me dance around nine and the time you left to go home?'

'I don't know.' Patsy was again growing confused, and feeling desperately tired. She longed to lie down and sleep, aching for these persistent, endless questions to stop. Why didn't someone help her? Was no one ready to ride to her rescue as she had done for Fran and Amy? 'I've told you that I went home early. The party was still in full swing when I went to bed. Oh, I had a bit of a walk, to get some air and a bit of peace then talked to Big Molly, and Ozzy for a while. They weren't very happy, bless them, something to do with—'

'Where did you walk?'

'I don't remember.'

'Then try harder. How long were you away from the market on this walk of yours?'

'I don't know. Not long.'

'Fifteen minutes? Twenty? Half an hour?'

'About that, yes. I remember that I went down Gartside Street, and back up Lower Byrom Street by the new Queen's Theatre. Just around the block, you might say. Then I talked to Big Molly.'

'Ample time in that half an hour to pop across the road, break in through the back kitchen window of the Bertalones' house, steal the Madonna and slip it into your wardrobe at number twenty-two.'

'I didn't. That's not what happened! Why would I do such a thing? I like the Bertalones.'

'Because you were angry with Marc Bertalone for dancing with another girl? Isn't he supposed to be your boyfriend? Has he cheated on you before with this girl?'

Patsy didn't answer.

'Has he?'

'I don't know. Maybe. He's not my boyfriend, anyway.'

The policeman smirked. 'And weren't the windows of the Georges' house broken just the other week? Did you do that too?'

Patsy stood up then, all pink-cheeked, and refused to answer another single question. 'That's it, I've had enough!'

'What my client means,' said Mr Fairbrother in a placatory manner, 'is that she would like a meal and a proper rest, before this investigation goes any further.'

And so here she was, stuck in a stinking prison cell while the police went round the market asking all manner of questions, determined to prove her guilt. But guilty or not, she would never be able to show her face there again. People would walk past her in the street without speaking, even those, like Winnie Watkins and Sam Beckett whom she'd come to look upon almost as friends; who'd appeared friendly enough to her. They would cut her dead after this, intending to take the side of the Bertalones. Why would they not?

And why would they believe that she'd been set up by Quinn? The police certainly didn't, for all the Irishman was known for his sharp dealings, and for operating on the wrong side of the law. She'd mentioned his possible role in this mess more than once, and each time her tale had been dismissed as nonsense. If only she hadn't burned that stupid note, as it might have helped to incriminate him. But there was nothing they could find to pin this on him, so where was the proof?

As for the Higginson sisters, they'd feel betrayed. Annie might rant and rave at the ham-handedness of the police, but they would have heard the worst about her by this time. Patsy had lied, told them the pie incident was a one-off. Now they knew that was not the case. They knew she was a thief and a liar. Why wouldn't they believe she was also a burglar?

Why would anyone ever trust her again? Patsy felt more of an outsider than ever.

Chapter Forty-Seven

Winnie Watkins was the first to come. She turned up at the police station in her woolly cardigan and bob cap, lips set tight as if challenging anyone not to take her seriously. She knocked on the counter with her knuckles, and demanded to speak to the sergeant.

'He's busy.'

'It may be none of my business but I have information regarding that burglary the other night in Champion Street. I saw something fishy and I reckon he ought to know about it, because he's got a friend of mine locked up for the offence, and I'm not leaving this spot till I've had my say.'

The sergeant came, an expression of weary resignation on his lugubrious features.

Winnie told how she'd seen two figures slinking into the shadows down the alley that led to the back of the Bertalones' place. 'I remember at the time thinking it was strange, and happen I should have investigated what they were up to, but I was waiting for my fried onions, to go with my hamburger. Eeh, it were right good, worth waiting for. Have you tasted Jimmy Ramsay's prime beef?' Seeing the officer's expression, she hurried on, 'Anyroad, there were so many people about, so much going on, I put it out of my mind. I clearly remember them. They were two big bruisers, the sort you might expect to act as bouncers at one of them nightclubs, but not our Patsy. She's nobbut size of two pennyworth of copper.'

The police sergeant asked her to go through her story again, but it was unvarying. Winnie was absolutely certain about what she'd seen. He couldn't budge her. 'I've told you once and I'll say it again, I'll tell the judge himself, them were two big bouncers, the sort that hang around with that Billy Quinn character. They were hovering about up that alley, clearly up to no good.'

The second person to turn up was Big Molly, who told some convoluted tale about recalcitrant daughters, anonymous letters, broken windows, and misguided attempts to involve Quinn in these affairs of the heart. The woman wept out her confession, claiming she couldn't stand by and see an innocent girl, particularly one who'd tried to help, be locked up for something that was none of her doing.

The sergeant warned Big Molly that she was cutting her own throat. 'Don't say any more, love. You're hanging yourself while you try to save her.'

'Well, I deserve to be,' Big Molly said, all wet eyed and snotty nosed, wringing her podgy hands as she beseeched him to let poor Patsy go.

He sent her away with a sharp warning not to get up to any of that sort of mischief ever again. 'Leave your girls to make their own mistakes in life, don't add to them with more of your own.'

'Oh, I won't. And Patsy?'

The sergeant sniffed. 'She hasn't been charged yet. We're still investigating. Go home, lady, before I have to charge you with something instead.'

These two were followed by Alec Hall, who claimed to have been dancing with Patsy; Sam Beckett, who apparently saw her talking to Big Molly and Ozzy; and the Higginson sisters who bored the pants off him by giving him the girl's entire life history, or at least as much as they knew of it.

Annie Higginson was adamant that the back kitchen window latch had been broken, even went so far as to demand fingerprints be taken, unheard of in anything but a murder enquiry, the procedure being fairly new and very expensive.

Even Papa Bertalone came, insisting Patsy would never do such a terrible thing. 'Mama Bertalone, my sons and my daughters all love her. She is the good girl, not the criminal you say she is. And my son Marc, he is potty about her, though he is getting nowhere, I'm sorry to say. She is very private, and cautious. Someone has a hurt that poor girl very badly in the past, I think. She not the nasty thief, you say she is, understand? I take my Madonna back and we put no charges. Okay?'

'Go home,' the sergeant told them all, wishing he'd never started down this road. 'Please go home. We'll give the matter our serious consideration.'

Last, but by no means least, came Marc himself, marching up to the sergeant's desk and demanding to see Patsy. 'And don't let her dare refuse to speak to me. I love her, do tell her that. It's not Fran Poulson I want, it's her. I mean to marry that lovely girl. You can tell her that too. I don't believe she's guilty of this heinous crime, not for a minute, but if you insist on banging her up, tell her I'll be waiting for her when she gets out, no matter how long it takes.'

'Oh, for pity's sake, don't expect me to do your courting for you. I'm not a go-between for lovelorn swains,' protested the sergeant. 'Actually, you can take her home now. Constable, go and tell that lass she's free to go, before I lose my mind. I can take no more information.'

–

They simply couldn't stop kissing. They did try to do a bit of talking in between, words of apology and explanation tumbling out of their mouths, all at the same time so that neither heard what the other was saying. Marc was struggling to say how he'd always meant to resist Fran Poulson and had succeeded.

Patsy at pains to apologise for being so self-absorbed, was saying she'd learned to be more patient with other people, and to understand that everyone has problems. But really, their kisses said so much more. Happiness was bubbling through her. To be free, and held in Marc's arms was all that mattered. It was intoxicating, and magical. Words were superfluous.

'I've been absolutely frantic to get you released, racing around the market, getting everyone to come into the police station and make a statement,' he said.

'That was your doing?'

'Mine and Annie's, she's worked hard too. Even got a piece in the local paper about rough justice and the police jumping to conclusions. She's marvellous, that woman.'

Patsy laughed, feeling joy and love flare through her veins, then grabbed him to kiss him again. No conclusive evidence had been found to connect her to the crime, other than the figurine in her wardrobe. In view of the fact that other characters had been seen in the neighbourhood acting suspiciously at around the time of the break-in, the back window of number twenty-two had clearly been tampered with; no motivation could be found for the alleged crime, so it was decided to drop the case. No charges would be made.

'I'm never going to let you go again,' Marc vowed.

'And if that Fran Poulson ever comes near you, I'll bat her one.'

'You aren't going to go on about leaving again, are you? Because if you ever do leave Champion Street, I'm coming with you.'

Patsy giggled as she kissed the tip of Marc's nose. 'I sincerely hope not. I mean to talk to Clara and Annie, just as soon as I get back home. Hopefully they'll let me stay on long enough to sort myself out, till I can find alternative accommodation, another job, whatever I need to stay.'

'Or marry me?'

Patsy became very still, but before she had the chance to speak, Marc rushed on. 'Don't say "over my dead body" or one of your other choice put-downs. And don't think I'm asking you out of pity or sympathy or any of those other daft things you've accused me of. I love you, and want you to be my wife. I can't imagine life without you. Is that plain enough for you?'

His kisses provided all the assurance Patsy needed to say yes.

She was welcomed back to Champion Street Market like a returning hero. People actually cheered as she made her way between the stalls. Many slapped her on the back, Winnie rushed up to hug her, and Jimmy Ramsay produced a string of sausages for her to enjoy for her tea. What a triumph! Patsy glowed with pride, surprised and touched by their reception. She hadn't realised they all cared, and it came to her in that moment with a sense of blinding joy, that she wasn't an outsider any longer. She was one of them.

Amy rushed over to hug her, and excitedly tell Patsy how just that morning her father-in-law had come to see them and offered Chris a job in the family firm.

'Chris had told him the other day that we were thinking of leaving. And then my brother Robert went round to pay off the money Mr George lent to Mam, and for the first time in years they sat down and talked. They've agreed to call an end to this dreadful feud, to leave it in the past. Robert hopes to win Mam round to this point of view. At the moment she's more concerned about our Fran, who seems to have done another of her disappearing acts, but we won't talk about that on your special day.'

Patsy couldn't agree more. 'Oh, Amy, I'm so pleased for you, I am really.'

'Best of all, we've heard of a house to rent in Hardman Street, which will be handy for the market. Chris has gone to see the landlord this morning. We hope one day to buy a place of our own, maybe one of the new houses they're building, and then start a family. Everything is turning out right for us, at last. I hope it does for you too, Patsy.'

'Don't you worry about me, I'll be fine.'

Having delivered her safely to the door of number twenty-two, Marc had to hurry back to work as he'd already overrun his lunch hour, but they promised to meet up again later that evening. They parted with a lingering kiss, Marc assuring her that all would be well and she was not to worry.

'We'll tell them our news tonight, together. Now I've got to go, or they'll be giving me the sack.' He blew her a kiss and ran.

Patsy watched with pride and love as his long legs carried him across the market, away from her, but he'd be back. He'd come to her rescue after all, and did everything he could to get her out of that place. He wasn't ashamed of her, he loved her. Oh, and she loved him! She really must remember to tell him so later.

–

Clara rushed about putting the kettle on, and Annie, having given Patsy what, for her, was a warm welcome, had to rush back to work too, to open up the stall again after lunch. Even on this red-letter day, they couldn't afford to lose business. But before she left, she said a surprising thing.

'I wish you to know, Patsy, that however things stood between us when you first came here, you are now an essential part of our lives. Arrangements can be made for you to attend a proper course in hat-making, if that is your wish. You could set up a little business, in association with our stall or on your own, whichever you prefer, to produce custom-made hats for clients, as you have already proved yourself capable of doing. You will have our full support, whatever you decide.

'But I do hope, and I know Clara agrees with me in this, that you will continue to reside here, at number twenty-two, with us. I trust you will continue to think of this house as your home, until such time as you choose to move into one of your own. If you can bear to tolerate our constantly listening to the *Third Programme*, I believe we can put up with a bit of rock 'n' roll.'

'Oh, Annie, thank you so much.' Patsy put her arms around her stiff figure and even felt it unbend just a little as she kissed her cheek. 'You don't know what it means to me to hear you say that.'

'There's more, but I'll leave all of that to Clara.'

Chapter Forty-Eight

'I have a confession to make,' Clara said, as they sat at the kitchen table sipping their tea. 'Just as you once snooped through my things, while you were in the police cell I looked through yours. In my own defence, I was trying unsuccessfully to find something to prove your innocence, which thankfully is now established. But what I did find was this.'

Clara took Shirley's letter from her pocket and smoothed it out on the table. 'I assume this is from a friend of yours, someone trying to help with your quest to find your mother?'

Patsy nodded, too puzzled to be offended by Clara's prying. What did it matter anyway? Shirley had found no proof, and all that nonsense about Clara possibly being her mother had been just that, a foolish hope, a silly dream.

'You never mentioned that you had any connection with Southport, or Felicity Matthews.'

'She was my grandmother, apparently,' Patsy said. 'Not that I knew she even existed until after she was dead. I wasn't aware I had a relative.'

Clara again smoothed out the letter, taking a moment before continuing. 'Actually she wasn't strictly speaking your grand-mother.'

Patsy stared. 'You sound as if you knew her? Oh, you did, as you lived next door. But how do you know she wasn't my grandmother? Shirley, who now lives in your old house, believed Mrs Matthews's son Rolf was my father.'

Clara smiled. 'And that I was his wife?'

'The neighbours said you were friends.'

'That's all we were. Rolf went to America after his wife left him, and took his baby daughter with him. I was not that wife, nor you that child.'

Patsy once again felt the same keen sense of loss, which had already been made clear. It was so silly of her. They'd had little more than gossip to base the theory on in the first place. 'I just wanted to know who I was, that's all.'

'Of course you do. Everyone has that right, and I think I can tell you, or at least make an accurate guess.'

Patsy was all attention, but was forced to wait while Clara brewed fresh tea and refilled their cups. Once she was seated again, she began talking.

'When our first attempt to escape from France failed, and fearing that Louis had indeed been killed, attempting to rescue his family from the Gestapo, Annie and I made a decision. It was Annie's idea, and I instantly agreed with her. She thought it would help my grieving process, as well as being a worthwhile thing to do, if we tried to help others who were trapped and wished to leave France. As I think I've explained to you already, it was terribly dangerous even to attempt to leave. But there were many people desperate enough to try for their children, at least to give them the chance to escape and survive.

'We learned of a movement which organised the travel and transfer of unaccompanied Jewish children. Some were transported to Switzerland, or taken through Spain and even as far as Portugal using secret mountain trails, forged documents and black-market money. Some were sent to Palestine, and many more were shipped to England. Something like 10–15,000 Jewish children were saved in this way from almost certain death. Some were fortunate enough to be smuggled out of internment camps by parents they never saw again. Many were Polish, while some came from Germany itself. There were several such organisations operating in France, England, Holland, and across Europe. And all of these children had to be found homes and shelter.

'When Annie and I became involved, raising money, smuggling children from A to B, according to our instructions, we also wanted to help secure a new life for them.'

Patsy said slowly, 'It must have been incredibly difficult and dangerous.'

'It was. But Annie is so brave, so strong, and I felt I had nothing to lose. I owed it to the memory of Louis, whose family I felt I'd betrayed and damaged.'

'I think you're being hard on yourself, Clara. He had some responsibility too. He chose to have an affair with you, just as you chose him.'

Clara smiled. 'I'm sure you're right, and I was very young, but that is how I felt. I needed to put something back, to ease my conscience, if you like, by helping other Jewish children in a similar situation. We couldn't just stand by and do nothing. Since we were ourselves caught up in the war in France, we needed to play a part, and do our bit.

'We contacted many old friends and neighbours in England, whom we thought might be prepared to help, including Felicity Matthews. Felicity, in fact, housed dozens of children for us over the course of two years. She placed many into foster care or arranged for them to be adopted. Annie and I surmise that you must have been one of those children.'

Patsy sat unmoving, hands clasped tight between her knees, saying nothing, her eyes wide, their expression intent.

'Sadly, it would appear that the Bowmans turned out to be less than perfect parents, and, once she realised that fact, feeling responsible for this mistake, Felicity sent money whenever she could in an effort to make your life a little more tolerable. Such an action would be typical of her,' Clara said with a smile.

'She wasn't supposed to get involved. Once children have been re-homed, such interference can create untold emotional problems. But I believe she did what she could to help out of the goodness of her heart. I suspect that since her own grandchild was so far away across a great ocean, and relations with her son not of the best, she thought of all those young refugees as her special grandchildren. Still saw them as her responsibility.

'She wasn't permitted to visit, or intervene in their lives, but I know she remained in contact with many of the foster parents, some of whom were not particularly well off. At first, funds would come through the system to assist them to cope with their charges, but when these dried up Felicity continued to use her own money, where necessary, till the day she died, practically in penury. Not that I think this troubled her in the slightest. Felicity Matthews was a small woman with a big heart.'

Clara looked more intently at Patsy. 'I dare say this has come as something of a shock to you. You'll need time to assimilate it, and think it through.'

Patsy tried to find her voice, to express something of the confusion of thoughts and emotions that were rattling around inside her head, but failed utterly. Clara was right. It would take time.

'And it's not a total solution. So many children, so many babies. Annie and I, like everyone else involved, did our best to keep control of the paperwork to learn the name of each child, their origin and nationality, as well as the names and locality of their parents. But it was not always possible. Sometimes children would be handed over to perfect strangers on the road, or smuggled out with no paperwork attached, for the sake of safety. Desperate women were known to throw their children on to trains as they drew out of stations, or on to boats. That is how it is when you love your child. Their survival, not your own, is all important.'

'Are you trying to tell me that you don't know exactly who I am, except that I'm one of these refugees?'

She gave a gentle smile. 'I've searched through copies of the registers we kept, but I can't, hand on heart, say that I could identify which of those children is you. As I say, they didn't all have names or identities. Many papers were forged, for the sake of the child's safety and of those who transported them. And if they were too young to know their own name, it could easily be lost forever. That may well have happened in your case.'

'I see.'

Clara's gaze was steady and warm. 'What I can say, however, with absolute certainty, is that wherever you came from, and whoever you once were, we know who you are now. You are Patsy, and we love you. I lost my own daughter, Marianne, and you lost your mother through a war not of your making. I am more than ready, would be honoured indeed, to take on that role, if you were willing to accept me as such?'

'Oh, Clara.' Tears were rolling unchecked down Patsy's cheeks, turning Clara's smiling face to a misty blur. 'I would be proud to be your daughter. I would, really.'

'Then welcome home, my dear. This is where you belong.'